THE
STRATEGY PROCESS

Concepts and Contexts

HENRY MINTZBERG
McGill University

and

JAMES BRIAN QUINN
Dartmouth College

PRENTICE HALL
Englewood Cliffs, New Jersey 07632

Library of Congress Cataloging-in-Publication Data

Mintzberg, Henry.
  The strategy process — concepts and contexts/Henry Mintzberg and
James Brian Quinn.
     p.   cm.
  Adapted from: The strategy process : concepts, contexts, cases/
Henry Mintzberg and James Brian Quinn. 2nd ed. © 1991.
  Includes bibliographical references and index.
  ISBN 0-13-855370-X (pbk.)
  1. Strategic planning. I. Quinn, James Brian, 1928–
II. Mintzberg, Henry. Strategy process. III. Title.
HD30.28.Q53 1992
658.4'012—dc20
                                   91-40954
                                       CIP

Acquisitions Editor: *Alison Reeves*
Production Editor: *Edith Pullman*
Interior design: *Linda Rosa*
Cover Design: *Ray Lundgren*
Manufacturing Buyers: *Trudy Pisciotti and Robert Anderson*
Editorial Assistant: *Diane Pierano*

© 1992 by Prentice-Hall, Inc.
a Simon & Schuster Company
Englewood Cliffs, New Jersey 07632

Printed in the United States of America

10 9 8 7 6 5 4 3 2

ISBN   0-13-855370-X

Prentice-Hall International (UK) Limited, *London*
Prentice-Hall of Australia Pty. Limited, *Sydney*
Prentice-Hall Canada Inc., *Toronto*
Prentice-Hall Hispanoamericana, S.A., *Mexico*
Prentice-Hall of India Private Limited, *New Delhi*
Prentice-Hall of Japan, Inc., *Tokyo*
Simon & Schuster Asia Pte. Ltd., *Singapore*
Editora Prentice-Hall do Brasil, Ltda., *Rio de Janeiro*

To All Our Thoughtful Students Past and Future

CONTENTS

Acknowledgments

Introduction

SECTION ONE STRATEGY

SECTION TWO ORGANIZATION

SECTION THREE CONTEXT

ACKNOWLEDGMENTS

We have been involved in the teaching and practice of strategy formation since the 1960s. What originally brought this book together was our firm belief that this field badly needed a new kind of text. We wanted one that looked at process issues as well as analysis; one that was built around critical strategy concepts and contexts instead of the overworked dichotomy of formulation and implementation; and one that accomplished these aims with writing that was intelligent, eclectic, and lively. We sought to combine theory and practice, and description and prescription, in new ways that offered insights none could achieve alone. All of these goals remain exactly the same in this text only, which offers the concept and context but not the cases.

In any work of this scope, there are far too many people involved to thank each one individually. We would, however, like to acknowledge the special assistance given us by those who went especially out of their way to be helpful. In the academic community, several people deserve special mention. Deans John Hennessey and Colin Blaydon at the Tuck School kindly arranged for time and funding support. Mr. Bohdan Hawrylyshyn of the Institute for Management Development of Lausanne, Switzerland generously contributed funding and contacts. At INSEAD, Sumantra Goshal offered especially valuable advice on new readings to consider.

The people who really make such a major project as this happen are the competent research associates and secretaries who undertake the major burden of the work. At the Amos Tuck School of Business Administration, Penny C. Paquette, Suzanne Sweet, and Tammy Stebbins deserve special praise. Mrs. Sweet and Stebbins very professionally provided secretarial and computer skills that were invaluable. At McGill David Myles helped in all kinds of little ways, while Kate Maguire-Devlin's untold numbers of little contributions, important though they were, do not stand up to her big one—to provide a good-natured order without which the portions of this book could never have been finished.

At Prentice Hall, Karen Bernhaut and other professionals worked industriously on the book. But our experience at Prentice Hall started much earlier, with Alison Reeves, who championed this book from the beginning and then worked vigorously to see it through to the publication of the original and the second edition as well as this text only version. It was never easy, and we appreciate her extensive efforts.

A special thanks must also be offered to those who worked with the book in both its preliminary stages and in revision and offered invaluable feedback: in Montreal, those 1985-86 "guinea pig" McGill MBA students, and for this edition, Jan Jorgensen, Cynthia Hardy, and Tom Powell, who made many useful suggestions based on their teaching. Pierre Brunet and Bill Taylor at Concordia gave helpful comments on both editions, as did Fritz Reiger at Windsor. Bill Joyce and Rich D'Aveni at Tuck and Bill Davidson at the University of Southern California made significant contributions. Further feedback of great use was provided by those users of the first edition book who returned the Prentice Hall questionnaire. We are deeply indebted to all of these people. A special mention should be made of John Voyer at the University of Southern Maine, whose excellent advice, provided since the beginning, has helped to shape this book. We are particularly grateful to him, not only for that feedback and his key role in the Teaching Manual, but for his capacity to get inside the book—to appreciate it for exactly what it is—and so to have provided us with the best indication of what it might be able to accomplish.

One last word; this book is not "finished." Our text, like the subject of so much of its content, is an ongoing process, not a static statement. So much of this book is so different from conventional strategy textbooks, indeed from our own text last time, that there are bound to be all kinds of opportunities for improvement. We would like to ask you to help us in this regard. We shall revise the text again to improve it to keep up with this exciting field. Please write to any of us with your suggestions on how to improve the readings, and the organization of the book at large and its presentation. Strategy making, we believe, is a learning process; we are also engaged in a learning process. And for that we need your feedback. Thank you and enjoy what follows.

Henry Mintzberg
James Brian Quinn

INTRODUCTION

In our original version of *The Strategy Process, Concepts, Contexts, Cases,* we tried to provide the reader with a richness of theory, a richness of practice, and a strong basis for linkage between the two. We collaborated on this book because we believe that in this complex world of organizations, a range of concepts is needed to cut through and illuminate particular aspects of that complexity. There is no "one best way" to create strategy, nor is there "one best form" of organization. Quite different forms work well in particular contexts. We believe that exploring a fuller variety systematically will create a deeper and more useful appreciation of the strategy process. In this *Concept and Contexts* only version, we remain loyal to those intentions allowing the classroom users to adopt their own cases or to build on other experiences, while also making the book more accessible to those who wish to read only the text.

This text, unlike most others, is eclectic. Presenting published articles and portions of other books in their original form, rather than filtered through our minds and pens, is one way to reinforce this variety. Each author has his or her own ideas and his or her own best way of expressing them (ourselves included!). Summarized by us, these readings would lose a good deal of their richness.

We do not apologize for contradictions among the ideas of leading thinkers. The world is full of contradictions. The real danger lies in using pat solutions to a nuanced reality, not in opening perspectives up to different interpretations. The effective strategist is one who can live with contradictions, learn to appreciate their causes and effects, and reconcile them sufficiently for effective action. The readings have, nonetheless, been ordered by chapter to suggest some ways in which that reconciliation can be considered. Our own chapter introductions are also intended to assist in this task and to help place the readings themselves in perspective.

ON THEORY

A word on theory is in order. We do not consider theory a dirty word, nor do we apologize for making it a major component of this book. To some people, to be theoretical is to be detached, impractical. But a bright social scientist once said that "there is nothing so practical as a good theory." And every successful doctor, engineer, and physicist would have to agree: they would be unable to practice their modern work without theories. Theories are useful because they shortcut the need to store masses of data. It is easier to remember a simple framework about some phenomenon that it is to consider every detail you ever observed. In a sense, theories are a bit like cataloging systems in libraries: the world would be impossibly confusing without them. They enable one to store and conveniently access his or her own experiences as well as those of others.

One can, however, suffer not just from an absence of theories, but also from being dominated by them without realizing it. To paraphrase the words of John Maynard Keynes, most "practical men" are the slaves of some defunct theorist. Whether we realize it or not, our behavior is guided by the systems of ideas that we have internalized over the years. Much can be learned by bringing these out in the open, examining them more carefully, and comparing them with alternative ways to view the world—including ones based on systematic study (that is, research). One of our prime intentions in this book is to expose the limitations of conventional theories and to offer alternate explanations that can be superior guides to understanding and taking action in specific contexts.

Prescriptive Versus Descriptive Theory

Unlike many books in this field, this one tries to explain the world as it is, rather than as someone thinks it is *supposed* to be. Although there has sometimes been a tendency to disdain such *descriptive* theories, *prescriptive* (or normative) ones have often been the problem, rather than the solution, in the field of management. There is no one best way in management; no prescription works for all organizations. Even when a prescription seems effective in some context, it requires a sophisticated understanding of exactly what that context is and how it functions. In other words, one cannot decide reliably what should be done in a system as complicated as a contemporary organization without a genuine understanding of how that organization really works. In engineering, no student ever questions having to learn physics, in medicine, having to learn anatomy. Imagine an engineering student's hand shooting up in a physics class: "Listen, prof, it's fine to tell us how the atom does work. But what we really want to know is how the atom *should* work." Why should a management student's similar demand in the realm of strategy or structure be considered any more appropriate? How can people manage complex systems they do not understand?

Nevertheless, we have not ignored prescriptive theory when it appears useful. A number of prescriptive techniques (industry analysis, portfolio analysis, experience curves, etc.) are discussed. But these are associated both with other readings and with cases that will help understand the context and limitations of their usefulness. The readings offer opportunities to pursue the full complexity of strategic situations, addressing a wide range of issues and perspectives. One of our main goals is to integrate a variety of views, rather than allow strategy to be fragmented into just "human issues" and "economics issues." The text provides a basis for treating the full complexity of strategic management.

ON SOURCES

How were all the readings selected and edited? One popular textbook boasted a few years back that all its readings were published since 1980 (except one dated 1979!). We make no such claim; indeed we would like to make quite a different boast; many of our readings have been around quite a while, long enough to mature, like fine wine. Our criterion for inclusion was not the newness of the piece so much as the quality of its insight—that is, its ability to explain some aspect of the strategy process better than any other article. Time does not age the really good articles.

Quite the opposite—it distinguishes their quality (but sometimes it brings us back to the old habits of masculine gender; we apologize to our readers for this). We are, of course, not biased toward old articles—just toward good ones. Hence, the materials in this book range from classics of the 1950s to some published just before our final selection was made (as well as a few hitherto unpublished pieces). You will find articles from the most serious academic journals, the best practitioner magazines, books, and some very obscure sources. The best can sometimes be found in strange places!

We have opted to include many shorter readings rather than fewer longer ones, and we have tried to present as wide a varitey of good ideas as possible while maintaining clarity. To do so we often had to cut within readings. We have, in fact, put a great deal of effort into the cutting in order to extract the key messages of each reading in as brief, concise, and clear a manner as possible. Unfortunately, our cutting sometimes forced us to eliminate interesting examples and side issues. (In the readings, as well as some of the case materials from published sources, dots . . . signify portions that have been deleted from the original, while [square brackets] signify our own insertions of minor clarifications into the original text.) We apologize to you, the reader, as well as to the authors, for having done this, but hope that the overall result has rendered these changes worthwhile.

We have also included a number of our own works. Perhaps we are biased, having less objective standards by which to judge what we have written. But we have messages to convey, too, and our own writings do examine the basic themes that we feel are important in policy and strategy courses today.

ON STRUCTURE

Not Formulation, Then Implementation

This book offers a chapter format that has been new to the policy or strategy field. Unlike most others, it has no specific chapter or section devoted to "implementation" per se. The assumption in other texts is that strategy is formulated and then implemented, with organizational structures, control systems, and the like following obediently behind strategy. In this book, as in reality, formulation and implementation are intertwined as complex interactive processes in which politics, values, organizational culture, and management styles determine or constrain particular strategic decisions. And strategy, structure, and systems mix together in complicated ways to influence outcomes. While strategy formulation and implementation may be separated in some situations—perhaps in crises, in some totally new ventures, as well as in organizations facing predictable futures—these events are rare. We certainly do not believe in building a whole book (let alone a whole field) around this conceptual distinction.

But Concepts, Then Contexts

The readings are divided roughly into two different parts. The first deals with *concepts,* the second with *contexts.* We introduce strategy and structure as well as power, culture, and several other concepts early in the book as equal partners in the complex web of ideas that make up what we call "the strategy process." In the second half of the book we weave these concepts together in a number of distinct situations, which we call *contexts.*

Our theme diagram illustrates this. Concepts, shown on top, are divided into two groups—strategy and organization—to represent the first two sections of the book. Contexts draw all these concepts together, in a variety of situations—covered in the third section—which we consider the key ones in the field of strategy today (though hardly the only ones). The outline of the book, chapter by chapter, proceeds as follows:

Section I: Strategy

The first section is called "*Strategy*"; it comprises five chapters (two introductory in nature and three on the processes by which strategy making takes place). Chapter 1 introduces *the strategy concept* and probes the meaning of this important word to broaden your view of it. Here the pattern is set of challenging the reader to question conventional views, especially when these act to narrow perspectives. The themes introduced in this chapter carry throughout the book and are worth care in understanding.

Chapter 2 introduces a very important character in this book, *the strategist* as general manager. This person may not be the only one who makes strategy in an organization, but he or she is clearly a key player. In examining the work of the general manager and the character of his or her job, we shall perhaps upset a number of widely accepted notions. We do this to help understand the very real complexities and difficulties of making strategy and managing in contemporary organizations.

Chapters 3, 4, and 5 take up a theme that is treated extensively in the book—to the point of being reflected in its title: the development of an understanding of the *processes* by which strategies are made. Chapter 3 looks at *formulating strategy,* specifically at some widely accepted prescriptive models for how organizations should go about developing their strategies. Chapter 4 extends these ideas to more formal ways of doing *strategy analysis* and considering what, if any, "generic" forms a strategy can take. While readings in later chapters will challenge some of these precepts, what will not be questioned is the importance of having to understand them. They are fundamental to appreciating the strategy process today.

Chapter 5 switches from a prescriptive to a descriptive approach. Concerned with understanding *strategy formation,* it considers how strategies actually *do* form in organizations (not necessarily by being formulated) and *why* different processes may be effective in specific circumstances. This book takes an unconventional stand by viewing planning and other formal approaches as not the only—and often indeed not even the most desirable—ways to make strategy. This emphasis on the descriptive process—as an equal partner with the more traditional concerns for technical and analytical issues—is one of the unifying themes of this book.

Section II: Organization

In Section I, the readings introduced strategy, the strategist, and various ways in which strategy might be formulated and does in fact form. In Section II, entitled *Organization,* we introduce other concepts that constitute part of the strategy process.

In Chapter 6, we consider *structure and systems,* where particular attention is paid to the various forms that structure can take as well as the mechanisms that comprise it. In Chapter 7, we consider *culture,* especially how strong systems of beliefs, called "ideologies," impact on organizations and their strategies and so influence their effectiveness. In Chapter 8, *power* is the focus. We consider two aspects of power: first, the distribution of power among the various actors within the organization and its links to political activity; second, the organization as a political entity in its own right and its power to pursue its own ends, whether or not respon-

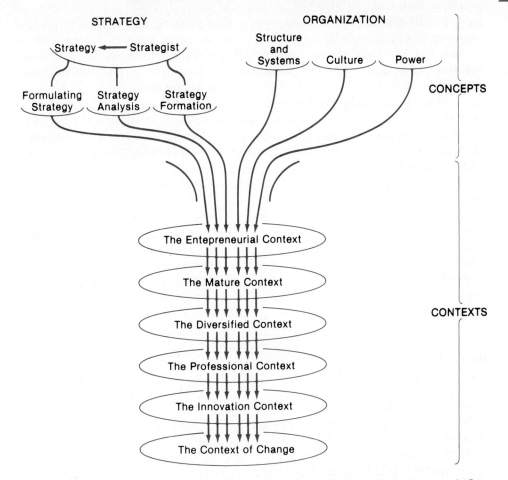

sibly, in the face of opposing forces in society. Both aspects will be seen to influence significantly the processes by which strategies are formulated or form.

Section III: Context

Section III is called *Context*. We consider how all of the elements introduced so far —strategy, the processes by which it is formulated and gets formed, the strategist, structure, systems, culture and power—combine to suit particular contexts, six in all.

Chapter 9 deals with the *entrepreneurial context*, where a rather simple organization comes under the close control of a strong leader, often a person with vision. Chapter 10 examines the *mature context*, one common to many large business and government organizations involved in the mass production or distribution of goods or services. Chapter 11 introduces the *diversified context*, and deals with organizations that have diversified their product or service lines and usually divisionalized their structures to deal with the greater varieties of environments they face.

Chapters 12 and 13 develop the contexts of professionalism and innovation, both involving organizations of high expertise. In the professional context, the experts work relatively independently in rather stable conditions, while in the innovation context, they combine in project teams under more dynamic conditions. What these two contexts have in common, however, is that they act in ways that upset many of the widely accepted notions about how organizations should be structured and make strategy.

In considering each of these widely different contexts, we seek to discuss (where appropriate material is available) the situations in which each is most likely to be found, the structures most suited to it, the kinds of strategies that tend to be pursued, the processes by which these strategies tend to be formed and might be formulated, and the social issues associated with the context.

Chapter 14 is devoted not so much to a specific context as to *managing change* between contexts, or within a context (which we can, of course, characterize as the context of change). The major concerns are how organizations can cope with crises, turnarounds, revitalizations, and new stages in their own life cycles or those of their key products.

The readings end in Chapter 15 on a provocative note, designed to encourage *thinking strategically,* about strategy itself and the whole process of management.

Well, there you have it. We have worked hard on this book to get it right. We have tried to think things through from the basics, with a resulting book that in style, format, and content is unusual for the field of policy or strategy. Our product may not be perfect, but we believe it is good—indeed better than any other text available. Now it's your turn to find out if you agree. Have fun doing so!

STRATEGY

THE STRATEGY CONCEPT

We open this text on its focal point: strategy. The first section is called "Strategy," the first chapter, "the Strategy Concept." Later chapters in this section describe the role of the general manager as strategist and consider the processes by which strategies get made from three perspectives: deliberate formulation, systematic analysis, and emergent formation. But in its opening chapter, we consider the central concept—strategy itself.

What is strategy anyway? There is no single, universally accepted definition. Different authors and managers use the term differently; for example, some include goals and objectives as part of strategy while others make firm distinctions between them. Our intention in including the following readings is not to promote any one view of strategy, but rather to suggest a number that seem useful. As will be evident throughout this text, our wish is not to narrow perspectives but to broaden them by trying to clarify issues. In pursuing these readings, it will be helpful to think about the meaning of strategy, to try to understand how different people have used the term, and, later, to see if certain definitions hold up better in particular contexts.

We have taken the opportunity to include in this first chapter readings by each of us, the two coauthors of the book. They set the tone for the material that follows and provide an indication of our own thinking. As you will see, our views are similar but certainly not identical; indeed in places we differ somewhat (for example, on the word "tactics"). But overall, we believe you will find these views complementary.

The first reading, by James Brian Quinn of the Amos Tuck Business School of Dartmouth College, provides a general overview by clarifying some of the vocabulary in this field and introducing a number of the themes that will appear throughout the text. In this reading from his book *Strategies for Change: Logical*

Incrementalism, Quinn places special emphasis on the military uses of the term and draws from this domain a set of essential "dimensions" or criteria for successful strategies. To derive these, he goes back to Philip and Alexander of Macedonia for his main example; he also provides a brief kaleidoscope of how similar concepts have influenced later military and diplomatic strategists.

Discussion of the military aspects of strategy must surely be among the oldest continuous literatures in the world. In fact, the origins of the word "strategy" go back even farther than this experience in Macedonia, to the Greeks whom Alexander and his father defeated. As Quinn notes and Roger Evered, in another article, elaborates,

> Initially *strategos* referred to a role (a general in command of an army). Later it came to mean "the art of the general," which is to say the psychological and behavioral skills with which he occupied the role. By the time of Pericles (450 B.C.) it came to mean managerial skill (administration, leadership, oration, power). And by Alexander's time (330 B.C.) it referred to the skill of employing forces to overcome opposition and to create a unified system of global governance. (1980:3)

The second reading, by Henry Mintzberg who teaches policy in the Faculty of Management at McGill University in Montreal, serves to open up the concept of strategy to a variety of views, some very different from traditional military or business writings (but suggested briefly in the Quinn reading). Mintzberg focuses on various distinct definitions of strategy—as plan (as well as ploy), pattern, position, and perspective. He uses the first two of these definitions to take us beyond *deliberate* strategy—beyond the traditional view of the term—to the notion of *emergent* strategy. This introduces the idea that strategies can *form* in an organization without being consciously intended, that is, without being *formulated.* This may seem to run counter to the whole thrust of the strategy literature, but Mintzberg argues that many people implicitly use the term this way even though they would not so define it.

Upon completion of these readings, we hope that you will be less sure of *the* use of the word strategy, but more ready to tackle the study of the strategy *process* with a broadened perspective and an open mind. There are no universally right answers in this field (any more than there are in most other fields), but there are interesting and constructive orientations.

• STRATEGIES FOR CHANGE*

BY JAMES BRIAN QUINN

SOME USEFUL DEFINITIONS

Because the words *strategy, objectives, goals, policy,* and *programs* . . . have different meanings to individual readers or to various organizational cultures, I [try] to

* Excerpted from James Brian Quinn, *Strategies for Change: Logical Incrementalism* (copyright © Richard D. Irwin, Inc., 1980), Chaps. 1 and 5; reprinted by permission of the publisher.

use certain definitions consistently ... For clarity—not pedantry—these are set forth as follows:

A **strategy** is the *pattern* or *plan* that *integrates* an organization's *major* goals, policies, and action sequences into a *cohesive* whole. A well-formulated strategy helps to *marshal* and *allocate* an organization's resources into a *unique and viable posture* based on its relative *internal competencies* and *shortcomings,* anticipated *changes in the environment,* and contingent moves by *intelligent opponents.*

Goals (or **objectives**) state *what* is to be achieved and *when* results are to be accomplished, but they do not state *how* the results are to be achieved. All organizations have multiple goals existing in a complex hierarchy (Simon, 1964): from value objectives, which express the broad value premises toward which the company is to strive; through overall organizational objectives, which establish the intended *nature* of the enterprise and the *directions* in which it should move; to a series of less permanent goals that define targets for each organizational unit, its subunits, and finally all major program activities within each subunit. Major goals —those that affect the entity's overall direction and viability—are called *strategic goals.*

Policies are rules or guidelines that express the *limits* within which action should occur. These rules often take the form of contingent decisions for resolving conflicts among specific objectives. For example: "Don't exceed three months' inventory in any item without corporate approval." Like the objectives they support, policies exist in a hierarchy throughout the organization. Major policies—those that guide the entity's overall direction and posture or determine its viability—are called *strategic policies.*

Programs specify the *step-by-step sequence of actions* necessary to achieve major objectives. They express *how* objectives will be achieved within the limits set by policy. They ensure that resources are committed to achieve goals, and they provide the dynamic track against which progress can be measured. Those major programs that determine the entity's overall thrust and viability are called *strategic programs.*

Strategic decisions are those that determine the overall direction of an enterprise and its ultimate viability in light of the predictable, the unpredictable, and the unknowable changes that may occur in its most important surrounding environments. They intimately shape the true goals of the enterprise. They help delineate the broad limits within which the enterprise operates. They dictate both the resources the enterprise will have accessible for its tasks and the principal patterns in which these resources will be allocated. And they determine the effectiveness of the enterprise—whether its major thrusts are in the right directions given its resource potentials—rather than whether individual tasks are performed efficiently. Management for efficiency, along with the myriad decisions necessary to maintain the daily life and services of the enterprise, is the domain of operations.

Strategies Versus Tactics

Strategies normally exist at many different levels in any large organization. For example, in government there are world trade, national economic, treasury department, military spending, investment, fiscal, monetary supply, banking, regional development, and local reemployment strategies—all related to each other somewhat hierarchically yet each having imperatives of its own. Similarly, businesses have numerous strategies from corporate levels to department levels within divisions. Yet if strategies exist at all these levels, how do strategies and tactics differ? Often the primary difference lies in the scale of action or the perspective of the leader. What appears to be a "tactic" to the chief executive officer (or general) may be a "strategy" to the marketing head (or lieutenant) if it determines the ultimate success and viability of his or her organization. In a more precise sense, tactics can occur at either level. They are the short-duration, adaptive, action-interaction realignments that opposing forces use to accomplish limited goals after their initial contact. Strategy defines a continuing basis for ordering these adaptations toward more broadly conceived purposes.

A genuine strategy is always needed when the potential actions or responses of intelligent opponents can seriously affect the endeavor's desired outcome—regardless of that endeavor's organizational level in the total enterprise. This condition almost always pertains to the important actions taken at the top level of competitive organizations. However, game theorists quickly point out that some important top-level actions—for example, sending a peacetime fleet across the Atlantic—merely require elaborate coordinative plans and programs (Von Neumann and Morgenstern, 1944; Shubik, 1975; McDonald, 1950). A whole new set of concepts, a true strategy, is needed if some people or nations decide to oppose the fleet's purposes. And it is these concepts that in large part distinguish strategic formulation from simpler programmatic planning.

Strategies may be looked at as either a priori statements to guide action or a posteriori results of actual decision behavior. In most complex organizations . . . one would be hard pressed to find a complete a priori statement of a total strategy that actually is followed. Yet often the existence of a strategy (or strategy change) may be clear to an objective observer, although it is not yet apparent to the executives making critical decisions. One, therefore, must look at the actual emerging *pattern* of the enterprise's operant goals, policies, and major programs to see what its true strategy is (Mintzberg, 1972). Whether it is consciously set forth in advance or is simply a widely held understanding resulting from a stream of decisions, this pattern becomes the real strategy of the enterprise. And it is changes in this pattern —regardless of what any formal strategic documents may say—that either analysts or strategic decision makers must address if they wish to comprehend or alter the concern's strategic posture. . . .

THE CLASSICAL APPROACH TO STRATEGY

Military-diplomatic strategies have existed since prehistoric times. In fact, one function of the earliest historians and poets was to collect the accumulated lore of these successful and unsuccessful life-and-death strategies and convert them into wisdom and guidance for the future. As societies grew larger and conflicts more complex, generals, statesmen, and captains studied, codified, and tested essential strategic concepts until a coherent body of principles seemed to emerge. In various forms these were ultimately distilled into the maxims of Sun Tzu (1963), Machiavelli (1950), Napoleon (1940), Von Clausewitz (1976), Foch (1970), Lenin (1927), Hart (1954), Montgomery (1958), or Mao Tse-Tung (1967). Yet with a few exceptions—largely introduced by modern technology—the most basic principles of strategy were in place and recorded long before the Christian era. More modern institutions primarily adapted and modified these to their own special environments.

Although one could choose any number of classical military-diplomatic strategies as examples, Philip and Alexander's actions at Chaeronea (in 338 B.C.) contain many currently relevant concepts (Varner and Alger, 1978; Green, 1970). . . .

A Grand Strategy

Philip and his young son, Alexander, had very *clear goals.* They sought to rid Macedonia of influence by the Greek city-states and to *establish dominance* over what was then essentially northern Greece. They also wanted Athens to *join a coalition* with them against Persia on their eastern flank. *Assessing their resources,* they *decided to avoid* the overwhelming superiority of the Athenian fleet and *chose to forego* attack on the powerful walled cities of Athens and Thebes where their superbly trained phalanxes and cavalry would not *have distinct advantages.*

Philip and Alexander *used an indirect approach* when an invitation by the Amphictyonic Council brought their army south to punish Amphissa. In a *planned sequence of actions and deceptive maneuvers,* they cut away from a direct line of march to Amphissa, *bypassed the enemy,* and *fortified a key base,* Elatea. They then took steps to *weaken their opponents politically and morally* by pressing restoration of the Phoenician communities earlier dispersed by the Thebans and by having Philip declared a champion of the Delphic gods. Then *using misleading messages* to make the enemy believe they had moved north to Thrace and also *using developed intelligence sources,* the Macedonians in a *surprise attack* annihilated the Greeks' positions near Amphissa. This *lured their opponents away from their defensive positions* in the nearby mountain passes to *consolidate their forces* near the town of Chaeronca.

There, *assessing the relative strengths* of their opponents, the Macedonians first *attempted to negotiate* to achieve their goals. When this was unsuccessful they had a *well-developed contingency plan* on how to *attack and overwhelm* the Greeks. Prior to this time, of course, the Macedonians had *organized* their troops into the famed phalanxes, and had *developed the full logistics* needed for their field support including a longer spear, which helped the Macedonian phalanxes penetrate the solid shield wall of the heavily massed Greek formations. *Using the natural advantages* of their grassy terrain, the Macedonians had developed cavalry support for their phalanxes' movements far beyond the Greek capability. Finally, using a *relative advantage*—the *command structure* their hierarchical *social system* allowed—against the more democratic Greeks, the Macedonian nobles had *trained their personnel* into one of the most *disciplined and highly motivated forces* in the world.

The Battle Strategy

Supporting this was the battle strategy at Chaeronea, which emerged as follows. Philip and Alexander first *analyzed their specific strengths and weaknesses and their opponents' current alignments and probable moves.* The Macedonian strength lay in their new spear technology, the *mobility* of their superbly disciplined phalanxes, and the powerful cavalry units led by Alexander. Their weaknesses were that they were badly outnumbered and faced—in the Athenians and the Theban Band—some of the finest foot troops in the world. However, their opponents had two weak points. One was the Greek left flank with lightly armed local troops placed near the Chaeronean Acropolis and next to some more heavily armed—but hastily assembled—hoplites bridging to the strong center held by the Athenians. The famed Theban Band anchored the Greek right wing near a swamp on the Cephissus River. [See Figure 1.]

Philip and Alexander *organized their leadership to command key positions;* Philip took over the right wing and Alexander the cavalry. They *aligned their forces* into *a unique posture* which *used their strengths* and *offset their weaknesses.* They decided on those spots at which they would *concentrate their forces,* what *positions to concede,* and what *key points* they *must take and hold.* Starting with their units angled back from the Greek lines (see map), they developed a *focused major thrust* against the Greek left wing and *attacked their opponents' weakness*—the troops near Chaeronea—with the most disciplined of the Macedonian units, the guards' brigade. After building up pressure and stretching the Greek line to its left, the guards' brigade abruptly began a *planned withdrawal.* This *feint* caused the Greek left to break ranks

FIGURE 1

The Battle of Chaeronea
Source: Modified with permission from P. Green, Alexander the Great, *Praeger Publishers, New York, 1970.*

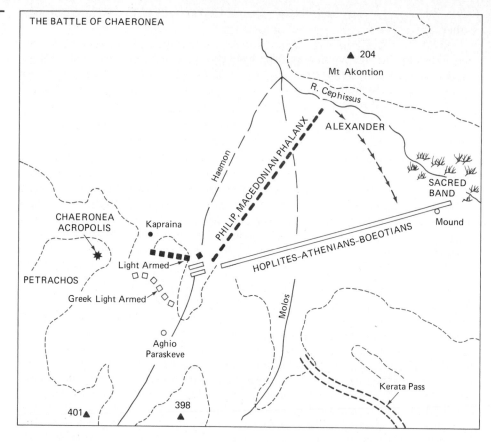

THE BATTLE OF CHAERONEA

and rush forward, believing the Macedonians to be in full retreat. This *stretched the opponents' resources* as the Greek center moved left to *maintain contact* with its flank and to attack the "fleeing" Macedonians.

Then *with predetermined timing,* Alexander's cavalry *attacked the exposure of* the stretched line at the same moment Philip's phalanxes *re-formed as planned* on the high ground at the edge of the Heamon River. Alexander *broke through* and *formed a bridgehead* behind the Greeks. He *refocused his forces against a segment* of the opponents' line; his cavalry *surrounded and destroyed* the Theban Band as the *overwhelming power* of the phalanxes poured through the gap he had created. From its *secured position,* the Macedonian left flank then turned and *attacked the flank* of the Athenians. With the help of Philip's *planned counterattack,* the Macedonians *expanded their dominance and overwhelmed the critical target,* i.e., the Greek center. . . .

Modern Analogies

Similar concepts have continued to dominate the modern era of formal strategic thought. As this period begins, Scharnhorst still points to the need to *analyze social forces and structures* as a basis for *understanding effective command styles* and *motivational stimuli* (Von Clausewitz, 1976:8). Frederick the Great proved this point in the field. Presumably based on such analyses, he adopted *training, discipline,* and *fast maneuvers* as the central concepts for a tightly disciplined German culture that had to be constantly ready to fight on two fronts (Phillips, 1940). Von Bülow (1806) continued to emphasize the dominant strategic roles of *geographical positioning* and *logistical support systems* in strategy. Both Jomini (1971) and Von Bülow (1806) stressed the concepts of *concentration, points of domination,* and *ra-*

pidity of movement as central strategic themes and even tried to develop them into mathematically precise principles for their time.

Still later Von Clausewitz expounded on the paramountcy of *clear major objectives* in war and on developing war strategies as a component of the nation's *broader goals* with *time horizons* extending beyond the war itself. Within this context he postulated that an effective strategy should be focused around a relatively *few central principles,* which can *create, guide,* and *maintain dominance* despite the enormous frictions that occur as one tries to position or maneuver large forces in war. Among these he included many of the concepts operant in Macedonian times: *spirit or morale, surprise, cunning, concentration in space, dominance of selected positions, use of strategic reserves, unification over time, tension and release,* and so on. He showed how these broad principles applied to a number of specific attack, defense, flanking, and retreat situations; but he always stressed the intangible of *leadership.* His basic positioning and organizational principles were to be mixed with boldness, perseverance, and genius. He constantly emphasized—as did Napoleon—the need for *planned flexibility* once the battle was joined.

Later strategic analysts adapted these classic themes for larger-scale conflicts. Von Schlieffen linked together the huge numerical and production *strengths* of Germany and the vast *maneuvering capabilities* of Flanders fields to pull the nation's might together conceptually behind a *unique alignment of forces* ("a giant hayrake"), which would *outflank* his French opponents, *attack weaknesses* (their supply lines and rear), capture and *hold key political centers* of France, and *dominate or destroy* its weakened army in the field (Tuchman, 1962). On the other side, Foch and Grandmaison saw *morale* ("élan"), *nerve* ("cran"), and continuous *concentrated attack* ("attaque à outrance") as *matching the values* of a volatile, recently defeated, and vengeful French nation, which had decided (for both moral and *coalition* reasons) to *set important limits* on its own actions in World War I— that is, not to attack first or through Belgium.

As these two strategies lost shape and became the head-on slaughter of trench warfare, Hart (1954) revitalized the *indirect approach,* and this became a central theme of British strategic thinking between the wars. Later in the United States, Matloff and Snell (1953) began to stress planning for *large-scale coalitions* as the giant forces of World War II developed. The Enigma group *moved secretly to develop the intelligence network* that was so crucial in the war's outcome (Stevenson, 1976). But once engaged in war, George Marshall still saw the only hope for Allied victory in *concentrating overwhelming forces* against one enemy (Germany) first, then after *conceding early losses* in the Pacific, *refocusing Allied forces* in a gigantic *sequential coordinated movement* against Japan. In the eastern theater, MacArthur first *fell back, consolidated a base* for operations, *built up his logistics, avoided his opponent's strengths, bypassed* Japan's established defensive positions, and in a *gigantic flanking maneuver* was ready to invade Japan after *softening its political and psychological will* through saturation bombing (James, 1970).

All these modern thinkers and practitioners utilized classical principles of strategy dating back to the Greek era, but perhaps the most startling analogies of World War II lay in Patton's and Rommel's battle strategies, which were almost carbon copies of the Macedonians' concepts of planned concentration, rapid breakthrough, encirclement, and attack on the enemy's rear (Essame, 1974; Farago, 1964; Irving, 1977; Young, 1974).

Similar concepts still pervade well-conceived strategies—whether they are government, diplomatic, military, sports, or business strategies. What could be more direct than the parallel between Chaeronea and a well-developed business strategy that first probes and withdraws to determine opponents' strengths, forces opponents to stretch their commitments, then concentrates resources, attacks a clear exposure, overwhelms a selected market segment, builds a bridgehead in that market, and then regroups and expands from that base to dominate a wider field? Many companies have followed just such strategies with great success. . . .

DIMENSIONS OF STRATEGY

Analysis of military-diplomatic strategies and similar analogies in other fields provides some essential insights into the basic dimensions, nature, and design of formal strategies.

First, effective formal strategies contain three essential elements: (1) the most important *goals* (or objectives) to be achieved, (2) the most significant *policies* guiding or limiting action, and (3) the major *action sequences* (or programs) that are to accomplish the defined goals within the limits set. Since strategy determines the overall direction and action focus of the organization, its formulation cannot be regarded as the mere generation and alignment of programs to meet predetermined goals. Goal development is an integral part of strategy formulation. . . .

Second, effective strategies develop around a *few key concepts and thrusts,* which give them cohesion, balance, and focus. Some thrusts are temporary; others are carried through to the end of the strategy. Some cost more per unit gain than others. Yet resources must be *allocated in patterns* that provide sufficient resources for each thrust to succeed regardless of its relative cost/gain ratio. And organizational units must be coordinated and actions controlled to support the intended thrust pattern or else the total strategy will fail. . . .

Third, strategy deals not just with the unpredictable but also with the *unknowable.* For major enterprise strategies, no analyst could predict the precise ways in which all impinging forces could interact with each other, be distorted by nature or human emotions, or be modified by the imaginations and purposeful counteractions of intelligent opponents (Braybrooke and Lindblom, 1963). Many have noted how large-scale systems can respond quite counterintuitively (Forrester, 1971) to apparently rational actions or how a seemingly bizarre series of events can conspire to prevent or assist success (White, 1978; Lindblom, 1959). . . .

Consequently, the essence of strategy—whether military, diplomatic, business, sports, (or) political . . .—is to *build a posture* that is so strong (and potentially flexible) in selective ways that the organization can achieve its goals despite the unforeseeable ways external forces may actually interact when the time comes.

Fourth, just as military organizations have multiple echelons of grand, theater, area, battle, infantry, and artillery strategies, so should other complex organizations have a number of hierarchically related and mutually supporting strategies (Vancil and Lorange, 1975; Vancil, 1976). Each such strategy must be more or less complete in itself, congruent with the level of decentralization intended. Yet each must be shaped as a cohesive element of higher-level strategies. Although, for reasons cited, achieving total cohesion among all of a major organization's strategies would be a superhuman task for any chief executive officer, it is important that there be a systematic means for testing each component strategy and seeing that it fulfills the major tenets of a well-formed strategy.

The criteria derived from military-diplomatic strategies provide an excellent framework for this, yet too often one sees purported formal strategies at all organizational levels that are not strategies at all. Because they ignore or violate even the most basic strategic principles, they are little more than aggregates of philosophies or agglomerations of programs. They lack the cohesiveness, flexibility, thrust, sense of positioning against intelligent opposition, and other criteria that historical analysis suggests effective strategies must contain. Whether formally or incrementally derived, strategies should be at least intellectually tested against the proper criteria.

Criteria for Effective Strategy

In devising a strategy to deal with the unknowable, what factors should one consider? Although each strategic situation is unique, are there some common criteria that tend to define a good strategy? The fact that a strategy worked in retrospect is not a sufficient criterion for judging any strategy. Was Grant really a greater strategist than Lee? Was Foch's strategy better than Von Schlieffen's? Was Xerxes's strategy superior to that of Leonidas? Was it the Russians' strategy that allowed them to roll over the Czechoslovaks in 1968? Clearly other factors than strategy—including luck, overwhelming resources, superb or stupid implementation, and enemy errors—help determine ultimate results. Besides, at the time one formulates a strategy, one cannot use the criterion of ultimate success because the outcome is still in doubt. Yet one clearly needs some guidelines to define an effective strategic structure.

A few studies have suggested some initial criteria for evaluating a strategy (Tilles, 1963; Christensen et al., 1978). These include its clarity, motivational impact, internal consistency, compatibility with the environment, appropriateness in light of resources, degree of risk, match to the personal values of key figures, time horizon, and workability. . . . In addition, historical examples—from both business and military-diplomatic settings—suggest that effective strategies should at a minimum encompass certain other critical factors and structural elements. . . .

- *Clear, decisive objectives:* Are all efforts directed toward clearly understood, decisive, and attainable overall goals? Specific goals of subordinate units may change in the heat of campaigns or competition, but the overriding goals of the strategy for all units must remain clear enough to provide continuity and cohesion for tactical choices during the time horizon of the strategy. All goals need not be written down or numerically precise, but they must be understood and be decisive—that is, if they are achieved they should ensure the continued viability and vitality of the entity vis-à-vis its opponents.

- *Maintaining the initiative:* Does the strategy preserve freedom of action and enhance commitment? Does it set the pace and determine the course of events rather than reacting to them? A prolonged reactive posture breeds unrest, lowers morale, and surrenders the advantage of timing and intangibles to opponents. Ultimately such a posture increases costs, decreases the number of options available, and lowers the probability of achieving sufficient success to ensure independence and continuity.

- *Concentration:* Does the strategy concentrate superior power at the place and time likely to be decisive? Has the strategy defined precisely what will make the enterprise superior in power—that is, "best" in critical dimensions—in relation to its opponents. A distinctive competency yields greater success with fewer resources and is the essential basis for higher gains (or profits) than competitors. . . .

- *Flexibility:* Has the strategy purposely built in resource buffers and dimensions for flexibility and maneuver? Reserved capabilities, planned maneuverability, and repositioning allow one to use minimum resources while keeping opponents at a relative disadvantage. As corollaries of concentration and concession, they permit the strategist to reuse the same forces to overwhelm selected positions at different times. They also force less flexible opponents to use more resources to hold predetermined positions, while simultaneously requiring minimum fixed commitment of one's own resources for defensive purposes.

- *Coordinated and committed leadership:* Does the strategy provide responsible, committed leadership for each of its major goals? . . . [Leaders] must be so chosen and motivated that their own interests and values match the needs of their roles. Successful strategies require commitment, not just acceptance.

- *Surprise:* Has the strategy made use of speed, secrecy, and intelligence to attack exposed or unprepared opponents at unexpected times? With surprise and correct timing, success can be achieved out of all proportion to the energy exerted and can decisively change strategic positions. . . .

- *Security:* Does the strategy secure resource bases and all vital operating points for the enterprise? Does it develop an effective intelligence system sufficient to prevent surprises by opponents? Does it develop the full logistics to support each of its major thrusts? Does it use coalitions effectively to extend the resource base and zones of friendly acceptance for the enterprise? . . .

These are critical elements of strategy, whether in business, government, or warfare.

- # FIVE Ps FOR STRATEGY*

HENRY MINTZBERG

Human nature insists on *a* definition for every concept. But the word *strategy* has long been used implicitly in different ways even if it has traditionally been defined in only one. Explicit recognition of multiple definitions can help people to maneuver through this difficult field. Accordingly, five definitions of strategy are presented here—as plan, ploy, pattern, position, and perspective—and some of their interrelationships are then considered.

STRATEGY AS PLAN

To almost anyone you care to ask, **strategy is a plan**—some sort of *consciously intended* course of action, a guideline (or set of guidelines) to deal with a situation. A kid has a "strategy" to get over a fence, a corporation has one to capture a market. By this definition, strategies have two essential characteristics: they are made in advance of the actions to which they apply, and they are developed consciously and purposefully. A host of definitions in a variety of fields reinforce this view. For example:

- in the military: Strategy is concerned with "draft[ing] the plan of war . . . shap[ing] the individual campaigns and within these, decid[ing] on the individual engagements" (Von Clausewitz, 1976:177).

- in Game Theory: Strategy is "a complete plan: a plan which specifies what

---

* Originally published in the *California Management Review* (Fall 1987), © 1987 by the Regents of the University of California. Reprinted with deletions by permission of the *California Management Review.*

choices [the player] will make in every possible situation" (von Newman and Morgenstern, 1944:79).

in management: "Strategy is a unified, comprehensive, and integrated plan . . . designed to ensure that the basic objectives of the enterprise are achieved" (Glueck, 1980:9).

As plans, strategies may be general or they can be specific. There is one use of the word in the specific sense that should be identified here. As plan, **a strategy can be a ploy,** too, really just a specific "maneuver" intended to outwit an opponent or competitor. The kid may use the fence as a ploy to draw a bully into his yard, where his Doberman pinscher awaits intruders. Likewise, a corporation may threaten to expand plant capacity to discourage a competitor from building a new plant. Here the real strategy (as plan, that is, the real intention) is the threat, not the expansion itself, and as such is a ploy.

In fact, there is a growing literature in the field of strategic management, as well as on the general process of bargaining, that views strategy in this way and so focuses attention on its most dynamic and competitive aspects. For example, in his popular book, *Competitive Strategy,* Porter (1980) devotes one chapter to "Market Signals" (including discussion of the effects of announcing moves, the use of "the fighting brand," and the use of threats of private antitrust suits) and another to "Competitive Moves" (including actions to preempt competitive response). And Schelling (1980) devotes much of his famous book, *The Strategy of Conflict,* to the topic of ploys to outwit rivals in a competitive or bargaining situation.

STRATEGY AS PATTERN

But if strategies can be intended (whether as general plans or specific ploys), surely they can also be realized. In other words, defining strategy as a plan is not sufficient; we also need a definition that encompasses the resulting behavior. Thus a third definition is proposed: **strategy is a pattern**—specifically, a pattern in a stream of actions (Mintzberg and Waters, 1985). By this definition, when Picasso painted blue for a time, that was a strategy, just as was the behavior of the Ford Motor Company when Henry Ford offered his Model T only in black. In other words, by this definition, strategy is *consistency* in behavior, *whether or not* intended.

This may sound like a strange definition for a word that has been so bound up with free will ("strategos" in Greek, the art of the army general[1]). But the fact of the matter is that while hardly anyone defines strategy in this way, many people seem at one time or another to so use it. Consider this quotation from a business executive: "Gradually the successful approaches merge into a pattern of action that becomes our strategy. We certainly don't have an overall strategy on this" (quoted in Quinn, 1980:35). This comment is inconsistent only if we restrict ourselves to one definition of strategy: what this man seems to be saying is that his firm has strategy as pattern, but not as plan. Or consider this comment in *Business Week* on a joint venture between General Motors and Toyota:

> The tentative Toyota deal may be most significant because it is another example of how GM's strategy boils down to doing a little bit of everything until the market decides where it is going. (*Business Week,* October 31, 1983)

---

[1] Evered (1983) discusses the Greek origins of the word and traces its entry into contemporary Western vocabulary through the military.

A journalist has inferred a pattern in the behavior of a corporation and labeled it strategy.

The point is that every time a journalist imputes a strategy to a corporation or to a government, and every time a manager does the same thing to a competitor or even to the senior management of his own firm, they are implicitly defining strategy as pattern in action—that is, inferring consistency in behavior and labeling it strategy. They may, of course, go further and impute intention to that consistency—that is, assume there is a plan behind the pattern. But that is an assumption, which may prove false.

Thus, the definitions of strategy as plan and pattern can be quite independent of each other: plans may go unrealized, while patterns may appear without preconception. To paraphrase Hume, strategies may result from human actions but not human designs (see Majone, 1976–77). If we label the first definition *intended* strategy and the second *realized* strategy, as shown in Figure 1, then we can distinguish *deliberate* strategies, where intentions that existed previously were realized, from *emergent* strategies, where patterns developed in the absence of intentions, or despite them (which went *unrealized*).

For a strategy to be truly deliberate—that is, for a pattern to have been intended *exactly* as realized—would seem to be a tall order. Precise intentions would have had to be stated in advance by the leadership of the organization; these would have had to be accepted as is by everyone else, and then realized with no interference by market, technological, or political forces and so on. Likewise, a truly emergent strategy is again a tall order, requiring consistency in action without any hint of intention. (No consistency means *no* strategy, or at least unrealized strategy.) Yet some strategies do come close enough to either form, while others—probably most—sit on the continuum that exists between the two, reflecting deliberate as well as emergent aspects. Table 1 lists various kinds of strategies along this continuum.

Strategies About What?

Labeling strategies as plans or patterns still begs one basic question: *strategies about what?* Many writers respond by discussing the deployment of resources, but the question remains: which resources and for what purposes? An army may plan to reduce the number of nails in its shoes, or a corporation may realize a pattern of

FIGURE 1
Deliberate and Emergent Strategies

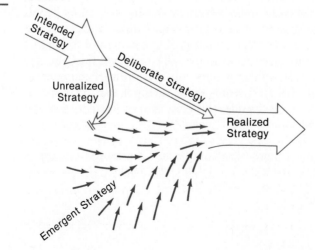

TABLE 1   Various Kinds of Strategies, from Rather Deliberate to Mostly Emergent*

Planned Strategy: Precise intentions are formulated and articulated by a central leadership, and backed up by formal controls to ensure their surprise-free implementation in an environment that is benign, controllable, or predictable (to ensure no distortion of intentions); these strategies are highly deliberate.

Entrepreneurial Strategy: Intentions exist as the personal, unarticulated vision of a single leader, and so are adaptable to new opportunities; the organization is under the personal control of the leader and located in a protected niche in its environment; these strategies are relatively deliberate but can emerge too.

Ideological Strategy: Intentions exist as the collective vision of all the members of the organization, controlled through strong shared norms; the organization is often proactive vis-à-vis its environment; these strategies are rather deliberate.

Umbrella Strategy: A leadership in partial control of organizational actions defines strategic targets or boundaries within which others must act (for example, that all new products be high priced and at the technological cutting edge, although what these actual products are to be is left to emerge); as a result, strategies are partly deliberate (the boundaries) and partly emergent (the patterns within them); this strategy can also be called deliberately emergent, in that the leadership purposefully allows others the flexibility to maneuver and form patterns within the boundaries.

Process Strategy: The leadership controls the process aspects of strategy (who gets hired and so gets a chance to influence strategy, what structures they work within, etc.), leaving the actual content of strategy to others; strategies are again partly deliberate (concerning process) and partly emergent (concerning content), and deliberately emergent.

Disconnected Strategy: Members or subunits loosely coupled to the rest of the organization produce patterns in the streams of their own actions in the absence of, or in direct contradiction to the central or common intentions of the organization at large; the strategies can be deliberate for those who make them.

Consensus Strategy: Through mutual adjustment, various members converge on patterns that pervade the organization in the absence of central or common intentions; these strategies are rather emergent in nature.

Imposed Strategy: The external environment dictates patterns in actions, either through direct imposition (say, by an outside owner or by a strong customer) or through implicitly preempting or bounding organizational choice (as in a large airline that must fly jumbo jets to remain viable); these strategies are organizationally emergent, although they may be internalized and made deliberate.

* Adapted from Mintzberg and Waters (1985:270).

marketing only products painted black, but these hardly meet the lofty label "strategy." Or do they?

As the word has been handed down from the military, "strategy" refers to the important things, "tactics" to the details (more formally, "tactics teaches the use of armed forces in the engagement, strategy the use of engagements for the object of the war," von Clausewitz, 1976:128). Nails in shoes, colors of cars; these are certainly details. The problem is that in retrospect details can sometimes prove "strategic." Even in the military: "For want of a Nail, the Shoe was lost; for want of a Shoe the Horse was lost . . . ," and so on through the rider and general to the battle, "all for want of Care about a Horseshoe Nail" (Franklin, 1977:280). Indeed one of the reasons Henry Ford lost his war with General Motors was that he refused to paint his cars anything but black.

Rumelt (1979) notes that "one person's strategies are another's tactics—that what is strategic depends on where you sit." It also depends on *when* you sit; what seems tactical today may prove strategic tomorrow. The point is that labels should not be used to imply that some issues are *inevitably* more important than others. There are times when it pays to manage the details and let the strategies emerge for themselves. Thus there is good reason to refer to issues as more or less "strategic," in other words, more or less "important" in some context, whether as intended before acting or as realized after it. Accordingly, the answer to the question, strategy about what, is: potentially about anything. About products and processes, customers and citizens, social responsibilities and self interests, control and color.

Two aspects of the content of strategies must, however, be singled out because they are of particular importance.

15

The fourth definition is that **strategy is a position**—specifically, a means of locating an organization in what organization theorists like to call an "environment." By this definition, strategy becomes the mediating force—or "match," according to Hofer and Schendel (1978:4)—between organization and environment, that is, between the internal and the external context. In ecological terms, strategy becomes a "niche"; in economic terms, a place that generates "rent" (that is "returns to [being] in a 'unique' place" (Bowman, 1974:47)); in management terms, formally, a product-market "domain" (Thompson, 1967), the place in the environment where resources are concentrated.

Note that this definition of strategy can be compatible with either (or all) of the preceding ones; a position can be preselected and aspired to through a plan (or ploy) and/or it can be reached, perhaps even found, through a pattern of behavior.

In military and game theory views of strategy, it is generally used in the context of what is called a "two-person game," better known in business as head-on competition (where ploys are especially common). The definition of strategy as position, however, implicitly allows us to open up the concept, to so-called n-person games (that is, many players), and beyond. In other words, while position can always be defined with respect to a single competitor (literally so in the military, where position becomes the site of battle), it can also be considered in the context of a number of competitors or simply with respect to markets or an environment at large. But strategy as position can extend beyond competition too, economic and otherwise. Indeed, what is the meaning of the word "niche" but a position that is occupied to *avoid* competition. Thus, we can move from the definition employed by General Ulysses Grant in the 1860s, "Strategy [is] the deployment of one's resources in a manner which is most likely to defeat the enemy," to that of Professor Richard Rumelt in the 1980s, "Strategy is creating situations for economic rents and finding ways to sustain them,"[2] that is, any viable position, whether or not directly competitive.

Astley and Fombrun (1983), in fact, take the next logical step by introducing the notion of "collective" strategy, that is, strategy pursued to promote cooperation between organizations, even would-be competitors (equivalent in biology to animals herding together for protection). Such strategies can range "from informal arrangements and discussions to formal devices such as interlocking directorates, joint ventures, and mergers" (p. 577). In fact, considered from a slightly different angle, these can sometimes be described as *political* strategies, that is strategies to subvert the legitimate forces of competition.

STRATEGY AS PERSPECTIVE

While the fourth definition of strategy looks out, seeking to locate the organization in the external environment, and down to concrete positions, the fifth looks inside the organization, indeed inside the heads of the collective strategist, but up to a broader view. Here, **strategy is a perspective,** its content consisting not just of a chosen position, but of an ingrained way of perceiving the world. There are organizations that favor marketing and build a whole ideology around that (an IBM); Hewlett-Packard has developed the "H-P way," based on its engineering culture,

---

[2] Expressed at the Strategic Management Society Conference, Montreal, October 1982.

while McDonald's has become famous for its emphasis on "quality, service, cleanliness, and value."

Strategy in this respect is to the organization what personality is to the individual. Indeed, one of the earliest and most influential writers on strategy (at least as his ideas have been reflected in more popular writings) was Philip Selznick (1957:47), who wrote about the "character" of an organization—distinct and integrated "commitments to ways of acting and responding" that are built right into it. A variety of concepts from other fields also capture this notion; anthropologists refer to the "culture" of a society and sociologists to its "ideology"; military theorists write of the "grand strategy" of armies; while management theorists have used terms such as the "theory of the business" and its "driving force" (Drucker, 1974; Tregoe and Zimmerman, 1980); and Germans perhaps capture it best with their word "Weltanschauung," literally "worldview," meaning collective intuition about how the world works.

This fifth definition suggests above all that strategy is a *concept*. This has one important implication, namely, that all strategies are abstractions which exist only in the minds of interested parties. It is important to remember that no one has ever seen a strategy or touched one; every strategy is an invention, a figment of someone's imagination, whether conceived of as intentions to regulate behavior before it takes place or inferred as patterns to describe behavior that has already occurred.

What is of key importance about this fifth definition, however, is that the perspective is *shared.* As implied in the words Weltanschauung, culture, and ideology (with respect to a society), but not the word personality, strategy is a perspective shared by the members of an organization, through their intentions and/or by their actions. In effect, when we are talking of strategy in this context, we are entering the realm of the *collective mind*—individuals united by common thinking and/or behavior. A major issue in the study of strategy formation becomes, therefore, how to read that collective mind—to understand how intentions diffuse through the system called organization to become shared and how actions come to be exercised on a collective yet consistent basis.

INTERRELATING THE Ps

As suggested above, strategy as both position and perspective can be compatible with strategy as plan and/or pattern. But, in fact, the relationships between these different definitions can be more involved than that. For example, while some consider perspective to *be* a plan (Lapierre, 1980, writes of strategies as "dreams in search of reality"), others describe it as *giving rise* to plans (for example, as positions and/or patterns in some kind of implicit hierarchy). But the concept of emergent strategy is that a pattern can emerge and be recognized so that it gives rise to a formal plan, perhaps within an overall perspective.

We may ask how perspective arises in the first place. Probably through earlier experiences: the organization tried various things in its formative years and gradually consolidated a perspective around what worked. In other words, organizations would appear to develop "character" much as people develop personality—by interacting with the world as they find it through the use of their innate skills and natural propensities. Thus pattern can give rise to perspective too. And so can position. Witness Perrow's (1970:161) discussion of the "wool men" and "silk men" of the textile trade, people who developed an almost religious dedication to the fibers they produced.

No matter how they appear, however, there is reason to believe that while plans and positions may be dispensable, perspectives are immutable (Brunsson,

1982). In other words, once they are established, perspectives become difficult to change. Indeed, a perspective may become so deeply ingrained in the behavior of an organization that the associated beliefs can become subconscious in the minds of its members. When that happens, perspective can come to look more like pattern than like plan—in other words, it can be found more in the consistency of behaviors than in the articulation of intentions.

Of course, if perspective is immutable, then change in plan and position within perspective is easy compared to change outside perspective. In this regard, it is interesting to take up the case of Egg McMuffin. Was this product when new— the American breakfast in a bun—a strategic change for the McDonald's fast-food chain? Posed in MBA classes, this earth-shattering (or at least stomach-shattering) question inevitably evokes heated debate. Proponents (usually people sympathetic to fast food) argue that of course it was: it brought McDonald's into a new market, the breakfast one, extending the use of existing facilities. Opponents retort that this is nonsense; nothing changed but a few ingredients: this was the same old pap in a new package. Both sides are, of course, right—and wrong. It simply depends on how you define strategy. Position changed; perspective remained the same. Indeed —and this is the point—the position could be changed easily because it was compatible with the existing perspective. Egg McMuffin is pure McDonald's, not only in product and package, but also in production and propagation. But imagine a change of position at McDonald's that would require a change of perspective—say, to introduce candlelight dining with personal service (your McDuckling à l'Orange cooked to order) to capture the late evening market. We needn't say more, except perhaps to label this the "Egg McMuffin syndrome."

THE NEED FOR ECLECTICISM IN DEFINITION

While various relationships exist among the different definitions, no one relationship, nor any single definition for that matter, takes precedence over the others. In some ways, these definitions compete (in that they can substitute for each other), but in perhaps more important ways, they complement. Not all plans become patterns nor are all patterns that develop planned; some ploys are less than positions, while other strategies are more than positions yet less than perspectives. Each definition adds important elements to our understanding of strategy, indeed encourages us to address fundamental questions about organizations in general.

As plan, strategy deals with how leaders try to establish direction for organizations, to set them on predetermined courses of action. Strategy as plan also raises the fundamental issue of cognition—how intentions are conceived in the human brain in the first place, indeed, what intentions really mean. The road to hell in this field can be paved with those who take all stated intentions at face value. In studying strategy as plan, we must somehow get into the mind of the strategist, to find out what is really intended.

As ploy, strategy takes us into the realm of direct competition, where threats and feints and various other maneuvers are employed to gain advantage. This places the process of strategy formation in its most dynamic setting, with moves provoking countermoves and so on. Yet ironically, strategy itself is a concept rooted not in change but in stability—in set plans and established patterns. How then to reconcile the dynamic notions of strategy as ploy with the static ones of strategy as pattern and other forms of plan?

As pattern, strategy focuses on action, reminding us that the concept is an empty one if it does not take behavior into account. Strategy as pattern also introduces the notion of convergence, the achievement of consistency in an organization's behavior. How does this consistency form, where does it come from? Realized strategy, when considered alongside intended strategy, encourages us to consider the notion that strategies can emerge as well as be deliberately imposed.

As position, strategy encourages us to look at organizations in their competitive environments—how they find their positions and protect them in order to meet competition, avoid it, or subvert it. This enables us to think of organizations in ecological terms, as organisms in niches that struggle for survival in a world of hostility and uncertainty as well as symbiosis.

And finally as perspective, strategy raises intriguing questions about intention and behavior in a collective context. If we define organization as collective action in the pursuit of common mission (a fancy way of saying that a group of people under a common label—whether a General Motors or a Luigi's Body Shop—somehow find the means to cooperate in the production of specific goods and services), then strategy as perspective raises the issue of how intentions diffuse through a group of people to become shared as norms and values, and how patterns of behavior become deeply ingrained in the group.

Thus, strategy is not just a notion of how to deal with an enemy or a set of competitors or a market, as it is treated in so much of the literature and in its popular usage. It also draws us into some of the most fundamental issues about organizations as instruments for collective perception and action.

To conclude, a good deal of the confusion in this field stems from contradictory and ill-defined uses of the term strategy. By explicating and using various definitions, we may be able to avoid some of this confusion, and thereby enrich our ability to understand and manage the processes by which strategies form.

CHAPTER

2

THE STRATEGIST

Every conventional strategy or policy textbook focuses on the job of the general manager as a main ingredient in understanding the process of strategy formation. The discussion of emergent strategy in the last chapter suggests that we do not take such a narrow view of the strategist. Anyone in the organization who happens to control key or precedent setting actions can be a strategist; the strategist can be a *collection* of people as well. Nevertheless, managers—especially senior general managers—are obviously prime candidates for such a role because their perspective is generally broader than any of their subordinates and because so much power naturally resides with them. Hence we focus in this chapter on the general manager as strategist.

We present three readings that describe the work of the manager. The one by Mintzberg challenges the conventional view of the manager as planner, organizer, coordinator, and controller. The point is not that managers do not do these things; it is that these words are too vague to capture the daily reality of managerial work. The image presented in this article is a very different one; a job characterized by pressure, interruption, orientation to action, oral rather than written communication, and working with outsiders and colleagues as much as with so-called subordinates. While the issue is not addressed at this point in any detail, one evident and important conclusion is that managers who work in such ways cannot possibly function as traditionally depicted strategists supposedly do—as leaders directing their organizations the way conductors direct their orchestras (at least the way it looks on the podium). We shall develop this point further in Chapter 5, when we consider how strategies really are formed in organizations.

The article by Edward Wrapp, of the University of Chicago and well known in management development circles, provides at least one widely referenced model illustrating how this does happen in large organizations. He depicts managers as somewhat political animals, providing broad guidance, but facilitating or pushing through their strategies, bit by bit, in rather unexpected ways. They rarely state specific goals. They practice "the art of imprecision," trying to "avoid policy straitjackets," while concentrating on only a few really significant issues. They move whenever possible through "corridors of comparative indifference" to avoid undue opposition, at the same time they are trying to ensure that the organization has a cohesive sense of direction. Wrapp's observations challenge the more prescriptive views of strategy formulation.

Philip Selznick, a famous Berkeley sociologist, offers another perspective on the manager as strategist in the third reading. It is not just his or her role in the *creation* of strategy so much as in its *institutionalization* that counts—the establishment of commitment among the people who make up the organization. In this reading, the full meaning of the view of strategy as perspective emerges—not as a calculated position but as a deep-rooted perspective. Selznick's brief but brilliant essay, written in the 1950s, introduced a number of concepts that subsequently became the foundation for much of our current thinking about business strategy (which, incidentally, both he and Wrapp refer to as "policy")—the selection of mission, the notion of distinctive competence, the definition of "organization character," and so on. Note also the differences between Selznick's and Wrapp's view of the manager, especially with regard to the articulation of purpose, or direction. Are they describing different contexts in which managers work? Might the two views sometimes be compatible in the same managerial job?

Selznick also discusses the role of values in managerial work, specifically the manager's role to "infuse [the organization] with value." Much strategy-making behavior is heavily influenced by values; individual managers looking at the same data may choose quite different strategies based on what they believe, that is, their values. Values provide the perceptive screen or "prism" through which individual managers sift and weigh different options, opportunities, or threats. They provide the "utility system" of the economist and the expectations of desired or unacceptable behavior that become the "culture" of an organization.

We introduce some of these concepts in our brief excerpts from Selznick's book to try to capture in his words ideas that will recur throughout the readings of this book. This reading is not always an easy one, and our editing of it may make it somewhat disjointed. But it is well worth your effort. The reading is brief, but it is an important premier statement on the role of leadership values in organizations. Peters and Waterman, in their book *In Search of Excellence,* refer to this "often-overlooked" book as "beautifully describ[ing]" these and other traits "basic to the success of the excellent companies" (1982:85, 98).

● THE MANAGER'S JOB: FOLKLORE AND FACT*

BY HENRY MINTZBERG

If you ask managers what they do, they will most likely tell you that they plan, organize, coordinate, and control. Then watch what they do. Don't be surprised if you can't relate what you see to these four words.

---

* Originally published in the *Harvard Business Review* (July–August 1975) and winner of the McKinsey prize for the best article in the *Review* in 1975. Copyright © 1975 by the President and Fellows of Harvard College; all rights reserved. Reprinted with deletions by permission of the *Harvard Business Review.*

When they are called and told that one of their factories has just burned down, and they advise the caller to see whether temporary arrangements can be made to supply customers through a foreign subsidiary, are they planning, organizing, coordinating, or controlling? How about when they present a gold watch to a retiring employee? Or when they attend a conference to meet people in the trade? Or on returning from that conference, when they tell one of their employees about an interesting product idea they picked up there?

The fact is that these four words, which have dominated management vocabulary since the French industrialist Henri Fayol first introduced them in 1916, tell us little about what managers actually do. At best, they indicate some vague objectives managers have when they work.

My intention in this article is simple: to break the reader away from Fayol's words and introduce him or her to a more supportable, and what I believe to be a more useful, description of managerial work. This description derives from my review and synthesis of the available research on how various managers have spent their time.

In some studies, managers were observed intensively ("shadowed" is the term some of them used); in a number of others, they kept detailed diaries of their activities; in a few studies, their records were analyzed. All kinds of managers were studied—foremen, factory supervisors, staff managers, field sales managers, hospital administrators, presidents of companies and nations, and even street gang leaders. These "managers" worked in the United States, Canada, Sweden, and Great Britain.

A synthesis of these findings paints an interesting picture, one as different from Fayol's classical view as a cubist abstract is from a Renaissance painting. In a sense, this picture will be obvious to anyone who has ever spent a day in a manager's office, either in front of the desk or behind it. Yet, at the same time, this picture may turn out to be revolutionary, in that it throws into doubt so much of the folklore that we have accepted about the manager's work.

I first discuss some of this folklore and contrast it with some of the findings of systematic research—the hard facts about how managers spend their time. Then I synthesize those research findings in a description of ten roles that seem to describe the essential content of all managers' jobs. In a concluding section, I discuss a number of implications of this synthesis for those trying to achieve more effective management.

SOME FOLKLORE AND FACTS ABOUT MANAGERIAL WORK

There are four myths about the manager's job that do not bear up under careful scrutiny of the facts.

Folklore: The manager is a reflective, systematic planner. The evidence on this issue is overwhelming, but not a shred of it supports this statement.

Fact: Study after study has shown that managers work at an unrelenting pace, that their activities are characterized by brevity, variety, and discontinuity, and that they are strongly oriented to action and dislike reflective activities. Consider this evidence:

- Half the activities engaged in by the five [American] chief executives [that I studied in my own research (Mintzberg, 1973a)] lasted less than nine minutes, and only 10% exceeded one hour. A study of 56 U.S. foremen found that they averaged 583 activities per eight-hour shift, an average of 1 every 48 seconds (Guest, 1956:478). The work pace for both chief executives and foremen was unrelenting. The chief executives met a steady stream of callers and mail from the moment they arrived in the morning until they left in the evening. Coffee breaks and lunches were inevitably work related, and ever-present subordinates seemed to usurp any free moment.

A diary study of 160 British middle and top managers found that they worked for a half hour or more without interruption only about once every two days (Stewart, 1967).

Of the verbal contacts of the chief executives in my study, 93% were arranged on an ad hoc basis. Only 1% of the executives' time was spent in open-ended observational tours. Only 1 out of 368 verbal contacts was unrelated to a specific issue and could be called general planning. Another researcher finds that "in *not one single case* did a manager report the obtaining of important external information from a general conversation or other undirected personal communication" (Aguilar, 1967:102).

No study has found important patterns in the way managers schedule their time. They seem to jump from issue to issue, continually responding to the needs of the moment.

Is this the planner that the classical view describes? Hardly. How, then, can we explain this behavior? The manager is simply responding to the pressures of the job. I found that my chief executives terminated many of their own activities, often leaving meetings before the end and interrupted their desk work to call in subordinates. One president not only placed his desk so that he could look down a long hallway but also left his door open when he was alone—an invitation for subordinates to come in and interrupt him.

Clearly, these managers wanted to encourage the flow of current information. But more significantly, they seemed to be conditioned by their own work loads. They appreciated the opportunity cost of their own time, and they were continually aware of their ever-present obligations—mail to be answered, callers to attend to, and so on. It seems that no matter what he or she is doing, the manager is plagued by the possibilities of what he or she might do and must do.

When the manager must plan, he or she seems to do so implicitly in the context of daily actions, not in some abstract process reserved for two weeks in the organization's mountain retreat. The plans of the chief executives I studied seemed to exist only in their heads—as flexible, but often specific, intentions. The traditional literature not-withstanding, the job of managing does not breed reflective planners; the manager is a real-time responder to stimuli, an individual who is conditioned by his or her job to prefer live to delayed action.

Folklore: The effective manager has no regular duties to perform. Managers are constantly being told to spend more time planning and delegating, and less time seeing customers and engaging in negotiations. These are not, after all, the true tasks of the manager. To use the popular analogy, the good manager, like the good conductor, carefully orchestrates everything in advance, then sits back to enjoy the fruits of his or her labor, responding occasionally to an unforeseeable exception. . . .

Fact: In addition to handling exceptions, managerial work involves performing a number of regular duties, including ritual and ceremony, negotiations, and proc-

essing of soft information that links the organization with its environment. Consider some evidence from the research studies:

- A study of the work of the presidents of small companies found that they engaged in routine activities because their companies could not afford staff specialists and were so thin on operating personnel that a single absence often required the president to substitute (Choran in Mintzberg, 1973a).
- One study of field sales managers and another of chief executives suggest that it is a natural part of both jobs to see important customers, assuming the managers wish to keep those customers (Davis, 1957; Copeman, 1963).
- Someone, only half in jest, once described the manager as that person who sees visitors so that everyone else can get his or her work done. In my study, I found that certain ceremonial duties—meeting visiting dignitaries, giving out gold watches, presiding at Christmas dinners—were an intrinsic part of the chief executive's job.
- Studies of managers' information flow suggest that managers play a key role in securing "soft" external information (much of it available only to them because of their status) and in passing it along to their subordinates.

Folklore: The senior manager needs aggregated information, which a formal management information system best provides. In keeping with the classical view of the manager as that individual perched on the apex of a regulated, hierarchical system, the literature's manager was to receive all important information from a giant, comprehensive MIS.

But this never proved true at all. A look at how managers actually process information makes the reason quite clear. Managers have five media at their command—documents, telephone calls, scheduled and unscheduled meetings, and observational tours.

Fact: Managers strongly favor the verbal media—namely, telephone calls and meetings. The evidence comes from every single study of managerial work: Consider the following:

- In two British studies, managers spent an average of 66% and 80% of their time in verbal (oral) communication (Stewart, 1967; Burns, 1954). In my study of five American chief executives, the figure was 78%.
- These five chief executives treated mail processing as a burden to be dispensed with. One came in Saturday morning to process 142 pieces of mail in just over three hours, to "get rid of all the stuff." This same manager looked at the first piece of "hard" mail he had received all week, a standard cost report, and put it aside with the comment, "I never look at this."
- These same five chief executives responded immediately to 2 of the 40 routine reports they received during the five weeks of my study and to four items in the 104 periodicals. They skimmed most of these periodicals in seconds, almost ritualistically. In all, these chief executives of good-sized organizations initiated on their own—that is, not in response to something else—a grand total of 25 pieces of mail during the 25 days I observed them.

An analysis of the mail the executives received reveals an interesting picture —only 13% was of specific and immediate use. So now we have another piece in the puzzle: not much of the mail provides live, current information—the action of a competitor, the mood of a government legislator, or the rating of last night's television show. Yet this is the information that drove the managers, interrupting their meetings and rescheduling their workdays.

Consider another interesting finding. Managers seem to cherish "soft" information, especially gossip, hearsay, and speculation. Why? The reason is its timeliness; today's gossip may be tomorrow's fact. The manager who is not accessible for the telephone call informing him or her that the firm's biggest customer was seen golfing with its main competitor may read about a dramatic drop in sales in the next quarterly report. But then it's too late.

Consider the words of Richard Neustadt, who studied the information-collecting habits of Presidents Roosevelt, Truman, and Eisenhower:

> It is not information of a general sort that helps a President see personal stakes; not summaries, not surveys, not the *bland amalgams*. Rather . . . it is the odds and ends of *tangible detail* that pieced together in his mind illuminate the underside of issues put before him. To help himself he must reach out as widely as he can for every scrap of fact, opinion, gossip, bearing on his interests and relationships as President. He must become his own director of his own central intelligence (1960:153–154; italics added).

The manager's emphasis on the verbal media raises two important points:

First, verbal information is stored in the brains of people. Only when people write this information down can it be stored in the files of the organization—whether in metal cabinets or on magnetic tape—and managers apparently do not write down much of what they hear. Thus the strategic data bank of the organization is not in the memory of its computers but in the minds of its managers.

Second, the managers' extensive use of verbal media helps to explain why they are reluctant to delegate tasks. When we note that most of the managers' important information comes in verbal form and is stored in their heads, we can well appreciate their reluctance. It is not as if they can hand a dossier over to someone; they must take the time to "dump memory"—to tell that someone all they know about the subject. But this could take so long that the managers may find it easier to do the task themselves. Thus the managers are damned by their own information systems to a "dilemma of delegation"—to do too much themselves or to delegate to their subordinates with inadequate briefing.

Folklore: Management is, or at least is quickly becoming, a science and a profession. By almost any definitions of *science* and *profession*, this statement is false. Brief observation of any manager will quickly lay to rest the notion that managers practice a science. A science involves the enaction of systematic, analytically determined procedures or programs. If we do not even know what procedures managers use, how can we prescribe them by scientific analysis? And how can we call management a profession if we cannot specify what managers are to learn?

Fact: The managers' programs—to schedule time, process information, make decisions, and so on—remain locked deep inside their brains. Thus, to describe these programs, we rely on words like *judgment* and *intuition,* seldom stopping to realize that they are merely labels for our ignorance.

I was struck during my study by the fact that the executives I was observing —all very competent by any standard—are fundamentally indistinguishable from their counterparts of a hundred years ago (or a thousand years ago, for that matter). The information they need differs, but they seek it in the same way—by word of mouth. Their decisions concern modern technology, but the procedures they use to make them are the same as the procedures of the nineteenth-century manager. In fact, the manager is in a kind of loop, with increasingly heavy work pressures but no aid forthcoming from management science.

Considering the facts about managerial work, we can see that the manager's job is enormously complicated and difficult. The manager is overburdened with obligations; yet he or she cannot easily delegate tasks. As a result, he or she is driven to overwork and is forced to do many tasks superficially. Brevity, fragmentation, and verbal communication characterize the work. Yet these are the very characteristics of managerial work that have impeded scientific attempts to improve it. As a result, the management scientists have concentrated their efforts on the specialized functions of the organization, where they could more easily analyze the procedures and quantify the relevant information. Thus the first step in providing managers with some help is to find out what their job really is.

BACK TO A BASIC DESCRIPTION OF MANAGERIAL WORK

Now let us try to put some of the pieces of this puzzle together. Earlier, I defined the manager as that person in charge of an organization or one of its subunits. Besides chief executive officers, this definition would include vice presidents, bishops, foremen, hockey coaches, and prime ministers. Can all of these people have anything in common? Indeed they can. For an important starting point, all are vested with formal authority over an organizational unit. From formal authority comes status, which leads to various interpersonal relations, and from these comes access to information. Information, in turn, enables the manager to make decisions and strategies for his or her unit.

The manager's job can be described in terms of various "roles," or organized sets of behaviors identified with a position. My description, shown in Figure 1, comprises ten roles.

Interpersonal Roles

Three of the manager's roles arise directly from formal authority and involve basic interpersonal relationships.

1. First is the *figurehead* role. By virtue of his or her position as head of an organizational unit, every manager must perform some duties of a ceremonial nature. The president greets the touring dignitaries, the foreman attends the wedding of a lathe operator, and the sales manager takes an important customer to lunch.

The chief executives of my study spend 12% of their contact time on ceremonial duties; 17% of their incoming mail dealt with acknowledgments and requests related to their status. For example, a letter to a company president requested free merchandise for a crippled schoolchild; diplomas were put on the desk of the school superintendent for his signature.

Duties that involve interpersonal roles may sometimes be routine, involving little serious communication and no important decision making. Nevertheless, they are important to the smooth functioning of an organization and cannot be ignored by the manager.

2. Because he or she is in charge of an organizational unit, the manager is responsible for the work of the people of that unit. His or her actions in this regard constitute the *leader* role. Some of these actions involve leadership directly—for

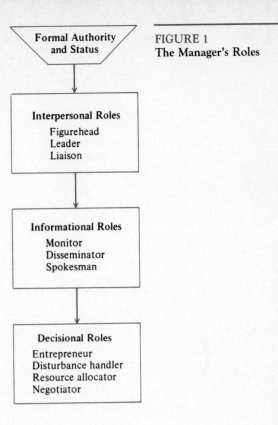

FIGURE 1
The Manager's Roles

example, in most organizations the manager is normally responsible for hiring and training his or her own staff.

In addition, there is the indirect exercise of the leader role. Every manager must motivate and encourage his or her employees, somehow reconciling their individual needs with the goals of the organization. In virtually every contact the manager has with these employees, subordinates seeking leadership clues probe his or her actions: "Does he approve?" "How would she like the report to turn out?" "Is he more interested in market share than high profits?"

The influence of managers is most clearly seen in the leader role. Formal authority vests them with great potential power; leadership determines in large part how much of it they will realize.

3. The literature of management has always recognized the leader role, particularly those aspects of it related to motivation. In comparison, until recently it has hardly mentioned the *liaison* role, in which the manager makes contacts outside his or her vertical chain of command. This is remarkable in light of the finding of virtually every study of managerial work that managers spend as much time with peers and other people outside their units as they do with their own subordinates —and, surprisingly, very little time with their own superiors (generally on the order of 45%, 45%, and 10% respectively).

The contacts the five CEOs made were with an incredibly wide range of people: subordinates; clients, business associates, and suppliers; and peers—managers of similar organizations, government and trade organization officials, fellow directors on outside boards, and independents with no relevant organizational affiliations. The chief executives' time with and mail from these groups is shown in Figure 2.

27

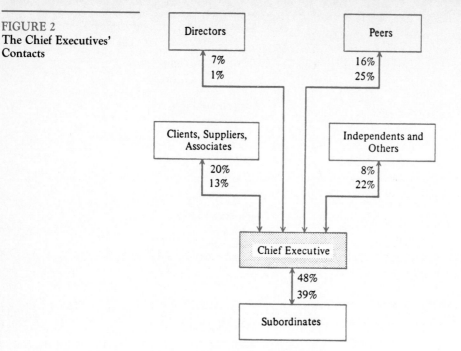

FIGURE 2
The Chief Executives' Contacts

As we shall see shortly, the manager cultivates such contacts largely to find information. In effect, the liaison role is devoted to building up the manager's own external information system—informal, private, verbal, but, nevertheless, effective.

Informational Roles

By virtue of their interpersonal contacts, both with subordinates and with their network of contacts, managers emerge as the nerve centers of their organizational units. They may not know everything, but they typically know more than any other member of their unit.

Studies have shown this relationship to hold for all managers, from street gang leaders to U.S. presidents. In *The Human Group,* George C. Homans (1950) explains how, because they were at the center of the information flow in their own gangs and were also in close touch with other gang leaders, street gang leaders were better informed than any of their followers. And Richard Neustadt describes the following account from his study of Franklin D. Roosevelt:

> The essence of Roosevelt's technique for information-gathering was competition. "He would call you in," one of his aides once told me, "and he'd ask you to get the story on some complicated business, and you'd come back after a couple of days of hard labor and present the juicy morsel you'd uncovered under a stone somewhere, and *then* you'd find out he knew all about it, along with something else you *didn't* know. Where he got this information from he wouldn't mention, usually, but after he had done this to you once or twice you got damn careful about *your* information." (1960:157).

We can see where Roosevelt "got this information" when we consider the relationship between the interpersonal and informational roles. As leaders, managers have formal and easy access to every member of their units. Hence, as noted earlier, they tend to know more about their own unit than anyone else does. In addition, their liaison contacts expose the managers to external information to which their subordinates often lack access. Many of these contacts are with other managers of equal status, who are themselves nerve centers in their own organization. In this way, managers develop powerful data bases of information.

The processing of information is a key part of the manager's job. In my study, the chief executives spent 40% of their contact time on activities devoted exclusively to the transmission of information; 70% of their incoming mail was purely informational (as opposed to requests for action). The manager does not leave meetings or hang up the telephone in order to get back to work. In large part, communication *is* his or her work. Three roles describe these informational aspects of managerial work.

4. As *monitor,* the manager perpetually scans the environment for information, interrogates his or her liaison contacts and subordinates, and receives unsolicited information, much of it as a result of the network of personal contacts he or she has developed. Remember that a good part of the information the manager collects in the monitor role arrives in verbal form, often as gossip, hearsay, and speculation. By virtue of his or her contacts, the manager has a natural advantage in collecting this soft information.

5. Managers must share and distribute much of this information. Information gleaned from outside personal contacts may be needed within the unit. In their *disseminator* roles, managers pass some of their privileged information directly to their subordinates, who would otherwise have no access to it. When their subordinates lack easy contact with one another, managers will sometimes pass information from one to another.

6. In their *spokesperson* roles, managers send some of their information to people outside their units—a president makes a speech to lobby for an organization cause, or a foreman suggests a product modification to a supplier. In addition, as part of their roles as spokesperson, every manager must inform and satisfy the influential people who control his or her organizational unit. Chief executives especially may spend great amounts of time with hosts of influencers. Directors and shareholders must be advised about financial performance; consumer groups must be assured that the organization is fulfilling its social responsibilities, and so on.

Decisional Roles

Information is not, of course, an end in itself; it is the basic input to decision making. One thing is clear in the study of managerial work: managers play the major role in their unit's decision-making system. As its formal authority, only they can commit the unit to important new courses of action; and as its nerve center, only they have full and current information to make the set of decisions that determine the unit's strategy. Four roles describe the manager as decision maker.

7. As *entrepreneur,* the manager seeks to improve the unit, to adapt it to changing conditions in the environment. In the monitor role, the president is constantly on the lookout for new ideas. When a good one appears, he or she initiates a development project that he or she may supervise himself or delegate to an employee (perhaps with the stipulation that he or she must approve the final proposal).

There are two interesting features about these development projects at the chief executive level. First, these projects do not involve single decisions or even unified clusters of decisions. Rather, they emerge as a series of small decisions and actions sequenced over time. Apparently, chief executives prolong each project so that they can fit it bit by bit into their busy, disjointed schedules and so that they can gradually come to comprehend the issue, if it is a complex one.

Second, the chief executives I studied supervised as many as 50 of these projects at the same time. Some projects entailed new products or processes; others involved public relations campaigns, improvement of the cash position, reorganization of a weak department, resolution of a morale problem in a foreign division, integration of computer operations, various acquisitions at different stages of development, and so on.

The chief executive appears to maintain a kind of inventory of the development projects that he or she supervises—projects that are at various stages of development, some active and some in limbo. Like a juggler, he or she keeps a number of projects in the air; periodically, one comes down, is given a new burst of energy, and is sent back into orbit. At various intervals, he or she puts new projects on-stream and discards old ones.

8. While the entrepreneur role describes the manager as the voluntary initiator of change, the *disturbance handler* role depicts the manager involuntarily responding to pressures. Here change is beyond the manager's control. A strike looms, a major customer has gone bankrupt, or a supplier reneges on his contract.

It has been fashionable, I noted earlier, to compare the manager to an orchestra conductor, just as Peter F. Drucker wrote in *The Practice of Management:*

> The manager has the task of creating a true whole that is larger than the sum of its parts, a productive entity that turns out more than the sum of the resources put into it. One analogy is the conductor of a symphony orchestra, through whose effort, vision and leadership individual instrumental parts that are so much noise by themselves become the living whole of music. But the conductor has the composer's score; he is only interpreter. The manager is both composer and conductor. (1954:341–342)

Now consider the words of Leonard R. Sayles, who has carried out systematic research on the manager's job:

> [The manager] is like a symphony orchestra conductor, endeavouring to maintain a melodious performance in which the contributions of the various instruments are co-ordinated and sequenced, patterned and paced, while the orchestra members are having various personal difficulties, stage hands are moving music stands, alternating excessive heat and cold are creating audience and instrument problems, and the sponsor of the concert is insisting on irrational changes in the program. (1964:162)

In effect, every manager must spend a good part of his or her time responding to high-pressure disturbances. No organization can be so well run, so standardized, that it has considered every contingency in advance. Disturbances arise not only because poor managers ignore situations until they reach crisis proportions, but also because good managers cannot possibly anticipate all the consequences of the actions they take.

9. The third decisional role is that of *resource allocator.* To the manager falls the responsibility of deciding who will get what in his or her organizational unit. Perhaps the most important resource the manager allocates is his or her own time. Access to the manager constitutes exposure to the unit's nerve center and decision-maker. The manager is also charged with designing the unit's structure, that pattern of formal relationships that determines how work is to be divided and coordinated.

Also, in his or her role as resource allocator, the manager authorizes the important decisions of the unit before they are implemented. By retaining this power, the manager can ensure that decisions are interrelated; all must pass through a single brain. To fragment this power is to encourage discontinuous decision making and a disjoined strategy.

10. The final decisional role is that of *negotiator.* Studies of managerial work at all levels indicate that managers spend considerable time in negotiations: the president of the football team is called in to work out a contract with the holdout superstar; the corporation president leads her company's contingent to negotiate a new stock issue; the foreman argues a grievance problem to its conclusion with the shop steward. As Leonard Sayles puts it, negotiations are a "way of life" for the sophisticated manager.

These negotiations are duties of the manager's job; perhaps routine, they are not to be shirked. They are an integral part of the job, for only the manager has the authority to commit organizational resources in "real time," and only he or she has the nerve center information that important negotiations require.

The Integrated Job

It should be clear by now that the ten roles I have been describing are not easily separable. In the terminology of the psychologist, they form a gestalt, an integrated whole. No role can be pulled out of the framework and the job be left intact. For example, a manager without liaison contacts lacks external information. As a result, he or she can neither disseminate the information employees need nor make decisions that adequately reflect external conditions. (In fact, this is a problem for the new person in a managerial position, since he or she cannot make effective decisions until he or she has built up his network of contacts.)

To say that the ten roles form a gestalt is not to say that all managers give equal attention to each role. In fact, I found in my review of the various research studies that

> . . . sales managers seem to spend relatively more of their time in the interpersonal roles, presumably a reflection of the extrovert nature of the marketing activity;
> . . . production managers give relatively more attention to the decisional roles, presumably a reflection of their concern with efficient work flow;
> . . . staff managers spend the most time in the informational roles, since they are experts who manage departments that advise other parts of the organization.

Nevertheless, in all cases the interpersonal, informational, and decisional roles remain inseparable.

CONCLUSION

No job is more vital to our society than that of the manager. It is the manager who determines whether our social institutions serve us well or whether they squander our talents and resources. It is time to strip away the folklore about managerial work, and time to study it realistically so that we can begin the difficult task of making significant improvements in its performance.

GOOD MANAGERS DON'T MAKE POLICY DECISIONS*

BY H. EDWARD WRAPP

The upper reaches of management are a land of mystery and intrigue. Very few people have ever been there, and the present inhabitants frequently send back messages that are incoherent both to other levels of management and to the world in general. This may account for the myths, illusions, and caricatures that permeate the literature of management—for example, such widely held notions as these:

- Life gets less complicated as a manager reaches the top of the pyramid.
- The manager at the top level knows everything that's going on in the organization, can command whatever resources he may need, and therefore can be more decisive.
- The general manager's day is taken up with making broad policy decisions and formulating precise objectives.
- The top executive's primary activity is conceptualizing long-range plans.
- In a large company, the top executive may be seen meditating about the role of his organization in society.

I suggest that none of these versions alone, or in combination, is an accurate portrayal of what a general manager does. Perhaps students of the management process have been overly eager to develop a theory and a discipline. As one executive I know puts it, "I guess I do some of the things described in the books and articles, but the descriptions are lifeless, and my job isn't."

What common characteristics, then, do successful executives exhibit *in reality?* I shall identify five skills or talents which, in my experience, seem especially significant. . . .

KEEPING WELL INFORMED

First, each of my heroes has a special talent for keeping himself informed about a wide range of operating decisions being made at different levels in the company. As he moves up the ladder, he develops a network of information sources in many different departments. He cultivates these sources and keeps them open no matter how high he climbs in the organization. When the need arises, he bypasses the lines on the organization chart to seek more than one version of a situation.

In some instances, especially when they suspect he would not be in total agreement with their decision, his subordinates will elect to inform him in advance, before they announce a decision. In these circumstances, he is in a position to defer the decision, or redirect it, or even block further action. However, he does not insist on this procedure. Ordinarily he leaves it up to the members of his organization to decide at what stage they inform him.

Top-level managers are frequently criticized by writers, consultants, and lower levels of management for continuing to enmesh themselves in operating

* Originally published in the *Harvard Business Review* (September–October 1967) and winner of the McKinsey prize for the best article in the *Review* in 1967. Copyright © 1967 by the President and Fellows of Harvard College; all rights reserved. Reprinted with deletions by permission of the *Harvard Business Review.*

problems, after promotion to the top, rather than withdrawing to the "big picture." Without any doubt, some managers do get lost in a welter of detail and insist on making too many decisions. Superficially, the good manager may seem to make the same mistake—but his purposes are different. He knows that only by keeping well informed about the decisions being made can he avoid the sterility so often found in those who isolate themselves from operations. If he follows the advice to free himself from operations, he may soon find himself subsisting on a diet of abstractions, leaving the choice of what he eats in the hands of his subordinates. As Kenneth Boulding puts it, "The very purpose of a hierarchy is to prevent information from reaching higher layers. It operates as an information filter, and there are little wastebaskets all along the way" (in *Business Week,* February 18, 1967:202). . . .

FOCUSING TIME AND ENERGY

The second skill of the good manager is that he knows how to save his energy and hours for those few particular issues, decisions, or problems to which he should give his personal attention. He knows the fine and subtle distinction between keeping fully informed about operating decisions and allowing the organization to force him into participating in these decisions or, even worse, making them. Recognizing that he can bring his special talents to bear on only a limited number of matters, he chooses those issues which he believes will have the greatest long-term impact on the company, and on which his special abilities can be most productive. Under ordinary circumstances he will limit himself to three or four major objectives during any single period of sustained activity.

What about the situations he elects *not* to become involved in as a decision maker? He makes sure (using the skill first mentioned) that the organization keeps him informed about them at various stages; he does not want to be accused of indifference to such issues. He trains his subordinates not to bring the matters to him for a decision. The communication to him from below is essentially one of: "Here is our sizeup, and here's what we propose to do." Reserving his hearty encouragement for those projects which hold superior promise of a contribution to total corporate strategy, he simply acknowledges receipt of information on other matters. When he sees a problem where the organization needs his help, he finds a way to transmit his know-how short of giving orders—usually by asking perceptive questions.

PLAYING THE POWER GAME

To what extent do successful top executives push their ideas and proposals through the organization? The rather common notion that the "prime mover" continually creates and forces through new programs, like a powerful majority leader in a liberal Congress, is in my opinion very misleading.

The successful manager is sensitive to the power structure in the organization. In considering any major current proposal, he can plot the position of the various individuals and units in the organization of a scale ranging from complete, outspoken support down to determined, sometimes bitter, and oftentimes well-cloaked opposition. In the middle of the scale is an area of comparative indifference. Usually, several aspects of a proposal will fall into this area, and *here is where he knows he can operate.* He assesses the depth and nature of the blocs in the organization. His perception permits him to move through what I call *corridors* of comparative indifference. He seldom challenges when a corridor is blocked, preferring to pause until it has opened up.

Related to this particular skill is his ability to recognize the need for a few trial-balloon launchers in the organization. He knows that the organization will tolerate only a certain number of proposals which emanate from the apex of the pyramid. No matter how sorely he may be tempted to stimulate the organization with a flow of his own ideas, he knows he must work through idea men in different parts of the organization. As he studies the reactions of key individuals and groups to the trial balloons these men send up, he is able to make a better assessment of how to limit the emasculation of the various proposals. For seldom does he find a proposal which is supported by all quarters of the organization. The emergence of strong support in certain quarters is almost sure to evoke strong opposition in others.

Value of Sense of Timing

Circumstances like these mean that a good sense of timing is a priceless asset for a top executive. . . . As a good manager stands at a point in time, he can identify a set of goals he is interested in, albeit the outline of them may be pretty hazy. His timetable, which is also pretty hazy, suggests that some must be accomplished sooner than others, and that some may be safely postponed for several months or years. He has a still hazier notion of how he can reach these goals. He assesses key individuals and groups. He knows that each has its own set of goals, some of which he understands rather thoroughly and others about which he can only speculate. He knows also that these individuals and groups represent blocks to certain programs or projects, and that these points of opposition must be taken into account. As the day-to-day operating decisions are made, and as proposals are responded to both by individuals and by groups, he perceives more clearly where the corridors of comparative indifference are. He takes action accordingly.

THE ART OF IMPRECISION

The fourth skill of the successful manager is knowing how to satisfy the organization that it has a sense of direction *without ever actually getting himself committed publicly to a specific set of objectives.* This is not to say that he does not have objectives—personal and corporate, long-term and short-term. They are significant guides to his thinking, and he modifies them continually as he better understands the resources he is working with, the competition, and the changing market demands. But as the organization clamors for statements of objectives, these are samples of what they get back from him:

> "Our company aims to be number one in its industry."
> "Our objective is growth with profit."
> "We seek the maximum return on investment."
> "Management's goal is to meet its responsibilities to stockholders, employees, and the public."

In my opinion, statements such as these provide almost no guidance to the various levels of management. Yet they are quite readily accepted as objectives by large numbers of intelligent people.

Why does the good manager shy away from precise statements of his objectives for the organization? The main reason is that he finds it impossible to set down specific objectives which will be relevant for any reasonable period into the future. Conditions in business change continually and rapidly, and corporate strategy must be revised to take the changes into account. The more explicit the statement of strategy, the more difficult it becomes to persuade the organization to turn to different goals when needs and conditions shift.

The public and the stockholders, to be sure, must perceive the organization as having a well-defined set of objectives and clear sense of direction. But in reality the good top manager is seldom so certain of the direction which should be taken. Better than anyone else, he senses the many, many threats to his company— threats which lie in the economy, in the actions of competitors, and, not least, within his own organization.

He also knows that it is impossible to state objectives clearly enough so that everyone in the organization understands what they mean. Objectives get communicated only over time by a consistency or pattern in operating decisions. Such decisions are more meaningful than words. In instances where precise objectives are spelled out, the organization tends to interpret them so they fit is own needs.

Subordinates who keep pressing for more precise objectives are in truth working against their own best interests. Each time the objectives are stated more specifically, a subordinate's range of possibilities for operating are reduced. The narrower field means less room to roam and to accommodate the flow of ideas coming up from his part of the organization.

Avoiding Policy Straitjackets

The successful manager's reluctance to be precise extends into the area of policy decisions. He seldom makes a forthright statement of policy. He may be aware that in some companies there are executives who spend more time in arbitrating disputes caused by stated policies than in moving the company forward. The management textbooks contend that well-defined policies are the sine qua non of a well-managed company. My research does not bear out this contention. For example,

> The president of one company with which I am familiar deliberately leaves the assignments of his top officers vague and refuses to define policies for them. He passes out new assignments with seemingly no pattern in mind and consciously sets up competitive ventures among his subordinates. His methods, though they would never be sanctioned by a classical organization planner, are deliberate—and, incidentally, quite effective.

Since able managers do not make policy decisions, does this mean that well-managed companies operate without policies? Certainly not. But the policies are those which evolve over time from an indescribable mix of operating decisions. From any single operating decision might have come a very minor dimension of the policy as the organization understands it; from a series of decisions comes a pattern of guidelines for various levels of the organization.

The skillful manager resists the urge to write a company creed or to compile a policy manual. Preoccupation with detailed statements of corporate objectives and departmental goals and with comprehensive organization charts and job descriptions—this is often the first symptom of an organization which is in the early stages of atrophy.

The "management by objectives" school, so widely heralded in recent years, suggests that detailed objectives be spelled out at all levels in the corporation. This method is feasible at lower levels of management, but it becomes unworkable at the upper levels. The top manager must think out objectives in detail, but ordinarily some of the objectives must be withheld, or at least communicated to the organization in modest doses. A conditioning process which may stretch over months or years is necessary in order to prepare the organization for radical departures from what it is currently striving to attain.

Suppose, for example, that a president is convinced his company must phase out of the principal business it has been in for 35 years. Although making this change of course is one of his objectives, he may well feel that he cannot disclose the idea even to his vice presidents, whose total know-how is in the present business. A blunt announcement that the company is changing horses would be too great a shock for most of them to bear. And so he begins moving toward this goal but without a full disclosure to his management group.

A detailed spelling out of objectives may only complicate the task of reaching them. Specific, detailed statements give the opposition an opportunity to organize its defenses.

MUDDLING WITH A PURPOSE

The fifth, and most important, skill I shall describe bears little relation to the doctrine that management is (or should be) a comprehensive, systematic, logical, well-programmed science. Of all the heresies set forth here, this should strike doctrinaires as the rankest of all!

The successful manager, in my observation, recognizes the futility of trying to push total packages or programs through the organization. He is willing to take less than total acceptance in order to achieve modest progress toward his goals. Avoiding debates on principles, he tries to piece together particles that may appear to be incidentals into a program that moves at least part of the way toward his objectives. His attitude is based on optimism and persistence. Over and over he says to himself, "There must be some parts of this proposal on which we can capitalize."

Whenever he identifies relationships among the different proposals before him, he knows that they present opportunities for combination and restructuring. It follows that he is a man of wide-ranging interests and curiosity. The more things he knows about, the more opportunities he will have to discover parts which are related. This process does not require great intellectual brilliance or unusual creativity. The wider ranging his interests, the more likely that he will be able to tie together several unrelated proposals. He is skilled as an analyst, but even more talented as a conceptualizer.

If the manager has built or inherited a solid organization, it will be difficult for him to come up with an idea which no one in the company has ever thought of before. His most significant contribution may be that he can see relationships which no one else has seen. . . .

Contrasting Pictures

It is interesting to note, in the writings of several students of management, the emergence of the concept that, rather than making decisions, the leader's principal task is maintaining operating conditions which permit the various decision-making systems to function effectively. The supporters of this theory, it seems to me, overlook the subtle turns of direction which the leader can provide. He cannot add purpose and structure to the balanced judgments of subordinates if he simply rubberstamps their decisions. He must weigh the issues and reach his own decision. . . .

Many of the articles about successful executives picture them as great thinkers who sit at their desks drafting master blueprints for their companies. The successful top executives I have seen at work do not operate this way. Rather than produce a full-grown decision tree, they start with a twig, help it grow, and ease themselves out on the limbs only after they have tested to see how much weight the limbs can stand.

In my picture, the general manager sits in the midst of a continuous stream of operating problems. His organization presents him with a flow of proposals to deal with the problems. Some of these proposals are contained in voluminous, well-documented, formal reports; some are as fleeting as the walk-in visit from a subordinate whose latest inspiration came during the morning's coffee break. Knowing how meaningless it is to say, "This is a finance problem," or, "That is a communications problem," the manager feels no compulsion to classify his problems. He is, in fact, undismayed by a problem that defies classification. As the late Gary Steiner, in one of his speeches, put it, "He has a high tolerance for ambiguity."

In considering each proposal, the general manager tests it against at least three criteria:

1. Will the total proposal—or, more often, will some part of the proposal— move the organization toward the objectives which he has in mind?

2. How will the whole or parts of the proposal be received by the various groups and sub-groups in the organization? Where will the strongest opposition come from, which group will furnish the strongest support, and which group will be neutral or indifferent?

3. How does the proposal relate to programs already in process or currently proposed? Can some parts of the proposal under consideration be added on to a program already under way, or can they be combined with all or parts of other proposals in a package which can be steered through the organization? . . .

CONCLUSION

To recapitulate, the general manager possesses five important skills. He knows how to

1. *Keep open many pipelines of information*—No one will quarrel with the desirability of an early warning system which provides varied viewpoints on an issue. However, very few managers know how to practice this skill, and the books on management add precious little to our understanding of the techniques which make it practicable.

2. *Concentrate on a limited number of significant issues*—No matter how skillful the manager is in focusing his energies and talents, he is inevitably caught up in a number of inconsequential duties. Active leadership of an organization demands a high level of personal involvement, and personal involvement brings with it many time-consuming activities which have an

infinitesimal impact on corporate strategy. Hence this second skill, while perhaps the most logical of the five, is by no means the easiest to apply.

3. *Identify the corridors of comparative indifference*—Are there inferences here that the good manager has no ideas of his own, that he stands by until his organization proposes solutions, that he never uses his authority to force a proposal through the organization? Such inferences are not intended. The message is that a good organization will tolerate only so much direction from the top; the good manager therefore is adept at sensing how hard he can push.

4. *Give the organization a sense of direction with open-ended objectives*—In assessing this skill, keep in mind that I am talking about top levels of management. At lower levels, the manager should be encouraged to write down his objectives, if for no other reason than to ascertain if they are consistent with corporate strategy.

5. *Spot opportunities and relationships in the stream of operating problems and decisions*—Lest it be concluded from the description of this skill that the good manager is more an improviser than a planner, let me emphasize that he is a planner and encourages planning by his subordinates. Interestingly, though, professional planners may be irritated by a good general manager. Most of them complain about his lack of vision. They devise a master plan, but the president (or other operating executive) seems to ignore it, or to give it minimum acknowledgment by borrowing bits and pieces for implementation. They seem to feel that the power of a good master plan will be obvious to everyone, and its implementation automatic. But the general manager knows that even if the plan is sound and imaginative, the job has only begun. The long, painful task of implementation will depend on his skill, not that of the planner. . . .

● LEADERSHIP IN ADMINISTRATION*

BY PHILIP SELZNICK

The nature and quality of leadership, in the sense of statesmanship, is an elusive but persistent theme in the history of ideas. Most writers have centered their attention on *political* statesmen, leaders of whole communities who sit in the high places where great issues are joined and settled. In our time, there is no abatement of the need to continue the great discussion, to learn how to reconcile idealism with expediency, freedom with organization.

But an additional emphasis is necessary. Ours is a pluralist society made up of many large, influential, relatively autonomous groups. The U.S. government itself consists of independently powerful agencies which do a great deal on their own initiative and are largely self-governing. These, and the institutions of industry, politics, education, and other fields, often command large resources; their leaders are inevitably responsible for the material and psychological well-being of numerous constituents; and they have become increasingly *public* in nature, attached to such interests and dealing with such problems as affect the welfare of the entire community. In our society the need for statesmanship is widely diffused and beset

---

* Excerpted from Philip Selznick, *Leadership in Administration: A Sociological Interpretation* (copyright © by Harper & Row, 1957); reprinted by permission of Harper & Row, Publishers, Inc.

by special problems. An understanding of leadership in both public and private organizations must have a high place on the agenda of social inquiry. . . .

The argument of this essay is quite simply stated: *The executive becomes a statesman as he makes the transition from administrative management to institutional leadership.* This shift entails a reassessment of his own tasks and of the needs of the enterprise. It is marked by a concern for the evolution of the organization as a whole, including its changing aims and capabilities. In a word, it means viewing the organization as an institution. To understand the nature of institutional leadership, we must have some notion of the meaning and significance of the term "institution" itself.

ORGANIZATIONS AND INSTITUTIONS

The most striking and obvious thing about an administrative organization is its formal system of rules and objectives. Here tasks, powers, and procedures are set out according to some officially approved pattern. This pattern purports to say how the work of the organization is to be carried on, whether it be producing steel, winning votes, teaching children, or saving souls. The organization thus designed is a technical instrument for mobilizing human energies and directing them toward set aims. We allocate tasks, delegate authority, channel communication, and find some way of coordinating all that has been divided up and parceled out. All this is conceived as an exercise in engineering; it is governed by the related ideals of rationality and discipline.

The term "organization" thus suggests a certain bareness, a lean, no-nonsense system of consciously coordinated activities (Barnard, 1938:73). It refers to an *expendable tool,* a rational instrument engineered to do a job. An "institution," on the other hand, is more nearly a natural product of social needs and pressures —a responsive, adaptive organism. This distinction is a matter of analysis, not of direct description. It does not mean that any given enterprise must be either one or the other. While an extreme case may closely approach either an "ideal" organization or an "ideal" institution, most living associations resist so easy a classification. They are complex mixtures of both designed and responsive behavior. . . .

In what is perhaps its most significant meaning, "to institutionalize" is to *infuse with value* beyond the technical requirements of the task at hand. The prizing of social machinery beyond its technical role is largely a reflection of the unique way in which it fulfills personal or group needs. Whenever individuals become attached to an organization or a way of doing things as persons rather than as technicians, the result is a prizing of the device for its own sake. From the standpoint of the committed person, the organization is changed from an expendable tool into a valued source of personal satisfaction. Some manifestations of this process are quite obvious; others are less easily recognized. It is commonplace that administrative changes are difficult when individuals have become habituated to and identified with long-established procedures. For example, the shifting of personnel is inhibited when business relations become personal ones and there is resistance to any change that threatens rewarding ties. A great deal of energy in organizations is expended in a continuous effort to preserve the rational, technical, impersonal system against such counterpressures. . . .

The test of infusion with value is *expendability.* If an organization is merely an instrument, it will be readily altered or cast aside when a more efficient tool becomes available. Most organizations are thus expendable. When value infusion takes place, however, there is a resistance to change. People feel a sense of personal loss; the "identity" of the group or community seems somehow to be violated; they bow to economic or technological considerations only reluctantly, with regret. A case in point is the perennial effort to save San Francisco's cable cars from replacement by more economical forms of transportation. The Marine Corps has this institutional halo, and it resists administrative measures that would submerge its identity. . . .

To summarize: organizations are technical instruments, designed as means to definite goals. They are judged on engineering premises; they are expendable. Institutions, whether conceived as groups or practices, may be partly engineered, but they have also a "natural" dimension. They are products of interaction and adaptation; they become the receptacles of group idealism; they are less readily expendable. . . .

THE DEFAULT OF LEADERSHIP

When institutional leadership fails, it is perhaps more often by default than by positive error or sin. Leadership is lacking when it is needed; and the institution drifts, exposed to vagrant pressures, readily influenced by short-run opportunistic trends. This default is partly a failure of nerve, partly a failure of understanding. It takes nerve to hold a course; it takes understanding to recognize and deal with the basic sources of institutional vulnerability.

One type of default is the failure to set goals. Once an organization becomes a "going concern," with many forces working to keep it alive, the people who run it can readily escape the task of defining its purposes. This evasion stems partly from the hard intellectual labor involved, a labor that often seems but to increase the burden of already onerous daily operations. In part, also, there is the wish to avoid conflicts with those in and out of the organization who would be threatened by a sharp definition of purpose, with its attendant claims and responsibilities. Even business firms find it easy to fall back on conventional phrases, such as that "our goal is to make profit," phrases which offer little guidance in the formulation of policy.

A critique of leadership, we shall argue, must include this emphasis on the leader's responsibility to define the mission of the enterprise. This view is not new. It is important because so much of administrative analysis takes the goal of the organization as given, whereas in many crucial instances this is precisely what is problematic. We shall also suggest that the analysis of goals is itself dependent on an understanding of the organization's social structure. In other words, the purposes we have or can have depend on what we are or what we can be. In statesmanship no less than in the search for personal wisdom, the Socratic dictum—know thyself—provides the ultimate guide.

Another type of default occurs when goals, however neatly formulated, enjoy only a superficial acceptance and do not genuinely influence the total structure of the enterprise. Truly accepted values must infuse the organization at many levels, affecting the perspectives and attitudes of personnel, the relative importance of staff activities, the distribution of authority, relations with outside groups, and many other matters. Thus if a large corporation asserts a wish to change its role in the community from a narrow emphasis on profit making to a larger social responsibility (even though the ultimate goal remains some combination of survival and profit-making ability), it must explore the implications of such a change for decision making in a wide variety of organizational activities. We shall stress that the task of building special values and a distinctive competence into the organization is a prime function of leadership. . . .

Finally, the role of the institutional leader should be clearly distinguished from that of the "interpersonal" leader. The latter's task is to smooth the path of human interaction, ease communication, evoke personal devotion, and allay anxiety. His expertness has relatively little to do with content; he is more concerned with persons than with policies. His main contribution is to the efficiency of the enterprise. The institutional leader, on the other hand, *is primarily an expert in the promotion and protection of values.* The interpretation that follows takes this idea as a starting point, exploring its meaning and implications. . . .

It is in the realm of policy—including the areas where policy formation and organization building meet—that the distinctive quality of institutional leadership is found. Ultimately, this is the quality of statesmanship which deals with current issues, not for themselves alone but according to their long-run implications for the role and meaning of the group. Group leadership is far more than the capacity to mobilize personal support; it is more than the maintenance of equilibrium through the routine solution of everyday problems; it is the function of the leader-statesman—whether of a nation or a private association—to define the ends of group existence, to design an enterprise distinctively adapted to these ends, and to see that that design becomes a living reality. These tasks are not routine; they call for continuous self-appraisal on the part of the leaders; and they may require only a few critical decisions over a long period of time. "Mere speed, frequency, and vigor in coming to decisions may have little relevance at the top executive level, where a man's basic contribution to the enterprise may turn on his making two or three significant decisions a year" (Learned, Ulrich, and Booz, 1951:57). This basic contribution is not always aided by the traits often associated with psychological leadership, such as aggressive self-confidence, intuitive sureness, ability to inspire. . . .

CHARACTER AS DISTINCTIVE COMPETENCE

In studying character we are interested in the *distinctive competence or inadequacy* that an organization has acquired. In doing so, we look beyond the formal aspects to examine the commitments that have been accepted in the course of adaptation to internal and external pressures. . . . Commitments to ways of acting and responding are built into the organization. When integrated, these commitments define the "character" of the organization. . . .

THE FUNCTIONS OF INSTITUTIONAL LEADERSHIP

We have argued that policy and administration are interdependent in the special sense that certain areas of organizational activity are peculiarly sensitive to policy matters. Because these areas exist, creative men are needed—more in some circumstances than in others—who know how to transform a neutral body of men into a committed polity. These men are called leaders; their profession is politics. . . .

Leadership sets goals, but in doing so takes account of the conditions that have already determined what the organization can do and to some extent what it must do. Leadership creates and molds an organization embodying—in thought and feeling and habit—the value premises of policy. Leadership reconciles internal strivings and environmental pressures, paying close attention to the way adaptive behavior brings about changes in organizational character. When an organization lacks leadership, these tasks are inadequately fulfilled, however expert the flow of paper and however smooth the channels of communication and command. And this fulfillment requires a continuous scrutiny of how the changing social structure affects the evolution of policy.

The relation of leadership to organizational character may be more closely explored if we examine some of the key tasks leaders are called on to perform:

1. *The definition of institutional mission and role.* The setting of goals is a creative task. It entails a self-assessment to discover the true commitments of the organization, as set by effective internal and external demands. The failure to set aims in the light of these commitments is a major source of irresponsibility in leadership.

2. *The institutional embodiment of purpose.* The task of leadership is not only to make policy but to build it into the organization's social structure. This, too, is a creative task. It means shaping the "character" of the organization, sensitizing it to ways of thinking and responding, so that increased reliability in the execution and elaboration of policy will be achieved according to its spirit as well as its letter.

3. *The defense of institutional integrity.* The leadership of any polity fails when it concentrates on sheer survival: institutional survival, properly understood, is a matter of maintaining values and distinctive identity. This is at once one of the most important and least understood functions of leadership. This area (like that of defining institutional mission) is a place where the intuitively knowledgeable leader and the administrative analyst often part company, because the latter has no tools to deal with it. The fallacy of combining agencies on the basis of "logical" association of functions is a characteristic result of the failure to take account of institutional integrity.

4. *The ordering of internal conflict.* Internal interest groups form naturally in large-scale organizations, since the total enterprise is in one sense a polity composed of a number of suborganizations. The struggle among competing interests always has a high claim on the attention of leadership. This is so because the direction of the enterprise as a whole may be seriously influenced by changes in the internal balance of power. In exercising control, leadership has a dual task. It must win the consent of constituent units, in order to maximize voluntary cooperation, and therefore must permit emergent interest blocs a wide degree of representation. At the same time, in order to hold the helm, it must see that a balance of power appropriate to the fulfillment of key commitments will be maintained.

FORMULATING STRATEGY

Most of what has been published in this field deals with how strategy *should* be designed or consciously *formulated.* On the prescription of how this should be accomplished, there has been a good deal of consensus, although, as we shall see later, this is now eroding. Perhaps we should more properly conclude that there have been two waves of consensus. The first, which developed in the 1960s, is presented in this chapter; the second, which emerged around 1980, did not challenge the first so much as build on it. This is presented in Chapter 4.

Ken Andrews of the Harvard Business School is the person most commonly associated with the first wave, although Bill Newman of Columbia wrote on some of these issues much earlier and Igor Ansoff simultaneously outlined very similar views while he was at Carnegie-Mellon. But the Andrews text became the best known, in part because it was so simply and clearly written, in part because it was embodied in a popular textbook (with cases) emanating from the Harvard Business School.

We reproduce parts of the Andrews text (as revised in its own publication in 1980, but based on the original 1965 edition). These serve to introduce the basic point that strategy, ultimately, requires the achievement of fit between the external situation (opportunities and threats) and internal capability (strengths and weaknesses). Note how the Andrews approach builds directly on some of the military concepts outlined earlier. Both seek to leverage the impact of resources by concentrating efforts within a defined zone of dominance while attempting to anticipate the effects of potentially damaging external forces. In reading the Andrews excerpts, you may also be struck by the relationship in spirit—and indeed sometimes in detail—to the Selznick material of the last chapter.

As you read the Andrews text, a number of basic premises will quickly become evident. Among these are: the clear distinction made between strategy formulation and strategy implementation (in effect, between thinking and action); the belief that strategy (or at least intended strategy) should be made explicit; the notion that structure should follow strategy (in other words, be designed in accordance with it); and the assumption that strategy emanates from the formal leadership of the organization. Similar premises underlie most of the prescriptive literature of strategic management.

This model (if we can call it that) has proven very useful in many circumstances as a broad way to analyze a strategic situation and to think about making strategy. A careful strategist should certainly touch all the bases suggested in this approach. But in many circumstances the model cannot or should not be followed to the letter, as shall be discussed in Chapter 5 and later ones.

The Rumelt reading elaborates on one element in this traditional model—the evaluation of strategies. While the Andrews text contains a similar discussion, Rumelt, a graduate of the Harvard Business School and policy professor at UCLA, develops it in a particularly elegant way, helping to round out this chapter on the classical view of formulating strategy.

● THE CONCEPT OF CORPORATE STRATEGY*

BY KENNETH R. ANDREWS

THE STRATEGY CONCEPT

What Strategy Is

Corporate strategy is the pattern of decisions in a company that determines and reveals its objectives, purposes, or goals, produces the principal policies and plans for achieving those goals, and defines the range of business the company is to pursue, the kind of economic and human organization it is or intends to be, and the nature of the economic and noneconomic contribution it intends to make to its shareholders, employees, customers, and communities. . . .

The strategic decision contributing to this pattern is one that is effective over long periods of time, affects the company in many different ways, and focuses and commits a significant portion of its resources to the expected outcomes. The pattern resulting from a series of such decisions will probably define the central character and image of a company, the individuality it has for its members and various publics, and the position it will occupy in its industry and markets. It will permit the specification of particular objectives to be attained through a timed sequence investment and implementation decisions and will govern directly the deployment or redeployment of resources to make these decisions effective.

Some aspects of such a pattern of decision may be in an established corporation unchanging over long periods of time, like a commitment to quality, or high technology, or certain raw materials, or good labor relations. Other aspects of a strategy must change as or before the world changes, such as product line, manu-

---

* Excerpted from Kenneth R. Andrews, *The Concept of Corporate Strategy*, rev. ed. (copyright © by Richard D. Irwin, Inc., 1980), Chaps. 2 and 3; reprinted by permission of the publisher.

facturing process, or merchandising and styling practices. The basic determinants of company character, if purposefully institutionalized, are likely to persist through and shape the nature of substantial changes in product-market choices and allocation of resources. . . .

It is important, however, not to take the idea apart in another way, that is, to separate goals from the policies designed to achieve those goals. The essence of the definition of strategy I have just recorded is *pattern.* The interdependence of purposes, policies, and organized action is crucial to the particularity of an individual strategy and its opportunity to identify competitive advantage. It is the unity, coherence, and internal consistency of a company's strategic decisions that position the company in its environment and give the firm its identity, its power to mobilize its strengths, and its likelihood of success in the marketplace. It is the interrelationship of a set of goals and policies that crystallizes from the formless reality of a company's environment a set of problems an organization can seize upon and solve.

What you are doing, in short, is never meaningful unless you can say or imply what you are doing it for: the quality of administrative action and the motivation lending it power cannot be appraised without knowing its relationship to purpose. Breaking up the system of corporate goals and the character-determining major policies for attainment leads to narrow and mechanical conceptions of strategic management and endless logic chopping. . . .

Summary Statements of Strategy

Before we proceed to clarification of this concept by application, we should specify the terms in which strategy is usually expressed. A summary statement of strategy will characterize the product line and services offered or planned by the company, the markets and market segments for which products and services are now or will be designed, and the channels through which these markets will be reached. The means by which the operation is to be financed will be specified, as will the profit objectives and the emphasis to be placed on the safety of capital versus level of return. Major policy in central functions such as marketing, manufacturing, procurement, research and development, labor relations, and personnel, will be stated where they distinguish the company from others, and usually the intended size, form, and climate of the organization will be included.

Each company, if it were to construct a summary strategy from what it understands itself to be aiming at, would have a different statement with different categories of decision emphasized to indicate what it wanted to be or do. . . .

Formulation of Strategy

Corporate strategy is an organization process, in many ways inseparable from the structure, behavior, and culture of the company in which it takes place. Nevertheless, we may abstract from the process two important aspects, interrelated in real life but separable for the purposes of analysis. The first of these we may call *formulation,* the second *implementation.* Deciding what strategy should be may be approached as a rational undertaking, even if in life emotional attachments . . . may complicate choice among future alternatives. . . .

The principal subactivities of strategy formulation as a logical activity include identifying opportunities and threats in the company's environment and attaching some estimate or risk to the discernible alternatives. Before a choice can be made, the company's strengths and weaknesses should be appraised together with the resources on hand and available. Its actual or potential capacity to take advantage of perceived market needs or to cope with attendant risks should be estimated as objectively as possible. The strategic alternative which results from matching opportunity and corporate capability at an acceptable level of risk is what we may call an *economic strategy.*

The process described thus far assumes that strategists are analytically objective in estimating the relative capacity of their company and the opportunity they see or anticipate in developing markets. The extent to which they wish to undertake low or high risk presumably depends on their profit objectives. The higher they set the latter, the more willing they must be to assume a correspondingly high risk that the market opportunity they see will not develop or that the corporate competence required to excel competition will not be forthcoming.

So far we have described the intellectual processes of ascertaining what a company *might do* in terms of environmental opportunity, of deciding what it *can do* in terms of ability and power, and of bringing these two considerations together in optimal equilibrium. The determination of strategy also requires consideration of what alternatives are preferred by the chief executive and perhaps by his or her immediate associates as well, quite apart from economic considerations. Personal values, aspirations, and ideals do, and in our judgment quite properly should, influence the final choice of purposes. Thus what the executives of a company *want to do* must be brought into the strategic decision.

Finally strategic choice has an ethical aspect—a fact much more dramatically illustrated in some industries than in others. Just as alternatives may be ordered in terms of the degree of risk that they entail, so may they be examined against the standards of responsiveness to the expectations of society that the strategist elects. Some alternatives may seem to the executive considering them more attractive than others when the public good or service to society is considered. What a company *should do* thus appears as a fourth element of the strategic decision. . . .

The Implementation of Strategy

Since effective implementation can make a sound strategic decision ineffective or a debatable choice successful, it is as important to examine the processes of implementation as to weigh the advantages of available strategic alternatives. The implementation of strategy is comprised of a series of subactivities which are primarily administrative. If purpose is determined, then the resources of a company can be mobilized to accomplish it. An organizational structure appropriate for the efficient performance of the required tasks must be made effective by information systems and relationships permitting coordination of subdivided activities. The organizational processes of performance measurement, compensation, management development—all of them enmeshed in systems of incentives and controls—must be directed toward the kind of behavior required by organizational purpose. The role of personal leadership is important and sometimes decisive in the accomplishment of strategy. Although we know that organization structure and processes of compensation, incentives, control, and management development influence and constrain the formulation of strategy, we should look first at the logical proposition that structure should follow strategy in order to cope later with the organizational reality that strategy also follows structure. When we have examined both tendencies, we will understand and to some extent be prepared to deal with the interdependence of the formulation and implementation of corporate purpose. Figure 1 may be useful in understanding the analysis of strategy as a pattern of interrelated decisions. . . .

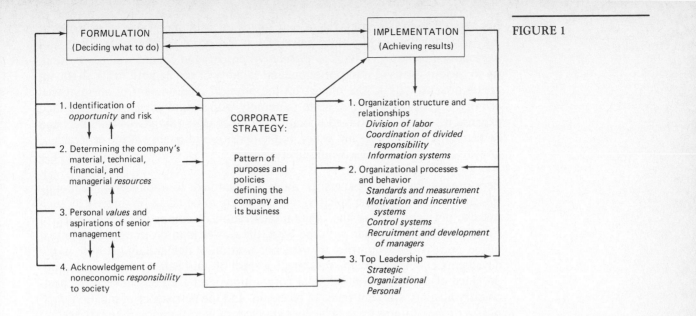

FIGURE 1

Figure 1 content:

FORMULATION (Deciding what to do)

IMPLEMENTATION (Achieving results)

1. Identification of *opportunity* and risk

2. Determining the company's material, technical, financial, and managerial *resources*

3. Personal *values* and aspirations of senior management

4. Acknowledgement of noneconomic *responsibility* to society

CORPORATE STRATEGY:

Pattern of purposes and policies defining the company and its business

1. Organization structure and relationships
   Division of labor
   Coordination of divided responsibility
   Information systems

2. Organizational processes and behavior
   Standards and measurement
   Motivation and incentive systems
   Control systems
   Recruitment and development of managers

3. Top Leadership
   Strategic
   Organizational
   Personal

RELATING OPPORTUNITIES TO RESOURCES

Determination of a suitable strategy for a company begins in identifying the opportunities and risks in its environment. This [discussion] is concerned with the identification of a range of strategic alternatives, the narrowing of this range by recognizing the constraints imposed by corporate capability, and the determination of one or more economic strategies at acceptable levels of risk. . . .

The Nature of the Company's Environment

The environment of an organization in business, like that of any other organic entity, is the pattern of all the external conditions and influences that affect its life and development. The environmental influences relevant to strategic decision operate in a company's industry, the total business community, its city, its country, and the world. They are technological, economic, physical, social, and political in kind. The corporate strategist is usually at least intuitively aware of these features of the current environment. But in all these categories change is taking place at varying rates—fastest in technology, less rapidly in politics. Change in the environment of business necessitates continuous monitoring of a company's definition of its business, lest it falter, blur, or become obsolete. Since by definition the formulation of strategy is performed with the future in mind, executives who take part in the strategic planning process must be aware of those aspects of their company's environment especially susceptible to the kind of change that will affect their company's future.

Technology: From the point of view of the corporate strategist, technological developments are not only the fastest unfolding but the most far-reaching in extending or contracting opportunity for an established company. They include the discoveries of science, the impact of related product development, the less dramatic machinery and process improvements, and the progress of automation and data processing. . . .

47

Ecology: It used to be possible to take for granted the physical characteristics of the environment and find them favorable to industrial development. Plant sites were chosen using criteria like availability of process and cooling water, accessibility to various forms of transportation, and stability of soil conditions. With the increase in sensitivity to the impact on the physical environment of all industrial activity, it becomes essential, often to comply with law, to consider how planned expansion and even continued operation under changing standards will affect and be perceived to affect the air, water, traffic density, and quality of life generally of any area which a company would like to enter. . . .

Economics: Because business is more accustomed to monitoring economic trends than those in other spheres, it is less likely to be taken by surprise by such massive developments as the internationalization of competition, the return of China and Russia to trade with the West, the slower than projected development of the Third World countries, the Americanization of demand and culture in the developing countries and the resulting backlash of nationalism, the increased importance of the large multinational corporations and the consequences of host-country hostility, the recurrence of recession, and the persistence of inflation in all phases of the business cycle. The consequences of world economic trends need to be monitored in much greater detail for any one industry or company.

Industry: Although the industry environment is the one most company strategists believe they know most about, the opportunities and risks that reside there are often blurred by familiarity and the uncritical acceptance of the established relative position of competitors. . . .

Society: Social development of which strategists keep aware include such influential forces as the quest for equality for minority groups, the demand of women for opportunity and recognition, the changing patterns of work and leisure, the effects of urbanization upon the individual, family, and neighborhood, the rise of crime, the decline of conventional morality, and the changing composition of world population.

Politics: The political forces important to the business firm are similarly extensive and complex—the changing relations between communist and noncommunist countries (East and West) and between prosperous and poor countries (North and South), the relation between private enterprise and government, between workers and management, the impact of national planning on corporate planning, and the rise of what George Lodge (1975) calls the communitarian ideology. . . .

Although it is not possible to know or spell out here the significance of such technical, economic, social, and political trends, and possibilities for the strategist of a given business or company, some simple things are clear. Changing values will lead to different expectations of the role business should perform. Business will be expected to perform its mission not only with economy in the use of energy but with sensitivity to the ecological environment. Organizations in all walks of life will be called upon to be more explicit about their goals and to meet the needs and aspirations (for example, for education) of their membership.

In any case, change threatens all established strategies. We know that a thriving company—itself a living system—is bound up in a variety of interrelationships with larger systems comprising its technological, economic, ecological, social, and political environment. If environmental developments are destroying and creating business opportunities, advance notice of specific instances relevant to a single company is essential to intelligent planning. Risk and opportunity in the last quarter of the twentieth century require of executives a keen interest in what is going on outside their companies. More than that, a practical means of tracking developments promising good or ill, and profit or loss, needs to be devised. . . .

For the firm that has not determined what its strategy dictates it needs to know or has not embarked upon the systematic surveillance of environmental change, a few simple questions kept constantly in mind will highlight changing opportunity and risk. In examining your own company or one you are interested in, these questions should lead to an estimate of opportunity and danger in the present and predicted company setting.

1. What are the essential economic, technical, and physical characteristics of the industry in which the company participates? . . .
2. What trends suggesting future change in economic and technical characteristics are apparent? . . .
3. What is the nature of competition both within the industry and across industries? . . .
4. What are the requirements for success in competition in the company's industry? . . .
5. Given the technical, economic, social, and political developments that most directly apply, what is the range of strategy available to any company in this industry? . . .

Identifying Corporate Competence and Resources

The first step in validating a tentative choice among several opportunities is to determine whether the organization has the capacity to prosecute it successfully. The capability of an organization is its demonstrated and potential ability to accomplish, against the opposition of circumstance or competition, whatever it sets out to do. Every organization has actual and potential strengths and weaknesses. Since it is prudent in formulating strategy to extend or maximize the one and contain or minimize the other, it is important to try to determine what they are and to distinguish one from the other.

It is just as possible, though much more difficult, for a company to know its own strengths and limitations as it is to maintain a workable surveillance of its changing environment. Subjectivity, lack of confidence, and unwillingness to face reality may make it hard for organizations as well as for individuals to know themselves. But just as it is essential, though difficult, that a maturing person achieve reasonable self-awareness, so an organization can identify approximately its central strength and critical vulnerability. . . .

To make an effective contribution to strategic planning, the key attributes to be appraised should be identified and consistent criteria established for judging them. If attention is directed to strategies, policy commitments, and past practices in the context of discrepancy between organization goals and attainment, an outcome useful to an individual manager's strategic planning is possible. The assessment of strengths and weaknesses associated with the attainment of specific objectives becomes in Stevenson's (1976) words a "key link in a feedback loop" which allows managers to learn from the success or failures of the policies they institute.

Although [a] study by Stevenson did not find or establish a systematic way of developing or using such knowledge, members of organizations develop judgments about what the company can do particularly well—its core of competence. If consensus can be reached about this capability, no matter how subjectively arrived at, its application to identified opportunity can be estimated.

Sources of Capabilities: The powers of a company constituting a resource for growth and diversification accrue primarily from experience in making and marketing a product line or providing a service. They inhere as well in (1) the developing strengths and weaknesses of the individuals comprising the organization, (2) the degree to which individual capability is effectively applied to the common task, and (3) the quality of coordination of individual and group effort.

The experience gained through successful execution of a strategy centered upon one goal may unexpectedly develop capabilities which could be applied to different ends. Whether they should be so applied is another question. For example, a manufacturer of salt can strengthen his competitive position by offering his customers salt-dispensing equipment. If, in the course of making engineering improvements in this equipment, a new solenoid principle is perfected that has application to many industrial switching problems, should this patentable and marketable innovation be exploited? The answer would turn not only on whether economic analysis of the opportunity shows this to be a durable and profitable possibility, but also on whether the organization can muster the financial, manufacturing, and marketing strength to exploit the discovery and live with its success. The former question is likely to have a more positive answer than the latter. In this connection, it seems important to remember that individual and unsupported flashes of strength are not as dependable as the gradually accumulated product and market-related fruits of experience.

Even where competence to exploit an opportunity is nurtured by experience in related fields, the level of that competence may be too low for any great reliance to be placed upon it. Thus a chain of children's clothing stores might well acquire the administrative, merchandising, buying, and selling skills that would permit it to add departments in women's wear. Similarly, a sales force effective in distributing typewriters might gain proficiency in selling office machinery and supplies. But even here it would be well to ask what *distinctive* ability these companies could bring to the retailing of soft goods or office equipment to attract customers away from a plethora of competitors.

Identifying Strengths: The distinctive competence of an organization is more than what it can do; it is what it can do particularly well. To identify the less obvious or by-product strengths of an organization that may well be transferable to some more profitable new opportunity, one might well begin by examining the organization's current product line and by defining the functions it serves in its markets. Almost any important consumer product has functions which are related to others into which a qualified company might move. The typewriter, for example, is more than the simple machine for mechanizing handwriting that it once appeared to be when looked at only from the point of view of its designer and manufacturer. Closely analyzed from the point of view of the potential user, the typewriter is found to contribute to a broad range of information processing functions. Any one of these might have suggested an area to be exploited by a typewriter manufacturer. Tacitly defining a typewriter as a replacement for a fountain pen as a writing instrument rather than as an input-output device for word processing is the explanation provided by hindsight for the failure of the old-line typewriter companies to develop before IBM did the electric typewriter and the computer-related input-output devices it made possible. The definition of product which would lead to identification of transferable skills must be expressed in terms of the market needs it may fill rather than the engineering specifications to which it conforms.

Besides looking at the uses or functions to which present products contribute, the would-be diversifier might profitably identify the skills that underlie whatever success has been achieved. The qualifications of an organization efficient at performing its long-accustomed tasks come to be taken for granted and considered humdrum, like the steady provision of first-class service. The insight required to identify the essential strength justifying new ventures does not come naturally. Its cultivation can probably be helped by recognition of the need for analysis. In any case, we should look beyond the company's capacity to invent new products. Product leadership is not possible for a majority of companies, so it is fortunate that patentable new products are not the only major highway to new opportunities. Other avenues include new marketing services, new methods of distribution, new values in quality-price combinations, and creative merchandising. The effort to find or to create a competence that is truly distinctive may hold the real key to a company's success or even to its future development. For example, the ability of a cement manufacturer to run a truck fleet more effectively than its competitors may constitute one of its principal competitive strengths in selling an undifferentiated product.

Matching Opportunity and Competence: The way to narrow the range of alternatives, made extensive by imaginative identification of new possibilities, is to match opportunity to competence, once each has been accurately identified and its future significance estimated. It is this combination which establishes a company's economic mission and its position in its environment. The combination is designed to minimize organizational weakness and to maximize strength. In every case, risk attends it. And when opportunity seems to outrun present distinctive competence, the willingness to gamble that the latter can be built up to the required level is almost indispensable to a strategy that challenges the organization and the people in it. Figure 2 diagrams the matching of opportunity and resources that results in an economic strategy.

Before we leave the creative act of putting together a company's unique internal capability and opportunity evolving in the external world, we should note that —aside from distinctive competence—the principal resources found in any company are money and people—technical and managerial people. At an advanced stage of economic development, money seems less a problem than technical competence, and the latter less critical than managerial ability. Do not assume that managerial capacity can rise to any occasion. The diversification of American industry is marked by hundreds of instances in which a company strong in one endeavor lacked the ability to manage an enterprise requiring different skills. The right to make handsome profits over a long period must be earned. Opportunism without competence is a path to fairyland.

Besides equating an appraisal of market opportunity and organizational capability, the decision to make and market a particular product or service should be accompanied by an identification of the nature of the business and the kind of company its management desires. Such a guiding concept is a product of many considerations, including the managers' personal values. . . .

Uniqueness of Strategy: In each company, the way in which distinctive competence, organizational resources, and organizational values are combined is or should be unique. Differences among companies are as numerous as differences among individuals. The combinations of opportunity to which distinctive compe-

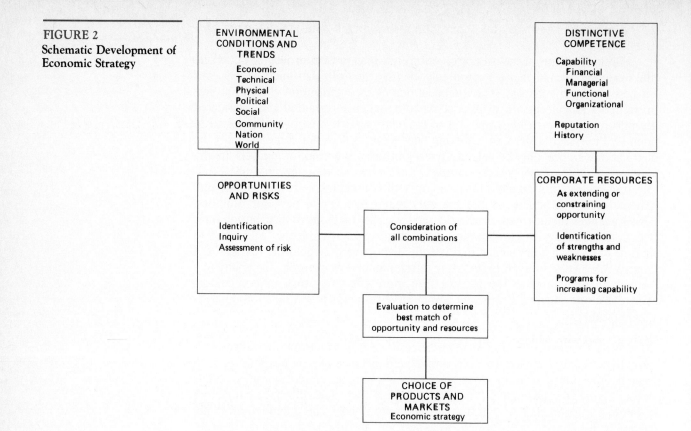

FIGURE 2
Schematic Development of
Economic Strategy

ENVIRONMENTAL CONDITIONS AND TRENDS

Economic
Technical
Physical
Political
Social
Community
Nation
World

DISTINCTIVE COMPETENCE

Capability
  Financial
  Managerial
  Functional
  Organizational

Reputation
History

OPPORTUNITIES AND RISKS

Identification
Inquiry
Assessment of risk

CORPORATE RESOURCES

As extending or
constraining
opportunity

Identification
of strengths and
weaknesses

Programs for
increasing capability

Consideration of
all combinations

Evaluation to determine
best match of
opportunity and resources

CHOICE OF PRODUCTS AND MARKETS
Economic strategy

tences, resources, and values may be applied are equally extensive. Generalizing about how to make an effective match is less rewarding than working at it. The effort is a highly stimulating and challenging exercise. The outcome will be unique for each company and each situation.

● THE EVALUATION OF BUSINESS STRATEGY*

BY RICHARD RUMELT

Strategy can neither be formulated nor adjusted to changing circumstances without a process of strategy evaluation. Whether performed by an individual or as part of an organizational review procedure, strategy evaluation forms an essential step in the process of guiding an enterprise.

For many executives strategy evaluation is simply an appraisal of how well a business performs. Has it grown? Is the profit rate normal or better? If the answers to these questions are affirmative, it is argued that the firm's strategy must be sound. Despite its unassailable simplicity, this line of reasoning misses the whole point of strategy—that the critical factors determining the quality of current results are often not directly observable or simply measured, and that by the time strategic opportunities or threats do directly affect operating results, it may well be too late

* Originally published in William F. Glueck, *Business Policy and Strategic Management,* 3rd ed. (McGraw-Hill, 1980); reprinted with deletions by permission of the publisher.

for an effective response. Thus, strategy evaluation is an attempt to look beyond the obvious facts regarding the short-term health of a business and appraise instead those more fundamental factors and trends that govern success in the chosen field of endeavor.

THE CHALLENGE OF EVALUATION

However it is accomplished, the products of a business strategy evaluation are answers to these three questions:

1. Are the objectives of the business appropriate?
2. Are the major policies and plans appropriate?
3. Do the results obtained to date confirm or refute critical assumptions on which the strategy rests?

Devising adequate answers to these questions is neither simple nor straightforward. It requires a reasonable store of situation-based knowledge and more than the usual degree of insight. In particular, the major issues which make evaluation difficult and with which the analyst must come to grips are these:

- Each business strategy is unique. For example, one paper manufacturer might rely on its vast timber holdings to weather almost any storm while another might place primary reliance in modern machinery and an extensive distribution system. Neither strategy is "wrong" nor "right" in any absolute sense; both may be right or wrong for the firms in question. Strategy evaluation must, then, rest on a type of situational logic that does not focus on "one best way" but which can be tailored to each problem as it is faced.
- Strategy is centrally concerned with the selection of goals and objectives. Many people, including seasoned executives, find it much easier to set or try to achieve goals than to evaluate them. In part this is a consequence of training in problem structuring. It also arises out of a tendency to confuse *values,* which are fundamental expressions of human personality, with objectives, which are *devices* for lending coherence to action.
- Formal systems of strategic review, while appealing in principle, can create explosive conflict situations. Not only are there serious questions as to who is qualified to give an objective evaluation, the whole idea of strategy evaluation implies management by "much more than results" and runs counter to much of currently popular management philosophy.

THE PRINCIPLES OF STRATEGY EVALUATION

. . . For our purposes a strategy is a set of objectives, policies, and plans that, taken together, define the scope of the enterprise and its approach to survival and success. Alternatively, we could say that the particular policies, plans, and objectives of a business express its strategy for coping with a complex competitive environment.

One of the fundamental tenets of science is that a theory can never be proven to be absolutely true. A theory can, however, be declared absolutely false if it fails to stand up to testing. Similarly, it is impossible to demonstrate conclusively that a particular business strategy is optimal or even to guarantee that it will work. One can, nevertheless, test it for critical flaws. Of the many tests which could be justifiably applied to a business strategy, most will fit within one of these broad criteria:

- *Consistency:* The strategy must not present mutually inconsistent goals and policies.
- *Consonance:* The strategy must represent an adaptive response to the external environment and to the critical changes occurring within it.
- *Advantage:* The strategy must provide for the creation and/or maintenance of a competitive advantage in the selected area of activity.
- *Feasibility:* The strategy must neither overtax available resources nor create unsolvable subproblems.

A strategy that fails to meet one or more of these criteria is strongly suspect. It fails to perform at least one of the key functions that are necessary for the survival of the business. Experience within a particular industry or other setting will permit the analyst to sharpen these criteria and add others that are appropriate to the situation at hand.

Consistency

Gross inconsistency within a strategy seems unlikely until it is realized that many strategies have not been explicitly formulated but have evolved over time in an ad hoc fashion. Even strategies that are the result of formal procedures may easily contain compromise arrangements between opposing power groups.

Inconsistency in strategy is not simply a flaw in logic. A key function of strategy is to provide coherence to organizational action. A clear and explicit concept of strategy can foster a climate of tacit coordination that is more efficient than most administrative mechanisms. Many high-technology firms, for example, face a basic strategic choice between offering high-cost products with high custom-engineering content and lower-cost products that are more standardized and sold at higher volume. If senior management does not enunciate a clear consistent sense of where the corporation stands on these issues, there will be continuing conflict between sales, design, engineering, and manufacturing people. A clear consistent strategy, by contrast, allows a sales engineer to negotiate a contract with a minimum of coordination—the trade-offs are an explicit part of the firm's posture.

Organizational conflict and interdepartmental bickering are often symptoms of a managerial disorder but may also indicate problems of strategic inconsistency. Here are some indicators that can help sort out these two different problems:

- If problems in coordination and planning continue despite changes in personnel and tend to be issue rather than people based, they are probably due to inconsistencies in strategy.
- If success for one organizational department means, or is interpreted to mean, failure for another department, the basic objective structure is inconsistent.
- If, despite attempts to delegate authority, operating problems continue to be brought to the top for the resolution of *policy* issues, the basic strategy is probably inconsistent.

A final type of consistency that must be sought in strategy is between organizational objectives and the values of the management group. Inconsistency in this area is more of a problem in strategy formulation than in the evaluation of a strategy that has already been implemented. It can still arise, however, if the future direction of the business requires changes that conflict with managerial values. The most frequent source of such conflict is growth. As a business expands beyond the scale that allows an easy informal method of operation, many executives experience a sharp sense of loss. While growth can of course be curtailed, it often will require special attention to a firm's competitive position if survival without growth is desired. The same basic issues arise when other types of personal or social values come into conflict with existing or apparently necessary policies: the resolution of the conflict will normally require an adjustment in the competitive strategy.

Consonance

The way in which a business relates to its environment has two aspects: the business must both match and be adapted to its environment and it must at the same time compete with other firms that are also trying to adapt. This dual character of the relationship between the firm and its environment has its analog in two different aspects of strategic choice and two different methods of strategy evaluation.

The first aspect of fit deals with the basic mission or scope of the business and the second with its special competitive position or "edge." Analysis of the first is normally done by looking at changing economic and social conditions over *time*. Analysis of the second, by contrast, typically focuses on the differences across firms at a given time. We call the first the "generic" aspect of strategy and the second "competitive" strategy. Table 1 summarizes the differences between these concepts.

The notion of consonance, or matching, therefore, invites a focus on generic strategy. The role of the evaluator in this case is to examine the basic pattern of economic relationships that characterize the business and determine whether or not sufficient value is being created to sustain the strategy. Most macroanalysis of changing economic conditions is oriented toward the formulation or evaluation of generic strategies. For example, a planning department forecasts that within 10 years home appliances will no longer use mechanical timers or logic. Instead, microprocessors will do the job more reliably and less expensively. The basic message here for the makers of mechanical timers is that their generic strategies are becoming obsolete, especially if they specialize in major home appliances. Note that the threat in this case is not to a particular firm, competitive position, or individual approach to the marketplace but to the basic generic mission.

One major difficulty in evaluating consonance is that most of the critical threats to a business are those which come from without, threatening an entire

TABLE 1 Generic Versus Competitive Strategy

	GENERIC	**COMPETITIVE**
Measure of success	Sales growth	Market share
Return to the firm	Value added	Return on investment
Function	Provision of value to the customer	Maintaining or obtaining a defensible position
Basic strategic tasks	Adapting to change and innovation	Creating barriers and deterring rivals
Method of expressing strategy	Product/market terms, functional terms	Policies leading to defensible position
Basic approach to analysis	Study of group of businesses over time	Comparision across rivals at a given time

group of firms. Management, however, is often so engrossed in competitive thinking that such threats are only recognized after the damage has reached considerable proportions. . . .

The key to evaluating consonance is an understanding of why the business, as it currently stands, exists at all and how it assumed its current pattern. Once the analyst obtains a good grasp of the basic economic foundation that supports and defines the business, it is possible to study the consequences of key trends and changes. Without such an understanding, there is no good way of deciding what kinds of changes are most crucial and the analyst can be quickly overwhelmed with data.

Advantage

It is no exaggeration to say that competitive strategy is the art of creating or exploiting those advantages that are most telling, enduring, and most difficult to duplicate.

Competitive strategy, in contrast with generic strategy, focuses on the differences among firms rather than their common missions. The problem it addresses is not so much "how can this function be performed" but "how can *we* perform it either better than, or at least instead of our rivals?" The chain supermarket, for example, represents a successful generic strategy. As a way of doing business, of organizing economic transactions, it has replaced almost all the smaller owner-managed food shops of an earlier era. Yet a potential or actual participant in the retail food business must go beyond this generic strategy and find a way of competing in this business. As another illustration, American Motors' early success in compact cars was generic—other firms soon copied the basic product concept. Once this happened, AMC had to try to either forge a strong competitive strategy in this area or seek a different type of competitive arena.

Competitive advantages can normally be traced to one of three roots:

- Superior resources
- Superior skills
- Superior position

The nature of the advantages produced by the first two are obvious. They represent the ability of a business to do more and/or do it better than its rivals. The critical analytical issue here is the question of which skills and resources represent advantages in which competitive arenas. The skills that make for success in the aerospace electronics industry, for instance, do not seem to have much to do with those needed in consumer electronics. Similarly, what makes for success in the early phases of an industry life cycle may be quite different than what ensures top performance in the later phases.

The idea that certain arrangements of one's resources can enhance their combined effectiveness, and perhaps even put rival forces in a state of disarray, is at the heart of the traditional notion of strategy. This kind of "positional" advantage is familiar to military theorists, chess players, and diplomats. Position plays a crucial role in business strategy as well. . . .

Positional advantage can be gained by foresight, superior skill and/or resources, or just plain luck. Once gained, a good position is defensible. This means that it (1) returns enough value to warrant its continued maintenance and (2) would be so costly to capture that rivals are deterred from full-scale attacks on the core of the business. Position, it must be noted, tends to be self-sustaining as long as the basic environmental factors that underlie it remain stable. Thus, entrenched firms can be almost impossible to unseat, even if their raw skill levels are only average. And when a shifting environment allows position to be gained by a new entrant or innovator, the results can be spectacular.

The types of positional advantage that are most well known are those associated with size or scale. As the scale of operations increases, most firms are able to reduce both the marginal and the total cost of each additional unit produced. Marginal costs fall due to the effects of learning and more efficient processes, and total costs per unit fall even faster as fixed overheads are spread over a larger volume of activity. The larger firm can simply take these gains in terms of increased profitability or it can invest some of the extra returns in position-maintaining activities. By engaging in more research and development, being first to go abroad, having the largest advertising budget, and absorbing the costs involved with acting as an industry spokesman, the dominant business is rechanneling the gains obtained from its advantages into activities designed to maintain those advantages. This kind of positive feedback is the source of the power of position-based advantages —the policies that act to enhance position do not require unusual skills; they simply work most effectively for those who are already in the position in the first place.

While it is not true that larger businesses always have the advantages, it is true that larger businesses will tend to operate in markets and use procedures that turn their size to advantage. Large national consumer-products firms, for example, will normally have an advantage over smaller regional firms in the efficient use of mass advertising, especially network TV. The larger firm will, then, tend to deal in those products where the marginal effect of advertising is most potent, while the smaller firms will seek product-market positions that exploit other types of advantage.

Not all positional advantages are associated with size, although some type of uniqueness is a virtual prerequisite. The principal characteristic of good position is that it permits the firm to obtain advantage from policies that would not similarly benefit rivals without the position. For example, Volkswagen in 1966 had a strong, well-defined position as the preeminent maker of inexpensive, well-engineered, functional automobiles. This position allowed it to follow a policy of not changing its body styling. The policy both enhanced VW's position and reduced costs. Rivals could not similarly benefit from such a policy unless they could also duplicate the other aspects of VW's position. At the other end of the spectrum, Rolls-Royce employed a policy of deliberately limiting its output, a policy which enhanced its unique position and which could do so only because of that position in the first place. Mintzberg (1973b) calls strongly defensible positions and the associated policies "gestalt strategies," recognizing that they are difficult to either analyze or attack in a piecemeal fashion.

Another type of positional advantage derives from successful trade names. These brands, especially when advertised, place retailers in the position of having to stock them which, in turn, reinforces the position and raises the barrier to entry still further. Such famous names as Sara Lee, Johnson & Johnson, and Kraft greatly reduce, for their holders, both the problems of gaining wide distribution for new products and obtaining trial use of new products by the buying public.

Other position-based advantages follow from such factors as:

- The ownership of special raw material sources or long-term supply contracts
- Being geographically located near key customers in a business involving significant fixed investment and high transport costs

- Being a leader in a service field that permits or requires the building of a unique experience base while serving clients
- Being a full-line producer in a market with heavy trade-up phenomena
- Having a wide reputation for providing a needed product or service trait reliably and dependably

In each case, the position permits competitive policies to be adopted that can serve to reinforce the position. *Whenever* this type of positive-feedback phenomena is encountered, the particular policy mix that creates it will be found to be a defensible business position. The key factors that sparked industrial success stories such as IBM and Eastman Kodak were the *early* and rapid domination of strong positions opened up by new technologies.

Feasibility

The final broad test of strategy is its feasibility. Can the strategy be attempted within the physical, human, and financial resources available? The financial resources of a business are the easiest to quantify and are normally the first limitation against which strategy is tested. It is sometimes forgotten, however, that innovative approaches to financing expansion can both stretch the ultimate limitations and provide a competitive advantage, even if it is only temporary. Devices such as captive finance subsidiaries, sale-leaseback arrangements, and tying plant mortgages to long-term contracts have all been used effectively to help win key positions in suddenly expanding industries.

The less quantifiable but actually more rigid limitation on strategic choice is that imposed by the individual and organizational capabilities that are available.

In assessing the organization's ability to carry out a strategy, it is helpful to ask three separate questions.

1. Has the organization demonstrated that it possesses the problem-solving abilities and/or special competences required by the strategy? A strategy, as such, does not and cannot specify in detail each action that must be carried out. Its purpose is to provide structure to the general issue of the business' goals and approaches to coping with its environment. It is up to the members and departments of the organization to carry out the tasks defined by strategy. A strategy that requires tasks to be accomplished which fall outside the realm of available or easily obtainable skill and knowledge cannot be accepted. It is either infeasible or incomplete.

2. Has the organization demonstrated the degree of coordinative and integrative skill necessary to carry out the strategy? The key tasks required of a strategy not only require specialized skill, but often make considerable demands on the organization's ability to integrate disparate activities. . . .

3. Does the strategy challenge and motivate key personnel and is it acceptable to those who must lend their support? The purpose of strategy is to effectively deploy the unique and distinctive resources of an enterprise. If key managers are unmoved by a strategy, not excited by its goals or methods, or strongly support an alternative, it fails in a major way. . . .

... In most medium- to large-size firms, strategy evaluation is not a purely intellectual task. The issues involved are too important and too closely associated with the distribution of power and authority for either strategy formulation or evaluation to take place in an ivory tower environment. In fact, most firms rarely engage in explicit formal strategy evaluation. Rather, the evaluation of current strategy is a continuing process and one that is difficult to separate from the normal planning, reporting, control, and reward systems of the firm. From this point of view, strategy evaluation is not so much an intellectual task as it is an organizational process.

As process, strategy evaluation is the outcome of activities and events which are strongly shaped by the firm's control and reward systems, its information and planning systems, its structure, and its history and particular culture. Thus, its performance is, in practice, tied more directly to the quality of the firm's strategic management than to any particular analytical scheme. In particular, organizing major units around the primary strategic tasks and making the extra effort required to incorporate measures of strategic success in the control system may play vital roles in facilitating strategy evaluation within the firm.

Ultimately, a firm's ability to maintain its competitive position in a world of rivalry and change may be best served by managers who can maintain a dual view of strategy and strategy evaluation—they must be willing and able to perceive the strategy within the welter of daily activity *and* to build and maintain structures and systems that make strategic factors the object of current activity.

CHAPTER

4

STRATEGY ANALYSIS

As noted in the introduction to Chapter 3, there is a second prescriptive view on the way strategy should be formulated, which developed in the 1980s. Its contribution is less as a new conceptual model—in fact it embraces most of the premises of the traditional model—than in carefully structuring the kinds of formal analyses that should be undertaken to develop a successful strategy. One outcome of this more formal approach is that its adherents have come to see many strategies as fitting certain "generic" classifications—not being created so much individually as selected from a limited set of options based on systematic study of the firm and the industry conditions it faces. This approach has proved to be powerful and useful in many situations.

A leader of this approach is Michael Porter of the Harvard Business School, who studied at the doctoral level in Harvard's economics department. By building intellectual bridges between the fields of management policy and industrial organization—the latter a branch of economics concerned with the performance of industries as a function of their competitive characteristics—Porter elaborated on the earlier views of Andrews, Ansoff, Newman, et al.

We open this chapter with Porter's basic model of competitive and industry analysis, probably his best known work in the area of strategy analysis. As presented in this award-winning *Harvard Business Review* article, it proposes a framework of five forces which in his view define the basic posture of competition in an industry—the bargaining power of existing suppliers and buyers, the threat of substitutes and new entrants, and the intensity of existing rivalry. The model is a powerful one, as you shall see in references to it in subsequent readings.

Porter is known for several other frameworks as well, for example, his concept of "generic strategies," of which he argues there are three in particular—cost leadership, differentiation, and focus (or scope); his discussion of the "value chain" as a way of decomposing the activities of a business to apply strategy analyses of various kinds; his notion of strategic groups, where firms with like sets of strategies compete in subsegments of an industry; and his concept of "generic industry environments," such as "fragmented" or "mature," which reflect similar characteristics.

We shall hear from Porter again on the last of these in our context section. But his three generic strategies as well as his value chain will be summarized in a second reading in this chapter, by Mintzberg, that seeks to present a more comprehensive picture of the various strategies that firms commonly pursue. Mintzberg's framework considers these at five levels—strategies concerned with locating the core business, distinguishing the core business (the heart of what is often referred to as "business"-level strategy, and where Porter's three generic strategies are found and where his value chain is best introduced), elaborating the core business, extending the core business (where so-called "corporate" level strategies are found), and reconceiving the core business(es).

Our third reading of this chapter, entitled "Developing Competitive Advantage" and authored by Xavier Gilbert and Paul Strebel, two professors at the International Institute for Management Development in Lausanne, Switzerland, draw on Porter's concept of industry analysis, generic strategies, and strategic groups (also including something akin to the value chain, which they call the "business system"), but knit them together in a unique way to suggest an integrated framework to formulate strategy. When Porter introduced his three generic strategies, he made a specific case for not being "stuck in the middle," particularly between cost leadership and differentiation. Gilbert and Strebel, in contrast, introduce "outpacing" strategies designed to do just that—get the best of both these worlds. They believe that over time, through a "dynamic path," some truly successful firms manage to be both efficient in their delivery of low-cost products and services and effective in their capacity to create high received value through differentiation. Consider this specific contradiction and these general views of strategy formulation as you read to help you decide for yourself which view better captures the realities of strategy.

In some ways, the strategy analysis frameworks of this chapter parallel those of Andrews. But these authors add a number of new systematic and analytical elements, often creating a result that is less broad, more focused. You should consider which approach will be more effective, at least under specific circumstances.

• HOW COMPETITIVE FORCES SHAPE STRATEGY*

BY MICHAEL E. PORTER

The essence of strategy formulation is coping with competition. Yet it is easy to view competition too narrowly and too pessimistically. While one sometimes hears

* Originally published in the *Harvard Business Review* (March–April, 1979) and winner of the McKinsey prize for the best article in the *Review* in 1979. Copyright © 1979 by the President and Fellows of Harvard College; all rights reserved. Reprinted with deletions by permission of the *Harvard Business Review*.

executives complaining to the contrary, intense competition in an industry is neither coincidence nor bad luck.

Moreover, in the fight for market share, competition is not manifested only in the other players. Rather, competition in an industry is rooted in its underlying economics, and competitive forces exist that go well beyond the established combatants in a particular industry. Customers, suppliers, potential entrants, and substitute products are all competitors that may be more or less prominent or active depending on the industry.

The state of competition in an industry depends on five basic forces, which are diagrammed in Figure 1. The collective strength of these forces determines the ultimate profit potential of an industry. It ranges from *intense* in industries like tires, metal cans, and steel, where no company earns spectacular returns on investment, to *mild* in industries like oil field services and equipment, soft drinks, and toiletries, where there is room for quite high returns.

In the economists' "perfectly competitive" industry, jockeying for position is unbridled and entry to the industry very easy. This kind of industry structure, of course, offers the worst prospect for long-run profitability. The weaker the forces collectively, however, the greater the opportunity for superior performance.

FIGURE 1
Elements of Industry Structure

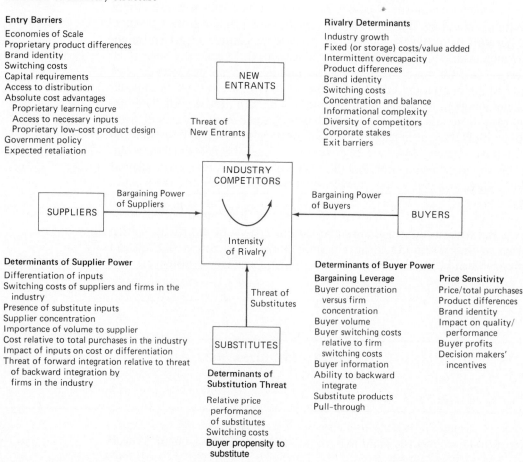

Whatever their collective strength, the corporate strategist's goal is to find a position in the industry where his or her company can best defend itself against these forces or can influence them in its favor. The collective strength of the forces may be painfully apparent to all the antagonists; but to cope with them, the strategist must delve below the surface and analyze the sources of each. For example, what makes the industry vulnerable to entry? What determines the bargaining power of suppliers?

Knowledge of these underlying sources of competitive pressure provides the groundwork for a strategic agenda of action. They highlight the critical strengths and weaknesses of the company, animate the positioning of the company in its industry, clarify the areas where strategic changes may yield the greatest payoff, and highlight the places where industry trends promise to hold the greatest significance as either opportunities or threats. Understanding these sources also proves to be of help in considering areas for diversification.

CONTENDING FORCES

The strongest competitive force or forces determine the profitability of an industry and so are of greatest importance in strategy formulation. For example, even a company with a strong position in an industry unthreatened by potential entrants will earn low returns if it faces a superior or lower-cost substitute product—as the leading manufacturers of vacuum tubes and coffee percolators have learned to their sorrow. In such a situation, coping with the substitute product becomes the number one strategic priority.

Different forces take on prominence, of course, in shaping competition in each industry. In the oceangoing tanker industry the key force is probably the buyers (the major oil companies), while in tires it is powerful OEM buyers coupled with tough competitors. In the steel industry the key forces are foreign competitors and substitute materials.

Every industry has an underlying structure, or a set of fundamental economic and technical characteristics, that gives rise to these competitive forces. The strategist, wanting to position his company to cope best with its industry environment or to influence that environment in the company's favor, must learn what makes the environment tick.

This view of competition pertains equally to industries dealing in services and to those selling products. To avoid monotony in this article, I refer to both products and services as "products." The same general principles apply to all types of business.

A few characteristics are critical to the strength of each competitive force. I shall discuss them in this section.

Threat of Entry

New entrants to an industry bring new capacity, the desire to gain market share, and often substantial resources. Companies diversifying through acquisition into the industry from other markets often leverage their resources to cause a shakeup, as Philip Morris did with Miller beer.

The seriousness of the threat of entry depends on the barriers present and on the reaction from existing competitors that the entrant can expect. If barriers to entry are high and a newcomer can expect sharp retaliation from the entrenched competitors, obviously he will not pose a serious threat of entering.

There are six major sources of barriers to entry:

1. *Economies of scale*—These economies deter entry by forcing the aspirant either to come in on a large scale or to accept a cost disadvantage. Scale economies in production, research, marketing, and service are probably the key barriers to entry in the mainframe computer industry, as Xerox and GE sadly discovered. Economies of scale can also act as hurdles in distribution, utilization of the sales force, financing, and nearly any other part of a business.

2. *Product differentiation*—Brand identification creates a barrier by forcing entrants to spend heavily to overcome customer loyalty. Advertising, customer service, being first in the industry, and product differences are among the factors fostering brand identification. It is perhaps the most important entry barrier in soft drinks, over-the-counter drugs, cosmetics, investment banking, and public accounting. To create high fences around their businesses, brewers couple brand identification with economies of scale in production, distribution, and marketing.

3. *Capital requirements*—The need to invest large financial resources in order to compete creates a barrier to entry, particulary if the capital is required for unrecoverable expenditures in up-front advertising or R&D. Capital is necessary not only for fixed facilities but also for customer credit, inventories, and absorbing start-up losses. While major corporations have the financial resources to invade almost any industry, the huge capital requirements in certain fields, such as computer manufacturing and mineral extraction, limit the pool of likely entrants.

4. *Cost disadvantages independent of size*—Entrenched companies may have cost advantages not available to potential rivals, no matter what their size and attainable economies of scale. These advantages can stem from the effects of the learning curve (and of its first cousin, the experience curve), proprietary technology, access to the best raw materials sources, assets purchased at preinflation prices, government subsidies, or favorable locations. Sometimes cost advantages are legally enforceable, as they are through patents. . . . [Editor's note: See Chapter 11 of this text for a discussion of the experience curve.]

5. *Access to distribution channels*—The new boy on the block must, of course, secure distribution of his product or service. A new food product, for example, must displace others from the supermarket shelf via price breaks, promotions, intense selling efforts, or some other means. The more limited the wholesale or retail channels are and the more that existing competitors have these tied up, obviously the tougher that entry into the industry will be. Sometimes this barrier is so high that, to surmount it, a new contestant must create its own distribution channels, as Timex did in the watch industry in the 1950s.

6. *Government policy*—The government can limit or even foreclose entry to industries with such controls as license requirements and limits on access to raw materials. Regulated industries like trucking, liquor retailing, and freight forwarding are noticeable examples; more subtle government restrictions operate in fields like ski-area development and coal mining. The government also can play a major indirect role by affecting entry barriers through controls such as air and water pollution standards and safety regulations.

The potential rival's expectations about the reaction of existing competitors also will influence its decision on whether to enter. The company is likely to have second thoughts if incumbents have previously lashed out at new entrants or if:

- The incumbents possess substantial resources to fight back, including excess cash and unused borrowing power, productive capacity, or clout with distribution channels and customers.

- The incumbents seem likely to cut prices because of a desire to keep market shares or because of industrywide excess capacity.

- Industry growth is slow, affecting its ability to absorb the new arrival and probably causing the financial performance of all the parties involved to decline.

Changing Conditions: From a strategic standpoint there are two important additional points to note about the threat of entry.

First, it changes, of course, as these conditions change. The expiration of Polaroid's basic patents on instant photography, for instance, greatly reduced its absolute cost entry barrier built by proprietary technology. It is not surprising that Kodak plunged into the market. Product differentiation in printing has all but disappeared. Conversely, in the auto industry economies of scale increased enormously with post–World War II automation and vertical integration—virtually stopping successful new entry.

Second, strategic decisions involving a large segment of an industry can have a major impact on the conditions determining the threat of entry. For example, the actions of many U.S. wine producers in the 1960s to step up product introductions, raise advertising levels, and expand distribution nationally surely strengthened the entry roadblocks by raising economies of scale and making access to distribution channels more difficult. Similarly, decisions by members of the recreational vehicle industry to vertically integrate in order to lower costs have greatly increased the economies of scale and raised the capital cost barriers.

Powerful Suppliers and Buyers

Suppliers can exert bargaining power on participants in an industry by raising prices or reducing the quality of purchased goods and services. Powerful suppliers can thereby squeeze profitability out of an industry unable to recover cost increases in its own prices. By raising their prices, soft drink concentrate producers have contributed to the erosion of profitability of bottling companies because the bottlers, facing intense competition from powdered mixes, fruit drinks, and other beverages, have limited freedom to raise *their* prices accordingly. Customers likewise can force down prices, demand higher quality or more service, and play competitors off against each other—all at the expense of industry profits.

The power of each important supplier or buyer group depends on a number of characteristics of its market situation and on the relative importance of its sales or purchases to the industry compared with its overall business.

A *supplier* group is powerful if:

- It is dominated by a few companies and is more concentrated than the industry it sells to.

- Its product is unique or at least differentiated, or if it has built up switching costs. Switching costs are fixed costs buyers face in changing suppliers. These arise because, among other things, a buyer's product specifications tie it to particular suppliers, it has invested heavily in specialized ancillary equipment or in learning how to operate a supplier's equipment (as in computer software), or its production lines are connected to the supplier's manufacturing facilities (as in some manufacture of beverage containers).

- It is not obliged to contend with other products for sale to the industry. For instance, the competition between the steel companies and the aluminum companies to sell to the can industry checks the power of each supplier.

- It poses a credible threat of integrating forward into the industry's business. This provides a check against the industry's ability to improve the terms on which it purchases.

- The industry is not an important customer of the supplier group. If the industry *is* an important customer, suppliers' fortunes will be closely tied to the industry, and they will want to protect the industry through reasonable pricing and assistance in activities like R&D and lobbying.

A *buyer* group is powerful if:

- It is concentrated or purchases in large volumes. Large-volume buyers are particularly potent forces if heavy fixed costs characterize the industry—as they do in metal containers, corn refining, and bulk chemicals, for example —which raise the stakes to keep capacity filled.

- The products it purchases from the industry are standard or undifferentiated. The buyers, sure that they can always find alternative suppliers, may play one company against another, as they do in aluminum extrusion.

- The products it purchases from the industry form a component of its product and represent a significant fraction of its cost. The buyers are likely to shop for a favorable price and purchase selectively. Where the product sold by the industry in question is a small fraction of buyers' costs, buyers are usually must less price sensitive.

- It earns low profits, which create great incentive to lower its purchasing costs. Highly profitable buyers, however, are generally less price sensitive (that is, of course, if the item does not represent a large fraction of their costs).

- The industry's product is unimportant to the quality of the buyers' products or services. Where the quality of the buyers' products is very much affected by the industry's product, buyers are generally less price sensitive. Industries in which this situation obtains include oil field equipment, where a malfunction can lead to large losses, and enclosures for electronic medical and test instruments, where the quality of the enclosure can influence the user's impression about the quality of the equipment inside.

- The industry's product does not save the buyer money. Where the industry's product or service can pay for itself many times over, the buyer is rarely price sensitive; rather, he is interested in quality. This is true in services like investment banking and public accounting, where errors in judgment can be costly and embarrassing, and in businesses like the logging of oil wells, where an accurate survey can save thousands of dollars in drilling costs.

- The buyers pose a credible threat of integrating backward to make the industry's product. The Big Three auto producers and major buyers of cars have often used the threat of self-manufacture as a bargaining lever. But sometimes an industry engenders a threat to buyers that its members may integrate forward.

Most of these sources of buyer power can be attributed to consumers as a group as well as to industrial and commercial buyers; only a modification of the frame of reference is necessary. Consumers tend to be more price sensitive if they are purchasing products that are undifferentiated, expensive relative to their incomes, and of a sort where quality is not particularly important.

The buying power of retailers is determined by the same rules, with one important addition. Retailers can gain significant bargaining power over manufacturers when they can influence consumers' purchasing decisions, as they do in audio components, jewelry, appliances, sporting goods, and other goods.

Strategic Action: A company's choice of suppliers to buy from or buyer groups to sell to should be viewed as a crucial strategic decision. A company can improve its strategic posture by finding suppliers or buyers who possess the least power to influence it adversely.

Most common is the situation of a company being able to choose whom it will sell to—in other words, buyer selection. Rarely do all the buyer groups a company sells to enjoy equal power. Even if a company sells to a single industry, segments usually exist within that industry that exercise less power (and that are therefore less price sensitive) than others. For example, the replacement market for most products is less price sensitive than the overall market.

As a rule, a company can sell to powerful buyers and still come away with above-average profitability only if it is a low-cost producer in its industry or if its product enjoys some unusual, if not unique, features. In supplying large customers with electric motors, Emerson Electric earns high returns because its low-cost position permits the company to meet or undercut competitors' prices.

If the company lacks a low-cost position or a unique product, selling to everyone is self-defeating because the more sales it achieves, the more vulnerable it becomes. The company may have to muster the courage to turn away business and sell only to less potent customers.

Buyer selection has been a key to the success of National Can and Crown Cork & Seal. They focus on the segments of the can industry where they can create product differentiation, minimize the threat of backward integration, and otherwise mitigate the awesome power of their customers. Of course, some industries do not enjoy the luxury of selecting "good" buyers.

As the factors creating supplier and buyer power change with time or as a result of a company's strategic decisions, naturally the power of these groups rises or declines. In the ready-to-wear clothing industry, as the buyers (department stores and clothing stores) have become more concentrated and control has passed to large chains, the industry has come under increasing pressure and suffered falling margins. The industry has been unable to differentiate its product or engender switching costs that lock in its buyers enough to neutralize these trends.

Substitute Products

By placing a ceiling on prices it can charge, substitute products or services limit the potential of an industry. Unless it can upgrade the quality of the product or differentiate it somehow (as via marketing), the industry will suffer in earnings and possibly in growth.

Manifestly, the more attractive the price-performance trade-off offered by substitute products, the firmer the lid placed on the industry's profit potential. Sugar producers confronted with the large-scale commercialization of high-fructose corn syrup, a sugar substitute, are learning this lesson today.

Substitutes not only limit profits in normal times; they also reduce the bonanza an industry can reap in boom times. In 1978 the producers of fiberglass insulation enjoyed unprecedented demand as a result of high energy costs and severe winter weather. But the industry's ability to raise prices was tempered by the plethora of insulation substitutes, including cellulose, rock wool, and styrofoam. These substitutes are bound to become an even stronger force once the current round of plant additions by fiberglass insulation producers has boosted capacity enough to meet demand (and then some).

Substitute products that deserve the most attention strategically are those that (1) are subject to trends improving their price-performance trade-off with the industry's product, or (2) are produced by industries earning high profits. Substitutes often come rapidly into play if some development increases competition in their industries and causes price reduction or performance improvement.

Jockeying for Position

Rivalry among existing competitors takes the familiar form of jockeying for position—using tactics like price competition, product introduction, and advertising slugfests. Intense rivalry is related to the presence of a number of factors:

- Competitors are numerous or are roughly equal in size and power. In many U.S. industries in recent years foreign contenders, of course, have become part of the competitive picture.

- Industry growth is slow, precipitating fights for market share that involve expansion-minded members.

- The product or service lacks differentiation or switching costs, which lock in buyers and protect one combatant from raids on its customers by another.

- Fixed costs are high or the product is perishable, creating strong temptation to cut prices. Many basic materials businesses, like paper and aluminum, suffer from this problem when demand slackens.

- Capacity is normally augmented in large increments. Such additions, as in the chlorine and vinyl chloride businesses, disrupt the industry's supply-demand balance and often lead to periods of overcapacity and price cutting.

- Exit barriers are high. Exit barriers, like very specialized assets or management's loyalty to a particular business, keep companies competing even though they may be earning low or even negative returns on investment. Excess capacity remains functioning, and the profitability of the healthy competitors suffers as the sick ones hang on. If the entire industry suffers from overcapacity, it may seek government help—particularly if foreign competition is present.

- The rivals are diverse in strategies, origins, and "personalities." They have different ideas about how to compete and continually run head on into each other in the process. . . .

While a company must live with many of these factors—because they are built into industry economics—it may have some latitude for improving matters through strategic shifts. For example, it may try to raise buyers' switching costs or increase product differentiation. A focus on selling efforts in the fastest-growing segments of the industry or on market areas with the lowest fixed costs can reduce the impact of industry rivalry. If it is feasible, a company can try to avoid confrontation with competitors having high exit barriers and can thus sidestep involvement in bitter price cutting.

Once the corporate strategist has assessed the forces affecting competition in his industry and their underlying causes, he can identify his company's strengths and weaknesses. The crucial strengths and weaknesses from a strategic standpoint are the company's posture vis-à-vis the underlying causes of each force. Where does it stand against substitutes? Against the sources of entry barriers?

Then the strategist can devise a plan of action that may include (1) positioning the company so that its capabilities provide the best defense against the competitive force; and/or (2) influencing the balance of the forces through strategic moves, thereby improving the company's position; and/or (3) anticipating shifts in the factors underlying the forces and responding to them, with the hope of exploiting change by choosing a strategy appropriate for the new competitive balance before opponents recognize it. I shall consider each strategic approach in turn.

Positioning the Company

The first approach takes the structure of the industry as given and matches the company's stengths and weaknesses to it. Strategy can be viewed as building defenses against the competitive forces or as finding positions in the industry where the forces are weakest.

Knowledge of the company's capabilities and of the causes of the competitive forces will highlight the areas where the company should confront competition and where avoid it. If the company is a low-cost producer, it may choose to confront powerful buyers while it takes care to sell them only products not vulnerable to competition from substitutes. . . .

Influencing the Balance

When dealing with the forces that drive industry competition, a company can devise a strategy that takes the offensive. This posture is designed to do more than merely cope with the forces themselves; it is meant to alter their causes.

Innovations in marketing can raise brand identification or otherwise differentiate the product. Capital investments in large-scale facilities or vertical integration affect entry barriers. The balance of forces is partly a result of external factors and partly in the company's control.

Exploiting Industry Change

Industry evolution is important strategically because evolution, of course, brings with it changes in the sources of competition I have identified. In the familiar product life-cycle pattern, for example, growth rates change, product differentiation is said to decline as the business becomes more mature, and the companies tend to integrate vertically.

These trends are not so important in themselves; what is critical is whether they affect the sources of competition. . . .

Obviously, the trends carrying the highest priority from a strategic standpoint are those that affect the most important sources of competition in the industry and those that elevate new causes to the forefront. . . .

The framework for analyzing competition that I have described can also be used to predict the eventual profitability of an industry. In long-range planning the task is to examine each competitive force, forecast the magnitude of each underlying cause, and then construct a composite picture of the likely profit potential of the industry. . . .

The key to growth—even survival—is to stake out a position that is less vulnerable to attack from head-to-head opponents, whether established or new, and less vulnerable to erosion from the direction of buyers, suppliers, and substitute goods. Establishing such a position can take many forms—solidifying relationships with favorable customers, differentiating the product either substantively or psychologically through marketing, integrating forward or backward, establishing technological leadership.

● GENERIC STRATEGIES*

BY HENRY MINTZBERG

Almost every serious author concerned with "content" issues in strategic management, not to mention strategy consulting "boutique," has his, her, or its own list of strategies commonly pursued by different organizations. The problem is that these lists almost always either focus narrowly on special types of strategies or else aggregate arbitrarily across all varieties of them with no real order.

In 1965, Igor Ansoff proposed a matrix of four strategies that became quite well known—market penetration, product development, market development, and diversification (1965:109). But this was hardly comprehensive. Fifteen years later, Michael Porter (1980) introduced what became the best known list of "generic strategies": cost leadership, differentiation, and focus. But the Porter list was also incomplete: while Ansoff focused on *extensions* of business strategy, Porter focused on *identifying* business strategy in the first place. This article seeks to outline in an orderly fashion the families of strategies widely represented in organizations in general, divided into five groupings:

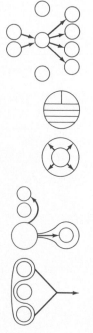

1. *locating* the core business, which will be shown as a single node—one circle —in a matrix of circles

2. *distinguishing* the core business, by looking inside that circle

3. *elaborating* the core business, considering how the circle may be enlarged or developed in various ways

4. *extending* the core business, leading the circle to link up with other circles (other businesses)

5. *reconceiving* the core business(es), in effect changing or combining the circles.

These will be presented as a logical hierarchy, although it should be emphasized that strategies do not necessarily develop that way in organizations.

---

* Abbreviated version prepared for this book of Henry Mintzberg, "Generic Strategies: Toward a Comprehensive Framework," in *Advances in Strategic Management,* Vol. 5 (Greenwich, CT: JAI Press, 1988), pp. 1–67.

A business can be thought to exist at a junction in a network of industries that take raw materials and through selling to and buying from each other produce various finished products (or services). Figure 1, for example, shows a hypothetical canoe business in such a network. Core location strategies can be described with respect to the stage of the business in the network and the particular industry in question.

Strategies of Stage of Operations

Traditionally, industries have been categorized as being in the primary (raw materials extraction and conversion), secondary (manufacturing), or tertiary (delivery or other service) stage of operations. More recently, however, stage in the "stream" has been the favored form of description:

Upstream Business Strategy: Upstream businesses function close to the raw material. As shown in the little figure, the flow of product tends to be divergent, from a basic material (wood, aluminum) to a variety of uses for it. Upstream business tends to be technology and capital intensive rather than people intensive, and more inclined to search for advantage through low costs than through high margins and to favor sales push over market pull (Galbraith, 1983:65–66).

Midstream Business Strategy: Here the organization sits at the neck of an hourglass, drawing a variety of inputs into a single production process out of which flows the product to a variety of users, much as the canoe business is shown in Figure 1.

Downstream Business Strategy: Here a wide variety of inputs converge into a narrow funnel, as in the many products sold by a department store.

Strategies of Industry

Many factors are involved in the identification of an industry, so many that it would be difficult to develop a concise set of generic labels. Moreover, change continually renders the boundaries between "industries" arbitrary. Diverse products get bundled together so that two industries become one while traditionally bundled products get separated so that one industry becomes two. Economists in government and elsewhere spend a great deal of time trying to pin these things down, via SIC codes and the like. In effect, they try to fix what strategists try to change: competitive advantage often comes from reconceiving the definition of an industry.

DISTINGUISHING THE CORE BUSINESS

Having located the circle that identifies the core business, the next step is to open it up—to distinguish the characteristics that enable an organization to achieve competitive advantage and so to survive in its own context.

The Functional Areas

This second level of strategy can encompass a whole host of strategies in the various functional areas. As shown in Figure 2, they may include input "sourcing"

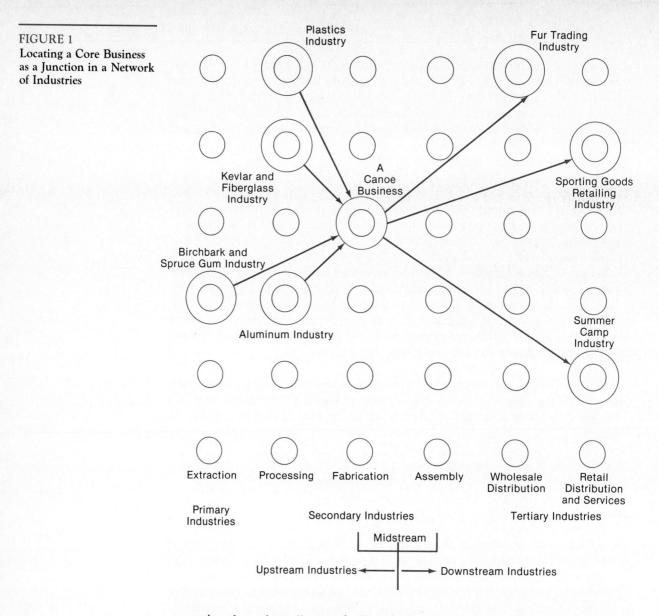

Plastics
Industry

Fur Trading
Industry

Kevlar and
Fiberglass
Industry

A
Canoe
Business

Sporting Goods
Retailing
Industry

Birchbark and
Spruce Gum Industry

Summer
Camp
Industry

Aluminum Industry

Extraction   Processing   Fabrication   Assembly   Wholesale
Distribution   Retail
Distribution
and Services

Primary
Industries

Secondary Industries

Tertiary Industries

Midstream

Upstream Industries ← → Downstream Industries

strategies, throughput "processing" strategies, and output "delivery" strategies, all reinforced by a set of "supporting" strategies.

It has been popular of late to describe organizations in this way, especially since Michael Porter built his 1985 book around the "generic value chain," shown in Figure 3. Porter presents it as "a systematic way of examining all the activities a firm performs and how they interact . . . for analyzing the sources of competitive advantage" (1985:33). Such a chain, and how it performs individual activities, reflects a firm's "history, its strategy, its approach to implementing its strategy, and the underlying economies of the activities themselves" (p. 36). According to Porter, "the goal of any generic strategy" is to "create value for buyers" at a profit. Accordingly,

> The value chain displays total value, and consists of *value activities* and *margin*. Value activities are the physically and technologically distinct activities a firm performs. These are the building blocks by which a firm creates a product valuable to its

FIGURE 2
**Functional Areas, in
Systems Terms**

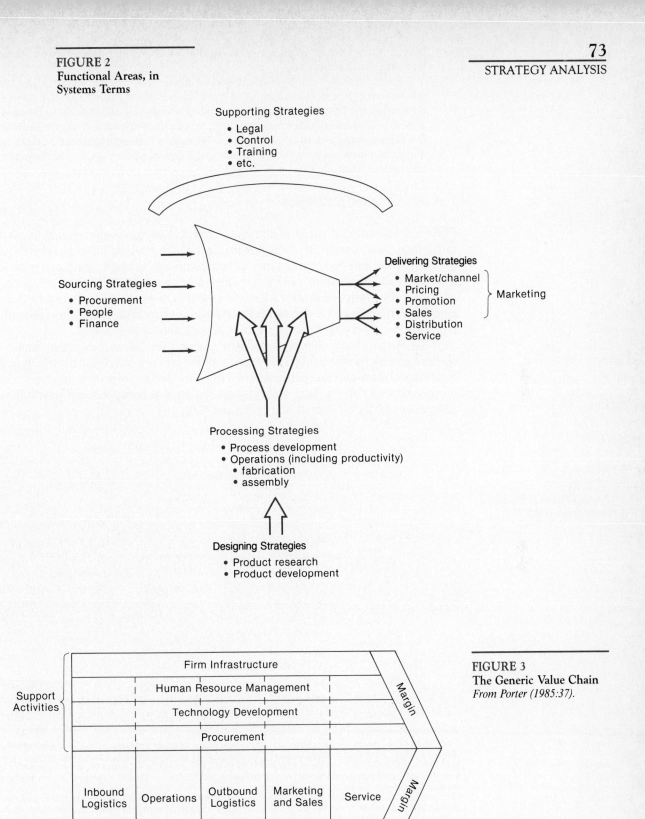

Supporting Strategies

- Legal
- Control
- Training
- etc.

Sourcing Strategies

- Procurement
- People
- Finance

Delivering Strategies

- Market/channel
- Pricing   } Marketing
- Promotion
- Sales
- Distribution
- Service

Processing Strategies

- Process development
- Operations (including productivity)
  - fabrication
  - assembly

Designing Strategies

- Product research
- Product development

FIGURE 3
The Generic Value Chain
From Porter (1985:37).

Support Activities

Firm Infrastructure					Margin
Human Resource Management					
Technology Development					
Procurement					
Inbound Logistics	Operations	Outbound Logistics	Marketing and Sales	Service	Margin

Primary Activities

buyers. Margin is the difference between total value and the collective cost of performing the value activities. . . .

Value activities can be divided into two broad types, *primary* activities and *support* activities. Primary activities, listed along the bottom of Figure 3 are the activities involved in the physical creation of the product and its sale and transfer to the buyer as well as after-sale assistance. In any firm, primary activities can be divided into the five generic categories shown in Figure 3. Support activities support the primary activities and each other by providing purchased inputs, technology, human resources, and various firmwide functions. (p. 38)[1]

Porter's Generic Strategies

Porter's framework of "generic strategies" has also become quite widely used. In our terms, these constitute strategies to distinguish the core business. Porter believes there are but two "basic types of competitive advantage a firm can possess: low cost or differentiation" (1985:11). These combine with the "scope" of a firm's operations (the range of market segments targeted) to produce "three *generic strategies* for achieving above-average performance in an industry: cost leadership, differentiation, and focus" (namely, narrow scope), shown in Figure 4.

To Porter, firms that wish to gain competitive advantage must "make a choice" among these: "being 'all things to all people' is a recipe for strategic mediocrity and below-average performance" (p. 12). Or in words that have become more controversial, "a firm that engages in each generic strategy but fails to achieve any of them is 'stuck in the middle' " (p. 16).

FIGURE 4
Porter's Generic Strategies
From Porter (1985:12)

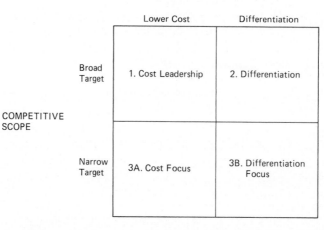

<hr>

[1] Our figure differs from Porter's in certain ways. Because he places his major emphasis on the flow of physical materials (for example, referring to "inbound logistics" as encompassing "materials handling, warehousing, inventory control, vehicle scheduling, and returns to suppliers"), he shows procurement and human resource management as support activities, whereas by taking more of a general system orientation, our Figure 2 shows them as inputs, among the sourcing strategies. Likewise, he considers technology development as support whereas Figure 2 considers it as part of processing. (Among the reasons Porter gives for doing this is that such development can pertain to "outbound logistics" or delivery as well as processing. While true, it also seems true that far more technology development pertains to operations than to delivery, especially in the manufacturing firms that are the focus of Porter's attention. Likewise, Porter describes procurement as pertaining to any of the primary activities, or other support activities for that matter. But in our terms that does not make it any less an aspect of sourcing on the inbound side.) In fact, Porter's description would relegate engineering and product design (not to mention human resources and purchasing) to staff rather than line activities, a place that would certainly be disputed in many manufacturing firms (with product design, for example, being mentioned only peripherally in his text (p. 42) alongside other "technology development" activities such as media research and servicing procedures).

The strategies we describe in this section take their lead from Porter, but depart in some respects. We shall distinguish scope and differentiation, as Porter did in his 1980 book (focus being introduced as narrow scope in his later book), but we shall include cost leadership as a form of differentiation (namely with regard to low price). If, as Porter argues, the intention of generic strategies is to seize and sustain competitive advantage, then it is not taking the leadership on cutting costs that matters so much as using that cost leadership to underprice competitors and so to attract buyers.[2]

Thus two types of strategies for distinguishing a core business are presented here. First is a set of increasingly extensive strategies of *differentiation,* shown on the face of the circle. These identify what is fundamentally distinct about a business in the marketplace, in effect as perceived by its customers. Second is a set of decreasingly extensive strategies of *scope,* shown as a third dimension, which converts the circle into a cylinder. These identify what markets the business is after, as perceived by itself.

Strategies of Differentiation

As is generally agreed in the literature of strategic management, an organization distinguishes itself in a competitive marketplace by differentiating its offerings in some way—by acting to distinguish its products and services from those of its competitors. Hence, differentiation fills the face of the circle used to identify the core business. An organization can differentiate its offerings in six basic ways:

Price Differentiation Strategy: The most basic way to differentiate a product (or service) is simply to charge a lower price for it. All things being equal, or not too unequal, some people at least will always beat a path to the door of the cheaper product. Price differentiation may be used with a product undifferentiated in any other way—in effect, a standard design, perhaps a commodity. The producer simply absorbs the lost margin, or makes it up through a higher volume of sales. But other times, backing up price differentiation is a strategy of design intended to create a product that is intrinsically cheaper.

Image Differentiation Strategy: Marketing is sometimes used to feign differentiation where it does not otherwise exist—an image is created for the product. This can also include cosmetic differences to a product that do not enhance its performance in any serious way, for example, putting fins on an automobile or a fancier package around yogurt. (Of course, if it is the image that is for sale, in other words if the product is intrinsically cosmetic, as, say, in "designer" jeans, then cosmetic differences would have to be described as design differentiation.)

Support Differentiation Strategy: More substantial, yet still having no effect on the product itself, is to differentiate on the basis of something that goes alongside the product, some basis of support. This may have to do with selling the product (such as special credit or 24-hour delivery), servicing the product (such as exceptional after-sales service), or providing a related product or service alongside the

---

[2] In other words, it is the differentiation of price that naturally drives the functional strategy of reducing costs just as it is the differentiation of product that naturally drives the functional strategies of enhancing quality or creating innovation. (To be consistent with the label of "cost leadership," Porter would have had to call his differentiation strategy "product leadership.") A company could, of course, cut costs while holding prices equivalent to competitors. But often that means less service, lower quality, fewer features, etc., and so the customers would have to be attracted by lower prices. [See Mintzberg (1988:14–17) for a fuller discussion of this point.]

basic one (paddling lessons with the canoe you buy). In an article entitled "Marketing Success Through Differentiation—of Anything," Theodore Levitt has argued the interesting point that "there is no such thing as a commodity" (1980:83). His basic point is that no matter how difficult it may be to achieve differentiation by design, there is always a basis to achieve another substantial form of differentiation, especially by support.

Quality Differentiation Strategy: Quality differentiation has to do with features of the product that make it better—not fundamentally different, just better. The product performs with (1) greater initial reliability, (2) greater long-term durability, and/or (3) superior performance.

Design Differentiation Strategy: Last but certainly not least is differentiation on the basis of design—offering something that is truly different, that breaks away from the "dominant design" if there is one, to provide unique features. While everyone else was making cameras whose pictures could be seen next week, Edwin Land went off and made one whose pictures could be seen in the next minute.

Undifferentiation Strategy: To have no basis for differentiation is a strategy too, indeed by all observation a common one, and in fact one that may be pursued deliberately. Hence there is a blank space in the circle. Given enough room in a market, and a management without the skill or the will to differentiate what it sells, there can be place for copycats.

Scope Strategies

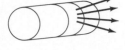

Customization
- standardized
- tailored
- pure

Increasing Selectivity

Unsegmented

Segmentation
- comprehensive
- selective
- focussed (niche)

The second dimension to distinguish the core business is by the *scope* of the products and services offered, in effect the extent of the markets in which they are sold. Scope is essentially a demand-driven concept, taking its lead from the market—what exists out there. Differentiation, in contrast, is a supply-driven concept, rooted in the nature of the product itself—what is offered to the market (Smith, 1956). Differentiation, by concentrating on the product offered, adopts the perspective of the customer, existing only when that person perceives some characteristic of the product that adds value. And scope, by focusing on the market served, adopts the perspective of the producer, existing only in the collective mind of the organization—in terms of how it diffuses and disaggregates its markets (in other words, what marketing people call segmentation).

Scope is shown here as a third dimension on our circle, converting it into a cylinder.

The disks of this figure represent the variety and range of products offered; arrows emanating from the cylinder, as shown, can represent the variety and range of markets served, as we shall do later. Scope strategies include the following:

Unsegmentation Strategy: "One size fits all": the Ford Model T, table salt. In fact, it is difficult to think of any product today that is not segmented in some way. What the unsegmented strategy really means then is that the organization tries to capture a wide chunk of the market with a basic configuration of the product.

Segmentation Strategies: The possibilities for segmentation are limitless, as are the possible degrees. We can, however, distinguish a range of this, from a simple segmentation strategy (three basic sizes of paper clips) to a hyperfine segmentation strategy (as in designer lighting). Also, some organizations seek to be *comprehen-*

sive, to serve all segments (department store, large cigarette manufacturers), others to be *selective,* targeting carefully only certain segments (e.g., "clean" mutual funds).

Niche Strategy: Niche strategies focus on a single segment. Just as the panda bear has found its biological niche in the consumption of bamboo shoots, so too is there the canoe company that has found its market niche in the fabrication of racing canoes, or the many firms which are distinguished only by the fact that they provide their highly standardized offerings in a unique place, a geographical niche—the corner grocery story, the regional cement producer, the national Red Cross office. All tend to follow "industry" recipes to the letter, providing them to their particular community. In a sense, all strategies are in some sense niche, characterized as much by what they exclude as by what they include. No organization can be all things to all people. The all-encompassing strategy is no strategy at all.

Customizing Strategies: Customization is the limiting case of segmentation: disaggregation of the market to the point where each customer constitutes a unique segment. *Pure* customization, in which the product is developed from scratch for each customer, is found in the architecturally designed house and the special purpose machine. It infiltrates the entire value chain: the product is not only delivered in a personalized way, not only assembled and even fabricated to order, but is also designed for the individual customer in the first place. Less ambitious but probably more common is *tailored* customization: a basic design is modified, usually in the fabrication stage, to the customer's needs or specifications (certain housing, protheses modified to fit the bone joints of each customer, and so on). *Standardized* customization means that final products are assembled to individual requests for standard components—as in automobiles in which the customer is allowed to choose color, engine, and various accessories. Advances in computer-aided design and manufacturing (CAD, CAM) will doubtlessly cause a proliferation of standardized customization, as well as tailored customization.

ELABORATING THE CORE BUSINESS

Given a core business with a distinguishing competitive posture, in terms of differentiation and scope, we now come to the question of what strategies of a generic nature are available to elaborate that core business.

An organization can elaborate a business in a number of ways. It can develop its product offerings within that business, it can develop its market via new segments, new channels, or new geographical areas, or it can simply push the same products more vigorously through the same markets. Back in 1965, Igor Ansoff showed these strategies (as well as one to be discussed in the next section) as presented in Figure 5.

	Existing Product	New Product
Existing Market	Penetration Strategies	Product Development Strategies
New Market	Market Development Strategies	Diversification Strategies

FIGURE 5
Ways to Elaborate a Given Business
From Ansoff (1965:109), with minor modifications; see also Johnson and Jones (1957:52).

Penetration Strategies: Penetration strategies work from a base of existing products and existing markets, seeking to penetrate the market by increasing the organization's share of it. This may be done by straight *expansion* or by the *takeover* of existing competitors. Trying to expand sales with no fundamental change in product or market (buying market share through more promotion, etc.) is at one and the same time the most obvious thing to do and perhaps the most difficult to succeed at, because, at least in a relatively stable market, it means extracting market share from other firms, which logically leads to increased competition. Takeover, where possible, obviously avoids this, but perhaps at a high cost. The harvesting strategy, popularized in the 1970s by the Boston Consulting Group, in some ways represents the opposite of the penetration strategies. The way to deal with "cash cows"—businesses with high market shares but low growth potential—was to harvest them, cease investment and exploit whatever potential remained. The mixing of the metaphors may have been an indication of the dubiousness of the strategy, since to harvest a cow is, of course, to kill it. (See the Seeger reading in Chapter 11).

Market Development Strategies: A predominant strategy here is *market elaboration,* which means promoting existing products in new markets—in effect broadening the scope of the business by finding new market segments, perhaps served by new channels. Product substitution is a particular case of market elaboration, where uses for a product are promoted that enable it to substitute for other products. *Market consolidation* is the inverse of market elaboration, namely reducing the number of segments. But this is not just a strategy of failure. Given the common tendency to proliferate market segments, it makes sense for the healthy organization to rationalize them periodically, to purge the excesses.

Geographic Expansion Strategies: An important form of market development can be geographic expansion—carrying the existing product offering to new geographical areas, anywhere from the next block to across the world. When this also involves a strategy of geographic rationalization—locating different business functions in different places—it is sometimes referred to as a "global strategy." The IKEA furniture company, for example, designs in Scandinavia, sources in Eastern Europe among other places, and markets in Western Europe and North America.

Product Development Strategies: Here we can distinguish a simple *product extention* strategy from a more extensive *product line proliferation* strategy, and their counterparts, *product line rationalization.* Offering new or modified products in the same basic business is another obvious way to elaborate a core business—from cornflakes to bran flakes and rice crispies, eventually offering every permutation and combination of the edible grains. This may amount to differentiation by design, if the products are new and distinctive, or else to no more than increased scope through segmentation, if standardized products are added to the line. Product line proliferation means aiming at comprehensive product segmentation—the complete coverage of a given business. Rationalization means culling products and thinning the line to get rid of overlaps or unprofitable excesses. Again we might expect cycles of product extension and rationalization, at least in businesses (such as cosmetics and textiles) predisposed to proliferation in their product lines.

EXTENDING THE CORE BUSINESS

Now we come to strategies designed to take organizations beyond their core business. This can be done in so-called vertical or horizontal ways, as well as combinations of the two. "Vertical" means backward or forward in the operating chain, the strategy being known formally as "vertical integration," although why this has been designated vertical is difficult to understand, especially since the flow of product and the chain itself are almost always drawn horizontally! Hence this will here be labeled chain integration. "Horizontal" diversification (its own geometry no more evident), which will be called here just plain diversification, refers to encompassing within the organization other, parallel businesses, not in the same chain of operations.

Chain Integration Strategies: Organizations can extend their operating chains downstream or upstream, encompassing within their own operations the activities of their customers on the delivery end or their suppliers on the sourcing end. In effect, they choose to "make" rather than to "buy" or sell. *Impartation* (Barreyre, 1984; Barreyre and Carle, 1983) is a label that has been proposed to describe the opposite strategy, where the organization chooses to buy what it previously made, or sell what it previously transferred.

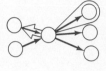

Diversification Strategies: *Diversification* refers to the entry into some business not in the same chain of operation. It may be *related* to some distinctive competence or asset of the core business itself (also called *concentric* diversification); otherwise, it is referred to as *unrelated* or *conglomerate,* diversification. In related diversification, there is evident potential synergy between the new business and the core one, based on a common facility, asset, channel, skill, even opportunity. Porter (1985:323–324) makes the distinction here between "intangible" and "tangible" relatedness. The former is based on some functional or managerial skill considered common across the businesses, as in a Philip Morris using its marketing capabilities in Kraft. The latter refers to businesses that actually "share activities in the value chain" (p. 323), for example, different products sold by the same sales force. It should be emphasized here that no matter what its basis, every related diversification is also fundamentally an unrelated one, as many diversifying organizations have discovered to their regret. That is, no matter what *is* common between two different businesses, many other things are not.

Strategies of Entry and Control: Chain integration or diversification may be achieved by *internal development* or *acquisition.* In other words, an organization can enter a new business by developing it itself or by buying an organization already in that business. Our little diagrams show the former as a circle growing out from the core business to envelope the new business, the latter as an arrow coming out from the core business to connect to the new but already established business. Both internal development and acquisition involve complete ownership and formal control of the diversified business. But there are a host of other possible strategies, as follows:

Strategies of Entry and Control

Full ownership and control	• Internal Development
	• Acquisition
Partial ownership and control	• Majority, minority
	• Partnership, including
	• Joint venture
	• Turnkey (temporary control)
Partial control without ownership	• Licencing
	• Franchising
	• Long-term contracting

Combined Integration-Diversification Strategies: Among the most interesting are those strategies that combine chain integration with business diversification, sometimes leading organizations into whole networks of new businesses. *By-product diversification* involves selling off the by-products of the operating chain in separate markets, as when an airline offers its maintenance services to other carriers. The new activity amounts to a form of market development at some intermediate point in the operating chain. *Linked diversification* extends by-product diversification: one business simply leads to another, whether integrated "vertically" or diversified "horizontally." The organization pursues its operating chain upstream, downstream, sidestream; it exploits preproducts, end products, and by-products of its core products as well as of each other, ending up with a network of businesses, as illustrated in the case of a supermarket chain in Figure 6. *Crystalline diversification* pushes the previous strategy to the limit, so that it becomes difficult and perhaps irrelevant to distinguish integration from diversification, core activities from peripheral activities, closely related businesses from distantly related ones. What were once clear links in a few chains now metamorphose into what looks like a form of crystalline growth, as business after business gets added literally right and left as well as up and down. Here businesses tend to be related, at least initially, through internal development of core competences, as in the "coating and bonding technologies" that are common to so many of 3M's products.

Withdrawal Strategies: Finally there are strategies that reverse all those of diversification: organizations cut back on the businesses they are in. "Exit" has been one popular label for this, withdrawal is another. Sometimes organizations *shrink* their activities, canceling long-term licenses, ceasing to sell by-products, reducing their crystalline networks. Other times they abandon or *liquidate* businesses (the

FIGURE 6
Linked Diversification on a Time Scale—the Case of the Steinberg chain
From Mintzberg and Waters (1982:490).

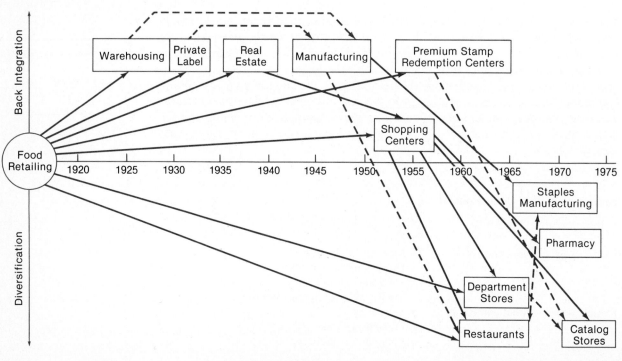

opposite of internal development), or else they *divest* them (the opposite of acquisition).

RECONCEIVING THE CORE BUSINESS(ES)

It may seem strange to end a discussion of strategies of ever more elaborate development of a business with ones involving reconception of the business. But in one important sense, there is a logic to this: after a core business has been identified, distinguished, elaborated, and extended, there often follows the need not just to consolidate it but also to redefine it and reconfigure it—in essence, to reconceive it. As they develop, through all the waves of expansion, integration, diversification, and so on, some organizations lose a sense of themselves. Then reconception becomes the ultimate form of consolidation: rationalizing not just excesses in product offerings or markets segments or even new businesses, but all of these things together and more—the essence of the entire strategy itself. We can identify three basic reconception strategies:

Business Redefinition Strategy: A business, as Abell (1980) has pointed out, may be defined in a variety of ways—by the function it performs, the market it serves, the product it produces. All businesses have popular conceptions. Some are narrow and tangible, such as the canoe business, others broader and vague, such as the financial services business. All such definitions, no matter how tangible, are ultimately concepts that exist in the minds of actors and observers. It therefore becomes possible, with a little effort and imagination, to *redefine* a particular business—reconceive the "recipe" for how that business is conducted (Grinyer and Spender, 1979; Spender, 1989)—as Edwin Land did when he developed the Polaroid camera.[3]

Business Recombination Strategies: As Porter notes, through the waves of diversification that swept American business in the 1960s and 1970s, "the concept of synergy has become widely regarded as passé"—a "nice idea" but one that rarely occurred in practice" (1985:317–318). Businesses were elements in a portfolio to be bought and sold, or, at best, grown and harvested. Deploring that conclusion, Porter devoted three chapters of his 1985 book to "horizontal strategy," which we shall refer to here (given our problems with the geometry of this field) as *business recombination* strategies—efforts to recombine different businesses in some way, at the limit to reconceive various businesses as one. Businesses can be recombined tangibly or only conceptually. The latter was encouraged by Levitt's "Marketing Myopia" (1960) article. By a stroke of the pen, railroads could be in the transportation business, ball bearing manufacturers in the friction reduction business. Realizing some practical change in behavior often proved much more difficult, however. But when some substantial basis exists for combining different activities, a strategy of business recombination can be very effective. There may never have been a transportation business, but 3M was able to draw on common technological capabilities to create a coating and bonding business.[4] Business recombination can

---

[3] MacMillan refers to the business redefinition strategy as "reshaping the industry infrastructure" (1983:18), while Porter calls it "reconfiguration" (1985:519–523), although his notion of product *substitution,* (273–314) could sometimes also constitute a form of business redefinition.

[4] Our suspicion, we should note, is that such labels often emerge after the fact, as the organization seeks a way to rationalize the diversification that has already taken place. In effect, the strategy is emergent. (See Chapter 1 on "Five Ps for Strategy.")

also be more tangible, based on shared activities in the value chain, as in a strategy of *bundling,* where complementary products are sold together for a single price (e.g., automobile service with the new car). Of course, *unbundling* can be an equally viable strategy, such as selling "term" insurance free of any investment obligation. Carried to their logical extreme, the more tangible recombination strategies lead to a "systems view" of the business, where all products and services are conceived to be tightly interrelated.

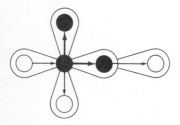

Core Relocation Strategies: Finally we come full circle by closing the discussion where we began, on the location of the core business. An organization, in addition to having one or more strategic positions in a marketplace, tends to have what Jay Galbraith (1983) calls a single "center of gravity" (see his article in Chapter 6), some conceptual place where is concentrated not only its core skills but also its cultural heart, as in a Procter & Gamble focusing its efforts on "branded consumer products," each "sold primarily by advertising to the homemaker and managed by a brand manager" (1984:13). But as changes in strategic position take place, shifts can also take place in this center of gravity, in various ways. First, the organization can move *along the operating chain,* upstream or downstream, as did General Mills "from a flour miller to a related diversified provider of products for the homemaker"; eventually the company sold off its flour milling operation altogether (Galbraith, 1983:76). Second, there can be a shift *between dominant functions,* say from production to marketing. Third is the shift *to a new business,* whether or not at the same stage of the operating chain. Such shifts can be awfully demanding, simply because each industry is a culture with its own ways of thinking and acting. Finally, is the shift *to a new core theme,* as in the reorientation from a single function or product to a broader concept, for example when Procter & Gamble changed from being a soap company to being in the personal care business.

This brings us to the end of our discussion of generic strategies—our loop from locating a business to distinguishing it, elaborating it, extending it, and finally reconceiving it. We should close with the warning that while a framework of generic strategies may help to think about positioning an organization, use of it as a pat list may put that organization at a disadvantage against competitors that develop their strategies in more creative ways.

• DEVELOPING COMPETITIVE ADVANTAGE*

BY XAVIER GILBERT AND PAUL STREBEL

Different industries offer different competitive opportunities and, as a result, successful strategies vary from one industry to another. Identifying which strategies can lead to competitive advantages in an industry may be done in three main steps:

1. *Industry definition:* This involves defining the boundaries of the industry, learning its rules of the game and identifying the other players.

---

* This article was prepared especially for the first edition of this book, and was also published with modifications in *The Handbook of Business Strategy: 1986–1987 Year Book,* William D. Guth (ed.), (Warrer, Gorham and Lamont, 1986), used with the permission of Xavier Gilbert and Paul Strebel.

2. *Identification of possible competitive moves:* Competitive moves exploit the possible sources of competitive advantages in the industry. Their degree of effectiveness evolves with the industry life cycle and is influenced by the moves of other competitors.

3. *Selecting among generic strategies:* Successful strategies rely on a sequence of competitive moves. There are only a few such successful sequences corresponding to different industry situations.

We shall discuss each of these steps in turn.

INDUSTRY DEFINITION

The arena of competition within which an industry member should fight will be described in terms of its boundaries, its rules of the game, and its players.

Identifying the Boundaries of the Industry

In identifying what constitutes the industry, we must take into account all the activities that are necessary to deliver a product or service that meets the expectations of a market. In this regard, many definitions of a company's business, or of its industry, have been too narrow: there is more to its business than a product, a process, and a market; there is in fact an entire chain of activities, from product design to product utilization by the final customer, that must be mobilized to meet certain market expectations.

The most commonly accepted term to designate this chain of activities is the *business system.* The concept, or some variation of it, has been used frequently under different names, such as "industry dynamics" or "value chain"; the term "business system" was coined in the Seventies by the consulting firm McKinsey & Company, from whom we borrow it. Some examples will illustrate why it is important to take into account the entire chain of activities represented by the business system when deciding how to compete.

The first example is provided by the personal computer industry (Figure 1). The business system of the personal computer industry includes a wide range of activities: product design, component manufacturing, different stages of assembly, software development, marketing, selling, distribution, service and support to the customer, and the utilization of the product by the customer. Each of these activities is expected to add value to the product so that it meets the needs of the customer. A view of all the activities necessary to serve customer expectations, as provided by the industry's business system, is thus the starting point of industry analysis.

Different competitors have made different choices with respect to how these activities should be dealt with. Some have designed their product around the "IBM industry standard" in order to have access to software, while others have been using a proprietary operating system. Some are designing their own components, while others are finding sources for them outside. Some have selectively authorized dealers to sell their products, while others use mass-retailing channels and others again sell directly to the final customer. This shows that there may be different ways to use the activities in the business system to provide value to the final customer.

Rather than considering the company as competing *in an industry,* it should thus be seen as competing *within a business system,* in the same way as a chess player uses the resources of a chessboard. A chess player does not try to win by

FIGURE 1
The PC Industry

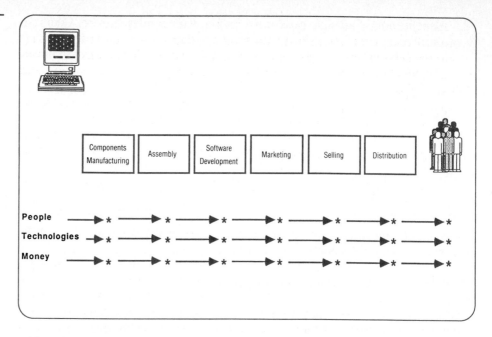

asking simply, "How do I win at chess?" Instead, the player asks, "How should I use my pawns, my rooks, my knights, my bishops, my queen, and even my king?" Similarly, each personal computer company should see itself as competing with other companies on design, on component manufacturing, on assembly of specific configurations, on software development, on marketing, on selling, on distribution, and on service support to the customer, and not simply as competing "in the personal computer industry."

Learning the Rules of the Game

Each activity in the business system adds perceived value to the product or service. Value,[1] for the customer, is the perceived stream of benefits that accrue from obtaining the product or service. Price is what the customer is willing to pay for that stream of benefits. If the price of a good or service is high, it must provide high value, otherwise it is driven out of the market. If the value of a good or service is low, its price must be low, otherwise it is also driven out of the market. Hence, in a competitive situation, and over a period of time, the price customers are willing to pay for a good or service is a good proxy measure of its value.

The "game" is to create a disequilibrium between the perceived value offered and the price asked by either increasing the former or by reducing the latter. This modifies the terms of competition and potentially drives competitors out of the market. Competitors will have to respond by either offering more perceived value for the same price or by offering the same value at a lower price.

At the same time, each activity in the business system is performed at a cost. Getting the stream of benefits that accrue from the good or service to the customer is thus done at a certain "delivered cost" which sets a lower limit to the price of the good or service if the business system is to remain profitable. Decreasing the price will thus imply that the delivered cost be first decreased by adjusting the business system. As a result, the rules of the game may also be described as providing the highest possible perceived value to the final customer, at the lowest possible delivered cost.

84

---

[1] "Value" is used here with the meaning it is given by economists in the utility theory.

In addition, the intrinsic logic of the business system must also be taken into account. This logic is dictated by the fact that the business-system activities must be coordinated to provide a specific final product. This requirement is best examined at the level of the resources needed for each activity: people, technologies and money.

The personal computer industry again illustrates the point. Among the resources needed to perform the various activities of the business system, the technologies will be used as an example. First, the final customers are not supposed to be computer experts. Their technological know-how might be in the areas of financial analysis, accounting or text processing, not in programming or establishing communication protocols with peripherals. This implies technological choices at the level of product and software design that will make the machine user friendly. It also implies that the technology required to service the machine and to assist customers, also selected at the time of product design, be compatible with the technology available in the distribution channels.

Similar consistency requirements could be observed with respect to the other resources: people and money. If these rules of the game were not respected, the business system could not deliver a product or service of desired perceived value. Laying out the activities of the business system and the resources required by each of them is thus necessary before the game can be played effectively.

Identifying the Other Players

"Players" in a business system do not consist only of competitors; they may be other participants in the business system that perform vital activities. For the provider of a product or service, managing the business system can be complicated by players up- and downstream in the system. By playing an optimal game from their perspective, these other participants may suboptimize the whole business system and put pressure on other activities.

Consider for example the Swiss watch industry (Figure 2). As long as competition was limited, the Swiss watch manufacturers, who were essentially fragmented assemblers, enjoyed satisfactory margins, even though their value added

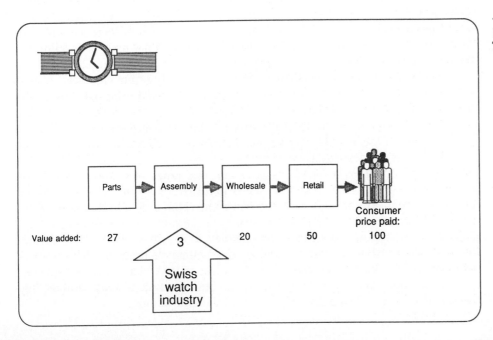

FIGURE 2
The Swiss Watch Industry

was small relative to the entire business system. But the industry experienced intense global competition during the Seventies and Eighties, leading to sharp price decreases. The first reaction was to believe that competition among watchmakers was the source of these difficulties. Attempts were made to restructure the Swiss watch industry so as to obtain economies of scale similar to those of global competitors.

However, the business system shows clearly that competition among watchmakers was not the biggest problem. Producing cheaper watches was necessary, but not sufficient. The Swiss watchmakers were competing fiercely for the consumers' money with costly distribution channels whose added value was questionable for a fast growing mass market. Developing a watch which would not only be inexpensive, but could also be sold through low-margin distribution channels with no service, such as the Swatch, was the way to circumvent this form of competition effectively.

COMPETITIVE MOVES

Competitive advantages are built on the ability to utilize the business system to provide final customers with the desired perceived value, at the lowest delivered cost. However, not all the activities of a business system offer the same potential to build these competitive advantages. In addition, their choice is affected by the stage of development of the industry as well as by the moves of other competitors. This leads to the identification of a limited number of generic moves to gain competitive advantages.

Competitive Advantages Offered by the Business System

Superior profitability requires either higher perceived value and/or lower delivered cost than the competition. This is achieved either through superior performance in at least one of the business-system activities, or through a creative and innovative combination of several activities. Such *competitive formulas* are the basis of all successful strategies.

For example, in the watch industry the main activities of the business system include design, manufacturing of movement parts, movement assembly, case manufacturing and assembly, wholesaling, and retail. Each of these activities can be performed to maximize the perceived value for the final user, or to minimize the delivered cost. Design, for example, can emphasize luxury and elegance, or it can ensure low-cost manufacturing. Traditional distribution channels through wholesalers and specialty stores will provide more perceived value, while mass distribution directly through low-margin outlets will contribute to a low delivered cost. A range of competitive formulas can thus be developed, combining the various activities of the business system in a manner that will provide the desired perceived value at the desired delivered cost.

Two observations, however, suggest that this range of possible competitive formulas is not very wide. The first one is that there is an internal logic to each business system. The balance between perceived value and delivered cost cannot be established for one activity independently of the others. For example, it is not possible to use traditional distribution channels to distribute the Swatch. Because of the high distribution margins and of the limited volume the delivered cost would be higher than the perceived value. This is indeed what is meant by a competitive formula. The various activities of the business system must combine high perceived value and low delivered cost in a coherent manner.

The second observation is that high perceived value and low delivered cost constitute the only possible generic competitive moves. Experience shows that there are no other possibilities. There are only variations around these two main themes, as allowed by the expectations of different market segments. Strategic advantages are obtained by combining them in a sequence, one being implemented preferably in a way that prepares the implementation of the other at a later time.

Many failures have been caused by the inability to put together coherent business systems, with respect to low delivered cost and high perceived value. This was exactly how the Swiss watch industry got into trouble, trying to compete in markets expecting low delivered cost with a business system designed for high perceived value. When the promoters of the Swatch saw that the biggest revolution in the industry was not a technological one, but a distribution one, they engineered a fine-tuned competitive formula in which each business-system activity contributed to delivering a watch for less than SFr50 (about $25). Even though the Swatch is very precise and carries an element of snobbish appeal, the move was quite clearly a low-delivered-cost one, with a formula that provided maximum perceived value within the low-delivered-cost constraint.

Stage of Development of the Industry

Although it would be theoretically feasible to choose either of these two moves—high perceived value or low delivered cost—at any point in time, the actual possibilities are in fact strongly influenced by the stage of industry development. The personal computer industry will be used as an example of the inferences that can be drawn from an industry life cycle to assist in the diagnosis of potential competitive advantages.

Consider first the personal computer industry in the second half of the Seventies. The characteristics of the product were in a state of flux, with many competing versions. The manufacturing process was not yet a matter of real concern, as the technology was still evolving. The business system of the industry had not stabilized. Competition was restricted to product innovation and development. These characteristics are typical of an *emerging industry* offering *high perceived value* to a limited market (Figure 3).

Consider now the personal computer industry after IBM's entry. Even though IBM's product was not regarded by seasoned users as particularly innovative on the technological side, it had the perhaps unintended advantage of embodying an acceptable common denominator of characteristics desired by a wide cross section of the market. Not the least of these characteristics was the image of IBM's reliability. The IBM PC was soon perceived as the industry standard.

Standardization marks the first important transition to another phase of industry evolution during which competitive advantages shift to *low delivered cost*. This new phase is characterized by *rapid market development*. The personal computer industry was no exception as it moved into a period of very rapid growth in unit sales. Attention had to be shifted to the production process, while most manufacturers were adopting the "IBM standard." Rather than further product development, resources were now directed towards the entire business system: process technology, market positioning, and distribution efficiency were key.

When IBM and others began to use prices strategically, many of the early competitors could not follow. Those who did survive had joined the industry-standard bandwagon and had the necessary resources to invest in the manufacturing process. The key competitors were now large, professional firms which followed a similar, low-delivered-cost industry discipline.

FIGURE 3
Industry Life Cycle

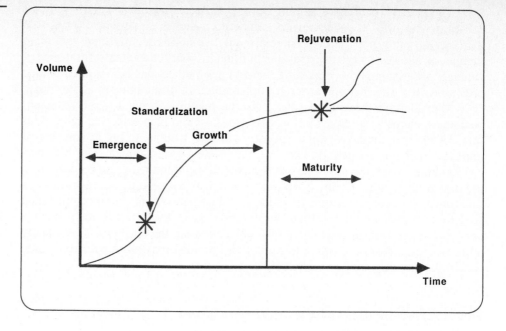

At the end of 1984 and in 1985, however, a new turn took place in the industry. Signs of *industry maturity* were appearing in the United States, while activity was starting again on the side of product improvement. IBM itself launched its PC-AT and the need for networks was receiving increasing attention from competitors. Such renewed interest in the perceived value of the product is typical at this stage of an industry's evolution, often called rejuvenation (Figure 3). However, the entire process that made the business system work was still getting much attention. Resources were now channeled both to the process and to a new product generation: integrated computer networks. These developments were in the hands of a few large competitors who could be active on two fronts, process and product.

In a *maturing industry, rejuvenation* is the second important evolutionary transition. It marks the shift to product differentiation and innovation, in addition to cost reduction and process efficiency. At this stage, competitive advantages must be maintained on two fronts: *low delivered cost* and, again, *high perceived value.* As a result of this combination, however, perceived-value advantages can only be marginal and short lived. This is a time when marketing activity is at its peak.

The effectiveness of high-perceived-value and low-delivered-cost advantages thus varies with the stage of development of the industry. The two generic moves that lead to these advantages must be implemented at the right stage of development of the industry, either to accelerate its evolution, or to follow it.

Identifying Strategic Groups

The competitors in an industry can be positioned according to which generic moves they are making at a given time. The resulting mapping may be examined for signs of strategic groups of competitors.

Identifying strategic groups can serve several purposes. An important one is to assess how the moves of competitors may affect the evolution of the industry. The life cycle of an industry is not only pulled by changes in market expectations. It is also pushed by the move of some of the competitors. For example, IBM's entry in the personal computer industry accelerated the transition to market development. Subsequently, IBM's low-delivered-cost move accompanied with decreasing prices accelerated the transition to maturity. As we have seen, assessing the industry evolution is an important input in deciding which competitive move to implement next.

In addition, the identification of strategic groups can serve two other purposes. First, by observing how the key competitors are playing the business system to obtain their competitive advantages, it is possible to develop a better understanding of the business system and of the possible competitive advantages it offers. Second, identifying which competitive positions are occupied and by whom helps decide which competitors may be confronted or avoided.

Although the movements of competitors can be assessed quantitatively, since both perceived value and delivered cost can be measured, an example of how it can be done qualitatively will be provided here. This example is based on the personal computer industry (Figure 4).

Three main groups could be identified in early 1986. The first group included the industry-standard competitors, of course led by IBM. A low-delivered-cost obsession was clear with this group, as indicated by the price decreases that marked 1985 and were continuing in 1986. In addition to IBM, the group included Compaq, Zenith, for example in the United States, Sharp, Epson and Toshiba from Japan, and Olivetti from Europe. All were offering basically the same commodity-like product. All were seeing low price as a necessary condition to stay in the game. However, and this is characteristic of a mature industry, all were also trying to offer something else in addition to low price, such as more speed, more capacity, more user friendliness, wider distribution. But none of these features could yield a lasting advantage.

There was a second group that was trying to exploit the fact that the rules of the game could perhaps be changed. If networking of personal computers, with each other and with mainframes, became critical, which seemed to be the case, the personal computer would become a standard workstation in a decentralized data processing system. It would no longer be the "force de frappe" and future competitive advantages would accrue from the ability to provide communication hardware and software.

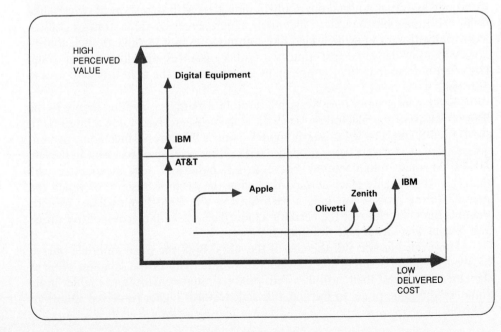

FIGURE 4
Strategic Groups: The PC Industry

Among the companies competing effectively in this direction were Digital Equipment and other minicomputer vendors, who had traditionally networked their machines. IBM was also trying to compete on this front, with its usual follower approach, but it was hampered by its traditionally centralized approach to data processing. AT&T and other telecommunication companies were other credible contenders. The strategies in this group were clearly on the side of the high perceived value. The battle of communication standards that was taking place at that time was characteristic of these strategies.

There was finally a third group of those who were beginning to look as if they had missed the boat. Apple was still its most successful member, fighting with low prices and product uniqueness, but a uniqueness of increasingly questionable relevance. However, Apple's statements of intention concerning a future compatibility of the Macintosh with IBM's personal-computer standard and with Digital Equipment's network architecture, demonstrated some understanding of the emerging new rules of the game.

GENERIC STRATEGIES

Two generic moves, leading either to high perceived value, or to low delivered cost advantages, have been identified and their relevance at different stages of evolution of an industry has been discussed. Successful competitors, however, appear to be combining these moves within overall strategies that allow them to maintain a superior competitive position throughout the evolution of their industry. Two types of generic strategies can be identified:

> One-dimensional strategies, either high perceived value or low delivered cost.
> Outpacing strategies, either preemptive or proactive.

One-dimensional Strategies

One-dimensional strategies rely on the continued repetition of one move, either a high-perceived-value one, or low-delivered-cost one. The situations where this seems possible are not numerous. Only in industries with very short life cycles, like fashion, is it possible to pursue indefinitely a high-perceived-value strategy. Only in industries with very long life cycles, like commodities, is it possible to stick continuously to a low-delivered-cost strategy. In other instances, one-dimensional strategies often hide an inability to implement a new move at the right time and lead to disasters.

The Japanese entry into Western automobile markets is an illustration. In the Sixties, Western manufacturers were pursuing high-perceived-value strategies. In the United States, this led to yearly model changes. In Europe, ingenious, overengineered small cars were being produced with rather primitive processes. In the late Sixties, Japanese manufacturers began to sell basic and very inexpensive cars thanks to their highly efficient way of playing the business system, of which the manufacturing process was only a part. Success was almost immediate. Western manufacturers failed to see the need for a radical change in their competitive thrust and several were never able to respond.

However, this was not the end of the story. Both the price umbrella offered by Western manufacturers and the superior productivity of the Japanese allowed the latter to reinvest their cash-flow into product improvements and to offer more value for the same price. In Europe, this shift towards higher perceived value was welcomed because it brought new attraction to a standardizing product entering the maturity stage. In the United States, it essentially met an unsatisfied need for a lower-value, lower-price car to which U.S. manufacturers could never respond. This is evidenced by the instant success achieved by Hyundai by providing the same value as a Japanese car maker, but for less money.

Outpacing Strategies

The example of the automobile industry showed clearly that the formulation of a successful strategy rarely relies on the repeated implementation of the same move to maintain a static position. Successful strategies generally consist of a planned sequence of moves from one position to another, at the right time. The sequential implementation of competitive moves should not be seen as strategy changes. It must be planned, one move creating the conditions for the implementation of the next. The dynamic nature of successful strategies is reflected in their description as *outpacing* strategies (Figure 5). Outpacing strategies can be preemptive or proactive.

A preemptive strategy is needed by an industry leader to prevent the occurrence of a situation such as the one in the automobile industry. If successful, this strategy will shift the industry life cycle from the emergence stage to the growth stage. Its purpose is to prevent followers from developing secure low-price positions. This is achieved by shifting at the right time from a high-perceived-value position to a low-delivered-cost one. This implies the establishment of a product standard and the development of a *pricing reserve.*

Establishing a standard is not only a matter of technology, as was well demonstrated by the IBM Personal Computer. It is rather a question of business system: establishing a formula that meets the expectations of a larger number of potential customers than do other competitive formulas. It is the desired outcome of a high-perceived-value move.

Developing a pricing reserve simply means investing in process improvements to enable the shift to a low-delivered-cost strategy, as soon as a standard is

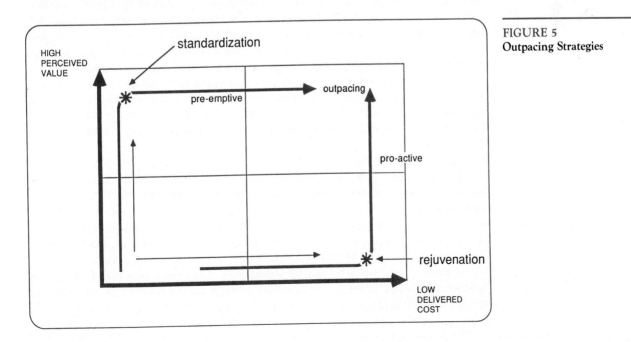

FIGURE 5
Outpacing Strategies

accepted. Experience shows that very few companies can make this shift effectively. It is nevertheless the condition for the tactical use of prices to prevent followers from generating the cash flow that will be necessary to go through the next industry transition, from low delivered cost, back to high perceived value, when the industry matures, if not to discourage them from entering at all. Such a strategy was followed by IBM, immediately after the IBM PC was accepted as a standard.

The timing of a preemptive, outpacing strategy is clearly critical. Launched too early, considerable investments in process improvement will be started before the formula is accepted as a standard. Should another standard emerge rapidly, the company will not be able to write off its previous process investments. Launched too late, further investments will have been made into product improvements which the market will not be willing to pay for. This will make it difficult to defend market share against the lower-priced standards and will waste resources that would otherwise be needed for process investments.

Proactive, outpacing strategies are required after the industry transition to lower growth and maturity. Their purpose is to escape the stalemate of maturity, so characteristic of many industries, where price wars often equate with self destruction. Often implemented by followers, they consist in building a solid low-delivered-cost position from which to launch a high-perceived-value move. While a preemptive strategy focuses on a mass market, a proactive one focuses on selected market segments to which more perceived value can be offered through a range of possibilities, from simple formula differentiation to rejuvenation of the industry. All these possibilities imply essentially the same approach: changing the rules of the game of the business system.

This is done by "unbundling" the perceived value added by each activity of the business system: what does each activity really provide to the selected market segment, and at what cost? The process of unbundling will identify elements of perceived value that are not worth their delivered cost. Then additional elements of perceived value, desirable for the market segment, can be included in the formula at an acceptable cost.

An example of this approach is the way in which the Swedish firm, IKEA, redesigned its business system in order to compete effectively in furniture mass distribution. IKEA eliminated or modified the activities that increased the delivered cost and did not add essential perceived value from the consumer point of view. Carefully monitored subcontracting of production to specialized manufacturers ensured quality at a lower cost. The furniture was no longer assembled, but flat-packed. It was not displayed in city-center stores, but in hyperstores, outside cities. A trade-off was made between minimum inventories, to decrease the delivered cost, and immediate availability. Furthermore, by doing its own product design, IKEA could ensure a low-delivered cost consistency throughout its business system.

On the other hand, perceived value was added where this could be done for a low-delivered cost. A very wide range of home products was offered under the same roof and could be looked at and tried by the consumer in the display section of the stores, rather than only seen in different stores or in catalogues. The furniture was normally available immediately and could be taken back home by car. Doing its own design, IKEA could offer a homogeneous, modular product range. The desirable image of Scandinavian furniture was skillfully exploited to add perceived value. Last but not least, by redesigning its entire business system, IKEA built an additional powerful competitive advantage: the know-how necessary to operate this formula.

Analysis of competitive advantage is thus an intrinsic part of strategic management, rather than a separate exercise, as it is often presented. Indeed, it cannot be performed linearly in a way that leads to one end product, the "knowledge of the industry." It is performed through an iterative process, leading to hypotheses concerning possible strategies, testing them against the company's capabilities and against the positions of competition, and going back to the drawing board to assess other possibilities. This iterative process is the foundation on which each move can lead to sustainable competitive advantages by being part of an overall strategy to fight in the dynamic battlefield of an industry. Bringing this iterative process to life is a permanent responsibility of the general manager of a business unit.

5

STRATEGY FORMATION

The readings of the last two chapters described how strategies are supposed to be made and thereby illustrated the *pre*scriptive side of the field. This chapter presents readings that describe how strategies really do seem to be made, the *de*scriptive side. We title this chapter "Strategy Formation" to emphasize the point introduced in Chapter 1 that strategies can *form* implicitly as well as be *formulated* explicitly.

The preceding chapters may seem to deal with an unreachable utopia, this one with an imperfect reality. But there may be a better conclusion: that *pre*scription offers useful guidelines for thinking about ends and how to order physical resources efficiently to achieve them, while *de*scription provides a useful frame of reference for considering how this must be related to real-world patterns of behavior in organizations. Another way to say this is that while the analytical tools and models prescribed earlier are vital to thinking about strategy intelligently, they must also be rooted in a genuine understanding of the realities of organizations. Unfortunately, management writers, especially in traditional strategy textbooks, have often been quick to prescribe without offering enough appreciation of why managers and organizations act in the ways they do.

Brian Quinn opens with a sharp focus on how managers really do seem to behave when they create strategy. This reading is drawn from his book *Strategies for Change, Logical Incrementalism,* and it develops a particular view of the strategy-making process based on intensive interviews in some of America's and Europe's best known corporations. Planning does not capture the essence of strategy formation, according to Quinn, although it does play an important role in developing new data and in confirming strategies derived in other ways. The traditional view of incrementalism does not fit observed behavior patterns either. The proc-

esses Quinn observed seem incremental on the surface, but a powerful logic underlies them. And, unlike the other incremental processes, these are not so much
*re*active as subtly *pro*active. Executives use incremental approaches to deal simultaneously with the informational, motivational, and political aspects of creating a
strategy.

Above all, Quinn depicts strategy formation as a managed interactive *learning* process in which the chief strategist gradually works out strategy in his or her
own mind and orchestrates the organization's acceptance of it. In emphasizing the
role of a central strategist—or small groups managing "subsystems" of strategy—
Quinn often seems close to Andrews's view. But the two differ markedly in other
important respects. In his emphasis on the political and motivational dimensions
of strategy, Quinn may be closer to Wrapp whose managers "don't make policy decisions." In fact, Quinn attempts to integrate his views with the traditional one,
noting that while the strategies themselves "emerge" from an incremental process,
they have many of the characteristics of the highly deliberate ones of Andrews's
strategists.

The following reading by Mintzberg complements that of Quinn. Called
"Crafting Strategy," it shows how managers mold strategies the way craftsmen
mold their clay. This reading also builds on Mintzberg's reading of Chapter 1 on
the different forms of strategy, developing further the concept of emergent strategy.

As you will see, the two authors of this book share a basic philosophy about
how organizations must go about the difficult process of setting basic direction in a
complex world. They also share a basic belief in the key role of the actual strategy-
making process in organizations. Hence the title of the book, *The Strategy Process*
and the particular importance of this chapter in it.

In a chapter that challenges many of the accepted notions about how strategy
should be made, the next reading may be the most upsetting of all. In it Richard
Pascale, a well-known consultant, writer, and lecturer at Stanford Business School,
challenges head on not only the whole approach to strategy analysis (as represented
in the last chapter), especially as practiced by the Boston Consulting Group (one of
the better known "strategy boutiques" whose ideas will be discussed in Chapters 10
and 11), but also the very concept of strategy formulation itself.

As his point of departure, Pascale describes a BCG study carried out for the
British government to explain how manufacturers in that country lost the American motorcycle market to the Japanese, and to the Honda Company in particular.
The analysis seems impeccable and eminently logical: The Japanese were simply
more clever, by thinking through a brilliant strategy before they acted. But then
Pascale flew to Japan and interviewed those clever executives who pulled off this
coup. We shall save the story for Pascale, who tells it with a great deal of color, except to note here its basic message: An openness to learning and a fierce commitment to an organization and its markets may count for more in strategy making
than all the brilliant analysis one can imagine. (Ask yourself while reading these accounts how the strategic behavior of the British motorcycle manufacturers who
received the BCG report might have differed if they had instead received Pascale's
second story.) Pascale in effect takes the arguments for incrementalism and strategy making as a crafting and learning process to their natural conclusions (or one
of them, at least).

No one who reads Pascale's account can ever feel quite so smug about rational strategy analysis again. We include this reading, however, not to encourage
rejection of that type of analysis, or the very solid thinking that has gone into the
works of Porter, Ansoff, and others. Rather, we wish to balance the message conveyed in so much of the strategy literature with the practical lessons from the field.
The point is that successful strategists can no more rely exclusively on such analy-

sis than they can do without it. Effective strategy formation, one must conclude from all these readings, is a sometimes deceptive and multifaceted affair, its complexity never to be underestimated.

We have mentioned the complementarity of the Quinn and Mintzberg views of strategy making. But there is one difference that is worth addressing. While both view the process as one of evolution and learning, Quinn tends to place greater emphasis on the role of the chief executive, and senior management team in general, as central strategist, while Mintzberg tends to place a little more emphasis on others who can feed strategy up the hierarchy, especially in his discussion of a "grass-roots" approach to the process. In effect, organizations may have senior managers sending their strategic visions down the hierarchy, while below creative people may be sending strategic initiatives back up. Effective organizations seem to do both, but that raises a major problem in the strategy process: the middle managers may get caught in the middle, between these two. How to reconcile the two opposing pressures? The Honda reading gives some indication of how they may deal with it, but it is restricted largely to a set of events in one part of a company. Thus we close this chapter on process with a reading that addresses in a rather sophisticated way this very issue. Written by Ikujiro Nonaka, dean of the Japanese strategy researchers and professor of management at Hitotsubashi University, it proposes as a reconciliation a form of "middle-up-down management."

• STRATEGIC CHANGE: "LOGICAL INCREMENTALISM"*

BY JAMES BRIAN QUINN

When I was younger I always conceived of a room where all these [strategic] concepts were worked out for the whole company. Later I didn't find any such room. . . . The strategy [of the company] may not even exist in the mind of one man. I certainly don't know where it is written down. It is simply transmitted in the series of decisions made. (Interview quote)

When well-managed major organizations make significant changes in strategy, the approaches they use frequently bear little resemblance to the rational-analytical systems so often touted in the planning literature. The full strategy is rarely written down in any one place. The processes used to arrive at the total strategy are typically fragmented, evolutionary, and largely intuitive. Although one can usually find embedded in these fragments some very refined *pieces* of formal strategic analysis, the real strategy tends to *evolve* as internal decisions and external events flow together to create a new, widely shared consensus for action among key members of the top management team. Far from being an abrogation of good management practice, the rationale behind this kind of strategy formulation is so powerful that it perhaps provides the normative model for strategic decision making—rather than the step-by-step "formal systems planning" approach so often espoused.

THE FORMAL SYSTEMS PLANNING APPROACH

A strong normative literature states what factors *should* be included in a systematically planned strategy and how to analyze and relate these factors step by step. While this approach is excellent for some purposes, it tends to focus unduly on

---

* Excerpted from an article originally published in *Sloan Management Review* I, no. 20 (Fall 1978), pp. 7–21. Copyright © 1978 by Sloan Management Review; reprinted by permission of the Review.

measurable quantitative factors and to underemphasize the vital qualitative, organizational, and power-behavioral factors which so often determine strategic success in one situation versus another. In practice, such planning is just one building block in a continuous stream of events that really determine corporate strategy.

THE POWER-BEHAVIORAL APPROACH

Other investigators have provided important insights on the crucial psychological, power, and behavioral relationships in strategy formulation. Among other things, these have enhanced understanding about: the *multiple goal structures* of organizations, the *politics* of strategic decisions, executive *bargaining* and *negotiation* processes, *satisficing* (as opposed to maximizing) in decision making, the role of *coalitions* in strategic management, and the practice of "muddling" in the public sphere. Unfortunately, however, many power-behavioral studies have been conducted in settings far removed from the realities of strategy formulation. Others have concentrated solely on human dynamics, power relationships, and organizational processes and ignored the ways in which systematic data analysis shapes and often dominates crucial aspects of strategic decisions. Finally, few have offered much normative guidance for the strategist.

THE STUDY

Recognizing the contributions and limitations of both approaches, I attempted to document the dynamics of actual strategic change processes in some ten major companies as perceived by those most knowledgeably and intimately involved in them. These companies varied with respect to products, markets, time horizons, technological complexities, and national versus international dimensions. . . .[1]

SUMMARY FINDINGS

Several important findings have begun to emerge from these investigations.

- Neither the "power-behavioral" nor the "formal systems planning" paradigm adequately characterizes the way successful strategic processes operate.
- Effective strategies tend to emerge from a series of "strategic subsystems," each of which attacks a specific class of strategic issue (e.g., acquisitions, divestitures, or major reorganizations) in a disciplined way, but which is blended incrementally and opportunistically into a cohesive pattern that becomes the company's strategy.
- The logic behind each "subsystem" is so powerful that, to some extent, it may serve as a normative approach for formulating these key elements of strategy in large companies.
- Because of cognitive and process limits, almost all of these subsystems—and the formal planning activity itself—must be managed and linked together by an approach best described as "logical incrementalism."

---

[1] Cooperating companies included General Motors Corp., Chrysler Corp., Volvo (AB), General Mills, Pillsbury Co., Xerox Corp., Texas Instruments, Exxon, Continental Group, and Pilkington Brothers.

- Such incrementalism is not "muddling." It is a purposeful, effective, proactive management technique for improving and integrating *both* the analytical and behavioral aspects of strategy formulation.

CRITICAL STRATEGIC ISSUES

Although certain "hard data" decisions (e.g., on product-market position or resource allocations) tend to dominate the analytical literature (Ansoff, 1965; Katz, 1970), executives identified other "soft" changes that have at least as much importance in shaping their concern's strategic posture. Most often cited were changes in the company's

1. Overall organizational structure or its basic management style
2. Relationships with the government or other external interest groups
3. Acquisition, divestiture, or divisional control practices
4. International posture and relationships
5. Innovative capabilities or personnel motivations as affected by growth
6. Worker and professional relationships reflecting changed social expectations and values
7. Past or anticipated technological environments

When executives were asked to "describe the processes through which their company arrived at its new posture" vis-à-vis each of these critical domains, several important points emerged. First, few of these issues lent themselves to quantitative modeling techniques or perhaps even formal financial analyses. Second, successful companies used a different "subsystem" to formulate strategy for each major class of strategic issues, yet these "subsystems" were quite similar among companies even in very different industries (see Figure 1). Finally, no single formal analytical process could handle all strategic variables simultaneously on a planned basis. Why?

Precipitating Events

Often external or internal events, over which managements had essentially no control, would precipitate urgent, piecemeal, interim decisions which inexorably shaped the company's future strategic posture. One clearly observes this phenomenon in: the decisions forced on General Motors by the 1973–1974 oil crisis, the shift in posture pressed upon Exxon by sudden nationalizations, or the dramatic opportunities allowed for Haloid Corporation and Pilkington Brothers, Ltd. by the unexpected inventions of xerography and float glass.

In these cases, analyses from earlier formal planning cycles did contribute greatly, as long as the general nature of the contingency had been anticipated. They broadened the information base available (as in Exxon's case), extended the options considered (Haloid-Xerox), created shared values to guide decisions about precipitating events in consistent directions (Pilkington), or built up resource bases, management flexibilities, or active search routines for opportunities whose specific nature could not be defined in advance (General Mills, Pillsbury). But no organization—no matter how brilliant, rational, or imaginative—could possibly foresee the timing, severity, or even the nature of all such precipitating events. Further, when these events did occur there might be neither time, resources, nor information enough to undertake a full formal strategic analysis of all possible options

FIGURE 1

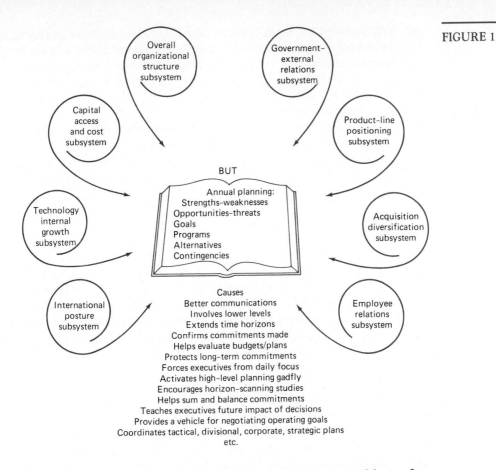

and their consequences. Yet early decisions made under stress conditions often meant new thrusts, precedents, or lost opportunities that were difficult to reverse later.

An Incremental Logic

Recognizing this, top executives usually consciously tried to deal with precipitating events in an incremental fashion. Early commitments were kept broadly formative, tentative, and subject to later review. In some case neither the company nor the external players could understand the full implications of alternative actions. All parties wanted to test assumptions and have an opportunity to learn from and adapt to the others' responses. Such behavior clearly occurred during the 1973–1974 oil crisis; the ensuing interactions improved the quality of decisions for all. It also recurred frequently in other widely different contexts. For example,

Neither the potential producer nor user of a completely new product or process (like xerography or float glass) could fully conceptualize its ramifications without interactive testing. All parties benefited from procedures which purposely delayed decisions and allowed mutual feedback. Some companies, like IBM or Xerox, have formalized this concept into "phase program planning" systems. They make concrete decisions only on individual phases (or stages) of new product developments, establish interactive testing procedures with customers, and postpone final configuration commitments until the latest possible moment.

Similarly, even under pressure, most top executives were extremely sensitive to organizational and power relationships and consciously managed decision processes to improve these dynamics. They often purposely delayed initial decisions, or kept such decisions vague, in order to encourage lower-level participation, to gain more information from specialists, or to build commitment to solutions. Even when a crisis atmosphere tended to shorten time horizons and make decisions more goal oriented than political, perceptive executives consciously tried to keep their options open until they understood how the crisis would affect the power bases and needs of their key constituents. . . .

Conscious incrementalism helps to (1) cope with both the cognitive and process limits on each major decision, (2) build the logical-analytical framework these decisions require, and (3) create the personal and organizational awareness, understanding, acceptance, and commitment needed to implement the strategies effectively.

The Diversification Subsystem

Strategies for diversification, either through R&D or acquisitions, provide excellent examples. The formal analytical steps needed for successful diversification are well documented (Mace and Montgomery, 1962). However, the precise directions that R&D may project the company can only be understood step by step as scientists uncover new phenomena, make and amplify discoveries, build prototypes, reduce concepts to practice, and interact with users during product introductions. Similarly, only as each acquisition is sequentially identified, investigated, negotiated for, and integrated into the organization can one predict its ultimate impact on the total enterprise.

A step-by-step approach is clearly necessary to guide and assess the strategic fit of each internal or external diversification candidate. Incremental processes are also required to manage the crucial psychological and power shifts that ultimately determine the program's overall direction and consequences. These processes help unify both the analytical and behavioral aspects of diversification decisions. They create the broad conceptual consensus, the risk-taking attitudes, the organizational and resource flexibilities, and the adaptive dynamism that determine both the timing and direction of diversification strategies. Most important among these processes are:

- *Generating a genuine, top-level psychological commitment to diversification.* General Mills, Pillsbury, and Xerox all started their major diversification programs with broad analytical studies and goal-setting exercises designed both to build top-level consensus around the need to diversify and to establish the general directions for diversification. Without such action, top-level bargaining for resources would have continued to support only more familiar (and hence apparently less risky) old lines, and this could delay or undermine the entire diversification endeavor.

- *Consciously preparing to move opportunistically.* Organizational and fiscal resources must be built up in advance to exploit candidates as they randomly appear. And a "credible activist" for ventures must be developed and backed by someone with commitment power. All successful acquirers created the potential for "profit-centered" divisions within their organizational structures, strengthened their financial-controllership capabilities, took action to create low-cost capital access, and maintained the shortest possible communication lines from the "acquisitions activist" to the resource-committing authority. All these actions integrally determined which diversifications actually could be made, the timing of their accession, and the pace they could be absorbed.

- *Building a "comfort factor" for risk taking.* Perceived risk is largely a function of one's knowledge about a field. Hence well-conceived diversification programs should anticipate a trial-and-error period during which top managers reject early proposed fields or opportunities until they have analyzed enough trail candidates to "become comfortable" with an initial selection. Early successes tend to be "sure things" close to the companies' past (real or supposed) expertise. After a few successful diversifications, managements tend to become more confident and accept other candidates—farther from traditional lines—at a faster rate. Again the way this process is handled affects both the direction and pace of the actual program.

- *Developing a new ethos.* If new divisions are more successful than the old—as they should be—they attract relatively more resources and their political power grows. Their most effective line managers move into corporate positions, and slowly the company's special competency and ethos change. Finally, the concepts and products which once dominated the company's culture may decline in importance or even disappear. Acknowledging these ultimate consequences to the organization at the beginning of a diversification program would clearly be impolitic, even if the manager both desired and could predict the probable new ethos. These factors must be handled adaptively, as opportunities present themselves and as individual leaders and power centers develop.

Each of the above processes interacts with all others (and with the random appearance of diversification candidates) to affect action sequences, elapsed time, and ultimate results in unexpected ways. Complexities are so great that few diversification programs end up as initially envisioned. Consequently, wise managers recognize the limits to systematic analysis in diversification, and use formal planning to build the "comfort levels" executives need for risk taking and to guide the program's early directions and priorities. They then modify these flexibly, step by step, as new opportunities, power centers, and developed competencies merge to create new potentials.

The Major Reorganization Subsystem

It is well recognized that major organizational changes are an integral part of strategy (Chandler, 1962). Sometimes they constitute a strategy themselves, sometimes they precede and/or precipitate a new strategy, and sometimes they help to implement a strategy. However, like many other important strategic decisions, macroorganizational moves are typically handled incrementally *and* outside of formal planning processes. Their effects on personal or power relationships preclude discussion in the open forums and reports of such processes.

In addition, major organizational changes have timing imperatives (or "process limits") all their own. In making any significant shifts, the executive must think through the new roles, capabilities, and probable individual reactions of the many principals affected. He may have to wait for the promotion or retirement of a valued colleague before consummating any change. He then frequently has to bring in, train, or test new people for substantial periods before he can staff key posts with confidence. During this testing period he may substantially modify his original concept of the reorganization, as he evaluates individuals' potentials, their performance in specific roles, their personal drives, and their relationships with other team members.

Because this chain of decisions affects the career development, power, affluence, and self-image of so many, the executive tends to keep close counsel in his discussions, negotiates individually with key people, and makes final commitments as late as possible in order to obtain the best matches between people's capabilities, personalities, and aspirations and their new roles. Typically, all these events do not come together at one convenient time, particularly the moment annual plans are due. Instead the executive moves opportunistically, step by step, selectively moving people toward a broadly conceived organizational goal, which is constantly modified and rarely articulated in detail until the last pieces fit together.

Major organizational moves may also define entirely new strategies the guiding executive cannot fully foresee. For example:

When Exxon began its regional decentralization on a worldwide basis, the Executive Committee placed a senior officer and board member with a very responsive management style in a vaguely defined "coordinative role" vis-à-vis its powerful and successful European units. Over a period of two years this man sensed problems and experimented with voluntary coordinative possibilities on a pan-European basis. Only later, with greater understanding by both corporate and divisional officers, did Exxon move to a more formal "line" relationship for what became Exxon Europe. Even then the move had to be coordinated in other areas of the world. All of these changes together led to an entirely new internal power balance toward regional and non-U.S. concerns and to a more responsive worldwide posture for Exxon. . . .

In such situations, executives may be able to predict the broad direction, but not the precise nature, of the ultimate strategy which will result. In some cases, such as Exxon, the rebalance of power and information relationships *becomes* the strategy, or at least its central element. In others, organizational shifts are primarily means of triggering or implementing new strategic concepts and philosophies. But in all cases, major organizational changes create unexpected new stresses, opportunities, power bases, information centers, and credibility relationships that can affect both previous plans and future strategies in unanticipated ways. Effective reorganization decisions, therefore, allow for testing, flexibility, and feedback. Hence, they should, and usually do, evolve incrementally.

FORMAL PLANNING IN CORPORATE STRATEGY

What role do classical formal planning techniques play in strategy formulation? All companies in the sample do have formal planning procedures embedded in their management direction and control systems. These serve certain essential functions. In a process sense, they

Provide a discipline forcing managers to take a careful look ahead periodically.

Require rigorous communications about goals, strategic issues, and resource allocations.

Stimulate longer-term analyses than would otherwise be made.

Generate a basis for evaluating and integrating short-term plans.

Lengthen time horizons and protect long-term investments such as R&D.

Create a psychological backdrop and an information framework about the future against which managers can calibrate short-term or interim decisions.

Fine-tune annual commitments.

Formalize cost reduction programs.

Help implement strategic changes once decided on (for example, coordinating all elements of Exxon's decision to change its corporate name).

In fact, formal planning practices actually institutionalize incrementalism. There are two reasons for this. *First,* in order to utilize specialized expertise and to obtain executive involvement and commitment, most planning occurs "from the bottom up" in response to broadly defined assumptions or goals, many of which are long standing or negotiated well in advance. Of necessity, lower-level groups have only a partial view of the corporation's total strategy, and command only a fragment of its resources. Their power bases, identity, expertise, and rewards also usually depend on their existing products or processes. Hence, these products or processes, rather than entirely new departures, should and do receive their primary attention. *Second,* most managements purposely design their plans to be "living" or "ever green." They are intended only as "frameworks" to guide and provide consistency for future decisions made incrementally. To act otherwise would be to deny that further information could have a value. Thus, properly formulated formal plans are also a part of an incremental logic.

In each case there were also important precursor events, analyses, and political interactions, and each was followed by organizational, power, and behavioral changes. But interestingly, such special strategic studies also represent a "subsystem" of strategy formulation distinct from both annual planning activities and the other subsystems exemplified above. Each of these develops some important aspect of strategy, incrementally blending its conclusions with those of other subsystems, and it would be virtually impossible to force all these together to crystallize a completely articulated corporate strategy at any one instant.

Total Posture Planning

Occasionally, however, managements do attempt very broad assessments of their companies' total posture. James McFarland of General Mills did this through taking the company's topmost managers away for a three day retreat to answer the questions on what defined a "great company" from the viewpoints of stockholders, employees, suppliers, the public, and society; how did the company's strengths and weaknesses compare with the defined posture of "greatness;" and finally how should they proceed to overcome the company's weaknesses and move it from "goodness to greatness." The strategies that characterized the McFarland era at General Mills flowed from these assessments.

Yet even such major endeavors are only portions of a total strategic process. Values which have been built up over decades stimulate or constrain alternatives. Precipitating events, acquisitions, divestitures, external relations, and organizational changes develop important segments of each strategy incrementally. Even the strategies articulated leave key elements to be defined as new information becomes available, polities permit, particular opportunities appear, or major product thrusts prove unsuccessful. Actual strategies therefore evolve as each company overextends, consolidates, makes errors, and rebalances various thrusts over time. And it is both logical and expected that this should be the case.

Strategic decisions do not lend themselves to aggregation into a single massive decision matrix where all factors can be treated relatively simultaneously in order to arrive at a holistic optimum. Many have spoken of the "cognitive limits" (March and Simon, 1958) which prevent this. Of equal importance are the "process limits"—that is, the timing and sequencing imperatives necessary to create awareness, build comfort levels, develop consensus, select and train people, and so on—which constrain the system, yet ultimately determine the decision itself.

A Strategy Emerges

Successful executives link together and bring order to a series of strategic processes and decisions spanning years. At the beginning of the process it is literally impossible to predict all the events and forces which will shape the future of the company. The best executives can do is to forecast the most likely forces which will impinge on the company's affairs and the ranges of their possible impact. They then attempt to build a resource base and a corporate *posture* that are so strong in selected areas that the enterprise can survive and prosper despite all but the most devastating events. They consciously select market/technological/product segments which the concern can "dominate" given its resource limits, and place some "side bets" (Ansoff, 1965) in order to decrease the risk of catastrophic failure or to increase the company's flexibility for future options.

They then proceed incrementally to handle urgent matters, start longer-term sequences whose specific future branches and consequences are perhaps murky, respond to unforeseen events as they occur, build on successes, and brace up or cut losses on failures. They constantly reassess the future, find new congruencies as events unfurl, and blend the organization's skills and resources into new balances of dominance and risk aversion as various forces intersect to suggest better—but never perfect—alignments. The process is dynamic, with neither a real beginning nor end. . . .

CONCLUSION

Strategy deals with the unknowable, not the uncertain. It involves forces of such great number, strength, and combinatory powers that one cannot predict events in a probabilistic sense. Hence logic dictates that one proceed flexibly and experimentally from broad concepts toward specific commitments, making the latter concrete as late as possible in order to narrow the bands of uncertainty and to benefit from the best available information. This is the process of "logical incrementalism."

"Logical incrementalism" is not "muddling," as most people use that word. It is conscious, purposeful, proactive, good management. Properly managed, it allows the executive to bind together the contributions of rational systematic analyses, political and power theories, and organizational behavior concepts. It helps the executive achieve cohesion and identity with new directions. It allows him to deal with power relationships and individual behavioral needs, and permits him to use the best possible informational and analytical inputs in choosing his major courses of action. . . .

CRAFTING STRATEGY*

BY HENRY MINTZBERG

Imagine someone planning strategy. What likely springs to mind is an image of orderly thinking: a senior manager, or a group of them, sitting in an office formulating courses of action that everyone else will implement on schedule. The keynote is reason—rational control, the systematic analysis of competitors and markets, of company strengths and weaknesses, the combination of these analyses producing clear, explicit, full-blown strategies.

Now imagine someone *crafting* strategy. A wholly different image likely results, as different from planning as craft is from mechanization. Craft evokes traditional skill, dedication, perfection through the mastery of detail. What springs to mind is not so much thinking and reason as involvement, a feeling of intimacy and harmony with the materials at hand, developed through long experience and commitment. Formulation and implementation merge into a fluid process of learning through which creative strategies evolve.

My thesis is simple: the crafting image better captures the process by which effective strategies come to be. The planning image, long popular in the literature, distorts these processes and thereby misguides organizations that embrace it unreservedly.

In developing this thesis, I shall draw on the experiences of a single craftsman, a potter, and compare them with the results of a research project that tracked the strategies of a number of corporations across several decades. Because the two contexts are so obviously different, my metaphor, like my assertion, may seem farfetched at first. Yet if we think of a craftsman as an organization of one, we can see that he or she must also resolve one of the great challenges the corporate strategist faces: knowing the organization's capabilities well enough to think deeply enough about its strategic direction. By considering strategy making from the perspective of one person, free of all the paraphernalia of what has been called the strategy industry, we can learn something about the formation of strategy in the corporation. For much as our potter has to manage her craft, so too managers have to craft their strategy.

At work, the potter sits before a lump of clay on the wheel. Her mind is on the clay, but she is also aware of sitting between her past experiences and her future prospects. She knows exactly what has and has not worked for her in the past. She has an intimate knowledge of her work, her capabilities, and her markets. As a craftsman, she senses rather than analyzes these things; her knowledge is "tacit." All these things are working in her mind as her hands are working the clay. The product that emerges on the wheel is likely to be in the tradition of her past work, but she may break away and embark on a new direction. Even so, the past is no less present, projecting itself into the future.

In my metaphor, managers are craftsmen and strategy is their clay. Like the potter, they sit between the past of corporate capabilities and a future of market opportunities. And if they are truly craftsmen, they bring to their work an equally intimate knowledge of the materials at hand. That is the essence of crafting strategy.

* Originally published in the *Harvard Business Review* (July–August 1987) and winner of McKinsey prize for second best article in the *Review* 1987. Copyright © 1987 by the President and Fellows of Harvard College; all rights reserved. Reprinted with deletions by permission of the *Harvard Business Review.*

1. STRATEGIES ARE BOTH PLANS FOR THE FUTURE AND PATTERNS FROM THE PAST.

Ask almost anyone what strategy is, and they will define it as a plan of some sort, an explicit guide to future behavior. Then ask them what strategy a competitor or a government or even they themselves have actually pursued. Chances are they will describe consistency in *past* behavior—a pattern in action over time. Strategy, it turns out, is one of those words that people define in one way and often use in another, without realizing the difference.

The reason for this is simple. Strategy's formal definition and its Greek military origins not withstanding, we need the word as much to explain past actions as to describe intended behavior. After all, if strategies can be planned and intended, they can also be pursued and realized (or not realized, as the case may be). And pattern in action, or what we call realized strategy, explains that pursuit. Moreover, just as a plan need not produce a pattern (some strategies that are intended are simply not realized), so too a pattern need not result from a plan. An organization can have a pattern (or realized strategy) without knowing it, let alone making it explicit.

Patterns, like beauty, are in the mind of the beholder, of course. But finding them in organizations is not very difficult. But what about intended strategies, those formal plans and pronouncements we think of when we use the term *strategy?* Ironically, here we run into all kinds of problems. Even with a single craftsman, how can we know what her intended strategies really were? If we could go back, would we find expressions of intention? And if we could, would we be able to trust them? We often fool ourselves, as well as others, by denying our subconscious motives. And remember that intentions are cheap, at least when compared with realizations.

Reading the Organization's Mind

If you believe all this has more to do with the Freudian recesses of a craftsman's mind than with the practical realities of producing automobiles, then think again. For who knows what the intended strategies of an organization really mean, let alone what they are? Can we simply assume in this collective context that the company's intended strategies are represented by its formal plans or by other statements emanating from the executive suite? Might these be just vain hopes or rationalizations or ploys to fool the competition? And even if expressed intentions do exist, to what extent do various people in the organization share them? How do we read the collective mind? Who is the strategist anyway?

The traditional view of strategic management resolves these problems quite simply, by what organizational theorists call attribution. You see it all the time in the business press. When General Motors acts, it's because its CEO has made a strategy. Given realization, there must have been intention, and that is automatically attributed to the chief.

In a short magazine article, this assumption is understandable. Journalists don't have a lot of time to uncover the origins of strategy, and GM is a large, complicated organization. But just consider all the complexity and confusion that gets tucked under this assumption—all the meetings and debates, the many people, the dead ends, the folding and unfolding of ideas. Now imagine trying to build a formal strategy-making system around that assumption. Is it any wonder that formal strategic planning is often such a resounding failure?

To unravel some of the confusion—and move away from the artificial complexity we have piled around the strategy-making process—we need to get back to some basic concepts. The most basic of all is the intimate connection between thought and action. That is the key to craft, and so also to the crafting of strategy.

2. STRATEGIES NEED NOT BE DELIBERATE—THEY CAN ALSO EMERGE, MORE OR LESS.

Virtually everything that has been written about strategy making depicts it as a deliberate process. First we think, then we act. We formulate, then we implement. The progression seems so perfectly sensible. Why would anybody want to proceed differently?

Our potter is in the studio, rolling the clay to make a waferlike sculpture. The clay sticks to the rolling pin, and a round form appears. Why not make a cylindrical vase? One idea leads to another, until a new pattern forms. Action has driven thinking: a strategy has emerged.

Out in the field, a salesman visits a customer. The product isn't quite right, and together they work out some modifications. The salesman returns to his company and puts the changes through; after two or three more rounds, they finally get it right. A new product emerges, which eventually opens up a new market. The company has changed strategic course.

In fact, most salespeople are less fortunate than this one or than our craftsman. In an organization of one, the implementor is the formulator, so innovations can be incorporated into strategy quickly and easily. In a large organization, the innovator may be ten levels removed from the leader who is supposed to dictate strategy and may also have to sell the idea to dozens of peers doing the same job.

Some salespeople, of course, can proceed on their own, modifying products to suit their customers and convincing skunkworks in the factory to produce them. In effect, they pursue their own strategies. Maybe no one else notices or cares. Sometimes, however, their innovations do get noticed, perhaps years later, when the company's prevalent strategies have broken down and its leaders are groping for something new. Then the salesperson's strategy may be allowed to pervade the system, to become organizational.

Is this story farfetched? Certainly not. We've all heard stories like it. But since we tend to see only what we believe, if we believe that strategies have to be planned, we're unlikely to see the real meaning such stories hold.

Consider how the National Film Board of Canada (NFB) came to adopt a feature-film strategy. The NFB is a federal government agency, famous for its creativity and expert in the production of short documentaries. Some years back, it funded a filmmaker on a project that unexpectedly ran long. To distribute his film, the NFB turned to theaters and so inadvertently gained experience in marketing feature-length films. Other filmmakers caught onto the idea, and eventually the NFB found itself pursuing a feature-film strategy—a pattern of producing such films.

My point is simple, deceptively simple: strategies can *form* as well as be *formulated.* A realized strategy can emerge in response to an evolving situation, or it can be brought about deliberately, through a process of formulation followed by implementation. But when these planned intentions do not produce the desired actions, organizations are left with unrealized strategies.

Today we hear a great deal about unrealized strategies, almost always in concert with the claim that implementation has failed. Management has been lax, controls have been loose, people haven't been committed. Excuses abound. At times, indeed, they may be valid. But often these explanations prove too easy. So some people look beyond implementation to formulation. The strategists haven't been smart enough.

While it is certainly true that many intended strategies are ill conceived, I believe that the problem often lies one step beyond, in the distinction we make between formulation and implementation, the common assumption that thought must be independent of and precede action. Sure, people could be smarter—but not only by conceiving more clever strategies. Sometimes they can be smarter by allowing their strategies to develop gradually, through the organization's actions and experiences. Smart strategists appreciate that they cannot always be smart enough to think through everything in advance.

Hands and Minds

No craftsman thinks some days and works others. The craftsman's mind is going constantly, in tandem with her hands. Yet large organizations try to separate the work of minds and hands. In so doing, they often sever the vital feedback link between the two. The salesperson who finds a customer with an unmet need may possess the most strategic bit of information in the entire organization. But that information is useless if he or she cannot create a strategy in response to it or else convey the information to someone who can—because the channels are blocked or because the formulators have simply finished formulating. The notion that strategy is something that should happen way up there, far removed from the details of running an organization on a daily basis, is one of the great fallacies of conventional strategic management. And it explains a good many of the most dramatic failures in business and public policy today.

Strategies like the NFB's that appear without clear intentions—or in spite of them—can be called emergent. Actions simply converge into patterns. They may become deliberate, of course, if the pattern is recognized and then legitimated by senior management. But that's after the fact.

All this may sound rather strange, I know. Strategies that emerge? Managers who acknowledge strategies already formed? Over the years, we have met with a good deal of resistance from people upset by what they perceive to be our passive definition of a word so bound up with proactive behavior and free will. After all, strategy means control—the ancient Greeks used it to describe the art of the army general.

Strategic Learning

But we have persisted in this usage for one reason: learning. Purely deliberate strategy precludes learning once the strategy is formulated; emergent strategy fosters it. People take actions one by one and respond to them, so that patterns eventually form.

Our craftsman tries to make a freestanding sculptural form. It doesn't work, so she rounds it a bit here, flattens it a bit there. The result looks better, but still isn't quite right. She makes another and another and another. Eventually, after days or months or years, she finally has what she wants. She is off on a new strategy.

In practice, of course, all strategy making walks on two feet, one deliberate, the other emergent. For just as purely deliberate strategy making precludes learning, so purely emergent strategy making precludes control. Pushed to the limit, neither approach makes much sense. Learning must be coupled with control. That is why we use the word *strategy* for both emergent and deliberate behavior.

Likewise, there is no such thing as a purely deliberate strategy or a purely emergent one. No organization—not even the ones commanded by those ancient Greek generals—knows enough to work everything out in advance, to ignore learning en route. And no one—not even a solitary potter—can be flexible enough to leave everything to happenstance, to give up all control. Craft requires control just as it requires responsiveness to the material at hand. Thus deliberate and emergent strategy form the end points of a continuum along which the strategies that are crafted in the real world may be found. Some strategies may approach either end, but many more fall at intermediate points.

3. EFFECTIVE STRATEGIES DEVELOP IN ALL KINDS OF STRANGE WAYS.

Effective strategies can show up in the strangest places and develop through the most unexpected means. There is no one best way to make strategy.

The form for a ceramic cat collapses on the wheel, and our potter sees a bull taking shape. Clay sticks to a rolling pin, and a line of cylinders results. Wafers come into being because of a shortage of clay and limited kiln space while visiting a studio in France. Thus errors become opportunities, and limitations stimulate creativity. The natural propensity to experiment, even boredom, likewise stimulates strategic change.

Organizations that craft their strategies have similar experiences. Recall the National Film Board with its inadvertently long film. Or consider its experiences with experimental films, which made special use of animation and sound. For 20 years, the NFB produced a bare but steady trickle of such films. In fact, every film but one in that trickle was produced by a single person, Norman McLaren, the NFB's most celebrated filmmaker. McLaren pursued a *personal strategy* of experimentation, deliberate for him perhaps (though who can know whether he had the whole stream in mind or simply planned one film at a time?) but not for the organization. Then 20 years later, others followed his lead and the trickle widened, his personal strategy becoming more broadly organizational.

While the NFB may seem like an extreme case, it highlights behavior that can be found, albeit in muted form, in all organizations. Those who doubt this might read Richard Pascale's account of how Honda stumbled into its enormous success in the American motorcyle market [the following article in this book].

Grass-roots Strategy Making

These strategies all reflect, in whole or part, what we like to call a grass-roots approach to strategic management. Strategies grow like weeds in a garden. They take root in all kinds of places, wherever people have the capacity to learn (because they are in touch with the situation) and the resources to support that capacity. These strategies become organizational when they become collective, that is, when they proliferate to guide the behavior of the organization at large.

Of course, this view is overstated. But it is no less extreme than the conventional view of strategic management, which might be labeled the hothouse approach. Neither is right. Reality falls between the two. Some of the most effective strategies we uncovered in our research combined deliberation and control with flexibility and organizational learning.

Consider first what we call the *umbrella strategy.* Here senior management sets out broad guidelines (say, to produce only high-margin products at the cutting edge of technology or to favor products using bonding technology) and leaves the specifics (such as what these products will be) to others lower down in the organization. This strategy is not only deliberate (in its guidelines) and emergent (in its specifics), but it is also deliberately emergent, in that the process is consciously managed to allow strategies to emerge en route. IBM used the umbrella strategy in the early 1960s with the impending 360 series, when its senior management approved a set of broad criteria for the design of a family of computers later developed in detail throughout the organization. [See the IBM case in this section.]

Deliberately emergent, too, is what we call the *process strategy.* Here management controls the process of strategy formation—concerning itself with the design of the structure, its staffing, procedures, and so on—while leaving the actual content to others.

Both process and umbrella strategies seem to be especially prevalent in businesses that require great expertise and creativity—a 3M, a Hewlett-Packard, a National Film Board. Such organizations can be effective only if their implementors are allowed to be formulators, because it is people way down in the hierarchy who are in touch with the situation at hand and have the requisite technical expertise. In a sense, these are organizations peopled with craftsmen, all of whom must be strategists.

4. STRATEGIC REORIENTATIONS HAPPEN IN BRIEF, QUANTUM LEAPS.

The conventional view of strategic management, especially in the planning literature, claims that change must be continuous: the organization should be adapting all the time. Yet this view proves to be ironic because the very concept of strategy is rooted in stability, not change. As this same literature makes clear, organizations pursue strategies to set direction, to lay out courses of action, and to elicit cooperation from their members around common, established guidelines. By any definition, strategy imposes stability on an organization. No stability means no strategy (no course to the future, no pattern from the past). Indeed, the very fact of having a strategy, and especially of making it explicit (as the conventional literature implores managers to do), creates resistance to strategic change!

What the conventional view fails to come to grips with, then, is how and when to promote change. A fundamental dilemma of strategy making is the need to reconcile the forces for stability and for change—to focus efforts and gain operating efficiencies on the one hand, yet adapt and maintain currency with a changing external environment on the other.

Quantum Leaps

Our own research and that of colleagues suggest that organizations resolve these opposing forces by attending first to one and then to the other. Clear periods of stability and change can usually be distinguished in any organization: while it is true that particular strategies may always be changing marginally, it seems equally true that major shifts in strategic orientation occur only rarely.

In our study of Steinberg, Inc., a large Quebec supermarket chain headquartered in Montreal, we found only two important reorientations in the 60 years from its founding to the mid-1970s: a shift to self-service in 1933 and the introduction of shopping centers and public financing in 1953. At Volkswagenwerk, we saw only one between the late 1940s and the 1970s, the tumultuous shift from the traditional Beetle to the Audi-type design. And at Air Canada, we found none over the airline's first four decades, following its initial positioning.

Our colleagues at McGill, Danny Miller and Peter Friesen (1984), found this pattern of change so common in their studies of large numbers of companies (especially the high-performance ones) that they built a theory around it, which they labeled the quantum theory of strategic change. Their basic point is that organizations adopt two distinctly different modes of behavior at different times.

Most of the time they pursue a given strategic orientation. Change may seem continuous, but it occurs in the context of that orientation (perfecting a given retailing formula, for example) and usually amounts to doing more of the same, perhaps better as well. Most organizations favor these periods of stability because they achieve success not by changing strategies but by exploiting the ones they have. They, like craftsmen, seek continuous improvement by using their distinctive competencies on established courses.

While this goes on, however, the world continues to change, sometimes slowly, occasionally in dramatic shifts. Thus gradually or suddenly, the organization's strategic orientation moves out of sync with its environment. Then what Miller and Friesen call a strategic revolution must take place. That long period of evolutionary change is suddenly punctuated by a brief bout of revolutionary turmoil in which the organization quickly alters many of its established patterns. In effect, it tries to leap to a new stability quickly to reestablish an integrated posture among a new set of strategies, structures, and culture.

But what about all those emergent strategies, growing like weeds around the organization? What the quantum theory suggests is that the really novel ones are generally held in check in some corner of the organization until a strategic revolution becomes necessary. Then, as an alternative to having to develop new strategies from scratch or having to import generic strategies from competitors, the organization can turn to its own emerging patterns to find its new orientation. As the old, established strategy disintegrates, the seeds of the new one begin to spread.

This quantum theory of change seems to apply particularly well to large established, mass-production companies, like a Volkswagenwerk. Because they are especially reliant on standardized procedures, their resistance to strategic reorientation tends to be especially fierce. So we find long periods of stability broken by short disruptive periods of revolutionary change. Strategic reorientations really are cultural revolutions.

In more creative organizations we see a somewhat different pattern of change and stability, one that is more balanced. Companies in the business of producing novel outputs apparently need to run off in all directions from time to time to sustain their creativity. Yet they also need to settle down after such periods to find some order in the resulting chaos—convergence following divergence.

Whether through quantum revolutions or cycles of convergence and divergence, however, organizations seem to need to separate in time the basic forces for change and stability, reconciling them by attending to each in turn. Many strategic failures can be attributed either to mixing the two or to an obsession with one of these forces at the expense of the other.

The problems are evident in the work of many craftsmen. On the one hand, there are those who seize on the perfection of a single theme and never change. Eventually the creativity disappears from their work and the world passes them by —much as it did Volkswagenwerk until the company was shocked into its strategic revolution. And then there are those who are always changing, who flit from one idea to another and never settle down. Because no theme or strategy ever emerges in their work, they cannot exploit or even develop any distinctive competence.

And because their work lacks definition, identity crises are likely to develop, with neither the craftsmen nor their clientele knowing what to make of it. Miller and Friesen (1978: 921) found this behavior in conventional business too; they label it "the impulsive firm running blind." How often have we seen it in companies that go on acquisition sprees?

5. TO MANAGE STRATEGY, THEN, IS TO CRAFT THOUGHT AND ACTION, CONTROL AND LEARNING, STABILITY AND CHANGE.

The popular view sees the strategist as a planner or as a visionary, someone sitting on a pedestal dictating brilliant strategies for everyone else to implement. While recognizing the importance of thinking ahead and especially of the need for creative vision in this pedantic world, I wish to propose an additional view of the strategist—as a pattern recognizer, a learner if you will—who manages a process in which strategies (and visions) can emerge as well as be deliberately conceived. I also wish to redefine that strategist, to extend that someone into the collective entity made up of the many actors whose interplay speaks an organization's mind. This strategist *finds* strategies no less than creates them, often in patterns that form inadvertently in its own behavior.

What, then, does it mean to craft strategy? Let us return to the words associated with craft: dedication, experience, involvement with the material, the personal touch, mastery of detail, a sense of harmony and integration. Managers who craft strategy do not spend much time in executive suites reading MIS reports or industry analyses. They are involved, responsive to their materials, learning about their organizations and industries through personal touch. They are also sensitive to experience, recognizing that while individual vision may be important, other factors must help determine strategy as well.

Manage stability: Managing strategy is mostly managing stability, not change. Indeed, most of the time senior managers should not be formulating strategy at all; they should be getting on with making their organizations as effective as possible in pursuing the strategies they already have. Like distinguished craftsmen, organizations become distinguished because they master the details.

To manage strategy, then, at least in the first instance, is not so much to promote change as to know *when* to do so. Advocates of strategic planning often urge managers to plan for perpetual instability in the environment (for example, by rolling over five-year plans annually). But this obsession with change is dysfunctional. Organizations that reassess their strategies continuously are like individuals who reassess their jobs or their marriages continuously—in both cases, they will drive themselves crazy or else reduce themselves to inaction. The formal planning process repeats itself so often and so mechanically that it desensitizes the organization to real change, programs it more and more deeply into set patterns, and thereby encourages it to make only minor adaptations.

So-called strategic planning must be recognized for what it is: a means, not to create strategy, but to program a strategy already created—to work out its implications formally. It is essentially analytic in nature, based on decomposition, while strategy creation is essentially a process of synthesis. That is why trying to create strategies through formal planning most often leads to extrapolating existing ones or copying those of competitors.

This is not to say that planners have no role to play in strategy formation. In addition to programming strategies created by other means, they can feed ad hoc analyses into the strategy-making process at the front end to be sure that the hard data are taken into consideration. They can also stimulate others to think strategi-cally. And of course people called planners can be strategists too, so long as they are creative thinkers who are in touch with what is relevant. But that has nothing to do with the technology of formal planning.

Detect discontinuity: Environments do not change on any regular or orderly basis. And they seldom undergo continuous dramatic change, claims about our "age of discontinuity" and environmental "turbulence" notwithstanding. (Go tell people who lived through the Great Depression or survivors of the siege of Lenin-grad during World War II that ours are turbulent times.) Much of the time, change is minor and even temporary and requires no strategic response. Once in a while there is a truly significant discontinuity or, even less often, a gestalt shift in the en-vironment, where everything important seems to change at once. But these events, while critical, are also easy to recognize.

The real challenge in crafting strategy lies in detecting the subtle discontinu-ities that may undermine a business in the future. And for that, there is no tech-nique, no program, just a sharp mind in touch with the situation. Such discontin-uities are unexpected and irregular, essentially unprecedented. They can be dealt with only by minds that are attuned to existing patterns yet able to perceive impor-tant breaks in them. Unfortunately, this form of strategic thinking tends to atrophy during the long periods of stability that most organizations experience. So the trick is to manage within a given strategic orientation most of the time yet be able to pick out the occasional discontinuity that really matters. The ability to make that kind of switch in thinking is the essence of strategic management. And it has more to do with vision and involvement than it does with analytic technique.

Know the business: Note the kind of knowledge involved in strategic thinking: not intellectual knowledge, not analytical reports or abstracted facts and figures (though these can certainly help), but personal knowledge, intimate understanding, equivalent to the craftsman's feel for the clay. Facts are available to anyone; this kind of knowledge is not. Wisdom is the word that captures it best. But wisdom is a word that has been lost in the bureaucracies we have built for ourselves, systems designed to distance leaders from operating details. Show me managers who think they can rely on formal planning to create their strategies, and I'll show you man-agers who lack intimate knowledge of their businesses or the creativity to do some-thing with it.

Craftsmen have to train themselves to see, to pick up things other people miss. The same holds true for managers of strategy. It is those with a kind of pe-ripheral vision who are best able to detect and take advantage of events as they un-fold.

Manage patterns: Whether in an executive suite in Manhattan or a pottery studio in Montreal, a key to managing strategy is the ability to detect emerging patterns and help them take shape. The job of the manager is not just to preconceive spe-cific strategies but also to recognize their emergence elsewhere in the organization and intervene when appropriate.

Like weeds that appear unexpectedly in a garden, some emergent strategies may need to be uprooted immediately. But management cannot be too quick to cut off the unexpected, for tomorrow's vision may grow out of today's aberration. (Europeans, after all, enjoy salads made from the leaves of the dandelion, Amer-ica's most notorious weed.) Thus some patterns are worth watching until their ef-fects have more clearly manifested themselves. Then those that prove useful can be made deliberate and be incorporated into the formal strategy, even if that means shifting the strategic umbrella to cover them.

To manage in this context, then, is to create the climate within which a wide variety of strategies can grow. In more complex organizations, this may mean building flexible structures, hiring creative people, defining broad umbrella strategies, and watching for the patterns that emerge.

Reconcile change and continuity: Finally, managers considering radical departures need to keep the quantum theory of change in mind. As Ecclesiastes reminds us, there is a time to sow and a time to reap. Some new patterns must be held in check until the organization is ready for a strategic revolution, or at least a period of divergence. Managers who are obsessed with either change or stability are bound eventually to harm their organizations. As pattern recognizer, the manager has to be able to sense when to exploit an established crop of strategies and when to encourage new strains to displace the old.

While strategy is a word that is usually associated with the future, its link to the past is no less central. As Kierkegaard once observed, life is lived forward but understood backward. Managers may have to live strategy in the future, but they must understand it through the past.

Like potters at the wheel, organizations must make sense of the past if they hope to manage the future. Only by coming to understand the patterns that form in their own behavior do they get to know their capabilities and their potential. Thus crafting strategy, like managing craft, requires a natural synthesis of the future, present, and past.

● THE HONDA EFFECT*

BY RICHARD T. PASCALE

At face value, "strategy" is an innocent noun. Webster defines it as the large-scale planning and direction of operations. In the business context, it pertains to a process by which a firm searches and analyzes its environment and resources in order to (1) select opportunities defined in terms of markets to be served and products to serve them and (2) make discrete decisions to invest resources in order to achieve identified objectives. (Bower, 1970: 7–8).

But for a vast and influential population of executives, planners, academics, and consultants, strategy is more than a conventional English noun. It embodies an implicit model of how organizations should be guided and consequently, proconfigures our way of thinking. Strategy formulation (1) is generally assumed to be driven by senior management whom we expect to set strategic direction, (2) has been extensively influenced by empirical models and concepts, and (3) is often associated with a laborious strategic planning process that, in some companies, has produced more paper than insight.

A $500-million-a-year "strategy" industry has emerged in the United States and Europe comprised of management consultants, strategic planning staffs, and business school academics. It caters to the unique emphasis that American and Eu-

---

* Excerpted from an article originally entitled "Perspectives on Strategy: The Real Story Behind Honda's Success," *California Management Review XXVI,* no. 3, pp. 47–72. Copyright © 1984 by the Regents of the University of California. Reprinted by permission of the Regents.

ropean companies place upon this particular aspect of managing and directing corporations.

Words often derive meaning from their cultural context. *Strategy* is one such word and nowhere is the contrast of meanings more pronounced than between Japan and the United States. The Japanese view the emphasis we place on "strategy" as we might regard their enthusiasm for Kabuki or sumo wrestling. They note our interest not with an intent of acquiring similar ones but for insight into our peculiarities. The Japanese are somewhat distrustful of a single "strategy" for in their view any idea that focuses attention does so at the expense of peripheral vision. They strongly believe that *peripheral vision* is essential to discerning changes in the customer, the technology or competition, and is the key to corporate survival over the long haul. They regard any prospensity to be driven by a single-minded strategy as a weakness.

The Japanese have particular discomfort with strategic concepts. While they do not reject ideas such as the experience curve or portfolio theory outright they regard them as a stimulus to perception. They have often ferreted out the "formula" of their concept-driven American competitors and exploited their inflexibility. In musical instruments, for example (a mature industry facing stagnation as birthrates in the United States and Japan declined), Yamaha might have classified its products as "cash cows" and gone on to better things (as its chief U.S. competitor, Baldwin United, had done). Instead, beginning with a negligible share of the U.S. market, Yamaha plowed ahead and destroyed Baldwin's seemingly unchallengeable dominance. YKK's success in zippers against Talon (a Textron division) and Honda's outflanking of Harley-Davidson (a former AMF subsidiary) in the motorcycle field provide parallel illustrations. All three cases involved American conglomerates, wedded to the portfolio concept, that had classified pianos, zippers, and motorcycles as mature businesses to be harvested rather than nourished and defended. Of course, those who developed portfolio theory and other strategic concepts protest that they were never intended to be mindlessly applied in setting strategic direction. But most would also agree that there is a widespread tendency in American corporations to misapply concepts and to otherwise become strategically myopic—ignoring the marketplace, the customer, and the problems of execution. This tendency toward misapplication, being both pervasive and persistent over several decades, is a phenomenon that the literature has largely ignored [for exceptions, see Hayes and Abernathy, 1980:67; Hayes and Garvin, 1982:71]. There is a need to identify explicitly the factors that influence how we conceptualize strategy —and which foster its misuse.

HONDA: THE STRATEGY MODEL

In 1975, Boston Consulting Group (BCG) presented the British government its final report: *Strategy Alternatives for the British Motorcycle Industry.* This 120-page document identified two key factors leading to the British demise in the world's motorcycle industry:

- Market share loss and profitability declines
- Scale economy disadvantages in technology, distribution, and manufacturing

During the period 1959 to 1973, the British share of the U.S. motorcycle industry had dropped from 49% to 9%. Introducing BCG's recommended strategy (of targeting market segments where sufficient production volumes could be attained to be price competitive) the report states:

> The success of the Japanese manufacturers originated with the growth of their domestic market during the 1950s. As recently as 1960, only 4 percent of Japanese motorcycle production was exported. By this time, however, the Japanese had developed huge production volumes in small motorcycles in their domestic market, and volume-related cost reductions had followed. This resulted in a highly competitive cost position which the Japanese used as a springboard for penetration of world markets with small motorcycles in the early 1960s (BCG, 1975:xiv).

The BCG study was made public by the British government and rapidly disseminated in the United States. It exemplifies the necessary (and, I argue, insufficient) strategist's perspective of

- examining competition primarily from an intercompany perspective,
- at a high level of abstraction,
- with heavy reliance on microeconomic concepts (such as the experience curve).

Case writers at Harvard Business School, UCLA, and the University of Virginia quickly condensed the BCG report for classroom use in case discussions. It currently enjoys extensive use in first-term courses in business policy.

Of particular note in the BCG study, and in the subsequent Harvard Business School rendition, is the historical treatment of Honda.

> The mix of competitors in the U.S. motorcycle market underwent a major shift in the 1960s. Motorcycle registrations increased from 575,000 in 1960 to 1,382,000 in 1965. Prior to 1960 the U.S. market was served mainly by Harley-Davidson of U.S.A., BSA, Triumph and Norton of U.K. and Moto-Guzzi of Italy. Harley was the market leader with total 1959 sales of $16.6 million. After the second world war, motorcycles in the U.S.A. attracted a very limited group of people other than police and army personnel who used motorcycles on the job. While most motorcyclists were no doubt decent people, groups of rowdies who went around on motorcycles and called themselves by such names as "Hell's Angels," "Satan's Slaves" gave motorcycling a bad image. Even leather jackets which were worn by motorcyclists as a protective device acquired an unsavory image. A 1953 movie called "The Wild Ones" starring a 650cc Triumph, a black leather jacket and Marlon Brando gave the rowdy motorcyclists wide media coverage. The stereotype of the motorcyclist was a leather-jacketed, teenage troublemaker.
>
> Honda established an American subsidiary in 1959—American Honda Motor Company. This was in sharp contrast to other foreign producers who relied on distributors. Honda's marketing strategy was described in the 1963 annual report as "With its policy of selling, not primarily to confirmed motorcyclists but rather to members of the general public who had never before given a second thought to a motorcycle. . . ." Honda started its push in the U.S. market with the smallest, lightweight motorcycles. It had a three-speed transmisson, an automatic clutch, five horsepower (the American cycle only had two and a half), an electric starter and step through frame for female riders. And it was easier to handle. The Honda machines sold for under $250 in retail compared with $1,000–$1,500 for the bigger American or British machines. Even at that early date Honda was probably superior to other competitors in productivity.
>
> By June 1960 Honda's Research and Development effort was staffed with 700 designers/engineers. This might be contrasted with 100 engineers/draftsmen employed by . . . (European and American competitors). In 1962 production per man-

year was running at 159 units, (a figure not reached by Harley-Davidson until 1974). Honda's net fixed asset investment was $8170 per employee . . . (more than twice its European and American competitors). With 1959 sales of $55 million Honda was already the largest motorcycle producer in the world.

Honda followed a policy of developing the market region by region. They started on the West Coast and moved eastward over a period of four–five years. Honda sold 2,500 machines in the U.S. in 1960. In 1961 they lined up 125 distributors and spent $150,000 on regional advertising. Their advertising was directed to the young families, their advertising theme was "You Meet the Nicest People on a Honda." This was a deliberate attempt to dissociate motorcycles from rowdy, Hell's Angels type people.

Honda's success in creating demand for lightweight motorcycles was phenomenal. American Honda's sales went from $500,000 in 1960 to $77 million in 1965. By 1966 the market share data showed the ascendancy of Japanese producers and their success in selling lightweight motorcycles. [Honda had 63% of the market.] . . . Starting from virtually nothing in 1960, the lightweight motorcycles had clearly established their lead (Purkayastha, 1981: 5, 10, 11, 12).

Quoting from the BCG report:

The Japanese motorcycle industry, and in particular Honda, the market leader, present a [consistent] picture. The basic philosophy of the Japanese manufacturers is that high volumes per model provide the potential for high productivity as a result of using capital intensive and highly automated techniques. Their marketing strategies are therefore directed towards developing these high model volumes, hence the careful attention that we have observed them giving to growth and market share.

The overall result of this philosophy over time has been that the Japanese have now developed an entrenched and leading position in terms of technology and production methods. . . . The major factors which appear to account for the Japanese superiority in both these areas are . . . (specialized production systems, balancing engineering and market requirements, and the cost efficiency and reliability of suppliers) (BCG, pp. 59, 40).

As evidence of Honda's strategy of taking position as low cost producer and exploiting economies of scale, other sources cite Honda's construction in 1959 of a plant to manufacture 30,000 motorcycles per month well ahead of existing demand at the time. (Up until then Honda's most popular models sold 2,000–3,000 units per month.) (Sakiya, 1982:119)

The overall picture as depicted by the quotes exemplifies the "strategy model." Honda is portrayed as a firm dedicated to being the low price producer, utilizing its dominant market position in Japan to force entry into the U.S. market, expanding that market by redefining a leisure class ("Nicest People") segment, and exploiting its comparative advantage via aggressive pricing and advertising. Rich-

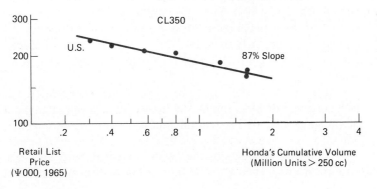

FIGURE 1
Source: BCG (1975) "Strategy Alternatives for the British Motorcycle Industry."

ard Rumelt, writing the teaching note for the UCLA adaptation of the case states: "The fundamental contribution of BCG is not the experience curve per se but the ever-present assumption that differences in cost (or efficiency) are the fundamental components of strategy." (Rumelt, 1980:2).

THE ORGANIZATIONAL PROCESS PERSPECTIVE

On September 10, 1982, the six Japanese executives responsible for Honda's entry into the U.S. motorcycle market in 1959 assembled in Honda's Tokyo headquarters. They had gathered at my request to describe in fine grain detail the sequence of events that had led to Honda's ultimate position of dominance in the U.S. market. All were in their sixties; three were retired. The story that unfolded, greatly abbreviated below, highlights miscalculation, serendipity, and organizational learning—counterpoints to the streamlined "strategy" version related earlier. . . .

Any account of Honda's successes must grasp at the outset the unusual character of its founder, Sochiro Honda, and his partner, Takeo Fujisawa. Honda was an inventive genius with a large ego and mercurial temperament, given to bouts of "philandering" (to use his expression) (Sakiya, 1979). . . .

Postwar Japan was in desperate need of transportation. Motorcycle manufacturers proliferated, producing clip-on engines that converted bicycles into makeshift "mopeds." Honda was among these but it was not until he teamed up with Fujisawa in 1949 that the elements of a successful enterprise began to take shape. Fujisawa provided money as well as financial and marketing strengths. In 1950 their first D-type motorcycle was introduced. They were, at that juncture, participating in a fragmented industry along with 247 other manufacturers. Other than its sturdy frame, this introductory product was unnoteworthy and did not enjoy great commercial success. (Sakiya, 1979, 1982).

Honda embodied a rare combination of inventive ability and ultimate self-confidence. His motivation was not primarily commercial. Rather, the company served as a vehicle to give expression to his inventive abilities. A successful company would provide a resource base to pursue, in Fujisawa's words, his "grandiose dream." Fujisawa continues, "There was no end to his pursuit of technology." (Sakiya, 1982).

Fujisawa, in an effort to save the faltering company, pressed Honda to abandon their noisy two-stroke engine and pursue a four-stroke design. The quieter four-stroke engines were appearing on competitive motorcycles, therefore threatening Honda with extinction. Mr. Honda balked. But a year later, Honda stunned Fujisawa with a breakthrough design that doubled the horsepower of competitive four-stroke engines. With this innovation, the firm was off and putting, and by 1951 demand was brisk. There was no organization, however, and the plant was chaotic (Sakiya, 1982). Strong demand, however, required early investment in a simplified mass production process. As a result, *primarily* due to design advantages, and secondarily to production methods, Honda became one of the four or five industry leaders by 1954 with 15 percent market share (data provided by company). . . .

For Fujisawa, the engine innovation meant increased sales and easier access to financing. For Mr. Honda, the higher horsepower engine opened the possibility of pursuing one of his central ambitions in life—to race his motorcycle and win. . . .

Fujisawa, throughout the fifties, sought to turn Honda's attention from his enthusiasm with racing to the more mundane requirements of running an enterprise. By 1956, as the innovations gained from racing had begun to pay off in vastly more efficient engines, Fujisawa pressed Honda to adapt this technology for a commercial motorcycle (Sakiya, 1979, 1982). Fujisawa had a particular segment in mind. Most motorcyclists in Japan were male and the machines were used primarily as an alternative form of transportation to trains and buses. There were, however, a vast number of small commercial establishments in Japan that still delivered goods and ran errands on bicycles. Trains and buses were inconvenient for these activities. The pursestrings of these small enterprises were controlled by the Japanese wife—who resisted buying conventional motorcycles because they were expensive, dangerous, and hard to handle. Fujisawa challenged Honda: Can you use what you've learned from racing to come up with an inexpensive, safe-looking motorcycle that can be driven with one hand (to facilitate carrying packages).

In 1958, the Honda 50cc Supercub was introduced—with an automatic clutch, three-speed transmission, automatic starter, and the safe, friendly look of a bicycle (without the stigma of the outmoded mopeds). Owing almost entirely to its high horsepower but *lightweight 50cc engine* (not to production efficiencies), it was affordable. Overnight, the firm was overwhelmed with orders. Engulfed by demand, they sought financing to build a new plant with a 30,000 unit per month capacity. "It wasn't a speculative investment," recalls one executive. "We had the proprietary technology, we had the market, and the demand was enormous." (The plant was completed in mid-1960.) Prior to its opening, demand was met through makeshift, high cost, company-owned assembly and farmed-out assembly through subcontractors. By the end of 1959, Honda had skyrocketed into first place among Japanese motorcycle manufacturers. Of its total sales that year of 285,000 units, 168,000 were Supercubs.

Fujisawa utilized the Supercub to restructure Honda's channels of distribution. For many years, Honda had rankled under the two-tier distribution system that prevailed in the industry. These problems had been exacerbated by the fact that Honda was a late entry and had been carried as secondary line by distributors whose loyalties lay with their older manufacturers. Further weakening Honda's leverage, all manufacturer sales were on a consignment basis.

Deftly, Fujisawa had characterized the Supercub to Honda's distributors as "something much more like a bicycle than a motorcycle." The traditional channels, to their later regret, agreed. Under amicable terms Fujisawa began selling the Supercub directly to retailers—and primarily through bicycle shops. Since these shops were small and numerous (approximately 12,000 in Japan), sales on consignment were unthinkable. A cash-on-delivery system was installed, giving Honda significantly more leverage over its dealerships than the other motorcycle manufacturers enjoyed.

The stage was now set for exploration of the U.S. market. Mr. Honda's racing conquests in the late 1950s had given substance to his convictions about his abilities. . . .

Two Honda executives—the soon-to-be-named president of American Honda, Kihachiro Kawashima, and his assistant—arrived in the United States in late 1958. Their itinerary: San Francisco, Los Angeles, Dallas, New York, and Columbus. Mr. Kawashima recounts his impressions:

> My first reaction after travelling across the United States was: How could we have been so stupid as to start a war with such a vast and wealthy country! My second reaction was discomfort. I spoke poor English. We dropped in on motorcycle dealers who treated us discourteously and in addition, gave the general impression of being motorcycle enthusiasts who, secondarily, were in business. There were only 3,000 motorcycle dealers in the United States at the time and only 1,000 of them were open five days a week. The remainder were open on nights and weekends. Inventory was

poor, manufacturers sold motorcycles to dealers on consignment, the retailers provided consumer financing; after-sales service was poor. It was discouraging.

My other impression was that everyone in the United States drove an automobile—making it doubtful that motorcycles could ever do very well in the market. However, with 450,000 motorcycle registrations in the U.S. and 60,000 motorcycles imported from Europe each year it didn't seem unreasonable to shoot for 10 percent of the import market. I returned to Japan with that report.

In truth, we had no strategy other than the idea of seeing if we could sell something in the United States. It was a new frontier, a new challenge, and it fit the "success against all odds" culture that Mr. Honda had cultivated. I reported my impressions to Fujisawa—including the seat-of-the-pants target of trying, over several years, to attain a 10 percent share of U.S. imports. He didn't probe that target quantitatively. We did not discuss profits or deadlines for breakeven. Fujisawa told me if anyone could succeed, I could and authorized $1 million for the venture.

The next hurdle was to obtain a currency allocation from the Ministry of Finance. They were extraordinarily skeptical. Toyota had launched the Toyopet in the U.S. in 1958 and had failed miserably. "How could Honda succeed?" they asked. Months went by. We put the project on hold. Suddenly, five months after our application, we were given the go-ahead—but at only a fraction of our expected level of commitment. "You can invest $250,000 in the U.S. market." they said, "but only $110,000 in cash." The remainder of our assets had to be in parts and motorcycle inventory.

We moved into frantic activity as the government, hoping we would give up on the idea, continued to hold us to the July 1959 start-up timetable. Our focus, as mentioned earlier, was to compete with the European exports. We knew our products at the time were good but not far superior. Mr. Honda was especially confident of the 250cc and 305cc machines. The shape of the handlebar on these larger machines looked like the eyebrow of Buddha, which he felt was a strong selling point. Thus, after some discussion and with no compelling criteria for selection, we configured our start-up inventory with 25 percent of each of our four products—the 50cc Supercub and the 125cc, 250cc, and 305cc machines. In dollar value terms, of course, the inventory was heavily weighted toward the larger bikes.

The stringent monetary controls of the Japanese government together with the unfriendly reception we had received during our 1958 visit caused us to start small. We chose Los Angeles where there was a large second and third generation Japanese community, a climate suitable for motorcycle use, and a growing population. We were so strapped for cash that the three of us shared a furnished apartment that rented for $80 per month. Two of us slept on the floor. We obtained a warehouse in a run-down section of the city and waited for the ship to arrive. Not daring to spare our funds for equipment, the three of us stacked the motorcycle crates three high—by hand, swept the floors, and built and maintained the parts bin.

We were entirely in the dark the first year. We were not aware the motorcycle business in the United States occurs during a seasonable April-to-August window—and our timing coincided with the closing of the 1959 season. Our hard-learned experiences with distributorships in Japan convinced us to try to go to the retailers direct. We ran ads in the motorcycle trade magazine for dealers. A few responded. By spring of 1960, we had forty dealers and some of our inventory in their stores—mostly larger bikes. A few of the 250cc and 305cc bikes began to sell. Then disaster struck.

By the first week of April 1960, reports were coming in that our machines were leaking oil and encountering clutch failure. This was our lowest moment. Honda's fragile reputation was being destroyed before it could be established. As it turned out, motorcycles in the United States are driven much farther and much faster than in Japan. We dug deeply into our precious cash reserves to air freight our motorcycles to the Honda testing lab in Japan. Through the dark month of April, Pan Am was the only enterprise in the U.S. that was nice to us. Our testing lab worked twenty-four-hour days bench testing the bikes to try to replicate the failure. Within a month, a redesigned head gasket and clutch spring solved the problem. But in the meantime, events had taken a surprising turn.

Throughout our first eight months, following Mr. Honda's and our own instincts, we had not attempted to move the 50cc Supercubs. While they were a smash success in Japan (and manufacturing couldn't keep up with demand there), they seemed wholly unsuitable for the U.S. market where everything was bigger and more luxurious. As a clincher, we had our sights on the import market—and the Europeans, like the American manufacturers, emphasized the larger machines.

We used the Honda 50s ourselves to ride around Los Angeles on errands. They attracted a lot of attention. One day we had a call from a Sears buyer. While persisting in our refusal to sell through an intermediary, we took note of Sears' interest. But we still hesitated to push the 50cc bikes out of fear they might harm our image in a heavily macho market. But when the larger bikes started breaking, we had no choice. We let the 50cc bikes move. And surprisingly, the retailers who wanted to sell them weren't motorcycle dealers, they were sporting goods stores.

The excitement created by the Honda Supercub began to gain momentum. Under restrictions from the Japanese government, we were still on a cash basis. Working with our initial cash and inventory, we sold machines, reinvested in inventory, and sunk the profits into additional inventory and advertising. Our advertising tried to straddle the market. While retailers continued to inform us that our Supercub customers were normal everyday Americans, we hesitated to target toward this segment out of fear of alienating the high margin end of our business—sold through the traditional motorcycle dealers to a more traditional "black leather jacket" customer.

Honda's phenomenal sales and share gains over the ensuing years have been previously reported. History has it that Honda "*redefined*" the U.S. motorcycle industry. In the view of American Honda's start-up team, this was an innovation they backed into—and reluctantly. It was certainly not the strategy they embarked on in 1959. As late as 1963, Honda was still working with its original Los Angeles advertising agency, its ad campaigns straddling all customers so as not to antagonize one market in pursuit of another.

In the spring of 1963, an undergraduate advertising major at UCLA submitted, in fulfillment of a routine course assignment, an ad campaign for Honda. Its theme: You Meet the Nicest People on a Honda. Encouraged by his instructor, the student passed his work on to a friend at Grey Advertising. Grey had been soliciting the Honda account—which with a $5 million a year budget was becoming an attractive potential client. Grey purchased the student's idea—on a tightly kept nondisclosure basis. Grey attempted to sell the idea to Honda.

Interestingly, the Honda management team, which by 1963 had grown to five Japanese executives, was badly split on this advertising decision. The president and treasurer favored another proposal from another agency. The director of sales, however, felt strongly that the Nicest People campaign was the right one—and his commitment eventually held sway. Thus, in 1963, through an inadvertent sequence of events, Honda came to adopt a strategy that directly identified and targeted that large untapped segment of the marketplace that has since become inseparable from the Honda legend.

The Nicest People campaign drove Honda's sales at an even greater rate. By 1964, nearly one out of every two motorcycles sold was a Honda. As a result of the influx of medium income leisure class consumers, banks and other consumer credit companies began to finance motorcycles—shifting away from dealer credit, which had been the traditional purchasing mechanism available. Honda, seizing the opportunity of soaring demand for its products, took a courageous and seemingly risky position. Late in 1964, they announced that thereafter, they would cease to ship on a consignment basis but would require cash on delivery. Honda braced itself for revolt. While nearly every dealer questioned, appealed, or complained, none relinquished his franchise. In one fell swoop, Honda shifted the power relationship from the dealer to the manufacturer. Within three years, this would become the pattern for the industry.

THE "HONDA EFFECT"

The preceding account of Honda's inroads in the U.S. motorcycle industry provides more than a second perspective on reality. It focuses our attention on different issues and raises different questions. What factors permitted two men as unlike one another as Honda and Fujisawa to function effectively as a team? What incentives and understandings permitted the Japanese executives at American Honda to respond to the market as it emerged rather than doggedly pursue the 250cc and 305 cc strategy that Mr. Honda favored? What decision process permitted the relatively junior sales director to overturn the bosses' preferences and choose the Nicest People campaign? What values or commitment drove Honda to take the enormous risk of alienating its dealers in 1964 in shifting from a consignment to cash? In hindsight, these pivotal events all seem ho-hum common sense. But each day, as organizations live out their lives without the benefit of hindsight, few choose so well and so consistently.

The juxtaposed perspectives reveal what I shall call the "Honda Effect." Western consultants, academics, and executives express a preference for oversimplifications of reality and cognitively linear explanations of events. To be sure, they have always acknowledged that the "human factor" must be taken into account. But extensive reading of strategy cases at business schools, consultants' reports, strategic planning documents as well as the coverage of the popular press, reveals a widespread tendency to overlook the process through which organizations experiment, adapt, and learn. We tend to impute coherence and purposive rationality to events when the opposite may be closer to the truth. How an organization deals with miscalculation, mistakes, and serendipitous events *outside its field of vision is often crucial to success over time.* It is this realm that requires better understanding and further research if we are to enhance our ability to guide an organization's destiny. . . .

An earlier section has addressed the shortcomings of the narrowly defined microeconomic strategy model. The Japanese avoid this pitfall by adopting a broader notion of "strategy." In our recent awe of things Japanese, most Americans forget that the original products of the Japanese automotive manufacturers badly missed the mark. Toyota's Toyopet was square, sexless, and mechanically defective. It failed miserably, as did Datsun's first several entries into the U.S. market. More recently, Mazda miscalculated badly with its first rotary engine and nearly went bankrupt. Contrary to myth, the Japanese did not from the onset embark on a strategy to seize the high-quality small-car market. They manufactured what they were accustomed to building in Japan and tried to sell it abroad. Their success, as any Japanese automotive executive will readily agree, did not result from a bold insight by a few big brains at the top. On the contrary, success was achieved by senior managers humble enough not to take their initial strategic positions too seriously. What saved Japan's near-failures was the cumulative impact of "little brains" in the form of salesmen and dealers and production workers, all contributing incrementally to the quality and market position these companies enjoy today. Middle and upper management saw their primary task as guiding and orchestrating this input from below rather than steering the organization from above along a predetermined strategic course.

The Japanese don't use the term "strategy" to describe a crisp business definition or competitive master plan. They think more in terms of "strategic accommodation," or "adaptive persistence," underscoring their belief that corporate direction evolves from an incremental adjustment to unfolding events. Rarely, in their view, does one leader (or a strategic planning group) produce a bold strategy that guides a firm unerringly. Far more frequently, the input is from below. It is this ability of an organization to move information and ideas from the bottom to the top and back again in continuous dialogue that the Japanese value above all things. As this dialogue is pursued, what in hindsight may be "strategy" evolves. In sum, "strategy" is defined as "all the things necessary for the successful functioning of organization as an adaptive mechanism." . . .

● TOWARD MIDDLE-UP-DOWN MANAGEMENT*

BY IKUJIRO NONAKA

The concepts of "top-down" and "bottom-up" management pervade management research and the popular business literature. Both center on information flow and information processing. Top-down management emphasizes the process of implementing and refining decisions made by top management as they are transmitted to the lower levels of the organization. Bottom-up management emphasizes the influence of information coming up from lower levels on management decision making. The management styles of individual firms are usually seen as located somewhere on the continuum between these two types.

However, organizations must not only process information; they must also create it. If we look closely at R&D activities, we find a pattern in some firms that does not fit on the continuum between top-down and bottom-up. It is a process that resolves the contradiction between the visionary but abstract concepts of top management and the experience-grounded concepts originating on the shopfloor by assigning a more central role to middle managers. This process, which is particularly well suited to the age of fierce market competition and rapid technological change, I call *middle-up-down management.* . . .

If we view the organization as a three-tiered structure—composed of the individual, the group, and the organization as a whole—then we can pinpoint the specific characteristics that are important to information creation at each tier of the organization (see Table 1).

TABLE 1   Levels of Organizational Information Creation

Level	Emergent Property	Factors Related to Information Creation
Organization	Structure	Competitive Resource Allocation
Group	Interaction	Direct Dialogue
Individual	Autonomy	Action and Deliberation

* Originally published in the *Sloan Management Review* (Spring 1988). Copyright © 1988 by the *Sloan Management Review;* all rights reserved. Reprinted with deletions by permission of the *Review.*

The Individual Level

The emergent, or critical, property of information creation at the individual level is autonomy. This level is characterized by action and deliberation: Only here is it possible to deliberate and act autonomously. Autonomy begins to be realized when individuals are given the freedom to combine thought and action at their own discretion, and are thereby able to guarantee the unity of knowledge and action. . . .

The Group Level

The emergent property at the group level is interaction—more concretely, open and frank dialogue. Human interaction is best realized within the organization at the group level.

The creation of information is the creation of a new perspective. The dynamic, complementary process that results in a shift to a new point of view requires interaction—a dialogue or debate—among people. The process is convoluted, involving a cycle of affirmation, denial, and resolution before new information is created. Since the significance of information is elastic during this process, individuals have the opportunity to interpret and reinterpret for themselves; this freedom allows group members to organize information individually. Unity and coherence are born from this group action. Coherence itself, however, can serve both to promote and to hinder the creation of information. Coherence often produces a pressure for conformity, and differing opinions are confined or limited with the birth of what Janis (1972) calls "group think." However, this tendency must be balanced against the fact that trust is the precondition for creative dialogue, as well as for the open exchange and cooperative possession of information.

The Organizational Level

The emergent property of the organization as a whole is structure. An organization's structure regulates the depth of the relationship between groups (sections) involved in information creation. From a macro perspective, structure produces the means for the distribution of resources among the various groups in the organization, and thereby contributes to a greater competitive capability. The structure of an organization is designed to be able to mediate between the desires of the group and of the individual in relation to information creation. It thus addresses the problem of allocating resources properly among competing interests. . . .

METHODOLOGIES OF ORGANIZATIONAL INFORMATION CREATION

Top-down management is essentially deductive; bottom-up management is essentially inductive. Let us briefly consider how these two managerial styles affect the "emergent properties" of resource allocation, interaction, and autonomy. Later we will propose middle-up-down management . . . as a methodology for information creation that can incorporate the strengths of both inductive and deductive management.

Deductive Management

Resource Allocation: The management methods used in deductive corporations are premised on the belief that information creation occurs mainly at the top. The role of top management is to clarify decision premises and to design organizational structures that can reduce individual information and decision burdens. Top management also allocates resources using sophisticated analytical techniques. Since decision making is concentrated at headquarters, a common set of clear-cut and measurable criteria that transcends the specific requirements of the various divisions is needed. ROI is typically used as such a criterion, with cash flow within and across individual strategic business units becoming the major concern with respect to resource allocation.

The underlying principle supporting such a management approach is the information-processing paradigm. But the hierarchy designed by top management in a deductive manner is not suited to allow organizational members at lower levels to create information in a flexible manner.

Interaction: Top-down, strong leadership is the basic policy adopted by deductive management. Information is processed; it moves from the upper levels to the lower levels, and variety reduction is the keystone. The elimination of "noise," "fluctuation," and "chaos" is the paramount concern. Information creation at the lower levels proceeds with great difficulty.

Information activity between divisions has a sequential relay pattern; work completed by one division is passed on to another division.

There is a tendency for the transformation of information into knowledge to occur with great intensity within the narrow areas of labor divisions. However, the amount of semantic information and knowledge absorbed and accumulated by the lower levels of the organization is small because of the lack of personal interaction.

Autonomy: Top managers and corporate staff possess the greatest autonomy. They are likely to adopt a hands-off, deductive methodology rather than a hands-on one. Consequently their information creation activities sometimes move far from the individual, shopfloor viewpoint. However, there is a potential for creating visionary concepts at the organizational level that could not be reached based on individual experience.

Inductive Management

Resource Allocation: Inductive management maintains that the organizational creation of information begins with the vision of the individual—the entrepreneurial individual—and that people who have an interest in a project will become the core of any long-term effort.

Technology is seen as the interaction between people and systems of information or knowledge. Thus the concept of synergy is basic to inductive management. Resources are allocated in a way that encourages interaction, allowing new concepts and theories to develop in the most natural way possible. The ideal inductive organization is "self-organizing." Autonomous information creation takes place by expanding from the individual level to the group level and then to the organizational level. At 3M, for example, a project can become a department and then a division if it is sufficiently successful.

Interaction: A supportive leadership that moves in step with the individual, the group, and the organization is necessary for information creation in an inductive-management organization. The support of an influential leader is necessary for individuals or self-organizing groups that have vision, since they will need help overcoming opposition from within the organization.

The need for a supporting sponsor to assist the intracompany entrepreneur is particularly emphasized at 3M. Before a daring and promising idea can stand on its own, it must be defined and supported by a sponsor willing to risk his or her reputation in order to advance or support changes in intracompany values. The leadership style of the sponsor can be summed up in the unspoken maxim, "The captain bites his tongue until it bleeds." On the basis of past experience, the leader relies on his or her own criteria (consciously and unconsciously) to guide the creation of new information.

Autonomy: Autonomy is given to those working as entrepreneurs at every organizational level. In many cases such individuals create meaningful information in the midst of interactive, tense relations, by testing and deepening their intuitive understanding through practice. Their information creation may be based on hunches or intuition, or on the ability to recognize the essence holistically in a moment.

Since the individual internalizes a great deal of tacit understanding, a career-path personnel policy that stresses promotions and transfers is used to support the organizational transfer of understanding. On the other hand, since the unlearning of acquired personal experience is difficult, inductive management may be unsuitable in instances where there are frequent large-scale reorganizations or replacements due to acquisitions or divestitures.

SYNTHESIZING INDUCTIVE AND DEDUCTIVE MANAGEMENT

Today, the intensity of market competition and the speed required for efficient information creation suggest a need to synthesize these two managerial styles. This synthesis involves the conceptualization of symbiotic management (Kagono et al., 1985) or what I call compressive management. . . . [It] can also be called middle-up-down management. The core of this managerial style is not the top managers or the entrepreneurial individuals, but rather the middle managers.

Middle management occupies a key position; it is equipped with the ability to combine strategic macro (context-free) information and hands-on micro (context-specific) information. In other words, middle management is in a position to forge the organizational link between deductive and inductive management.

Middle management is able most effectively to eliminate the noise, fluctuation, and chaos within an organization's information creation structure by serving as the starting point for action to be taken by upper and lower levels. Therefore, middle managers are also able to serve as the agent for change in the organization's self-renewal process.

Resource Allocation: Top management is responsible for determining the overall direction of the company and for establishing the time limits on realizing that vision. Time is the key resource. Each individual performing day-to-day tasks has his or her own vision. It is the middle manager who works, within a certain time limit, as a "translator" in charge of unifying individual visions and creating a larger vision, which will in turn be reflected in future individual visions. The group functions as the field for the realization of this process. In order to achieve this vision, middle managers work with upper- and lower-level personnel. However, it is the top that selects the middle, and selecting the right people becomes the most important foundation of an effective corporate strategy. In addition to deciding who will formulate and implement a strategy, the top serves as a catalyst that creates fluctuation or chaos.

Consequently, in compressive management, the entrepreneurial middle receives broad direction from the top and begins the process of information creation within the group, working to involve relevant individuals and carrying out information creation intensively within a compressed period of time. Through interaction with top management, middle management secures the resources required to achieve its vision. In this process, both deductive strategic planning and inductive emanation of information from the needs of the market are integrated to establish a definite direction for resource deployment and to create a practical concept which follows that direction.

The unit for resource allocation should be designed by the top so that the middle can create meaningful concepts. The structure of this unit can take a variety of forms, but usually consists of a multidisciplinary team led by middle management.

Interaction: Before the entrepreneurial middle can realize its vision, it must first confront and survive the criticism of other members of the group through intensive communication. As a result of this criticism, a more concrete concept will be formed. In order to realize a vision, an idea must successfully challenge the stability of the organization, involving people from both top and bottom, left and right.

This process often involves the following steps. The first stage is establishing creative chaos (Nonaka, 1989). Top management offers a challenging goal and creates tension. As the organization moves in the direction of innovation, creative chaos is amplified to focus on specific contradictions in order to solve the problem. These contradictions produce a demand for a new perspective, speeding up information creation activity. This approach is exemplified by the Honda R&D manager's statement, "Creativity is born by pushing people against the wall and pressuring them almost to the extreme."

The second stage involves the formation of a self-organizing team that tries to create a new order (meaning) out of the chaos. This self-organizing group has the following characteristics: it is autonomous; it is multidisciplinary, so as to encourage cross-fertilization among its members; and it creates challenging goals that force it to transcend the existing contradictions. This team forms the core for an intense level of activity and works independently of other divisions within the corporation.

The third stage is the synchronization of concept creation. This stage is the embodiment of the spiral in which information creation moves from middle management to the top and bottom. These movements resemble the punting and passing that occur in a rugby match as the opposing teams attempt to win ground (Takeuchi and Nonaka, 1986). The realization of a concept is made possible by the intraorganizational divisions pulling together in a "shared division of labor" and by promoting "active cooperative phenomena" (Imai et al., 1985).

The fourth stage involves the transfer of learning and unlearning. Innovation that aims at a distant and vaguely defined goal goes through apparently redundant phases of shared division of labor. The natural consequence of this process is to activate the information creation activities at all levels of the organization. The successful innovation generates a new order and gives birth to organizational learning and unlearning.

Autonomy: A group is given both autonomy (freedom) and a time limitation (constraint). Middle management becomes the logical center for the fusion of the deductive and inductive styles of management. Although it may be possible to balance the use of stored syntactic information and of tacit understanding, the need for a rapid response to changing conditions will not allow middle management to concentrate exclusively on the creation of information. The requirement simultaneously to expand the knowledge base and process information may eventually place an excessive burden upon the middle management group. If these people are not allowed to recharge their batteries from time to time, the long-term capacity for organizational information creation will weaken.

PROPER MANAGEMENT OF ORGANIZATIONAL INFORMATION CREATION

I have spoken of three methodologies for information creation—deductive, inductive, and compressive. Their approximate patterns are sketched in Figure 1 and Table 2.

One cannot make an unqualified choice of methodology until one has considered the special environmental characteristics present. The relationship between the environment and the appropriate management methodology is perhaps best illustrated in Figure 2.

FIGURE 1
A Comparison of
Organizational Information
Creation Patterns

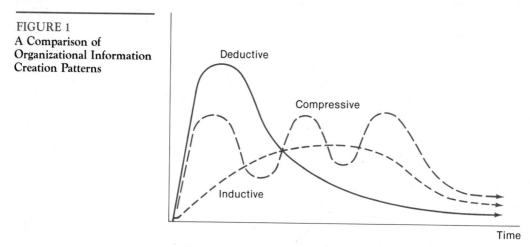

Fluctuation in Organizational
Information Creation Activity

TABLE 2 Comparison of Methodology of Organizational Information Creation

	DEDUCTIVE MANAGEMENT	INDUCTIVE MANAGEMENT	COMPRESSIVE MANAGEMENT
Resource Allocation			
• Key Resource	Money	People	Time
• Time Management	Periodical Planning	Self-management	Deadline
• Unit of Resource Allocation	SBU	Individual	Self-organizing Team
Interaction			
• Top Management	Leader	Sponsor	Catalyst
• Context of Interaction	Within Headquarters	Among Voluntary Individuals	Among Designated Individuals within the Group
• Direction	Top down	Bottom up	Middle up and down
Autonomy			
• Methodology	Deductive, Hands off	Inductive, Hands on	Hands on and off
• Knowledge	Articulate	Tacit	Articulate/Tacit
Problem	Analysis Paralysis	Inductive Ambiguity	Exhaustion

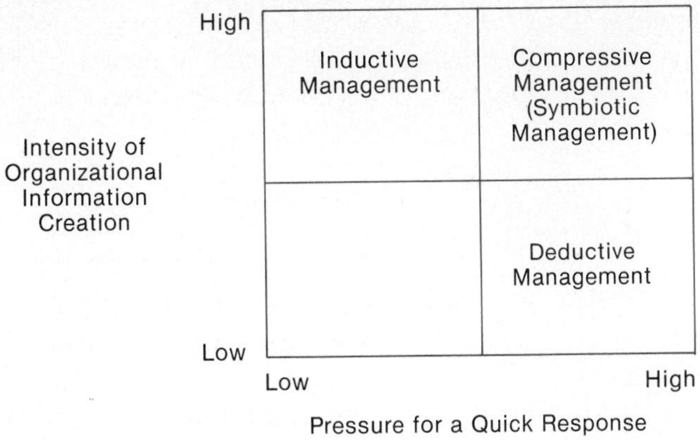

FIGURE 2
The Relationship between
Organizational Information
Creation and
Environmental
Characteristics

High
Inductive
Management

Compressive
Management
(Symbiotic
Management)

Intensity of
Organizational
Information
Creation

Deductive
Management

Low

Low   High

Pressure for a Quick Response

As environmental uncertainty increases, the organization can adapt itself more effectively with a high level of information creation occurring at all levels of the organization, rather than with a low level of information creation. In this sense, as the need for information creation increases, companies will probably make a shift from deductive management to inductive or compressive management, which have higher information creativity.

In the meantime, as market reactions speed up as a result of intense competition, companies will likely shift from inductive or deductive management to compressive management to cope with that problem. However, compressive management must come to grips with the problem of placing a great deal of pressure on middle management to process an expanding base of information within a limited time period. Therefore, whether or not information creation that is both high in quality and well coordinated can occur will depend largely on how entrepreneurial middle management really is.

CONCLUSION

The essential logic of compressive management is that top management creates a vision or dream, and middle management creates and implements concrete concepts to solve and transcend the contradictions arising from gaps between what exists at the moment and what management hopes to create. In other words, top management creates an overall theory, while middle management creates a middle-range theory and tests it empirically within the framework of the entire organization.

Mr. Tadashi Kume, president of Honda, expresses the role of middle management as follows: "I continually create dreams, but people run in different directions unless they are able to directly interact with reality. Top management doesn't know what bottom management is doing. The opposite is also true. For example, John at Honda Ohio is not able to see the company's overall direction. We at corporate headquarters see the world differently, think differently, and face a different environment. It is middle management that is charged with integrating the two viewpoints emanating from top and bottom management. There can be no progress without such integration." . . .

Middle-up-down management is a type of organizational information creation that involves the total organization. It may best embody the essence of an organization spontaneously surviving in the business environment's ceaseless generation of changes.

ORGANIZATION

DEALING WITH STRUCTURE AND SYSTEMS

Chapter 5 has completed Section 1, which introduced the concepts related to our central theme, strategy—what it is, how it should and does get made, and the nature of the work of one of its key makers, the general manager. Chapter 6 begins Section 2, which deals with another set of concepts that every student of general management must come to understand. We group these under the title *Organization* because they all pertain to the basic design and running of the organization.

In this chapter we examine the design of organizational *structure* and the development of *systems* for coordination and control. In Chapter 7, we consider *culture,* that ideological glue that holds organizations together, enhancing their ability to pursue strategies on one hand, but sometimes impeding strategic change on the other. And in Chapter 8, we turn to the questions of *power*—how it flows within the organization and how the organization uses it in its external environment.

Structure, in our view, no more follows strategy than the left foot follows the right in walking. The two exist *inter*dependently, each influencing the other. There are certainly times when a structure is redesigned to carry out a new strategy. But the choice of any new strategy is likewise influenced by the realities and potentials of the existing structure. Indeed, the classical model of strategy formulation (discussed in Chapter 3) implicitly recognizes this by showing the strengths and weaknesses of the organization as an input to the creation of strategies. Surely these strengths and weaknesses are deeply rooted within the existing structure, indeed often part and parcel of it. Hence, we introduce here structure and the associated administrative systems which make it work as essential factors to consider in the strategy process. Later when we present the various contexts within which organizations function, we shall consider the different ways in which strategy and structure interact.

All of the readings of this chapter reinforce these points. The Waterman, Peters, and Phillips article originally published under the title "Structure Is Not Organization," introduces the well-known "7-S" framework that was developed at the McKinsey consulting firm, where all three authors worked when this article was published. (This framework was, in fact, one of the antecedents of the best-selling management book *In Search of Excellence* by two of these authors.) This framework explicitly considers how structure, systems, style, and other organizational factors interrelate with strategy; as such, many practicing executives and students have found this a most valuable construct in thinking about organizations. (Note that what the authors call "superordinate goals" were renamed "shared values" in the *Excellence* book. We discuss them in some depth under the label "culture" in Chapter 7, noting that these were first introduced in this book in the Selznick reading of Chapter 2.)

The second reading approaches conventional concepts of strategy and its relationship to structure, but does so in an unconventional way. In his article "Strategy and Organization Planning," Jay Galbraith, a former MIT and Wharton Business School professor who worked as an independent management consultant for several years and now teaches at the University of Southern California, also views structure broadly as encompassing support systems of various kinds. Building on concepts such as "driving force" and "center of gravity," Galbraith links various strategies (of vertical integration and diversification) to forms of structure, ranging from the functional to the increasingly diversified. Galbraith covers a wide body of important literature in the field and uses visual imagery to make his points. The result is one of the best articles in print on the relationship between the strategy of diversification and the structure of divisionalization.

Unconventional, too, but in a very different way, is the following article by Quinn, Doorley, and Paquette. Whereas Galbraith discusses vertical integration and diversification, they focus in a sense on vertical *de*integration; whereas Galbraith discusses moving upstream and downstream, they in a sense recommend taking many internal activities *off*stream. Interestingly, however, these authors focus their discussion on a concept very close to Galbraith's "center of gravity," which they call an organization's "core activities."

The subject here is a rather new concept of organization for the 1990s, facilitated by new information technologies, what the authors call the "intellectual holding company." By concentrating strategic analyses on each element in the value chain, companies can target their own resources towards those things they do best, and outsource those activities others can perform better. In this way they can lower their investments, flatten their organizations, and improve the quality and flexibility of their outputs. (See the associated reading by two of these authors in Chapter 12 on "Spider's Web," "Infinitely Flat," and "Inverted" Organizations.) The authors suggest how these innovative new forms can act to restructure entire industries. When coupled with concepts from the Professional Context chapter, this reading provides powerful new insights.

The fourth reading, excerpted originally from Mintzberg's book *The Structuring of Organizations,* comprehensively probes the design of organizational structures, including their formal systems. It seeks to do two things: first to delineate the basic dimensions or organizations and then to combine these to identify various basic types of organizations, called "configurations." The dimensions introduced include mechanisms used to coordinate work in organizations, parameters to consider in designing structures, and situational factors which influence choices among these design parameters. This reading also introduces a somewhat novel diagram to depict organizations, not as the usual organizational chart or cybernetic flow process, but as a visual combination of the critical parts of an organization. This reading then clusters all these dimensions into a set of configurations, each introduced briefly here and discussed at length in later chapters. In fact, the choice of the chapters on context—entrepreneurial, mature, diversified, professional, and innovative (leaving aside the last on strategic change)—was really based on five of these types, so that reading the conclusion to this article will help to introduce you to Section 3.

● THE 7-S FRAMEWORK*

BY ROBERT H. WATERMAN, JR., THOMAS J. PETERS, AND JULIEN R. PHILLIPS

The Belgian surrealist René Magritte painted a series of pipes and titled the series *Ceci n'est pas une pipe:* this is not a pipe. The picture of the thing is not the thing. In the same way, a structure is not an organization. We all know that, but like as not, when we reorganize, what we do is to restructure. Intellectually all managers and consultants know that much more goes on in the process of organizing than the charts, boxes, dotted lines, position descriptions, and matrices can possibly depict. But all too often we behave as though we didn't know it; if we want change we change the structure. . . .

Our assertion is that productive organization change is not simply a matter of structure, although structure is important. It is not so simple as the interaction between strategy and structure, although strategy is critical too. Our claim is that effective organizational change is really the relationship between structure, strategy, systems, style, skills, staff, and something we call superordinate goals. (The alliteration is intentional: it serves as an aid to memory.)

Our central idea is that organization effectiveness, stems from the interaction of several factors—some not especially obvious and some underanalyzed. Our framework for organization change, graphically depicted in Figure 1, suggests several important ideas:

- First is the idea of a multiplicity of factors that influence an organization's ability to change and its proper mode of change. Why pay attention to only one or two, ignoring the others? Beyond structure and strategy, there are at least five other identifiable elements. The division is to some extent arbitrary, but it has the merit of acknowledging the complexity identified in the research and segmenting it into manageable parts.

- Second, the diagram is intended to convey the notion of the interconnectedness of the variables—the idea is that it's difficult, perhaps impossible, to make significant progress in one area without making progress in the others as well. Notions of organization change that ignore its many aspects or their interconnectedness are dangerous.

* Originally published as "Structure is Not Organization" in *Business Horizons* (June 1980); copyright © 1980 by the Foundation for the School of Business at Indiana University; all rights reserved. Reprinted with deletions by permission of the publisher.

FIGURE 1
A New View of
Organization

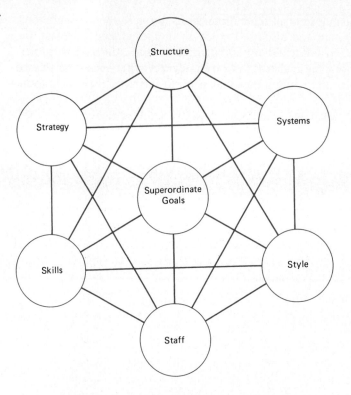

- In [an] article on strategy, *Fortune* commented that perhaps as many as 90% of carefully planned strategies don't work. If that is so, our guess would be that the failure is a failure in execution, resulting from inattention to the other S's. Just as a logistics bottleneck can cripple a military strategy, inadequate systems or staff can make paper tigers of the best-laid plans for clobbering competitors.

- Finally, the shape of the diagram is significant. It has no starting point or implied hierarchy. A priori, it isn't obvious which of the seven factors will be the driving force in changing a particular organization at a particular point in time. In some cases, the critical variable might be strategy. In others, it could be systems or structure.

STRUCTURE

To understand this model of organization change better, let us look at each of its elements, beginning—as most organization discussions do—with structure. What will the new organization of the 1980s be like? If decentralization was the trend of the past, what is next? Is it matrix organization? What will "Son of Matrix" look like? Our answer is that those questions miss the point. . . .

The central problem in structuring today . . . is not the one on which most organization designers spend their time—that is, how to divide up tasks. It is one of emphasis and coordination—how to make the whole thing work. The challenge lies not so much in trying to comprehend all the possible dimensions of organization structure as in developing the ability to focus on those dimensions which are currently important to the organization's evolution—and to be ready to refocus as the crucial dimensions shift.

If structure is not enough, what is? Obviously, there is strategy. It was Alfred Chandler (1962) who first pointed out that structure follows strategy, or more precisely, that a strategy of diversity forces a decentralized structure. Throughout the past decade, the corporate world has given close attention to the interplay between strategy and structure. Certainly, clear ideas about strategy make the job of structural design more rational.

By "strategy" we mean those actions that a company plans in response to or anticipation of changes in its external environment—its customers, its competitors. Strategy is the way a company aims to improve its position vis-à-vis competition—perhaps through low-cost production or delivery, perhaps by providing better value to the customer, perhaps by achieving sales and service dominance. It is, or ought to be, an organization's way of saying: "Here is how we will create unique value."

As the company's chosen route to competitive success, strategy is obviously a central concern in many business situations—especially in highly competitive industries where the game is won or lost on share points. But "structure follows strategy" is by no means the be-all and end-all of organization wisdom. We find too many examples of large, prestigious companies around the world that are replete with strategy and cannot execute any of it. There is little if anything wrong with their structures; the causes of their inability to execute lie in other dimensions of our framework. When we turn to nonprofit and public sector organizations, moreover, we find that the whole meaning of "strategy" is tenuous—but the problem of organizational effectiveness looms as large as ever.

Strategy, then, is clearly a critical variable in organization design—but much more is at work.

By systems we mean all the procedures, formal and informal, that make the organization go, day by day and year by year: capital budgeting systems, training systems, cost accounting procedures, budgeting systems. If there is a variable in our model that threatens to dominate the others, it could well be systems. Do you want to understand how an organization really does (or doesn't) get things done? Look at the systems. Do you want to change an organization without disruptive restructuring? Try changing the systems.

A large consumer goods manufacturer was recently trying to come up with an overall corporate strategy. Textbook portfolio theory seemed to apply: find a good way to segment the business, decide which segments in the total business portfolio are most attractive, invest most heavily in those. The only catch: reliable cost data by segment were not to be had. The company's management information system was not adequate to support the segmentation. . . .

[One] intriguing aspect of systems is the way they mirror the state of an organization. Consider a certain company we'll call International Wickets. For years management has talked about the need to become more market oriented. Yet astonishingly little time is spent in their planning meetings on customers, marketing, market share, or other issues having to do with market orientation. One of their key systems, in other words, remains *very* internally oriented. Without a change in this key system, the market orientation goal will remain unattainable no matter how much change takes place in structure and strategy.

To many business managers the word "systems" has a dull, plodding, middle-management sound. Yet it is astonishing how powerfully systems changes can enhance organizational effectiveness—without the disruptive side effects that so often ensue from tinkering with structure.

STYLE

It is remarkable how often writers, in characterizing a corporate management for the business press, fall back on the word "style." . . . The trouble we have with style is not in recognizing its importance, but in doing much about it. Personalities don't change, or so the conventional wisdom goes.

We think it is important to distinguish between the basic personality of a top-management team and the way that team comes across to the organization. Organizations may listen to what managers say, but they believe what managers do. Not words, but patterns of actions are decisive. The power of style, then, is essentially manageable.

One element of a manager's style is how he or she chooses to spend time. As Henry Mintzberg has pointed out managers don't spend their time in the neatly compartmentalized planning, organizing, motivating, and controlling modes of classical management theory. Their days are a mess—or so it seems. There's a seeming infinity of things they might devote attention to. No top executive attends to all of the demands of his time; the median time spent on any one issue is nine minutes.

What can a top manager do in nine minutes? Actually, a good deal. He can signal what's on his mind; he can reinforce a message; he can nudge people's thinking in a desired direction. Skillful management of his inevitably fragmented time is, in fact, an immensely powerful change lever. . . .

Another aspect of style is symbolic behavior. Companies most successful in finding mineral deposits typically have more people on the board who understand exploration or have headed exploration departments. Typically they fund exploration more consistently (that is, their year-to-year spending patterns are less volatile). They define fewer and more consistent exploration targets. Their exploration activities typically report at a higher organizational level. And they typically articulate better reasons for exploring in the first place.

STAFF

Staff (in the sense of people, not line/staff) is often treated in one of two ways. At the hard end of the spectrum, we talk of appraisal systems, pay scales, formal training programs, and the like. At the soft end, we talk about morale, attitude, motivation, and behavior.

Top management is often, and justifiably, turned off by both these approaches. The first seems too trivial for their immediate concern ("Leave it to the personnel department"), the second too intractable ("We don't want a bunch of shrinks running around, stirring up the place with more attitude surveys").

Our predilection is to broaden and redefine the nature of the people issue. What do the top-performing companies do to foster the process of developing managers? How, for example, do they shape the basic values of their management cadre? Our reason for asking the question at all is simply that no serious discussion of organization can afford to ignore it (although many do). Our reason for framing the question around the development of managers is our observation that the superbly performing companies pay extraordinary attention to managing what might be called the socialization process in their companies. This applies especially to the way they introduce young recruits into the mainstream of their organizations and to the way they manage their careers as the recruits develop into tomorrow's managers. . . .

Considering people as a pool of resources to be nurtured, developed, guarded, and allocated is one of the many ways to turn the "staff" dimension of our 7-S framework into something not only amenable to, but worthy of practical control by senior management.

We are often told, "Get the structure 'right' and the people will fit" or "Don't compromise the 'optimum' organization for people considerations." At the other end of the spectrum we are earnestly advised, "The right people can make any organization work." Neither view is correct. People do count, but staff is only one of our seven variables.

SKILLS

We added the notion of skills for a highly practical reason: It enables us to capture a company's crucial attributes as no other concept can do. A strategic description of a company, for example, might typically cover markets to be penetrated or types of products to be sold. But how do most of us characterize companies? Not by their strategies or their structures. We tend to characterize them by what they do best. We talk of IBM's orientation to the marketplace, its prodigious customer service capabilities, or its sheer market power. We talk of Du Pont's research prowess, Procter & Gamble's product management capability, ITT's financial controls, Hewlett-Packard's innovation and quality, and Texas Instruments' project management. These dominating attributes, or capabilities, are what we mean by skills.

Now why is this distinction important? Because we regularly observe that organizations facing big discontinuities in business conditions must do more than shift strategic focus. Frequently they need to add a new capability, that is to say, a new skill. . . . These dominating capability needs, unless explicitly labeled as such, often get lost as the company "attacks a new market" (strategy shift) or "decentralizes to give managers autonomy" (structure shift).

Additionally, we frequently find it helpful to *label* current skills, for the addition of a new skill may come only when the old one is dismantled. Adopting a newly "flexible and adaptive marketing thrust," for example, may be possible only if increases are accepted in certain marketing or distribution costs. Dismantling some of the distracting attributes of an old "manufacturing mentality" (that is, a skill that was perhaps crucial in the past) may be the only way to ensure the success of an important change program. Possibly the most difficult problem in trying to organize effectively is that of weeding out old skills—and their supporting systems, structures, and so on—to ensure that important new skills can take root and grow.

SUPERORDINATE GOALS

The word "superordinate" literally means "of higher order." By superordinate goals, we mean guiding concepts—a set of values and aspirations, often unwritten, that goes beyond the conventional formal statement of corporate objectives.

Superordinate goals are the fundamental ideas around which a business is built. They are its main values. But they are more as well. They are the broad notions of future direction that the top management team wants to infuse throughout the organization. They are the way in which the team wants to express itself, to leave its own mark. Examples would include Theodore Vail's "universal service" objective, which has so dominated AT&T; the strong drive to "customer service" which guides IBM's marketing. . . .

In a sense, superordinate goals are like the basic postulates in a mathematical system. They are the starting points on which the system is logically built, but in themselves are not logically derived. The ultimate test of their value is not their logic but the usefulness of the system that ensues. Everyone seems to know the importance of compelling superordinate goals. The drive for their accomplishment pulls an organization together. They provide stability in what would otherwise be a shifting set of organization dynamics.

Unlike the other six S's, superordinate goals don't seem to be present in all, or even most, organizations. They are, however, evident in most of the superior performers.

To be readily communicated, superordinate goals need to be succinct. Typically, therefore, they are expressed at high levels of abstraction and may mean very little to outsiders who don't know the organization well. But for those inside, they are rich with significance. Within an organization, superordinate goals, if well articulated, make meanings for people. And making meanings is one of the main functions of leadership.

CONCLUSION

We have passed rapidly through the variables in our framework. What should the reader have gained from the exercise?

We started with the premise that solutions to today's thorny organizing problems that invoke only structure—or even strategy and structure—are seldom adequate. The inadequacy stems in part from the inability of the two-variable model to explain why organizations are so slow to adapt to change. The reasons often lie among the other variables: systems that embody outdated assumptions, a management style that is at odds with the stated strategy, the absence of a superordinate goal that binds the organization together in pursuit of a common purpose, the refusal to deal concretely with "people problems" and opportunities.

At its most trivial, when we merely use the framework as a checklist, we find that it leads into new terrain in our efforts to understand how organizations really operate or to design a truly comprehensive change program. At a minimum, it gives us a deeper bag in which to collect our experiences.

More importantly, it suggests the wisdom of taking seriously the variables in organizing that have been considered soft, informal, or beneath the purview of top management interest. We believe that style, systems, skills, superordinate goals can be observed directly, even measured—if only they are taken seriously. We think that these variables can be at least as important as strategy and structure in orchestrating major change; indeed, that they are almost critical for achieving necessary, or desirable change. A shift in systems, a major retraining program for staff, or the generation of top-to-bottom enthusiasm around a new superordinate goal could take years. Changes in strategy and structure, on the surface, may happen more quickly. But the pace of real change is geared to all seven S's.

At its most powerful and complex, the framework forces us to concentrate on interactions and fit. The real energy required to redirect an institution comes when all the variables in the model are aligned. One of our associates looks at our diagram as a set of compasses. "When all seven needles are all pointed the same way," he comments, "you're looking at an *organized* company."

• STRATEGY AND ORGANIZATION PLANNING*

BY JAY R. GALBRAITH

... There has been a great deal of progress in the knowledge base supporting organization planning in the last twenty-five years. Modern research on corporate structures probably started with Chandler's *Strategy and Structure*. Subsequent research has been aimed at expanding the number of attributes of an organization beyond that of just structure. I have used the model shown in Figure 1 to indicate that organization consists of structure, processes that cut the structural lines like budgeting, planning, teams, and so on, reward systems like promotions and compensation, and finally people practices like selection and development (Galbraith, 1977). The trend lately is to expand to more attributes like the 7-S's (Waterman, 1980) and to "softer" attributes like culture.

All of these models are intended to convey the same ideas. First, organization is more than just structure. And, second, all of the elements must "fit" to be in "harmony" with each other. The effective organization is one that has blended its structure, management practices, rewards, and people into a package that in turn fits with its strategy. However, strategies change and therefore the organization must change.

The research of the past few years is creating some evidence by which organizations and strategies are matched. Some of the strategies are proving more successful than others. One of the explanations is organizational in nature. Also the evidence shows that for any strategy, the high performers are those who have achieved a fit between their strategy and their organization.

These findings give organization planning a base from which to work. The organization planner should become a member of the strategic team in order to guide management to choose the appropriate strategies for which the organization is developed or to choose the appropriate organization for the new strategy.

In the sections that follow, the strategic changes that are made by organizations are described. Then the strategy and organization evidence is presented. Finally the data on economic performance and fit is discussed.

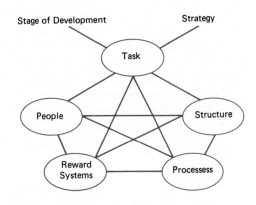

FIGURE 1
Model of Organization Structure

---

* Originally published in *Human Resource Management* (Spring-Summer 1983). Copyright © 1983 John Wiley & Sons, Inc. Reprinted with deletions by permission of John Wiley & Sons, Inc.

There has been a good deal of recent attention given to the match between strategy and organization. Much of this work consists of empirical tests of Chandler's ideas presented in *Strategy and Structure* (1962). Most of this material is reviewed elsewhere (Galbraith and Nathanson, 1978). However, some recent work and ideas hold out considerable potential for understanding how different patterns of strategic change lead to different organization structures, management systems, and company cultures. In addition, some good relationships with economic performance are also attained.

The ideas rest on the concept of an organization having a center of gravity or driving force. (Tregoe and Zimmerman, 1980). This center of gravity arises from the firm's initial success in the industry in which it grew up. Let us first explore the concept of center of gravity, then the patterns of strategic change that have been followed by American enterprises.

The center of gravity of a company depends on where in the industry supply chain the company started. In order to explain the concept, manufacturing industries will be used. Figure 2 depicts the stages of supply in an industry chain. Six stages are shown here. Each industry may have more or fewer stages. Service industries typically have fewer stages.

The chain begins with a raw material extraction stage which supplies crude oil, iron ore, logs, or bauxite to the second stage of primary manufacturing. The second stage is a variety-reducing stage to produce a standardized output (petrochemicals, steel, paper pulp, or aluminum ingots). The next stage fabricates commodity products from this primary material. Fabricators produce polyethylene, cans, sheet steel, cardboard cartons, and semiconductor components. The next stage is the product producers who add value, usually through product development, patents, and proprietary products. The next stage is the marketer and distributor. These are the consumer branded product manufacturers and various distributors. Finally, there are the retailers who have the direct contact with the ultimate consumer.

The line splitting the chain into two segments divides the industry into upstream and downstream halves. While there are differences between each of the stages, the differences between the upstream and downstream stages are striking. The upstream stages add value by reducing the variety of raw materials found on the earth's surface to a few standard commodities. The purpose is to produce flexible, predictable raw materials and intermediate products from which an increasing variety of downstream products are made. The downstream stages add value through producing a variety of products to meet varying customer needs. The downstream value is added through advertising, product positioning, marketing channels, and R&D. Thus, the upstream and downstream companies face very different business problems and tasks.

The reason for distinguishing between upstream and downstream companies is that the factors for success, the lessons learned by managers, and the organizations used are fundamentally different. The successful, experienced manager has

FIGURE 2
Supply Stages in an
Industry Chain

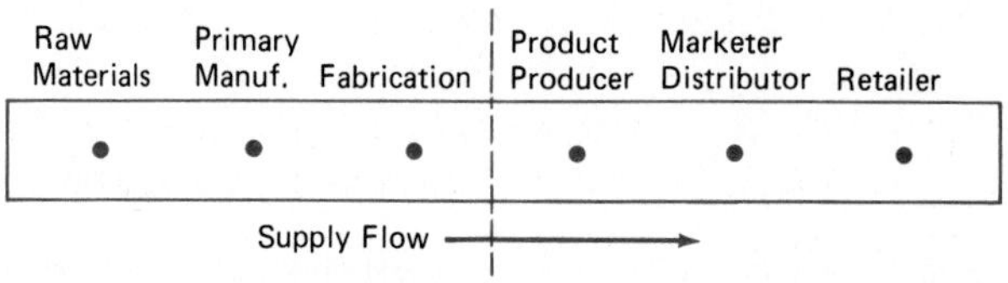

been shaped and formed in fundamentally different ways in the different stages. The management processes are different, as are the dominant functions. In short, the company's culture is shaped by where it began in the industry chain. Listed are some fundamental differences that illustrate the contrast:

Upstream	*Downstream*
Standardize/homogenize	Customize/segment
Low-cost producer	High margins/proprietary positions
Process innovation	Product innovation
Capital budget	R&D/advertising budget
Technology/capital intensive	People intensive
Supply/trader/engineering	R&D/marketing dominated
Line driven	Line/staff
Maximize end users	Target end users
⋮	⋮
Sales push	Market pull

The mind set of the upstream manager is geared toward standardization and efficiency. They are the producers of standardized commodity products. In contrast, downstream managers try to customize and tailor output to diverse customer needs. They segment markets and target individual users. The upstream company wants to standardize in order to maximize the number of end users and get volume to lower costs. The downstream company wants to target particular sets of end users. Therefore, the upstreamers have a divergent view of the world based on their commodity. For example, the cover of the 1981 annual report of Intel (a fabricator of commodity semiconductors) is a listing of the 10,000 uses to which microprocessors have been put. The downstreamers have a convergent view of the world based on customer needs and will select whatever commodity will best serve that need. In the electronics industry there is always a conflict between the upstream component types and the downstream systems types because of this contrast in mind sets.

The basis of competition is different in the two stages. Commodities compete on price since the products are the same. Therefore, it is essential that the successful upstreamer be the low-cost producer. Their organizations are the lean and mean ones with a minimum of overheads. Low cost is also important for the downstreamer, but it is proprietary features that generate high margins. That feature may be a brand image, such as Maxwell House, a patented technology, an endorsement (such as the American Dental Association's endorsement of Crest toothpaste), customer service policy, and so on. Competition revolves around product features and product positioning and less on price. This means that marketing and product management sets prices. Products move by marketing pull. In contrast, the upstream company pushes the product through a strong sales force. Often salespeople negotiate prices within limits set by top management.

The organizations are different as well. The upstream companies are functional and line driven. They seek a minimum of staff, and even those staffs that are used are in supporting roles. The downstream company with multiple products and multiple markets learns to manage diversity early. Profit centers emerge and resources need to be allocated across products and markets. Larger staffs arise to assist top management in priority setting across competing product/market advocates. Higher margins permit the overhead to exist.

Both upstream and downstream companies use research and development. However, the upstream company invests in process development in order to lower costs. The downstream company invests primarily in product development in order to achieve proprietary positions.

The key managerial processes also vary. The upstream companies are driven by the capital budget and have various capital appropriations controls. The downstream companies also have a capital budget but are driven by the R&D budget (product producers) or the advertising budget (marketers). Further downstream it is working capital that becomes paramount. Managers learn to control the business by managing the turnover of inventory and accounts receivable. Thus, the upstream company is capital intensive and technological "know-how" is critical. Downstream companies are more people intensive. Therefore, the critical skills revolve around human resources management.

The dominant functions also vary with stages. The raw material processor is dominated by geologists, petroleum engineers, and traders. The supply and distribution function which searches for the most economical end use is powerful. The manufacturers of commodities are dominated by engineers who come up through manufacturing. The downstream companies are dominated first by technologists in research and product development. Farther downstream, it is marketing and then merchandising that emerge as the power centers. The line of succession to the CEO usually runs through this dominant function.

In summary, the upstream and downstream companies are very different entities. The differences, a bit exaggerated here because of the dichotomy, lead to differences in organization structure, management processes, dominant functions, succession paths, management beliefs and values or, in short, the management way of life. Thus, companies can be in the same industry but be very different because they developed from a beginning at a particular stage of the industry. This beginning, and the initial successes, teaches management the lessons of that stage. The firm develops an integrated organization (structure, processes, rewards, and people) which is peculiar to that stage and forms the center of gravity.

STRATEGIC CHANGE

The first strategic change that an organization makes is to vertically integrate within its industry. At a certain size, the organization can move backward to prior stages to guarantee sources of supply and secure bargaining leverage on vendors. And/or it can move forward to guarantee markets and volume for capital investments and become a customer to feed back data for new products. This initial strategic move does not change the center of gravity because the prior and subsequent stages are usually operated for the benefit of the center-of-gravity stage.

The paper industry is used to illustrate the concepts of center of gravity and vertical integration. Figure 3 depicts five paper companies which operate from different centers of gravity. The first is Weyerhauser. Its center of gravity is at the land and timber stage of the industry. Weyerhauser seeks the highest return use for a log. They make pulp and paper rolls. They make containers and milk cartons. But they are a timber company. If the returns are better in lumber, the pulp mills get fed with sawdust and chips. International Paper (the name of the company tells it all), by contrast, is a primary manufacturer of paper. It also has timber lands, container plants, and works on new products around aseptic packaging. However, if the pulp mills ran out of logs, the manager of the woodlands used to be fired. The raw material stage is to supply the manufacturing stage, not seek the highest return for its

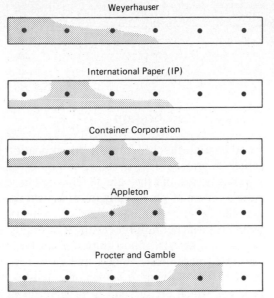

timber. The Container Corporation (again, the name describes the company) is the example of the fabricator. It also has woodlands and pulp mills, but they are to supply the container making operations. The product producer is Appleton. It makes specialty paper products. For example, Appleton produces a paper with globules of ink imbedded in it. The globules burst and form a letter or number when struck with an impact printer.

The last company is Procter & Gamble. P&G is a consumer products company. And, like the other companies, it operates pulp mills and owns timber lands. However, it is driven by the advertising or marketing function. If one wanted to be CEO of P&G, one would not run a pulp mill or the woodlands. The path to CEO is through the brand manager for Charmin or Pampers.

Thus, each of these companies is in the paper industry. Each operates at a number of stages in the industry. Yet each is a very different company because it has its center of gravity at a different stage. The center of gravity establishes a base from which subsequent strategic changes take place. That is, as a company's industry matures, the company feels a need to change its center of gravity in order to move to a place in the industry where better returns can be obtained, or move to a new industry but use its same center of gravity and skills in that industry, or make some combination of industry and center of gravity change. These options lead to different patterns of corporate developments.

By-products Diversification

One of the first diversification moves that a vertically integrated company makes is to sell by-products from points along the industry chain. Figure 4 depicts this strategy. These companies appear to be diversified if one attributes revenue to the various industries in which the company operates. But the company has changed neither its industry nor its center of gravity. The company is behaving intelligently by seeking additional sources of revenue and profit. However, it is still psychologically committed to its center of gravity and to its industry. Alcoa is such a firm. Even though they operate in several industries, their output varies directly with the aluminum cycle. They have not reduced their dependence on a single industry, as one would with real diversification.

145

FIGURE 4
By-product Diversification

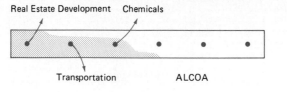

Related Diversification

Another strategic change is the diversification into new industries but at the same center of gravity. This is called related diversification." The firm diversifies into new businesses, but they are all related. The relationship revolves around the company's center of gravity. Figure 5 depicts the diversification moves of Procter & Gamble. After beginning in the soap industry, P&G vertically integrated back into doing its own chemical processing (fatty acids) and seed crushing. Then, in order to pursue new growth opportunities, it has been diversifying into paper, food, beverages, pharmaceuticals, coffee, and so on. But each move into a new industry is made at the company's center of gravity. The new businesses are all consumer products which are driven out of advertising by brand managers. The 3M Company also follows a related diversification strategy, but theirs is based on technology. They have 40,000 different products which are produced by some seventy divisions. However, 95% of the products are based on coating and bonding technologies. Its center of gravity is a product producer, and it adds value through R&D.

Linked Diversification

A third type of diversification involves moving into new industries and operating at different centers of gravity in those new industries. However, there is a linkage of some type among various businesses. Figure 6 depicts Union Camp as following this pattern of corporate development. Union Camp is a primary producer of paper products. As such, it vertically integrated backwards to own woodlands. From there, it moved downstream within the wood products industry by running sawmills and fabricating plants. However, they recently purchased a retail lumber business.

They also moved into the chemical business by selling by-products from the pulping process. This business was successful and expanded. Recently, Union Camp was bidding for a flavors and fragrances (F & F) company. The F&F company is a product producer which adds value through creating flavors and fragrances for mostly consumer products companies.

Thus, Union Camp is an upstream company that is acquiring downstream companies. However, these new companies are in industries in which the company

FIGURE 5
Related Diversification

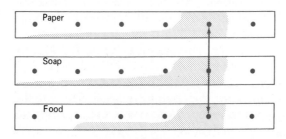

Procter and Gamble

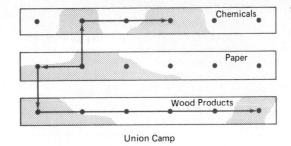

FIGURE 6
Linked Diversification

Union Camp

already diversified from its upstream center of gravity. But these new acquisitions are not operated for the benefit of the center of gravity but are stand-alone profit centers.

Unrelated Diversification

The final type of strategic change is to diversify into unrelated businesses. Like the linked diversifiers, unrelated diversifiers move into new industries often at different centers of gravity. They almost always use acquisition, while related and linked companies will use some acquisitions but rely heavily on internal development. There is often very little relation between the industries into which the unrelated company diversifies. Textron and Teledyne have been the paradigm examples. They operate in industrial equipment, aerospace, consumer products, insurance, and so on. Others have spread into retailing, services, and entertainment. The purpose is to insulate the company's earnings from the uncertainties of any one industry or from the business cycle.

Center of Gravity Change

Another possibility is for an organization to stay in the same industry but change its center of gravity in that industry. Recent articles describe the attempts of chemical companies to move downstream into higher margin, proprietary products. They went to move away from the overcapacity/undercapacity cycles of commodity businesses with their low margins and high capital intensity. In aerospace, some of the system integration houses are moving backward into making electronic components. For example, there are going to be fewer airplanes and more effort on the avionics, radars, weapons, and so on that go into airplanes. In either case, it means a shift in the center of gravity of the company.

In summary, several patterns of strategic change can occur in a company. These involve changes to the company's industry of origination, changes to the center of gravity of the company, or some combination of the two. For some of the strategic changes there are appropriate organizations and measures of their economic performance.

STRATEGY, ORGANIZATION, AND PERFORMANCE

For a number of years now, studies have been made of strategy and structure of the *Fortune* 500. Most of these were conducted by the Harvard Business School. These studies were reviewed in previous work (Galbraith and Nathanson, 1978). The current view is illustrated in Table 1. If one samples the *Fortune* 500 and categorizes them by strategy and structure, the following relationships hold.

147

TABLE 1

STRATEGY	STRUCTURE
Single business	Functional
Vertical by-products	Functional with P&Ls
Related businesses	Divisional
Linked businesses	Mixed structures
Unrelated businesses	Holding company

One can still find organizations staying in their same original business. Such a single business is Wrigley Chewing Gum. These organizations are run by centralized functional organizations. The next strategic type is the vertically integrated by-product seller. Again, these companies have some diversification but remain committed to their industry and center of gravity. The companies are also functional, but the sequential stages are often operated as profit and loss divisions. The companies are usually quite centralized and run by collegial management groups. The profit centers are not true ones in being independent to run their own businesses. These are almost all upstream companies.

The related businesses are those that move into new industries at their center of gravity. Usually these are downstream companies. They adopt the decentralized profit center divisions. However, the divisions are not completely decentralized. There are usually strong corporate staffs and some centralized marketing, manufacturing, and R&D. There may be several thousand people on the corporate payroll.

The clearest contrast to the related diversifier is the unrelated business company. These companies enter a variety of businesses at several centers of gravity. The organization they adopt is the very decentralized holding company. Their outstanding feature is the small corporate staff. Depending on their size, the numbers range between fifty and two hundred. Usually these are support staffs. All of the marketing, manufacturing, and R&D is decentralized to the divisions. Group executives have no staffs and are generally corporate oriented.

The linked companies are neither of these extremes. Often linked forms are transitory. The organizations that they utilize are usually mixed forms that are not easily classified. Some divisions are autonomous, while others are managed out of the corporate HQ. Still others have strong group executives with group staffs. Some work has been done on classifying these structures (Allen, 1978).

There has been virtually no work done on center of gravity changes and their changes in structure. Likewise, there has been nothing done on comparisons for economic performance. But for the other categories and structures, there is emerging some good data on relative economic performance.

The studies of economic performance have compared the various strategic patterns and the concept of fit between strategy and organization. Both sets of results have organization design implications. The economic studies use return on equity as the performance measure. If one compares the strategic categories listed in Table 1, there are distinct performance differences. The high performers are consistently the related diversifiers (Rumelt, 1974; Galbraith and Nathanson, 1978; Nathanson and Cassano, 1982; Bettis, 1981; Rumelt, 1982). There are several explanations for this performance difference. One explanation is that the related diversifiers are all downstream companies in businesses with high R&D and advertising expenditures. These businesses have higher margins and returns than other businesses. Thus, it may not be the strategy but the businesses the relateds happen to be in. However, if the unrelateds are good acquirers, why do they not enter the high-return businesses?

The other explanation is that the relateds learn a set of core skills and design an organization to perform at a particular center of gravity. Then, when they diversify, they take on the task of learning a new business, but at the same center of gravity. Therefore, they get a diversified portfolio of businesses but each with a system of management and an organization that is understood by everyone. The management understands the business and is not spread thin.

The unrelateds, however, have to learn new industries and also how to operate to a different center of gravity. This latter change is the most difficult to accomplish. One upstream company diversified via acquisition into downstream companies. It consistently encountered control troubles. It instituted a capital appropriation process for each investment of $50,000 or more. It still had problems, however. The retail division opened a couple of stores with leases for $40,000. It didn't use the capital process. The company got blindsided because the stores required $40 million in working capital for inventory and receivables. Thus, the management systems did not fit the new downstream business. It appears that organizational fit makes a difference. . . .

One additional piece of evidence results from the studies of economic performance. This result is that the poorest performer of the strategic categories is the vertically integrated by-product seller. Recall these companies are all upstream, raw material, and primary manufacturers. They make up a good portion of "Smokestack America." In some respects, these companies made their money early in the century, and their value added is shifting to lesser developed countries in the natural course of industrial development. However, what is significant here is their inability to change. It is no secret to anyone that they have been underperformers, yet they have continued to put money back into the same business.

My explanation revolves around the center of gravity. These previously successful companies put together an organization that fit their industry and stage. When the industry declined, they were unable to change as well as the downstream companies. The reason is that upstream companies were functional organizations with few general managers. Their resource allocation was within a single business, not across multiple products. The management skill is partly technological know-how. This technology does not transfer across industries at the primary manufacturing center of gravity. The knowledge of paper making does not help very much in glass making. Yet both might be combined in a package company. Also, the capital intensity of these industries limits the diversification. Usually one industry must be chosen and capital invested to be the low-cost producer. So there are a number of reasons why these companies have been notoriously poor diversifiers.

In addition, it appears to be very difficult to change centers of gravity no matter where an organization is along the industry chain. The reason is that a center of gravity shift requires a dismantling of the current power structure, rejection of parts of the old culture, and establishing all new management systems. The related diversification works for exactly the opposite reasons. They can move into new businesses with minimal change to the power structure and accepted ways of doing things. Changes in the center of gravity usually occur by new start-ups at a new center of gravity rather than a shift in the center of established firms. . . .

There are some exceptions that prove the rule. Some organizations have shifted from upstream commodity producers to downstream product producers and consumer product firms. General Mills moved from a flour miller to a related diversified provider of products for the homemaker. Over a long period of time they shifted downstream into consumer food products from their cake mix product beginnings. From there, they diversified into related areas after selling off the milling operations, the old core of the company. . . . [In these cases], however, new management was brought in and acquisition and divestment used to make the transition. So, even though vestiges of the old name remain, these are substantially different companies. . . .

The vast majority of our research has examined one kind of strategic change —diversification. The far more difficult one, the change in center of gravity, has received far less [attention]. For the most part, the concept is difficult to measure and not publicly reported like the number of industries in which a company operates. Case studies will have to be used. But there is a need for more systematic knowledge around this kind of strategic change.

• THE INTELLECTUAL HOLDING COMPANY: STRUCTURING AROUND CORE ACTIVITIES*

BY JAMES BRIAN QUINN, THOMAS L. DOORLEY, AND PENNY C. PAQUETTE

Most companies primarily produce a chain of services and integrate these into a form most useful to certain customers. So dominant is this consideration that one questions whether many companies—like those in pharmaceuticals, computers, clothing, oil and gas, foods, office or automation equipment—should really be classified as "manufacturers" anymore. The vast majority of their systems costs, value-added profits, and competitive advantage grows out of service activities.

For example, the strategies of virtually all pharmaceutical companies are critically dependent on service functions. This is especially true of the top performers like $5-billion Merck and £1.7-billion Glaxo, and less true for lower profit generic drug producers. The direct manufacturing cost of most patented ethical drugs is trivial relative to their sale price. Value is added primarily by service activities— discovery of a drug through R&D, a carefully constructed patent and legal defense, rapid and thorough clinical clearance through regulatory bodies, or a strong pre-emptive distribution system. Recognizing this, in recent years Merck's strategy has focused on one portion of the value chain, a powerful research-based patent position. Glaxo has successfully targeted rapid clinical clearance as its key activity. Both strategies rest primarily on adding value through service activities. Merck and Glaxo outperform the industry in gross margins (71.5% and 79.6% versus an industry composite of 66.9%), in operating income margins (27.1% and 38.2% versus 21.2%), and in profits as a percentage of shareholders' equity (48% of 35% versus an industry average of 23%).

As manufacturing becomes more universally automated, the major value added to a product increasingly moves away from the point where raw materials are converted into useful form (that is, steel into an auto "body in white" or grain into edible cereals) and toward the styling features, perceived quality, subjective taste, and marketing presentation that service activities provide at all levels of the value chain. At each stage, technology had increased the relative power of services to the point where they dominate virtually all companies' value chains (see Figure 1).

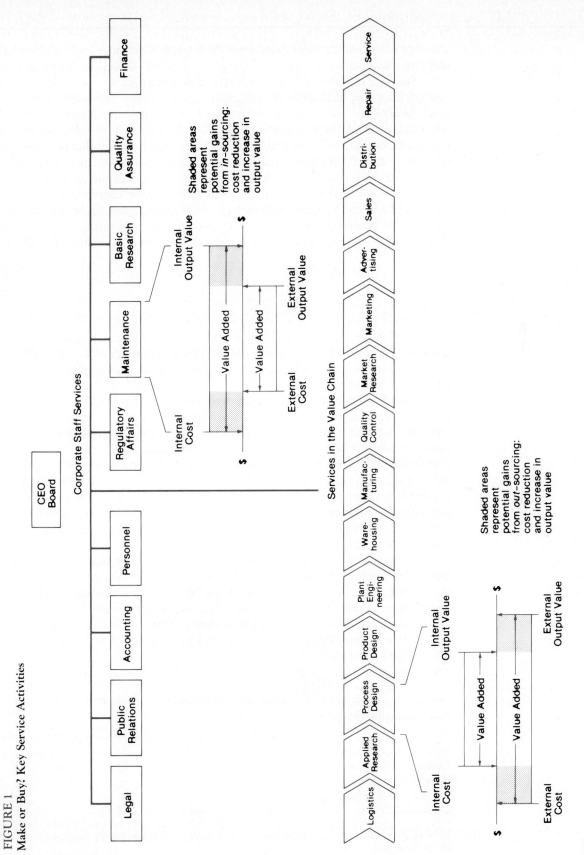

FIGURE 1
Make or Buy? Key Service Activities

151

The fact is that many large companies, like Apple Computer and IBM, initially succeeded by recognizing and leveraging this concept—becoming essentially "intellectual holding companies," purposely manufacturing or producing as little product internally as possible. For example, until the early 1960s IBM was known as an "assembler," outsourcing up to 80 percent of its manufacturing costs. And Apple succeeded by masterminding the highly sophisticated interconnection of architectural, design, software, and hardware supply relationships that became its explosively successful Apple II system. This strategy may have been essential for Apple in its early years when it lacked both the time and capital to build factories or hire a salesforce. But even today—with three to four times the sales per employee and a third to a quarter the fixed investment per sales dollar of its competitors—Apple is structured less like a traditional "manufacturing" company and more like a $4-billion "service" company that happens to have three manufacturing facilities (see Table 1).

SMASHING OVERHEADS THROUGH OUTSOURCING

Because of the scale economies they permit, new service technologies also make it possible to achieve major economies of scale by purchasing not just manufactured parts, but also crucial services, externally—and also to manage such outsourcing effectively on a global basis.

Outside service groups can often provide greater economies of scale, flexibility, and levels of expertise for specialize overhead services than virtually any company can achieve internally. To thoroughly develop these potentials one should consider each overhead category—whether in the value chain or in a staff function—as a service that the company could either "make" internally or "buy" externally. This perspective will, at a minimum, introduce a new objectivity into overhead evaluations and create some strong competitive pressures for internal productivity. In many cases, companies find that specialized outside service sources can be much more cost effective than their internal groups. And they start outsourcing to lower costs or to improve value-added.

For example, $3-billion ServiceMaster Company can take over many of its customers' equipment and facilities maintenance functions, simultaneously improving the quality and lowering the costs of these activities through system economies and specialized management skills. So effective are its systems that ServiceMaster can not only lower absolute maintenance costs, it can often jointinvest in new equipment with its customers, sharing productivity gains to the benefit of both parties.

TABLE 1   Apple, Which Outsources Extensively, Is Structured Less Like a Manufacturing than Like a Service Company

	APPLE	IBM	DEC	DATA GENERAL
Sales per employee	$369,593	$139,250	$84,972	$81,243
Net plant, property, and equipment as % of sales[a]	18.4	63.0	44.6	56.7

[a] Net property, plant, and equipment figures have been adjusted to account for leased assets by multiplying the annual rental expense by 8.

Whenever a company produces a service internally that others buy or produce more efficiently or effectively externally, it sacrifices competitive advantage. Conversely, the key to strategic success for many firms has been their coalitions with the world's best service providers—their external product designers, advertising agencies, distribution channels, financial houses, and so on. How can companies best exploit such opportunities?

LEARNING TO LOVE THE "HOLLOW CORPORATION"

Considering the enterprise as an intellectual holding company (à la Apple Computer) restructures the entire way one attacks strategy. One needs to ask, activity by activity, "Are we really competitive with the world's best here? If not, can intelligent outsourcing improve our long-term position?" Competitive analyses of service activities should not consider just the company's own industry, but should benchmark each service against "best in class" performance among all potential service providers and industries that might cross-compete within the analyzed category—both in the United States and abroad.

As companies begin to outsource nonstrategic activities—particularly overheads—they often discover important secondary benefits. Managements concentrate more on their businesses' core strategic activities. Other internal costs and time delays frequently drop as long-standing bureaucracies disappear and political pressures decrease for annual increments to each department's budget. All this leads to a more compact organization, with fewer hierarchical levels. It also leads to a much sharper focus on recruiting, developing, and motivating the people who create most value in those areas where the company has special competencies.

DOMINATING THOSE ACTIVITIES CRUCIAL TO STRATEGY

Many have expressed concerns about the hollowing out and loss of strategic capability outsourcing could cause (*Business Week,* 1986). However, if the process is approached properly, careful outsourcing should increase both productivity and strategic focus. A company must maintain command of those activities crucial to its strategic position. If it does not, it has essentially redefined the business it is in. For all other activities, if the company cannot see its way to strategic superiority, or if the activity is not essential to areas where it can attain such superiority, the company should consider outsourcing. But it is essential that the company plan and manage its outsourcing coalitions so that it does not become overly dependent on —and hence dominated by—its partner. In some cases this means consciously developing and maintaining alternate competitive sources or even strategically controlling critical stages in an overall process that might otherwise be totally outsourced.

HIGHEST ACTIVITY SHARE, NOT MARKET SHARE, FOR PROFITS

Once a company develops great depth in certain selected service activities as its strategic focus, many individual products can spring off these "core" activities to give the firm a consistent corporate strategy for decades. Unfortunately, the true nature of these core capabilities is usually obscured by the tendency of organizations to think of their strengths in product—not activity or service—terms. The key point is that a few *selected activities should drive strategy.* Knowledge bases, skills sets, and service activities are the things that generally can create continuing added value and competitive advantage.

Too much strategic attention has been paid to having a high share of the market. High share can be bought by inappropriate pricing or other short-term strategies. High market share and high profitability together come from having the highest relevant *activity* share in the marketplace—in other words, having the most effective presence in a service activity the market desires and thus gaining the experience curve and other benefits accruing to that high activity share.

To be most effective, this service-activity dominance needs truly global development. As noted, the major value-added in most products today comes not from direct production or conversion processes, but from the technological improvements, styling, quality, marketing, timing, and financing contributions of service activities. Since these are knowledge-based intangibles that can be shipped cost-free anywhere, producers who expand their scope worldwide to tap the best knowledge and service sources available anywhere can obtain significant competitive advantage.

AVOIDING VERTICAL INTEGRATION

Since most firms cannot afford to own or internally dominate all needed service activities, they tend to form coalitions, linking their own and their partners' capabilities through information, communication, and contract arrangements—rather than through ownership (that is, vertical or horizontal integration). Because of their high value-added potentials, service companies and service activities within companies are central to many of these coalitions. An entirely new form of enterprise seems to be emerging, with a carefully conceived and limited set of "core strategic activities" (usually services) at its center, that allows a company to command and coordinate a constantly changing network of the world's best production and service suppliers on a global basis. This is a logical and most powerful extension of the Kieretsu concept (linked networks of banks, producers, suppliers, and support-distribution companies) that has long been at the heart of Japan's trading success.

Given today's rapid technological advances, many enterprises find they can lower their risks and leverage their assets substantially by *avoiding* investments in vertical integration and managing "intellectual systems" instead of workers and machines. The core strategy of a coordinating or systems company becomes: "Do only those things in-house that contribute to your competitive advantage, and try to source the rest from the world's best suppliers."

MANUFACTURING INDUSTRIES BECOME "SERVICE NETWORKS"

Many industries are becoming loosely structured networks of service enterprises that join together temporarily for one purpose—yet are each other's suppliers, competitors, or customers elsewhere.

Biotechnology, where highly specialized companies are developing at each level, providing "service" activities for one another and the industry, is becoming structured as a number of multiple-level consortia, offers an interesting example of this phenomenon. The semiconductor and electronics industries are moving toward a similar structure. Independent design, foundry, packaging, assembly, industrial distribution, kitting, configuration, systems analysis, networking, and value-added distributor groups do more than $15 billion worth of customized development, generating almost $140,000 of revenue per employee (*Electronic Business,* 1988). Even large OEMs are finding that these groups' specialization, fast turnarounds, advanced designs, and independent perspectives can lower costs, decrease investments, and increase value at all levels.

STRATEGICALLY REDEFINING THE "FOCUSED COMPANY"

Given the vast changes being wrought by new technologies, and the resulting potential for worldwide strategic outsourcing, the whole notion of what constitutes an "industry" or a "focused company" needs to be reexamined. True focus in strategy means the capacity to bring more power to bear on a selected sector than anyone else can.

Properly developed, a broad product or service line does not necessarily signify loss of focus if a firm can deploy especially potent service skills against selected marketplaces in a coordianated fashion. (In fact, a broad line may represent the leveraging of a less obvious strategic focus.) The key question is whether a company dominates a set of service skills that has importance to its customers—in other words, can bring more power to bear on this activity than anyone in the world. If so, the company can be a strategic success, provided it focuses its attention on that activity, obtains at least strategic parity through outsourcing elsewhere, and then blocks others from entering its markets by leveraging its skills across as broad a product line or customer base as it can dominate. Competitors must be defined as those with substitutable skill bases, not those with similar product lines. Product lines can be remarkably broad when the service skill base is deep enough to be dominating. Toys R Us, Procter & Gamble, McKesson, Matsushita, and 3M provide only a few of many excellent cases in point.

For example, Procter and Gamble (P&G) created a $15-billion corporation largely based on two central sets of service skills: its R&D capabilities in eight core technologies, and its superb marketing-distribution skills. Today its extremely broad product line flows naturally from the interaction of these two service activities. Figure 2 shows how skills associated with bar soap could lead P&G naturally to flaked soaps, Tide detergent, and many of its later products. P&G's research depth in surfactant chemistry provided the central linkage among products apparently as diverse as soap and acne or bone disease control drugs, while its marketing and distribution strength allowed P&G to move powerfully, but incrementally, from market to market.

CONCLUSIONS

Most companies create a major portion of their incremental value and gain their real competitive advantage from a relatively few—generally service—activities. Much of the remaining enterprise exists primarily to permit these activities to take place. Yet managements typically spend an inordinate amount of their time, energy, and company resources dealing with these latter support functions—all of which decrease their attention to the company's truly crucial areas of strategic focus. Virtually all managers can benefit from a more carefully structured approach to managing their service activities strategically. Doing so involves defining each activity in the value-creation system as a service; carefully analyzing each such service activity to determine whether the company can become the best in the world at it; and eliminating, outsourcing, or joint venturing the activity to achieve "best in world" status when this is impossible internally. Perhaps most important,

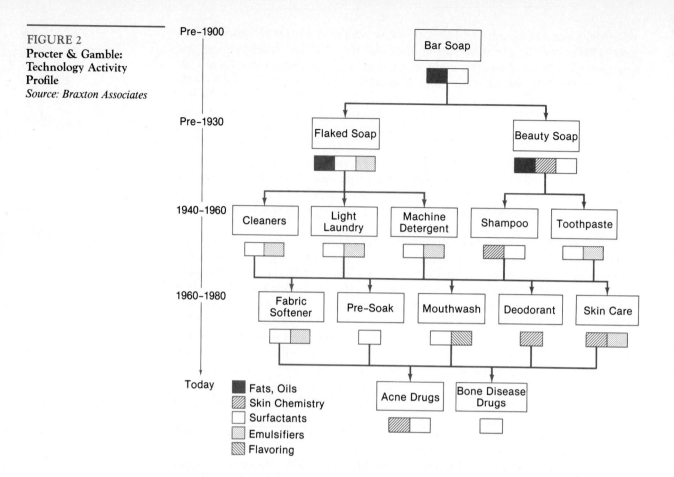

FIGURE 2
Procter & Gamble:
Technology Activity
Profile
Source: Braxton Associates

Pre–1900

Bar Soap

Pre–1930

Flaked Soap · Beauty Soap

1940–1960

Cleaners · Light Laundry · Machine Detergent · Shampoo · Toothpaste

1960–1980

Fabric Softener · Pre-Soak · Mouthwash · Deodorant · Skin Care

Today

■ Fats, Oils
▨ Skin Chemistry
☐ Surfactants
▦ Emulsifiers
▧ Flavoring

Acne Drugs · Bone Disease Drugs

managers must recognize the cold reality that *not* achieving a strong enough competitive performance in each critical service activity will relegate the company to an inevitable loss of strategic advantage, provide lower profitability, and create a higher risk of takeover by those who do see the missed potentials.

● THE STRUCTURING OF ORGANIZATIONS*

BY HENRY MINTZBERG

The "one best way" approach has dominated our thinking about organizational structure since the turn of the century. There is a right way and a wrong way to design an organization. A variety of failures, however, has made it clear that organizations differ, that, for example, long-range planning systems or organizational development programs are good for some but not others. And so recent management theory has moved away from the "one best way" approach, toward an "it all depends" approach, formally known as "contingency theory." Structure should re-

* Excerpted originally from *The Structuring of Organizations* (Prentice Hall, 1979), with added sections from *Power in and Around Organizations* (Prentice Hall, 1983). This chapter was rewritten for this edition of the text, based on two other excerpts: "A Typology of Organizational Structure," published as Chapter 3 in Danny Miller and Peter Friesen, *Organizations: A Quantum View* (Prentice Hall, 1984) and "Deriving Configurations," Chapter 6 in *Mintzberg on Management: Inside Our Strange World of Organizations* (Free Press, 1989).

flect the organization's situation—for example, its age, size, type of production system, the extent to which its environment is complex and dynamic.

This reading argues that the "it all depends" approach does not go far enough, that structures are rightfully designed on the basis of a third approach, which might be called the "getting it all together" or, "configuration" approach. Spans of control, types of formalization and decentralization, planning systems, and matrix structures should not be picked and chosen independently, the way a shopper picks vegetables at the market. Rather, these and other elements of organizational design should logically configure into internally consistent groupings.

When the enormous amount of research that has been done on organizational structure is looked at in the light of this conclusion, much of its confusion falls away, and a convergence is evident around several configurations, which are distinct in their structural designs, in the situations in which they are found, and even in the periods of history in which they first developed.

To understand these configurations, we must first understand each of the elements that make them up. Accordingly, the first four sections of this reading discuss the basic parts of organizations, the mechanisms by which organizations coordinate their activities, the parameters they use to design their structures, and their contingency, or situational, factors. The final section introduces the structural configurations, each of which will be discussed at length in Section Three of this text.

SIX BASIC PARTS OF THE ORGANIZATION

At the base of any organization can be found its operators, those people who perform the basic work of producing the products and rendering the services. They form the *operating core*. All but the simplest organizations also require at least one full-time manager who occupies what we shall call the *strategic apex*, where the whole system is overseen. And as the organization grows, more managers are needed—not only managers of operators but also managers of managers. A *middle line* is created, a hierarchy of authority between the operating core and the strategic apex.

As the organization becomes still more complex, it generally requires another group of people, whom we shall call the analysts. They, too, perform administrative duties—to plan and control formally the work of others—but of a different nature, often labeled "staff." These analysts form what we shall call the *technostructure*, outside the hierarchy of line authority. Most organizations also add staff units of a different kind, to provide various internal services, from a cafeteria or mailroom to a legal counsel or public relations office. We call these units and the part of the organization they form the *support staff*.

Finally, every active organization has a sixth part, which we call its *ideology* (by which is meant a strong "culture"). Ideology encompasses the traditions and beliefs of an organization that distinguish it from other organizations and infuse a certain life into the skeleton of its structure.

This gives us six basic parts of an organization. As shown in Figure 1, we have a small strategic apex connected by a flaring middle line to a large, flat operating core at the base. These three parts of the organization are drawn in one uninterrupted sequence to indicate that they are typically connected through a single chain of formal authority. The technostructure and the support staff are shown off to either side to indicate that they are separate from this main line of authority, influencing the opening core only indirectly. The ideology is shown as a kind of halo that surrounds the entire system.

FIGURE 1
The Six Basic Parts of the
Organization

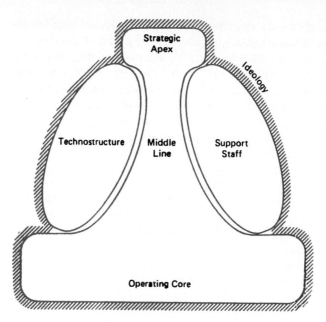

These people, all of whom work inside the organization to make its decisions and take its actions—full-time employees or, in some cases, committed volunteers—may be thought of as *influencers* who form a kind of *internal coalition.* By this term, we mean a system within which people vie among themselves to determine the distribution of power.

In addition, various outside people also try to exert influence on the organization, seeking to affect the decisions and actions taken inside. These external influencers, who create a field of forces around the organization, can include owners, unions and other employee associations, suppliers, clients, partners, competitors, and all kinds of publics, in the form of governments, special interest groups, and so forth. Together they can all be thought to form an *external coalition.*

Sometimes the external coalition is relatively *passive* (as in the typical behavior of the shareholders of a widely held corporation or the members of a large union). Other times it is *dominated* by one active influencer or some group of them acting in concert (such as an outside owner of a business firm or a community intent on imposing a certain philosophy on its school system). And in still other cases, the external coalition may be *divided,* as different groups seek to impose contradictory pressures on the organization (as in a prison buffeted between two community groups, one favoring custody, the other rehabilitation).

SIX BASIC COORDINATING MECHANISMS

Every organized human activity—from the making of pottery to the placing of a man on the moon—gives rise to two fundamental and opposing requirements: the *division of labor* into various tasks to be performed and the *coordination* of those tasks to accomplish the activity. The structure of an organization can be defined simply as the total of the ways in which its labor is divided into distinct tasks and then its coordination achieved among those tasks.

1. *Mutual adjustment* achieves coordination of work by the simple process of informal communication. The people who do the work interact with one another to coordinate, much as two canoeists in the rapids adjust to one an-

other actions. Figure 2a shows mutual adjustment in terms of an arrow between two operators. Mutual adjustment is obviously used in the simplest of organizations—it is the most obvious way to coordinate. But, paradoxically, it is also used in the most complex, because it is the only means that can be relied upon under extremely difficult circumstances, such as trying to figure out how to put a man on the moon for the first time.

2. *Direct supervision* in which one person coordinates by giving orders to others, tends to come into play after a certain number of people must work together. Thus, fifteen people in a war canoe cannot coordinate by mutual

(a) Mutual Adjustment

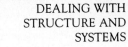

FIGURE 2

The Basic Mechanisms of Coordination

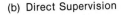

(b) Direct Supervision

(c) Standardization of Work

(d) Standardization of Outputs

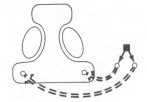

(e) Standardization of Skills

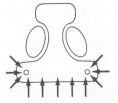

(f) Standardization of Norms

adjustment; they need a leader who, by virtue of instructions, coordinates their work, much as a football team requires a quarterback to call the plays. Figure 2b shows the leader as a manager with the instructions as arrows to the operators.

Coordination can also be achieved by *standardization*—in effect, automatically, by virtue of standards that predetermine what people do and so ensure that their work is coordinated. We can consider four forms—the standardization of the work processes themselves, of the outputs of the work, of the knowledge and skills that serve as inputs to the work, or of the norms that more generally guide the work.

3. *Standardization of work processes* means the specification—that is, the programming—of the content of the work directly, the procedures to be followed, as in the case of the assembly instructions that come with many children's toys. As shown in Figure 2c, it is typically the job of the analysts to so program the work of different people in order to coordinate it tightly.

4. *Standardization of outputs* means the specification not of what is to be done but of its results. In that way, the interfaces between jobs is predetermined, as when a machinist is told to drill holes in a certain place on a fender so that they will fit the bolts being welded by someone else, or a division manager is told to achieve a sales growth of 10% so that the corporation can meet some overall sales target. Again, such standards generally emanate from the analysts, as shown in Figure 2d.

5. *Standardization of skills,* as well as knowledge, is another, though looser way to achieve coordination. Here, it is the worker rather than the work or the outputs that is standardized. He or she is taught a body of knowledge and a set of skills which are subsequently applied to the work. Such standardization typically takes place outside the organization—for example in a professional school of a university before the worker takes his or her first job—indicated in Figure 2e. In effect, the standards do not come from the analyst; they are internalized by the operator as inputs to the job he or she takes. Coordination is then achieved by virtue of various operators' having learned what to expect of each other. When an anesthetist and a surgeon meet in the operating room to remove an appendix, they need hardly communicate (that is, use mutual adjustment, let alone direct supervision); each knows exactly what the other will do and can coordinate accordingly.

6. *Standardization of norms* means that the workers share a common set of beliefs and can achieve coordination based on it, as implied in Figure 2f. For example, if every member of a religious order shares a belief in the importance of attracting converts, then all will work together to achieve this aim.

These coordinating mechanisms can be considered the most basic elements of structure, the glue that holds organizations together. They seem to fall into a rough order: As organizational work becomes more complicated, the favored means of coordination seems to shift from mutual adjustment (the simplest mechanism) to direct supervision, then to standardization, preferably of work processes or norms, otherwise of outputs or of skills, finally reverting back to mutual adjustment. But no organization can rely on a single one of those mechanisms; all will typically be found in every reasonably developed organization.

Still, the important point for us here is that many organizations do favor one mechanism over the others, at least at certain stages of their lives. In fact, organizations that favor none seem most prone to becoming politicized, simply because of the conflicts that naturally arise when people have to vie for influence in a relative vacuum of power.

161

DEALING WITH
STRUCTURE AND
SYSTEMS

THE ESSENTIAL PARAMETERS OF DESIGN

The essence of organizational design is the manipulation of a series of parameters that determine the division of labor and the achievement of coordination. Some of these concern the design of individual positions, others the design of the super-structure (the overall network of subunits, reflected in the organizational chart), some the design of lateral linkages to flesh out that superstructure, and a final group concerns the design of the decision-making system of the organization. Listed as follows are the main parameters of structural design, with links to the co-ordinating mechanisms.

- **Job specialization** refers to the number of tasks in a given job and the workers's control over these tasks. A job is *horizontally* specialized to the extent that it encompasses a few narrowly defined tasks, *vertically* specialized to the extent that the worker lacks control of the tasks performed. *Unskilled* jobs are typically highly specialized in both dimensions; skilled or *professional* jobs are typically specialized horizontally but not vertically. "Job enrichment" refers to the enlargement of jobs in both the vertical and horizontal dimension.

- **Behavior formalization** refers to the standardization of work processes by the imposition of operating instructions, job descriptions, rules, regulations, and the like. Structures that rely on any form of standardization for coordination may be defined as *bureaucratic,* those that do not as *organic.*

- **Training** refers to the use of formal instructional programs to establish and standardize in people the requisite skills and knowledge to do particular jobs in organizations. Training is a key design parameter in all work we call professional. Training and formalization are basically substitutes for achieving the standardization (in effect, the bureaucratization) of behavior. In one, the standards are learned as skills, in the other they are imposed on the job as rules.

- **Indoctrination** refers to programs and techniques by which the norms of the members of an organization are standardized, so that they become responsive to its ideological needs and can thereby be trusted to make its decisions and take its actions. Indoctrination too is a substitute for formalization, as well as for skill training, in this case the standards being internalized as deeply rooted beliefs.

- **Unit grouping** refers to the choice of the bases by which positions are grouped together into units, and those units into higher-order units (typically shown on the organization chart). Grouping encourages coordination by putting different jobs under common supervision, by requiring them to share common resources and achieve common measures of performance, and by using proximity to facilitate mutual adjustment among them. The various bases for grouping—by work process, product, client, place, and so on—can be reduced to two fundamental ones—the *function* performed and the *market* served. The former (illustrated in Fig. 3) refers to means, that is to a single link in the chain of processes by which products or services are produced, the latter (in Fig. 4) to ends, that is, the whole chain for specific end products,

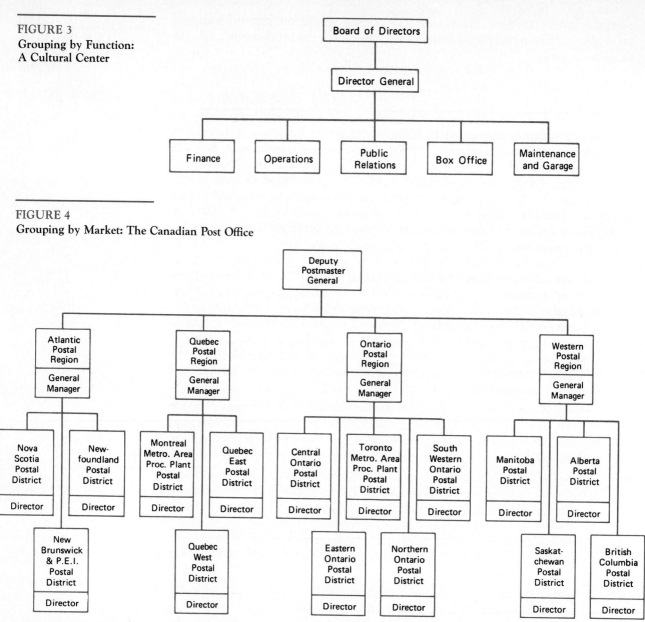

FIGURE 3
Grouping by Function:
A Cultural Center

Board of Directors

Director General

Finance | Operations | Public Relations | Box Office | Maintenance and Garage

FIGURE 4
Grouping by Market: The Canadian Post Office

Deputy Postmaster General

Atlantic Postal Region — General Manager

Quebec Postal Region — General Manager

Ontario Postal Region — General Manager

Western Postal Region — General Manager

Nova Scotia Postal District — Director
New-foundland Postal District — Director
New Brunswick & P.E.I. Postal District — Director

Montreal Metro. Area Proc. Plant Postal District — Director
Quebec East Postal District — Director
Quebec West Postal District — Director

Central Ontario Postal District — Director
Toronto Metro. Area Proc. Plant Postal District — Director
South Western Ontario Postal District — Director
Eastern Ontario Postal District — Director
Northern Ontario Postal District — Director

Manitoba Postal District — Director
Alberta Postal District — Director
Saskatchewan Postal District — Director
British Columbia Postal District — Director

*Headquarter staff groups deleted.

services, or markets. On what criteria should the choice of a basis for grouping be made? First, there is the consideration of workflow linkages, or "interdependencies." Obviously, the more tightly linked are positions or units in the workflow, the more desirable that they be grouped together to facilitate their coordination. Second is the consideration of process interdependencies —for example, across people doing the same kind of work but in different workflows (such as maintenance men working on different machines). It sometimes makes sense to group them together to facilitate their sharing of equipment or ideas, to encourage the improvement of their skills, and so on. Third is the question of scale interdependencies. For example, all maintenance people in a factory may have to be grouped together because no single department has enough maintenance work for one person. Finally, there are

162

the social interdependencies, the need to group people together for social reasons, as in coal mines where mutual support under dangerous working conditions can be a factor in deciding how to group people. Clearly, grouping by function is favored by process and scale interdependencies, and to a lesser extent by social interdependecies (in the sense that people who do the same kind of job often tend to get along better). Grouping by function also encourages specialization, for example, by allowing specialists to come together under the supervision of one of their own kind. The problem with functional grouping, however, is that it narrows perspectives, encouraging a focus on means instead of ends—the way to do the job instead of the reason for doing the job in the first place. Thus grouping by market is used to favor coordination in the workflow at the expense of process and scale specialization. In general, market grouping reduces the ability to do specialized or repetitive tasks well and is more wasteful, being less able to take advantage of economies of scale and often requiring the duplication of resources. But it enables the organization to accomplish a wider variety of tasks and to change its tasks more easily to serve the organization's end markets. And so if the workflow interdependencies are the important ones and if the organization cannot easily handle them by standardization, then it will tend to favor the market bases for grouping in order to encourage mutual adjustment and direct supervision. But if the workflow is irregular (as in a "job shop"), if standardization can easily contain the important workflow interdependencies, or if the process or scale interdependencies are the important ones, then the organization will be inclined to seek the advantages of specialization and group on the basis of function instead. Of course in all but the smallest organizations, the question is not so much *which* basis of grouping, but in what *order.* Much as fires are built by stacking logs first one way and then the other, so too are organizations built by varying the different bases for grouping to take care of various interdependencies.

- **Unit size** refers to the number of positions (or units) contained in a single unit. The equivalent term, *span of control,* is not used here, because sometimes units are kept small despite an absence of close supervisory control. For example, when experts coordinate extensively by mutual adjustment, as in an engineering team in a space agency, they will form into small units. In this case, unit size is small and span of control is low despite a relative absence of direct supervision. In contrast, when work is highly standardized (because of either formalization or training), unit size can be very large, because there is little need for direct supervision. One foreman can supervise dozens of assemblers, because they work according to very tight instructions.

- **Planning and control systems** are used to standardize outputs. They may be divided into two types: *action planning* systems, which specify the results of specific actions before they are taken (for example, that holes should be drilled with diameters of 3 centimeters); and *performance control* systems, which specify the desired results of whole ranges of actions after the fact (for example, that sales of a division should grow by 10% in a given year).

- **Liaison devices** refer to a whole series of mechanisms used to encourage mutual adjustment within and between units. Four are of particular importance:

  - *Liaison positions* are jobs created to coordinate the work of two units directly, without having to pass through managerial channels, for example, the purchasing engineer who sits between purchasing and engineering or the sales liaison person who mediates between the sales force and the factory. These positions carry no formal authority per se; rather, those who serve in them must use their powers of persuasion, negotiation, and so on to bring the two sides together.

- *Task forces and standing committees* are institutionalized forms of meetings which bring members of a number of different units together on a more intensive basis, in the first case to deal with a temporary issue, in the second, in a more permanent and regular way to discuss issues of common interest.

- *Integrating managers*—essentially liaison personnel with formal authority —provide for stronger coordination. These "managers" are given authority not over the units they link, but over something important to those units, for example, their budgets. One example is the brand manager in a consumer goods firm who is responsible for a certain product but who must negotiate its production and marketing with different functional departments.

- *Matrix structure* carries liaison to its natural conclusion. No matter what the bases of grouping at one level in an organization, some interdependencies always remain. Figure 5 suggests various ways to deal with these "residual interdependencies": a different type of grouping can be used at the next level in the hierarchy; staff units can be formed next to line units to advise on the problems; or one of the liaison devices already discussed can be overlaid on the grouping. But in each case, one basis of grouping is favored over the others. The concept of matrix structure is balance between two (or more) bases of grouping, for example functional with market (or for that matter, one kind of market with another—say, regional with product). This is done by the creation of a dual authority structure—two (or more) managers, units, or individuals are made jointly and equally responsible for the same decisions. We can distinguish a *permanent* form of matrix structure,

FIGURE 5
Structures to Deal with Residual Interdependencies

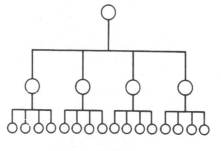

(a) Hierarchical Structure

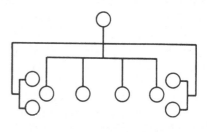

(b) Line and Staff Structure

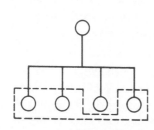

(c) Liaison Overlay Structure
(e.g., Task Force)

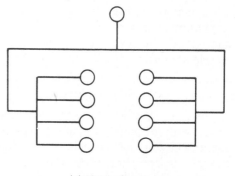

(d) Matrix Structure

where the units and the people in them remain more or less in place, as shown in the example of a whimsical multinational firm in Figure 6, and a *shifting* form, suited to project work, where the units and the people in them move around frequently. Shifting matrix structures are common in high-technology industries, which group specialists in functional departments for housekeeping purposes (process interdependencies, etc.) but deploy them from various departments in project teams to do the work, as shown for NASA in Figure 7.

- **Decentralization** refers to the diffusion of decision-making power. When all the power rests at a single point in an organization, we call its structure centralized; to the extent that the power is dispersed among many individuals,

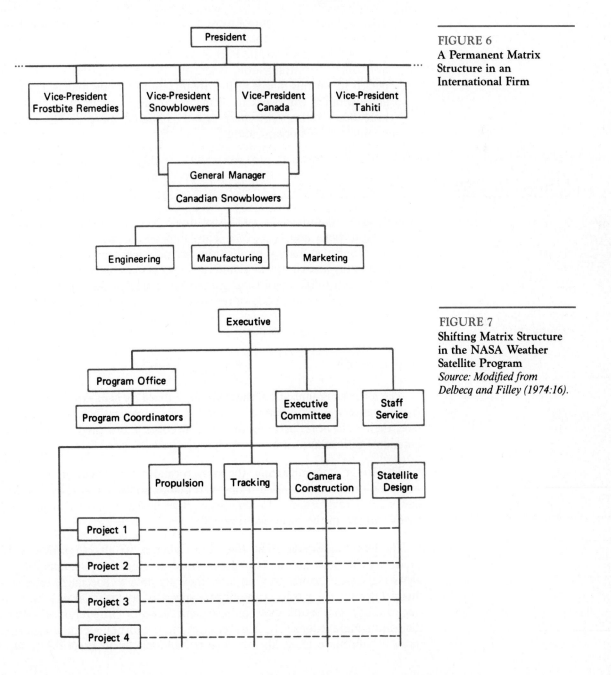

FIGURE 6
A Permanent Matrix Structure in an International Firm

FIGURE 7
Shifting Matrix Structure in the NASA Weather Satellite Program
Source: Modified from Delbecq and Filley (1974:16).

we call it relatively decentralized. We can distinguish *vertical decentralization* —the delegation of formal power down the hierarchy to line managers— from *horizontal decentralization*—the extent to which formal or informal power is dispersed out of the line hierarchy to nonmanagers (operators, analysts, and support staffers). We can also distinguish *selective* decentralization —the dispersal of power over different decisions to different places in the organization—from *parallel* decentralization—where the power over various kinds of decisions is delegated to the same place. Six forms of decentralization may thus be described: (1) vertical and horizontal centralization, where all the power rests at the strategic apex; (2) limited horizontal decentralization (selective), where the strategic apex shares some power with the technostructure that standardizes everybody else's work; (3) limited vertical decentralization (parallel), where managers of market-based units are delegated the power to control most of the decisions concerning their line units; (4) vertical and horizontal decentralization, where most of the power rests in the operating core, at the bottom of the structure; (5) selective vertical and horizontal decentralization, where the power over different decisions is dispersed to various places in the organization, among managers, staff experts, and operators who work in teams at various levels in the hierarchy; and (6) pure decentralization, where power is shared more or less equally by all members of the organization.

THE SITUATIONAL FACTORS

A number of "contingency" or "situational" factors influence the choice of these design parameters, and vice versa. They include the age and size of the organization; its technical system of production; various characteristics of its environment, such as stability and complexity; and its power system, for example, whether or not it is tightly controlled by outside influencers. Some of the effects of these factors, as found in an extensive body of research literature, are summarized below as hypotheses.

Age and Size

• **The older an organization, the more formalized its behavior.** What we have here is the "we've-seen-it-all-before" syndrome. As organizations age, they tend to repeat their behaviors: as a result, these become more predictable and so more amenable to formalization.

• **The larger an organization, the more formalized its behavior.** Just as the older organization formalizes what it has seen before, so the larger organization formalizes what it sees often. ("Listen mister, I've heard that story at least five times today. Just fill in the form like it says.")

• **The larger an organization, the more elaborate its structure; that is, the more specialized its jobs and units and the more developed its administrative components.** As organizations grow in size, they are able to specialize their jobs more finely. (The big barbershop can afford a specialist to cut children's hair; the small one cannot.) As a result, they can also specialize—or "differentiate"—the work of their units more extensively. This requires more effort at coordination. And so the larger organization tends also to enlarge its hierarchy to effect direct supervision and to make greater use of its technostructure to achieve coordination by standardization, or else to encourage more coordination by mutual adjustment.

- **The larger the organization, the larger the size of its average unit.** This finding relates to the previous two, the size of units growing larger as organizations themselves grow larger because (1) as behavior becomes more formalized, and (2) as the work of each unit becomes more homogeneous, managers are able to supervise more employees.

- **Structure reflects the age of the industry from its founding.** This is a curious finding, but one that we shall see holds up remarkably well. An organization's structure seems to reflect the age of the industry in which it operates, no matter what its own age. Industries that predate the industrial revolution seem to favor one kind of structure, those of the age of the early railroads another, and so on. We should obviously expect different structures in different periods; the surprising thing is that these structures seem to carry through to new periods, old industries remaining relatively true to earlier structures.

Technical System

Technical system refers to the instruments used in the operating core to produce the outputs. (This should be distinguished from "technology," which refers to the knowledge base of an organization.)

- **The more regulating the technical system—that is, the more it controls the work of the operators—the more formalized the operating work and the more bureaucratic the structure of the operating core.** Technical systems that regulate the work of the operators—for example, mass production assembly lines—render that work highly routine and predictable, and so encourage its specialization and formalization, which in turn create the conditions for bureaucracy in the operating core.

- **The more complex the technical system, the more elaborate and professional the support staff.** Essentially, if an organization is to use complex machinery, it must hire staff experts who can understand that machinery—who have the capability to design, select, and modify it. And then it must give them considerable power to make decisions concerning that machinery, and encourage them to use the liaison devices to ensure mutual adjustment among them.

- **The automation of the operating core transforms a bureaucratic administrative structure into an organic one.** When unskilled work is coordinated by the standardization of work processes, we tend to get bureaucratic structure throughout the organization, because a control mentality pervades the whole system. But when the work of the operating core becomes automated, social relationships tend to change. Now it is machines, not people, that are regulated. So the obsession with control tends to disappear—machines do not need to be watched over—and with it go many of the managers and analysts who were needed to control the operators. In their place come the support specialists to look after the machinery, coordinating their own work by mutual adjustment. Thus, automation reduces line authority in favor of staff expertise and reduces the tendency to rely on standardization for coordination.

Environment

Environment refers to various characteristics of the organization's outside context, related to markets, political climate, economic conditions, and so on.

- **The more dynamic an organization's environment, the more organic its structure.** It stands to reason that in a stable environment—where nothing changes—an organization can predict its future conditions and so, all other things being equal, can easily rely on standardization for coordination. But when conditions become dynamic—when the need for product change is frequent, labor turnover is high, and political conditions are unstable—the organization cannot standardize but must instead remain flexible through the use of direct supervision or mutual adjustment for coordination, and so it must use a more organic structure. Thus, for example, armies, which tend to be highly bureaucratic institutions in peacetime, can become rather organic when engaged in highly dynamic, guerilla-type warfare.

- **The more complex an organization's environment, the more decentralized its structure.** The prime reason to decentralize a structure is that all the information needed to make decisions cannot be comprehended in one head. Thus, when the operations of an organization are based on a complex body of knowledege, there is usually a need to decentralize decision-making power. Note that a simple environment can be stable or dynamic (the manufacturer of dresses faces a simple environment yet cannot predict style from one season to another), as can a complex one (the specialist in perfected open heart surgery faces a complex task, yet knows what to expect).

- **The more diversified an organization's markets, the greater the propensity to split it into market-based units, or divisions, given favorable economies of scale.** When an organization can identify distinct markets—geographical regions, clients, but especially products and services—it will be predisposed to split itself into high-level units on that basis, and to give each a good deal of control over its own operations (that is, to use what we called "limited vertical decentralization"). In simple terms, diversification breeds divisionalization. Each unit can be given all the functions associated with its own markets. But this assumes favorable economies of scale: If the operating core cannot be divided, as in the case of an aluminum smelter, also if some critical function must be centrally coordinated, as in purchasing in a retail chain, then full divisionalization may not be possible.

- **Extreme hostility in its environment drives any organization to centralize its structure temporarily.** When threatened by extreme hostility in its environment, the tendency for an organization is to centralize power, in other words, to fall back on its tightest coordinating mechanism, direct supervision. Here a single leader can ensure fast and tightly coordinated response to the threat (at least temporarily).

Power

- **The greater the external control of an organization, the more centralized and formalized its structure.** This important hypothesis claims that to the extent that an organization is controlled externally, for example by a parent firm or a government that dominates its external coalition—it tends to centralize power at the strategic apex and to formalize its behavior. The reason is that the two most effective ways to control an organization from the outside are to hold its chief executive officer responsible for its actions and to impose clearly defined standards on it. Moreover, external control forces the organization to be especially careful about its actions.

- **A divided external coalition will tend to give rise to a politicized internal coalition, and vice versa.** In effect, conflict in one of the coalitions tends to spill over to the other, as one set of influencers seeks to enlist the support of the others.

Fashion favors the structure of the day (and of the culture), sometimes even when inappropriate. Ideally, the design parameters are chosen according to the dictates of age, size, technical system, and environment. In fact, however, fashion seems to play a role too, encouraging many organizations to adopt currently popular design parameters that are inappropriate for themselves. Paris has its salons of haute couture; likewise New York has its offices of "haute structure," the consulting firms that sometimes tend to oversell the latest in structural fashion.

THE CONFIGURATIONS

We have now introduced various attributes of organizations—parts, coordinating mechanisms, design paramaters, situational factors. How do they all combine?

We proceed here on the assumption that a limited number of configurations can help explain much of what is observed in organizations. We have introduced in our discussion six basic parts of the organization, six basic mechanisms of coordination, as well as six basic types of decentralization. In fact, there seems to be a fundamental correspondence between all of these sixes, which can be explained by a set of pulls exerted on the organization by each of its six parts, as shown in Figure 8. When conditions favor one of these pulls, the associated part of the organization becomes key, the coordinating mechanism appropriate to itself becomes prime, and the form of decentralization that passes power to itself emerges. The organization is thus drawn to design itself as a particular configuration. We list here and then introduce briefly the six resulting configurations, together with a seventh that tends to appear when no one pull or part dominates.

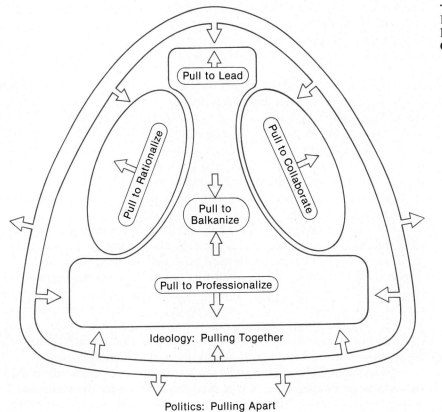

FIGURE 8
Basic Pulls on the Organization

CONFIGURATION	PRIME COORDINATING MECHANISM	KEY PART OF ORGANIZATION	TYPE OF DECEN-TRALIZATION
Entrepreneurial organization	Direct supervision	Strategic apex	Vertical and horizontal centralization
Machine organization	Standardization of work processes	Technostructure	Limited horizontal decentralization
Professional organization	Standardization of skills	Operating core	Horizontal decentralization
Diversified organization	Standardization of outputs	Middle line	Limited vertical decentralization
Innovative organization	Mutual adjustment	Support staff	Selected decentralization
Missionary organization	Standardization of norms	Ideology	Decentralization
Political organization	None	None	Varies

The Entrepreneurial Organization

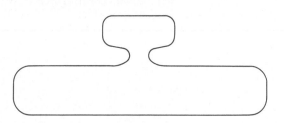

The name tells it all. And the figure above shows it all. The structure is simple, not much more than one large unit consisting of one or a few top managers, one of whom dominates by the pull to lead, and a group of operators who do the basic work. Little of the behavior in the organization is formalized and minimal use is made of planning, training, or the liaison devices. The absence of standardization means that the structure is organic and has little need for staff analysts. Likewise there are few middle line managers because so much of the coordination is handled at the top. Even the support staff is minimized, in order to keep the structure lean, the organization flexible.

The organization must be flexible because it operates in a dynamic environment, often by choice since that is the only place where it can outsmart the bureaucracies. But that environment must be simple, as must the production system, or else the chief executive could not for long hold on to the lion's share of the power. The organization is often young, in part because time drives it toward bureaucracy, in part because the vulnerability of its simple structure often causes it to fail. And many of these organizations are often small, since size too drives the structure toward bureaucracy. Not infrequently the chief executive purposely keeps the organization small in order to retain his or her personal control.

The classic case is of course the small entrepreneurial firm, controlled tightly and personally by its owner. Sometimes, however, under the control of a strong leader, the organization can grow large. Likewise, entrepreneurial organizations can be found in other sectors too, like government, where strong leaders personally control particular agencies, often ones they have founded. Sometimes under crisis conditions, large organizations also revert temporarily to the entrepreneurial form to allow forceful leaders to try to save them.

The Machine Organization

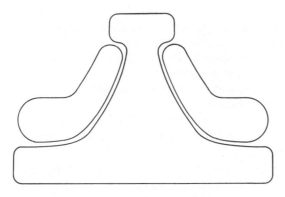

The machine organization is the offspring of the industrial revolution, when jobs became highly specialized and work became highly standardized. As can be seen in the figure above, in contrast to entrepreneurial organizations, the machine one elaborates is administration. First, it requires a large technostructure to design and maintain its systems of standardization, notably those that formalize its behaviors and plan its actions. And by virtue of the organization's dependence on these systems, the technostructure gains a good deal of informal power, resulting in a limited amount of horizontal decentralization, reflecting the pull to rationalize. A large hierarchy of middle-line managers emerges to control the highly specialized work of the operating core. But the middle line hierarchy is usually structured on a functional basis all the way up to the top, where the real power of coordination lies. So the structure tends to be rather centralized in the vertical sense.

To enable the top managers to maintain centralized control, both the environment and the production system of the machine organization must be fairly simple, the latter regulating the work of the operators but not itself automated. In fact, machine organizations fit most naturally with mass production. Indeed it is interesting that this structure is most prevalent in industries that date back to the period from the Industrial Revolution to the early part of this century.

The Professional Organization

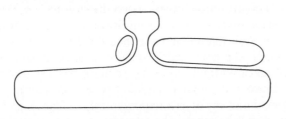

There is another bureaucratic configuration, but because this one relies on the standardization of skills rather than of work processes or outputs for its coordination, it emerges as dramatically different from the machine one. Here the pull to professionalize dominates. In having to rely on trained professionals—people highly specialized, but with considerable control over their work, as in hospitals or universities—to do its operating tasks, the organization surrenders a good deal of its power not only to the professionals themselves but also to the associations and institutions that select and train them in the first place. So the structure emerges as highly decentralized horizontally; power over many decisions, both operating and strategic, flows all the way down the hierarchy, to the professionals of the operating core.

Above the operating core we find a rather unique structure. There is little need for a technostructure, since the main standardization occurs as a result of training that takes place outside the organization. Because the professionals work so independently, the size of operating units can be very large, and few first line managers are needed. The support staff is typically very large too, in order to back up the high-priced professionals.

The professional organization is called for whenever an organization finds itself in an environment that is stable yet complex. Complexity requires decentralization to highly trained individuals, and stability enables them to apply standardized skills and so to work with a good deal of autonomy. To ensure that autonomy, the production system must be neither highly regulating, complex, nor automated.

The Diversified Organization

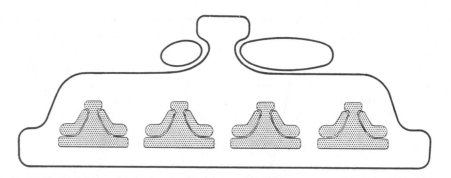

Like the professional organization, the diversified one is not so much an integrated organization as a set of rather independent entities coupled together by a loose administrative structure. But whereas those entities of the professional organization are individuals, in the diversified one they are units in the middle line, generally called "divisions," exerting a dominant pull to Balkanize. This configuration differs from the others in one major respect: it is not a complete structure, but a partial one superimposed on the others. Each division has its own structure.

An organization divisionalizes for one reason above all, because its product lines are diversified. And that tends to happen most often in the largest and most mature organizations, the ones that have run out of opportunities—or have become bored—in their traditional markets. Such diversification encourages the organization to replace functional by market-based units, one for each distinct product line (as shown in the diversified organization figure), and to grant considerable autonomy to each to run its own business. The result is a limited form of decentralization down the chain of command.

How does the central headquarters maintain a semblance of control over the divisions? Some direction supervision is used. But too much of that interferes with the necessary divisional autonomy. So the headquarters relies on performance control systems, in other words, the standardization of outputs. To design these control systems, headquarters creates a small technostructure. This is shown in the figure, across from the small central support staff that headquarters sets up to provide certain services common to the divisions such as legal counsel and public relations. And because headquarters' control constitutes external control, as discussed in the first hypothesis on power, the structure of the divisions tend to be drawn toward the machine form.

The Innovative Organization

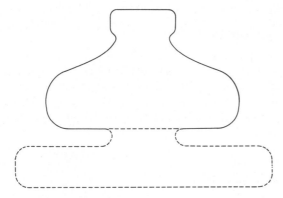

None of the structures so far discussed suits the industries of our age, industries such as aerospace, petrochemicals, think tank consulting, and film making. These organizations need above all to innovate in very complex ways. The bureaucratic structures are too inflexible, and the entrepreneurial one too centralized. These industries require "project structures," ones that can fuse experts drawn from different specialties into smoothly functioning creative teams. That is the role of our fifth configuration, the innovative organization, which we shall also call "adhocracy," dominated by the experts' pull to collaborate.

Adhocracy is an organic structure that relies for coordination on mutual adjustment among its highly trained and highly specialized experts, which it encourages by the extensive use of the liaison devices—integrating managers, standing committees, and above all task forces and matrix structure. Typically the experts are grouped in functional units for housekeeping purposes but deployed in small market based project teams to do their work. To these teams, located all over the structure in accordance with the decisions to be made, is delegated power over different kinds of decisions. So the structure becomes decentralized selectively in the vertical and horizontal dimensions, that is, power is distributed unevenly, all over the structure, according to expertise and need.

All the distinctions of conventional structure disappear in the innovative organization, as can be seen in the figure above. With power based on expertise, the line-staff distinction evaporates. With power distributed throughout the structure, the distinction between the strategic apex and the rest of the structure blurs.

These organizations are found in environments that are both complex and dynamic, because those are the ones that require sophisticated innovation, the type that calls for the cooperative efforts of many different kinds of experts. One type of adhocracy is often associated with a production system that is very complex, sometimes automated, and so requires a highly skilled and influential support staff to design and maintain the technical system of the operating core. (The dashed lines of the figure designate the separation of the operating core from the adhocratic administrative structure.) Here the projects take place in the administration to bring new operating facilities on line (as when a new complex is designed in a petro-chemicals firm). Another type of adhocracy produces its projects directly for its clients (as in a think tank consulting firm or manufacturer of engineering proto-types). Here, as a result, the operators also take part in the projects, bringing their expertise to bear on them; hence the operating core blends into the administrative structure (as indicated in the figure above the dashed line). This second type of ad-hocracy tends to be young on average, because with no standard products or serv-ices, many tend to fail while others escape their vulnerability by standardizing some products or services and so converting themselves to a form of bureaucracy.[1]

The Missionary Organization

Our sixth configuration forms another rather distinct combination of the elements we have been discussing. When an organization is dominated by its ideology, its members are encouraged to pull together, and so there tends to be a loose division of labor, little job specialization, as well as a reduction of the various forms of dif-ferentiation found in the other configurations—of the strategic apex from the rest, of staff from line or administration from operations, between operators, between divisions, and so on.

What holds the missionary together—that is, provides for its coordination—is the standardization of norms, the sharing of values and beliefs among all its members. And the key to ensuring this is their socialization, effected through the design parameter of indoctrination. Once the new member has been indoctrinated into the organization—once he or she identifies strongly with the common beliefs —then he or she can be given considerable freedom to make decisions. Thus the result of effective indoctrination is the most complete form of decentralization. And because other forms of coordination need not be relied upon, the missionary organization formalizes little of its behavior as such and makes minimal use of planning and control systems. As a result, it has little technostructure. Likewise, external professional training is not relied upon, because that would force the or-ganization to surrender a certain control to external agencies.

Hence, the missionary organization ends up as an amorphous mass of mem-

---

[1] We shall clarify in a later reading these two basic types of adhocracies. Toffler employed the term adhocracy is his popular book *Future Shock,* but it can be found in print at least as far back as 1964.

bers, with little specialization as to job, differentiation as to part, division as to status.

Missionaries tend not to be very young organizations—it takes time for a set of beliefs to become institutionalized as an ideology. Many missionaries do not get a chance to grow very old either (with notable exceptions, such as certain long-standing religious orders). Missionary organizations cannot grow very large per se —they rely on personal contacts among their members—although some tend to spin off other enclaves in the form of relatively independent units sharing the same ideology. Neither the environment nor the technical system of the missionary organization can be very complex, because that would require the use of highly skilled specialists, who would hold a certain power and status over others and thereby serve to differentiate the structure. Thus we would expect to find the simplest technical systems in these organizations, usually hardly any at all, as in religious orders or in the primitive farm cooperatives.

The Political Organization

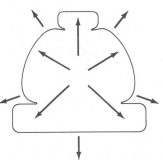

Finally, we come to a form of organization characterized, structurally at least, by what it lacks. When an organization has no dominate part, no dominant mechanism of coordination, and no stable form of centralization or decentralization, it may have difficulty tempering the conflicts within its midst, and a form of organization called the *political* may result. What characterizes its behavior is the pulling apart of its different parts, as shown in the figure above.

Political organizations can take on different forms. Some are temporary, reflecting difficult transitions in strategy or structure that evoke conflict. Others are more permanent, perhaps because the organization must face competing internal forces (say, between necessarily strong marketing and production departments), perhaps because a kind of political rot has set in but the organization is sufficiently entrenched to support it (being, for example, a monopoly or a protected government unit).

Together, all these configurations seem to encompass and integrate a good deal of what we know about organizations. It should be emphasized however, that as presented, each configuration is idealized—a simplification, really a caricature of reality. No real organization is ever exactly like any one of them, although some do come remarkably close, while others seem to reflect combinations of them, sometimes in transition from one to another.

The first five represent what seem to be the most common forms of organizations; thus these will form the basis for the "context" section of this book—labeled entrepreneurial, mature, diversified, innovation, and professional. There, a reading in each chapter will be devoted to each of these configurations, describing its structure, functioning, conditions, strategy-making process, and the issues that surround it. Other readings in these chapters will look at specific strategies in each of these contexts, industry conditions, strategy techniques, and so on.

The other two configurations—the missionary and the political—seem to be less common, represented more by the forces of culture and conflict that exist in all organizations than by distinct forms as such. Hence they will be discussed in the two chapters that immediately follow this one, on "Dealing with Power" and "Dealing with Culture." But because all these configurations themselves must not be taken as hard and fast, indeed because ideology and politics work within different configurations in all kinds of interesting ways, a final chapter in the context section, on managing change, will include a reading called "Beyond Configuration: Forces and Forms in Effective Organizations," that seeks to broaden this view of organizations.

DEALING WITH CULTURE

Culture arrived on the management scene in the 1980s like a typhoon blowing in from the Far East. It suddenly became fashionable in consulting circles to sell culture like some article of organizational clothing, much as "management by objectives" or "total information systems" were once sold. What gave this subject most impetus was Peter and Waterman's book *In Search of Excellence.* This depicted successful organizations as being rich in culture—permeated with strong and sustaining systems of beliefs. In our view—as in theirs—culture is not an article of fashion, but an intrinsic part of a deeper organizational "character," as Selznick described it (in Chapter 2). To draw on definitions introduced earlier, strategy is not just an arbitrarily chosen *position,* nor an analytically developed *plan,* but a deeply entrenched *perspective* which influences the way an organization develops new ideas, considers and weights options, and responds to changes in its environment.

Culture thus permeates many critical aspects of strategy making. But perhaps the most crucial realm is the way people are chosen, developed, nurtured, interrelated, and rewarded in the organization. The kinds of people attracted to an organization and the way they can most effectively deal with problems and each other are largely a function of the culture a place builds—and the practices and systems which support it.

In some organizations, the culture may become so strong that it is best referred to as an "ideology" that dominates all else—as in the "missionary" configuration introduced in the Mintzberg reading on structure in Chapter 6. But culture is generally an influencing force in all organizations, and so it is appropriately considered in this book as an element of organization, alongside structure, systems, and power. In a way, culture may be considered the mirror opposite of power exercised as politics. While the latter focuses on self-interest and the building of one's own power base through individual initiative, culture concentrates on the collective interest and the building of a unified organization, through shared systems of beliefs, habits, and traditions.

The readings in this chapter tend to focus on rich cultures—ideologies—and how these may promote "excellence" in certain situations. Later we shall consider how culture and ideology can discourage excellence by making organizations resistant to strategic change.

The first reading, drawn originally from two chapters of Mintzberg's book *Power in and Around Organizations,* traces how ideologies evolve through three stages: their rooting in a sense of mission, their development through traditions and sagas, and their reinforcement through various forms of identifications. Mintzberg then briefly considers the missionary type organization introduced in Chapter 6 and then shows how other organizations, for example regular business firms, sometimes overlay rich cultures on their more conventional ways of operating.

The second reading, by Pucik and Hatvany, focuses on one well-known example of this, the norm-driven Japanese business firm. The authors first investigate this much discussed organization's particular ways of functioning, its management practices and techniques. The authors then show how this organization's favored objectives and strategies—for example, its emphasis on market share, internal growth, and longer-term returns—grow directly out of its culture.

● IDEOLOGY AND THE MISSIONARY ORGANIZATION*

By Henry Mintzberg

We all know that $2 + 2 = 4$. But general systems theory, through the concept of synergy, suggests that it can also equal 5, that the parts of a system may produce more working together than they can apart. A flashlight and a battery add up to just so many pieces of hardware; together they form a working system. Likewise an organization is a working system that can entice from its members more than they would produce apart—more effort, more creativity, more output (or, of course, less). This may be "strategic"—deriving from the way components have been combined in the organization. Or it may be motivational: The group is said to develop a "mood," an "atmosphere," to have some kind of "chemistry." In organizations, we talk of a "style," a "culture," a "character." One senses something unique when one walks into the offices of IBM; the chemistry of Hewlett-Packard just doesn't feel the same as that of Texas Instruments, even though the two have operated in some similar businesses.

---

* Adapted from Henry Mintzberg, *Power in and Around Organizations* (copyright © Prentice-Hall, 1983), Chaps. 11 and 21; used by permission of the publisher; based on a summary that appeared in *Mintzberg on Management: Inside Our Strange World of Organizations* (New York: Free Press, 1989).

All these words are used to describe something—intangible yet very real, over and above the concrete components of an organization—that we refer to as its *ideology*. Specifically, an ideology is taken here to mean a rich system of values and beliefs about an organization, shared by its members, that distinguishes it from other organizations. For our purposes, the key feature of such an ideology is its unifying power: It ties the individual to the organization, generating an "esprit de corps," a "sense of mission," in effect, an integration of individual and organizational goals that can produce synergy.

THE DEVELOPMENT OF AN ORGANIZATIONAL IDEOLOGY

The development of an ideology in an organization will be discussed here in three stages. The roots of the ideology are planted when a group of individuals band together around a leader and, through a sense of mission, found a vigorous organization, or invigorate an existing one. The ideology then develops over time through the establishment of traditions. Finally, the existing ideology is reinforced when new members enter the organization and identify with its system of beliefs.

Stage 1: The Rooting of Ideology in a Sense of Mission

Typically, an organization is founded when a single prime mover identifies a mission—some product to be produced, service to be rendered—and collects a group around him or her to accomplish it. Some organizations are, of course, founded by other means, as when a new agency is created by a government or a subsidiary by a corporation. But a prime mover often can still be identified behind the founding of the organization.

The individuals who come together don't do so at random, but coalesce because they share some values associated with the fledgling organization. At the very least they see something in it for themselves. But in some cases, in addition to the mission per se there is a "sense of mission," that is, a feeling that the group has banded together to create something unusual and exciting. This is common in new organizations for a number of reasons.

First, unconstrained by procedure and tradition, new organizations offer wide latitude for maneuver. Second, they tend to be small, enabling the members to establish personal relationships. Third, the founding members frequently share a set of strong basic beliefs, sometimes including a sense that they wish to work together. Fourth, the founders of new organizations are often "charismatic" individuals, and so energize the followers and knit them together. Charisma, as Weber (1969:12) used the term, means a sense of "personal devotion" to the leader for the sake of his or her personal qualities rather than formal position. People join and remain with the organization because of dedication to the leader and his or her mission. Thus the roots of strong ideologies tend to be planted in the founding of organizations.

Of course, such ideologies can also develop in existing organizations. But a review of the preceding points suggests why this should be much more difficult to accomplish. Existing organizations *are* constrained by procedures and traditions, many are *already* large and impersonal, and their *existing* beliefs tend to impede the establishment of new ones. Nonetheless, with the introduction of strong charismatic leadership reinforced by a strong new sense of mission, an existing organization can sometimes be invigorated by the creation of a new ideology.

A key to the development of an organizational ideology, in a new or existing organization, is a leadership with a genuine belief in mission and an honest dedication to the people who must carry it out. Mouthing the right words might create the veneer of an organizational ideology, but it is only an authentic feeling on the part of the leadership—which followers somehow sense—that sets the roots of the ideology deep enough to sustain it when other forces, such as impersonal administration (bureaucracy) or politics, challenge it.

Stage 2: The Development of Ideology Through Traditions and Sagas

As a new organization establishes itself or an existing one establishes a new set of beliefs, it makes decisions and takes actions that serve as commitments and establish precedents. Behaviors reinforce themselves over time, and actions become infused with value. When those forces are strong, ideology begins to emerge in its own right. That ideology is strengthened by stories—sometimes called "myths"—that develop around important events in the organization's past. Gradually the organization establishes its own unique sense of history. All of this—the precedents, habits, myths, history—form a common base of tradition, which the members of the organization share, thus solidifying the ideology. Gradually, in Selznick's (1957) terms, the organization is converted from an expendable "instrument" for the accomplishment of externally imposed goals into an "institution," a system with a life of its own. It "acquires a self, a distinctive identity."

Thus Clark described the "distinctive college," with reference particularly to Reed, Antioch, and Swarthmore. Such institutions develop, in his words, an "organizational saga," "a collective understanding of a unique accomplishment based on historical exploits," which links the organization's present with its past and "turns a formal place into a beloved institution." (1972:178). The saga captures allegiance, committing people to the institution (Clark 1970:235).

Stage 3: The Reinforcement of Ideology Through Identifications

Our description to this point makes it clear that an individual entering an organization does not join a random collection of individuals, but rather a living system with its own culture. He or she may come with a certain set of values and beliefs, but there is little doubt that the culture of the organization can weigh heavily on the behavior he or she will exhibit once inside it. This is especially true when the culture is rich—when the organization has an emerging or fully developed ideology. Then the individual's *identification* with and *loyalty* to the organization can be especially strong. Such identification can develop in a number of ways:

- Most simply, identification occurs *naturally* because the new member is attracted to the organization's system of beliefs.
- Identification may also be *selected*. New members are chosen to "fit in" with the existing beliefs, and positions of authority are likewise filled from among the members exhibiting the strongest loyalty to those beliefs.
- Identification may also be *evoked*. When the need for loyalty is especially great, the organization may use informal processes of *socialization* and formal programs of *indoctrination* to reinforce natural or selected commitment to its system of beliefs.
- Finally, and most weakly, identification can be *calculated*. In effect, individuals conform to the beliefs not because they identify naturally with them nor because they even necessarily fit in with them, not because they have been

socialized or indoctrinated into them, but simply because it pays them to identify with the beliefs. They may enjoy the work or the social group, may like the remuneration, may work to get ahead through promotion and the like. Of course, such identification is fragile. It disappears as soon as an opportunity calculated to be better appears.

Clearly, the higher up this list an organization's member identifications tend to be, the more likely it is to sustain a strong ideology, or even to have such an ideology in the first place. Thus, strong organizational belief systems can be recognized above all by the presence of much natural identification. Attention to selected identification indicates the presence of an ideology, since it reflects an organization's efforts to sustain its ideology, as do efforts at socialization and indoctrination. Some organizations require a good deal of the latter two, because of the need to instill in their new members a complex system of beliefs. When the informal processes of socialization tend to function naturally, perhaps reinforced by more formal programs of indoctrination, then the ideology would seem to be strong. But when an organization is forced to rely almost exclusively on indoctrination, or worse to fall back on forms of calculated identification, then its ideology would appear to be weakening, if not absent to begin with.

THE MISSIONARY ORGANIZATION

While some degree of ideology can be found in virtually every organization, that degree can vary considerably. At one extreme are those organizations, such as religious orders or radical political movements, whose ideologies tend to be strong and whose identifications are primarily natural and selected. Edwards (1977) refers to organizations with strong ideologies as "stylistically rich," Selznick (1957) as "institutions." It is the presence of such an ideology that enables an organization to have "a life of its own," to emerge as "a living social institution" (Selznick 1949:10). At the other extreme are those organizations with relatively weak ideologies, "stylistically barren," in some cases business organizations with strongly utilitarian reward systems. History and tradition have no special value in these organizations. In the absence of natural forms of identification on the part of their members, these organizations sometimes try to rely on the process of indoctrination to integrate individual and organizational goals. But usually they have to fall back on calculated identifications and especially formal controls.

We can refer to "stylistically rich" organizations as *missionaries,* because they are somewhat akin in their beliefs to the religious organizations by that name. Mission counts above all—to preserve it, extend it, or perfect it. That mission is typically (1) clear and focused, so that its members are easily able to identify with it; (2) inspiring, so that the members do, in fact, develop such identifications; and (3) distinctive, so that the organization and its members are deposited into a unique niche where the ideology can flourish. As a result of their attachment to its mission, the members of the organization resist strongly any attempt to change it, to interfere with tradition. The mission and the rest of the ideology must be preserved at all costs.

The missionary organization is a distinct configuration of the attributes of structure, internally highly integrated yet different from other configurations. What holds this organization together—that is, provides for its coordination—is the standardization of its norms, in other words, the sharing of values and beliefs among its members. As was noted, that can happen informally, either through natural selection or else the informal process of socialization. But from the perspective of structural design the key attribute is indoctrination, meaning formalized programs to develop or reinforce identification with the ideology. And once the new member has been selected, socialized, and indoctrinated, he or she is accepted into the system as an equal partner, able to participate in decision making alongside everyone else. Thus, at the limit, the missionary organization can achieve the purest form of decentralization: All who are accepted into the system share its power.

But that does not mean an absence of control. Quite the contrary. No matter how subtle, control tends to be very powerful in this organization. For here, the organization controls not just people's behavior but their very souls. The machine organization buys the "workers'" attention through imposed rules; the missionary organization captures the "members'" hearts through shared values. As Jay noted in his book *Management and Machiavelli* (1970), teaching new Jesuit recruits to "love God and do what you like" is not to do what they like at all but to act in strict conformance with the order's beliefs (1970:70).

Thus, the missionary organization tends to end up as an amorphous mass of members all pulling together within the common ideology, with minimum specialization as to job, differentiation as to part, division as to status. At the limit, managers, staffers, and operators, once selected, socialized, and indoctrinated, all seem rather alike and may, in fact, rotate into each other's positions.

The traditional Israeli kibbutz is a classic example of the missionary organization. In certain seasons, everyone pitches in and picks fruit in the fields by day and then attends the meetings to decide administrative issues by night. Managerial positions exist but are generally filled on a rotating basis so that no one emerges with the status of office for long. Likewise, staff support positions exist, but they too tend to be filled on a rotating basis from the same pool of members, as are the operating positions in the fields. (Kitchen duty is, for example, considered drudgery that everyone must do periodically.) Conversion to industry has, however, threatened that ideology. As suggested, it was relatively easy to sustain the egalitarian ideology when the work was agricultural. Industry, in contrast, generally called for greater levels of technology, specialization, and expertise, with a resulting increase in the need for administrative hierarchy and functional differentiation, all a threat to the missionary orientation. The kibbutzim continue to struggle with this problem.

A number of our points about the traditional kibbutz are summarized in a table developed by Rosner, which contrasts the "principles of kibbutz organization"—classic missionary—with those of "bureaucratic organization," in our terms, the classic machine.

Principles of Bureaucratic Organization	*Principles of Kibbutz Organization*
1. Permanency of office	Impermanency of office
2. The office carries with it impersonal, fixed privileges and duties.	The definition of office is flexible—privileges and duties are not formally fixed and often depend on the personality of the official.
3. A hierarchy of functional authorities expressed in the authority of the officials.	A basic assumption of the equal value of all functions without a formal hierarchy of authority
4. Nomination of officials is based on formal objective qualifications.	Officials are elected, not nominated. Objective qualifications are not decisive, personal qualities are more important in election.

| 5. The office is a full-time occupation. | The office is usually supplementary to the full-time occupation of the official. (Rosner, 1969) | **183**
DEALING WITH CULTURE |

We can distinguish several forms of the pure missionary organization. Some are *reformers* that set out to change the world directly—anything from overthrowing a government to ensuring that all domestic animals are "decently" clothed. Other missionaries can be called *converters,* their mission being to change the world indirectly, by attracting members and changing them. The difference between the first two types of missionaries is the difference between the Women's Christian Temperance Union and Alcoholics Anonymous. Their ends were similar, but their means differed, seeking to reduce alcoholism in one case by promoting a general ban on liquor sales, in the other by discouraging certain individuals, namely joined members, from drinking. Third are the *cloister* missionaries that seek not to change things so much as to allow their members to pursue a unique style of life. The monasteries that close themselves off from the outside world are good examples, as are groups that go off to found new isolated colonies.

Of course, no organization can completely seal itself off from the world. All missionary organizations, in fact, face the twin opposing pressures of isolation and assimilation. Together these make them vulnerable. On one side is the threat of *isolation,* of growing ever inward in order to protect the unique ideology from the pressures of the ordinary world until the organization eventually dies for lack of renewal. On the other side is the threat of *assimilation,* of reaching out so far to promote the ideology that it eventually gets compromised. When this happens, the organization may survive but the ideology dies, and so the configuration changes (typically to the machine form).

IDEOLOGY AS AN OVERLAY ON CONVENTIONAL ORGANIZATIONS

So far we have discussed what amounts to the extreme form of ideological organization, the missionary. But more organizations have strong ideologies that can afford to structure themselves in this way. The structure may work for an Israeli kibbutz in a remote corner of the Negev desert, but this is hardly a way to run a Hewlett-Packard or a McDonald's, let alone a kibbutz closer to the worldly pressures of Tel Aviv.

What such organizations tend to do is overlay ideological characteristics on a more conventional structure—perhaps machinelike in the case of McDonald's and that second kibbutz, innovative in the case of Hewlett-Packard. The mission may sometimes seem ordinary—serving hamburgers, producting instruments and computers—but it is carried out with a good dose of ideological fervor by employees firmly committed to it.

Best known for this are, or course, certain of the Japanese corporations, Toyota being a prime example. Ouchi and Jaeger (1978:308) contrast in the table reproduced below the typical large American corporation (Type A) with its Japanese counterpart (Type J):

Type A (for American)	*Type J (for Japanese)*
Short-term employment	Lifetime employment
Individual decision making	Consensual decision making
Individual responsibility	Collective responsibility
Rapid evaluation and promotion	Slow evaluation and promotion

Explicit, formalized control	Implicit, informal control
Specialized career path	Nonspecialized career path
Segmented concern	Holistic concern

Ouchi and Jaeger (1978) in fact make their point best with an example in which a classic Japanese ideological orientation confronts a conventional American bureaucratic one:

> [D]uring one of the author's visits to a Japanese bank in California, both the Japanese president and the American vice-presidents of the bank accused the other of being unable to formulate objectives. The Americans meant that the Japanese president could not or would not give them explicit, quantified targets to attain over the next three or six months, while the Japanese meant that the Americans could not see that once they understood the company's philosophy, they would be able to deduce for themselves the proper objective for any conceivable situation. (p. 309)

In another study, however, Ouchi together with Johnson (1978) discussed a native American corporation that does resemble the Type J firm (labeled "Type Z"; Ouchi (1981) later published a best seller about such organizations). In it, they found greater loyalty, a strong collective orientation, less specialization, and a greater reliance on informal controls. For example, "a new manager will be useless for at least four or five years. It takes that long for most people to decide whether the new person really fits in, whether they can really trust him." That was in sharp contrast to the "auction market" atmosphere of a typical American firm: It "is almost as if you could open up the doors each day with 100 executives and engineers who had been randomly selected from the country, and the organization would work jut as well as it does now" (1978:302).

The trends in American business over several decades—"professional" management, emphasis on technique and rationalization, "bottom-line" mentality—have worked against the development of organizational ideologies. Certainly the missionary configuration has hardly been fashionable in the West, especially the United States. But ideology may have an important role to play there, given the enormous success many Japanese firms have had in head-on competition with American corporations organized in machine and diversified ways, with barren cultures. At the very least, we might expect more ideological overlays on the conventional forms of organizations in the West. But this, as we hope our discussion has made clear, may be both for better and for worse.

• MANAGEMENT PRACTICES IN JAPAN AND THEIR IMPACT ON BUSINESS STRATEGY*

BY VLADIMIR PUCIK AND NINA HATVANY

. . . we propose that a basic organizational paradigm in large Japanese organizations is the *focus on human resources*. Our understanding of this paradigm follows Kuhn's (1970) definition of it as an amalgamation of shared rules and common in-

* Originally published in *Advances in Strategic Management,* Vol. 1 (JAI Press, Inc., 1983), pp. 103–131. Copyright © 1983 by JAI Press, Inc. Reprinted with deletions by permission of JAI Press, Inc.

tuitions. The focus on human resources in Japanese firms reflects an explicit preference for the maximum utilization of available human assets as well as an implicit understanding of how an organization ought to be managed.

This paradigm translates into the three main interrelated strategic thrusts [which are in turn expressed in specific management techniques, as shown in Figure 1 and discussed in turn in the paragraphs that follow].

STRATEGIES

The Organization as an Internal Labor Market

As a rule, large Japanese companies hire a male employee just after graduation from high school or university with the expectation of retaining him for the rest of his working life (Yoshino, 1968). The policy of lifetime employment is not extended to females, who are generally expected to leave the company and the job market once they are married. The temporary nature of the female work force, as well as the use of part-time workers, gives employers flexibility in adjusting the size of their work force to adapt to current economic conditions and still maintain employment for regular workers. The widespread use of subcontracting serves a similar purpose. . . .

Such a set of employment practices that price and allocate labor according to intraorganizational rules and procedures rather than according to external demand and supply conditions is described in the economic literature as an internal labor market (ILM) (Doeringer and Piore, 1971). . . .

The maintenance of a stable ILM requires that sufficient training is provided within the firm so that the company does not have to hire outside to satisfy its need for qualified personnel. Yet, when skills are learned on the job, they are largely "company specific," the employee cannot realize their full value outside the firm, and inter-firm mobility is again discouraged (Becker, 1964).

. . . job security has advantages for the organization. One, for example, is the reduction of employee hostility to the introduction of labor-saving technology or to organizational changes (Vogel, 1979). Employees know that they may be trans-

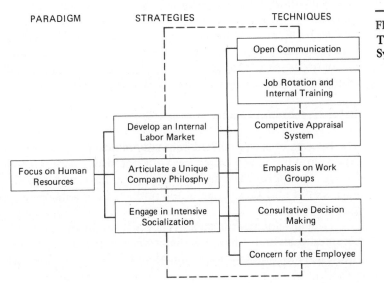

FIGURE 1

The Japanese Management System

ferred to new jobs but do not fear losing their jobs altogether. Another advantage . . . is that long tenure is positively associated with commitment to the organization. . . .

Articulated and Unique Company Philosophy

A philosophy that is both articulated and enacted may facilitate [the transformation of commitment to the organization into a productive effort] as it presents a clear picture of the organization's goals, norms, and values. Familiarity with the goals of an organization provides direction for individuals' actions, sets constraints on their behavior, and enhances their motivation (Scott, 1966). . . .

The personnel departments of large Japanese firms as well as many chief executives are actively engaged in promoting their company's philosophy of work and management (Rohlen, 1974). These philosophies frequently describe the firm as a family, unique and distinct from any other firm. This "family" is a social group into which one is carefully selected, but which, as in a real family, one is not supposed to leave, even if one becomes dissatisfied with this or that aspect of "family" life. The cultivation of a sense of "uniqueness" may provide an ideological justification of the limited possibilities for interfirm mobility.

At the same time, the articulation of concepts, such as "the family" embedded in a company philosophy, may change over time in order to fit the shifting values of a broader social environment. . . .

Among the norms of company life, *wa* (harmony), is still the single most popular component in company philosophies. The concept of *wa* expresses a "quality of relationship, particularly within working groups and it refers to the cooperation, trust, sharing, warmth, morale, and hard work of efficient, pleasant, and purposeful fellowship. Teamwork comes to mind as a suitable approximation" (Rohlen, 1974:74). *Wa* is the watchword for developing the group consciousness of the employees and enhancing cooperation within the work group. The ideal is to integrate two objectives: pursuit of profits and perpetuation of the company as a primary social group. The employees are asked to devote substantial effort to the company's well-being, and in return the company is expected to avoid layoffs and to contribute generously to its employees' welfare. Without reasonable employment security, the fostering of team spirit and cooperation would be a nearly impossible task.

The understanding of shared meanings and beliefs expressed in the company philosophy binds the individual to the collectivity (Pfeffer, 1979b) and at the same time stimulates the emergence of goals that are shared within an organization. This goal congruence provides one of the principal defenses against opportunistic behavior on the part of those members who, endowed with special skills, might be inclined to bargain for special rewards (Ouchi, 1980). . . .

Intensive Socialization

The benefits of an articulated company philosophy are lost, however, if not properly communicated to employees or if not visibly supported in management's behavior. Therefore, ensuring that employees have understood the philosophy and have seen it in action is one of the primary functions of the company's socialization effort.

The development of cohesiveness within the firm, based on the acceptance of common goals and values, is a major focus of personnel policies in a Japanese firm throughout the whole working life of an employee. . . . The basic criteria for hiring are moderate views and a harmonious personality. Ability on the job is obviously also a requirement, but at the same time applicants may be eliminated during the selection process if they arouse suspicion that they cannot get along with people, possess radical views, or come from an unfavorable home environment (Rohlen, 1974). It is only natural that, when employees are expected to remain the firm for most of their working lives, even top executives become intimately involved in the interviewing and assessment of new hires. To encourage recruitment into the company, employees' referrals are often actively solicited.

The socialization process begins with the initial training program, which is geared toward familiarizing new employees with the company, sometimes for as long as six months. During the course of the program the recruits learn about the business philosophy of the company and experience work on the factory floor as well as in the sales offices, disregarding their final vocational specialization. They are expected to assume the identity of a "company man," and in such a case their specialization becomes of secondary importance. Both careful screening and introductory training are designed to develop the homogeneity of the people in the firm.

In addition to this initial socialization, a "resocialization" (Katz, 1980) takes place each time the employee enters a new position, as he has to familiarize himself with a new set of people and tasks. Employees are transferred for two main reasons. First, they are assigned to new positions to learn additional skills in on-the-job training programs. Second, transfers are part of a long-range experience-building program, through which the organization grooms its future managers, which usually takes the form of periodic, lateral, interdepartmental transfers. (Yoshino, 1968). While employees rotate semilaterally from job to job, they become increasingly socialized into the organization, immersed in the company's philosophy and culture, as well as bound to a set of shared goals. It should be noted that such transfers are the prerogative of management, and unions are usually not involved. . . .

TECHNIQUES

The basic management orientation and strategies are closely interrelated with [the following] management techniques used in Japanese firms. . . .

Open Communication

If we had to stress one technique . . . it would be management's commitment to developing a climate of trust in the corporation, through sharing information across departmental boundaries. The emphasis on team spirit embodied in corporate philosophies and the network of contacts that employees develop during their long socialization in the organization encourage . . . extensive face-to-face communication. . . . Frequent and open communication is also an inherent part of the Japanese work setting. Work spaces are crowded with individuals at different levels of the hierarchy. Subordinates can do little that the supervisor is not aware of and vice versa. Even high-ranking office managers seldom have separate private offices. . . . Even senior plant managers spend as much time as possible on the shop floor.

Open communication is not limited to vertical exchanges. Periodic job rotation is instrumental in building extensive informal lateral communication networks across departmental boundaries. . . .

Job Rotation, Slow Promotion, and Internal Training

Under conditions of lifetime employment . . . [p]romotion is . . . unlikely to be rapid unless an organization is expanding dramatically. . . . [nevertheless] early informal identification of the "elite" is not unusual (Rohlen, 1974), and carefully planned lateral job transfers thereafter may add substantial flexibility to job reward and recognition (Ono, 1976). . . .

An additional feature adding flexibility to the promotion system is the emergence of a dual promotion system in many Japanese companies (Haitani, 1978). Promotion in "status" is based on the results of past evaluations and seniority within the firm; promotion in "position" is based on evaluation results and the availability of vacancies in the level above. Therefore, even if immediate upper-level positions are blocked by a cohort of seniors, promotion in status will provide an employe with more respect and money. Delegation of authority is also frequent, so a position of responsibility can be assigned to an outstanding employee who does not fulfill the seniority requirements for promotion in status (Tsurumi, 1977). . . .

The emphasis on job rotation creates an environment in which an employee becomes a "generalist," rather than a "specialist" in any functional area. . . .

Competitive Appraisal System

Employee evaluations in Japanese firms are usually conducted on an annual or semiannual basis. The evaluation criteria include not only "bottom-line" individual performance measures but also various desirable personality traits and behaviors, such as creativity, emotional maturity, and cooperation with others. . . . the employee is not made to feel that the "bottom-line," which may sometimes be beyond his control, is the key dimension of evaluation. Occasional mistakes, particularly for lower-level employees, are considered part of the learning process (Tsurumi, 1977).

At the same time, evaluations do clearly discriminate among employees, as each employee is compared to other members of an appropriate group (in age and status); and the competition is keen. Year after year, all managers at a given level are ranked according to their performance and future potential. This is done by the personnel department based on raw scores submitted by line superiors. For each manager, the scores from at last two superiors are required to assure objectivity, but the scores seldom differ substantially. . . .

A future- rather than a past-oriented evaluation system serves, however, as a powerful check in divisive competitiveness. What is rewarded is the credibility and ability to get things done in cooperation with others. Thus, the focal point of competition is building cooperative networks with the same people who are rivals for future promotions (Pucik, 1981). . . .

The Emphasis on Work Groups

Not only evaluation but many other company policies revolve around groups. Tasks are assigned to groups rather than individuals. (Rohlen, 1974). Group cohesion is stimulated by the delegation of responsibility to work groups as well as by other job design features such as job rotation and group-based performance feedback. . . .

Work-group autonomy is enhanced by not using experts to solve operational problems for specific groups. This would be regarded as outside interference, and the result would be to undermine morale and leadership (Rohlen, 1974). One widely used group-based technique is quality control (QC) circles (Cole, 1979). A QC circle has as its major function the uncovering and solving of a particular workshop's problem. However, fostering motivation by direct participation in the design of the work process is also a major consideration in the introduction of QC circles and similar activities to the factory floor. In principle, participation is voluntary, but in practice refusal to participate is unusual. The team operates autonomously, with an emphasis on self-improvement activities that will help the achievement of group goals. . . .

Consultative Decision Making

The extensive face-to-face communication observed in Japanese companies is often confused with participative decision making. . . . The usual procedure is that a formal proposal will be initiated by a middle manager, but often under the directive of top management (Hattori, 1977). Some observers of the Japanese decision-making process argue . . . that this process is not "bottom-up" but rather a top-down or interactive consultative process, especially when long-term planning and strategy are concerned (Kono, 1980).

The middle manager will usually engage in informal discussion and consultation about the decisions with his subordinates, peers, and supervisors. When all are familiar with the proposal, a request for a decision is made formally at an appropriate level, and because of the earlier discussions it is almost inevitably ratified, often in a ceremonial group meeting or through the *ringi* procedure. All this does not imply unanimous approval of the proposed decision, but it does imply consent to its implementation.

This kind of decision making is not "participative" in the Western sense of the word, which includes ideas of negotiations and bargaining between a manager and his subordinates. In the Japanese context the negotiations are primarily lateral, between the departments concerned with the decision. Within the work group, the emphasis is on inclusion of all group members in the process of decision making rather than on a consensus about the alternatives. However, the manager will usually not state his position "until others who will be affected have had sufficient time to offer their views, feel that they have been fairly heard, and are willing to support the decision even though they may not feel that it is the best one." (Rohlen, 1974:308). . . .

A frequently mentioned consequence of decision making in Japan is the avoidance of identifying responsibility for eventual mistakes. (Yoshino, 1968; Tsuji, 1968). However, Clark (1979) calls this "misleading," citing the large number of Japanese firms managed by a strong and powerful chief executive. . . .

Concern for the Employee

Informal communication not only facilitates decision making but it also forms a channel to express management concern for the well-being of employees. Managers invest a great deal of time in talking to employees about everyday matters, (Cole, 1971), and the quality of their relationships with subordinates is also an important part of their evaluation. They thus develop a feeling for their employees' personal needs and problems, as well as their performance. Obviously this intimate knowledge of each employe is facilitated by the employees' long tenure, but managers do consciously and explicitly attempt to get to know their employees and place a premium on having time to talk.

Deepening the company's involvement with employees' lives is the sponsoring of various cultural, athletic, and other recreational activities. There is usually a heavy schedule of company social affairs. These activities are ostensibly voluntary, but virtually all members participate. Rohlen (1974) describes an annual calendar of office events: it typically includes two overnight trips, monthly Saturday afternoon recreation, and an average of six office parties, all at company expense. At these events a great deal of drinking goes on and much good fellowship is expressed. Discussion in an informal atmosphere is also characteristic of evening social activities of the work team which are often subsidized by the manger's budget.

Finally, the company allocates substantial financial resources to pay for benefits that are given all employees such as a family allowance and commuting and other job-related allowances. Furthermore, there are various welfare systems that "penetrate every crack of workers' lives." (Hazama, 1978:43). These range from company housing, dormitories, and housing loans through company nurseries and company scholarships for employees' children, to credit extension, savings, and insurance. Thus, employees perceive their own welfare and the financial welfare of their company as being identical (Tsurumi, 1977). . . .

DISCUSSION

. . . There are indeed many cultural differences between people in Japan and Western countries. However, this should not distract our attention from the fact that people in any country also have a lot in common. In the workplace, they value decent treatment, security, and an opportunity for emotional fulfillment. It goes to the credit of Japanese managers that they have developed organizational systems which, even though far from perfect, respond to these needs to a great extent.

The strategies and techniques we have reviewed constitute a remarkably well-integrated system. The management practices are highly congruent with the way tasks are structured, with the goals of individual members, and with the climate of the organization. Such a "fit" is expected to result in a high degree of organizational effectiveness or productivity (Nadler and Lawler, 1977). . . .

There are, however, [certain] contingencies that may limit the applicability of [these] techniques. As we have indicated, the practices described and the resulting efficiency can be observed primarily in large Japanese manufacturing corporations. In the service industries, even among large firms as well as in parts of the public sector, the effectiveness of the system is markedly lower. . . .

The system also implicitly assumes the near equality of rights between the employees, management, and owners. The institutional arrangements in some countries may in fact operate against such equality. Moreover, general economic conditions are also obviously an important additional intervening variable. During recessions the system's stability in many Japanese firms relies to some degree on a reduction in a "buffer" labor force, be it women, reemployed retirees, or subscontractors. This pattern may be difficult to replicate in other countries, but, as the evidence shows, that does not preclude the emergence of the ILM structure (Doeringer and Piore, 1971). In addition, less overtime, hiring freezes, reduced bonuses, and temporary transfers are other effective and often used measures protecting basic job security while keeping labor costs flexible (Rohlen, 1979). . . .

IMPLICATIONS FOR BUSINESS STRATEGY

So far we have focused primarily on the relationship between Japanese human resource management practices and employee commitment and productivity. However, several important organizational characteristics directly tied to the area of business strategy are also heavily influenced by the management style described in detail above. . . .

Competitive Spirit

First of all, the long-term socialization of employees in combination with the articulated "distinct" company philosophy is conducive to the development of organizational culture emphasizing competition. The world outside of the firm is perceived in terms of foes and friends, markets to be captured or defended. The purpose of the organization is to survive as a group, a task possible only through besting its current and potential rivals, both in Japan and overseas.

Japanese managers are brought up in an atmosphere of a competitive rivalry that gradually permeates every action and decision they make. The activities of the firm are continuously scrutinized with respect to its impact on its major competitors (Ohmae, 1982). . . . gathered intelligence is distributed widely throughout the organization, accompanied by summaries pointing out its consequences for future market battles (Tsurumi, 1977).

Contrary to the popular image of "Japan, Inc." where the government and the private industry support each other in an oligopolistic collusion, competition in Japan is very keen. Often the foreign market strategies of Japanese firms are products of the competitive circumstances at home. For example, the heavy emphasis on export by relative newcomers in their respective fields, such as Sony on consumer electronics and Honda in automobiles, was to a large degree made imperative by the difficulties encountered in competition with the established domestic producers. . . .

Long-Term Perspective

It is not, as often thought, superior planning that enables the Japanese to execute consistent business strategies. Rather, it is the absence of short-term incentives that may otherwise distract managers from pursuing long-term corporate objectives. Although bonuses are usually tied to current performance, the fact that one cannot escape the consequences of one's decisions, as most employees are expected to remain in the organization for most of their working lives, tends to minimize the danger of taking advantage of the current circumstances at the expense of future goals.

In addition, the reliance on future company well-being to provide for individual welfare, coupled with the future-oriented appraisal system, makes it easier to incorporate long-term strategic objectives into the management of everyday operations, with a minimum of formality and complexity. There is no need for "sophisticated" reporting systems which attempt to use complex formulas to direct executives and managers in a proper direction. In this respect, "perseverance" and "commitment" are equal to "harmony" and "team spirit" in the arsenal of desired, and rewarded, corporate values.

The impact of a long-term strategic perspective is clearly visible in the way the Japanese on the one hand, and many Western firms on the other, view joint ventures and other kinds of technological and marketing tie-ups. Japanese perceive such relationships as a temporary arrangement to rectify some of their competitive weakness, and that should, in the long run, lead to their dominance in the partnership; the foreign firms are generally content with short-term gains from such endeavors, without considering the long-term competitive consequences. . . .

Emphasis on Market Share

. . . a market share orientation fits well into the system of Japanese management practices, as it provides an objective measure of competitive standing . . . clear and understandable to anyone in the organization. At the same time, it has been shown that market share over the long run is a good predictor of corporate performance expressed in more traditional financial terms (Buzzell, Gale, and Sultan, 1975).

For most Japanese firms, driven by their competitive orientation, market share is ultimately a worldwide concept. To retreat from a market territory or product segment under challenge from a Japanese competitor will therefore do nothing more than buy time before the remaining markets also fall under siege. Just as self-defeating is attempting to piggyback onto Japanese manufacturing prowess and use them as OEM (original equipment manufacturer) suppliers for domestically well-established brands. Sooner or later they will go independent, with only crumbs left for their former partner. . . . maintaining competitive parity is the only way to ensure fruitful long-term cooperation.

Internal Growth

The value system of Japanese managers and executives places a premium on maintaining the corporation as a semipermanent group of individuals tied together with lasting bonds. For that reason, divestitures, mergers, and acquisitions, especially affecting unrelated firms, are unusual in Japan, and hostile takeovers are for all practical purposes next to impossible (Clark, 1979).

This might be detrimental to the efficiency of resource allocation in the economy to some degree, but once it is clearly established that the only way to grow is from internal competitive strength, the strategic implications are clear: there is no shortcut, no other way, than concentrating on making a product which fits customers' needs and is cheaper and of better quality than the competitors'.

Under such conditions it is natural that production becomes a major strategic concern, resulting in an emphasis on continuous product and process innovation, on upgrading quality, and on lowering costs (Wheelwright, 1981). The production area is viewed as a key to corporate survival in the long run and is staffed by high-quality managers with good chances of advancing eventually to top executive positions.

Usually top management is also closely involved with production, and their staff are free from spending their time planning takeover strategies or putting together defenses against them. Given the limits on executive time, a contrast with the Japanese suggests that the acquisition route to growth may suffer from rather substantial opportunity costs.

In addition the focus on internal growth permits the organization to pursue strategic changes incrementally, so they can be more easily absorbed by the organization. The "logical incrementalism" advocated by Quinn (1980) is a concept familiar in practice to managers in many Japanese firms. Moreover, internal growth allows the organization to satisfy the career aspirations of many employees by opening additional vacancies in new areas of business to be staffed from within.

Aggressive Innovation

It was pointed out earlier that the nature of the competitive appraisal system in Japanese firms and the rapid reception and dissemination of new ideas possible in an "organic" firm should encourage innovation. This notion is contrary to the stereotypical image of the Japanese as poor innovators constrained in the exploration of new frontiers by a group desire to maintain consensus and harmony (Lohr, 1982). In this respect the evidence is clear: Japanese do innovate, and probably as fast, if not faster, than most businesses in other countries (Moritani, 1981).

One reason for the discrepancy between the stereotype and the reality is the misunderstanding of innovation processes in the organization. It is not only the bright idea that counts, it is also the process of bringing the product based on the new idea to market. In terms of winning the competitive game, the origin of the idea is often secondary. After all, computers, jet engines, or scanners were not invented in the United States. It is in the implementation process that the Japanese have an advantage with their carefully built worldwide monitoring systems on the outside, and high level of interface, coordination, and teamwork on the inside, which involve all those concerned with development, design, and manufacturing.

Second, it is widely believed that a lack of venture capital in Japan limits incentives for innovation, as it is very difficult for research and development (R&D) personnel to quit their employers and strike out on their own, a pattern common in the United States (*Business Week,* December 14, 1981). However, a closer look at the problem reveals this also to be to the advantage of the Japanese.

With their stable research teams shielded from the temptation of windfall profits as independent entrepreneurs, Japanese companies are well poised to capitalize quickly on newly acquired knowledge. Rather than working in the secrecy of the family garage, the Japanese engineer is working on a new invention in the corporate laboratory, in regular communication with those responsible for its future commercial adaptation. Then, once an innovative idea is proven to be potentially promising, the organization can move on very quickly to the adoption phase, as everyone concerned is already familiar with the new product's characteristics.

The close cooperation and communication between the research engineers on the one side, and production and market personnel on the other, built into the Japanese management system, greatly facilitates the commercialization of new innovations and assures the integration of research and development with other critical corporate functions. A steady feedback of market information to the research personnel makes it more likely that research and development result in products that will meet market needs. Participation of production engineers in the development process increases the likelihood that the newly designed product can be built efficiently with available production technologies or that new technologies will be available shortly. Thus, rather than remaining an exclusive domain of R&D professionals, the innovation process is diffused widely throughout the organization, enlarging the strategic alternatives available to the firm, especially in the high-technology area.

CONCLUSIONS

In many countries it is possible to observe firms as committed as the Japanese to growth through a superior product and process innovation. Well-run U.S. firms use management practices to a large degree similar to those we have pointed out as typical for the Japanese. What make the Japanese special, but by no means unique, is their concentrated effort to develop systemic solutions to managerial problems, to match cultural, organizational, and strategic imperatives in an integrated management system. . . .

. . . In our opinion . . . the Japanese will remain the principal challengers of any Western firm serious about world markets. There is no shortcut other than to meet this challenge. No concession bargaining, marketing gimmicks, or shuffling of assets through acquisitions will do more than provide a bit of breathing space. In the long run the only feasible response is to do better what the Japanese are doing well already—developing management systems that motivate employees from the top to the bottom to pursue growth-oriented, innovation-focused competitive strategies.

DEALING WITH POWER

The readings to this point have, for the most part, dealt with organizations as rather rational and cooperative instruments. Strategies, whether formulated analytically or allowed to emerge in some kind of learning process, have nonetheless served for the good of the organization at large in a purely economic and competitive sense, as have the associated structures and systems. True, Wrapp's and Quinn's managers, for example, have consciously considered and dealt with potential resistance in creating and implanting their strategies. In doing so, they may have been forced to think in political terms. But the overt use of power and organized political action has largely been absent from our discussion.

An important group of thinkers in the field, however, have come to view the strategy process as an interplay of the forces of power, sometimes highly politicized. Rather than assuming that organizations are consistent, coherent and cooperative systems, tightly integrated to pursue certain traditional ends (namely the delivery of their products and services in the pursuit of profit, at least in the private sector), these writers start with quite different premises. They believe that organizations' goals and directions are determined primarily by the power needs of those who populate them. Their analyses raise all kinds of interesting and unsettled questions, such as: For whom does the organization really exist? For what purposes? If the organization is truly a political entity, how does one manage effectively in it? And so on.

No work in the literature sets this into perspective better than the famous study of the United States' response to the Cuban Missile Crisis by Graham Allison (1971) of Harvard's Kennedy School of Government. Allison believes that our conception of how decision making proceeds in organizations can be considered from three perspectives: a "rational actor" model (which is the concept he believes the American leaders had of the Soviets), an "organizations process" model, and a "bureaucratic politics" model (both of which Allison thinks could have been used as well to improve America's understanding of the Soviets' behavior). In the first model, power is embedded in a relatively rational and calculating center of action, much as strategy making was described in Chapters 3 and 4. In the second, it is entrenched in various organizational departments, each using power to further its own particular purposes. In the third model, "politics" comes into full play as individuals and groups exercise their influence to determine outcomes for their own benefits.

Our first reading focuses especially on the third model, but also incorporates aspects of the second. In parallel with Mintzberg's reading in the last chapter (and likewise based on two related chapters of his *Power In and Around Organizations* book), it considers first the general force of politics in organizations, what it is and what political "games" people play in organizations, and then the various forms taken by organizations that are dominated by such politics, the extreme one labeled the "political arena." This reading concludes with a discussion of when and why politics sometimes plays a functional role in organizations.

The second reading of the chapter brings us back to strategy, but in a kind of political way. You may recall one of the definitions of strategy introduced in Chapter 1 that was not heard from since—that of ploy. In this second reading, ploy comes to life in the context of "competitive maneuvering," various means strategists use to outwit competitors. This reading is based on two short articles entitled "Brinkmanship in Business" and "The Nonlogical Strategy" by Bruce Henderson, drawn from his book *Henderson on Corporate Strategy,* a collection of short, pithy, and rather opinionated views on management issues. Henderson founded the Boston Consulting Group, one of the early so-called "strategy boutiques," and built it into a major international force in management consulting. Now retired from there, he teaches strategy at the Vanderbilt University School of Management.

While the Mintzberg reading considers power and politics inside the organization, in terms of the maneuverings of various actors to gain influence, the Henderson one looks at the maneuverings of organizations at large, vis-à-vis their competitors. This second theme is pursued in the last two readings of this chapter, except that the context is extended beyond competitors to all of an organization's influencers (sometimes called "stakeholders," in contrast to only "shareholders"). To some observers, organizations are not merely instruments to produce goods and services, but also political systems that seek to enhance their own power. We might refer to this as *macro* politics, in contrast to the *micro* politics that takes place within organizations.

Some writers (e.g., Astley and Fombrun, 1983) have discussed the notion of *collective* strategy, concerning the management of external relationships in ways that are more cooperative (and perhaps social) than strictly competitive (and economic). This has become an important aspect of the strategy process in a world increasingly influenced by large multinational (or "global") corporations and by the joint ventures and other partnerships among such corporations and their associated coalitions with governments. The third reading of this chapter, by Jeffrey Pfeffer, a Stanford Business School professor and the researcher perhaps most identified with what we are here calling macro politics, goes beyond just the idea of collective strategy. It considers not only such legal, cooperative alignments, but also overt political behaviors for ends such as market collusion.

Note that Pfeffer is writing about *generic* strategies too, indeed some of the very same ones introduced earlier as competitive (such as acquisitions, or mergers, and joint ventures.) But in his work they are presented as *political* devices. Pfeffer's work, in some respects, can be viewed as a mirror image of Porter's. Perhaps you may want to go back to Chapter 4 and reread Porter, this time between the lines, about barriers to entry, bargaining power of suppliers, and so on—from Pfeffer's perspective. You may discover that "political" and "competitive" are not so distinct as they might at first seem.

You may not agree with Pfeffer who challenges some of the most cherished precepts about business. But it is difficult to deny the need to consider his point of view, which serves at the very least to balance the often overstated economic and competitive perspective. Pfeffer's views also deserve attention because they lie at the heart of many people's fears and concerns about business and the perceived need to regulate the behavior of large corporations.

The final reading of this chapter introduces another major theme about macro power, perhaps one that is really a composite of the issues raised in the other articles: For whom does or should the large business corporation exist? Mintzberg proposes a whole portfolio of answers around a "conceptual horseshoe." In so doing, he perhaps helps to reconcile some of the basic differences between those who view organizations as agents of economic competition and those who consider them to be instruments of the public will, or else as political systems in their own right. This reading also discusses the concept of *social responsibility*, one of the traditional topics covered in policy or strategy courses. But here the subject is treated not in a philanthropic or ethical sense, but as a managerial or organizational one. It also reviews the issues of corporate democracy, of regulation and pressure campaigns, and of "freedom" as described by Milton Friedman.

● POLITICS AND THE POLITICAL ORGANIZATION*

By Henry Mintzberg

How does conflict arise in an organization, why, and with what consequences? Years ago, the literature of organizations avoided such questions. But in the last decade or so, conflict and politics that go along with it have become not just acceptable topics but fashionable ones. Yet these topics, like most others in the field, have generally been discussed in fragments. Here we seek to consider them somewhat more comprehensively, first by themselves and then in the context of what will be called the political organization—the organization that comes to be dominated by politics and conflict.

---

* Adapted from Henry Mintzberg, *Power in and Around Organizations* (Copyright © Prentice-Hall, 1983), Chaps. 13 and 23, used by permission of the publisher; based on a summary that appeared in *Mintzberg on Management: Inside Our Strange World of Organizations* (Free Press, 1989).

What do we mean by "politics" in organizations? An organization may be described as functioning on the basis of a number of systems of influence: authority, ideology, expertise, politics. The first three can be considered legitimate in some sense: Authority is based on legally sanctioned power, ideology on widely accepted beliefs, expertise on power that is officially certified. The system of politics, in contrast, reflects power that is technically illegitimate (or, perhaps more accurately, *a*legitimate), in the means it uses, and sometimes also in the ends it promotes. In other words, political power in the organization (unlike government) is not formally authorized, widely accepted, or officially certified. The result is that political activity is usually divisive and conflictive, pitting individuals or groups against the more legitimate systems of influence and, when those systems are weak, against each other.

POLITICAL GAMES IN ORGANIZATIONS

Political activity in organizations is sometimes described in terms of various "games." The political scientist Graham Allison, for example, has described political games in organizations and government as "intricate and subtle, simultaneous, overlapping," but nevertheless guided by rules: "some rules are explicit, others implicit, some rules are quite clear, others fuzzy. Some are very stable; others are ever changing. But the collection of rules, in effect, defines the game" (1971:170). I have identified thirteen political games in particular, listed here together with their main players, the main reasons they seem to be played, and how they relate to the other systems of influence.

- *Insurgency game:* usually played to resist authority, although can be played to resist expertise or established ideology or even to effect change in the organization; ranges "from protest to rebellion" (Zald and Berger, 1978:841), and is usually played by "lower participants" (Mechanic, 1962), those who feel the greatest weight of formal authority

- *Counterinsurgency game:* played by those with legitimate power who fight back with political means, perhaps with legitimate means as well (e.g., excommunication in the church)

- *Sponsorship game:* played to build power base, in this case by using superiors; individual attaches self to someone with more status, professing loyalty in return for power

- *Alliance-building game:* played among peers—often line managers, sometimes experts—who negotiate implicit contracts of support for each other in order to build power base to advance selves in the organization

- *Empire-building game:* played by line managers, in particular, to build power bases, not cooperatively with peers but individually with subordinates

- *Budgeting game:* played overtly and with rather clearly defined rules to build power base; similar to last game, but less divisive, since prize is resources, not positions or units per se, at least not those of rivals

- *Expertise game:* nonsanctioned use of expertise to build power base, either by flaunting it or by feigning it; true experts play by exploiting technical skills and knowledge, emphasizing the uniqueness, criticality, and irreplaceability of the expertise (Hickson et al., 1971), also by seeking to keep skills from being programmed, by keeping knowledge to selves; nonexperts play by attempting to have their work viewed as expert, ideally to have it declared professional so they alone can control it

- *Lording game:* played to build power base by "lording" legitimate power over those without it or with less of it (i.e., using legitimate power in illegitimate ways); manager can lord formal authority over subordinate or civil servant over a citizen; members of missionary configuration can lord its ideology over outsiders; experts can lord technical skills over the unskilled

- *Line versus staff game:* a game of sibling-type rivalry, played not just to enhance personal power but to defeat a rival; pits line managers with formal decision-making authority against staff advisers with specialized expertise; each side tends to exploit legitimate power in illegitimate ways

- *Rival camps game:* again played to defeat a rival; typically occurs when alliance or empire-building games result in two major power blocs, giving rise to two-person, zero-sum game in place of n-person game; can be most divisive game of all; conflict can be between units (e.g., between marketing and production in manufacturing firm), between rival personalities, or between two competing missions (as in prisons split between custody and rehabilitation orientations)

- *Strategic candidates game:* played to effect change in an organization; individuals or groups seek to promote through political means their own favored changes of a strategic nature; many play—analysts, operating personnel, lower-level managers, even senior managers and chief executives (especially in the professional configurations), who must promote own candidates politically before they can do so formally; often combines elements of other games —empire-building (as purpose of game), alliance-building (to win game), rival camps, line versus staff, expertise, and lording (evoked during game), insurgency (following game), and so on

- *Whistle-blowing game:* a typically brief and simple game, also played to effect organizational change; privileged information is used by an insider, usually a lower participant, to "blow the whistle" to an influential outsider on questionable or illegal behavior by the organization

- *Young Turks game:* played for highest stakes of all, not to effect simple change or to resist legitimate power per se, but to throw the latter into question, perhaps even to overthrow it, and institute major shift; small group of "young Turks," close to but not at center of power, seeks to reorient organization's basic strategy, displace a major body of its expertise, replace its ideology, or rid it of its leadership; Zald and Berger discuss a form of this game they call "organizational coup d'état," where the object is "to effect an unexpected succession"—to replace *holders* of authority while maintaining *system* of authority intact (1978:833).

Some of these games, such as sponsorship and lording, while themselves technically illegitimate, can nevertheless *coexist with* strong legitimate systems of influence, as found for example in the machine and missionary type organizations; indeed, they could not exist without these systems of influence. Other political games, such as insurgency and young Turks—usually highly divisive games—arise in the presence of legitimate power but are *antagonistic to it,* designed to destroy or at least weaken it. And still others, such as rival camps, often arise when legitimate power is weak and *substitute for* it, for example in the professional and innovative type organizations.

The implication of this is that politics and conflict may exist at two levels in an organization. They may be present but not dominant, existing as an overlay in a more conventional organization, perhaps a kind of fifth column acting on behalf of some challenging power. Or else politics may be the dominant system of influence, and conflict strong, having weakened the legitimate systems of influence or having arisen in their weakness. It is this second level that gives rise to the type of organization we call *political.*

FORMS OF POLITICAL ORGANIZATIONS

What characterizes the organization dominated by politics is a lack of any of the forms of order found in conventional organizations. In other words, the organization is best described in terms of power, not structure, and that power is exercised in ways not legitimate in conventional organizations. Thus, there is no preferred method of coordination, no single dominant part of the organization, no clear type of decentralization. Everything depends on the fluidity of informal power, marshaled to win individual issues.

How does such an organization come to be? There is little published research on the question. But some ideas can be advanced tentatively. First, conflict would seem to arise in a circumscribed way in an organization, say between two units (such as marketing and production) or between an influential outside group and a powerful insider (such as between a part owner and the CEO). That conflict may develop gradually or it may flare up suddenly. It may eventually be resolved, but when it becomes intense, it may tend to spread, as other influencers get drawn in on one side or the other. But since few organizations can sustain intense political activity for long, that kind of conflict must eventually moderate itself (unless it kills off the organization first). In moderated form, however, the conflict may endure, even when it pervades the whole system, so long as the organization can make up for its losses, perhaps by being in a privileged position (as in the case of a conflict-ridden regulatory agency that is sustained by a government budget, or a politicized corporation that operates in a secure cartel).

What we end up with are two dimensions of conflict, first moderate or intense and second confined or pervasive. A third dimension—enduring or brief—really combines with the first (intense conflict having to be typically brief, moderate conflict possibly enduring). Combining these dimensions, we end up with four forms of the political organization:

- *Confrontation,* characterized by conflict that is *intense, confined,* and *brief* (unstable)
- *Shaky alliance,* characterized by conflict that is *moderate, confined,* and possibly *enduring* (relatively stable)
- *Politicized organization,* characterized by conflict that is *moderate, pervasive,* and possibly *enduring* (relatively stable, so long as it is sustained by privileged position)
- *Complete political arena,* characterized by conflict that is *intense, pervasive,* and *brief* (unstable)[1]

---

[1] I do not consider conflict that is moderate, confined, and brief to merit inclusion under the label of political organization.

One of these forms is called *complete* because its conflict is both intense and pervasive. In this form, the external influencers disagree among themselves; they try to form alliances with some insiders, while clashing with others. The internal activities are likewise conflictive, permeated by divisive political games. Authority, ideology, and expertise are all subordinated to the play of political power. An organization so politicized can pursue no goal with any consistency. At best, it attends to a number of goals inconsistently over time, at worst it consumes all its energy in disputes and never accomplishes anything. In essense, the complete political arena is less a coherent organization than a free-for-all of individuals. As such, it is probably the form of political organization least commonly found in practice, or, at least, the most unstable when it does appear.

In contrast, the other three forms of political organization manage to remain partial, one by moderating its conflict, a second by containing it, and the third by doing both. As a result, these forms are more stable than the complete form and so are probably more common, with two of them in particular appearing to be far more viable.

In the *confrontational* form, conflict may be intense, but it is also contained, focusing on two parties. Typical of this is the takeover situation, where, for example, an outside stockholder tries to seize control of a closed system corporation from its management. Another example is the situation, mentioned earlier, of two rival camps in and around a prison, one promoting the mission of custody, the other that of rehabilitation.

The *shaky alliance* commonly emerges when two or more major systems of influence or centers of power must coexist in roughly equal balance. The symphony orchestra, for example, must typically combine the strong personal authority of the conductor (entrepreneurial orientation) with the extensive expertise of the musicians (professional orientation). As Fellini demonstrated so well in his film *Orchestra Rehearsal,* this alliance, however uncomfortable (experts never being happy in the face of strong authority), is nevertheless a necessary one. Common today is the professional organization operating in the public sector, which must somehow sustain an alliance of experts and government officials, one group pushing upward for professional autonomy, the other downward for technocratic control.

Our final form, the *politicized organization,* is characterized by moderate conflict that pervades the entire system of power. This would appear to describe a number of today's largest organizations, especially ones in the public sector whose mandates are visible and controversial—many regulatory agencies, for example, and some public utilities. Here it is government protection, or monopoly power, that sustains organizations captured by conflict. This form seems to be increasingly common in the private sector too, among some of the largest corporations that are able to sustain the inefficiencies of conflict through their market power and sometimes by their ability to gain government support as well.

THE FUNCTIONAL ROLE OF POLITICS IN ORGANIZATIONS

Little space need be devoted to the dysfunctional influence of politics in organizations. Politics is divisive and costly; it burns up energies that could instead go into the operations. It can also lead to all kinds of aberrations. Politics is often used to sustain outmoded systems of power, and sometimes to introduce new ones that are not justified. Politics can also paralyze an organization to the point where its effective functioning comes to a halt and nobody benefits. The purpose of an organization, after all, is to produce goods and services, not to provide an arena in which people can fight with one another.

What does deserve space, however, because they are less widely appreciated, are those conditions in which politics and the political organization serve a functional role.

In general, the system of politics is necessary in an organization to correct certain deficiencies in its other, legitimate systems of influence—above all to provide for certain forms of flexibility discouraged by those other systems. The other systems of influence were labeled legitimate because their *means*—authority, ideology, or expertise—have some basis of legitimacy. But sometimes those means are used to pursue *ends* that are illegitimate (as in the example of the lording game, where legitimate power is flaunted unreasonably). In contrast, the system of politics, whose *means* are (by definition) illegitimate, can sometimes be used to pursue *ends* that are in fact legitimate (as in certain of the whistle-blowing and young Turks games, where political pressures are used against formal authority to correct irresponsible or ineffective behaviors). We can elaborate on this in terms of four specific points.

First, politics as a system of influence can act in a Darwinian way to ensure that the strongest members of an organization are brought into positions of leadership. Authority favors a single chain of command; weak leaders can suppress strong subordinates. Politics, on the other hand, can provide alternate channels of information and promotion, as when the sponsorship game enables someone to leap over a weak superior (McClelland, 1970). Moreover, since effective leaders have been shown to exhibit a need for power, the political games can serve as tests to demonstrate the potential for leadership. The second-string players may suffice for the scrimmages, but only the stars can be allowed to meet the competition. Political games not only suggest who those players are but also help to remove their weak rivals from contention.

Second, politics can also ensure that all sides of an issue are fully debated, whereas the other systems of influence may promote only one. The system of authority, by aggregating information up a central hierarchy, tends to advance only a single point of view, often the one already known to be favored above. So, too, does the system of ideology, since every issue is interpreted in terms of "the word," the prevailing set of beliefs. As for the system of expertise, people tend to defer to the expert on any particular issue. But experts are often closed to new ideas, ones that developed after they received their training. Politics, however, by obliging "responsible men . . . to fight for what they are convinced is right" (Allison, 1971:145) encourages a variety of voices to be heard on any issue. And, because of attacks by its opponents, each voice is forced to justify its conclusions in terms of the broader good. That means it must marshal arguments and support proposals that can at least be justified in terms of the interests of the organization at large rather than the parochial needs of a particular group. As Burns has noted in an amusing footnote:

> It is impossible to avoid some reference from the observations made here to F. M. Cornford's well known "Guide for the Young Academic Politician." Jobs "fall into two classes, My Jobs and Your Jobs. My Jobs are public-spirited proposals, which happen (much to my regret) to involve the advancement of a personal friend, or (still more to my regret) of myself. Your Jobs are insidious intrigues for the advancement of yourself and your friends, spuriously disguised as public-spirited proposals." (1961–62:260)

Third, the system of politics is often required to stimulate necessary change that is blocked by the legitimate systems of influence. Internal change is generally threatening to the "vested interest" of an organization. The system of authority concentrates power up the hierarchy, often in the hands of those who were responsible for initiating the existing strategies in the first place. It also contains the established controls, which are designed to sustain the status quo. Similarly, the system of expertise concentrates power in the hands of senior and established experts, not junior ones who may possess newer, more necessary skills. Likewise, the system of ideology, because it is rooted in the past, in tradition, acts as a deterrent to change. In the face of these resistances, it is politics that is able to work as a kind of "invisible hand"—"invisible underhand" would be a better term—to promote necessary change, through such games as strategic candidates, whistle-blowing, and young Turks.

Fourth and finally, the system of politics can ease the path for the execution of decisions. Senior managers, for example, often use politics to gain acceptance for their decisions, playing the strategic candidates game early in promoting proposals to avoid having to play the more divisive and risky counterinsurgency game later in the face of resistance to them. They persuade, negotiate, and build alliances to smooth the path for the decisions they wish to make.

To conclude our discussion, while I am not personally enthusiastic about organizational politics and have no desire to live in a political organization, I do accept, and hope I have persuaded the reader to accept, that politics does have useful roles to play in a society of organizations. Organizational politics may irritate us, but it can also serve us.

• COMPETITIVE MANEUVERING*

BY BRUCE HENDERSON

BRINKMANSHIP IN BUSINESS

A businessman often convinces himself that he is completely logical in his behavior when in fact the critical factor is his emotional bias compared to the emotional bias of his opposition. Unfortunately, some businessmen and students perceive competition as some kind of impersonal, objective, colorless affair, with a company competing against the field as a golfer competes in medal play. A better case can be made that business competition is a major battle in which there are many contenders, each of whom must be dealt with individually. Victory, if achieved, is more often won in the mind of a competitor than in the economic arena.

I shall emphasize two points. The first is that the management of a company must persuade each competitor voluntarily to stop short of a maximum effort to acquire customers and profits. The second point is that persuasion depends on emotional and intuitive factors rather than on analysis or deduction.

The negotiator's skill lies in being as arbitrary as necessary to obtain the best possible compromise without actually destroying the basis for voluntary mutual cooperation of self-restraint. There are some commonsense rules for success in such an endeavor:

---

* "Brinkmanship in Business" and "The Nonlogical Strategy," in *Henderson on Corporate Strategy* (Cambridge, MA, Abt Books, 1979), pp. 27–33, title selected for this book; section on "Rules for the Strategist" originally at the end of "Brinkmanship in Business" moved to the end of "The Nonlogical Strategy;" reprinted by permission of publisher.

1. Be sure that your rival is fully aware of what he can gain if he cooperates and what it will cost him if he does not.
2. Avoid any action which will arouse your competitor's emotions, since it is essential that he behave in a logical, reasonable fashion.
3. Convince your opponent that you are emotionally dedicated to your position and are completely convinced that it is reasonable.

It is worth emphasizing that your competitor is under the maximum handicap if he acts in a completely rational, objective, and logical fashion. For then he will cooperate as long as he thinks he can benefit. In fact, if he is completely logical, he will not forgo the profit of cooperation as long as there is *any* net benefit.

Friendly Competitors

It may strike most businessmen as strange to talk about cooperation with competitors. But it is hard to visualize a situation in which it would be worthwhile to pursue competition to the utter destruction of a competitor. In every case there is a greater advantage to reducing the competition on the condition that the competitor does likewise. Such mutual restraint is cooperation, whether recognized as such or not.

Without cooperation on the part of competitors, there can be no stability. We see this most clearly in international relationships during times of peace. There are constant encroachments and aggressive acts. And the eventual consequence is always either voluntarily imposed self-restraint or mutual destruction. Thus, international diplomacy has only one purpose: to stabilize cooperation between independent nations on the most favorable basis possible. Diplomacy can be described as the art of being stubborn, arbitrary, and unreasonable without arousing emotional responses.

Businessmen should notice the similarity between economic competition and the peacetime behavior of nations. The object in both cases is to achieve a voluntary, cooperative restraint on the part of otherwise aggressive competitors. Complete elimination of competition is almost inconceivable. The goal of the hottest economic war is an agreement for coexistence, not annihilation. The competition and mutual encroachment do not stop; they go on forever. But they do so under some measure of mutual restraint.

"Cold War" Tactics

A breakdown in negotiations is inevitable if both parties persist in arbitrary positions which are incompatible. Yet there are major areas in business where some degree of arbitrary behavior is essential for protecting a company's self-interest. In effect, a type of brinkmanship is necessary. The term was coined to describe cold war international diplomacy, but it describes a normal pattern in business, too.

In a confrontation between parties who are in part competitors and in part cooperators, deciding what to accept is essentially emotional or arbitrary. Deciding what is attainable requires an evaluation of the other party's degree of intransigence. The purpose is to convince him that you are arbitrary and emotionally committed while trying to discover what he would really accept in settlement. The competitor known to be coldly logical is at a great disadvantage. Logically, he can afford to compromise until there is no advantage left in cooperation. If, instead, he is emotional, irrational, and arbitrary, he has a great advantage.

The heart of business strategy for a company is to promote attitudes on the part of its competitors that will cause them either to restrain themselves or to act in a fashion which management deems advantageous. In diplomacy and military strategy the key to success is very much the same.

The most easily recognized way of enforcing cooperation is to exhibit obvious willingness to use irresistible or overwhelming force. This requires little strategic skill, but there is the problem of convincing the competing organization that the force will be used without actually resorting to it (which would be expensive and inconvenient).

In industry, however, the available force is usually not overwhelming, although one company may be able to inflict major punishment on another. In the classic case, each party can inflict such punishment on the other. If there were open conflict, then both parties would lose. If they cooperate, both parties are better off, but not necessarily equally so—particularly if one is trying to change the status quo.

When each party can punish the other, the prospects of agreement depend on three things:

1. Each party's willingness to accept the risk of punishment
2. Each party's belief that the other party is willing to accept the risk of punishment
3. The degree of rationality in the behavior of each party

If these conclusions are correct, what can we deduce about how advantages are gained and lost in business competition?

First, management's unwillingness to accept the risk of punishment is almost certain to produce either the punishment or progressively more onerous conditions for cooperation—provided the competition recognized the attitude.

Second, beliefs about a competitor's future behavior or response are all that determine competitive cooperation. In other words, it is the judgment not of actual capability but of probable use of capability that counts.

Third, the less rational or less predictable the behavior of a competitor appears to be, the greater the advantage he possesses in establishing a favorable competitive balance. This advantage is limited only by his need to avoid forcing his competitors into an untenable position or creating an emotional antagonism that will lead them to be unreasonable and irrational (as he is).

The Nonlogical Strategy

The goal of strategy in business, diplomacy, and war is to produce a stable relationship favorable to you with the consent of your competitors. By definition, restraint by a competitor is cooperation. Such cooperation from a competitor must seem to be profitable to him. *Any competition which does not eventually eliminate a competitor requires his cooperation to stabilize the situation.* The agreement is usually that of tacit nonaggression; the alternative is death for all but one competitor. A stable competitive situation requires an agreement between competing parties to maintain self-restraint. Such agreement cannot be arrived at by logic. It must be achieved by an emotional balance of forces. This is why it is necessary to appear irrational to competitors. For the same reason, you must seem unreasonable and arbitrary in negotiations with customers and suppliers.

Competition and cooperation go hand in hand in all real-life situations. Otherwise, conflict could only end in extermination of the competitor. There is a point in all situations of conflict where both parties gain more or lose less from peace than they can hope to gain from any foreseeable victory. Beyond that point cooperation is more profitable than conflict. But how will the benefits be shared?

In negotiated conflict situations, the participant who is coldly logical is at a great disadvantage. Logically, he can afford to compromise until there is no advantage left in cooperation. The negotiator/competitor whose behavior is irrational or arbitrary has a great advantage if he can depend upon his opponent being logical and unemotional. The arbitrary or irrational competitor can demand far more than a reasonable share and yet his logical opponent can still gain by compromise rather than breaking off the cooperation.

Absence of monopoly in business requires voluntary restraint of competition. At some point there must be a tacit agreement not to compete. Unless this restraint of trade were acceptable to all competitors, the resulting aggression would inevitably eliminate the less efficient competitors leaving only one. Antitrust laws represent a formal attempt to limit competition. All antimonopoly and fair trade laws constitute restraint of competition.

Utter destruction of a competitor is almost never profitable unless the competitor is unwilling to accept peace. In our daily social contacts, in our international affairs, and in our business affairs, we have far more ability to damage those around us than we ever dare use. Others have the same power to damage us. The implied agreement to restrain our potential aggression is all that stands between us and eventual elimination of one by the other. Both war and diplomacy are mechanisms for establishing or maintaining this self-imposed restraint on all competitors. The conflict continues, but within the implied area of cooperative agreement.

There is a definite limit to the range within which competitors can expect to achieve an equilibrium or negotiate a shift in equilibrium even by implication. Arbitrary, uncooperative, or aggressive attitudes will produce equally emotional reactions. These emotional reactions are in turn the basis for nonlogical and arbitrary responses. Thus, nonlogical behavior is self-limiting.

This is why the art of diplomacy can be described as the ability to be unreasonable without arousing resentment. It is worth remembering that the objective of diplomacy is to induce cooperation on terms that are relatively more favorable to you than to your protagonist without actual force being used.

More business victories are won in the minds of competitors than in the laboratory, the factory or the marketplace. The competitor's conviction that you are emotional, dogmatic, or otherwise nonlogical in your business strategy can be a great asset. This conviction on his part can result in an acceptance of your actions without retaliation, which would otherwise be unthinkable. More important, the anticipation of nonlogical or unrestrained reactions on your part can inhibit his competitive aggression.

Rules for the Strategist

If I were asked to distill the conditions and forces described into advice for the business-strategist, I would suggest five rules:

1. You must know as accurately as possible just what your competition has at stake in his contact with you. It is not what you gain or lose, but what he gains or loses that sets the limit on his ability to compromise with you.

2. The less the competition knows about your stakes, the less advantage he has. Without a reference point, he does not even know whether you are being unreasonable.

3. It is absolutely essential to know the character, attitudes, motives, and habitual behavior of a competitor if you wish to have a negotiating advantage.

4. The more arbitrary your demands are, the better your relative competitive position—provided you do not arouse an emotional reaction.

5. The less arbitrary you seem, the more arbitrary you can in fact be.

These rules make up the art of business brinkmanship. They are guidelines for winning a strategic victory in the minds of competitors. Once this victory has been won, it can be converted into a competitive victory in terms of sales volume, costs, and profits.

● THE INSTITUTIONAL FUNCTION OF MANAGEMENT*

BY JEFFREY PFEFFER

Theory, research, and education in the field of organizational behavior and management have been dominated by a concern for the management of people *within* organizations. The question of how to make workers more productive has stood as the foundation for management theory and practice since the time of Frederick Taylor. Such an emphasis neglects the institutional function of management. While managing people within organizations is critical, managing the organization's relationships with other organizations such as competitors, creditors, suppliers, and governmental agencies is frequently as critical to the firm's success.

Parsons (1960) noted that there were three levels of organizations: (1) the technical level, where the technology of the organization was used to produce some product or service; (2) the administrative level, which coordinated and supervised the technical level; and (3) the institutional level, which was concerned with the organization's legitimacy and with organization-environment relations. Organization and management theory has primarily concentrated on administrative level problems, frequently at very low hierarchical levels in organizations.

Practicing managers and some researchers do recognize the importance of the institutional context in which the firm operates. There is increasing use of institutional advertising, and executives from the oil industry, among others, have been active in projecting their organizations' views in a variety of contexts. Mintzberg (1973a) has identified the liaison role as one of ten roles managers fill. Other authors explicitly have noted the importance of relating the organization to other organizations (Pfeffer and Nowak, n.d., Whyte, 1955). . . .

The purposes of this article are: (a) to present evidence of the importance of the institutional function of management, and (b) to review data consistent with a model of institutional management. This model argues that managers behave as if they were seeking to manage and reduce uncertainty and interdependence arising

---

* Originally published as "Beyond Management and the Worker: The Institutional Function of Management," in the *Academy of Management Review* (April 1976); copyright © *Academy of Management Review*. Reprinted with deletions by the permission of the *Academy of Management Review* and the author.

from the firm's relationships with other organizations. Several strategic responses to interorganizational exchange, including their advantages and disadvantages, are considered.

INSTITUTIONAL PROBLEMS OF ORGANIZATIONS

Organizations are open social systems, engaged in constant and important transactions with other organizations in their environments. Business firms transact with customer and supplier organizations, and with sources of credit; they interact on the federal and local level with regulatory and legal authorities which are concerned with pollution, taxes, antitrust, equal employment, and myriad other issues. Because firms do interact with these other organizations, two consequences follow. First, organizations face uncertainty. If an organization were a closed system so that it could completely control and predict all the variables that affected its operation, the organization could make technically rational, maximizing decisions and anticipate the consequences of its actions. As an open system, transacting with important external organizations, the firm does not have control over many of the important factors that affect its operations. Because organizations are open, they are affected by events outside their boundaries.

Second, organizations are interdependent with other organizations with which they exchange resources, information or personnel, and thus open to influence by them. The extent of this influence is likely to be a function of the importance of the resource obtained, and inversely related to the ease with which the resource can be procured from alternative sources (Jacobs, 1974; Thompson, 1967). Interdependence is problematic and troublesome. Managers do not like to be dependent on factors outside their control. Interdependence is especially troublesome if there are few alternative sources, so the external organization is particularly important to the firm.

Interdependence and uncertainty interact in their effects on organizations. One of the principal functions of the institutional level of the firm is the management of this interdependence and uncertainty.

THE IMPORTANCE OF INSTITUTIONAL MANAGEMENT

Katz and Kahn (1966) noted that organizations may pursue two complementary paths to effectiveness. The first is to be as efficient as possible, and thereby obtain a competitive advantage with respect to other firms. Under this strategy, the firm succeeds because it operates so efficiently that it achieves a competitive advantage in the market. The second strategy, termed "political," involves the establishment of favorable exchange relationships based on considerations that do not relate strictly to price, quality, service, or efficiency. Winning an order because of the firm's product and cost characteristics would be an example of the strategy of efficiency; winning the order because of interlocks in the directorates of the organizations involved, or because of family connections between executives in the two organizations, would illustrate political strategies.

The uses and consequences of political strategies for achieving organizational success have infrequently been empirically examined. Hirsch (1975) has . . . compared the ethical drug and record industries, noting great similarities between them. Both sell their products through gatekeepers or intermediaries—in the case of pharmaceuticals, through doctors who must write the prescriptions, and in the case of records, through disc jockeys who determine air time and, consequently, exposure. Both sell products with relatively short life cycles, and both industries place great emphasis on new products and product innovation. Both depend on the legal environment of patents, copyrights, and trademarks for market protection.

Hirsch noted that the rate of return for the average pharmaceutical firm during the period 1956–1966 was more than double the rate of return for the average firm in the record industry. Finding no evidence that would enable him to attribute the striking differences in profitability to factors associated with internal structural arrangements, Hirsch concluded that at least one factor affecting the relative profitability of the two industries is the ability to manage their institutional environments, and more specifically, the control over distribution, patent and copyright protection, and the prediction of adoption by the independent gatekeepers.

In a review of the history of both industries, Hirsch indicated that in pharmaceuticals, control over entry was achieved by (a) amending the patent laws to permit the patenting of naturally occurring substances, antibiotics and (b) instituting a long and expensive licensing procedure required before drugs could be manufactured and marketed, administered by the Food and Drug Administration (FDA). In contrast, record firms have much less protection under the copyright laws; as a consequence, entry is less controlled, leading to more competition and lower profits. While there are other differences between the industries, including size and expenditures on research and development, Hirsch argued that at least some of the success of drug firms derives from their ability to control entry and their ability to control information channels relating to their product through the use of detail personnel and advertising in the American Medical Association Journals. Retail price maintenance, tariff protection, and licensing to restrict entry are other examples of practices that are part of the organization's institutional environment and may profoundly affect its success.

MANAGING UNCERTAINTY AND INTERDEPENDENCE

The organization, requiring transactions with other organizations and uncertain about their future performance, has available a variety of strategies that can be used to manage uncertainty and interdependence. Firms face two problems in their institutional relationships: (a) managing the uncertainty caused by the unpredictable actions of competitors and (b) managing the uncertainty resulting from noncompetitive interdependence with suppliers, creditors, government agencies, and customers. In both instances, the same set of strategic responses is available: merger, to completely absorb the interdependence and resulting uncertainty; joint ventures; interlocking directorates, to partially absorb interdependence; the movement and selective recruiting of executives and other personnel, to develop interorganizational linkages; regulation, to provide government enforced stability; and other political activity to reduce competition, protect markets, and sources of supply, and otherwise manage the organization's environment.

Because organizations are open systems, each strategy is limited in its effect. While merger or some other interorganizational linkage may manage one source of organizational dependence, it probably at the same time makes the organizations dependent on yet other organizations. For example, while regulation may eliminate effective price competition and restrict entry into the industry (Jordan, 1972;

Pfeffer, 1974a; Posner, 1974), the regulated organizations then face the uncertainties involved in dealing with the regulatory agency. Moreover, in reducing uncertainty for itself, the organization must bargain away some of its own discretion (Thompson, 1967). One can view institutional management as an exchange process—the organization assures itself of needed resources, but at the same time, must promise certain predictable behaviors in return. Keeping these qualifications in mind, evidence on use of the various strategies of institutional management is reviewed.

Merger

There are three reasons an organization may seek to merge—first, to reduce competition by absorbing an important competitor organization; second, to manage interdependence with either sources of input or purchasers of output by absorbing them; and third, to diversify operations and thereby lessen dependence on the present organizations with which it exchanges (Pfeffer, 1972b). While merger among competing organizations is presumably proscribed by the antitrust laws, enforcement resources are limited, and major consolidations do take place. . . .

The classic expressed rationale for merger has been to increase the profits or the value of the shares of the firm. In a series of studies beginning as early as 1921, researchers have been unable to demonstrate that merger active firms are more profitable or have higher stock prices following the merger activity. This literature has been summarized by Reid (1968), who asserts that mergers are made for growth, and that growth is sought because of the relationship between firm size and managerial salaries.

Growth, however, does not provide information concerning the desired characteristics of the acquired firm. Under a growth objective, any merger is equivalent to any other of the same size. Pfeffer (1972b) has argued that mergers are undertaken to manage organizational interdependence. Examining the proportion of merger activity occurring within the same two-digit SIC industry category, he found that the highest proportion of within-industry mergers occurred in industries of intermediate concentration. The theoretical argument was that in industries with many competitors, the absorption of a single one did little to reduce competitive uncertainty. At the other extreme, with only a few competitors, merger would more likely be scrutinized by the antitrust authorities and coordination could instead be achieved through more informal arrangements, such as price leadership.

The same study investigated the second reason to merge: to absorb the uncertainty among organizations vertically related to each other, as in a buyer-seller relationship. He found that it was possible to explain 40% of the variation in the distribution of merger activity over industries on the basis of resource interdependence, measured by estimates of the transactions flows between sectors of the economy. On an individual industry basis, in two-thirds of the cases a measure of transactions interdependence accounted for 65% or more of the variation in the pattern of merger activity. The study indicated that it was possible to account for the industry of the likely merger partner firm by considering the extent to which firms in the two industries exchanged resources.

While absorption of suppliers or customers will reduce the firm's uncertainty by bringing critical contingencies within the boundaries of the organization, this strategy has some distinct costs. One danger is that the process of vertical integration creates a larger organization which is increasingly tied to a single industry.

The third reason for merger is diversification. Occasionally, the organization is confronted by interdependence it cannot absorb, either because of resource or legal limitations. Through diversifying its activities, the organization does not reduce the uncertainty, but makes the particular contingency less critical for its success and well-being. Diversification provides the organization with a way of avoiding, rather than absorbing, problematic interdependence.

Merger represents the most complete solution to situations of organizational independence, as it involves the total absorption of either a competitor or a vertically related organization, or the acquisition of an organization operating in another area. Because it does involve total absorption, merger requires more resources and is a more visible and substantial form of interorganizational linkage.

Joint Ventures

Closely related to merger is the joint venture: the creation of a jointly owned, but independent organization by two or more separate parent firms. Merger involves the total pooling of assets by two or more organizations. In a joint venture, some assets of each of several parent organizations are used, and thus only a partial pooling of resources is involved (Bernstein, 1965). For a variety of reasons, joint ventures have ben prosecuted less frequently and less successfully than mergers, making joint ventures particularly appropriate as a way of coping with competitive interdependence.

The joint subsidiary can have several effects on competitive interdependence and uncertainty. First, it can reduce the extent of new competition. Instead of both firms entering a market, they can combine some of their assets and create a joint subsidiary to enter the market. Second, since joint subsidiaries are typically staffed, particularly at the higher executive levels, with personnel drawn from the parent firms, the joint subsidiary becomes another location for the management of competing firms to meet. Most importantly, the joint subsidiary must set price and output levels, make new product development and marketing decisions and decisions about its advertising policies. Consequently, the parent organizations are brought into association in a setting in which exactly those aspects of the competitive relationship must be jointly determined.

In a study of joint ventures among the manufacturing and oil and gas companies during the period 1960–1971, Pfeffer and Nowak (1976a, 1976b) found that 56% involved parent firms operating in the same two-digit industry. Further, in 36% of the 166 joint ventures studied, the joint subsidiary operated in the same industry as both parent organizations. As in the case of mergers, the proportion of joint venture activities undertaken with other firms in the same industry was related to the concentration of the firm's industry being intermediate. The relationship between concentration and the proportion of joint ventures undertaken within the same industry accounted for some 25% of the variation in the pattern of joint venture activities.

In addition to considering the use of joint ventures in coping with competitive interdependence, the Pfeffer and Nowak study of joint ventures examined the extent to which the creation of joint subsidiaries was related to patterns of transaction interdependence across industries. While the correlations between the proportion of transactions and the proportion of joint ventures undertaken between industry pairs were lower than in the case of mergers, statistically significant relationships between this form of interorganizational linkage activity and patterns of resource exchange were observed. The difference between mergers and joint ventures appears to be that mergers are used relatively more to cope with buyer–seller interdependence, and joint ventures are more highly related to considerations of coping with competitive uncertainty.

Cooptation is a venerable strategy for managing interdependence between organizations. Cooptation involves the partial absorption of another organization through the placing of a representative of that organization on the board of the focal organization. Corporations frequently place bankers on their boards; hospitals and universities offer trustee positions to prominent business leaders; and community action agencies develop advisory boards populated with active and strong community political figures. . . .

Interlocks in the boards of directors of competing organizations provide a possible strategy for coping with competitive interdependence and the resulting uncertainty. The underlying argument is that in order to manage interorganizational relationships, information must be exchanged, usually through a joint subsidiary or interlocking directorate. While interlocks among competitors are ostensibly illegal, until very recently there was practically no prosecution of this practice. In a 1965 study, a subcommittee of the House Judiciary Committee found more than 300 cases in which direct competitors had interlocking boards of directors (House of Representatives, 1965). In a study of the extent of interlocking among competing organizations in a sample of 109 manufacturing organizations, Pfeffer and Nowak (n.d.) found that the proportion of directors on the board from direct competitors was higher for firms operating in industries in which concentration was intermediate. This result is consistent with the result found for joint ventures and mergers as well. In all three instances, linkages among competing organizations occurred more frequently when concentration was in an intermediate range.

Analyses of cooptation through the use of boards of directors have not been confined to business firms. Price (1963) argued that the principal function of the boards of the Oregon Fish and Game Commissions was to link the organizations to their environments. Zald (1967) found that the composition of YMCA boards in Chicago matched the demography of their operating areas, and affected the organizations' effectiveness, particularly in raising money. Pfeffer (1973) examined the size, composition, and function of hospital boards of directors, finding that variables of organizational context, such as ownership, source of funds, and location, were important explanatory factors. He also found a relationship between cooptation and organizational effectiveness. In 1972, Pfeffer (1972a) found that regulated firms, firms with a higher proportion of debt in their capital structures, and larger firms tended to have more outside directors. Allen (1974) also found that size of the board and the use of cooptation was predicted by the size of the firm, but did not replicate Pfeffer's earlier finding of a relationship between the organization's capital structure and the proportion of directors from financial institutions. In a study of utility boards, Pfeffer (1974b) noted that the composition of the board tended to correlate with the demographics of the area in which the utility was regulated.

The evidence is consistent with the strategy of organizations using their boards of directors to coopt external organizations and manage problematic interdependence. The role of the board of directors is seen not as the provision of management expertise or control, but more generally as a means of managing problematic aspects of an organization's institutional environment.

Executive Recruitment

Information also is transferred among organizations though the movement of personnel. The difference between movement of executives between organizations and cooptation is that in the latter case, the person linking the two organizations retains membership in both organizations. In the case of personnel movement, dual organizational membership is not maintained. When people change jobs, they take with themselves information about the operations, policies, and values of their previous employers, as well as contacts in the organization. In a study of the movement of faculty among schools of business, Baty et al. (1971) found that similar orientations and curricula developed among schools exchanging personnel. The movement of personnel is one method by which new techniques of management and new marketing and product ideas are diffused through a set of organizations.

Occasionally, the movement of executives between organizations has been viewed as intensifying, rather than reducing, competition. Companies have been distressed by the raiding of trade secrets and managerial expertise by other organizations. While this perspective must be recognized, the exchange of personnel among organizations is a revered method of conflict *reduction* between organizations (Stern, Sternthal, and Craig, 1973). Personnel movement inevitably involves sharing information among a set of organizations.

If executive movement is a form of interfirm linkage designed to manage competitive relationships, the proportion of executives recruited from within the same industry should be highest at intermediate levels of industrial concentration. Examining the three top executive positions in twenty different manufacturing industries, the evidence on executive backgrounds was found to be consistent with this argument (Pfeffer and Leblebici, 1973). The proportion of high level executives with previous jobs in the same industry but in a different company was found to be negatively related to the number of firms in the industry. The larger the number of firms, the less likely that a single link among competitors will substantially reduce uncertainty, but the larger the available supply of external executive talent. The data indicated no support for a supply argument, but supported the premise that interorganizational linkages are used to manage interdependence and uncertainty.

The use of executive movement to manage noncompetitive interorganizational relationships is quite prevalent. The often-cited movement of personnel between the Defense Department and major defense contractors is only one example, because there is extensive movement of personnel between many government departments and industries interested in the agencies decisions. The explanation is frequently proposed that organizations are acquiring these personnel because of their expertise. The expertise explanation is frequently difficult to separate from the alternative that personnel are being exchanged to enhance interorganizational relationships. Regardless of the motivation, exchanging personnel inevitably involves the transfer of information and access to the other organization.

Regulation

Occasionally, institutional relationships are managed through recourse to political intervention. The reduction of competition and its associated uncertainty may be accomplished through regulation. Regulation, however, is a risky strategy for organizations to pursue. While regulation most frequently benefits the regulated industry (Jordan, 1972; Pfeffer, 1974a), the industry and firms have no assurance that regulatory authority will not be used against their interests. Regulation is very hard to repeal. Successful use of regulation requires that the firm and industry face little or no powerful political opposition, and that the political future can be accurately forecast.

The benefits of regulation to those being regulated have been extensively reviewed (Posner, 1974; Stigler, 1971). Regulation frequently has been sought by the regulated industry. . . . Estimates of the effects of regulation on prices in electric utilities, airlines, trucking, and natural gas have indicated that regulation either increases price or has no effect.

The theory behind these outcomes is still unclear. One approach suggests that regulation is created for the public benefit, but after the initial legislative attention, the regulatory process is captured by the firms subject to regulation. Another approach proposes that regulation, like other goods, is acquired subject to supply and demand considerations (Posner, 1974). Political scientists, focusing on the operation of interest groups, argue that regulatory agencies are "captured" by organized and well-financed interests. Government intervention in the market can solve many of the interdependence problems faced by firms. Regulation is most often accompanied by restriction of entry and the fixing of prices, which tend to reduce market uncertainties. Markets may be actually allocated to firms, and with the reduction of risk, regulation may make access to capital easier. Regulation may alter the organization's relationships with suppliers and customers. One theory of why the railroads were interested in the creation of the Interstate Commerce Commission (ICC) in 1887 was that large users were continually demanding and winning discriminatory rate reductions, disturbing the price stability of railroad price fixing cartels. By forbidding price discrimination and enforcing this regulation, the ICC strengthened the railroads' position with respect to large customers (MacAvoy, 1965).

Political Activity

Regulation is only one specific form of organizational activity in governmental processes. Business attempts to affect competition through the operation of the tariff laws date back to the 1700's (Bauer et al., 1968). Epstein (1969) provided one of the more complete summaries of the history of corporate involvement in politics and the inevitability of such action. The government has the power of coercion, possessed legally by no other social institution. Furthermore, legislation and regulation affect most of our economic institutions and markets, either indirectly through taxation, or more directly through purchasing, market protection or market creation. For example, taxes on margarine only recently came to an end. Federal taxes, imposed in 1886 as a protectionist measure for dairy interests, were removed in 1950, but a law outlawing the sale of oleo in its colored form lasted until 1967 in Wisconsin.

As with regulation, political activities carry both benefits and risks. The risk arises because once government intervention in an issue on behalf of a firm or industry is sought, then political intervention becomes legitimated, regardless of whose interests are helped or hurt. The firm that seeks favorable tax legislation runs the risk of creating a setting in which it is equally legitimate to be exposed to very unfavorable legislation. After an issue is opened to government intervention, neither side will find it easy to claim that further government action is illegitimate.

In learning to cope with a particular institutional environment, the firm may be unprepared for new uncertainties caused by the change of fundamental institutional relationships, including the opening of price competition, new entry and the lack of protection from overseas competition.

CONCLUSION

. . . Considering its probable importance to the firm, the institutional function of management has received much less concern than it warrants. It is time that this aspect of management receives the systematic attention long reserved for motiva-

tional and productivity problems associated with relationships between management and workers.

• WHO SHOULD CONTROL THE CORPORATION?*

BY HENRY MINTZBERG

Who should control the corporation? How? And for the pursuit of what goals? Historically, the corporation was controlled by its owners—through direct control of
the managers if not through direct management—for the pursuit of economic
goals. But as shareholding became dispersed, owner control weakened; and as the
corporation grew to very large size, its economic actions came to have increasing
social consequences. The giant, widely held corporation came increasingly under
the implicit control of its managers, and the concept of social responsibility—the
voluntary consideration of public social goals alongside the private economic ones
—arose to provide a basis of legitimacy for their actions.

To some, including those closest to the managers themselves, this was accepted as a satisfactory arrangement for the large corporation. "Trust it" to the
goodwill of the managers was their credo; these people will be able to achieve an
appropriate balance between social and economic goals.

But others viewed this basis of control as fundamentally illegitimate. The corporation was too large, too influential, its actions too pervasive to be left free of the
direct and concerted influence of outsiders. At the extreme were those who believed that legitimacy could be achieved only by subjecting managerial authority to
formal and direct external control. "Nationalize it," said those at one end of the
political spectrum, to put ultimate control in the hands of the government so that
it will pursue public social goals. No, said those at the other end, "restore it" to direct shareholder control, so that it will not waiver from the pursuit of private economic goals.

Other people took less extreme positions. "Democratize it" became the rally-
ing cry for some, to open up the governance of the large, widely held corporation
to a variety of affected groups—if not the workers, then the customers, or conservation interests, or minorities. "Regulate it" was also a popular position, with its
implicit premise that only by sharing their control with government would the corporation's managers attend to certain social goals. Then there were those who accepted direct management control so long as it was tempered by other, less formal
types of influence. "Pressure it," said a generation of social activists, to ensure that
social goals are taken into consideration. But others argued that because the corporation is an economic instrument, you must "induce it" by providing economic
incentives to encourage the resolution of social problems.

Finally, there were those who argued that this whole debate was unnecessary,
that a kind of invisible hand ensures that the economic corporation acts in a socially responsible manner. "Ignore it" was their implicit conclusion.

This article is written to clarify what has become a major debate of our era,
the major debate revolving around the private sector: Who should control the corporation, specifically the large, widely held corporation, how, and for the pursuit of

* Originally published in the *California Management Review* (Fall 1984), pp. 90–115, based on a section of Henry
Mintzberg, *Power in and Around Organizations* (Prentice-Hall, 1983). Copyright © 1984 by The Regents of the University of California. Reprinted with deletions by permission of The Regents.

what goals? The answers that are eventually accepted will determine what kind of society we and our children shall live in. . . .

As implied earlier, the various positions of who should control the corporation, and how, can be laid out along a political spectrum, from nationalization at one end to the restoration of shareholder power at the other. From the managerial perspective, however, those two extremes are not so far apart. Both call for direct control of the corporation's managers by specific outsiders, in one case the government to ensure the pursuit of social goals, in the other case the shareholders to ensure the pursuit of economic ones. It is the moderate positions—notably, trusting the corporation to the social responsibility of its managers—that are farthest from the extremes. Hence, we can fold our spectrum around so that it takes the shape of a horseshoe.

Figure 1 shows our "conceptual horseshoe," with "nationalize it" and "restore it" at the two ends. "Trust it" is at the center, because it postulates a natural balance of social and economic goals. "Democratize it," "regulate it," and "pressure it" are shown on the left side of the horseshoe, because all seek to temper economic goals with social ones. "Induce it" and "ignore it," both of which favor the exclusive pursuit of economic goals, are shown on the right side.

This conceptual horseshoe provides a basic framework to help clarify the issues in this important debate. We begin by discussing each of these positions in turn, circling the horseshoe from left to right. Finding that each (with one exception) has a logical context, we conclude—in keeping with our managerial perspective—that they should be thought of as forming a portfolio from which society can draw to deal with the issue of who should control the corporation and how.

FIGURE 1
The Conceptual Horseshoe

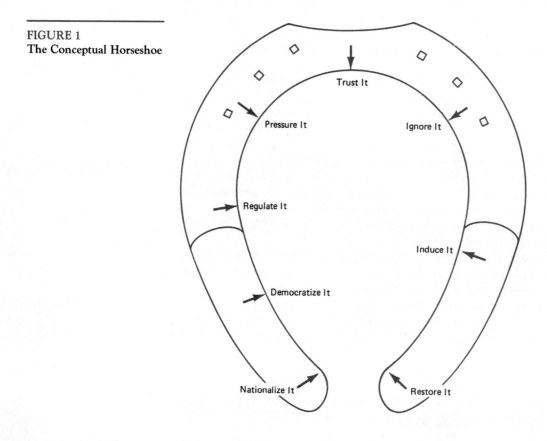

Nationalization of the corporation is a taboo subject in the United States—in general, but not in particular. Whenever a major corporation runs into serious difficulty (i.e., faces bankruptcy with possible loss of many jobs), massive government intervention, often including direct nationalization, inevitably comes up as an option. This option has been exercised: U.S. travelers now ride on Amtrak; Tennessee residents have for years been getting their power from a government utility; indeed, the Post Office was once a private enterprise. Other nations have, of course, been much more ambitious in this regard.

From a managerial and organizational perspective, the question is not whether nationalization is legitimate, but whether it works—at least in particular, limited circumstances. As a response to concerns about the social responsibility of large corporations, the answer seems to be no. The evidence suggests that social difficulties arise more from the size of an organization and its degree of bureaucratization than from its form of ownership (Epstein, 1977; Jenkins, 1976). On the other hand, contrary to popular belief in the United States, nationalization does not necessarily harm economic efficiency. Over the years, Renault has been one of the most successful automobile companies outside Japan; it was nationalized by the French government shortly after World War II. . . . When people believe that government ownership leads to interference, politicization, and inefficiency, that may be exactly what happens. However, when they believe that nationalization *has* to work, then state-owned enterprises may be able to attract the very best talent in the country and thereby work well.

But economic efficiency is no reason to favor nationalization any more than is concern about social responsibility. Nationalization does, however, seem to make sense in at least two particular circumstances. The first is when a mission deemed necessary in a society will not be provided adequately by the private sector. That is presumably why America has its Amtrak [and why Third World nations often create state enterprises]. . . . The second is when the activities of an organization must be so intricately tied to government policy that it is best managed as a direct arm of the state. The Canadian government created Petrocan to act as a "window" and a source of expertise on the sensitive oil industry.

Thus, it is not rhetoric but requirement that should determine the role of this position as a solution to who should control the corporation. "Nationalize it" should certainly not be embraced as a panacea, but neither should it be rejected as totally inapplicable.

"DEMOCRATIZE IT"

A less extreme position—at least in the context of the American debate—is one that calls for formal devices to broaden the governance of the corporation. The proponents of this position either accept the legal fiction of shareholder control and argue that the corporation's power base is too narrow, or else they respond to the emergent reality and question the legitimacy of managerial control. Why, they ask, do stockholders or self-selected managers have any greater right to control the profound decisions of these major institutions than do workers or customers or the neighbors downstream.

This stand is not to be confused with what is known as "participative management." The call to "democratize it" is a legal, rather than ethical one and is based on power, not generosity. Management is not asked to share its power voluntarily; rather, that power is to be reallocated constitutionally. That makes this position a fundamental and important one, *especially* in the United States with its strong tradition of pluralist control of its institutions.

The debate over democratization of the corporation has been confusing in part because many of the proposals have been so vague. We can bring some order to it by considering, in organizational terms, two basic means of democratization and two basic constituencies that can be involved. As shown in Figure 2, they suggest four possible forms of corporate democracy. One means is through the election of representatives to the board of directors, which we call *representative democracy.* The other is through formal but direct involvement in internal decision making processes, which we call *participatory democracy.* Either can focus on the *workers* ... or else on a host of outside interest groups, the latter giving rise to a *pluralistic* form of democracy. These are basic forms of corporate democracy in theory. With one exception, they have hardly been approached—let alone achieved—in practice. But they suggest where the "democratize it" debate may be headed.

The European debate has focused on worker representative democracy. This has, in some sense, been achieved in Yugoslavia, where the workers of all but the smallest firms elect the members of what is the equivalent of the American board of directors. In Germany, under the so-called *Mitbestimmung* ("codetermination"), the workers and the shareholders each elect half of the directors.

The evidence on this form of corporate democracy has been consistent, and it supports neither its proponents nor its detractors. Workers representation on the board seems to make relatively little difference one way or the other. The worker representatives concern themselves with wage and welfare issues but leave most other questions to management. Worker-controlled firms (not unlike the state-owned ones) appear to be no more socially responsible than private ones....

On the other hand, worker representative democracy may have certain positive benefits. German Chancellor Helmut Schmidt is reported to have said that "the key to [his] country's postwar economic miracle was its sophisticated system of workers' participation" (in Garson, 1977:63). While no one can prove this statement, codetermination certainly does not seem to have done the German economy much harm. By providing an aura of legitimacy to the German corporation and by involving the workers (at least officially) in its governance, codetermination may perhaps have enhanced the spirit of enterprise in Germany (while having little real effect on how decisions are actually made). More significantly, codetermination may have fostered greater understanding and cooperation between the managers and the union members who fill most of the worker seats on the boards....

... the embryonic debate over representative democracy in the United States

FIGURE 2
Four Basic Forms of Corporate Democracy

		GROUPS INVOLVED	
		Internal Employees	External Interest Groups
FOCUS OF ATTENTION	Board of Directors	Worker Representative Democracy (European style, e.g., "co-determination" or worker ownership)	Pluralistic Representative Democracy (American style, e.g., "public interest" directors)
	Internal Decision-Making Process	Worker Participatory Democracy (e.g., works councils)	Pluralistic Participatory Democracy (e.g., outsiders on new product committees)

has shown signs of moving in a different direction. Consistent with the tradition of pluralism in America's democratic institutions, there has been increasing pressure to elect outside directors who represent a wide variety of special interest groups— that is, consumers, minorities, environmentalists, and so on. . . .

Critics . . . have pointed out the problems of defining constituencies and finding the means to hold elections. "One-person, one-vote" may be easily applied to electing representatives of the workers, but no such simple rule can be found in the case of the consumer or environmental representatives, let alone ones of the "public interest." Yet it is amazing how quickly things become workable in the United States when Americans decide to put their collective mind to it. Indeed, the one case of public directors that I came across is telling in this regard. According to a Conference Board report, the selection by the Chief Justice of the Supreme Court of New Jersey of 6 of the 24 members of the board of Prudential Insurance as public directors has been found by the company to be "quite workable" (Bacon and Brown, 1975:48). . . . [Note—see the associated box on "The Power of the Board."]

THE POWER OF THE BOARD

Proposals for representative democracy, indeed those for nationalization and the restoration of shareholder control as well, rest on assumptions about the power of the board of directors. It may, therefore, be worth considering at this point the roles that boards of directors play in organizations and the board's resulting powers.

In law, traditionally, the business of a corporation was to be "managed" by its board. But of course, the board does no such thing. Managers manage, although some may happen to sit on the board. What, then, are the roles of the board, particularly of its "outside" directors?

The most tangible role of the board, and clearly provided for in law, is to name, and of course to dismiss as well, the chief executive officer, that person who in turn names the rest of the management. A second role may be to exercise direct control during periods of crisis, for example when the management has failed to provide leadership. And a third is to review the major decisions of the management as well as its overall performance.

These three constitute the board's roles of control, in principal at least because there is no shortage of evidence that boards have difficulty doing even these effectively, especially outside directors. Their job is, after all, part-time, and in a brief meeting once in a while they face a complex organization led by a highly organized management that deals with it every day. The result is that board control tends to reduce to naming and replacing the chief executive, and that person's knowledge of that fact, nothing more. Indeed, even that power is circumscribed, because a management cannot be replaced very often. In a sense, the board is like a bee hovering near a person picking flowers. The person must proceed carefully, so as not to provoke the bee, but can proceed with the task. But if the bee does happen to be provoked, it only gets to sting once. Thus many boards try to know only enough to know when the management is not doing its job properly, so that they can replace it.

But if boards tend to be weaker than expected in exercising *control over* the organization, they also tend perhaps to be stronger than expected in providing *service to* the organization. Here board membership plays at least four other roles. First, it "co-opts" influential outsiders: The organization uses the status of a seat on its board to gain the support of people important to it (as in the case of the big donors who sit on university boards). Second, board membership may be used to establish contacts for the organization (as when retired military officers sit on the boards of weapons manufacturing firms). This may be done to help in such things as the securing of contracts and the raising of funds. Third, seats on the board can be used to enhance an organization's reputation (as when an astronaut or some other type of celebrity is given a seat). And fourth, the board can be used to provide advice for the organization (as in the case of many of the bankers and lawyers who sit on the boards of corporations).

How much do boards serve organizations, and how much do they control them? Some boards do, of course, exercise control, particularly when their members represent a well-defined constituency, such as the substantial owner of a corporation. But, as noted, this tends to be a loose control at best. And other boards hardly do even that, especially when their constituencies are widely dispersed.

To represent everyone is ultimately to represent no one, especially when faced with a highly organized management that knows exactly what it wants. (Or from the elector's point of view, having some distant representative sitting on a board somewhere hardly brings him or her closer to control over the things that impinge on daily life—the work performed, the products consumed, the rivers polluted.) In corporations, this has been shown to be true of the directors who represent many small shareholders no less than those who represent many workers or many customers, perhaps even those who represent government, since that can be just a confusing array of pressure groups. These boards become, at best, tools of the organization, providing it with the variety of the services discussed above, at worst mere façades of formal authority.

Despite its problems, representative democracy is crystal clear compared with participatory democracy. What the French call "autogestion" (as opposed to "cogestion," or codetermination) seems to describe a kind of bottom-up, grassroots democracy in which the workers participate directly in decision making (instead of overseeing management's decisions from the board of directors) and also elect their own managers (who then become more administrators than bosses). Yet such proposals are inevitably vague, and I have heard of no large mass production or mass service firm—not even one owned by workers or a union—that comes close to this. . . .

What has impeded worker participatory democracy? In my opinion, something rather obvious has stood in its way; namely, the structure required by the very organizations in which the attempts have been made to apply it. Worker participatory democracy—and worker representative democracy too, for that matter —has been attempted primarily in organizations containing large numbers of workers who do highly routine, rather unskilled jobs that are typical of most mass production and service—what I have elsewhere called Machine Bureaucracies. The overriding requirement in Machine Bureaucracy is for tight coordination, the kind that can only be achieved by central administrators. For example, the myriad of decisions associated with producing an automobile at Volvo's Kalmar works in Sweden cannot be made by autonomous groups, each doing as it pleases. The whole car must fit together in a particular way at the end of the assembly process. These decisions require a highly sophisticated system of bureaucratic coordination. That is why automobile companies are structured into rigid hierarchies of authority. . . .

Participatory democracy *is* approached in other kinds of organizations . . . the autonomous professional institutions such as universities and hospitals, which have very different needs for central coordination. . . . But the proponents of democracy in organizations are not lobbying for changes in hospitals or universities. It is the giant mass producers they are after, and unless the operating work in these corporations becomes largely skilled and professional in nature, nothing approaching participative democracy can be expected.

In principal, the pluralistic form of participatory democracy means that a variety of groups external to the corporation can somehow control its decision-making processes directly. In practice, of course, this concept is even more elusive than the worker form of participatory democracy. To fully open up the internal decision-making processes of the corporation to outsiders would mean chaos. Yet certain very limited forms of outside participation would seem to be not only feasible but perhaps even desirable. . . . Imagine telephone company executives resolving rate conflicts with consumer groups in quiet offices instead of having to face them in noisy public hearings.

To conclude, corporate democracy—whether representative or participatory in form—may be an elusive and difficult concept, but it cannot be dismissed. It is not just another social issue, like conservation or equal opportunity, but one that strikes at the most fundamental of values. Ours has become a society of organizations. Democracy will have decreasing meaning to most citizens if it cannot be extended beyond political and judicial processes to those institutions that impinge upon them in their daily lives—as workers, as consumers, as neighbors. This is why we shall be hearing a great deal more of "democratize it."

"REGULATE IT"

In theory, regulating the corporation is about as simple as democratizing it is complex. In practice, it is, of course, another matter. To the proponents of "regulate it," the corporation can be made responsive to social needs by having its actions subjected to the controls of a higher authority—typically government, in the form of a regulatory agency or legislation backed up by the courts. Under regulation, constraints are imposed externally on the corporation while its internal governance is left to its managers.

Regulation of business is at least as old as the Code of Hammurabi. In America, it has tended to come in waves. . . .

To some, regulation is a clumsy instrument that should never be relied upon; to others, it is a panacea for the problems of social responsibility. At best, regulation sets minimum and usually crude standards of acceptable behavior; when it works, it does not make any firm socially responsible so much as stop some from being grossly irresponsible. Because it is inflexible, regulation tends to be applied slowly and conservatively, usually lagging public sentiment. Regulation often does not work because of difficulties in enforcement. The problems of the regulatory agencies are legendary—limited resources and information compared with the industries they are supposed to regulate, the cooptation of the regulators by industries, and so on. When applied indiscriminately, regulation either fails dramatically or else succeeds and creates havoc.

Yet there are obvious places for regulation. A prime one is to control tangible "externalities"—costs incurred by corporations that are passed on to the public at large. When, for example, costly pollution or worker health problems can be attributed directly to a corporation, then there seems to be every reason to force it (and its customers) to incur these costs directly, or else to terminate the actions that generate them. Likewise, regulation may have a place where competition encourages the unscrupulous to pull all firms down to a base level of behavior, forcing even the well-intentioned manager to ignore the social consequences of his actions. Indeed, in such cases, the socially responsible behavior is to encourage sensible regulation. "Help us to help others," businessmen should be telling the government. . . .

Most discouraging, however, is Theodore Levitt's revelation some years ago that business has fought every piece of proposed regulatory or social legislation throughout this century, from the Child Labor Acts on up. In Levitt's opinion, much of that legislation has been good for business—dissolving the giant trusts, creating a more honest and effective stock market, and so on. Yet, "the computer is programmed to cry wolf" (Levitt, 1968:83). . . .

In summary, regulation is a clumsy instrument but not a useless one. Were the business community to take a more enlightened view of it, regulation could be applied more appropriately, and we would not need these periodic housecleanings to eliminate the excesses.

"PRESSURE IT"

"Pressure it" is designed to do what "regulate it" fails to do: provoke corporations to act beyond some base level of behavior, usually in an area that regulation misses entirely. Here, activists bring ad hoc campaigns of pressure to bear on one or a group of corporations to keep them responsive to the activists' interpretation of social needs. . . .

"Pressure it" is a distinctively American position. While Europeans debate the theories of nationalization and corporate democracy in their cafés, Americans read about the exploits of Ralph Nader et al. in their morning newspapers. Note that "pressure it," unlike "regulate it," implicitly accepts management's right to make the final decisions. Perhaps this is one reason why it is favored in America.

While less radical than the other positions so far discussed, "pressure it" has nevertheless proved far more effective in eliciting behavior sensitive to social needs . . . [activist groups] have pressured for everything from the dismemberment of diversified corporations to the development of day care centers. Of special note is the class action suit, which has opened up a whole new realm of corporate social issues. But the effective use of the pressure campaign has not been restricted to the traditional activist. President Kennedy used it to roll back U.S. Steel price increases in the early 1960s, and business leaders in Pittsburgh used it in the late 1940s by threatening to take their freight-haulage business elsewhere if the Pennsylvania Railroad did not replace its coal burning locomotives to help clean up their city's air.

"Pressure it" as a means to change corporate behavior is informal, flexible, and focused; hence, it has been highly successful. Yet it is irregular and ad hoc, with different pressure campaigns sometimes making contradictory demands on management. Compared to the positions to its right on the horseshoe, "pressure it," like the other positions to its left, is based on confrontation rather than cooperation.

To a large and vocal contingent, which parades under the banner of "social responsibility," the corporation has no need to act irresponsibly, and therefore there is no reason for it to either be nationalized by the state, democratized by its different constituencies, regulated by the government, or pressured by activists. This contingent believes that the corporation's leaders can be trusted to attend to social goals for their own sake, simply because it is the noble thing to do. (Once this position was known as *nobelesse oblige,* literally "nobility obliges.")

We call this position "trust it," or, more exactly, "trust the corporation to the goodwill of its managers," although looking from the outside in, it might just as well be called "socialize it." We place it in the center of our conceptual horseshoe because it alone postulates a natural balance between social and economic goals—a balance which is to be attained in the heads (or perhaps the hearts) of responsible businessmen. And, as a not necessarily incidental consequence, power can be left in the hands of the managers; the corporation can be trusted to those who reconcile social and economic goals.

The attacks on social responsibility, from the right as well as the left, boil down to whether corporate managers should be trusted when they claim to pursue social goals; if so, whether they are capable of pursuing such goals; and finally, whether they have any right to pursue such goals.

The simplest attack is that social responsibility is all rhetoric, no action. E. F. Cheit refers to the "Gospel of Social Responsibility" as "designed to justify the power of managers over an ownerless system" (1964:172). . . .

Others argue that businessmen lack the personal capabilities required to pursue social goals. Levitt claims that the professional manager reaches the top of the hierarchy by dedication to his firm and his industry; as a result, his knowledge of social issues is highly restricted (Levitt, 1968:83). Others argue that an orientation to efficiency renders business leaders inadept at handling complex social problems (which require flexibility and political finesse, and sometimes involve solutions that are uneconomic). . . .

The most far reaching criticism is that businessmen have no right to pursue social goals. "Who authorized them to do that?" asks Braybrooke (1967:224), attacking from the left. What business have they—self-selected or at best appointed by shareholders—to impose *their* interpretation of the public good on society. Let the elected politicians, directly responsible to the population, look after the social goals.

But this attack comes from the right, too. Milton Friedman writes that social responsibility amounts to spending other people's money—if not that of shareholders, then of customers or employees. Drawing on all the pejorative terms of right-wing ideology, Friedman concludes that social responsibility is a "fundamentally subversive doctrine," representing "pure and unadulterated socialism," supported by businessmen who are "unwitting puppets of the intellectual forces that have been undermining the basis of a free society these past decades." To Friedman, "there is one and only one social responsibility of business—to use its resources and engage in activities designed to increase its profits so long as it stays within the rules of the game" (1970). Let businessmen, in other words, stick to their own business, which is business itself.

The empirical evidence on social responsibility is hardly more encouraging. Brenner and Molander, comparing their 1977 survey of *Harvard Business Review* readers with one conducted fifteen years earlier, concluded that the "respondents are somewhat more cynical about the ethical conduct of their peers" than they were previously (1977:59). Close to half the respondents agreed with the statement that "the American business executive tends not to apply the great ethical laws immediately to work. He is preoccupied chiefly with gain" (p. 62). Only 5% listed social responsibility as a factor "influencing ethical standards" whereas 31% and 20% listed different factors related to pressure campaigns and 10% listed regulation. . . .

The modern corporation has been described as a rational, amoral institution —its professional managers "hired guns" who pursue "efficiently" any goals asked of them. The problem is that efficiency really means measurable efficiency, so that the guns load only with goals that can be quantified. Social goals, unlike economic ones, just don't lend themselves to quantification. As a result, the performance control systems—on which modern corporations so heavily depend—tend to drive out social goals in favor of economic ones (Ackerman, 1975). . . .

In the contemporary large corporation, professional amorality turns into economic morality. When the screws of the performance control systems are turned tight . . . economic morality can turn into social immorality. And it happens often: A *Fortune* writer found that "a surprising number of [big companies] have been involved in blatant illegalities" in the 1970s, at least 117 of 1,043 firms studied (Ross, 1980:57). . . .

How, then, is anyone to "trust it"?

The fact is that we have to trust it, for two reasons. First, the strategic decisions of large organizations inevitably involve social as well as economic consequences that are inextricably intertwined. The neat distinction between economic goals in the private sector and social goals in the public sector just doesn't hold up in practice. Every important decision of the large corporation—to introduce a new product line, to close an old plant, whatever—generates all kinds of social consequences. There is no such thing as purely economic decisions in big business. Only a conceptual ostrich, with his head deeply buried in the abstractions of economic theory, could possibly use the distinction between economic and social goals to dismiss social responsibility.

The second reason we have to "trust it" is that there is always some degree of discretion involved in corporate decision making, discretion to thwart social needs or to attend to them. Things could be a lot better in today's corporation, but they could also be an awful lot worse. It is primarily our ethics that keep us where we are. If the performance control systems favored by diversified corporations cut too deeply into our ethical standards, then our choice is clear; to reduce these standards or call into question the whole trend toward diversification.

To dismiss social responsibility is to allow corporate behavior to drop to the lowest level, propped up only by external controls such as regulation and pressure campaigns. Solzhenitsyn, who has experienced the natural conclusion of unrestrained bureaucratization, warns us (in sharp contrast to Friedman) that "a society with no other scale but the legal one is not quite worthy of man. . . . A society which is based on the letter of the law and never reaches any higher is scarcely taking advantage of the high level of human possibilities" (1978:B1).

This is not to suggest that we must trust it completely. We certainly cannot trust it unconditionally by accepting the claim popular in some quarters that only business can solve the social ills of society. Business has no business using its resources without constraint in the social sphere—whether to support political candidates or to dictate implicitly through donations how nonprofit institutions should allocate their efforts. But where business is inherently involved, where its decisions have social consequences, that is where social responsibility has a role to play: where business creates externalities that cannot be measured and attributed to it (in other words, where regulation is ineffective); where regulation would work if only business would cooperate with it; where the corporation can fool its customers, or suppliers, or government through superior knowledge; where useful products can be marketed instead of wasteful or destructive ones. In other words, we have to realize that in many spheres we must trust it, or at least socialize it (and perhaps change it) so that we can trust it. Without responsible and ethical people in important places, our society is not worth very much.

225

DEALING WITH POWER

"IGNORE IT"

"Ignore it" differs from the other positions on the horseshoe in that explicitly or implicitly it calls for no change in corporate behavior. It assumes that social needs are met in the course of pursuing economic goals. We include this position in our horseshoe because it is held by many influential people and also because its validity would preempt support for the other positions. We must, therefore, investigate it alongside the others.

It should be noted at the outset the "ignore it" is not the same position as "trust it." In the latter, to be good is the right thing to do; in the present case, "it pays to be good." The distinction is subtle but important, for now it is economics, not ethics, that elicits the desired behavior. One need not strive to be ethical; economic forces will ensure that social needs fall conveniently into place. Here we have moved one notch to the right on our horseshoe, into the realm where the economic goals dominate. . . .

"Ignore it" is sometimes referred to as "enlightened self-interest," although some of its proponents are more enlightened than others. Many a true believer in social responsibility has used the argument that it pays to be good to ward off the attacks from the right that corporations have no business pursuing social goals. Even Milton Friedman must admit that they have every right to do so if it pays them economically. The danger of such arguments, however—and a prime reason "ignore it" differs from "trust it"—is that they tend to support the status quo: corporations need not change their behavior because it already pays to be good.

Sometimes the case for "ignore it" is made in terms of corporations at large, that the whole business community will benefit from socially responsible behavior. Other times the case is made in terms of the individual corporation, that it will benefit directly from its own socially responsible actions. . . . Others make the case for "ignore it" in "social investment" terms, claiming that socially responsible behavior pays off in a better image for the firm, a more positive relationship with customers, and ultimately a healthier and more stable society in which to do business.

Then, there is what I like to call the "them" argument: "If we're not good, *they* will move in"—"they" being Ralph Nader, the government, whoever. In other words, "Be good or else." The trouble with this argument is that by reducing social responsibility to simply a political tool for sustaining managerial control of the corporation in the face of outside threats, it tends to encourage general pronouncements instead of concrete actions (unless of course, "they" actually deliver with pressure campaigns). . . .

The "ignore it" position rests on some shaky ground. It seems to encourage average behavior at best; and where the average does not seem to be good enough, it encourages the status quo. In fact, ironically, "ignore it" makes a strong case for "pressure it," since the whole argument collapses in the absence of pressure campaigns. Thus while many influential people take this position, we question whether in the realities of corporate behavior it can really stand alone.

Continuing around to the right, our next position drops all concern with social responsibility per se and argues, simply, "pay it to be good," or, from the corporation's point of view, "be good only where it pays." Here, the corporation does not actively pursue social goals at all, whether as ends in themselves or as means to economic ends. Rather, it undertakes socially desirable programs only when induced economically to do so—usually through government incentives. If society wishes to clean up urban blight, then let its government provide subsidies for corporations that renovate buildings; if pollution is the problem, then let corporations be rewarded for reducing it.

"Induce it" faces "regulate it" on the opposite side of the horseshoe for good reason. While one penalizes the corporation for what it does do, the other rewards it for doing what it might not otherwise do. Hence these two positions can be direct substitutes: pollution can be alleviated by introducing penalties for the damage done or by offering incentives for the improvements rendered.

Logic would, however, dictate a specific role for each of these positions. Where a corporation is doing society a specific, attributable harm—as in the case of pollution—then paying it to stop hardly seems to make a lot of sense. If society does not wish to outlaw the harmful behavior altogether, then surely it must charge those responsible for it—the corporation and, ultimately, its customers. Offering financial incentives to stop causing harm would be to invite a kind of blackmail—for example, encouraging corporations to pollute so as to get paid to stop. And every citizen would be charged for the harm done by only a few.

On the other hand, where social problems exist which cannot be attributed to specific corporations, yet require the skills of certain corporations for solution, then financial incentives clearly make sense (so long, of course, as solutions can be clearly defined and tied to tangible economic rewards). Here, and not under "trust it," is where the "only business can do it" argument belongs. When it is true that only business can do it (and business has not done it to us in the first place), then business should be encouraged to do it. . . .

"RESTORE IT"

Our last position on the horseshoe tends to be highly ideological, the first since "democratize it" to seek a fundamental change in the governance and the goals of the corporation. Like the proponents of "nationalize it," those of this position believe that managerial control is illegitimate and must be replaced by a more valid form of external control. The corporation should be restored to its former status, that is, returned to its "rightful" owners, the shareholders. The only way to ensure the relentless pursuit of economic goals—and that means the maximization of profit, free of the "subversive doctrine" of social responsibility—is to put control directly into the hands of those to whom profit means the most.

A few years ago this may have seemed to be an obsolete position. But thanks to its patron saint Milton Friedman . . . , it has recently come into prominence. Also, other forms of restoring it, including the "small is beautiful" theme, have also become popular in recent years.

Friedman has written,

In a free-enterprise, private-property system, a corporate executive is an employee of the owners of the business. He has direct responsibility to his employers. That responsibility is to conduct the business in accordance with their desires, which generally will be to make as much money as possible while conforming to the basic rules of the society, both those embodied in law and those embodied in ethical custom. (1970:33)

Interestingly, what seems to drive Friedman is a belief that the shift over the course of this century from owner to manager control, with its concerns about social responsibility, represents an unstoppable skid around our horseshoe. In the opening chapter of his book *Capitalism and Freedom,* Friedman seems to accept only two possibilities—traditional capitalism and socialism as practiced in Eastern Europe. The absence of the former must inevitably lead to the latter:

> The preservation and expansion of freedom are today threatened from two directions. The one threat is obvious and clear. It is the external threat coming from the evil men in the Kremlin who promised to bury us. The other threat is far more subtle. It is the internal threat coming from men of good intentions and good will who wish to reform us. (1962:20)

The problem of who should control the corporation thus reduces to a war between two ideologies—in Friedman's terms, "subversive" socialism and "free" enterprise. In this world of black and white, there can be no middle ground, no moderate position between the black of "nationalize it" and the white of "restore it," none of the gray of "trust it." Either the owners will control the corporation of else the government will. Hence: " 'restore it' or else." Anchor the corporation on the right side of the horseshoe, Friedman seems to be telling us, the only place where "free" enterprise and "freedom" are safe.

All of this, in my view, rests on a series of assumptions—technical, economic, and political—which contain a number of fallacies. First is the fallacy of the technical assumption of shareholder control. Every trend in ownership during this century seems to refute the assumption that small shareholders are either willing or able to control the large, widely held corporation. The one place where free markets clearly still exist is in stock ownership, and that has served to detach ownership from control. When power is widely dispersed—among stockholders no less than workers or customers—those who share it tend to remain passive. It pays no one of them to invest the effort to exercise their power. Hence, even if serious shareholders did control the boards of widely held corporations (and one survey of all the directors of the *Fortune* 500 in 1977 found that only 1.6% of them represented significant shareholder interests, [Smith, 1978]), the question remains open as to whether they would actually try to control the management. (This is obviously not true of closely held corporations, but these—probably a decreasing minority of the *Fortune* 500—are "restored" in any event.)

The economic assumptions of free markets have been discussed at length in the literature. Whether there exists vibrant competition, unlimited entry, open information, consumer sovereignty, and labor mobility is debatable. Less debatable is the conclusion that the larger the corporation, the greater is its ability to interfere with these processes. The issues we are discussing center on the giant corporation. It is not Luigi's Body Shop that Ralph Nader is after, but General Motors, a corporation that employs more than half a million people and earns greater revenues than many national governments.

Those who laid the foundation for conventional economic theory—such as Adam Smith and Alfred Marshall—never dreamed of the massive amounts now spent for advertising campaigns, most of them designed as much for affect as for effect; of the waves of conglomeration that have combined all kinds of diverse businesses into single corporate entities; of chemical complexes that cost more than a billion dollars; and of the intimate relationships that now exist between giant corporations and government, as customer and partner not to mention subsidizer. The concept of arm's length relationships in such conditions is, at best, nostalgic. What happens to consumer sovereignty when Ford knows more about its gas tanks than do its customers? And what does labor mobility mean in the presence of an inflexible pension plan, or commitment to a special skill, or a one-factory town? It is an ironic twist of conventional economic theory that the worker is the one who typically stays put, thus rendering false the assumption of labor mobility, while the shareholder is the mobile one, thus spoiling the case for owner control.

The political assumptions are more ideological in nature, although usually implicit. These assumptions are that the corporation is essentially amoral, society's instrument for producing goods and services, and, more broadly, that a society is "free" and "democratic" so long as its governmental leaders are elected by universal suffrage and do not interfere with the legal activities of businessmen. But many people—a large majority of the general public, if polls are to be believed—seem to subscribe to one or more assumptions that contradict these "free enterprise" assumptions.

One assumption is that the large corporation is a social and political institution as much as an economic instrument. Economic activities, as noted previously, produce all kinds of social consequences. Jobs get created and rivers get polluted, cities get built and workers get injured. These social consequences cannot be factored out of corporate strategic decisions and assigned to government.

Another assumption is that society cannot achieve the necessary balance between social and economic needs so long as the private sector attends only to economic goals. Given the pervasiveness of business in society, the acceptance of Freidman's prescriptions would drive us toward a one-dimensional society—a society that is too utilitarian and too materialistic. Economic morality, as noted earlier, can amount to a social immorality.

Finally, the question is asked: Why the owners? In a democratic society, what justifies owner control of the corporation any more than worker control, or consumer control, or pluralistic control? Ours is not Adam Smith's society of small proprietors and shopkeepers. His butcher, brewer, and baker have become Iowa Beef Packers, Anheuser-Bush, and ITT Continental Baking. What was once a case for individual democracy now becomes a case for oligarchy. . . .

I see Friedman's form of "restore it" as a rather quaint position in a society of giant corporations, managed economies, and dispersed shareholders—a society in which the collective power of corporations is coming under increasing scrutiny and in which the distribution between economic and social goals is being readdressed.

Of course, there are other ways [than Friedman's] to "restore it." "Divest it" could return the corporation to the business or central theme it knows best, restoring the role of allocating funds between different businesses to capital markets instead of central headquarters. Also, boards could be restored to positions of influence by holding directors legally responsible for their actions and by making them more independent of managers (for example, by providing them with personal staffs and by precluding full-time managers from their ranks, especially the position of chairman). We might even wish to extend use of "reduce it" where possible, to decrease the size of those corporations that have grown excessively large on the basis of market or political power rather than economies of scale, and perhaps to eliminate certain forms of vertical integration. In many cases it may prove advantageous, economically as well as socially, to have the corporation trade with its suppliers and customers instead of being allowed to ingest them indiscriminately.[1]

I personally doubt that these proposals could be any more easily realized in today's society than those of Friedman, even though I believe them to be more desirable. "Restore it" is the nostalgic position on our horseshoe, a return to our fantasies of a glorious past. In this society of giant organizations, it flies in the face of powerful economic and political forces.

CONCLUSION: IF THE SHOE FITS . . .

I believe that today's corporation cannot ride on any one position any more than a horse can ride on part of a shoe. In other words, we need to treat the conceptual horseshoe as a portfolio of positions from which we can draw, depending on circumstances. Exclusive reliance on one position will lead to a narrow and dogmatic society, with an excess concentration of power . . . the use of a variety of positions can encourage the pluralism I believe most of us feel is necessary to sustain democracy. If the shoe fits, then let the corporation wear it.

I do not mean to imply that the eight positions do not represent fundamentally different values and, in some cases, ideologies as well. Clearly they do. But I also believe that anyone who makes an honest assessment of the realities of power in and around today's large corporations must conclude that a variety of positions have to be relied upon [even if they themselves might tilt to the left, right or center of our horseshoe]. . . .

I tilt to the left of center, as has no doubt been obvious in my comments to this point. Let me summarize my own prescriptions as follows, and in the process provide some basis for evaluating the relevant roles of each of the eight positions.

First "trust it," or at least "socialize it." Despite my suspicions about much of the rhetoric that passes for social responsibility and the discouraging evidence about the behavior of large contemporary organizations (not only corporations), I remain firmly convinced that without honest and responsible people in important places, we are in deep trouble. We need to trust it because, no matter how much we rely on the other positions, managers will always retain a great deal of power. And that power necessarily has social no less than economic consequences. The positions on the right side of our horseshoe ignore these social consequences while some of those on the left fail to recognize the difficulties of influencing these consequences in large, hierarchical organizations. Sitting between these two sets of positions, managers can use their discretion to satisfy or to subvert the wishes of the public. Ultimately, what managers do is determined by their sense of responsibility as individual members of society.

Although we must "trust it," we cannot *only* "trust it." As I have argued, there is an appropriate and limited place for social responsibility—essentially to get the corporation's own house in order and to encourage it to act responsibly in its own sphere of operations. Beyond that, social responsibility needs to be tempered by other positions around our horseshoe.

Then "pressure it," ceaselessly. As we have seen, too many forces interfere with social responsibility. The best antidote to these forces is the ad hoc pressure campaign, designed to pinpoint unethical behavior and raise social consciousness

---

[1] A number of these proposals would be worthwhile to pursue in the public and parapublic sectors as well, to divide up overgrown hospitals, school systems, social service agencies, and all kinds of government departments.

about issues. The existence of the "pressure it" position is what most clearly distinguishes the western from the eastern "democracies." Give me one Ralph Nader to all those banks of government accountants.

In fact, "pressure it" underlies the success of most of the other positions. Pressure campaigns have brought about necessary new regulations and have highlighted the case for corporate democracy. As we have seen, the "ignore it" position collapses without "pressure it". . . .

After that, try to "democratize it." A somewhat distant third in my portfolio is "democratize it," a position I view as radical only in terms of the current U.S. debate, not in terms of fundamental American values. Democracy matters most where it affects us directly—in the water we drink, the jobs we perform, the products we consume. How can we call our society democratic when many of its most powerful institutions are closed to governance from the outside and are run as hierarchies of authority from within?

As noted earlier, I have no illusions about having found the means to achieve corporate democracy. But I do know that Americans can be very resourceful when they decide to resolve a problem—and this is a problem that badly needs resolving. Somehow, ways must be found to open the corporation up to the formal influence of the constituencies most affected by it—employees, customers, neighbors, and so on—without weakening it as an economic institution. At stake is nothing less than the maintenance of basic freedoms in our society.

Then, only where specifically appropriate, "regulate it" and "induce it." Facing each other on the horseshoe are two positions that have useful if limited roles to play. Regulation is neither a panacea nor a menace. It belongs where the corporation can abuse the power it has and can be penalized for that abuse—notably where externalities can be identified with specific corporations. Financial inducements belong, not where a corporation has created a problem, but where it has the capability to solve a problem created by someone else.

Occasionally, selectively, "nationalize it" and "restore it," but not in Friedman's way. The extreme positions should be reserved for extreme problems. If "pressure it" is a scalpel and "regulate it" a cleaver, then "nationalize it" and "restore it" are guillotines.

Both these positions are implicitly proposed as alternatives to "democratize it." One offers public control, the other "shareholder democracy." The trouble is that control by everyone often turns out to be control by no one, while control by the owners—even if attainable—would remove the corporation even further from the influence of those most influenced by it.

Yet, as noted earlier, nationalization sometimes makes sense—when private enterprise cannot provide a necessary mission, at least in a sufficient or appropriate way, and when the activities of a corporation must be intricately tied in to government policy.

As for "restore it," I believe Friedman's particular proposals will aggrevate the problems of political control and social responsibility, strengthening oligarchical tendencies in society and further tilting what I see as the current imbalance between social and economic goals. In response to Friedman's choice between "subversive" socialism and "free" enterprise, I say "a pox on both your houses." Let us concentrate our efforts on the intermediate positions around the horseshoe. However, other forms of "restore it" are worth considering—to "divest it" where diversification has interfered with capital markets, competition, and economic efficiency; to "*dis*integrate it" vertically where a trading network is preferable to a managerial hierarchy; to strengthen its board so that directors can assess managers objectively; and to "reduce it" where size represents a power game rather than a means to provide better and more efficient service to the public. I stand with Friedman in wishing to see competitive markets strengthened; it is just that I believe his proposals lead in exactly the opposite direction.

Finally, above all, don't "ignore it." I leave one position out of my portfolio altogether, because it contradicts the others. The one thing we must not do is ignore the large, widely held corporation. It is too influential a force in our lives. Our challenge is to find ways to distribute the power in and around our large organizations so that they will remain responsive, vital, and effective.

CONTEXT

THE ENTREPRENEURIAL CONTEXT

The text of this book really divides into two basic parts, although there are three sections. The first, encompassing Chapters 1 through 8 and Sections I and II, introduces a variety of important *concepts* of organizations—strategy, the strategist, process, structure, systems, culture, power. The second, beginning here with Section 3 and Chapter 9, considers how these concepts combine to form major *contexts* of organizations. In effect, a context is a type of situation wherein can be found particular structures, power relationships, processes, competitive settings, and so on.

Traditionally, policy and strategy textbooks divided themselves into two very different parts—a first on the "formulation" of strategy, a second on its "implementation" (including discussion of structure, systems, culture, etc.). As some of the readings of Chapter 5 have already made clear, we believe this is often a false dichotomy: in many situations (that is, contexts), formulation and implementation can be so intertwined that it makes no sense to separate them. To build a textbook around a questionable dichotomy likewise makes no sense to us, and so we have instead proceeded by introducing all the concepts related to the strategy process first and then considering the various ways in which they might interact in specific situations.

There is no "one best way" to manage the strategy process. The notion that there are several possible "good ways" however—various contexts appropriate to strategic management—was first developed in the Mintzberg reading in Chapter 6. In fact, his *configurations* of structure served as the basis for determining the set of contexts we include here. These are as follows:

We begin here in Chapter 9 with what seems to be the simplest context, certainly one that has had much good press in America since Horatio Alger first went into business—the *entrepreneurial* context. Here a single leader takes personal charge in a highly dynamic situation, as in a new firm or a small one operating in a growing market, or even sometimes in a large organization facing crisis.

We next consider in Chapter 10 a contrasting context that often dominates large business as well as big government. We label it the *mature* context, although it might equally be referred to as the stable context or the mass-production or mass-service context. Here rather formal structures combine with strategy-making processes that are heavily planning and technique oriented.

Third, we consider the context of the *diversified* organization, which has become increasingly important as waves of mergers have swept across various Western economies. Because product-market strategies are diversified, the structures tend to get divisionalized, and the focus of strategy shifts to two levels: the corporate or portfolio level and the divisional or business level.

Our fourth and fifth contexts are those of organizations largely dependent on specialists or experts. These contexts are called *professional* when the environment is stable, *innovation* when it is dynamic. Here responsibility for strategy making tends to diffuse throughout the organization, sometimes even lodging itself at the bottom of the hierarchy. The strategy process tends to become rather emergent in nature.

We complete our discussion of contexts with consideration of the problems of managing *change* from one of these contexts to another (often "cultural revolution") or from one major strategy and structure to another within a particular context.

In the chapter on each context, our intention was to include material that would describe all the basic concepts as they take shape in that context. We wished to describe the form of organizational structure and of strategic leadership found there, the nature of its strategy-making process, including its favored forms of strategy analysis and its most appropriate types of strategies (generic and otherwise), its natural power relationships and preferred culture, and the nature of its competition and industry structure as well as the social issues that surround it. Unfortunately, appropriate readings on all this are not available—in part we do not yet know all that we must about each context. But we believe that the readings that we have included in this section do cover a good deal of the ground, enough to give a real sense of each different context.

Before beginning, we should warn you of one danger in focusing this discussion on contexts such as these: it may make the world of organizations appear to be more pat and ordered than it really is. Many organizations certainly seem to fit one context or another, as numerous examples will make clear. But none ever does so quite perfectly—the world is too nuanced for that. And then there are the many organizations that do not fit any single context at all. We believe, and have included arguments in a concluding chapter to this section, that in fact the set of contexts altogether form a framework by which to understand better all kinds of organizations. But until we get there, you should bear in mind that much of this material caricatures reality as much as it mirrors it.

Of course, such caricaturing is a necessary part of formal learning: like the librarian's need for a cataloguing system to store books, we all need frameworks of categories in which to store the confusing set of experiences that the world throws at us. That is what theory is. Without it, we would simply be overwhelmed—and paralyzed. Managers, for example, would never get anything done if they could not use such simplified frameworks to comprehend their experiences in order to act on them. As we suggested in the introduction to this book, paraphrasing Keynes, the "practical" person who believes him or herself free of theory is simply the prisoner of some old theory buried deep in the subconscious mind. Moreover, as Miller and Mintzberg have argued in a paper called "The Case for Configuration," managers are attracted to a particular, well-defined context because that allows them to achieve a certain consistency and coherence in the design of their organization and so to facilitate its effective performance. Each context, as you will see, has its own logic, its own integrated way of dealing with its part of the world—that makes things more manageable.

This chapter of Section 3 discusses the entrepreneurial context. At least in its traditional form, this encompasses situations in which a single individual, typically with a clear and distinct vision of purpose, directs an organization that is structured to be as responsive as possible to his or her personal wishes. Strategy making thus revolves around a single brain, unconstrained by the forces of bureaucratic momentum.

Such entrepreneurship is typically found in young organizations, especially ones in new or emerging industries. Entrepreneurial vision tends to have a high potential payoff in these situations and may indeed be essential when there are long delays between the conception of an idea and its commercial success. In addition, in crisis situations a similar type of strong and visionary leadership may offer the only hope for successful turnaround. And it can thrive as well in highly fragmented industries, where small flexible organizations can move quickly into and out of specialized market niches, and so outmaneuver the big bureaucracies.

The word entrepreneurship has also been associated recently with change and innovation inside of larger, more bureaucratic organizations—sometimes under the label "intrapreneurship." In these situations, it is often not the boss, but someone in an odd corner of the organization—a "champion" for some technology or strategic issue—who takes on the entrepreneurial role. We believe, however, for reasons that will later become evident, that intrapreneurship better fits into our chapter on the innovation context.

To describe the structure that seems to be most logically associated with the traditional form of entrepreneurship, we open with material on the simple structure in Mintzberg's book *The Structuring of Organizations.* Combined with this is a discussion of strategy making in the entrepreneurial context, especially with regard to strategic vision, based on two sets of research projects carried out at McGill University. In one, the strategies of visionary leadership were studied through biographies and autobiographies; in the other, the strategies of entrepreneurial firms were tracked across several decades of their histories.

Then, to investigate the external situations that seem to be most commonly (although not exclusively) associated with the entrepreneurial context, we present excerpts from two chapters of Michael Porter's book *Competitive Strategy,* one on emerging industries, the other on fragmented industries.

A final reading of this chapter looks specifically at niche strategies, those most commonly associated with younger and smaller firms. Written by Cooper, Willard, and Woo of the Krannet Graduate School of Management at Purdue University, it "reexamines" this concept, suggesting some characteristics under which small and new firms can also compete directly with the larger bureaucracies.

• THE ENTREPRENEURIAL ORGANIZATION*

BY HENRY MINTZBERG

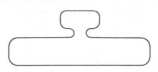

Consider an automobile dealership with a flamboyant owner, a brand-new government department, a corporation or even a nation run by an autocratic leader, or a school system in a state of crisis. In many respects, those are vastly different organizations. But the evidence suggests that they share a number of basic characteristics. They form a configuration we shall call the *entrepreneurial organization.*

THE BASIC STRUCTURE

The structure of the entrepreneurial organization is often very simple, characterized about all by what it is not: elaborated. As shown in the opening figure, typically it has little or no staff, a loose division of labor, and a small managerial hierarchy. Little of its activity is formalized, and it makes minimal use of planning procedures or training routines. In a sense, it is nonstructure; in my "structuring" book, I called it *simple structure.*

Power tends to focus on the chief executive, who exercises a high personal profile. Formal controls are discouraged as a threat to the chief's flexibility. He or she drives the organization by sheer force of personality or by more direct interventions. Under the leader's watchful eye, politics cannot easily arise. Should outsiders, such as particular customers or suppliers, seek to exert influence, such leaders are as likely as not to take the organizations to a less exposed niche in the marketplace.

Thus, it is not uncommon in small entrepreneurial organizations for everyone to report to the chief. Even in ones not so small, communication flows informally, much of it between the chief executive and others. As one group of McGill MBA students commented in their study of a small manufacturer of pumps: "It is not unusual to see the president of the company engaged in casual conversation with a machine shop mechanic. [That way he is] informed of a machine breakdown even before the shop superintendent is advised."

Decision making is likewise flexible, with a highly centralized power system allowing for rapid response. The creation of strategy is, of course, the responsibility of the chief executive, the process tending to be highly intuitive, often oriented to the aggressive search for opportunities. It is not surprising, therefore, that the re-

* Adapted from *The Structuring of Organizations* (Prentice Hall, 1979, Chap. 17 on "The Simple Structure"), *Power In and Around Organizations* (Prentice Hall, 1983, Chap. 20 on "The Autocracy"), and the material on strategy formation from "Visionary Leadership and Strategic Management," *Strategic Management Journal,* (1989, coauthored with Frances Westley); see also, "Tracking Strategy in an Entrepreneurial Firm," *Academy of Management Journal* (1982), and "Researching the Formation of Strategies: The History of a Canadian Lady, 1939–1976," in R. B. Lamb, ed., *Competitive Strategic Management* (Prentice Hall, 1984), the last two coauthored with James A. Waters. A chapter similar to this appeared in *Mintzberg on Management: Inside Our Strange World of Organizations* (Free Press, 1989).

sulting strategy tends to reflect the chief executive's implicit vision of the world, often an extrapolation of his or her own personality.

Handling disturbances and innovating in an entrepreneurial way are perhaps the most important aspects of the chief executive's work. In contrast, the more formal aspects of managerial work—figurehead duties, for example, receive less attention, as does the need to disseminate information and allocate resources internally, since knowledge and power remain at the top.

CONDITIONS OF THE ENTREPRENEURIAL ORGANIZATION

A centrist entrepreneurial configuration is fostered by an external context that is both simple and dynamic. Simpler environments (say, retailing food as opposed to designing computer systems) enable one person at the top to retain so much influence, while it is a dynamic environment that requires flexible structure, which in turn enables the organization to outmaneuver the bureaucracies. Entrepreneurial leaders are naturally attracted to such conditions.

The classic case of this is, of course, the entrepreneurial firm, where the leader is the owner. Entrepreneurs often found their own firms to escape the procedures and control of the bureaucracies where they previously worked. At the helm of their own enterprises, they continue to loathe the ways of bureaucracy, and the staff analysts that accompany them, and so they keep their organizations lean and flexible. Figure 1 shows the organigram for Steinberg's, a supermarket chain we shall be discussing shortly, during its most classically entrepreneurial years. Notice the identification of people above positions, the simplicity of the structure (the firm's sales by this time were on the order of $27 million), and the focus on the chief executive (not to mention the obvious family connections).

Entrepreneurial firms are often young and aggressive, continually searching for the risky markets that scare off the bigger bureaucracies. But they are also careful to avoid the complex markets, preferring to remain in niches that their leaders can comprehend. Their small size and focused strategies allow their structures to remain simple, so that the leaders can retain tight control and maneuver flexibly.

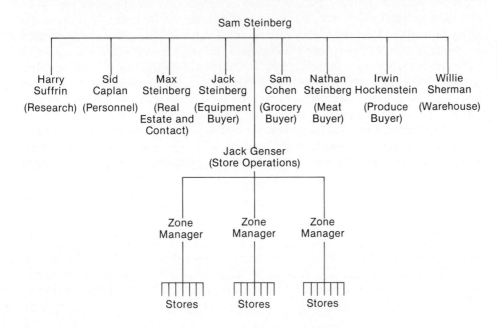

FIGURE 1
Organization of Steinberg's, an Entrepreneurial Firm (circa 1948)

Moreover, business entrepreneurs are often visionary, sometimes charismatic or autocratic as well (sometimes both, in sequence!). Of course, not all "entrepreneurs" are so aggressive or visionary; many settle down to pursue common strategies in small geographic niches. Labeled the *local producers,* these firms can include the corner restaurant, the town bakery, the regional supermarket chain.

But an organization need not be owned by an entrepreneur, indeed need not even operate in the profit sector, to adopt the configuration we call entrepreneurial. In fact, most new organizations seem to adopt this configuration, whatever their sector, because they generally have to rely on personalized leadership to get themselves going—to establish their basic direction, or *strategic vision,* to hire their first people and set up their initial procedures. Of course, strong leaders are likewise attracted to new organizations, where they can put their own stamp on things. Thus, we can conclude that most organizations in business, government, and not-for-profit areas pass through the entrepreneurial configuration in their formative years, during *start-up.*

Moreover, while new organizations that quickly grow large or that require specialized forms of expertise may make a relatively quick transition to another configuration, many others seem to remain in the entrepreneurial form, more or less, as long as their founding leaders remain in office. This reflects the fact that the structure has often been built around the personal needs and orientation of the leader and has been staffed with people loyal to him or her.

This last comment suggests that the personal power needs of a leader can also, by themselves, give rise to this configuration in an existing organization. When a chief executive hoards power and avoids or destroys the formalization of activity as an infringement on his or her right to rule by fiat, then an autocratic form of the entrepreneurial organization will tend to appear. This can been seen in the cult of personality of the leader, in business (the last days of Henry Ford) no less than in government (the leadership of Stalin in the Soviet Union). Charisma can have a similar effect, though different consequences, when the leader gains personal power not because he or she hoards it but because the followers lavish it on the leader.

The entrepreneurial configuration also tends to arise in any other type of organization that faces severe crisis. Backed up against a wall, with its survival at stake, an organization will typically turn to a strong leader for salvation. The structure thus becomes effectively (if not formally) simple, as the normal powers of existing groups—whether staff analysts, line managers, or professional operators, and so on, with their perhaps more standardized forms of control—are suspended to allow the chief to impose a new integrated vision through his or her personalized control. The leader may cut costs and expenses in an attempt to effect what is known in the strategic management literature as an *operating turnaround,* or else reconceive the basic product and service orientation, to achieve *strategic turnaround.* Of course, once the turnaround is realized, the organization may revert to its traditional operations, and, in the bargain, spew out its entrepreneurial leader, now viewed as an impediment to its smooth functioning.

STRATEGY FORMATION IN THE ENTREPRENEURIAL ORGANIZATION

How does strategy develop in the entrepreneurial organization? And what role does that mysterious concept known as "strategic vision" play? We know something of the entrepreneurial mode of strategy making, but less of strategic vision itself, since it is locked in the head of the individual. But some studies we have done at McGill do shed some light on both these questions. Let us consider strategic vision first.

Visionary Leadership

In a paper she coauthored with me, my McGill colleague Frances Westley contrasted two views of visionary leadership. One she likened to a hypodermic needle, in which the active ingredient (vision) is loaded into a syringe (words) which is injected into the employees to stimulate all kinds of energy. There is surely some truth to this, but Frances prefers another image, that of drama. Drawing from a book on theater by Peter Brook (1968), the legendary director of the Royal Shakespeare Company, she conceives strategic vision, like drama, as becoming magical in that moment when fiction and life blend together. In drama, this moment is the result of endless "rehearsal," the "performance" itself, and the "attendance" of the audience. But Brook prefers the more dynamic equivalent words in French, all of which have English meanings—"repetition," "representation," and "assistance." Frances likewise applies these words to strategic vision.

"Repetition" suggests that success comes from deep knowledge of the subject at hand. Just as Sir Laurence Olivier would repeat his lines again and again until he had trained his tongue muscles to say them effortlessly (Brook, p. 154), so too Lee Iococca "grew up" in the automobile business, going to Chrysler after Ford because cars were "in his blood" (Iococca, 1984:141). The visionary's inspiration stems not from luck, although chance encounters can play a role, but from endless experience in a particular context.

"Representation" means not just to perform but to make the past live again, giving it immediacy, vitality. To the strategist, that is vision articulated, in words and actions. What distinguishes visionary leaders is their profound ability with language, often in symbolic form, as metaphor. It is not just that they "see" things from a new perspective but that they get others to so see them.

Edwin Land, who built a great company around the Polaroid camera he invented, has written of the duty of "the inventor to build a new gestalt for the old one in the framework of society" (1975:50). He himself described photography as helping "to focus some aspect of [your] life"; as you look through the viewfinder, "it's not merely the camera you are focusing: you are focusing yourself . . . when you touch the button, what is inside of you comes out. It's the most basic form of creativity. Part of you is now permanent" (*Time*, 1972:84). Lofty words for 50 tourists filing out of a bus to record some pat scene, but powerful imagery for someone trying to build an organization to promote a novel camera. Steve Jobs, visionary (for a time) in his promotion, if not invention, of the personal computer, placed a grand piano and a BMW in Apple's central foyer, with the claim that "I believe people get great ideas from seeing great products" (in Wise, 1984:146).

"Assistance" means that the audience for drama, whether in the theater or in the organization, empowers the actor no less than the actor empowers the audience. Leaders become visionary because they appeal powerfully to specific constituencies at specific periods of time. That is why leaders once perceived as visionary can fall so dramatically from grace—a Steve Jobs, a Winston Churchill. Or to take a more dramatic example, here is how Albert Speer, arriving skeptical, reacted to the first lecture he heard by his future leader: "Hitler no longer seemed to be speaking to convince; rather, he seemed to feel that he was experiencing what the audience, by now transformed into a single mass, expected of him" (1970:16).

Of course, management is not theater; the leader who becomes a stage actor, playing a part he or she does not live, is destined to fall from grace. It is integrity—a genuine feeling behind what the leader says and does—that makes leadership truly visionary, and that is what makes impossible the transition of such leadership into any formula.

This visionary leadership is style and strategy, coupled together. It is drama, but not playacting. The strategic visionary is born and made, the product of a historical moment. Brook closes his book with the following quotation:

> In everyday life, "if" is a fiction, in the theatre "if" is an experiment.
> In everyday life, "if" is an evasion, in the theatre "if" is the truth.
> When we are persuaded to believe in this truth, then the theatre and life are one.
> This is a high aim. It sounds like hard work.
> To play needs much work. But when we experience the work as play, then it is not work any more.
> A play is play. (p. 157)

In the entrepreneurial organization, at best, "theater," namely strategic vision, becomes one with "life," namely organization. That way leadership creates drama; it turns work into play.

Let us now consider the entrepreneurial approach to strategy formation in terms of two specific studies we have done, one of a supermarket chain, the other of a manufacturer of women's undergarments.

The Entrepreneurial Approach to Strategy Formation in a Supermarket Chain

Steinberg's is a Canadian retail chain that began with a tiny food store in Montreal in 1917 and grew to sales in the billion-dollar range during the almost 60-year reign of its leader. Most of that growth came from supermarket operations. In many ways, Steinberg's fits the entrepreneurial model rather well. Sam Steinberg, who joined his mother in the first store at the age of 11 and personally made a quick decision to expand it 2 years later, maintained complete formal control of the firm (including every single voting share) to the day of his death in 1978. He also exercised close managerial control over all its major decisions, at least until the firm began to diversify after 1960, primarily into other forms of retailing.

It has been popular to describe the "bold stroke" of the entrepreneur (Cole, 1959). In Steinberg's we saw only two major reorientations of strategy in the sixty years, moves into self-service in the 1930s and into the shopping center business in the 1950s. But the stroke was not bold so much as tested. The story of the move into self-service is indicative. In 1933 one of the company's eight stores "struck it bad," in the chief executive's words, incurring "unacceptable" losses ($125 a week). Sam Steinberg closed the store one Friday evening, converted it to self-service, changed its name from "Steinberg's Service Stores" to "Wholesale Groceteria," slashed its prices by 15–20%, printed handbills, stuffed them into neighborhood mailboxes, and reopened on Monday morning. That's strategic change! But only once these changes proved successful did he convert the other stores. Then, in his words, "We grew like Topsy."

This anecdote tells us something about the bold stroke of the entrepreneur—"controlled boldness" is a better expression. The ideas were bold, the execution careful. Sam Steinberg could have simply closed the one unprofitable store. Instead he used it to create a new vision, but he tested that vision, however ambitiously, before leaping into it. Notice the interplay here of problems and opportunities. Steinberg took what most businessmen would probably have perceived as a *problem* (how to cut the losses in one store) and by treating it as a *crisis* (what is wrong with our *general* operation that produces these losses) turned it into an *opportunity* (we can grow more effectively with a new concept of retailing). That was how he got energy behind actions and kept ahead of his competitors. He "oversolved" his problem and thereby remade his company, a characteristic of some of the most effective forms of entrepreneurship.

But absolutely central to this form of entrepreneurship is intimate, detailed knowledge of the business or of analogous business situations, the "repetition" discussed earlier. The leader as conventional strategic "planner"—the so-called architect of strategy—sits on a pedestal and is fed aggregate data that he or she uses to "formulate" strategies that are "implemented" by others. But the history of Steinberg's belies that image. It suggests that clear, imaginative, integrated strategic vision depends on an involvement with detail, an intimate knowledge of specifics. And by closely controlling "implementation" personally, the leader is able to reformulate en route, to adapt the evolving vision through his or her own process of learning. That is why Steinberg tried his new ideas in one store first. And that is why, in discussing his firm's competitive advantage, he told us: "Nobody knew the grocery business like we did. Everything has to do with your knowledge." He added: "I knew merchandise, I knew cost, I knew selling, I knew customers, I knew everything . . . and I passed on all my knowledge; I kept teaching my people. That's the advantage we had. They couldn't touch us."

Such knowledge can be incredibly effective when concentrated in one individual who is fully in charge (having no need to convince others, not subordinates below, not superiors at some distant headquarters, nor market analysts looking for superficial pronouncements) and who retains a strong, long-term commitment to the organization. So long as the business is simple and focused enough to be comprehended in one brain, the entrepreneurial approach is powerful, indeed unexcelled. Nothing else can provide so clear and complete a vision, yet also allow the flexibility to elaborate and rework that vision when necessary. The conception of a new strategy is an exercise in synthesis, which is typically best carried out in a single, informed brain. That is why the entrepreneurial approach is at the center of the most glorious corporate successes.

But in its strength lies entrepreneurship's weakness. Bear in mind that strategy for the entrepreneurial leader is not a formal, detailed plan on paper. It is a personal vision, a concept of the business, locked in a single brain. It may need to get "represented," in words and metaphors, but that must remain general if the leader is to maintain the richness and flexibility of his or her concept. But success breeds a large organization, public financing, and the need for formal planning. The vision must be articulated to drive others and gain their support, and that threatens the personal nature of the vision. At the limit, as we shall see later in the case of Steinberg's, the leader can get captured by his or her very success.

In Steinberg's, moreover, when success in the traditional business encouraged diversification into new ones (new regions, new forms of retailing, new industries), the organization moved beyond the realm of its leader's personal comprehension, and the entrepreneurial mode of strategy formation lost its viability. Strategy making became more decentralized, more analytic, in some ways more careful, but at the same time less visionary, less integrated, less flexible, and ironically, less deliberate.

Conceiving a New Vision in a Garment Firm

The genius of an entrepreneur like Sam Steinberg was his ability to pursue one vision (self-service and everything that entailed) faithfully for decades and then, based on a weak signal in the environment (the building of the first small shopping center in Montreal), to realize the need to shift that vision. The planning literature makes a big issue of forecasting such discontinuities, but as far as I know there are no formal techniques to do so effectively (claims about "scenario analysis" notwithstanding). The ability to perceive a sudden shift in an established pattern and then to conceive a new vision to deal with it appears to remain largely in the realm of informed intuition, generally the purview of the wise, experienced, and energetic leader. Again, the literature is largely silent on this. But another of our studies, also concerning entrepreneurship, did reveal some aspects of this process.

Canadelle produces women's undergarments, primarily brassieres. It too was a highly successful organization, although not on the same scale at Steinberg's. Things were going well for the company in the late 1960s, under the personal leadership of Larry Nadler, the son of its founder, when suddenly everything changed. A sexual revolution of sorts was accompanying broader social manifestations, with bra burning a symbol of its resistance. For a manufacturer of brassieres the threat was obvious. For many other women the miniskirt had come to dominate the fashion scene, obsoleting the girdle and giving rise to pantyhose. As the executives of Canadelle put it, "the bottom fell out of the girdle business." The whole environment—long so receptive to the company's strategies—seemed to turn on it all at once.

At the time, a French company had entered the Quebec market with a light, sexy, molded garment called "Huit," using the theme, "just like not wearing a bra." Their target market was 15–20-year-olds. Though the product was expensive when it landed in Quebec and did not fit well in Nadler's opinion, it sold well. Nadler flew to France in an attempt to license the product for manufacture in Canada. The French firm refused, but, in Nadler's words, what he learned in "that one hour in their offices made the trip worthwhile." He realized that what women wanted was a more natural look, not no bra but less bra. Another trip shortly afterward, to a sister American firm, convinced him of the importance of market segmentation by age and life-style. That led him to the realization that the firm had two markets, one for the more mature customer, for whom the brassiere was a cosmetic to look and feel more attractive, and another for the younger customer who wanted to look and feel more natural.

Those two events led to a major shift in strategic vision. The CEO described it as sudden, the confluence of different ideas to create a new mental set. In his words, "all of a sudden the idea forms." Canadelle reconfirmed its commitment to the brassiere business, seeking greater market share while its competitors were cutting back. It introduced a new line of more natural brassieres for the younger customers, for which the firm had to work out the molding technology as well as a new approach to promotion.

We can draw on Kurt Lewin's (1951) three-stage model of unfreezing, changing, and refreezing to explain such a gestalt shift in vision. The process of *unfreezing* is essentially one of overcoming the natural defense mechanisms, the established "mental set" of how an industry is supposed to operate, to realize that things have changed fundamentally. The old assumptions no longer hold. Effective managers, especially effective strategic managers, are supposed to scan their environments continually, looking for such changes. But doing so continuously, or worse, trying to use technique to do so, may have exactly the opposite effect. So much attention may be given to strategic monitoring when nothing important is happening that when something really does, it may not even be noticed. The trick, of course, is to pick out the discontinuities that matter, and as noted earlier that seems to have more to do with informed intuition than anything else.

A second step in unfreezing is the willingness to step into the void, so to speak, for the leader to shed his or her conventional notions of how a business is supposed to function. The leader must above all avoid premature closure—seizing on a new thrust before it has become clear what its signals really mean. That takes a special kind of management, one able to live with a good deal of uncertainty and discomfort. "There is a period of confusion," Nadler told us, "you sleep on it . . . start looking for patterns . . . become an information hound, searching for [explanations] everywhere."

Strategic *change* of this magnitude seems to require a shift in mind-set before a new strategy can be conceived. And the thinking is fundamentally conceptual and inductive, probably stimulated (as in this case) by just one or two key insights. Continuous bombardment of facts, opinions, problems, and so on may prepare the mind for the shift, but it is the sudden *insight* that is likely to drive the synthesis—to bring all the disparate elements together in one "eureka"-type flash.

Once the strategist's mind is set, assuming he or she has read the new situation correctly and has not closed prematurely, then the *refreezing* process begins. Here the object is not to read the situation, at least not in a global sense, but in effect to block it out. It is a time to work out the consequences of the new strategic vision.

It has been claimed that obsession is an ingredient in effective organizations (Peters, 1980). Only for the period of refreezing would we agree, when the organization must focus on the pursuit of the new orientation—the new mind-set—with full vigor. A management that was open and divergent in its thinking must now become closed and convergent. But that means that the uncomfortable period of uncertainty has passed, and people can now get down to the exciting task of accomplishing something new. Now the organization knows where it is going; the object of the exercise is to get there using all the skills at its command, many of them formal and analytic. Of course, not everyone accepts the new vision. For those steeped in old strategies, *this* is the period of discomfort, and they can put up considerable resistance, forcing the leader to make greater use of his or her formal powers and political skills. Thus, refreezing of the leader's mind-set often involves the unfreezing, changing, and refreezing of the organization itself! But when the structure is simple, as it is in the entrepreneurial organization, that problem is relatively minor.

Leadership Taking Precedence in the Entrepreneurial Configuration

To conclude, entrepreneurship is very much tied up with the creation of strategic vision, often with the attainment of a new concept. Strategies can be characterized as largely deliberate, since they reside in the intentions of a single leader. But being largely personal as well, the details of those strategies can emerge as they develop. In fact, the vision can change too. The leader can adapt en route, can learn, which means new visions can emerge too, sometimes, as we have seen, rather quickly.

In the entrepreneurial organization, as shown in Figure 2, the focus of attention is on the leader. The organization is malleable and responsive to that person's initiatives, while the environment remains benign for the most part, the result of the leader's selecting (or "enacting") the correct niche for his or her organization. The environment can, of course, flare up occasionally to challenge the organization, and then the leader must adapt, perhaps seeking out a new and more appropriate niche in which to operate.

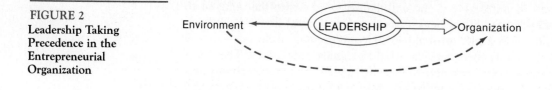

SOME ISSUES ASSOCIATED WITH THE ENTREPRENEURIAL ORGANIZATION

We conclude briefly with some broad issues associated with the entrepreneurial organization. In this configuration, decisions concerning both strategy and operations tend to be centralized in the office of the chief executive. This centralization has the important advantage of rooting strategic response in deep knowledge of the operations. It also allows for flexibility and adaptability: Only one person need act. But this same executive can get so enmeshed in operating problems that he or she loses sight of strategy; alternatively, he or she may become so enthusiastic about strategic opportunities that the more routine operations can wither for lack of attention and eventually pull down the whole organization. Both are frequent occurrences in entrepreneurial organizations.

This is also the riskiest of organizations, hinging on the activities of one individual. One heart attack can literally wipe out the organization's prime means of coordination. Even a leader in place can be risky. When change becomes necessary, everything hinges on the chief's response to it. If he or she resists, as is not uncommon where that person developed the existing strategy in the first place, then the organization may have no means to adapt. Then the great strength of the entrepreneurial organization—the vision of its leader plus its capacity to respond quickly—becomes its chief liability.

Another great advantage of the entrepreneurial organization is its sense of mission. Many people enjoy working in a small, intimate organization where the leader—often charismatic—knows where he or she is taking it. As a result, the organization tends to grow rapidly, with great enthusiasm. Employees can develop a solid identification with such an organization.

But other people perceive this configuration as highly restrictive. Because one person calls all the shots, they feel not like the participants on an exciting journey, but like cattle being led to market for someone else's benefit. In fact, the broadening of democratic norms into the sphere of organizations has rendered the entrepreneurial organization unfashionable in some quarters of contemporary society. It has been described as paternalistic and sometimes autocratic, and accused of concentrating too much power at the top. Certainly, without countervailing powers in the organization the chief executive can easily abuse his or her authority.

Perhaps the entrepreneurial organization is an anachronism in societies that call themselves democratic. Yet there have always been such organizations, and there always will be. This was probably the only structure known to those who first discovered the benefits of coordinating their activities in some formal way. And it probably reached its heyday in the era of the great American trusts of the late nineteenth century, when powerful entrepreneurs personally controlled huge empires. Since then, at least in Western society, the entrepreneurial organization has been on the decline. Nonetheless, it remains a prevalent and important configuration, and will continue to be so as long as society faces the conditions that require it: the prizing of entrepreneurial initiative and the resultant encouragement of new organizations, the need for small and informal organizations in some spheres and of strong personalized leadership despite larger size in others, and the need periodically to turn around ailing organizations of all types.

• COMPETITIVE STRATEGY IN EMERGING INDUSTRIES*

BY MICHAEL E. PORTER

Emerging industries are newly formed or reformed industries that have been created by technological innovations, shifts in relative cost relationships, emergence of new consumer needs, or other economic and sociological changes that elevate a new product or service to the level of a potentially viable business opportunity. . . .

The essential characteristic of an emerging industry from the viewpoint of formulating strategy is that there are no rules of the game. The competitive problem in an emerging industry is that all the rules must be established such that the firm can cope with and prosper under them.

THE STRUCTURAL ENVIRONMENT

Although emerging industries can differ a great deal in their structures, there are some common structural factors that seem to characterize many industries in this stage of their development. Most of them relate either to the absence of established bases for competition or other rules of the game or to the initial small size and newness of the industry.

Common Structural Characteristics

Technological Uncertainty: There is usually a great deal of uncertainty about the technology in an emerging industry: What product configuration will ultimately prove to be the best? Which production technology will prove to be the most efficient? . . .

Strategic Uncertainty: . . . No "right" strategy has been clearly identified, and different firms are groping with different approaches to product/market positioning, marketing, servicing, and so on, as well as betting on different product configurations or production technologies. . . . Closely related to this problem, firms often have poor information about competitors, characteristics of customers, and industry conditions in the emerging phase. No one knows who all the competitors are, and reliable industry sales and market share data are often simply unavailable, for example.

High Initial Costs but Steep Cost Reduction: Small production volume and newness usually combine to produce high costs in the emerging industry relative to those the industry can potentially achieve. . . . Ideas come rapidly in terms of improved procedures, plant layout, and so on, and employees achieve major gains in

---

productivity as job familiarity increases. Increasing sales make major additions to the scale and total accumulated volume of output produced by firms. . . .

Embryonic Companies and Spin-Offs: The emerging phase of the industry is usually accompanied by the presence of the greatest proportion of newly formed companies (to be contrasted with newly formed units of established firms) that the industry will ever experience. . . .

First-Time Buyers: Buyers of the emerging industry's product or service are inherently first-time buyers. The marketing task is thus one of inducing substitution, or getting the buyer to purchase the new product or service instead of something else. . . .

Short Time Horizon: In many emerging industries the pressure to develop customers or produce products to meet demand is so great that bottlenecks and problems are dealt with expediently rather than as a result of an analysis of future conditions. At the same time, industry conventions are often born out of pure chance. . . .

Subsidy: In many emerging industries, especially those with radical new technology or that address areas of societal concern, there may be subsidization of early entrants. Subsidy may come from a variety of government and nongovernment sources. . . . Subsidies often add a great degree of instability to an industry, which is made dependent on political decisions that can be quickly reversed or modified. . . .

Early Mobility Barriers

In an emerging industry, the configuration of mobility barriers is often predictably different from that which will characterize the industry later in its development. Common early barriers are the following:

- proprietary technology
- access to distribution channels
- access to raw materials and other inputs (skilled labor) of appropriate cost and quality
- cost advantages due to experience, made more significant by the technological and competitive uncertainties
- risk, which raises the effective opportunity cost of capital and thereby effective capital barriers

. . . The nature of the early barriers is a key reason why we observe newly created companies in emerging industries. The typical early barriers stem less from the need to command massive resources than from the ability to bear risk, be creative technologically, and make forward-looking decisions to garner input supplies and distribution channels. . . . There may be some advantages to late entry, however. . . .

Strategic Choices

Formulation of strategy in emerging industries must cope with the uncertainty and risk of this period of an industry's development. The rules of the competitive game are largely undefined, the structure of the industry unsettled and probably changing, and competitors hard to diagnose. Yet all these factors have another side—the emerging phase of an industry's development is probably the period when the strategic degrees of freedom are the greatest and when the leverage from good strategic choices is the highest in determining performance.

Shaping Industry Structure: The overriding strategic issue in emerging industries is the ability of the firm to shape industry structure. Through its choices, the firm can try to set the rules of the game in areas like product policy, marketing approach, and pricing strategy. . . .

Externalities in Industry Development: In an emerging industry, a key strategic issue is the balance the firm strikes between industry advocacy and pursuing its own narrow self-interest. Because of potential problems with industry image, credibility, and confusion of buyers . . . in the emerging phase the firm is in part dependent on others in the industry for its own success. The overriding problem for the industry is inducing substitution and attracting first-time buyers, and it is usually in the firm's interest during this phase to help promote standardization, police substandard quality and fly-by-night producers, and present a consistent front to suppliers, customers, government, and the financial community. . . .

It is probably a valid generalization that the balance between industry outlook and firm outlook must shift in the direction of the firm as the industry begins to achieve significant penetration. Sometimes firms who have taken very high profiles as industry spokespersons, much to their and the industry's benefit, fail to recognize that they must shift their orientation. As a result, they can be left behind as the industry matures. . . .

Changing Role of Suppliers and Channels: Strategically, the firm in an emerging industry must be prepared for a possible shift in the orientation of its suppliers and distribution channels as the industry grows in size and proves itself. Suppliers may become increasingly willing (or can be forced) to respond to the industry's special needs in terms of varieties, service, and delivery. Similarly, distribution channels may become more receptive to investing in facilities, advertising, and so forth in partnership with the firms. Early exploitation of these changes in orientation can give the firm strategic leverage.

Shifting Mobility Barriers: As outlined earlier . . . the early mobility barriers may erode quickly in an emerging industry, often to be replaced by very different ones as the industry grows in size and as the technology matures. This factor has a number of implications. The most obvious is that the firm must be prepared to find new ways to defend its position and must not rely solely on things like proprietary technology and a unique product variety on which it has succeeded in the past. Responding to shifting mobility barriers may involve commitments of capital that far exceed those that have been necessary in the early phases.

Another implication is that the *nature of entrants* into the industry may shift to more established firms attracted to the larger and increasingly proven (less risky) industry, often competing on the basis of the newer forms of mobility barriers, like scale and marketing clout. . . .

Timing Entry

A crucial strategic choice for competing in emerging industries is the appropriate timing of entry. Early entry (or pioneering) involves high risk but may involve otherwise low entry barriers and can offer a large return. Early entry is appropriate when the following general circumstances hold:

- Image and reputation of the firm are important to the buyer, and the firm can develop an enhanced reputation by being a pioneer.
- Early entry can initiate the learning process in a business in which the learning curve is important, experience is difficult to imitate, and it will not be nullified by successive technological generations.
- Customer loyalty will be great, so that benefits will accrue to the firm that sells to the customer first.
- Absolute cost advantages can be gained by early commitment to supplies of raw materials, distribution channels, and so on. . . .

Tactical Moves: The problems limiting development of an emerging industry suggest some tactical moves that may improve the firm's strategic position:

- Early commitments to suppliers of raw materials will yield favorable priorities in times of shortages.
- Financing can be timed to take advantage of a Wall Street love affair with the industry if it happens, even if financing is ahead of actual needs. This step lowers the firm's cost of capital. . . .

The choice of which emerging industry to enter is dependent on the outcome of a predictive exercise such as the one described above. An emerging industry is attractive if its ultimate structure (not its *initial* structure) is one that is consistent with above-average returns and if the firm can create a defendable position in the industry in the long run. The latter will depend on its resources relative to the mobility barriers that will evolve.

Too often firms enter emerging industries because they are growing rapidly, because incumbents are currently very profitable, or because ultimate industry size promises to be large. These may be contributing reasons, but the decision to enter must ultimately depend on a structural analysis. . . .

• COMPETITIVE STRATEGY IN FRAGMENTED INDUSTRIES*

BY MICHAEL E. PORTER

An important structural environment in which many firms compete is the fragmented industry, that is, an industry in which no firm has a significant market share and can strongly influence the industry outcome. Usually fragmented industries are populated by a large number of small- and medium-sized companies, many of them privately held. . . . The essential notion that makes these industries a unique environment in which to compete is the absence of market leaders with the power to shape industry events. . . .

Some fragmented industries, such as computer software and television program syndication, are characterized by products or services that are differentiated, whereas others, such as oil tanker shipping, electronic component distribution, and fabricated aluminum products, involve essentially undifferentiated products. Fragmented industries also vary greatly in their technological sophistication, ranging from high technology businesses like solar heating to garbage collection and liquor retailing. . . .

251

THE
ENTREPRENEURIAL
CONTEXT

WHAT MAKES AN INDUSTRY FRAGMENTED?

. . . in many industries there are underlying economic causes [of fragmentation] and the principal ones seem to be as follows:

Low Overall Entry Barriers: Nearly all fragmented industries have low overall entry barriers. Otherwise they could not be populated by so many small firms. . . .

Absence of Economies of Scale or Experience Curve: Most fragmented industries are characterized by the absence of significant scale economies or learning curves in any major aspect of the business. . . .

High Transportation Costs: High transportation costs limit the size of an efficient plant or production location despite the presence of economies of scale. . . .

High Inventory Costs or Erratic Sales Fluctuations: Although there may be intrinsic economies of scale in the production process, they may be reaped if inventory carrying costs are high and sales fluctuate. . . . Small-scale, less specialized facilities or distribution systems are usually more flexible in absorbing output shifts than large, more specialized ones, even though they may have higher operating costs at a steady operating rate.

No Advantages of Size in Dealing with Buyers or Suppliers: . . . Buyers, for example, might be so large that even a large firm in the industry would only be marginally better off in bargaining with them than a smaller firm. . . .

Diseconomies of Scale in Some Important Aspect: [Rapid product changes or style changes, need to maintain low overhead, a highly diverse product line, heavy creative content, need for close local control (as in restaurants), personal service or local image or contacts are key.]

Diverse Market Needs: In some industries buyers' tastes are fragmented, with different buyers each desiring special varieties of a product and willing (and able) to pay a premium for it rather than accept a more standardized version. . . .

High Product Differentiation, Particularly if Based on Image: . . . Performing artists, for example, may prefer dealing with a small booking agency or record label that carries the image they desire to cultivate.

Exit Barriers: If there are exit barriers, marginal firms will tend to stay in the industry and thereby hold back consolidation. . . .

Local Regulation: Local regulation, by forcing the firm to comply with standards that may be particularistic, or to be attuned to a local political scene, can be a major source of fragmentation in an industry, even where the other conditions do not hold. . . .

Government Prohibition of Concentration: Legal restrictions prohibit consolidation in industries such as electric power and television and radio stations. . . .

Newness: An industry can be fragmented because it is new and no firm or firms have yet developed the skills and resources to command a significant market share, even though there are no other impediments to consolidation. . . .

COPING WITH FRAGMENTATION

It takes the presence of only one of these characteristics to block the consolidation of an industry. . . .

In many situations, industry fragmentation is . . . the result of underlying industry economics that cannot be overcome. Fragmented industries are characterized not only by many competitors but also by a generally weak bargaining position with suppliers and buyers. Marginal profitability can be the result. In such an environment, strategic *positioning* is of particularly crucial significance. The strategic challenge is to cope with fragmentation by becoming one of the most successful firms, although able to garner only a modest market share.

Since every industry is ultimately different, there is no generalized method for competing most effectively in a fragmented industry. However, there are a number of possible strategic alternatives for coping with a fragmented structure that should be considered when examining any particular situation. These are specific approaches to pursuing the low cost, differentiate, or focus generic strategies. . . .

Tightly Managed Decentralization: Since fragmented industries often are characterized by the need for intense coordination, local management orientation, high personal service, and close control, an important alternative for competition is tightly managed decentralization. Rather than increasing the scale of operations at one or a few locations, this strategy involves deliberately keeping individual operations small and as autonomous as possible. This approach is supported by tight central control and performance-oriented compensation for local managers. . . .

"Formula" Facilities: Another alternative, related to the previous one, is to view the key strategic variable in the business as the building of efficient, low-cost facilities at multiple locations. This strategy involves designing a standard facility, whether it be a plant or a service establishment, and polishing to a science the process of constructing and putting the facility into operation at minimum cost. . . .

Increased Value Added: Many fragmented industries produce products or services that are commodities or otherwise difficult to differentiate; many distribution businesses, for example, stock similar if not identical product lines to their competitors'. In cases such as these, an effective strategy may be to increase the value added of the business by providing more service with sale, by engaging in some final fabrication of the product (like cutting to size or punching holes), or by doing subassembly or assembly of components before they are sold to the customer. . . .

Specialization by Product Type or Product Segment: When industry fragmentation results from or is accompanied by the presence of numerous items in the product line, an effective strategy for achieving above-average results can be to specialize on a tightly constrained group of products. . . . [This] can allow the firm to achieve some bargaining power with suppliers by developing a significant volume of their products. It may also allow the enhancement of product differentiation with the customer as a result of the specialist's perceived expertise and image in the particular product area. . . .

Specialization by Customer Type: If competition is intense because of a fragmented structure, a firm can potentially benefit by specialization on a particular category of customer in the industry. . . .

Specialization by Type of Order: Regardless of the customer, the firm can specialize in a particular type of order to cope with intense competitive pressure in a fragmented industry. One approach is to service only small orders for which the customer wants immediate delivery and is less price sensitive. Or the firm can service only custom orders to take advantage of less price sensitivity or to build switching costs. Once again, the cost of such specialization may be some limitation in volume.

A Focused Geographic Area: Even though a significant industry-wide share is out of reach or there are no national economies of scale (and perhaps even diseconomies), there may be substantial economies in blanketing a given geographic area by concentrating facilities, marketing attention, and sales activity. This policy can economize on the use of the sales force, allow more efficient advertising, allow a single distribution center, and so on. . . .

Bare Bones/No Frills: Given the intensity of competition and low margins in many fragmented industries, a simple but powerful strategic alternative can be intense attention to maintaining a bare bones/no frills competitive posture—that is, low overhead, low-skilled employees, tight cost control, and attention to detail. This policy places the firm in the best position to compete on price and still make an above-average return.

Backward Integration: Although the causes of fragmentation can preclude a large share of the market, selective backward integration may lower costs and put pressure on competitors who cannot afford such integration. . . .

● A REEXAMINATION OF THE NICHE CONCEPT*

ARNOLD C. COOPER, GARY E. WILLARD, AND CAROLYN Y. WOO

. . . Despite the number and importance of new and small firms, there has been little explicit examination of their strategies. Founders of new firms must find ways to compete in a world which had gotten along without them before. Starting with no reputation and limited financial and human resources, they must seek out opportunities and develop strategies which enable them to compete, sometimes in industries dominated by large, established companies. Since almost any strategy involves competing with someone, they need to consider which established competitors might be challenged and whether sustainable competitive advantages could be achieved.

The extant literature generally advises small firms not to meet larger competitors head on. They should concentrate on specialized products, localize business

* Originally published in the *Journal of Business Venturing* (1986) under the title "Strategies of High-Performing New and Small Firms: A Reexamination of the Niche Concept." Copyright © 1986 by Elsevier Science Publishing Company, New York; reprinted with deletions by permission of the authors and publisher.

operations, and provide products which require a high degree of craftsmanship (Hosmer, 1957; Gross, 1967). Small businesses are also seen to benefit from the provision of customer service, product customization, and other factors which are inimical to large-scale production (Cohn and Lindberg, 1972). The above recommendations would often limit the opportunities open to new and small firms to "niches" too small to be of interest to larger firms. . . . We suggest that this concept of the niche, although descriptive of the strategies of many small firms, is unduly limiting; in fact, it does not describe the strategies of some of the most successful new and small companies. Under some conditions, and for some firms, exceptional opportunities exist for *competing directly* with large established companies. These smaller challengers pursue "niche" strategies in the sense of being focused and directed at serving the needs of a particular group of customers. However, they do not avoid direct competition with market leaders or confine themselves to segments of no interest to them. If we were to apply the test of asking who the young firm takes customers away from, the answer would be clear. It is the largest, the most established, often the most successful firms in the industry that the smaller firm is competing with. . . .

The objective of this article is to reexamine the concept of the niche strategy with particular attention to the new firms challenging industry leaders. In no sense do we argue that such strategies of direct competition are feasible under all conditions or should be undertaken by all new firms. In this article we will discuss what conditions might support the choice of this strategy. . . .

The concepts discussed will be illustrated by reference to five successful challenges which developed strategies of direct competition against much larger established industry leaders. These are

1. MCI, which competed directly with AT&T
2. Amdahl Corporation, which competed directly with IBM
3. Iowa Beef Processors, which competed directly against large meat packers such as Armour and Wilson
4. People Express Airline, which competed directly against larger airlines such as Eastern
5. Nucor, which competed directly against old-line steel companies such as US Steel and Bethlehem

CONDITIONS UNDER WHICH SUCCESSFUL DIRECT COMPETITION MAY BE POSSIBLE

Opportunities to compete directly with large firms vary widely across industries. Of particular importance is whether an industry is changing, the nature of those changes, and whether the managements of the leading firms recognize their implications. In any industry the leading companies have been the most successful in developing strategies to exploit previously existing opportunities. Over time they have mastered existing technologies, fine-tuned their strategies, and developed organizations trained and committed to these ways of competing. If there are no changes, there are few opportunities for challengers.

However, changes in the form of deregulation, new technology, organizational and management innovations, and changing consumer preferences create opportunities for new firms. Thus, deregulation in air transportation and telecommunications enabled People Express Airline and MCI to confront established firms not attuned to competing against new entrants. Nucor took advantage of technology in the form of electric furnaces and continuous casting which permitted it to compete directly against steel mills locked into old technology. . . .

Although change can create opportunities, other industry conditions may make it easier for a small firm to achieve advantages or to keep from being overwhelmed by larger competitors. If there are opportunities for differentiation, for offering a product or service which is somewhat different, then the small firm may be able to achieve an advantage in serving some segment of the market. Frequently, differentiation is perceived to be the process of adding services or product features which some customers value. But, differentiation may also be achieved by subtracting a feature or service included by large firms in their standard offering, but which a segment of the market does not value highly. People Express Airline, for example, eliminated the "meals-in-flight" feature and baggage handling from the standard airline product, reduced the price, and found a ready market from among the major airlines' price-sensitive passengers.

By contrast, if products are nondifferentiated—"commodity-like"—then alternative ways of competing are more limited. Although established firms may already be organized to compete on the basis of price, the new firm can, in certain cases, adopt a different (and inherently lower cost) technology for providing the commodity-like product. Nucor, a successful "mini-mill," adopted the electric furnace technology for making steel directly from scrap-iron, and avoided the heavy capital investments associated with making steel from ore. Low-cost technology similarly enabled Iowa Beef to undercut prices of industry leaders.

The relative importance of economies of scale and/or experience curve effects also bears upon the opportunities for direct competition. If it is possible to compete on a small scale or with little experience and not incur a substantial cost disadvantage, then small firms (with little volume) or new firms (with little experience) may be able to compete directly with success. Nucor and other mini-mills positioned themselves in a segment of the steel industry in which small scale was not a disadvantage. Mini-mills can achieve cost advantage despite annual tonnages of only 250,000 tons per year, a mere "drop in the ladle" in the steel industry.

NATURE OF SUCCESSFUL CHALLENGERS

Even within industries offering opportunities for direct competition, only some new firms may be in a position to adopt such strategies. There must be the right combination of insight, assets, and commitment.

Central to success is a concept, a strategy, which enables the new firm to earn a competitive advantage. Although all of the small firms considered here confronted much large companies, none competed in exactly the same way as their larger competitors. All were headed by entrepreneurs who innovated and challenged the conventional wisdom within their industries. At first, their strategies were untested and their potential was unclear. However, all saw possibilities not evident to others and all served as champions of the new strategies which their firms developed.

Financial and managerial resources are critical to all firms, but particularly to those following these strategies. The emphasis on innovation, the development of larger markets, and direct confrontation with powerful competitors all require more resources than needed for many small businesses. In addition, these strategies are characterized by experimentation, by feedback from the marketplace, and by adaptation to competitive response. All require time and sufficient capital to stay in the game. Some new firms run out of money (or credibility with investors) before they can perfect and implement their strategy. Thus, Amdahl, after developing its initial product line, but before market introduction, was confronted by a newly introduced IBM product in 1972. It was necessary for Amdahl to go back to its investors for an additional $16 million in order to upgrade its product line before it had realized any revenues.

The early capital of these five firms (after initial public offerings) ranged from $956 thousand to $105 million. Although these amounts were substantially more than the capitalization of most new firms, they were far less than those of their major competitors. For example, the initial capital of People Express Airline was $28 million versus $2 billion for Eastern Airline at that time, and that for MCI was $105 million, compared to $29 billion for AT&T. In no way were these challengers in a position to outspend their major competitors.

Those small competitors suited for strategies of direct confrontation must also be able to capitalize upon their potential for achieving organizational commitment and for shaping organizations attuned to these innovative strategies. A young firm, such as those considered here, does not have a stake in the status quo. Employees' security and influence are not tied to traditional ways of competing. If the young firm is led by management with vision and leadership ability, it may be possible to recruit, train, and motivate a cadre of people dedicated to the new strategy. Thus, the new employees of People Express knew they would be operating out of dingy headquarters in Newark, with "previously owned" aircraft, and a work schedule in which jobs would be rotated. An enthusiastic management, which led by example, was able to achieve a high degree of organizational commitment to the new strategy.

BARRIERS TO RESPONSE

In each of the five examples considered here, these young companies competed directly with established large firms. Despite limited finances, reputation, and organizations, they developed and implemented strategies which captured customers away from large, established competitors. We might have expected direct and massive retaliation. Yet, in many cases, this did not occur.

The literature on barriers that prevent response to competitive challenge offers some insights worth noting. MacMillan and Jones (1984) suggest that response will be difficult in situations in which the challenged firm is organized around a particular activity/output configuration. To the extent that response will divert the challenged firm from "doing what it does best," violate existing product-market boundary charters, or result in cannibalization of existing product offering, the competitive reaction will likely be delayed (Coyne, 1986; Kotter and Schlesinger, 1979; McIntyre, 1982).

If the response requires fundamental changes in the organizational or reporting relationships within the challenged firm, the response lag is likely to be greater (MacMillan, McCaffery, and Van Wijk, 1985). Coyne (1986) suggests that response may be delayed if "capability gaps" exist because of facility locations or regulatory/legal restrictions. MacMillan (1982) and Coyne (1986) refer to inertia barriers which may prevent competitive response.

The literature above suggests several reasons why the challenged firm may be unable to answer the competitive attack promptly. In our study of five focal firms, we found some support for these, as well as some additional considerations.

Standardized Products: Large firms often develop a common approach to serving broad markets, even though customer preferences may not be uniform. This practice enables firms to simplify the structure of their supporting organizations and to standardize policies with respect to production, customer services, distribution, pricing, and other functional activities. Thus, established airlines had developed strategies of providing full services for all of their customers. Organizations were developed and employees trained to provide ticketing assistance, baggage handling, and meals inflight. Having defined their "product" in this fashion, and having developed the supporting logistic structure, it was difficult for them to "unbundle" these services for those passengers who would rather not pay for them.

Pricing Distortions: Similar distortions may occur when one product is priced to recover the cost of another product. The unprofitable product may be justified on the basis of social benefits, attempt to gain distribution power, utilization of excess capacity or other reasons. AT&T, for example, had long used the profits from long-distance service to subsidize local telephone rates. As a regulated monopoly, it had been considered "in the public interest" to provide this subsidy, which was estimated to be as high as 35% of long-distance revenues. When MCI was permitted to compete in the long distance market, paying a much lower subsidy to local phone service than AT&T, the latter faced a competitive challenge which was difficult to respond to. This disparity was reported to account for 70% of MCI's ability to undercut AT&T. AT&T [was] bound to this local subsidy until 1988, when it [began to] be phased out. Meanwhile, they must rely on the short-term solution of emphasizing nonprice characteristics in the face of 15–50% price discounts offered by MCI and other new competitors.

Cannibalization of Existing Products: In meeting a confrontation, established firms are constrained by the extent to which their response would affect sales of products which are not directly challenged. Efforts to protect a particular product may lead to loss of sales on other products.

At IBM, the pricing policy reflected a constant price/performance ratio across the entire family of computers. This policy paid off for IBM inasmuch as the lineup of products was developed to derive maximum revenues. While still employed at IBM, Gene Amdahl proposed to IBM a large central processor which would be profitable under two conditions. First, to gain market acceptance, this machine would have to be priced lower than that stipulated by the existing pricing strategy. Second, two additional machines would have to be placed between the IBM 370 family and the largest processor to generate sufficient volume. These steps, however, would upset IBM's overall pricing ratio and threaten the demand for those machines for which the price/performance ratio would become less attractive. Thus, IBM rejected this proposal, and Amdahl subsequently left to found his own firm. He eventually gained success by offering an advanced central processor (the 470 V/6) priced at a level consistent with market demand and not hampered by consideration of whether it would cannibalize smaller machines.

Manufacturing Barriers

The challengers in our examples all demonstrated superior cost advantages. These became feasible through a combination of policies which departed from traditional industry practice. However, the established firms found themselves "locked into" higher cost positions, which reflected historic decisions about wages, work rules, locations, processes, and the skills needed to compete.

Wage Rates and Work Rules: At People Express, the salary structure was substantially lower than that of the established airlines. Initially, its pilots earned $30,000 per year and worked 70 hours per month, compared with industry averages of $60,000 and 45 hours.

Operating by work rules which were much more flexible than those of the industry, People Express promoted efficiency by rotating all its employees through different job assignments This practice extended to managers, pilots, maintenance personnel, and flight attendants (known as customer service managers at People Express). Hence, People Express "produced" at significantly lower costs than would have been the case had they accepted the high salary structures and rigid job classifications of their larger rivals. Its labor costs were about 20% of revenues, compared with 37% for major airlines as a group. The competing major airlines had wage contracts in place; they also had pilots and managers who would regard the rotation of job assignments as demeaning and unacceptable.

Existing Facilities and Processes: IBP's decision to locate its cattle slaughtering facilities in the heart of cattle feeding country, rather than only in the traditional stockyard terminal cities of Kansas City, St. Louis, or Chicago, not only resulted in lower wage rates, but also lower real estate and building costs. Moreover, this strategy drastically reduced the shrinkage normally experienced when livestock were transported long distances from the feedlot to the slaughter site.

And redefining the manner in which slaughter cattle were processed, IBP introduced the moving "disassembly" line. Unskilled or semiskilled laborers were used to perform simple repetitive tasks, replacing the skilled butchers required by the traditional meat packing process. The combination of efficient, one-story plants, redefined process operations and lower wage rates gave IBP a "kill" cost of around $18 per head compared to $30–35 per head for old-line packers.

IBP led the industry in cleaving and trimming carcasses into loins, ribs, and other cuts and boxing the pieces at the plant, which further reduced the transportation costs by removing excess weight. The innovative plastic packaging introduced by IBP virtually eliminated shrinkage due to refrigeration and quadrupled the shelf-life of fresh meat from 7 to 28 days. In fact, IBP claimed it could deliver boxed beef to a supermarket at prices as much as $36 less per head than the retailer could buy and process carcasses himself.

The established meat packers had commitments to existing plants and facilities. They had already trained skilled butchers, and were paying them accordingly. Their entire organizations were oriented toward the traditional way of slaughtering and shipping beef.

Joint Manufacturing: Components shared across product lines can give rise to economies of scale in production, lower design, engineering, and service costs. On the other hand, this practice often promotes standardization and exacts a compromise in product performance.

In IBM's case, the component division recognized that the largest mainframe computers represented only a small market. To attain economies of scale, components for the large processor would also be designed for use in the smaller computers in the company's line. This commonality would lead to lower production costs, particularly across the entire family of products, but also would lead to sacrifices in product performance. When Gene Amdahl proposed the development of a large cental processing unit, he could not obtain assurances that the components needed would not be downgraded. Yet without such guarantees, he felt that the desired performance specifications would be compromised. When Amdahl later left IBM and developed his own central processor, utilizing only those components appropriate to its design, IBM was faced with a dilemma. Should it retain emphasis on commonality, leading to lower development, manufacturing, and service costs across a family of products, or should it seek to match the price/performance ratios of the Amdahl computers through using components uniquely suited to large central processors?

Organizational Structure and Culture

Organizational Structures: The organizational structures of large companies influence their ability to respond to direct competition by small firms. High degrees of centralization and thick policy manuals make it more difficult to modify policies or respond quickly to the moves of smaller competitors. Layers of organization also are often associated with high overhead rates. AT&T was characterized by strong central staff groups, careful and deliberate study of proposed policy changes —including pricing, and concern about systemwide consistency. The corporation was noted for many strengths, but not for internal entrepreneurship. Thus, MCI's development of a lean, stripped-down organization with innovative pricing and marketing techniques, was difficult for AT&T to match.

Organization Cultures: The organizational cultures of established firms evolve through long periods of hiring, training, and motivating employees to implement particular strategies. Employees become proud of organizational capabilities, such as offering a full product line or excellent service.

The integrated steel companies competed on the basis of offering broad product lines. Many major steel companies had integrated backward to the point of iron and coal mining and forward to the point of steel service centers where structural shapes were prepared for individual customers. The traditional "big steel" claim of "If it's done in steel, we do it" required a large investment in metallurgical skills and facilities which had come to be accepted as a necessary requirement of being in the steel business.

But, at Nucor Steel, Iverson did not need or want a full product line. Hence, he had no requirement for the extensive staff, large-capacity furnaces, rolling equipment, reheating facilities, and other investments required of an integrated steel producer. In fact, the investment cost of Nucor's "mini-mills" ran only about $150 per ton of annual output, compared to the nearly $1400 per ton of annual output for an integrated mill.

The young firms in this study created cultures which were difficult for the large firms to replicate. In the early days of Amdahl, Gene Amdahl visited customers and closed the sale himself—an approach that was difficult for IBM to match. Nucor created a culture in which every employee was made to feel important. They even listed the name of every employee on the back page of their annual report!

Ability to Innovate: Innovation can vary widely across established firms. Often, they are well equipped to deal with incremental innovations leading to gradual improvements in cost or performance. However, dramatic changes in the concept of the products, services, or production systems may encounter significant organizational barriers. Initially, it is not clear whether the new concepts will be successful or how large their market potential might be. The methods of analysis used in large corporations often emphasize "hard data" and systematic analysis more suited to incremental innovation than to major changes in strategy. Moreover, innovative strategies often call into question the long-established success formula of the corporation. Such changes threaten managers whose power bases depend on the existing strategy and who may have spent careers developing skills which would no longer be valued.

By contrast, the entrepreneurs within these new companies were the product champions. Gene Amdahl of Amdahl Corporation and Gitner and Burr of People Express Airline had dreams of what they hoped to bring about through their new companies. They could rely upon their "feel" for the technology and marketplace based upon personal experience. Unencumbered by high administrative overhead and large organizations, they could achieve success at relatively low sales volumes. Thus, their small firms were almost ideal settings for experimentation with innovative strategies.

Barriers to Response: In examining these barriers to response, we should not underestimate the role of *government regulation* and *union contracts.* Established firms are visible and accumulate, over time, a history of agreements. AT&T certainly was subject to regulatory constraints, such as the requirement to provide low-cost local service. MCI was faced with no such requirement. Major airlines and old-line beef packers were obligated to labor agreements which restricted flexible work assignments and called for much higher hourly wage rates than those faced by competitors such as People Express or Iowa Beef.

FACTORS BEARING ON WHETHER CHALLENGER ADVANTAGES MAY BE ERODED

Young firms engaged in strategies of direct competition may achieve initial success, based upon some of the advantages just considered. The firms illustrated in this study . . . all achieved substantial growth. . . . Their 1984 sales ranged from more than $500 million to over $5 billion.

This is not to suggest that the conditions which give rise to this success, and the effectiveness of strategies which exploited these opportunities will persist permanently [as, for example, in the case of People Express]. Much depends on how the industry evolves and how established competitors respond. Responses may be of a short-term tactical nature, or they may involve basic changes in the large firms' strategies and organization structures.

Small firms must also be aware that, as they grow, they may lose some of the characteristics which contributed to their success. New players, encouraged by the visible success of challengers, may enter and crowd the markets. Managements of challenging firms must assess these developments and how they may threaten their competitive advantage.

The previous literature clearly notes that early success may not endure and that "sustainable competitive advantage" is required for continuing success (Coyne, 1986; Porter, 1985). The ability to sustain advantage may depend, in part, upon how well the new firm deals with the continuing crises of growth (Buchele, 1967; Baumback and Mancuso, 1975). Even as the firm grows to substantial size, management confronts a series of internal challenges, of evolutions and revolutions (Greiner, 1972). Outside the firm, continuing industry development may shift the focus of competition (Porter, 1980). In some cases early success may attract excessive numbers of competitors, which coupled with rapid change and customer instability, can lead to disappointing performance for many participants (Sahlman and Stevenson, 1985).

The five challengers considered here all had to deal with a succession of responses by established competitors, internal changes, and confrontations with new entrants.

Responses by Established Firms

Responses by established firms can be tactical or strategic. Tactical responses do not stem from fundamental changes in the firm's policies. They represent short term responses by established firms to protect critical segments, to test the commitment of challengers, or to buy time to implement new strategies or organizational changes. In certain key markets, established airlines slashed ticket prices by over 50% to meet People Express's low fares in an all-out price war. One United ad directly attacked the upstart with the slogan, "You can fly or you can be shipped." Established airlines also lobbied the CAB to eliminate subsidies relating to the lower penalties People Express faced if luggage was lost or confirmed passengers were bumped.

Strategic actions, on the other hand, involve major adjustments in the large competitors' products, processes, and organizational structures. Two years after Amdahl sold its first 470 V/6, IBM announced a radical new product, Model 3033, which would bring a price/performance improvement of some 140% over its predecessor. . . . Major efforts were also undertaken by leading airlines to pare down operations, evaluate route structures, and negotiate with unions for lower wage rates.

When faced with these tactical and strategic countermoves, what might challengers do? They must choose their battlefields carefully, taking into account their more limited resources. . . .

Challenging firms must also be prepared to compete more aggressively as established firms react. As MCI's cost advantage over AT&T began to slide, MCI increased its marketing emphasis and expanded its sales force to contact wavering customers. Moreover, it continued to adopt an aggressive posture, spending heavily to expand capacity, work force, and upgrade microwave transmitters.

Evolution of Small Firms

If challengers are successful in developing markets, they will eventually evolve into larger organizations. As these firms grow, they become more complex and the necessary administrative processes may cause such firms to take on characteristics of larger competitors, slowing response time and dulling the competitive edge they once held. . . .

Challengers must recognize those dimensions of their cultures which were relevant not only to their past success, but would be critical to their future performance as well. Only half-jokingly, McGowan said he would abolish the existing MCI to build a new company "to keep employees on their toes." This statement, albeit made in jest, reflected his acknowledgment of the need to maintain MCI's fighting spirit despite experiences of success. Nucor, to affirm its belief in the importance of its workers, has continued to print the names of employees on its annual reports. Only now the organization has grown so large that even the front cover is used for this purpose. Nucor's workers have always enjoyed generous bonuses based on production levels. The base levels on which such bonuses are calculated have remained unchanged despite significant technology-driven productivity gains.

Entrance of Other Firms

In the beginning, it is usually not clear whether innovative small firms are developing strategies with great potential. However, as their success becomes visible, other competitors, both established corporations and new ventures, may begin to copy their strategies. For example, MCI and AT&T subsequently competed not only with each other, but also with Sprint, Allnet, US Telephone, and SBS. In the meatpacking industry, IBP competed not only against the old-line packers, but also against such firms as MBPXL and Monfort, which were following strategies similar to their own. Suppliers of supercomputers subsequently included not only IBM and Amdahl, but Cray Research and Control Data as well.

The innovative small firm may thus confront a variety of competitors, with different strategies and strengths. Management must anticipate these competitive pressures. This may include being careful not to overextend the firm and developing the financial strength or competitive alliances needed to survive under more difficult conditions. It also means sharpening the distinctive skills which led to their early successes and being careful not to let creeping changes in strategy take the firm away from its core strengths. . . .

CONCLUSIONS

. . . The strategies considered here are niche strategies in the sense that they concentrate on serving the needs of limited groups of customers. They are also "focus strategies" as described by Porter (1980), in the sense of emphasizing lower costs, differentiation, or both, in dealing with a portion of the market. However, contrary to the prevailing thinking in much of the literature, these niche or focus strategies do not limit young firms to markets that are of no interest to leading competitors. Those firms with the right combination of corporate resources and industry opportunity may be able to develop strategies of direct competition which lead to continuing and enviable success.

In no way do we suggest that a direct confrontation strategy is appropriate for all small businesses. The sample considered is small and may not be broadly representative. However, these observations may challenge the dominant perspective and hopefully, invite future entrepreneurs and researchers to think more broadly and aggressively about the distinctive competencies of small and new businesses.

THE MATURE CONTEXT

In this chapter, we focus on one of the more common contexts for today's organizations. Whether we refer to this by its form of operations (usually mass production or the mass provision of services), by the form of structure adopted (machine-like bureaucracy), by the type of environment it prefers (a stable one in a mature industry), or by the specific generic strategy often found there (low cost), the context tends to be common and to give rise to a relatively well-defined configuration.

The readings on what we shall refer to as the *mature* context cover these different aspects and examine some of the problems and opportunities of functioning in this realm. The first reading, on the machine organization, from Mintzberg's work, describes the structure for this context as well as the environment in which it tends to be found, and also investigates some of the social issues surrounding this particular form of organization. This reading also probes the nature of the strategy making process in this context. Here we can see what happens when large organizations accustomed to stability suddenly have to change their strategies dramatically. The careful formal planning, on which they tend to rely so heavily in easier times, seems ill suited to dealing with changes that may require virtual revolutions in their functioning. A section of this reading thus considers what can be the role of planners when their formal procedures fail to come to grips with the needs of strategy making.

A second reading of this chapter probes more deeply into the nature of formal planning. A highly sophisticated piece by Brian Loasby who teaches management at the University of Sterling in the United Kingdom, considers in a balanced way the advantages of formal planning and a number of its dangers.

The third reading is a chapter from Michael Porter's book *Competitive Strategy* on how to deal with the transition to industry maturity. It describes the environment of this context and also probes some of its favored strategies, notably what Porter calls cost leadership.

A particular technique designed for use with this strategy, and the mature context in general, is the subject of the last reading. Called *Cost Dynamics: Scale and Experience Effects* and written by Derek Abell and John Hammond for a marketing textbook, it probes the "experience curve." Developed by the Boston Consulting Group some years ago, this technique became quite popular in the 1970s. Although its limitations are now widely recognized, it still has certain applicability to firms operating in the mature context.

● THE MACHINE ORGANIZATION*

BY HENRY MINTZBERG

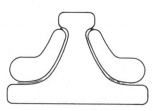

A national post office, a custodial prison, an airline, a giant automobile company, even a small security agency—all these organizations appear to have a number of characteristics in common. Above all, their operating work is routine, the greatest part of it rather simple and repetitive; as a result, their work processes are highly standardized. These characteristics give rise to the machine organizations of our society, structures fine-tuned to run as integrated, regulated, highly bureaucratic machines.

THE BASIC STRUCTURE

A clear configuration of the attributes has appeared consistently in the research: highly specialized, routine operating tasks; very formalized communication throughout the organization; large-size operating units; reliance on the functional

---

* Adapted from *The Structure of Organizations* (Prentice Hall, 1979), Chap. 18 on "The Machine Bureaucracy"; also *Power In and Around Organizations* (Prentice Hall, 1983), Chaps. 18 and 19 on "The Instrument" and "The Closed System"; the material on strategy formation from "Patterns in Strategy Formation," *Management Science* (1978); Does Planning Impede Strategic Thinking? Tracking the Strategies of Air Canada, from 1937–1976" (coauthored with Pierre Brunet and Jim Waters), in R. B. Lamb and P. Shrivastava, eds., *Advances in Strategic Management*, Volume IV (JAI press, 1986); and "The Mind of the Strategist(s)" (coauthored with Jim Waters), in S. Srivastva, ed., *The Executive Mind* (Jossey-Bass, 1983); the section on the role of planning, plans, and planners is drawn from a book in process on strategic planning. A chapter similar to this appeared in *Mintzberg on Management: Inside Our Strange World of Organizations* (Free Press, 1989).

basis for grouping tasks; relatively centralized power for decision making; and an elaborate administrative structure with a sharp distinction between line and staff.

The Operating Core and Administration

The obvious starting point is the operating core, with its highly rationalized work flow. This means that the operating tasks are made simple and repetitive, generally requiring a minimum of skill and training, the latter often taking only hours, seldom more than a few weeks, and usually in-house. This in turn results in narrowly defined jobs and an emphasis on the standardization of work processes for coordination, with activities highly formalized. The workers are left with little discretion, as are their supervisors, who can therefore handle very large spans of control.

To achieve such high regulation of the operating work, the organization has need for an elaborate administrative structure—a fully developed middle-line hierarchy and technostructure—but the two clearly distinguished.

The managers of the middle line have three prime tasks. One is to handle the disturbances that arise in the operating core. The work is so standardized that when things fall through the cracks, conflict flares, because the problems cannot be worked out informally. So it falls to managers to resolve them by direct supervision. Indeed, many problems get bumped up successive steps in the hierarchy until they reach a level of common supervision where they can be resolved by authority (as with a dispute in a company between manufacturing and marketing that may have to be resolved by the chief executive). A second task of the middle-line managers is to work with the staff analysts to incorporate their standards down into the operating units. And a third task is to support the vertical flows in the organization—the elaboration of action plans flowing down the hierarchy and the communication of feedback information back up.

The technostructure must also be highly elaborated. In fact this structure was first identified with the rise of technocratic personnel in early-nineteenth-century industries such as textiles and banking. Because the machine organization depends primarily on the standardization of its operating work for coordination, the technostructure—which houses the staff analysts who do the standardizing—emerges as the key part of the structure. To the line managers may be delegated the formal authority for the operating units, but without the standardizers—the cadre of work-study analysts, schedulers, quality control engineers, planners, budgeters, accountants, operations researchers, and many more—these structures simply could not function. Hence, despite their lack of formal authority, considerable informal power rests with these staff analysts, who standardize everyone else's work. Rules and regulations permeate the entire system: The emphasis on standardization extends well beyond the operating core of the machine organization, and with it follows the analysts' influence.

A further reflection of this formalization of behavior are the sharp divisions of labor all over the machine organization. Job specialization in the operating core and the pronounced formal distinction between line and staff have already been mentioned. In addition, the administrative structure is clearly distinguished from the operating core; unlike the entrepreneurial organization, here managers seldom work alongside operators. And they themselves tend to be organized along functional lines, meaning that each runs a unit that performs a single function in the chain that produces the final outputs. Figure 1 shows this, for example, in the organigram of a large steel company, traditionally machinelike in structure.

All this suggests that the machine organization is a structure with an obsession—namely, control. A control mentality pervades it from top to bottom. At the

266

FIGURE 1
Organigram of a Large Steel Company

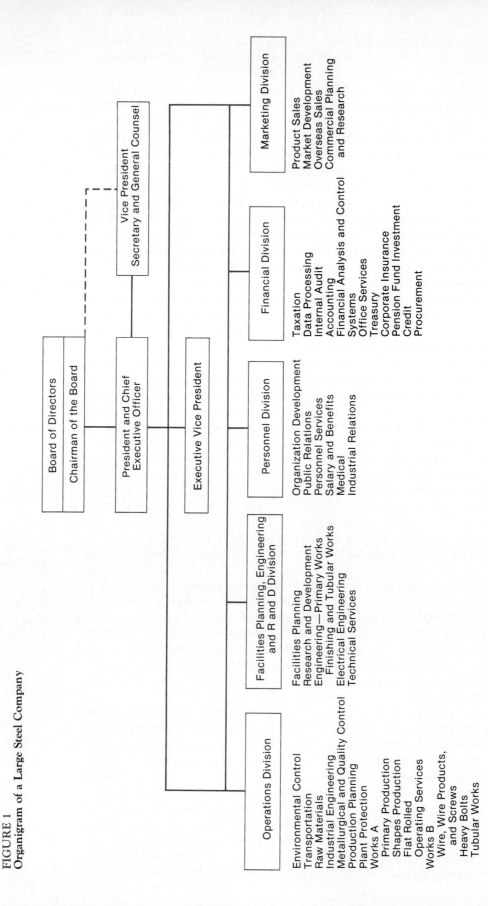

bottom, consider how a Ford Assembly Division general foreman described his work:

> I refer to my watch all the time. I check different items. About every hour I tour my line. About six thirty, I'll tour labor relations to find out who is absent. At seven, I hit the end of the line. I'll check paint, check my scratches and damage. Around ten I'll start talking to all the foremen. I make sure they're all awake. We can't have no holes, no nothing.

And at the top, consider the words of a chief executive:

> When I was president of this big corporation, we lived in a small Ohio town, where the main plant was located. The corporation specified who you could socialize with, and on what level. (His wife interjects: "Who were the wives you could play bridge with."). In a small town they didn't have to keep check on you. Everybody knew. There are certain sets of rules. (Terkel, 1972:186, 406)

The obsession with control reflects two central facts about these organizations. First, attempts are made to eliminate all possible uncertainty, so that the bureaucratic machine can run smoothly, without interruption, the operating core perfectly sealed off from external influence. Second, these are structures ridden with conflict; the control systems are required to contain it. The problem in the machine organization is not to develop an open atmosphere where people can talk the conflicts out, but to enforce a closed, tightly controlled one where the work can get done despite them.

The obsession with control also helps to explain the frequent proliferation of support staff in these organizations. Many of the staff services could be purchased from outside suppliers. But that would expose the machine organization to the uncertainties of the open market. So it "makes" rather than "buys," that is, it envelops as many of the support services as it can within its own structure in order to control them, everything from the cafeteria in the factory to the law office at headquarters.

The Strategic Apex

The managers at the strategic apex of these organizations are concerned in large part with the fine-tuning of their bureaucratic machines. Theirs is a perpetual search for more efficient ways to produce the given outputs.

But not all is strictly improvement of performance. Just keeping the structure together in the face of its conflicts also consumes a good deal of the energy of top management. As noted, conflict is not resolved in the machine organization; rather it is bottled up so that the work can get done. And as in the case of a bottle, the cork is applied at the top: Ultimately, it is the top managers who must keep the lid on the conflicts through their role of handling disturbances. Moreover, the managers of the strategic apex must intervene frequently in the activities of the middle line to ensure that coordination is achieved there. The top managers are the only generalists in the structure, the only managers with a perspective broad enough to see all the functions.

All this leads us to the conclusion that considerable power in the machine organization rests with the managers of the strategic apex. These are, in other words, rather centralized structures: The formal power clearly rests at the top; hierarchy and chain of authority are paramount concepts. But so also does much of the informal power, since that resides in knowledge, and only at the top of the hierarchy does the formally segmented knowledge of the organization come together.

Thus, our introductory figure shows the machine organization with a fully elaborated administrative and support structure—both parts of the staff component being focused on the operating core—together with large units in the operating core but narrower ones in the middle line to reflect the tall hierarchy of authority.

CONDITIONS OF THE MACHINE ORGANIZATION

Work of a machine bureaucratic nature is found, above all, in environments that are simple and stable. The work associated with complex environments cannot be rationalized into simple tasks, and that associated with dynamic environments cannot be predicted, made repetitive, and so standardized.

In addition, the machine configuration is typically found in mature organizations, large enough to have the volume of operating work needed for repetition and standardization, and old enough to have been able to settle on the standards they wish to use. These are the organizations that have seen it all before and have established standard procedures to deal with it. Likewise, machine organizations tend to be identified with technical systems that regulate the operating work, so that it can easily be programmed. Such technical systems cannot be very sophisticated or automated (for reasons that will be discussed later).

Mass production firms are perhaps the best-known machine organizations. Their operating work flows through an integrated chain, open at one end to accept raw materials, and after that functioning as a sealed system that processes them through sequences of standardized operations. Thus, the environment may be stable because the organization has acted aggressively to stabilize it. Giant firms in such industries as transportation, tobacco, and metals are well known for their attempts to influence the forces of supply and demand by the use of advertising, the development of long-term supply contacts, sometimes the establishment of cartels. They also tend to adopt strategies of "vertical integration," that is, extend their production chains at both ends, becoming both their own suppliers and their own customers. In that way they can bring some of the forces of supply and demand within their own planning processes.

Of course, the machine organization is not restricted to large, or manufacturing, or even private enterprise organizations. Small manufacturers—for example producers of discount furniture or paper products—may sometimes prefer this structure because their operating work is simple and repetitive. Many service firms use it for the same reason, such as banks or insurance companies in their retailing activities. Another condition often found with machine organizations is external control. Many government departments, such as post offices and tax collection agencies, are machine bureaucratic not only because their operating work is routine but also because they must be accountable to the public for their actions. Everything they do—treating clients, hiring employees, and so on—must be seen to be fair, and so they proliferate regulations.

Since control is the forte of the machine bureaucracy, it stands to reason that organizations in the business of control—regulatory agencies, custodial prisons, police forces—are drawn to this configuration, sometimes in spite of contradictory conditions. The same is true for the special need for safety. Organizations that fly airplanes or put out fires must minimize the risks they take. Hence they formalize their procedures extensively to ensure that they are carried out to the letter: A fire crew cannot arrive at a burning house and then turn to the chief for orders or discuss informally who will connect the hose and who will go up the ladder.

Control raises another issue about machine organizations. Being so pervasively regulated, they themselves can easily be controlled externally, as the *instruments* of outside influencers. In contrast, however, their obsession with control runs not only up the hierarchy but beyond, to control of their own environments, so that they can become *closed systems* immune to external influence. From the perspective of power, the instrument and the closed system constitute two main types of machine organizations.

In our terms, the instrument form of machine organization is dominated by one external influencer or by a group of them acting in concert. In the "closely held" corporation, the dominant influencer is the outside owner; in some prisons, it is a community concerned with the custody rather than the rehabilitation of prisoners.

Outside influencers render an organization their instrument by appointing the chief executive, charging that person with the pursuit of clear goals (ideally quantifiable, such as return on investment or prisoner escape measures), and then holding the chief responsible for performance. That way outsiders can control an organization without actually having to manage it. And such control, by virtue of the power put in the hands of the chief executive and the numerical nature of the goals, acts to centralize and bureaucratize the internal structure, in other words, to drive it to the machine form.

In contrast to this, Charles Perrow, the colorful and outspoken organizational sociologist, does not quite see the machine organization as anyone's instrument:

> Society is adaptive to organizations, to the large, powerful organizations controlled by a few, often overlapping, leaders. To see these organizations as adaptive to a "turbulent," dynamic, very changing environment is to indulge in fantasy. The environment of most powerful organizations is well controlled by them, quite stable, and made up of other organizations with similar interests, or ones they control. (1972:199)

Perrow is, of course, describing the closed system form of machine organization, the one that uses its bureaucratic procedures to seal itself off from external control and control others instead. It controls not only its own people but its environment as well: perhaps its suppliers, customers, competitors, even government and owners too.

Of course, autonomy can be achieved not only by controlling others (for example, buying up customers and suppliers in so-called vertical integration) but simply by avoiding the control of others. Thus, for example, closed system organizations sometimes form cartels with ostensible competitors or, less blatantly, diversify markets to avoid dependence on particular customers, finance internally to avoid dependence on particular financial groups, and even buy back their own shares to weaken the influence of their own owners. Key to being a closed system is to ensure wide dispersal, and therefore pacification, of all groups of potential external influence.

What goals does the closed system organization pursue? Remember that to sustain centralized bureaucracy the goals should be operational, ideally quantifiable. What operational goals enable an organization to serve itself, as a system closed to external influence? The most obvious answer is growth. Survival may be an indispensable goal and efficiency a necessary one, but beyond those what really matters here is making the system larger. Growth serves the system by providing greater rewards for its insiders—bigger empires for managers to run or fancier private jets to fly, greater programs for analysts to design, even more power for unions to wield by virtue of having more members. (The unions may be external influencers, but the management can keep them passive by allowing them more of the spoils of the closed system.) Thus the classic closed system machine organization, the large, widely held industrial corporation, has long been described as oriented far more to growth than to the maximization of profit per se (Galbraith, 1967).

Of course, the closed system form of machine organization can exist outside the private sector too, for example in the fundraising agency that, relatively free to external control, becomes increasingly charitable to itself (as indicated by the plushness of its managers' offices), the agricultural or retail cooperative that ignores those who collectively own it, even government that becomes more intent on serving itself than the citizens for which it supposedly exists.

The communist state, at least up until very recently, seemed to fit all the characteristics of the closed system bureaucracy. It had no dominant external influencer (at least in the case of the Soviet Union, if not the other East European states, which were its "instruments"). And the population to which it is ostensibly responsible had to respond to its own plethora of rules and regulations. Its election procedures, traditionally offering a choice of one, were similar to those for the directors of the "widely held" Western corporation. The government's own structure was heavily bureaucratic, with a single hierarchy of authority and a very elaborate technostructure, ranging from state planners to KGB agents. (As James Worthy [1959:77] noted, Frederick Taylor's "Scientific Management had its fullest flowering not in America but in Soviet Russia.") All significant resources were the property of the state—the collective system—not the individual. And, as in other closed systems, the administrators tend to take the lion's share of the benefits.

SOME ISSUES ASSOCIATED WITH THE MACHINE ORGANIZATION

No structure has evoked more heated debate than the machine organization. As Michel Crozier, one of its most eminent students, has noted,

> On the one hand, most authors consider the bureaucratic organization to be the embodiment of rationality in the modern world, and, as such, to be intrinsically superior to all other possible forms of organizations. On the other hand, many authors—often the same ones—consider it a sort of Leviathan, preparing the enslavement of the human race. (1964:176)

Max Weber, who first wrote about this form of organization, emphasized its rationality; in fact, the word *machine* comes directly from his writings (see Gerth and Mills, 1958). A machine is certainly precise; it is also reliable and easy to control; and it is efficient—at least when restricted to the job it has been designed to do. Those are the reasons many organizations are structured as machine bureaucracies. When an integrated set of simple, repetitive tasks must be performed precisely and consistently by human beings, this is the most efficient structure—indeed, the only conceivable one.

But in these same advantages of machinelike efficiency lie all the disadvantages of this configuration. Machines consist of mechanical parts; organizational structures also include human beings—and that is where the analogy breaks down.

James Worthy, when he was an executive of Sears, wrote a penetrating and scathing criticism of the machine organization in his book *Big Business and Free Men.* Worthy traced the root of the human problems in these structures to the "scientific management" movement led by Frederick Taylor that swept America early in this century. Worthy acknowledged Taylor's contribution to efficiency, narrowly defined. Worker initiative did not, however, enter into his efficiency equation. Taylor's pleas to remove "all possible brain work" from the shop floor also removed all possible initiative from the people who worked there: the "machine has no will of its own. Its parts have no urge to independent action. Thinking, direction—even purpose—must be provided from outside or above." This had the "consequence of destroying the meaning of work itself," which has been "fantastically wasteful for industry and society," resulting in excessive absenteeism, high worker turnover, sloppy workmanship, costly strikes, and even outright sabotage (1959:67, 79, 70). Of course, there are people who like to work in highly structured situations. But increasing numbers do not, at least not *that* highly structured.

Taylor was fond of saying, "In the past the man has been first; in the future the system must be first" (in Worthy 1959:73). Prophetic words, indeed. Modern man seems to exist for his systems; many of the organizations he created to serve him have come to enslave him. The result is that several of what Victor Thompson (1961) has called "bureaupathologies"—dysfunctional behaviors of these structures—reinforce each other to form a vicious circle in the machine organization. The concentration on means at the expense of ends, the mistreatment of clients, the various manifestations of worker alienation—all lead to the tightening of controls on behavior. The implicit motto of the machine organization seems to be, "When in doubt, control." All problems have to be solved by the turning of the technocratic screws. But since that is what caused the bureaupathologies in the first place, increasing the controls serves only to magnify the problems, leading to the imposition of further controls, and so on.

Coordination Problems in the Administrative Center

Since the operating core of the machine organization is not designed to handle conflict, many of the human problems that arise there spill up and over, into the administrative structure.

It is one of the ironies of the machine configuration that to achieve the control it requires, it must mirror the narrow specialization of its operating core in its administrative structure (for example, differentiating marketing managers from manufacturing managers, much as salesmen are differentiated from factory workers). This, in turn, means problems of communication and coordination. The fact is that the administrative structure of the machine organization is also ill suited to the resolution of problems through mutual adjustment. All the communication barriers in these structures—horizontal, vertical, status, line/staff—impede informal communication among managers and with staff people. "Each unit becomes jealous of its own prerogatives and finds ways to protect itself against the pressure or encroachments of others" (Worthy, 1950:176). Thus narrow functionalism not only impedes coordination; it also encourages the building of private empires, which tends to produce top-heavy organizations that can be more concerned with the political games to be won than with the clients to be served.

Adaptation Problems in the Strategic Apex

But if mutual adjustment does not work in the administrative center—generating more political heat than cooperative light—how does the machine organization resolve its coordination problems? Instinctively, it tries standardization, for example, by tightening job descriptions or proliferating rules. But standardization is not suited to handling the nonroutine problems of the administrative center. Indeed, it only aggravates them, undermining the influence of the line managers and increasing the conflict. So to reconcile these coordination problems, the machine organization is left with only one coordinating mechanism, direct supervision from above. Specifically, nonroutine coordination problems between units are "bumped" up the line hierarchy until they reach a common level of supervision, often at the top of the structure. The result can be excessive centralization of power, which in turn produces a host of other problems. In effect, just as the human problems in the operating core become coordination problems in the administrative center, so too do the coordination problems in the administrative center become adaptation problems at the strategic apex. Let us take a closer look at these by concluding with a discussion of strategic change in the machine configuration.

STRATEGY FORMATION IN THE MACHINE ORGANIZATION

Strategy in the machine organization is supposed to emanate from the top of the hierarchy, where the perspective is broadest and the power most focused. All the relevant information is to be sent up the hierarchy, in aggregated, MIS-type form, there to be formulated into integrated strategy (with the aid of the technostructure). Implementation then follows, with the intended strategies sent down the hierarchy to be turned into successively more elaborated programs and action plans. Notice the clear division of labor assumed between the formulators at the top and the implementors down below, based on the assumption of perfectly deliberate strategy produced through a process of planning.

That is the theory. The practice has been shown to be another matter. Drawing on our strategy research at McGill University, we shall consider first what planning really proved to be in one machinelike organization, how it may in fact have impeded strategic thinking in a second, and how a third really did change its strategy. From there we shall consider the problems of strategic change in machine organizations and their possible resolution.

Planning as Programming in a Supermarket Chain

What really is the role of formal planning? Does it produce original strategies? Let us return to the case of Steinberg's in the later years of its founder, as large size drove this retailing chain toward the machine form, and as is common in that form, toward a planning mode of management at the expense of entrepreneurship.

One event in particular encouraged the start of planning at Steinberg's: the company's entry into capital markets in 1953. Months before it floated its first bond issue (stock, always nonvoting, came later), Sam Steinberg boasted to a newspaper reporter that "not a cent of any money outside the family is invested in the company." And asked about future plans, he replied: "Who knows? We will try to go everywhere there seems to be a need for us." A few months later he announced a $5 million debt issue and with it a $15 million five-year expansion program, one new store every two months for a total of thirty, the doubling of sales, new stores to average double the size of existing ones.

What happened in those ensuing months was Sam Steinberg's realization, after the opening of Montreal's first shopping center, that he needed to enter the shopping center business himself to protect his supermarket chain and that he could not do so with the company's traditional methods of short-term and internal financing. And, of course, no company is allowed to go to capital markets without a plan. You can't just say: "I'm Sam Steinberg and I'm good," though that was really the issue. In a "rational" society, you have to plan (or at least appear to do so).

But what exactly was that planning? One thing for certain: It did not formulate a strategy. Sam Steinberg already had that. What planning did was justify, elaborate, and articulate the strategy that already existed in Sam Steinberg's mind. Planning operationalized his strategic vision, programmed it. It gave order to that vision, imposing form on it to comply with the needs of the organization and its environment. Thus, planning followed the strategy-making process, which had been essentially entrepreneurial.

But its effect on that process was not incidental. By specifying and articulation the vision, planning constrained it and rendered it less flexible. Sam Steinberg retained formal control of the company to the day of his death. But his control over strategy did not remain so absolute. The entrepreneur, by keeping his vision personal, is able to adapt it at will to a changing environment. But by being forced to program it, the leader loses that flexibility. The danger, ultimately, is that the planning mode forces out the entrepreneurial one; procedure replaces vision. As its structure became more machinelike, Steinberg's required planning in the form of strategic programming. But that planing also accelerated the firm's transition toward the machine form of organization.

Is there, then, such a thing as "strategic planning"? I suspect not. To be more explicit, I do not find that major new strategies are formulated through any formal procedure. Organizations that rely on formal planning procedures to formulate strategies seem to extrapolate existing strategies, perhaps with marginal changes in them, or else copy the strategies of other organizations. This came out most clearly in another of our McGill studies.

Planning as an Impediment to Strategic Thinking in an Airline

From about the mid-1950s, Air Canada engaged heavily in planning. Once the airline was established, particularly once it developed its basic route structure, a number of factors drove it strongly to the planning mode. Above all was the need for coordination, both of flight schedules with aircraft, crews, and maintenance, and of the purchase of expensive aircraft with the structure of the route system. (Imagine someone calling out in the hangar: "Hey, Fred, this guy says he has two 747s for us; do you know who ordered them?") Safety was another factor: The intense need for safety in the air breeds a mentality of being very careful about what the organization does on the ground, too. This is the airlines' obsession with control. Other factors included the lead times inherent in key decisions, such as ordering new airplanes or introducing new routes, the sheer cost of the capital equipment, and the size of the organization. You don't run an intricate system like an airline, necessarily very machinelike, without a great deal of formal planning.

But what we found to be the consequence of planning at Air Canada was the absence of a major reorientation of strategy during our study period (up to the mid-1970s). Aircraft certainly changed—they became larger and faster—but the basic route system did not, nor did markets. Air Canada gave only marginal attention, for example, to cargo, charter, and shuttle operations. Formal planning, in our view, impeded strategic thinking.

The problem is that planning, too, proceeds from the machine perspective, much as an assembly line or a conventional machine produces a product. It all depends on the decomposition of analysis: You split the process into a series of steps or component parts, specify each, and then by following the specifications in sequence you get the desired product. There is a fallacy in this, however. Assembly lines and conventional machines produce standardized products, while planning is supposed to produce a novel strategy. It is as if the machine is supposed to design the machine; the planning machine is expected to create the original blueprint—the strategy. To put this another way, planning is analysis oriented to decomposition, while strategy making depends on synthesis oriented to integration. That is why the term "strategic planning" has proved to be an oxymoron.

Roles of Planning, Plans, Planners

If planning does not create strategy, then what purpose does it serve? We have suggested a role above, which has to do with the programming of strategies already created in other ways. This is shown in Figure 2, coming out of a box labeled strategy formation—meant to represent what is to planning a mysterious "black box." But if planning is restricted to programming strategy, plans and planners nonetheless have other roles in play, shown in Figure 2 and discussed alongside that of planning itself.

FIGURE 2
Specific Roles of Planning, Plans, Planners

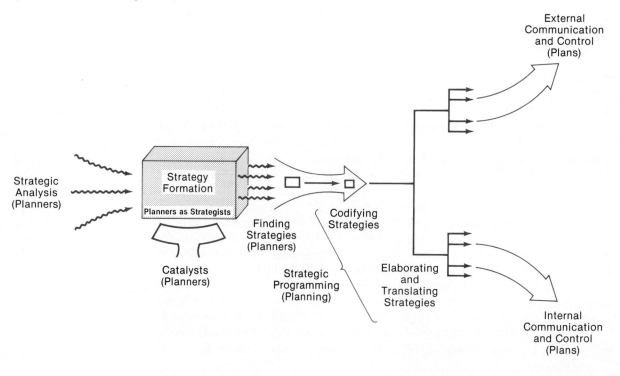

Role of Planning: Why do organizations engage in formal planning? The answer seems to be: not to create strategies, but to program the strategies they already have, that is, to elaborate and operationalize the consequences of those strategies formally. We should really say that *effective* organizations so engage in planning, at least when they require the formalized implementation of their strategies. Thus strategy is not the *consequence* of planning but its starting point. Planning helps to translate the intended strategies into realized ones, taking the first step that leads ultimately to implementation.

This *strategic programming,* as it might properly be labeled, can be considered to involve a series of steps, namely the *codification* of given strategy, including its clarification and articulation, the *elaboration* of that strategy into substrategies, ad hoc action programs, and plans of various kinds, and the *translation* of those substrategies, programs, and plans into routine budgets and objectives. In these steps, we see planning as an analytical process that takes over after the synthesis of strategic formation is completed.

Thus formal planning properly belongs in the *implementation* of strategy, not in its formulation. But it should be emphasized that strategic programming makes sense when viable intended strategies are available, in other words when the world is expected to hold still while these strategies unfold, so that formulation can logically precede implementation, and when the organization that does the implementing in fact requires clearly codified and elaborated strategies. In other circumstances, strategic programming can do organizations harm by preempting the flexibility that managers and others may need to respond to changes in the environment, or to their own internal processes of learning.

Roles of Plans: If planning is programming, then plans clearly serve two roles. They are a medium for communication and a device for control. Both roles draw on the analytical character of plans, namely, that they represent strategies in decomposed and articulated form, if not quantified then often at least quantifiable.

Why program strategy? Most obviously for coordination, to ensure that everyone in the organization pulls in the same direction, a direction that may have to be specified as precisely as possible. In Air Canada, to use our earlier example, that means linking the acquisition of new aircraft with the particular routes that are to be flown, and scheduling crews and planes to show up when the flights are to take off, and so on. Plans, as they emerge from strategic programming as programs, schedules, budgets, and so on, can be prime media to communicate not just strategic intention but also the role each individual must play to realize it.

Plans, as communication media, inform people of intended strategy and its consequences. But as control devices they can go further, specifying what role departments and individuals must play in helping to realize strategy and then comparing that with performance in order to feed control information back into the strategy-making process.

Plans can help to effect control in a number of ways. The most obvious is control of the strategy itself. Indeed what has long paraded under the label of "strategy planning" has probably had more to do with "strategic control" than many people may realize. Strategic control has to do with keeping organizations on their strategic tracks: to ensure the realization of intended strategy, its implementation as expected, with resources appropriately allocated. But there is more to strategic control than this. Another aspect includes the assessment of the realization of strategies in the first place, namely, whether the patterns realized corresponded to the intentions specified beforehand. In other words, strategic control must assess behavior as well as performance. Then the more routine and traditional form of control can come in to consider whether the strategies that were in fact realized proved effective.

Roles of Planners: Planners, of course, play key roles in planning (namely, strategic programming), and in using the resulting plans for purposes of communication and control. But many of the most important things planners do have little to do with planning or even plans per se. Three roles seem key here.

First, planners can play a role in finding strategies. This may seem curious, but if strategies really do emerge in organizations, then planners can help to identify the patterns that are becoming strategies, so that consideration can be given to formalizing them, that is, making them deliberate. Of course, finding the strategies of competitors—for assessment and possible modified adoption—is also important here.

Second, planners play the roles of analysts, carrying out ad hoc studies to feed into the black box of strategy making. Indeed, one could argue that this is precisely what Michael Porter proposes with his emphasis on industry and competitive analysis. The ad hoc nature of such studies should, however, be emphasized because they feed into a strategy-making process that is itself irregular, proceeding on no schedule and following no standard sequence of steps. Indeed, regularity in the planning process can interfere with strategic thinking, which must be flexible, responsive, and creative.

The third role of the planner is as a catalyst. This refers not to the traditional role long promoted in the literature of selling formal planning as some kind of religion, but to encourage strategic *thinking* throughout the organization. Here the planner encourages *informal* strategy making, trying to get others to think about the future in a creative way. He or she does not enter the block box of strategy making so much as ensure that the box is occupied with active line managers.

A Planner For Each Side of the Brain: We have discussed various roles for planning, plans, and planners, summarized around the block box of strategy formation in Figure 2. These roles suggest two different orientations for planners.

On one hand (so to speak), the planner must be a highly analytic, convergent type of thinker, dedicated to bringing order to the organization. Above all, this planner programs intended strategies and sees to it that they are communicated clearly and used for purposes of control. He or she also carries out studies to ensure that the managers concerned with strategy formation take into account the necessary hard data that they may be inclined to miss and that the strategies they formulate are carefully and systematically evaluated before they are implemented.

On the other hand, there is another type of planner, less conventional a creative, divergent thinker, rather intuitive, who seeks to open up the strategy-making process. As a "soft analyst," he or she tends to conduct "quick and dirty" studies, to find strategies in strange places, and to encourage others to think strategically. This planner is inclined toward the intuitive processes identified with the brain's right hemisphere. We might call him or her a *left-handed planner.* Some organizations need to emphasize one type of planner, others the other type. But most complex organizations probably need some of both.

Strategic Change in an Automobile Firm

Given planning itself is not strategic, how does the planning-oriented machine bureaucracy change its strategy when it has to? Volkswagenwerk was an organization that had to. We interpreted its history from 1934 to 1974 as one long cycle of a single strategic perspective. The original "people's car," the famous "Beetle," was conceived by Ferdinand Porsche; the factory to produce it was built just before the war but did not go into civilian automobile production until after. In 1948, a man named Heinrich Nordhoff was given control of the devastated plant and began the rebuilding of it, as well as of the organization and the strategy itself, rounding out Porsche's original conception. The firm's success was dramatic.

By the late 1950s, however, problems began to appear. Demand in Germany was moving away from the Beetle. The typically machine-bureaucratic response was not to rethink the basic strategy—"it's okay" was the reaction—but rather to graft another piece onto it. A new automobile model was added, larger than the Beetle but with a similar no-nonsense approach to motoring, again air-cooled with the engine in the back. Volkswagenwerk added position but did not change perspective.

But that did not solve the basic problem, and by the mid-1960s the company was in crisis. Nordhoff, who had resisted strategic change, died in office and was replaced by a lawyer from outside the business. The company then underwent a frantic search for new models, designing, developing, or acquiring a whole host of them with engines in the front, middle, and rear; air and water cooled; front- and rear-wheel drive. To paraphrase the humorist Stephen Leacock, Volkswagenwerk leaped onto its strategic horse and rode off in all directions. Only when another leader came in, a man steeped in the company and the automobile business, did the firm consolidate itself around a new strategic perspective, based on the stylish front-wheel drive, water-cooled designs of one of its acquired firms, and thereby turn its fortunes around.

What this story suggests, first of all, is the great force of bureaucratic momentum in the machine organization. Even leaving planning aside, the immense effort of producing and marketing a new line of automobiles locks a company into a certain posture. But here the momentum was psychological, too. Nordhoff, who had been the driving force behind the great success of the organization, became a major liability when the environment demanded change. Over the years, he too had been captured by bureaucratic momentum. Moreover, the uniqueness and tight integration of Volkswagenwerk's strategy—we labeled it *gestalt*—impeded strategic change. Change an element of a tightly integrated gestalt and it *dis*integrates. Thus does success eventually breed failure.

Bottleneck at the Top

Why the great difficulty in changing strategy in the machine organization? Here we take up that question and show how changes generally have to be achieved in a different configuration, if at all.

As discussed earlier, unanticipated problems in the machine organization tend to get bumped up the hierarchy. When these are few, which means conditions are relatively stable, things work smoothly enough. But in times of rapid change, just when new strategies are called for, the number of such problems magnifies, resulting in a bottleneck at the top, where senior managers get overloaded. And that tends either to impede strategic change or else to render it ill considered.

A major part of the problem is information. Senior managers face an organization decomposed into parts, like a machine itself. Marketing information comes up one channel, manufacturing information up another, and so on. Somehow it is the senior managers themselves who must integrate all that information. But the very machine bureaucratic premise of separating the administration of work from the doing of it means that the top managers often lack the intimate, detailed knowledge of issues necessary to effect such an integration. In essence, the necessary power is at the top of the structure, but the necessary knowledge is often at the bottom.

Of course, there is a machinelike solution to that problem too—not surprisingly in the form of a system. It is called a management information system, or MIS, and what it does is combine all the necessary information and package it neatly so that top managers can be informed about what is going on—the perfect solution for the overloaded executive. At least in theory.

Unfortunately, a number of real-world problems arise in the MIS. For one thing, in the tall administrative hierarchy of the machine organization, information must pass through many levels before it reaches the top. Losses take place at each one. Good news gets highlighted while bad news gets blocked on the way up. And "soft" information, so necessary for strategy information, cannot easily pass through, while much of the hard MIS-type information arrives only slowly. In a stable environment, the manager may be able to wait; in a rapidly changing one, he or she cannot. The president wants to be told right away that the firm's most important customer was seen playing golf yesterday with a main competitor, not to find out six months later in the form of a drop in a sales report. Gossip, hearsay, speculation—the softest kinds of information—warn the manager of impeding problems; the MIS all too often records for posterity ones that have already been felt. The manager who depends on an MIS in a changing environment generally finds himself or herself out of touch.

The obvious solution for top managers is to bypass the MIS and set up their own informal information systems, networks of contacts that bring them the rich, tangible, instant information they need. But that violates the machine organization's presuppositions of formality and respect for the chain of authority. Also, that takes the managers' time, the lack of which caused the bottleneck in the first place. So a fundamental dilemma faces the top managers of the machine organization as a result of its very own design: in times of change, when they most need the time to inform themselves, the system overburdens them with other pressures. They are thus reduced to acting superficially, with inadequate, abstract information.

The Formulation/Implementation Dichotomy

The essential problem lies in one of the chief tenets of the machine organization, that strategy formation must be sharply separated from strategy implementation. One is thought out at the top, the other then acted out lower down. For this to work assume two conditions: first, that the formulator has full and sufficient information, and second, that the world will hold still, or at least change in predictable ways, during the implementation, so that there is no need for *re*formulation.

Now consider why the organization needs a new strategy in the first place. It is because its world has changed in an unpredictable way, indeed may continue to do so. We have just seen how the machine bureaucratic structure tends to violate the first condition—it misinforms the senior manager during such times of change. And when change continues in an unpredictable way (or at least the world unfolds in a way not yet predicted by an ill-informed management), then the second condition is violated too—it hardly makes sense to lock in by implementation a strategy that does not reflect changes in the world around it.

What all this amounts to is a need to collapse the formulation/implementation dichotomy precisely when the strategy of machine bureaucracy must be changed. This can be done in one of two ways.

In one case, the formulator implements. In other words, power is concentrated at the top, not only for creating the strategy but also for implementing it, step by step, in a personalized way. The strategist is put in close personal touch with the situation at hand (more commonly a strategist is appointed who has or can develop that touch) so that he or she can, on one hand, be properly informed and, on the other, control the implementation en route in order to reformulate when necessary. This, of course, describes the entrepreneurial configuration, at least at the strategic apex.

In the other case, the implementers formulate. In other words, power is concentrated lower down, where the necessary information resides. As people who are naturally in touch with the specific situations at hand take individual actions—approach new customers, develop new products, et cetera—patterns form, in other words, strategies emerge. And this describes the innovative configuration, where strategic initiatives often originate in the grass roots of the organization, and then are championed by managers at middle levels who integrate them with one another or with existing strategies in order to gain their acceptance by senior management.

We conclude, therefore, that the machine configuration is ill suited to change its fundamental strategy, that the organization must in effect change configuration temporarily in order to change strategy. Either it reverts to the entrepreneurial form, to allow a single leader to develop vision (or proceed with one developed earlier), or else it overlays an innovative form on its conventional structure (for example, creates an informed network of lateral teams and task forces) so that the necessary strategies can emerge. The former can obviously function faster than the latter; that is why it tends to be used for drastic *turnaround,* while the latter tends to proceed by the slower process of *revitalization.* (Of course, quick turnaround may be necessary because there has been no slow revitalization.) In any event, both are characterized by a capacity to *learn*—that is the essence of the entrepreneurial and innovative configurations, in one case learning centralized for the simpler context, in the other, decentralized for the more complex one. The machine configuration is not so characterized.

This, however, should come as no surprise. After all, machines are specialized instruments, designed for productivity, not for adaptation. In Hunt's (1970) words, machine bureaucracies are performance systems, not problem-solving ones. Efficiency is their forte, not innovation. An organization cannot put blinders on its personnel and then expect peripheral vision. Managers here are rewarded for cutting costs and improving standards, not for taking risks and ignoring procedures. Change makes a mess of the operating systems: change one link in a carefully coupled system, and the the whole chain must be reconceived. Why, then, should we be surprised when our bureaucratic machines fail to adapt?

Of course, it is fair to ask why we spend so much time trying to make them adapt. After all, when an ordinary machine becomes redundant, we simply scrap it, happy that it served us for as long and as well as it did. Converting it to another use generally proves more expensive than simply starting over. I suspect the same is often true for bureaucratic machines. But here, of course, the context is social and political. Mechanical parts don't protest, nor do displaced raw materials. Workers, suppliers, and customers do, however, protest the scrapping of organizations, for obvious reasons. But that the cost of this is awfully high in a society of giant machine organizations will be the subject of the final chapter of this book.

Strategic Revolutions in Machine Organizations

Machine organizations do sometimes change, however, at times effectively but more often it would seem at great cost and pain. The lucky ones are able to overlay an innovative structure for periodic revitalization, while many of the other survivors somehow manage to get turned around in entrepreneurial fashion.

Overall, the machine organizations seem to follow what my colleagues Danny Miller and Peter Friesen (1984) call a "quantum theory" of organization change. They pursue their set strategies through long periods of stability (naturally occurring or created by themselves as closed systems), using planning and other procedures to do so efficiently. Periodically these are interrupted by short bursts of change, which Miller and Friesen characterize as "strategic revolutions" (although another colleague, Mihaela Firsirotu [1985], perhaps better labels it "strategic turn-around as cultural revolution").

Organization Taking Precedence in the Machine Organization

To conclude, as shown in Figure 3, it is organization—with its systems and procedures, its planning and its bureaucratic momentum—that takes precedence over leadership and environment in the machine configuration. Environment fits organization, either because the organization has slotted itself into a context that matches its procedures, or else because it has forced the environment to do so. And leadership generally falls into place too, supporting the organization, indeed often becoming part of its bureaucratic momentum.

This generally works effectively, though hardly nonproblematically, at least in times of stability. But in times of change, efficiency becomes ineffective and the organization will falter unless it can find a different way to organize for adaptation.

All of this is another way of saying that the machine organization is a configuration, a species, like the others, suited to its own context but ill suited to others. But unlike the others, it is the dominant configuration in our specialized societies. As long as we demand inexpensive and so necessarily standardized goods and services, and as long as people continue to be more efficient than real machines at providing them, and remain willing to do so, then the machine organization will remain with us—and so will all its problems.

FIGURE 3
Organization Takes Precedence

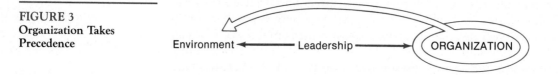

Environment ←——— Leadership ———→ (ORGANIZATION)

● LONG-RANGE FORMAL PLANNING IN PERSPECTIVE*

BY BRIAN J. LOASBY

Planning has become a fashionable subject in American management literature, and shows some signs of becoming a fashionable managerial preoccupation in Britain. But the word 'planning' is currently used in so many and various senses that it is in some danger of degenerating into an emotive noise. . . . instead of succumbing to the slogan that "The Future Is Planning," [1] let us attempt to restore some content to the idea by examining the purposes of a formal procedure for long-range planning. . . .

---

* Originally published in *The Journal of Management Studies* (October 1967). Copyright © 1967 *The Journal of Management Studies;* reprinted by permission of the publishers.
[1]"The Past is History . . . The Future is Planning" is the title of an article (Rickard, 1965).

The basic question in considering any sort of planning is: why should a firm attempt to look into the future? Why not wait until it arrives? There seem to be three basic reasons.

The first reason for looking into the future in a systematic way is to understand the future implications of present decisions. What must a firm be prepared to do next year in order to gain the full advantage from what it decides to do now; what will be the effect of its current choice on the range of options available to it in the future; what problems may be created later on by choosing a particular course of action now? These questions need to be asked on a project-by-project basis; but the major advantage of a systematic procedure is that it also requires various projects to be looked at simultaneously. This is important if individual projects have important "external effects," that is, if one project is likely to assist or impede another—whether by their combined effects on the demand for the firm's resources (or the efficiency with which they are used), or by their effects outside the firm. The process by which two or more projects assist each other has been christened synergy (Ansoff, 1965:75); perhaps the opposite process by which they impede each other could be called allergy. It is hard to imagine a situation in which such effects are completely absent; if they are significant, then the agenda for considering one project is not wide enough unless it includes the implications of competitive or complementary projects. A formal procedure, by informing various levels and various sections of the firm of what other levels and other sections are proposing to do, and requiring such information to be taken into account when decisions are made, may be the most effective way of securing the necessary width.

The second reason for looking into the future in a systematic way is in a sense the obverse of the first. As well as considering the future implications of present decisions, it is necessary to examine the present implications of the future events. The question here is: 'What needs to be decided now in order to be prepared for what is expected to happen later on?' If the first question is concerned with the width of the agenda, the second is concerned with its length. When James P. McFarland of General Mills says that "effective long-range planning will probably be more useful in making problems apparent than in solving them"[2] he is pointing to the second purpose of looking into the future in a formal kind of way. The systematic attempt to forecast the future should help to reveal problems in time to anticipate them.

The future implications of present decisions and the present implications of future events cannot, obviously, be thoroughly considered every day; but without some specific motivation and mechanism they may never be adequately considered at all. The third reason for looking into the future in a systematic way is to provide such motivation and such a mechanism. The formal planning process should require an explicit review of the assumptions which underlie the limited agendas which are necessarily used for day-to-day decisions, in order to reduce the danger that "what look like rational decisions under limited agendas . . . (may) turn out to be disastrous." (Boulding, 1966:167).

Too many major issues, though obviously important, seem easily postponable in favor of immediate minor problems; they are therefore liable to be postponed either until they are decided by default, or, at best, until they have to be resolved by improvisation instead of by thoughtful and wide-ranging study. The

---

[2] James P. McFarland, "Planning and Control at General Mills," unpublished lecture notes, Harvard Business School, Cambridge, MA.

formal planning process should ensure an adequate commitment of management resources to these issues, and a commitment in time to allow such study. It should encourage the proper exploration of a range of genuine options, not merely a single proposal. A time to make choices is a time to offer alternatives: the final decision maker, of course, has the power to veto, but the power of veto is a very limited form of the power to choose.

It is not always easy for a manager to combine efficient day-to-day operation of a system with the review and redesign of that system; that he should be encouraged and assisted to combine them is clearly desirable for the reasons already given. There is another reason: this exercise of both widening and lengthening his agenda is the part of a manager's job that is most relevant to the requirements of a higher position, and is thus particularly useful in preparing him for greater responsibilities and in indicating his capacity to undertake them.

POTENTIAL DANGERS OF FORMAL PLANNING

It should be emphasized that the purposes identified so far all relate to present decisions for present action. ("I use long-range planning," says a senior I.C.I. manager, "to decide what to do tomorrow.") They imply no commitment to any future action, and do not in themselves require any planning document to be kept after the immediate decisions have been made. Short-term plans will presumably be prepared in the normal budgeting process, and performance will be evaluated against these. Why should managers be required to make decisions now about action to be taken in the future?

One obvious reason is that a comparison of performance with plan may be useful in revealing possible problems or opportunities—in other words, as a means of getting topics on the agenda. This is clearly useful in itself, though one must remember the danger with any incomplete automatic warning system—that it tends to divert attention from the danger that it does not signal.

Another possible reason is to secure a manager's commitment to an objective. But one must be very careful here. Commitment to making a proper job of today's decisions, based on careful and imaginative evaluation of their future implications, is certainly desirable. Some commitment to next year's plans may be desirable too—but not unquestioning commitment, because conditions may change. It is far from clear that any commitment that is at all precise is desirable beyond that. The fact that a firm should not, for example, start to develop a new product unless it is, at the time of the decision, prepared to launch a marketing effort at the appropriate time does not mean that is should decide now to launch that future effort. The attempt to develop a new product may fail; and even if it succeeds, the situation may have so changed by the time the decision to market needs to be taken that it may be best not to market. Just as by then the costs of development are sunk costs, so the earlier intention to market is a bygone intention; and sunk costs and bygone intentions are a poor basis for present decisions.

The third reason why a firm might want managers to make decisions now about future actions is to provide a basis for evaluation of their performance. This reason is subject to the same criticism as that advance against commitment, that action in accordance with a plan prepared long beforehand may well not be the action that is best for the firm.

It is not surprising that some companies should make the apparently natural progression for the annual budget to the "five-year forward look." It is not surprising, but it is dangerous. Any attempt to use a long-term plan for control purposes is liable to frustrate the valuable purposes of the planning process. Budgetary control is intended to ensure, by a system of rewards and penalties, the attainment of forecast results. As the penalty for failure is usually greater than the reward for success, the control system motivates a manager to promise no more than he is confident of performing.

This is quite the wrong apparatus for securing the advantages of formal planning. These advantages lie in the stimulus to fresh thought and imaginative ideas; but imaginative ideas involve risk, and risk implies the possibility of failure. To ask a man to commit himself, under threat of penalty, to the success of his proposed action is to ask him never to take a risk. It is therefore quite natural that, as Charles O. Rossotti (n.d.) observes, "one objection to action planning is that it makes an insufficient contribution to, or even hinders, the vital process of generating proposals for major policy changes and new opportunities" (p. 6). The allure of an integrated planning and control system should be resisted.

The fourth reason for requiring managers to decide now what they will do at specific points in the future is that it facilitates future decision making in other groups where external effects are important. Short-term decisions are made on the basis of two kinds of assumptions: one kind is about the outside world, the other is about what is happening in other parts of the organization. Whether the first kind of assumption turns out to be right or wrong cannot be controlled by the firm; but it does have the power to ensure that the assumptions of the second kind are right, by insisting that they be spelled out well in advance and adhered to. Thus the assurance which may be given in an action plan of what other parts of the organization will be doing helps to narrow the agenda for other decisions. It does not improve communications between parts of the organization; it eliminates the need for them. It makes it possible to allocate responsibilities in a pretty watertight way. This kind of planning is not an aid, but an alternative, to good communications.

Of course, the price of improving the compatibility between a decision made in one part of an organization and simultaneous decisions made elsewhere may be the reduction of compatibility between the decision and the outside environment. One way of dealing with this is to draw up a set of contingency plans, or conditional decisions, based on several different sets of assumptions; provided that the facts fit one set reasonably well, it is necessary only to make sure that everyone knows which set they are all to use. In some circumstances this may be a good method. But just how necessary is it to secure this coordination in advance? If these conditional decisions are to be intelligently prepared, with due regard for the interaction between various sections of the business, then while they are being prepared there has to be close contact between the sections (unless, of course, as may be the case, there really is very little cross-effect, in which case this reason for decisions about future action disappears). Why, then, should one design a system which appears to postulate very little contact in the intervals between the formulation of these decisions? Might one not get both better-integrated decision making and better-coordinated response to changing conditions by abandoning compartmentalization and not specifying responsibility so narrowly?

The apparent need to improve (but in fact to dispense with) communication and coordination is likely to be associated with what has been called a "mechanistic system of management" (Burns and Stalker, 1961), that is a system characterized by a well-ordered hierarchy of clearly defined responsibilities, so that everyone knows precisely what is—and also what is not—his business. In a situation where the interrelationships ignored by this formal structure are nevertheless important, the structure may appear to require equally formal planning procedures; and these procedures may appear to be facilitated by the structure. But instead of using formal planning procedures to reconcile the organization structure to the real needs of the company, it might be better to encourage the growth of a network structure of relationships, in which the active contacts at any time are determined by the task in hand, instead of being specified in advance. Such an "organic system" (Burns and Stalker, 1961) will be more responsive to changing circumstances, and might well produce better results for the organization than an attempt to predetermine future decisions.

An important virtue of a systematic look into the future is that it forces a company to make its forecasts more explicit. But even this virtue is not without its accompanying dangers. It is often argued that to make better decisions we need better information. Now it is certainly true that information can be improved. To take two examples: few firms apparently attempt to improve the accuracy of their forecasts by analyzing the reasons for past forecasting errors—even when the errors are as notorious as those made by American television manufacturers in the early days of color television; and few firms do as much as they could to assess the impact of known technological change. Better information is both desirable and obtainable. But—and here is a major source of error—better information does not necessarily mean more precise information. The demand for better information is often a demand for false certainty; and the institution of formal procedures for looking into the future may encourage this demand. Certainly one cannot make sensible decisions in ignorance; but uncertainty is not ignorance—it is knowledge. A seemingly precise forecast hides uncertainties, and therefore actually provides less information than a forecast which shows a range of possible values.

Thus the search for more information may be perverted into a search for false certainty. This is particularly likely if managers are asked to commit themselves to results at all far ahead. Such a pervasion may have two unfortunate consequences. Decisions may be made that do not properly reflect the possibility of error in the forecasts on which they are based; and overconfidence may produce excessive commitment to future action, and therefore a reluctance to take new decisions in the light of new information—indeed sometimes a reluctance even to notice new information.

The risk of domination by sophisticated techniques is serious. As a consequence of the emphasis on perfection of calculations, "computerized data processing rather than planning has (sometimes) become the major concern. Figures (have been) accepted without sufficient questioning" ("Little, Inc., 1966). At least one major British company has rejected the use of discounted cash flow for investment calculations because of the fear that its use will divert resources and attention from improving the quality of the basic data.

But these dangers are not inevitable. Instead of attempting to produce an optimum solution under given assumptions, formal procedures can be designed to force a "broadening of the planning agenda, . . . giving a means for exploring the meaning of changed assumptions and effects of changes in policy" (Magee, 1966). Its power to compel a systematic search, in situations where sequential search procedures may be inadequate, or even disastrous, is perhaps the most important virtue of the "decision tree" as an aid to management (Magee, 1964).

FORMAL PLANNING AND THE MANAGEMENT SYSTEM

Even if planning procedures are properly designed, however, there remains a deeper danger. Improving the quality of information is not the only way of improving the quality of decisions. If one asks what information is needed now to make the decisions that must be made now, one sometimes finds that some of the desired information is not really necessary. Some decisions are made too soon, even within the management system that a firm has at present. Others could be made later if the system were changed. Rossotti's statement that "the more efficiently . . . information is made available, presumably the more flexible the organization can be in adapting to it quickly" (p. 13) is precisely the reverse of the truth. Rossotti is confusing the speed of response with its timing. If reliable information is available well in advance, the organization can start to prepare well in advance. If one sets out early, one doesn't need to go very fast. Flexibility is not the result of good early warning, it is an alternative to it.

If one looks at the whole sequence between the emergence of information and the fruition of decisions, one may well see greater possibilities in reducing the delays in the system than in improving the quality of information. The Industrial Dynamics Group at M.I.T., investigating a successful company that was worried about the problem of predicting success for a new product, found not only that there were ways of reducing the interval between ordering equipment and getting it into production, but that half the total lapse of time between information and production was consumed in the decision process itself. In another instance, a company's production scheduling was improved by making more frequent but less accurate forecasts. A consulting team from Arthur D. Little, Inc., found a complex PERT chart, prepared for a highway agency, which showed a lead time of ten years between the results of traffic survey and the engineering drawing for the road; and not one input during that ten years represented any further information about traffic. A formal procedure which is directed at producing more information for earlier decisions is liable to channel efforts into refining forecasts and elaborating future action which could be better used in other ways.

The dangers of formal procedures outlined in the previous section may be summarized in two points: they may reduce the organization's flexibility (or in other words inhibit that initiation of a new decision process and reduce the speed with which new decisions can be made), and they may divert attention away from recognizing the need for flexibility. Perhaps the best way for firms to approach formal long-range planning is as something they should try to avoid. This does not mean as something they should try to dodge: it means so arranging the way they do things that as little as possible needs to be decided in advance. Of course, "as little as possible" will still be a good deal, but if, instead of asking how they can more accurately foresee future events and thus make better decisions further ahead, firms were to ask first what they can do to avoid the need to decide so far ahead, they might be led to discover important ways of improving their performance.

What is needed is not action planning but system planning: the question at issue is not only the adequacy of formal procedures but also the effectiveness (and especially the speed) of the decision process: these are by no means the same. The effectiveness of the decision process depends on information and organization. In assembling information, more emphasis should be placed on surveillance rather than sophistication. The valid arguments for sophistication should not be ignored, but nor should it be forgotten that effective monitoring is more useful than elaborate manipulation of data which is out of date before the manipulation is complete.

. . . the real problem is to design an organization that can cope with the amount of uncertainty that is inherent in its situation. To deal effectively with this problem requires a shift of emphasis for organizational structure to the decision process. . . . It is easy to become so absorbed in the details of devising an elaborate planning procedure as to forget that redesign of the information flow and of the management system may be more effective ways of achieving some of the objectives of formal long-range planning.

This article has been concerned with the purposes of formal planning, not with techniques. The great value of formal procedures—and their value can be very great—is in the raising and broadening of important issues that are liable otherwise to be inadequately considered. Much of this value can, however, be lost if these formal procedures are at all closely connected with the conflicting objective of controlling managerial performance. Planning procedures should be designed to illuminate, rather than obscure, the existence and implications of uncertainty. Finally, planning procedures should not concentrate on management action at the expense of the management system, and in particular should not be used to reconcile organization structure with the real situation: the design of a management system which facilitates quicker and more direct responses can be a better answer to some of the problems for which formal procedures offer only a second-best solution.

● THE TRANSITION TO INDUSTRY MATURITY*

BY MICHAEL E. PORTER

As part of their evolutionary process, many industries pass from periods of rapid growth to the more modest growth of what is commonly called industry maturity. . . . industry maturity does not occur at any fixed point in an industry's development, and it can be delayed by innovations or other events that fuel continued growth for industry participants. Moreover, in response to strategic breakthroughs, mature industries may regain their rapid growth and thereby go through more than one transition to maturity. With these important qualifications in mind, however, let us consider the case in which a transition to maturity is occurring. . . . .

INDUSTRY CHANGE DURING TRANSITION

Transition to maturity can often signal a number of important changes in an industry's competitive environment. Some of the probable tendencies for change are as follows:

1. *Slowing growth means more competition for market share.* With companies unable to maintain historical growth rates merely by holding market share, competitive attention turns inward toward attacking the shares of the others. . . . Not only are competitors probably going to be more aggressive, but also the likelihood of misperceptions and "irrational" retaliation is great. Outbreaks of price, service, and promotional warfare are common during transition to maturity.

2. *Firms in the industry increasingly are selling to experienced, repeat buyers.* The product is no longer new but an established legitimate item. Buyers are often increasingly knowledgeable and experienced, having already purchased the product, sometimes repeatedly. The buyers' focus shifts from deciding whether to purchase the product at all to making choices among brands. Approaching these differently oriented buyers requires a fundamental reassessment of strategy.

* Excerpted from *Competitive Strategy: Techniques for Analyzing Industries and Competitors,* by Michael E. Porter. Copyright © by The Free Press, a division of Macmillan, Inc.; reprinted by permission of the publisher.

3. *Competition often shifts toward greater emphasis on cost and service.* As a result of slower growth, more knowledgeable buyers, and usually greater technological maturity, competition tends to become more cost and service-oriented. . . .

4. *There is a topping-out problem in adding industry capacity and personnel.* As the industry adjusts to slower growth, the rate of capacity addition in the industry must slow down as well or overcapacity will occur. . . . [But the necessary] shifts in perspective rarely occur in maturing industries, and overshooting of industry capacity relative to demand is common. Overshooting leads to a period of overcapacity, accentuating the tendency during transition toward price warfare. . . .

5. *Manufacturing, marketing, distributing, selling, and research methods are often undergoing change.* These changes are caused by increased competition for market share, technological maturity, and buyer sophistication. . . .

6. *New products and applications are harder to come by.* Whereas the growth phase may have been one of rapid discovery of new products and applications, the ability to continue product change generally becomes increasingly limited, or the costs and risks greatly increase, as the industry matures. This change requires, among other things, a reorientation of attitude toward research and new product development.

7. *International competition increases.* As a consequence of technological maturity, often accompanied by product standardization and increasing emphasis on costs, transition is often marked by the emergence of significant international competition. . . .

8. *Industry profits often fall during the transition period, sometimes temporarily and sometimes permanently.* Slowing growth, more sophisticated buyers, more emphasis on market share, and the uncertainties and difficulties of the required strategic changes usually mean that industry profits fall in the short run from the levels of the pretransition growth phase. . . . Whether or not profits will rebound depends on the level of mobility barriers and other elements of industry structure. . . .

9. *Dealers' margins fall, but their power increases.* For the same reasons that industry profits are often depressed, dealers' margins may be squeezed, and many dealers may drop out of business—often *before* the effect on manufacturers' profits is noticeable. . . . Such trends tighten competition among industry participants for dealers, who may have been easy to find and hold in the growth phase but not upon maturity. Thus, dealers' power may increase markedly.

SOME STRATEGIC IMPLICATIONS OF TRANSITION

. . . Some characteristic strategic issues often arise in transition. These are presented as issues to examine rather than generalizations that will apply to all industries; like humans, all industries mature a little differently. Many of these approaches can be a basis for the entry of new firms into an industry even though it is mature.

Overall Cost Leadership Versus Differentiate Versus Focus
—The Strategic Dilemma Made Acute by Maturity

Rapid growth tends to mask strategic errors and allow most, if not all, companies in the industry to survive and even to prosper financially. Strategic experimentation is high, and a wide variety of strategies can coexist. Strategic sloppiness is generally exposed by industry maturity, however. Maturity may force companies to confront, often for the first time, the need to choose among the three generic strategies described (in Chapter 4 of this text). It becomes a matter of survival.

Sophisticated Cost Analysis

Cost analysis becomes increasingly important in maturity to (1) rationalize the product mix and (2) price correctly.

Rationalizing the Product Mix: . . . a quantum improvement in the sophistication of product costing is necessary to allow pruning of unprofitable items from the line and to focus attention on items either that have some distinctive advantage (technology, cost, image, etc.) or whose buyers are "good" buyers. . . .

Correct Pricing: Related to product line rationalization is the change in pricing methodology that is often necessary in maturity. Although average-cost pricing, or pricing the line as a whole rather than as individual items, may have been sufficient in the growth era, maturity often requires increased capability to measure costs on individual items and to price accordingly. . . .

We might summarize this and the other points in this section by saying that an enhanced level of "financial consciousness" along a variety of dimensions is often necessary in maturity, whereas in the developmental period of the industry areas such as new products and research may have rightly held center stage. . . .

Process Innovation and Design for Manufacture

The relative importance of process innovations usually increases in maturity, as does the payoff for designing the product and its delivery system to facilitate lower-cost manufacturing and control. . . .

Increasing Scope of Purchases: Increasing purchases of existing customers may be more desirable than seeking new customers. . . . Such a strategy may take the firm out of the industry into related industries. This strategy is often less costly than finding new customers. In a mature industry, winning new customers usually means battling for market share with competitors and is consequently quite expensive. . . .

Buy Cheap Assets

Sometimes assets can be acquired very cheaply as a result of the company distress that is caused by transition to maturity. A strategy of acquiring distressed companies or buying liquidated assets can improve margins and create a low-cost position if the rate of technological change is not too great. . . .

Buyer Selection

As buyers become more knowledgeable and competitive pressures increase in maturity, buyer selection can sometimes be a key to continued profitability. Buyers who may not have exercised their bargaining power in the past, or had less power because of limited product availability, will usually not be bashful about exercising their power in maturity. Identifying "good" buyers and locking them in . . . becomes crucial.

Different Cost Curves

There is often more than one cost curve possible in an industry. The firm that is *not* the overall cost leader in a mature market can sometimes find new cost curves which may actually make it a lower-cost producer for certain types of buyers, product varieties, or order sizes. This step is key to implementing the generic strategy of focus. . . .

Competing Internationally

A firm may escape maturity by competing internationally where the industry is more favorably structured. Sometimes equipment that is obsolete in the home market can be used quite effectively in international markets, greatly lowering the costs of entry there. . . .

STRATEGIC PITFALLS IN TRANSITION

In addition to failure to recognize the strategic implications of transition described above, there is the tendency for firms to fall prey to some characteristic strategic pitfalls:

1. *A company's self-perceptions and its perception of the industry.* Companies develop perceptions or images of themselves and their relative capabilities ("we are the quality leader"; "we provide superior customer service"), which are reflected in the implicit assumptions that form the basis of their strategies. . . . These self-perceptions may be increasingly inaccurate as transition proceeds, buyers' priorities adjust, and competitors respond to new industry conditions. Similarly, firms have assumptions about the industry, competitors, buyers, and suppliers which may be invalidated by transition. Yet altering these assumptions, built up through actual past experience, is sometimes a difficult process.

2. *Caught in the middle.* The problem of being caught in the middle described [earlier] is particularly acute in transition to maturity. Transition often squeezes out the slack that has made this strategy viable in the past.

3. *The cash trap—investments to build share in a mature market.* Cash should be invested in a business only with the expectation of being able to remove it later. In a mature, slow-growing industry, the assumptions required to justify investing new cash in order to build market share are often heroic. Maturity of the industry works against increasing or maintaining margins long enough to recoup cash investments down the road, by making the present value of cash inflows justify the outflows. Thus businesses in maturity can be cash traps, particularly when a firm is not in a strong market position but is attempting to build a large market share in a maturing market. The odds are against it.

A related pitfall is placing heavy attention on revenues in the maturing market instead of on profitability. This strategy may have been desirable in the growth phase, but it usually faces diminishing returns in maturity. . . .

4. *Giving up market share too easily in favor of short-run profits.* In the face of the profit pressures in transition, there seems to be a tendency for some companies to try to maintain the profitability of the recent past—which is done at the expense of market share or by foregoing marketing, R&D, and other needed investments, which in turn hurts future market position. . . . A period of lower profits may be inevitable while industry rationalization occurs, and a cool head is necessary to avoid overreaction.

5. *Resentment and irrational reaction to price competition (*"we will not compete on price"*).* It is often difficult for firms to accept the need for price competition after a period in which it has not been necessary. . . .

6. *Resentment and irrational reaction to changes in industry practices (*"they are hurting the industry"*).* Changes in industry practices, such as marketing techniques, production methods, and the nature of distributor contracts are often an inevitable part of transition. They may be important to the industry's long-run potential, but there is often resistance to them. . . .

7. *Overemphasis on* "creative," "new" *products rather than improving and aggressively selling existing ones.* Although past success in the early and growth phases of an industry may have been built on research and on new products, the onset of maturity often means that new products and applications are harder to come by. It is usually appropriate that the focus of innovative activity should change, putting standardization rather than newness and fine tuning at a premium. Yet this development is not satisfying to some companies and is often resisted.

8. *Clinging to* "higher quality" *as an excuse for not meeting aggressive pricing and marketing moves of competitors.* High quality can be a crucial company strength, but quality differentials have a tendency to erode as an industry matures. . . . Yet it is difficult for many companies to accept the fact that they do not possess the highest-quality product or that their quality is unnecessarily high.

9. *Overhanging excess capacity.* As a result of capacity overshooting demand, or because of capacity increases that inevitably accompany the plant modernization required to compete in the mature industry, some firms may have some excess capacity. Its mere presence creates both subtle and unsubtle pressures to utilize it, and it can be used in ways that will undermine the firm's strategy. . . .

• COST DYNAMICS: SCALE AND EXPERIENCE EFFECTS*

BY DEREK F. ABELL AND JOHN S. HAMMOND

Market share is one of the primary determinants of business profitability; other things being equal, businesses with a larger share of a market are more profitable than their smaller-share competitors. For instance, a study by the PIMS Program (Buzzell, Gale and Sultan, 1975) . . . found that, on average, a difference of 10 percentage points in market share is accompanied by a difference of about 5 points in pretax ROI ("pretax operating profits" divided by "long-term debt plus equity"). Additional evidence is that companies having large market shares in their primary product markets—such as General Motors, IBM, Gillette, Eastman Kodak, and Xerox—tend to be highly profitable.

An important reason for the increase in profitability with market share is that large-share firms usually have *lower costs*. The lower costs are due in part to econ-

---

* Originally published in *Strategic Market Planning: Problems and Analytical Approaches* (Prentice Hall, 1979), Chap. 3. Copyright © Prentice Hall, 1979; reprinted with deletions by permission of the publisher.

omies of scale; for instance, very large plants cost less per unit of production to build and are often more efficient than smaller plants. Lower costs are also due in part to the so-called *experience effect,* whereby the cost of many (if not most) products declines by 10–30 percent each time a company's experience at producing and selling them doubles. In this context *experience* has a precise meaning: it is the cumulative number of units produced to date. Since at any point in time, businesses with large market shares typically (but not always) have more experience than their smaller-share competitors, they would be expected to have lower costs. . . .

This [reading] considers how costs decline due to scale and to experience, practical problems in analyzing the experience effect, strategic implications of scale and experience, and limitations of strategies based on cost reduction. . . .

SCALE EFFECT

As mentioned earlier, scale effect refers to the fact that large businesses have the potential to operate at lower unit costs than their smaller counterparts. The increased efficiency due to size is often referred to as "economy of scale"; it could equally be called "economy of size."

Most people think of economy of scale as a manufacturing phenomenon because large manufacturing facilities can be constructed at a lower cost per unit of capacity and can be operated more efficiently than smaller ones. . . .

Just as they cost less to build, large-scale plants have lower *operating* costs per unit of output. . . . While substantial in manufacturing, scale effect is also significant in other cost elements, such as marketing, sales, distribution, administration, R&D, and service. For instance, a chain with 30 supermarkets in a metropolitan area needs much less than three times as much advertising as a chain of 10 stores. . . . Economies of scale are also achieved with purchased items such as raw material and shipping. . . .

Although scale economies potentially exist in all cost elements of a business in both the short and long run, large size alone doesn't assure the benefits of scale. It is evident from the above illustrations that size provides an *opportunity* for scale economies; to achieve them requires strategies and actions consciously designed to seize the opportunity, especially with operating costs. . . .

EXPERIENCE EFFECT

The experience effect, whereby costs fall with cumulative production, is measurable and predictable; it has been observed in a wide range of products including automobiles, semiconductors, petrochemicals, long-distance telephone calls, synthetic fibers, airline transportation, the cost of administering life insurance, and crushed limestone, to mention a few. Note that this list ranges from high technology to low technology products, service to manufacturing industries, consumer to industrial products, new to mature products, and process to assembly oriented products, indicating the wide range of applicability. . . .

. . . it is only comparatively recently that this phenomenon has been carefully measured and quantified; at first it was thought to apply only to the labor portion of *manufacturing* costs. . . . In the 1960s evidence mounted that the phenomenon was broader. Personnel from the Boston Consulting Group and others showed that each time cumulative volume of a product doubled, total value added costs—including administration, sales, marketing, distribution, and so on in addition to manufacturing—fell by a constant and predictable percentage. In addition, the costs of purchased items usually fell as suppliers reduced prices as their costs fell, due also to the experience effect. The relationship between costs and experience was called the *experience curve* (Boston Consulting Group, 1972).

An experience curve is plotted with the cumulative units produced on the horizontal axis, and cost per unit on the vertical axis. An "85%" experience curve is shown in Figure 1. The "85%" means that every time experience doubles, costs per unit drop to 85% of the original level. It is known as the *learning rate*. Stated differently, costs per unit decrease 15 percent for every doubling of cumulative production. For example, the cost of the 20th unit produced is about 85% of the cost of the 10th unit. . . .

An experience curve appears as a straight line when plotted on a double log paper (logarithmic scale for both the horizontal and vertical axes). Figure 2 shows the "85 percent" experience curve from Figure 1 on the double logarithmic scale. . . . Figure 3 provides illustrations for [some specific] products.

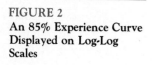

FIGURE 1
A Typical Experience Curve [85%]

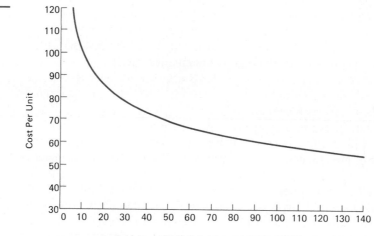

Experience (Cumulative Units of Production)

FIGURE 2
An 85% Experience Curve Displayed on Log-Log Scales

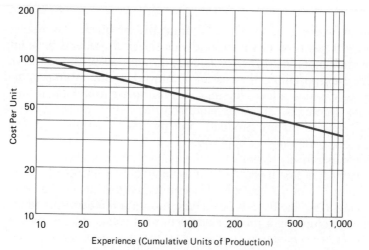

Experience (Cumulative Units of Production)

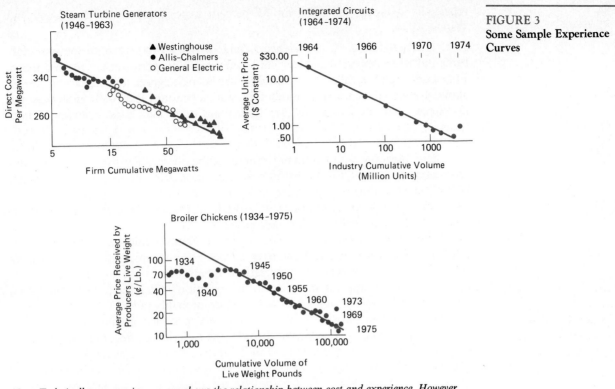

FIGURE 3
Some Sample Experience Curves

Note: *Technically an experience curve shows the relationship between cost and experience. However, cost figures are seldom publicly available; therefore most of the above experience curves show industry price (in constant dollars) vs. experience.*

Source: The Boston Consulting Group.

SOURCES OF THE EXPERIENCE EFFECT

The experience effect has a variety of sources; to capitalize on it requires knowledge of why it occurs. Sources of the experience effect are outlined as follows:

1. *Labor efficiency.* . . . As workers repeat a particular production task, they become more dextrous and learn improvements and shortcuts which increase their collective efficiency. The greater the number of worker-paced operations, the greater the amount of learning which can accrue with experience. . . .

2. *Work specialization and methods improvements.* Specialization increases worker proficiency at a given task. . . .

3. *New production processes.* Process innovations and improvements can be an important source of cost reductions, especially in capital-intensive industries. . . .

4. *Getting better performance from production equipment.* When first designed, a piece of production equipment may have a conservatively rated output. Experience may reveal innovative ways of increasing its output. . . .

5. *Changes in the resource mix.* As experience accumulates, a producer can often incorporate different or less expensive resources in the operation. . . .

6. *Product standardization.* Standardization allows the replication of tasks necessary for worker learning. Production of the Ford Model T, for example, followed a strategy of deliberate standardization; as a result, from 1909 to 1923 its price was repeatedly reduced, following an 85 percent experience curve (Abernathy and Wayne, 1974). . . .

7. *Product redesign.* As experience is gained with a product, both the manufacturer and customers gain a clearer understanding of its performance requirements. This understanding allows the product to be redesigned to conserve material, allows greater efficiency in manufacture, and substitutes less costly materials and resources, while at the same time improving performance on relevant dimensions. . . .

The foregoing list of sources dramatizes the observation that cost reductions due to experience don't occur by natural inclination; they are the result of substantial, concerted effort and pressure to lower costs. In fact, left unmanaged, costs rise. Thus, experience does not cause reductions but rather provides an opportunity that alert managements can exploit. . . .

The list of reasons for the experience effect raises perplexing questions on the difference between experience and scale effects. For instance, isn't it true that work specialization and project standardization, mentioned in the experience list, become possible because of the *size* of an operation? Therefore, aren't they each really scale effects? The answer is that they are probably both.

The confusion arises because growth in experience usually coincides with growth in size of an operation. We consider the experience effect to arise primarily due to ingenuity, cleverness, skill, and dexterity derived from experience as embodied in the adages "practice makes perfect" or "experience is the best teacher." On the other hand, scale effect comes from capitalizing on the size of an operation. . . .

Usually the overlap between the two effects is so great that it is difficult (and not too important) to separate them. This is the practice we will adopt from here on. . . .

PRICES AND EXPERIENCE

In stable competitive markets, one would expect that as costs decrease due to experience, prices will decrease similarly. (The price-experience curves in Figure 3 are examples of prices falling with experience.) If profit margins remain at a constant percentage of price, average industry costs and prices should follow identically sloped experience curves (on double logarithmic scales). The constant gap separating them will equal the profit margin percentage; Figure 4 illustrates such an idealized situation.

In many cases, however, prices and costs exhibit a relationship similar to the one shown in Figure 5, where prices start briefly below cost, then cost reductions exceed price reductions until prices suddenly tumble. Ultimately the price and cost curves parallel, as they do in Figure 4. Specifically, in the development phase, new product prices are below average industry costs due to pricing based on anticipated costs. In the price umbrella phase, when demand exceeds supply, prices remain firm under a price umbrella supported by the market leader. This is unstable. At some point a shakeout phase starts; one producer will almost certainly reduce prices to gain share. If this does not precipitate a price decline, the high profit margins will attract enough new entrants to produce temporary overcapacity, causing prices to tumble faster than costs, and marginal producers to be forced out of the market. The stability phase starts when profit margins return to normal levels and prices begin to follow industry costs down the experience curve. . . .

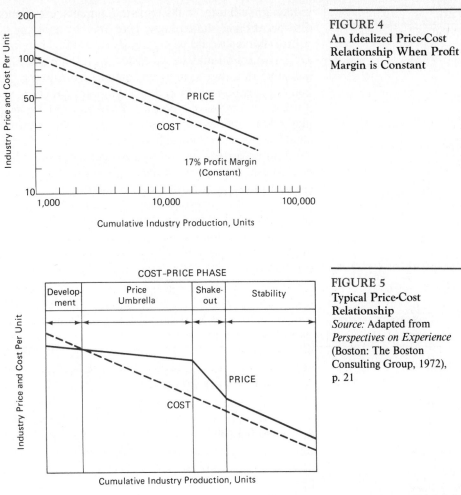

FIGURE 4
An Idealized Price-Cost
Relationship When Profit
Margin is Constant

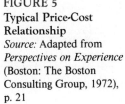

FIGURE 5
Typical Price-Cost
Relationship
Source: Adapted from
Perspectives on Experience
(Boston: The Boston
Consulting Group, 1972),
p. 21

STRATEGIC IMPLICATIONS

In industries where a significant portion of total cost can be reduced due to scale or experience, important cost advantages can usually be achieved by pursuing a strategy geared to accumulating experience faster than competitors. (Such a strategy will ultimately require that the firm acquire the largest market share relative to competition.).

The dominant producer can greatly influence industry profitability. The rate of decline of competitors' costs must at least keep pace with the leader if they are to maintain profitability. If their costs decrease more slowly, either because they are pursuing cost reductions less aggressively or are growing more slowly than the leader, then their profits will eventually disappear, thus eliminating them from the market.

... the advantage of being the leader is obvious. Leadership is usually best seized at the start when experience doubles quickly (e.g., experience increases tenfold as you move from the 20th to the 2,000th unit, but only doubles as you move from the 2,000th to the 4,000th unit.) Then a firm can build an unassailable cost advantage and at the same time gain price leadership. The best course of action for a product depends on a number of factors, one of the most important being the

295

market growth rate. In fast-growing markets, experience can be gained by taking a disproportionate share of new sales, thereby avoiding taking sales away from competitors (which would be vigorously resisted). Therefore, with high rates of growth, aggressive action may be called for. But, share-gaining tactics are usually costly in the short run, due to reduced margins from lower prices, added advertising and marketing expense, new product development costs, and the like. This means that if it lacks the resources (product, financial, and other) for leadership and in particular if it is opposed by a very aggressive competitor, a firm may find it wise to abandon the market entirely or focus on a segment it can dominate. On the other hand, in no-growth or slowly growing markets it is hard to take share from competitors and the time it takes to acquire superior experience is usually too long and the cost too great to favor aggressive strategies.

In stable competitive markets, usually the firm with the largest share of market has the greatest experience and it is often the case that each firm's experience is roughly proportional to market share. A notable exception occurs when a late entrant to a market quickly obtains a commanding market share. It may have less experience than some early entrants. . . .

EFFICIENCY VERSUS EFFECTIVENESS: LIMITATIONS TO STRATEGIES BASED ON EXPERIENCE OR SCALE

The selection of a competitive strategy based on cost reduction due to experience or scale often involves a fundamental choice. It is the selection of cost-price *efficiency* over noncost-price marketing *effectiveness*. However, when the market is more concerned with product and service features and up-to-date technology, a firm pursuing efficiency can find itself offering a low-priced product that few customers want. Thus two basic questions arise: (1) when to use an efficiency strategy and (2) if used, how far to push it before running into dangers of losing effectiveness. . . .

Whether to pursue an efficiency strategy depends on answers to questions such as,

1. Does the industry offer significant cost advantages from experience or scale (as in semiconductors or chemicals)?

2. Are there significant market segments that will reward competitors with low prices?

3. Is the firm well equipped (financially, managerially, technologically, etc.) for or already geared up for strategies relying heavily on having the lowest cost . . .?

If the answer is "yes" to all these questions, then "efficiency" strategies should probably be pursued.

Once it decided to pursue an "efficiency" strategy a firm must guard against going so far that it loses effectiveness, primarily through inability to respond to changes. For instance, experience-based strategies frequently require a highly specialized work force, facilities and organization, making it difficult to respond to changes in consumer demand, to respond to competitors' innovations, or to initiate them. In addition, large-scale plants are vulnerable to changes in process technology, and the heavy cost of operation below capacity.

For example, Ford's Motel T automobile ultimately suffered the consequences of inflexibility due to overemphasizing "efficiency" (Abernathy and

Wayne, 1974). Ford followed a classic experience-based strategy; over time it slashed its product line to a single model (the Model T), built modern plants, pushed division of labor, introduced the continuous assembly line, obtained economies in purchased parts through high volume, backward integrated, increased mechanization, and cut prices as costs fell. The lower prices increased Ford's share of a growing market to a high of 55.4% by 1921.

In the meantime, consumer demand began shifting to heavier, closed-body cars and to more comfort. Ford's chief rival, General Motors, had the flexibility to respond quickly with new designs. Ford responded by adding features to its existing standard design. While the features softened the inroads of GM, the basic Model T design, upon which Ford's "efficiency" strategy was based, inadequately met the market's new performance standards. To make matters worse, the turmoil in production due to constant design changes slowed experience-based efficiency gains. Finally Ford was forced, at enormous cost, to close for a whole year beginning May 1927 while it retooled to introduce its Model A. Hence experience or scale-based *efficiency* was carried too far and thus it ultimately limited *effectiveness* to meet consumer needs, to innovate, and to respond.

Thus the challenge is to decide when to emphasize efficiency and when to emphasize effectiveness, and further to design efficiency strategies that maintain effectiveness and vice versa. . . .

11

THE DIVERSIFIED CONTEXT

A good deal of evidence has accumulated on the relationship between diversification and divisionalization. Once organizations diversify their product or service lines, they tend to create distinct structural divisions to deal with each distinct business. This relationship was perhaps first carefully documented in the classic historical study by Alfred D. Chandler, *Strategy and Structure: Chapters in the History of the Great American Enterprise.* Chandler traced the origins of diversification and divisionalization in Du Pont and General Motors in the 1920s which were followed later by other major firms. A number of other studies elaborated on Chandler's conclusions; these are discussed in the readings of this chapter.

The first reading, drawn from Mintzberg's work on structuring, probes the structure of divisionalization—how it works, what brings it about, what intermediate variations of it exist, and what problems it poses for organizations that use it and for society at large. It concludes on a rather pessimistic note about conglomerate diversification and about the purer forms of divisionalization.

The next set of readings on the diversified context probe issues of its strategy, generally referred to as "corporate," to be distinguished from the "business" strategies of specific divisions. This has to do with managing the "portfolio" of businesses—which to develop and acquire, which to close or divest, but more important as one of these readings makes clear, how to knit them into a viable corporate entity.

As diversification became an especially popular strategy among large corporations in the 1960s and 1970s, a number of techniques were developed to analyze strategies at the corporate level. Among the most widely used were a number labeled "portfolio," which viewed the businesses of a diversified company as a collection of investments whose return could be optimized by properly balancing their growth and maturity characteristics and by redeploying investments and cash flows among them.

To describe this, we turn to the words of Bruce Henderson, who built up the Boston Consulting Group in good part on the basis of the best known of these techniques, its "growth-share matrix." This offered corporate executives a way to think of managing an array of businesses, but it also came in for some sharp criticism, not the least of which came from John Seeger, a professor at Bentley College, who used his earlier journalistic skills to turn around BCG's images of businesses as question marks, cash cows, stars, and dogs. We reprint Seeger's article here not only to present another perspective on a famous technique but also to convey his broader message, one well worth bearing in mind throughout management education. "No management model can safely substitute for analysis and common sense." While techniques such as the experience curve and competitive and portfolio analysis can be very useful in understanding critical relationships and in making sure one touches all the right bases, they provide no substitutes for a thorough-going intellectual and intuitive understanding of the full complexity of a company's unique capabilities in its particular environments. Many of these cannot be captured in numerical analyses, but abide in the minds and motivations of the people in the organization.

Aspects of the diversified organization, particularly in its more conglomerate form, thus come in for some heavy criticism in this chapter. The next reading takes up that torch too, but it quickly turns to the more constructive questions of how to use strategy to combine a cluster of different businesses into an effective corporate entity. This is Michael Porter's award-winning *Harvard Business Review* article "From Competitive Advantage to Corporate Strategy." Porter discusses in a most insightful way various types of overall corporate strategies, including portfolio management, restructuring, transferring skills, and sharing activities (the last two referred to in his 1985 book *Competitive Advantage* as "horizontal strategies," the former dealing with "intangible," the latter "tangible" interrelationships among business units, and conceived in terms of his value chain [see pages 72–74]).

Finally, we close this chapter with a look at what might be thought of as an important subcontext of the diversified one. That is the so-called "global" context —diversification geographically across many parts of the globe with the various activities rationalized among many different countries. The recent article by George Yip, who now teaches management at Georgetown University after working for several years as a management consultant, provides an excellent summary of the issues surrounding "global strategies."

THE DIVERSIFIED ORGANIZATION*

BY HENRY MINTZBERG

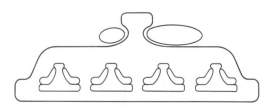

THE BASIC DIVISIONALIZED STRUCTURE

The diversified organization is not so much an integrated entity as a set of semiautonomous units coupled together by a central administrative structure. The units are generally called *divisions,* and the central administration, the *headquarters.* This is a widely used configuration in the private sector of the industrialized economy; the vast majority of the *Fortune* 500, America's largest corporations, use this structure or a variant of it. But, as we shall see, it is also found in other sectors as well.

In what is commonly called the "divisionalized" form of structure, units, called "divisions," are created to serve distinct markets and are given control over the operating functions necessary to do so, as shown in Figure 1. Each is therefore relatively free of direct control by headquarters or even of the need to coordinate

FIGURE 1

**Typical Organigram
for a Divisionalized
Manufacturing Firm**

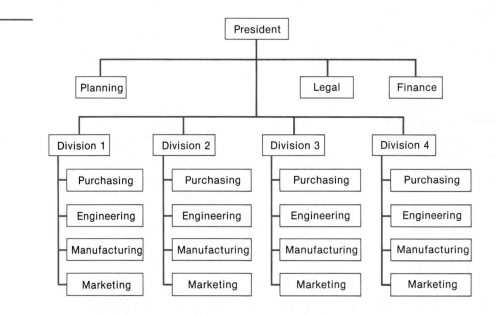

* Adapted from *The Structuring of Organizations* (Prentice Hall, 1979), Chap. 20 on "The Divisionalized Form". A chapter similar to this appeared in *Mintzberg on Management: Inside Our Strange World of Organizations* (Free Press, 1989).

activities with other divisions. Each, in other words, appears to be a self-standing business. Of course, none is. There *is* a headquarters, and it has a series of roles that distinguish this overall configuration from a collection of independent businesses providing the same set of products and services.

Roles of the Headquarters

Above all, the headquarters exercises performance control. It sets standards of achievement, generally in quantitative terms (such as return on investment or growth in sales), and then monitors the results. Coordination between headquarters and the divisions thus reduces largely to the standardization of outputs. Of course, there is some direct supervision—headquarters' managers have to have personal contact with and knowledge of the divisions. But that is largely circumscribed by the key assumption in this configuration that if the division managers are to be responsible for the performance of their divisions, they must have considerable autonomy to manage them as they see fit. Hence there is extensive delegation of authority from headquarters to the level of division manager.

Certain important tasks do, however, remain for the headquarters. One is to develop the overall *corporate* strategy, meaning to establish the portfolio of businesses in which the organization will operate. The headquarters establishes, acquires, divests, and closes down divisions in order to change its portfolio. Popular in the 1970s in this regard was the Boston Consulting Group's "growth share matrix," where corporate managers were supposed to allocate funds to divisions on the basis of their falling into the categories of dogs, cash cows, wildcats, and stars. But enthusiasm for that technique waned, perhaps mindful of Pope's warning that a little learning can be a dangerous thing.

Second, the headquarters manages the movement of funds between the divisions, taking the excess profits of some to support the greater growth potential of others. Third, of course, the headquarters, through it own technostructure, designs and operates the performance control system. Fourth, it appoints and therefore retains the right to replace the division managers. For a headquarters that does not directly manage any division, its most tangible power when the performance of a division lags—short of riding out an industry downturn or divesting the division—is to replace its leader. Finally, the headquarters provides certain support services that are common to all the divisions—a corporate public relations office or legal counsel, for example.

Structure of the Divisions

It has been common to label divisionalized organizations "decentralized." That is a reflection of how *certain* of them came to be, most notably Du Pont early in this century. When organizations that were structured functionally (for example, in departments of marketing, manufacturing, and engineering, etc.) diversified, they found that coordination of their different product lines across the functions became increasingly complicated. The central managers had to spend great amounts of time intervening to resolve disputes. But once these corporations switched to a divisionalized form of structure, where all the functions for a given business could be contained in a single unit dedicated to that business, management became much simpler. In effect, their structures became *more* decentralized, power over distinct businesses being delegated to the division managers.

But more decentralized does not mean *decentralized.* That word refers to the dispersal of decision-making power in an organization, and in many of the diversified corporations much of the power tended to remain with the few managers who ran the businesses. Indeed, the most famous case of divisionalization was one of relative *centralization:* Alfred P. Sloan introduced the divisionalized structure to General Motors in the 1920s to *reduce* the power of its autonomous business units, to impose systems of financial controls on what had been a largely unmanaged agglomeration of different automobile businesses.

In fact, I would argue that it is the *centralization* of power within the divisions that is most compatible with the divisionalized form of structure. In other words, the effect of having a headquarters over the divisions is to drive them toward the machine configuration, namely a structure of centralized bureaucracy. That is the structure most compatible with headquarters control, in my opinion. If true, this would seem to be an important point, because it means that the proliferation of the diversified configuration in many spheres—business, government, and the rest—has the effect of driving many suborganizations toward machine bureaucracy, even where that configuration may be inappropriate (school systems, for example, or government departments charged with innovative project work).

The explanation for this lies in the standardization of outputs, the key to the functioning of the divisionalized structure. Bear in mind the headquarters' dilemma: to respect divisional autonomy while exercising control over performance. This it seeks to resolve by after-the-fact monitoring of divisional results, based on clearly defined performance standards. But two main assumptions underlie such standards.

First, each division must be treated as a single integrated system with a single, consistent set of goals. In other words, although the divisions may be loosely coupled with each other, the assumption is that each is tightly coupled internally.[1]

Second, these goals must be operational ones, in other words, lend themselves to quantitative measurement. But in the less formal configurations—entrepreneurial and innovative—which are less stable, such performance standards are difficult to establish, while in the professional configuration, the complexity of the work makes it difficult to establish such standards. Moreover, while the entrepreneurial configuration may lend itself to being integrated around a single set of goals, the innovative and professional configurations do not. Thus, only the machine configuration of the major types fits comfortably into the conventional divisionalized structure, by virtue of its integration and its operational goals.

In fact, when organizations with another configuration are drawn under the umbrella of a divisionalized structure, they tend to be forced toward the machine bureaucratic form, to make them conform with *its* needs. How often have we heard stories of entrepreneurial firms recently acquired by conglomerates being descended upon by hordes of headquarters technocrats bemoaning the loose controls, the absence of organigrams, the informality of the systems? In many cases, of course, the very purpose of the acquisition was to do just this, tighten up the organization so that its strategies can be pursued more pervasively and systematically. But other times, the effect is to destroy the organization's basic strengths, sometimes including its flexibility and responsiveness. Similarly, how many times have we heard tell of government administrators complaining about being unable to control public hospitals or universities through conventional (meaning machine bureaucratic) planning systems?

This conclusion is, in fact, a prime manifestation of the hypothesis [discussed in Chapter 6] that concentrated external control of an organization has the effect of formalizing and centralizing its structure, in other words, of driving it toward the

---

[1] Unless, of course, there is a second layer of divisionalization, which simply takes this conclusion down another level in the hierarchy.

machine configuration. Headquarters' control of divisions is, of course, concentrated; indeed, when the diversified organization is itself a *closed system,* as I shall argue later many tend to be, then it is a most concentrated form of control. And, the effect of that control is to render the divisions its *instruments.*

There is, in fact, an interesting irony in this, in that the less society controls the overall diversified organization, the more the organization itself controls its individual units. The result is increased autonomy for the largest organizations coupled with decreased autonomy for their many activities.

To conclude this discussion of the basic structure, the diversified configuration is represented in the opening figure, symbolically in terms of our logo, as follows. Headquarters has three parts: a small strategic apex of top managers, a small technostructure to the left concerned with the design and operation of the performance control system, and a slightly larger staff support group to the right to provide support services common to all the divisions. Each of the divisions is shown below the headquarters as a machine configuration.

CONDITIONS OF THE DIVERSIFIED ORGANIZATION

While the diversified configuration may arise from the federation of different organizations, which come together under a common headquarters umbrella, more often it appears to be the structural response to a machine organization that has diversified its range of product or service offerings. In either case, it is the diversity of markets above all that drives an organization to use this configuration. An organization faced with a single integrated market simply cannot split itself into autonomous divisions; the one with distinct markets, however, has an incentive to create a unit to deal with each.

There are three main kinds of market diversity—product and service, client, and region. In theory, all three can lead to divisionalization. But when diversification is based on variations in clients or regions as opposed to products or services, divisionalization often turns out to be incomplete. With identical products or services in each region or for each group of clients, the headquarters is encouraged to maintain central control of certain critical functions, to ensure common operating standards for all the divisions. And that seriously reduces divisional autonomy, and so leads to a less than complete form of divisionalization.

Thus, one study found that insurance companies concentrate at headquarters the critical function of investment, and retailers concentrate that of purchasing, also controlling product range, pricing, and volume (Channon, 1975). One need only look at the individual outlets of a typical retail chain to recognize the absence of divisional autonomy: usually they all look alike. The same conclusion tends to hold for other businesses organized by regions, such as bakeries, breweries, cement producers, and soft drink bottlers: Their "divisions," distinguished only by geographical location, lack the autonomy normally associated with ones that produce distinct products or services.

What about the conditions of size? Although large size itself does not bring on divisionalization, surely it is not coincidental that most of America's largest corporations use some variant of this configuration. The fact is that as organizations grow large, they become inclined to diversify and then to divisionalize. One reason is protection: large organizations tend to be risk averse—they have too much to lose—and diversification spreads the risk. Another is that as firms grow large, they come to dominate their traditional market, and so must often find growth opportunities elsewhere, through diversification. Moreover, diversification feeds on itself. It creates a cadre of aggressive general managers, each running his or her own division, who push for further diversification and further growth. Thus, most of the giant corporations—with the exception of the "heavies," those with enormously high fixed-cost operating systems, such as the oil or aluminum producers —not only were able to reach their status by diversifying but also feel great pressures to continue to do so.

Age is another factor associated with this configuration, much like size. In larger organizations, the management runs out of places to expand in its traditional markets; in older ones, the managers sometimes get bored with the traditional markets and find diversion through diversification. Also, time brings new competitors into old markets, forcing the management to look elsewhere for growth opportunities.

As governments grow large, they too tend to adopt a kind of divisionalized structure. The central administrators, unable to control all the agencies and departments directly, settle for granting their managers considerable autonomy and then trying to control their results through planning and performance controls. Indeed, the "accountability" buzzword so often heard in governments these days reflects just this trend—to move closer to a divisionalized structure.

One can, in fact, view the entire government as a giant diversified configuration (admittedly an oversimplification, since all kinds of links exist among the departments), with its three main coordinating agencies corresponding to the three main forms of control used by the headquarters of the large corporation. The budgetary agency, technocratic in nature, concerns itself with performance control of the departments; the public service commission, also partly technocratic, concerns itself with the recruiting and training of government managers; and the executive office, top management in nature, reviews the principal proposals and initiatives of the departments.

In the preceding chapter, the communist state was described as a closed-system machine bureaucracy. But it may also be characterized as the ultimate closed system diversified configuration, with the various state enterprises and agencies its instruments, machine bureaucracies tightly regulated by the planning and control systems of the central government.

STAGES IN THE TRANSITION TO THE DIVERSIFIED ORGANIZATION

There has been a good deal of research on the transition of the corporation from the functional to the diversified form. Figure 2 and the discussion that follows borrow from this research to describe four stages in that transition.

At the top of Figure 2 is the pure *functional* structure, used by the corporation whose operating activities form one integrated, unbroken chain from purchasing through production to marketing and sales. Only the final output is sold to the customers.[2] Autonomy cannot, therefore, be granted to the units, so the organization tends to take on the form of one overall machine configuration.

As an integrated firm seeks wider markets, it may introduce a variety of new end products and so shift all the way to the pure diversified form. A less risky alternative, however, is to start by marketing its intermediate products on the open market. This introduces small breaks in its processing chain, which in turn calls for a measure of divisionalization in its structure, giving rise to the *by-product* form.

---

[2] It should be noted that this is in fact the definition of a functional structure: Each activity contributes just one step in a chain toward the creation of the final product. Thus, for example, engineering is a functionally organized unit in the firm that produces and markets its own designs, while it would be a market organized unit in a consulting firm that sells its design services, among other, directly to clients.

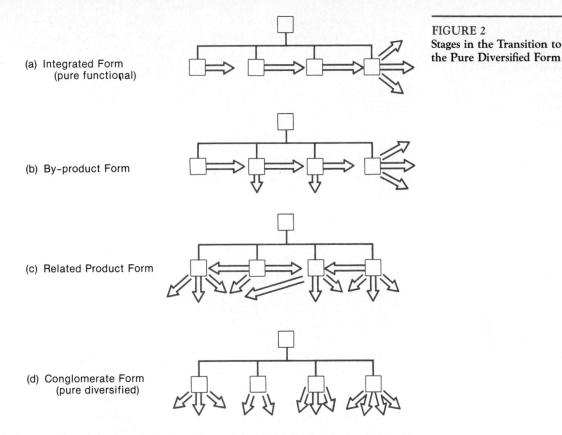

FIGURE 2
Stages in the Transition to
the Pure Diversified Form

(a) Integrated Form
    (pure functional)

(b) By-product Form

(c) Related Product Form

(d) Conglomerate Form
    (pure diversified)

But because the processing chain remains more or less intact, central coordination must largely remain. Organizations that fall into this category tend to be vertically integrated, basing their operations on a single raw material, such as wood, oil, or aluminum, which they process to a variety of consumable end products. The example of Alcoa is shown in Figure 3.

Some corporations further diversify their by-product markets, breaking down their processing chain until what the divisions sell on the open market becomes more important than what they supply to each other. The organization then moves to the *related-product* form. For example, a firm manufacturing washing machines may set up a division to produce the motors. When the motor division sells more motors to outside customers than to its own sister division, a more serious form of divisionalization is called for. What typically holds the divisions of these firms together is some common thread among their products, perhaps a core skill or technology, perhaps a central market theme, as in a corporation such as 3M that likes to describe itself as being in the coating and bonding business. A good deal of the control over the specific product-market strategies can now revert to the divisions, such as research and development.

As a related-product firm expands into new markets or acquires other firms with less regard to a central strategic theme, the organization moves to the *conglomerate* form and so adopts a pure diversified configuration, the one described at the beginning of this reading. Each division serves its own markets, producing products unrelated to those of the other divisions—chinaware in one, steam shovels in a second, and so on.* The result is that the headquarters planning and

---

* I wrote this example here somewhat whimsically before I encountered a firm in Finland with divisions that actually produce, among other things, the world's largest icebreaker ships and fine pottery!

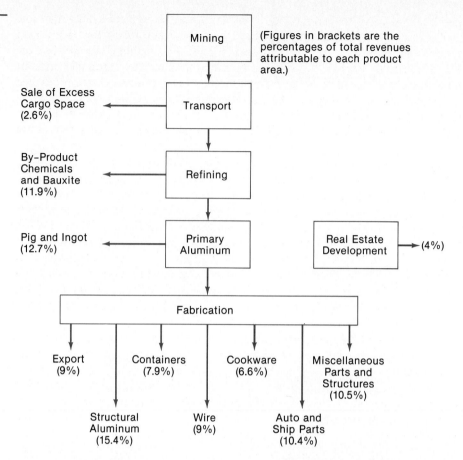

FIGURE 3
By-Product and End-Product Sales of Alcoa (from Rumelt, 1974:21)
Note: Percentages for 1969 prepared by Richard Rumelt from data in company's annual reports.

control system becomes simply a vehicle for regulating performance, and the headquarters staff can diminish to almost nothing—a few general and group managers supported by a few financial analysts with a minimum of support services.

SOME ISSUES ASSOCIATED WITH THE DIVERSIFIED ORGANIZATION

The Economic Advantages of Diversification?

It has been argued that the diversified configuration offers four basic advantages over the functional structure with integrated operations, namely an overall machine configuration. First, it encourages the efficient allocation of capital. Headquarters can choose where to put its money and so can concentrate on its strongest markets, milking the surpluses of some divisions to help others grow. Second, by opening up opportunities to run individual businesses, the diversified configuration helps to train general managers. Third, this configuration spreads its risk across different markets, whereas the focused machine bureaucracy has all its strategic eggs in one market basket, so to speak. Fourth, and perhaps most important, the diversified configuration is strategically responsive. The divisions can fine-tune their bureaucratic machines while the headquarters can concentrate on the strategic portfolio. It can acquire new businesses and divest itself of old, unproductive ones.

But is the single machine organization the correct basis of comparison? Is not the real alternative, at least from society's perspective, the taking of a further step

306

along the same path, to the point of eliminating the headquarters altogether and allowing the divisions to function as independent organization? Beatrice Foods, described in a 1976 *Fortune* magazine article, had 397 different divisions (Martin, 1976). The issue is whether this arrangement was more efficient than 397 separate corporations.[3] In this regard, let us reconsider the four advantages discussed earlier.

In the diversified corporation, headquarters allocates the capital resources among the divisions. In the case of 397 independent corporations, the capital markets do that job instead. Which does it better? Studies suggest that the answer is not simple.

Some people, such as the economist Oliver Williamson (1975, 1985), have argued that the diversified organization may do a better job of allocating money because the capital markets are inefficient. Managers at headquarters who know their divisions can move the money around faster and more effectively. But others find that arrangement more costly and, in some ways, less flexible. Moyer (1970), for example, argued early on that conglomerates pay a premium above stock market prices to acquire businesses, whereas the independent investor need pay only small brokerage fees to diversify his or her own portfolio, and can do so easier and more flexibly. Moreover, that provides the investor with full information on all the businesses owned, whereas the diversified corporation provides only limited information to stockholders on the details inside its portfolio.

On the issue of management development, the question becomes whether the division managers receive better training and experience than they would as company presidents. The diversified organization is able to put on training courses and to rotate its managers to vary their experience; the independent firm is limited in those respects. But if, as the proponents of diversification claim, autonomy is the key to management development, then presumably the more autonomy the better. The division managers have a headquarters to lean on—and to be leaned on by. Company presidents, in contrast, are on their own to make their own mistakes and to learn from them.

On the third issue, risk, the argument from the diversified perspective is that the independent organization is vulnerable during periods of internal crisis or economic slump; conglomeration offers support to see individual businesses through such periods. The counter-argument, however, is that diversification may conceal bankruptcies, that ailing divisions are sometimes supported longer than necessary, whereas the market bankrupts the independent firm and is done with it. Moreover, just as diversification spreads the risk, so too does it spread the consequences of that risk. A single division cannot go bankrupt; the whole organization is legally responsible for its debts. So a massive enough problem in one division can pull down the whole organization. Loose coupling may turn out to be riskier than no coupling!

Finally, there is the issue of strategic responsiveness. Loosely coupled divisions may be more responsive than tightly coupled functions. But how responsive do they really prove to be? The answer appears to be negative: this configuration appears to inhibit, not encourage, the taking of strategic initiatives. The problem seems to lie, again, in its control system. It is designed to keep the carrot just the right distance in front of the divisional managers, encouraging them to strive for better and better financial performance. At the same time, however, it seems to dampen their inclination to innovate. It is that famous "bottom line" that creates

---

[3] The example of Beatrice was first written as presented here in the 1970s, when the company was the subject of a good deal of attention and praise in the business press. At the time of this revision, in 1988, the company is being disassembled. It seemed appropriate to leave the example as first presented, among other reasons to question the tendency to favor fashion over investigation in the business press.

the problem, encouraging short-term thinking and shortsightedness; attention is focused on the carrot just in front instead of the fields of vegetables beyond. As Bower has noted,

> [T]he risk to the division manager of a major innovation can be considerable if he is measured on short-run, year-to-year, earnings performance. The result is a tendency to avoid big risk bets, and the concomitant phenomenon that major new developments are, with few exceptions, made outside the major firms in the industry. Those exceptions tend to be single-product companies whose top managements are committed to true product leadership. . . . Instead, the diversified companies give us a steady diet of small incremental change. (1970:194)

Innovation requires entrepreneurship, or intrapreneurship, and these, as we have already argued, do not thrive under the diversified configuration. The entrepreneur takes his or her own risks to earn his or her own rewards; the intrapreneur (as we shall see) functions best in the loose structure of the innovative adhocracy. Indeed, many diversified corporations depend on those configurations for their strategic responsiveness, since they diversify not by innovating themselves but by acquiring the innovative results of independent firms. Of course, that may be their role—to exploit rather than create those innovations—but we should not, as a result, justify diversification on the basis of its innovative capacity.

The Contribution of Headquarters

To assess the effectiveness of conglomeration, it is necessary to assess what actual contribution the headquarters makes to the divisions. Since what the headquarters does in a diversified organization is otherwise performed by the various boards of directors of a set of independent firms, the question then becomes, what does a headquarters offer to the divisions that the independent board of directors of the autonomous organization does not?

One thing that neither can offer is the management of the individual business. Both are involved with it only on a part-time basis. The management is, therefore, logically left to the full-time managers, who have the required time and information. Among the functions a headquarters *does* perform, as noted earlier, are the establishment of objectives for the divisions, the monitoring of their performance in terms of these objectives, and the maintenance of limited personal contacts with division managers, for example to approve large capital expenditures. Interestingly, those are also the responsibilities of the directors of the individual firm, at least in theory.

In practice, however, many boards of directors—notably, those of widely held corporations—do those things rather ineffectively, leaving business managements carte blanche to do what they like. Here, then, we seem to have a major advantage to the diversified configuration. It exists as an administrative mechanism to overcome another prominent weakness of the free-market system, the ineffective board.

There is a catch in this argument, however, for diversification by enhancing an organization's size and expanding its number of markets, renders the corporation more difficult to understand and so to control by its board of part-time directors. Moreover, as Moyer has noted, one common effect of conglomerate acquisition is to increase the number of shareholders, and so to make the corporation more widely held, and therefore less amenable to director control. Thus, the diversified configuration in some sense resolves a problem of its own making—it offers the control that its own existence has rendered difficult. Had the corporation remained in one business, it might have been more narrowly held and easier to understand, and so its directors might have been able to perform their functions more effectively. Diversification thus helped to create the problem that divisionalization is said to solve. Indeed, it is ironic that many a diversified corporation that does such a vigorous job of monitoring the performance of its own divisions is itself so poorly monitored by its own board of directors!

All of this suggests that large diversified organizations tend to be classic closed systems, powerful enough to seal themselves off from much external influence while able to exercise a good deal of control over not only their own divisions, as instruments, but also their external environments. For example, one study of all 5,995 directors of the *Fortune* 500 found that only 1.6 percent of them represented major shareholder interests (Smith, 1978) while another survey of 855 corporations found that 84 percent of them did not even formally require their directors to hold any stock at all! (Bacon, 1973:40).

What does happen when problems arise in a division? What can a headquarters do that various boards of directors cannot? The chairman of one major conglomerate told a meeting of the New York Society of Security Analysts, in reference to the headquarters vice presidents who oversee the divisions, that "it is not too difficult to coordinate five companies that are well run" (in Wrigley, 1970:V78). True enough. But what about five that are badly run? What could the small staff of administrators at a corporation's headquarters really do to correct problems in that firm's thirty operating divisions or in Beatrice's 397? The natural tendency to tighten the control screws does not usually help once the problem has manifested itself, nor does exercising close surveillance. As noted earlier, the headquarters managers cannot manage the divisions. Essentially, that leaves them with two choices. They can either replace the division manager, or they can divest the corporation of the division. Of course, a board of directors can also replace the management. Indeed, that seems to be its only real prerogative; the management does everything else.

On balance, then, the economic case for one headquarters versus a set of separate boards of directors appears to be mixed. It should, therefore, come as no surprise that one important study found that corporations with "controlled diversity" had better profits than those with conglomerate diversity (Rumelt, 1974). Overall, the pure diversified configuration (the conglomerate) may offer some advantages over a weak system of separate boards of directors and inefficient capital markets, but most of those advantages would probably disappear if certain problems in capital markets and boards of directors were rectified. And there is reason to argue, from a social no less than an economic standpoint, that society would be better off trying to correct fundamental inefficiencies in its economic system rather than encourage private administrative arrangements to circumvent them, as we shall now see.

The Social Performance of the Performance Control System

This configuration requires that headquarters control the divisions primarily by quantitative performance criteria, and that typically means financial ones—profit, sales growth, return on investment, and the like. The problem is that these performance measures often become virtual obsessions in the diversified organization, driving out goals that cannot be measured—product quality, pride in work, customers well served. In effect, the economic goals drive out the social ones. As the chief of a famous conglomerate once remarked, "We, in Textron, worship the god of New Worth" (in Wrigley, 1970:V86).

That would pose no problem if the social and economic consequences of decisions could easily be separated. Governments would look after the former, corporations the latter. But the fact is that the two are intertwined; every strategic decision of every large corporation involves both, largely inseparable. As a result, its control systems, by focusing on economic measures, drive the diversified organization to act in ways that are, at best, socially unresponsive, at worst, socially irresponsible. Forced to concentrate on the economic consequences of decisions, the division manager is driven to ignore their social consequences. (Indeed, that manager is also driven to ignore the intangible economic consequences as well, such as product quality or research effort, another manifestation of the problem of the short-term, bottom-line thinking mentioned earlier.) Thus, Bower found that "the best records in the race relations area are those of single-product companies whose strong top managements are deeply involved in the business" (1970:193).

Robert Ackerman, in a study carried out at the Harvard Business School, investigated this point. He found that social benefits such as "a rosier public image . . . pride among managers . . . an attractive posture for recruiting on campus" could not easily be measured and so could not be plugged into the performance control system. The result was that

> . . . the financial reporting system may actually inhibit social responsiveness. By focusing on economic performance, even with appropriate safeguards to protect against sacrificing long-term benefits, such a system directs energy and resources to achieving results measured in financial terms. It is the only game in town, so to speak, at least the only one with an official scoreboard. (1975:55, 56)

Headquarters managers who are concerned about legal liabilities or the public relations effects of decisions, or even ones personally interested in broader social issues, may be tempted to intervene directly in the divisions' decision-making process to ensure proper attention to social matters. But they are discouraged from doing so by this configuration's strict division of labor: divisional autonomy requires no meddling by the headquarters in specific business decisions.

As long as the screws of the performance control system are not turned too tight, the division managers may retain enough discretion to consider the social consequences of their actions, if they so choose. But when those screws are turned tight, as they often are in the diversified corporation with a bottom-line orientation, then the division managers wishing to keep their jobs may have no choice but to act socially unresponsively, if not actually irresponsibly. As Bower has noted of the General Electric price-fixing scandal of the 1960s, "a very severely managed system of reward and punishment that demanded yearly improvements in earnings, return and market share, applied indiscriminately to all divisions, yielded a situation which was—at the very least—conducive to collusion in the oligopolistic and mature electric equipment markets" (1970:193).

The Diversified Organization in the Public Sphere

Ironically, for a government intent on dealing with these social problems, solutions are indicated in the very arguments used to support the diversified configuration. Or so it would appear.

For example, if the administrative arrangements are efficient while the capital markets are not, then why should a government hesitate to interfere with the capital markets? And why shouldn't it use those same administrative arrangements to deal with the problems? If Beatrice Foods really can control those 397 divisions, then what is to stop Washington from believing it can control 397 Beatrices? After all, the capital markets don't much matter. In his book on "countervailing power,"

John Kenneth Galbraith (1952) argued that bigness in one sector, such as business, promotes bigness in other sectors, such as unions and government. That has already happened. How long before government pursues the logical next step and exercises direct controls?

While such steps may prove irresistible to some governments, the fact is that they will not resolve the problems of power concentration and social irresponsibility but rather will aggravate them, but not just in the ways usually assumed in Western economics. All the existing problems would simply be bumped up to another level, and there increase. By making use of the diversified configuration, government would magnify the problems of size. Moreover, government, like the corporation, would be driven to favor measurable economic goals over intangible social ones, and that would add to the problems of social irresponsibility—a phenomenon of which we have already seen a good deal in the public sector.

In fact, these problems would be worse in government, because its sphere is social, and so its goals are largely ill suited to performance control systems. In other words, many of the goals most important for the public sector—and this applies to not-for-profit organizations in spheres such as health and education as well—simply do not lend themselves to measurement, no matter how long and how hard public officials continue to try. And without measurement, the conventional diversified configuration cannot work.

There are, of course, other problems with the application of this form of organization in the public sphere. For example, government cannot divest itself of subunits quite so easily as can corporations. And public service regulations on appointments and the like, as well as a host of other rules, preclude the degree of division manager autonomy available in the private sector. (It is, in fact, these central rules and regulations that make governments resemble integrated machine configurations as much as loosely coupled diversified ones, and that undermine their efforts at "accountability.")

Thus, we conclude that, appearances and even trends notwithstanding, the diversified configuration is generally not suited to the public and not-for-profit sectors of society. Governments and other public-type institutions that wish to divisionalize to avoid centralized machine bureaucracy may often find the imposition of performance standards an artificial exercise. They may thus be better off trying to exercise control of their units in a different way. For example, they can select unit managers who reflect their desired values, or indoctrinate them in those values, and then let them manage freely, the control in effect being normative rather than quantitative. But managing ideology, even creating it in the first place, is no simple matter, especially in a highly diversified organization.

In Conclusion: A Structure on the Edge of a Cliff

Our discussion has led to a "damned if you do, damned if you don't" conclusion. The pure (conglomerate) diversified configuration emerges as an organization perched symbolically on the edge of the cliff, at the end of a long path. Ahead, it is one step away from disintegration—breaking up into separate organizations on the rocks below. Behind it is the way back to a more stable integration, in the form of the machine configuration at the start of that path. And ever hovering above is the eagle, representing the broader social control of the state, attracted by the organization's position on the edge of the cliff and waiting for the chance to pull it up to a higher cliff, perhaps more dangerous still. The edge of the cliff is an uncomfortable place to be, perhaps even a temporary one that must inevitably lead to disintegration on the rocks below, a trip to that cliff above, or a return to a safer resting place somewhere on that path behind.

THE PRODUCT PORTFOLIO* (GROWTH-SHARE MATRIX OF THE BOSTON CONSULTING GROUP)

BY BRUCE D. HENDERSON

To be successful, a company should have a portfolio of products with different growth rates and different market shares. The portfolio composition is a function of the balance between cash flows. High-growth products require cash inputs to grow. Low-growth products should generate excess cash. Both kinds are needed simultaneously.

Four rules determine the cash flow of a product:

Margins and cash generated are a function of market share. High margins and high market share go together. This is a matter of common observation, explained by the experience curve effect.

Growth requires cash input to finance added assets. The added cash required to hold share is a function of growth rates.

High market share must be earned or bought. Buying market share requires additional investment.

No product market can grow indefinitely. The payoff from growth must come when the growth slows, or it will not come at all. The payoff is cash that cannot be reinvested in that product.

Products with high market share and slow growth are "cash cows." (See Figure 1.) Characteristically, they generate large amounts of cash, in excess of the reinvestment required to maintain share. This excess need not, and should not, be reinvested in those products. In fact, if the rate of return exceeds the growth rate, the cash *cannot* be reinvested indefinitely, except by depressing returns.

Products with low market share and slow growth are "dogs." They may show an accounting profit, but the profit must be reinvested to maintain share, leaving no cash throwoff. The product is essentially worthless, except in liquidation.

All products eventually become either a "cash cow" or a "dog." The value of a product is completely dependent upon obtaining a leading share of its market before the growth slows.

Low-market-share, high-growth products are the "problem children." They almost always require far more cash than they can generate. If cash is not supplied, they fall behind and die. Even when the cash is supplied, if they only hold their share, they are still dogs when the growth stops. The "problem children" require large added cash investment for market share to be purchased. The low-market-share, high-growth product is a liability unless it becomes a leader. It requires very large cash inputs that it cannot generate itself.

The high-share, high-growth product is the "star." It nearly always shows reported profits, but it may or may not generate all of its own cash. If it stays a leader, however, it will become a large cash generator when growth slows and its reinvestment requirements diminish. The star eventually becomes the cash cow—providing high volume, high margin, high stability, security—and cash throwoff for reinvestment elsewhere.

* Originally published in *Henderson on Corporate Strategy* (Cambridge, MA; Abt Books, Copyright © 1979); reprinted by permission of the author and the publisher. pp. 163–166.

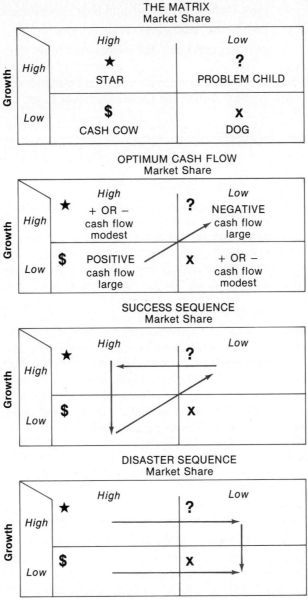

FIGURE 1
Boston Consulting Group
Growth-Share Matrix

The payoff for leadership is very high indeed, if it is achieved early and maintained until growth slows. Investment in market share during the growth phase can be very attractive—if you have the cash. Growth in market is compounded by growth in share. Increases in share increase the margin. Higher margin permits higher leverage with equal safety. The resulting profitability permits higher payment of earning after financing normal growth. The return on investment is enormous.

The need for a portfolio of businesses becomes obvious. Every company needs products in which to invest cash. Every company needs products that generate cash. And every product should eventually be a cash generator; otherwise, it is worthless.

Only a diversified company with a balanced portfolio can use its strengths to truly capitalize on its growth opportunities. The balanced portfolio has

313

"stars," whose high share and high growth assure the future.

"cash cows," that supply funds for that future growth.

"problem children," to be converted into "stars" with the added funds.

"Dogs" are not necessary. They are evidence of failure either to obtain a leadership position during the growth phase, or to get out and cut the losses.

• REVERSING THE IMAGES OF BCG'S GROWTH SHARE MATRIX*

BY JOHN A. SEEGER

. . . Simple concepts can easily be oversimplified, and graphic descriptors can become stereotypes. Few current business concepts are more prone to oversimplification than the growth/share model, with its labeling of products or divisions or whole companies as "dogs," "question marks," "stars" or "cash cows." Three-quarters of those labels are subject to dangerous misapplication, because popularized versions of the BCG philosophy and its derivatives carry a handy prescription for each category: we should kick the dogs, cloister the cows, and throw our money at the stars. Only the question mark category demands management thought.

This commentary attempts to counter these superficial prescriptions by turning the BCG model's own images back upon themselves. If the tendency to oversimplify comes from the language's imagery, then we must make the images do double duty; they must remind the student and manager of the growth/share matrix's pitfalls as well as its presumptions.

EVERY DOG HAS ITS DAY

Consider the "dogs." In the BCG model these are the portfolio components which have low market shares and whose markets themselves are matured or shrinking; these are components we should dispose of, for they are going nowhere. The image conveyed by BCG's term is that of a feral beast preying on our resources or of a mangy cur slinking off with our picnic hotdogs.

But there are other kinds of dogs—warm, loving companions of humanity since the time of the caves. These dogs give unquestioning loyalty to their managers, serving as scouts or watchdogs, to spread the alarm if intruders threaten. By establishing a presence—with bared teeth if necessary—these friendly dogs prevent their wild cousins from approaching our picnic at all. They protect our weaker members and occupy the territory so that attackers will keep their distance. Our own dogs can repay handsomely a small investment in dog food and flea powder. . . .

"It's a dog," says [one CEO of his key] retail product line. "I only wish I could get rid of it." Such attitudes are easily sensed, by canines or humans. It is

---

* Originally published in the *Strategic Management Journal* Copyright © 1984 John Wiley & Sons; reprinted with deletions by permission of John Wiley & Sons Limited.

predictable that the managers of his company regard its retail division as the least attractive assignment in the company. Good managers do not willingly stay with an organization which is defined in the boss's eyes as hopeless.

Divesting this retail division would be analogous to a fire engine company's disposing of its Dalmation hound. The dog does not contribute much to the direct function of putting out fires. But it looks good in photographs; it makes life more pleasant for the firefighters during their boring waits for alarms; and it keeps other dogs from pissing on the equipment.

WHAT DO YOU GET FROM A CASH COW?

Consider the "cash cow." In the BCG model this is a business component which does dominate its market, but whose market is not growing. Since growth cannot logically be expected here, the consultant's advice is to operate the business as a cash flow generator. Management should deny requests for new resources from a cash cow component, and concentrate on milking it for the highest possible returns.

The imagery conveyed by this term is doubly unfortunate. In oversimplified form, the "cash cow" brand can result in the gradual wastage of both the physical and human resources of an organization, as operating management learns not to request new resources and top management learns not to demand continual replenishment of the unit's productive capacities. Where operations are measured in current profitability and growth aspirations are systematically throttled, it is natural for growth-oriented managers to leave the organization. They are replaced by people content to operate the business as it stands but uninterested and unskilled at changing the business. The creative energy required for continual renewal can decay as natural attrition suits the culture of the organization to its "cash cow" role.

In effect, classification as a cash cow may be the equivalent, over time, of placing the unit in a cloister where distractions of the outside world are minimized and all attentions are focused on the single goal, generation of high cash flows. "Milking managers" will be expert at feeding the cow and keeping it healthy in the short run. They may not be adept at maintaining the barn, however. Particularly where large outlays are needed for long term improvements, the cash cow manager is likely to postpone investments which would hurt cash flow in the short run.

Keeping creativity, innovation and energy at high levels in an organization designated as a cash cow is an unsolved problem. One possible solution is suggested by another look at the BCG symbolism. A cow can give more than milk; properly exposed to outside influences and environmental forces, a cow can also give calves.

The investment needed to produce a calf, given that you already have a cow, is incredibly small; without a cow, no amount of investment will do the job. Similarly, the investment needed to produce creative ideas, given a creative workforce, is small; where natural energy has burned out, however, no amount of effort will produce innovation. Recognition of the importance of new projects—even though the business unit itself lacks the resources to exploit them—might help retain the creativity needed in a naturally adaptive organization. Provision of exploitation channels outside the business unit itself—through transfer to other corporate units, new subsidiaries, joint ventures, or entrepreneurial sabbatical leaves—could help the unit's people see the utility of continued idea generation. In a time of diminished general economic growth, no company can afford to reject a good idea because it comes from a unit which is not "supposed to" grow. Neither can we afford to let the "cash cow" label stifle the creativity and adaptability which are vital to survival in increasingly competitive times.

The dairying analogy is appropriate for these organizations, so long as we resist the urge to oversimplify it. On the farm, even the best producing cows eventually begin to dry up. The farmer's solution to this is euphemistically called "freshening" the cow: he arranges a date with a bull; she has a calf; the milk begins flowing again. Cloistering the cow—isolating her from everything but the feed trough and the milking machines—assures that she will go dry.

THE FAULT LIES NOT IN OUR STARS, BUT IN OURSELVES . . .

Consider the "stars." In the BCG model, these are the business units with major shares of growing markets. These are the units which need resources and investments in order to exploit their opportunities. These are the units sought by aggressive, ambitious people, who crave the excitement and challenges of growth. It is in the stars that people blaze career reputations and become recognized as winners.

Unfortunately, however, not all stars turn out to be winners over the long term. Current market share and market growth rates are not sufficient criteria to justify investment, although they suffice to label the business unit as a star. Oversimplification of the BCG prescription can result in investing in situations whose growth rates cannot be sustained in the future for a variety of reasons not apparent in backward scanning market analysis. . . .

Investment based on growth rate and share, without regard for environmental constraints or market saturation, is encouraged by the oversimplification inherent in the popular two-by-two matrices.

Still, with proper qualification, the "star" analogy is appropriate. Think, for example, about the stars themselves. What we know of them is based on old information. When we observe a star through the telescope, we see evidence of an energetic past, but we have no knowledge of whether that same star is still producing energy now. The light we observe has been traveling towards us for eons—billions of years in some cases—and its source may have long since degenerated into a white dwarf or even a black hole, which would absorb any amount of resources we would care to throw at it without ever permitting any return.

Organizational stars, to, take their place in the BCG matrix based on their past performance. Whether they merit additional investment depends on their future potential, not upon their past.

CONCLUSION

I have no quarrel with the fourth BCG category, the "question mark" business unit. This unit, a nondominant participator in a growing market, requires management thought, says the BCG model. All the categories require management thought.

No management model can safely substitute for analysis and common sense. Models are useful to managers, to the extent that they can help provide order to the thinking process. Models are dangerous to managers, to the extent that they bias judgement or substitute for analysis. . . .

FROM COMPETITIVE ADVANTAGE TO CORPORATE STRATEGY*

BY MICHAEL E. PORTER

Corporate strategy, the overall plan for a diversified company, is both the darling and the stepchild of contemporary management practice—the darling because CEOs have been obsessed with diversification since the early 1960s, the stepchild because almost no consensus exists about what corporate strategy is, much less about how a company should formulate it.

A diversified company has two levels of strategy: business unit (or competitive) strategy and corporate (or companywide) strategy. Competitive strategy concerns how to create competitive advantage in each of the businesses in which a company competes. Corporate strategy concerns two different questions: what businesses the corporation should be in and how the corporate office should manage the array of business units.

Corporate strategy is what makes the corporate whole add up to more than the sum of its business unit parts.

The track record of corporate strategies has been dismal. I studied the diversification records of 33 large, prestigious U.S. companies over the 1950–1986 period and found that most of them had divested many more acquisitions than they had kept. The corporate strategies of most companies have dissipated instead of created shareholder value.

The need to rethink corporate strategy could hardly be more urgent. By taking over companies and breaking them up, corporate raiders thrive on failed corporate strategy. Fueled by junk bond financing and growing acceptability, raiders can expose any company to takeover, no matter how large or blue chip. . . .

A SOBER PICTURE

. . . My study of 33 companies, many of which have reputations for good management, is a unique look at the track record of major corporations. . . . Each company entered an average of 80 new industries and 27 new fields. Just over 70% of the new entries were acquisitions, 22% were start-ups, and 8% were joint ventures. IBM, Exxon, Du Pont, and 3M, for example, focused on startups, while ALCO Standard, Beatrice, and Sara Lee diversified almost solely through acquisitions. . . .

My data paint a sobering picture of the success ratio of these moves. . . . I found that on average corporations divested more than half their acquisitions in new industries and more than 60% of their acquisitions in entirely new fields. Fourteen companies left more than 70% of all the acquisitions they had made in new fields. The track record in unrelated acquisitions is even worse—the average divestment rate is startling 74%. Even a highly respected company like General Electric divested a very high percentage of its acquisitions, particularly those in new fields. . . . Some [companies] bear witness to the success of well-thought-out corporate strategies. Others, however, enjoy a lower rate simply because they have not faced up to their problem units and divested them. . . .

* Originally published in the *Harvard Business Review* (May–June 1987) and winner of the McKinsey Prize for the best in the *Review* in 1987. Copyright © 1987 by the President and Fellows of Harvard College; all rights reserved. Reprinted with deletions by permission of the Harvard Business Review.

I would like to make one comment on the use of shareholder value to judge performance. Linking shareholder value quantitatively to diversification performance only works if you compare the shareholder value that is with the shareholder value that might have been without diversification. Because such a comparison is virtually impossible to make, my own measure of diversification success—the number of units retained by the company—seems to be as good an indicator as any of the contribution of diversification to corporate performance.

My data give a stark indication of the failure of corporate strategies.[1] Of the 33 companies, 6 had been taken over as my study was being completed. . . . Only the lawyers, investment bankers, and original sellers have prospered in most of these acquisitions, not the shareholders.

PREMISES OF CORPORATE STRATEGY

Any successful corporate strategy builds on a number of premises. These are facts of life about diversification. They cannot be altered, and when ignored, they explain in part why so many corporate strategies fail.

Competition Occurs at the Business Unit Level: Diversified companies do not compete; only their business units do. Unless a corporate strategy places primary attention on nurturing the success of each unit, the strategy will fail, no matter how elegantly constructed. Successful corporate strategy must grow out of and reinforce competitive strategy.

Diversification Inevitably Adds Costs and Constraints to Business Units: Obvious costs such as the corporate overhead allocated to a unit may not be as important or subtle as the hidden costs and constraints. A business unit must explain its decisions to top management, spend time complying with planning and other corporate systems, live with parent company guidelines and personnel policies, and forgo the opportunity to motivate employees with direct equity ownership. These costs and constraints can be reduced but not entirely eliminated.

Shareholders Can Readily Diversify Themselves: Shareholders can diversify their own portfolios of stocks by selecting those that best match their preferences and risk profiles (Salter and Weinhold, 1979). Shareholders can often diversify more cheaply than a corporation because they can buy shares at the market price and avoid hefty acquisition premiums.

These premises mean that corporate strategy cannot succeed unless it truly adds value—to business units by providing tangible benefits that offset the inherent costs of lost independence and to shareholders by diversifying in a way they could not replicate.

---

[1] Some recent evidence also supports the conclusion that acquired companies often suffer eroding performance after acquisition. See Frederick M. Scherer, "Mergers, Sell-Offs and Managerial Behavior," in *The Economics of Strategic Planning,* ed. Lacy Glenn Thomas (Lexington, MA: Lexington Books, 1986), p. 143, and David A. Ravenscraft and Frederick M. Scherer, "Mergers and Managerial Performance," paper presented at the Conference on Takeovers and Contests for Corporate Control, Columbia Law School, 1985.

To understand how to formulate corporate strategy, it is necessary to specify the conditions under which diversification will truly create shareholder value. These conditions can be summarized in three essential tests:

1. *The attractiveness test.* The industries chosen for diversification must be structurally attractive or capable of being made attractive.
2. *The cost-of-entry test.* The cost of entry must not capitalize all the future profits.
3. *The better-off test.* Either the new unit must gain competitive advantage from its link with the corporation or vice versa.

Of course, most companies will make certain that their proposed strategies pass some of these tests. But my study clearly shows that when companies ignored one or two of them, the strategic results were disastrous.

How Attractive Is the Industry?

In the long run, the rate of return available from competing in an industry is a function of its underlying structure [see Porter reading in Chapter 4]. An attractive industry with a high average return on investment will be difficult to enter because entry barriers are high, suppliers and buyers have only modest bargaining power, substitute products or services are few, and the rivalry among competitors is stable. An unattractive industry like steel will have structural flaws, including a plethora of substitute materials, powerful and price-sensitive buyers, and excessive rivalry caused by high fixed costs and a large group of competitors, many of whom are state supported.

Diversification cannot create shareholder value unless new industries have favorable structures that support returns exceeding the cost of capital. If the industry doesn't have such returns, the company must be able to restructure the industry or gain a sustainable competitive advantage that leads to returns well above the industry average. An industry need not be attractive before diversification. In fact, a company might benefit from entering before the industry shows its full potential. The diversification can then transform the industry's structure.

In my research, I often found companies had suspended the attractiveness test because they had a vague belief that the industry "fit" very closely with their own businesses. In the hope that the corporate "comfort" they felt would lead to a happy outcome, the companies ignored fundamentally poor industry structures. Unless the close fit allows substantial competitive advantage, however, such comfort will turn into pain when diversification results in poor returns. Royal Dutch Shell and other leading oil companies have had this unhappy experience in a number of chemicals businesses, where poor industry structures overcame the benefits of vertical integration and skills in process technology.

Another common reason for ignoring the attractiveness test is a low entry cost. Sometimes the buyer has an inside track or the owner is anxious to sell. Even if the price is actually low, however, a one-shot gain will not offset a perpetually poor business. Almost always, the company finds it must reinvest in the newly acquired unit, if only to replace fixed assets and fund working capital.

Diversifying companies are also prone to use rapid growth or other simple indicators as a proxy for a target industry's attractiveness. Many that rushed into fast-growing industries (personal computers, video games, and robotics, for example) were burned because they mistook early growth for long-term profit potential. Industries are profitable not because they are sexy or high tech; they are profitable only if their structures are attractive.

What Is the Cost of Entry?

Diversification cannot build shareholder value if the cost of entry into a new business eats up its expected returns. Strong market forces, however, are working to do just that. A company can enter new industries by acquisition or start-up. Acquisitions expose it to an increasingly efficient merger market. An acquirer beats the market if it pays a price not fully reflecting the prospects of the new unit. Yet multiple bidders are commonplace, information flows rapidly, and investment bankers and other intermediaries work aggressively to make the market as efficient as possible. In recent years, new financial instruments such a junk bonds have brought new buyers into the market and made even large companies vulnerable to takeover. Acquisition premiums are high and reflect the acquired company's future prospects—sometimes too well. Philip Morris paid more than four times book value for Seven-Up Company, for example. Simple arithmetic meant that profits had to more than quadruple to sustain the preacquisition ROI. Since there proved to be little Philip Morris could add in marketing prowess to the sophisticated marketing wars in the soft drink industry, the result was the unsatisfactory financial performance of Seven-Up and ultimately the decision to divest.

In a start-up, the company must overcome entry barriers. It's a real catch-22 situation, however, since attractive industries are attractive because their entry barriers are high. Bearing the full cost of the entry barriers might well dissipate any potential profits. Otherwise, other entrants to the industry would have already eroded its profitability.

In the excitement of finding an appealing new business, companies sometimes forget to apply the cost-of-entry test. The more attractive a new industry, the more expensive it is to get into.

Will the Business Be Better Off?

A corporation must bring some significant competitive advantage to the new unit, or the new unit must offer potential for significant advantage to the corporation. Sometimes, the benefits to the new unit accrue only once, near the time of entry, when the parent instigates a major overhaul of its strategy or installs a first-rate management team. Other diversification yields ongoing competitive advantage if the new unit can market its product, through the well-developed distribution system of its sister units, for instance. This is one of the important underpinnings of the merger of Baxter Travenol and American Hospital Supply.

When the benefit to the new unit comes only once, the parent company has no rationale for holding the new unit in its portfolio over the long term. Once the results of the one-time improvement are clear, the diversified company no longer adds value to offset the inevitable costs imposed on the unit. It is best to sell the unit and free up corporate resources.

The better-off test does not imply that diversifying corporate risk creates shareholder value in and of itself. Doing something for shareholders that they can do themselves is not a basis for corporate strategy. (Only in the case of a privately held company, in which the company's and the shareholder's risk are the same, is diversification to reduce risk valuable for its own sake.) Diversification of risk should only be a by-product of corporate strategy, not a prime motivator.

Executives ignore the better-off test most of all or deal with it through arm waving or trumped-up logic rather than hard strategic analysis. One reason is that they confuse company size with shareholder value. In the drive to run a bigger company, they lose sight of their real job. They may justify the suspension of the better-off test by pointing to the way they manage diversity. By cutting corporate staff to the bone and giving business units nearly complete autonomy, they believe they avoid the pitfalls. Such thinking misses the whole point of diversification, which is to create shareholder value rather than to avoid destroying it.

CONCEPTS OF CORPORATE STRATEGY

The three tests for successful diversification set the standards that any corporate strategy must meet; meeting them is so difficult that most diversification fails. Many companies lack a clear concept of corporate strategy to guide their diversification or pursue a concept that does not address the tests. Others fail because they implement a strategy poorly.

My study has helped me identify four concepts of corporate strategy that have been put into practice—portfolio management, restructuring, transferring skills, and sharing activities. While the concepts are not always mutually exclusive, each rests on a different mechanism by which the corporation creates shareholder value and each requires the diversified company to manage and organize itself in a different way. The first two require no connections among business units; the second two depend on them. . . . While all four concepts of strategy have succeeded under the right circumstances, today some make more sense than others. Ignoring any of the concepts is perhaps the quickest road to failure.

Portfolio Management

The concept of corporate strategy most in use is portfolio management, which is based primarily on diversification through acquisition. The corporation acquires sound, attractive companies with competent managers who agree to stay on. While acquired units do not have to be in the same industries as existing units, the best portfolio managers generally limit their range of businesses in some way, in part to limit the specific expertise needed by top management.

The acquired units are autonomous, and the teams that run them are compensated according to unit results. The corporation supplies capital and works with each to infuse it with professional management techniques. At the same time, top management provides objective and dispassionate review of business unit results. Portfolio managers categorize units by potential and regularly transfer resources from units that generate cash to those with high potential and cash needs. . . .

In most countries, the days when portfolio management was a valid concept of corporate strategy are past. In the face of increasingly well-developed capital markets, attractive companies with good managements show up on everyone's computer screen and attract top dollar in terms of acquisition premium. Simply contributing capital isn't contributing much. A sound strategy can easily be funded; small to medium-size companies don't need a munificent parent.

Other benefits have also eroded. Large companies no longer corner the market for professional management skills; in fact, more and more observers believe managers cannot necessarily run anything in the absence of industry-specific knowledge and experience. . . .

But it is the sheer complexity of the management task that has ultimately defeated even the best portfolio managers. As the size of the company grows, portfolio managers need to find more and more deals just to maintain growth. Supervising dozens or even hundreds of disparate units and under chain-letter pressures to add more, management begins to make mistakes. At the same time, the inevitable costs of being part of a diversified company take their toll and unit performance slides while the whole company's ROI turns downward. Eventually, a new management team is installed that initiates wholesale divestments and pares down the company to its core businesses. . . .

In developing countries, where large companies are few, capital markets are undeveloped, and professional management is scarce, portfolio management still works. But it is no longer a valid model for corporate strategy in advanced economies. . . . Portfolio management is no way to conduct corporate strategy.

Restructuring

Unlike its passive role as a portfolio manager, when it serves as banker and reviewer, a company that bases its strategy on restructuring becomes an active restructurer of business units. The new businesses are no necessarily related to existing units. All that is necessary is unrealized potential.

The restructuring strategy seeks out undeveloped, sick, or threatened organizations or industries on the threshold of significant change. The parent intervenes, frequently changing the unit management team, shifting strategy, or infusing the company with new technology. Then it may make follow-up acquisitions to build a critical mass and sell off unneeded or unconnected parts and thereby reduce the effective acquisition cost. The result is a strengthened company or a transformed industry. As a coda, the parent sells off the stronger unit once results are clear because the parent is no longer adding value, and top management decides that its attention should be directed elsewhere. . . .

When well implemented, the restructuring concept is sound, for it passes the three tests of successful diversification. The restructurer meets the cost-of-entry test through the types of company it acquires. It limits acquisition premiums by buying companies with problems and lackluster images or by buying into industries with as yet unforeseen potential. Intervention by the corporation clearly meets the better-off test. Provided that the target industries are structurally attractive, the restructuring model can create enormous shareholder value. . . . Ironically, many of today's restructurers are profiting from yesterday's portfolio management strategies.

To work, the restructuring strategy requires a corporate management team with the insight to spot undervalued companies or positions in industries ripe for transformation. The same insight is necessary to actually turn the units around even though they are in new and unfamiliar businesses. . . .

Perhaps the greatest pitfall . . . is that companies find it very hard to dispose of business units once they are restructured and performing well. . . .

Transferring Skills

The purpose of the first two concepts of corporate strategy is to create value through a company's relationship with each autonomous unit. The corporation's role is to be a selector, a banker, and an intervenor.

The last two concepts exploit the interrelationships between businesses. In articulating them, however, one comes face-to-face with the often ill-defined concept of synergy. If you believe the text of the countless corporate annual reports, just about anything is related to just about anything else! But imagined synergy is much more common than real synergy. GM's purchase of Hughes Aircraft simply because cars were going electronic and Hughes was an electronics concern demonstrates the folly of paper synergy. Such corporate relatedness is an ex post facto rationalization of a diversification undertaken for other reasons.

Even synergy that is clearly defined often fails to materialize. Instead of cooperating, business units often compete. A company that can define the synergies it is pursuing still faces significant organizational impediments in achieving them.

But the need to capture the benefits of relationships between businesses has never been more important. Technological and competitive developments already link many businesses and are creating new possibilities for competitive advantage. In such sectors as financial services, computing, office equipment, entertainment, and health care, interrelationships among previously distinct businesses are perhaps the central concern of strategy.

To understand the role of relatedness in corporate strategy, we must give new meaning to this often ill-defined idea. I have identified a good way to start—the value chain. [See pp. 72–74] Every business unit is a collection of discrete activities ranging from sales to accounting that allow it to compete. I call them value activities. It is at this level, not in the company as a whole, that the unit achieves competitive advantage.

I group these activities in nine categories. *Primary* activities create the product or service, deliver and market it, and provide after-sale support. The categories of primary activities are inbound logistics, operations, outbound logistics, marketing and sales, and service. *Support* activities provide the input and infrastructure that allow the primary activities to take place. The categories are company infrastructure, human resource management, technology development, and procurement.

The value chain defines the two types of interrelationships that may create synergy. The first is a company's ability to transfer skills or expertise among similar value chains. The second is the ability to share activities. Two business units, for example, can share the same sales force or logistics network.

The value chain helps expose the last two (and most important) concepts of corporate strategy. The transfer of skills among business units in the diversified company is the basis for one concept. While each business unit has a separate value chain, knowledge about how to perform activities is transferred among the units. For example, a toiletries business unit, expert in the marketing of convenience products, transmits ideas on new positioning concepts, promotional techniques, and packaging possibilities to a newly acquired unit that sells cough syrup. Newly entered industries can benefit from the expertise of existing units, and vice versa.

These opportunities arise when business units have similar buyers or channels, similar value activities like government relations or procurement, similarities in the broad configuration of the value chain (for example, managing a multisite service organization), or the same strategic concept (for example, low cost). Even though the units operate separately, such similarities allow the sharing of knowledge. . . .

Transferring skills leads to competitive advantage only if the similarities among businesses meet three conditions:

1. The activities involved in the businesses are similar enough that sharing expertise is meaningful. Broad similarities (marketing intensiveness, for example, or a common core process technology such as bending metal) are not a sufficient basis for diversification. The resulting ability to transfer skills is likely to have little impact on competitive advantage.

2. The transfer of skills involves activities important to competitive advantage. Transferring skills in peripheral activities such as government relations or real estate in consumer goods units may be beneficial but is not a basis for diversification.

3. The skills transferred represent a significant source of competitive advantage for the receiving unit. The expertise or skills to be transferred are both advanced and proprietary enough to be beyond the capabilities of competitors. . . .

Transferring skills meets the tests of diversification if the company truly mobilizes proprietary expertise across units. This makes certain the company can offset the acquisition premium or lower the cost of overcoming entry barriers.

The industries the company chooses for diversification must pass the attractiveness test. Even a close fit that reflects opportunities to transfer skills may not overcome poor industry structure. Opportunities to transfer skills, however, may help the company transform the structures of newly entered industries and send them in favorable directions.

The transfer of skills can be one time or ongoing. If the company exhausts opportunities to infuse new expertise into a unit after the initial post-acquisition period, the unit should ultimately be sold. . . .

By using both acquisitions and internal development, companies can build a transfer-of-skills strategy. The presence of a strong base of skills sometimes creates the possibility for internal entry instead of the acquisition of a going concern. Successful diversifiers that employ the concept of skills transfer may, however, often acquire a company in the target industry as a beachhead and then build on it with their internal expertise. By doing so, they can reduce some of the risks of internal entry and speed up the process. Two companies that have diversified using the transfer-of-skills concept are 3M and PepsiCo.

Sharing Activities

The fourth concept of corporate strategy is based on sharing activities in the value chains among business units. Procter & Gamble, for example, employs a common physical distribution system and sales force in both paper towels and disposable diapers. McKesson, a leading distribution company, will handle such diverse lines as pharmaceuticals and liquor through superwarehouses.

The ability to share activities is a potent basis for corporate strategy because sharing often enhances competitive advantage by lowering cost or raising differentiation. . . .

Sharing activities inevitably involves costs that the benefits must outweigh. One cost is the greater coordination required to manage a shared activity. More important is the need to compromise the design or performance of an activity so that it can be shared. A salesperson handling the products of two business units, for example, must operate in a way that is usually not what either unit would choose were it independent. And if compromise greatly erodes the unit's effectiveness, then sharing may reduce rather than enhance competitive advantage. . . .

Despite . . . pitfalls, opportunities to gain advantage from sharing activities have proliferated because of momentous developments in technology, deregulation, and competition. The infusion of electronics and information systems into many industries creates new opportunities to link businesses. . . .

Following the shared-activities model requires and organizational context in which business unit collaboration is encouraged and reinforced. Highly autonomous business units are inimical to such collaboration. The company must put into place a variety of what I call horizontal mechanisms—a strong sense of corporate identity, a clear corporate mission statement that emphasizes the importance of integrating business unit strategies, an incentive system that rewards more than just business unit results, cross-business-unit task forces, and other methods of integrating.

A corporate strategy based on shared activities clearly meets the better-off test because business units gain ongoing tangible advantages from others within the corporation. It also meets the cost-of-entry test by reducing the expense of surmounting the barriers to internal entry. Other bids for acquisitions that do not share opportunities will have lower reservation prices. Even widespread opportunities for sharing activities do not allow a company to suspend the attractiveness test, however. Many diversifiers have made the critical mistake of equating the close fit of a target industry with attractive diversification. Target industries must pass the strict requirement test of having an attractive structure as well as a close fit in opportunities if diversification is to ultimately succeed.

CHOOSING A CORPORATE STRATEGY

. . . Both the strategic logic and the experience of the companies I studied over the last decade suggest that a company will create shareholder value through diversification to a greater and greater extent as its strategy moves from portfolio management toward sharing activities. . . .

Each concept of corporate strategy is not mutually exclusive of those that come before, a potent advantage of the third and fourth concepts. A company can employ a restructuring strategy at the same time it transfers skills or shares activities. A strategy based on shared activities becomes more powerful if business units can also exchange skills. . . .

My study supports the soundness of basing a corporate strategy on the transfer of skills or shared activities. The data on the sample companies' diversification programs illustrate some important characteristics of successful diversifiers. They have made a disproportionately low percentage of unrelated acquisitions, *unrelated* being defined as having no clear opportunity to transfer skills or share important activities. . . . Even successful diversifiers such as 3M, IBM, and TRW have terrible records when they strayed into unrelated acquisitions. Successful acquirers diversify into fields, each of which is related to many others. Procter & Gamble and IBM, for example, operate in 18 and 19 interrelated fields respectively and so enjoy numerous opportunities to transfer skills and share activities.

Companies with the best acquisition records tend to make heavier-than-average use of start-ups and joint ventures. Most companies shy away from modes of entry besides acquisition. My results cast doubt on the conventional wisdom regarding start-ups. . . . successful companies often have very good records with start-up units, as 3M, P&G, Johnson & Johnson, IBM, and United Technologies illustrate. When a company has the internal strength to start up a unit, it can be safer and less costly to launch a company than to rely solely on an acquisition and then have to deal with the problem of integration. Japanese diversification histories support the soundness of start-up as an entry alternative.

My data also illustrate that none of the concepts of corporate strategy works when industry structure is poor or implementation is bad, no matter how related the industries are. Xerox acquired companies in related industries, but the businesses had poor structures and its skills were insufficient to provide enough competitive advantage to offset implementation problems.

An Action Program

. . . A company can choose a corporate strategy by:

1. Identifying the interrelationships among already existing business units. . . .
2. Selecting the core businesses that will be the foundation of the corporate strategy. . . .
3. Creating horizontal organizational mechanisms to facilitate interrelationships among the core businesses and lay the groundwork for future related diversification. . . .
4. Pursuing diversification opportunities that allow shared activities. . . .
5. Pursing diversification through the transfer of skills if opportunities for sharing activities are limited or exhausted. . . .
6. Pursuing a strategy restructuring if this fits the skills of management or no good opportunities exist for forging corporate interrelationships. . . .
7. Paying dividends so that the shareholders can be the portfolio managers. . . .

Creating a Corporate Theme

Defining a corporate theme is a good way to ensure that the corporation will create shareholder value. Having the right theme helps unite the efforts of business units and reinforces the ways they interrelate as well as guides the choice of new businesses to enter. NEC Corporation, with its "C&C" theme, provides a good example. NEC integrates its computer, semiconductor, telecommunications, and consumer electronics businesses by merging computers and communication.

It is all too easy to create a shallow corporate theme. CBS wants to be an "entertainment company," for example, and built a group of businesses related to leisure time. It entered such industries as toys, crafts, musical instruments, sports teams, and hi-fi retailing. While this corporate theme sounded good, close listening revealed its hollow ring. None of these businesses had any significant opportunity to share activities or transfer skills among themselves or with CBS's traditional broadcasting and record businesses. They were all sold, often at significant losses, except for a few of CBS's publishing-related units. Saddled with the worst acquisition record in my study, CBS has eroded the shareholder value created through its strong performance in broadcasting and records.

Moving from competitive strategy to corporate strategy is the business equivalent of passing through the Bermuda Triangle. The failure of corporate strategy reflects the fact that most diversified companies have failed to think in terms of how they really add value. A corporate strategy that truly enhances the competitive advantage of each business unit is the best defense against the corporate raider. With a sharper focus on the tests of diversification and the explicit choice of a clear concept of corporate strategy, companies' diversification track records from now on can look a lot different.

GLOBAL STRATEGY . . . IN A WORLD OF NATIONS?*[1]

BY GEORGE S. YIP

Whether to globalize, and how to globalize, have become two of the most burning strategy issues for managers around the world. Many forces are driving companies around the world to globalize by expanding their participation in foreign markets. Almost every product market in the major world economies—computers, fast food, nuts and bolts—has foreign competitors. Trade barriers are also falling; the recent United States/Canada trade agreement and the impending 1992 harmonization in the European Community are the two most dramatic examples. Japan is gradually opening up its long barricaded markets. Maturity in domestic markets is also driving companies to seek international expansion. This is particularly true of U.S. companies that, nourished by the huge domestic market, have typically lagged behind their European and Japanese rivals in internationalization.

Companies are also seeking to globalize by integrating their worldwide strategy. Such global integration contrasts with the multinational approach whereby companies set up country subsidiaries that design, produce, and market products or services tailored to local needs. This multinational model (also described as a "multidomestic strategy") is now in question (Hout et al., 1982). Several changes seem to increase the likelihood that, in some industries, a global strategy will be more successful than a multidomestic one. One of these changes, as argued forcefully and controversially by Levitt (1983) is the growing similarity of what citizens of different countries want to buy. Other changes include the reduction of tariff and nontariff barriers, technology investments that are becoming too expensive to amortize in one market only, and competitors that are globalizing the rules of the game.

Companies want to know how to globalize—in other words, expand market participation—and how to develop an integrated worldwide strategy. As depicted in Figure 1, three steps are essential in developing a total worldwide strategy:

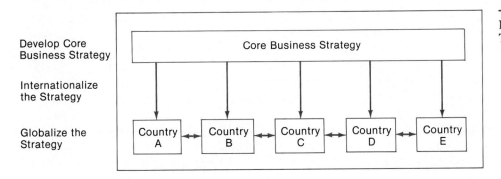

Develop Core Business Strategy

Internationalize the Strategy

Globalize the Strategy

FIGURE 1
Total Global Strategy

[1] My framework, developed in this article, is based in part on M. E. Porter's (1986) pioneering work on global strategy. Bartlett and Ghoshal (1987) define a "transnational industry" that is somewhat similar to Porter's "global industry."
* Originally published in the *Sloan Management Review* (Fall 1989). Copyright © *Sloan Management Review* 1989; reprinted with deletions by permission of the *Review*.

- Developing the core strategy—the basis of sustainable competitive advantage. It is usually developed for the home country first.
- Internationalizing the core strategy through international expansion of activities and through adaptation.
- Globalizing the international strategy by integrating the strategy across countries.

Multinational companies know the first two steps well. They know the third step less well since globalization runs counter to the accepted wisdom of tailoring for national markets (Douglas and Wind, 1987).

This article makes a case for how a global strategy might work and directs managers toward opportunities to exploit globalization. It also presents the drawbacks and costs of globalization. Figure 2 lays out a framework for thinking through globalization issues.

Industry globalization drivers (underlying market, cost, and other industry conditions) are externally determined, while global strategy levers are choices available to the worldwide business. Drivers create the potential for a multinational business to achieve the benefits of global strategy. To achieve these benefits, a multinational business needs to set its *global strategy levers* (e.g., use of product standardization) appropriately to industry drivers, and to the position and resources of the business and its parent company. The organization's ability to implement the strategy affects how well the benefits can be achieved.

WHAT IS GLOBAL STRATEGY?

Setting strategy for a worldwide business requires making choices along a number of strategic dimensions. Table 1 lists five such dimensions or "global strategy levels" and their respective positions under a pure multidomestic strategy and a pure global strategy. Intermediate positions are, of course, feasible. For each dimension, a multidomestic strategy seeks to maximize worldwide performance by maximizing local competitive advantage, revenues, or profits; a global strategy seeks to maximize worldwide performance through sharing and integration.

FIGURE 2
Framework of Global
Strategy Forces

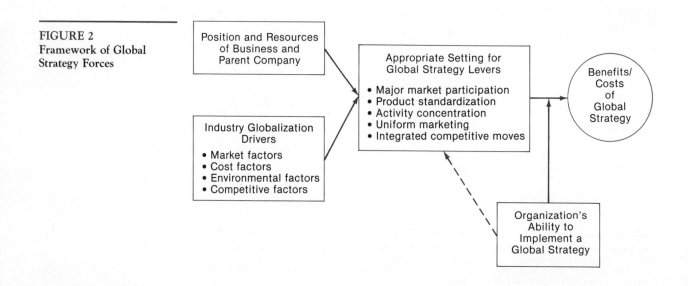

TABLE 1   Globalization Dimensions/Global Strategy Levers

DIMENSION	SETTING FOR PURE MULTIDOMESTIC STRATEGY	SETTING FOR PURE GLOBAL STRATEGY
Market Participation	No particular pattern	Significant share in major markets
Product Offering	Fully customized in each country	Fully standardized worldwide
Location of Value-Added Activities	All activities in each country	Concentrated—one activity in each (different) country
Marketing Approach	Local	Uniform worldwide
Competitive Moves	Stand-alone by country	Integrated across countries

Market Participation

In a multidomestic strategy, countries are selected on the basis of their stand-alone potential for revenues and profits. In a global strategy, countries need to be selected for their potential contribution to globalization benefits. This may mean entering a market that is unattractive in its own right, but has global strategic significance, such as the home market of a global competitor. Or it may mean building share in a limited number of key markets rather than undertaking more widespread coverage. . . . The Electrolux Group, the Swedish appliance giant, is pursuing a strategy of building significant share in major world markets. The company aims to be the first global appliance maker. . . .

Product Offering

In a multidomestic strategy, the products offered in each country are tailored to local needs. In a global strategy, the ideal is a standardized core product that requires minimal local adaptation. Cost reduction is usually the most important benefit of product standardization. . . . Differing worldwide needs can be met by adapting a standardized core product. In the early 1970s, sales of the Boeing 737 began to level off. Boeing turned to developing countries as an attractive new market, but found initially that its product did not fit the new environments. Because of the shortness of runways, their greater softness, and the lower technical expertise of their pilots, the planes tended to bounce a great deal. When the planes bounced on landing, the brakes failed. To fix this problem, Boeing modified the design by adding thrust to the engines, redesigning the wings and landing gear, and installing tires with lower pressure. These adaptations to a standardized core product enabled the 737 to become the best selling plane in history.

Location of Value Added Activities

In a multidomestic strategy, all or most of the value chain is reproduced in every country. In another type of international strategy—exporting—most of the value chain is kept in one country. In a global strategy, costs are reduced by breaking up the value chain so each activity may be conducted in a different country. . . .

329

Marketing Approach

In a multidomestic strategy, marketing is fully tailored for each country, being developed locally. In a global strategy, a uniform marketing approach is applied around the world, although not all elements of the marketing mix need be uniform. Unilever achieved great success with a fabric softener that used a globally common positioning, advertising theme, and symbol (a teddy bear), but a brand name that varied by country. Similarly, a product that serves a common need can be geographically expanded with a uniform marketing program, despite differences in marketing environments.

Competitive Moves

In a multidomestic strategy, the managers in each country make competitive moves without regard for what happens in other countries. In a global strategy, competitive moves are integrated across countries at the same time or in a systematic sequence: a competitor is attacked in one country in order to drain its resources for another country, or a competitive attack in one country is countered in a different country. Perhaps the best example is the counterattack in a competitor's home market as a parry to an attack on one's own home market. Integration of competitive strategy is rarely practiced, except perhaps by some Japanese companies.

Bridgestone Corporation, the Japanese tire manufacturer, tried to integrate its competitive moves in response to global consolidation by its major competitors. . . . These competitive actions forced Bridgestone to establish a presence in the major U.S. market in order to maintain its position in the world tire market. To this end, Bridgestone formed a joint venture to own and manage Firestone Corporation's worldwide tire business. This joint venture also allowed Bridgestone to gain access to Firestone's European plants.

BENEFITS OF A GLOBAL STRATEGY

Companies that use global strategy levers can achieve one or more of these benefits. . . .

- cost reductions
- improved quality of products and programs
- enhanced customer preference
- increased competitive leverage

Cost Reductions

An integrated global strategy can reduce worldwide costs in several ways. A company can increase the benefits from economies of scale by *pooling production or other activities* for two or more countries. Understanding the potential benefit of these economies of scale, Sony Corporation has concentrated its compact disc production in Terre Haute, Indiana, and Salzburg, Austria.

A second way to cut costs is by *exploiting lower factor costs* by moving manufacturing or other activities to low-cost countries. This approach has, of course, motivated the recent surge of offshore manufacturing, particularly by U.S. firms. For example, the Mexican side of the U.S.-Mexico border is now crowded with "maquiladoras"—manufacturing plants set up and run by U.S. companies using Mexican labor.

Global strategy can also cut costs by *exploiting flexibility.* A company with manufacturing locations in several countries can move production from location to location on short notice to take advantage of the lowest costs at a given time. Dow Chemical takes this approach to minimize the cost of producing chemicals. Dow uses a linear programming model that takes account of international differences in exchange rates, tax rates, and transportation and labor costs. The model comes up with the best mix of production volume by location for each planning period.

An integrated global strategy can also reduce costs by *enhancing bargaining power.* A company whose strategy allows for switching production among different countries greatly increases its bargaining power with suppliers, workers, and host governments. . . .

Improved Quality of Products and Programs

Under a global strategy, companies focus on a smaller number of products and programs than under a multidomestic strategy. This concentration can improve both product and program quality. Global focus is one reason for Japanese success in automobiles. Toyota markets a far smaller number of models around the world than does General Motors, even allowing for its unit sales being half that of General Motors's. . . .

Enhanced Customer Preference

Global availability, serviceability, and recognition can enhance customer preference through reinforcement. Soft drink and fast food companies are, of course, leading exponents of this strategy. Many suppliers of financial services, such as credit cards, must have a global presence because their service is travel related. . . .

Increased Competitive Leverage

A global strategy provides more points from which to attack and counterattack competitors. In an effort to prevent the Japanese from becoming a competitive nuisance in disposable syringes, Becton Dickinson, a major U.S. medical products company, decided to enter three markets in Japan's backyard. Becton entered the Hong Kong, Singapore, and Philippine markets to prevent further Japanese expansion (Var, 1986).

DRAWBACKS OF GLOBAL STRATEGY

Globalization can incur significant management costs through increased coordination, reporting requirements, and even added staff. It can also reduce the firm's effectiveness in individual countries if overcentralization hurts local motivation and morale. In addition, each global strategy lever has particular drawbacks.

A global strategy approach to *market participation* can incur an earlier or greater commitment to a market than is warranted on its own merits. Many American companies, such as Motorola, are struggling to penetrate Japanese markets, more in order to enhance their global competitive position than to make money in Japan for its own sake.

Product standardization can result in a product that does not entirely satisfy *any* customers. When companies first internationalize, they often offer their standard domestic product without adapting it for other countries, and suffer the consequences. . . .

A globally standardized product is designed for the global market but can seldom satisfy all needs in all countries. For instance, Canon, a Japanese company, sacrificed the ability to copy certain Japanese paper sizes when it first designed a photocopier for the global market.

Activity concentration distances customers and can result in lower responsiveness and flexibility. It also increases currency risk by incurring costs and revenues in different countries. Recently volatile exchange rates have required companies that concentrate their production to hedge their currency exposure.

Uniform marketing can reduce adaptation to local customer behavior. For example, the head office of British Airways mandated that every country use the "Manhattan Landing" television commercial developed by advertising agency Saatchi and Saatchi. While the commercial did win many awards, it has been criticized for using a visual image (New York City) that was not widely recognized in many countries.

Integrated competitive moves can mean sacrificing revenues, profits, or competitive position in individual countries, particularly when the subsidiary in one country is asked to attack a global competitor in order to send a signal or to divert that competitor's resources from another country.

FINDING THE BALANCE

The most successful worldwide strategies find a balance between overglobalizing and underglobalizing. The ideal strategy matches the level of strategy globalization to the globalization potential of the industry. . . .

INDUSTRY GLOBALIZATION DRIVERS

To achieve the benefits of globalization, the managers of a worldwide business need to recognize when industry globalization drivers (industry conditions) provide the opportunity to use global strategy levers. These drivers can be grouped in four categories: market, cost, governmental, and competitive. Each industry globalization driver affects the potential use of global strategy levers. . . .

Market Drivers

Market globalization drivers depend on customer behavior and the structure of distribution channels. These drivers affect the use of all five global strategy levers.

Homogeneous Customer Needs: When customers in different countries want essentially the same type of product or service (or can be so persuaded), opportunities arise to market a standardized product. Understanding which aspects of the product can be standardized and which should be customized is key. In addition, homogeneous needs make participation in a large number of markets easier because fewer different product offerings need to be developed and supported.

Global Customers: Global customers buy on a centralized or coordinated basis for decentralized use. The existence of global customers both allows and requires a uniform marketing program. There are two types of global customers: national and multinational. A national global customer searches the world for suppliers but uses the purchased product or service in one country. National defense agencies are a good example. A multinational global customer also searches the world for suppliers, but uses the purchased product or service in many countries. The World Health Organization's purchase of medical products is an example. Multinational global customers are particularly challenging to serve and often require a global account management program. . . .

Global Channels: Analogous to global customers, channels of distribution may buy on a global or at least a regional basis. Global channels or middlemen are also important in exploiting differences in prices by buying at a lower price in one country and selling at a higher price in another country. Their presence makes it more necessary for a business to rationalize its worldwide pricing. Global channels are rare, but regionwide channels are increasing in number, particularly in European grocery distribution and retailing.

Transferable Marketing: The buying decision may be such that marketing elements, such as brand names and advertising, require little local adaptation. Such transferability enables firms to use uniform marketing strategies and facilitates expanded participation in markets. A worldwide business can also adapt its brand names and advertising campaigns to make them more transferable, or, even better, design global ones to start with. Offsetting risks include the blandness of uniformly acceptable brand names or advertising, and the vulnerability of relying on a single brand franchise.

Cost Drivers

Cost drivers depend on the economics of the business; they particularly affect activity concentration.

Economies of Scale and Scope: A single-country market may not be large enough for the local business to achieve all possible economies of scale or scope. Scale at a given location can be increased through participation in multiple markets combined with product standardization or concentration of selected value activities. Corresponding risks include rigidity and vulnerability to disruption. . . .

Learning and Experience: Even if economies of scope and scale are exhausted, expanded market participation and activity concentration can accelerate the accumulation of learning and experience. The steeper the learning and experience curves, the greater the potential benefit will be. Managers should beware, though, of the usual danger in pursuing experience curve strategies—overaggressive pricing that destroyed not just the competition but the market as well. Prices get so low that profit is insufficient to sustain any competitor.

Sourcing Efficiencies: Centralized purchasing of new materials can significantly lower costs. . . .

Favorable Logistics: A favorable ratio of sales value to transportation cost enhances the company's ability to concentrate production. Other logistical factors include nonperishability, the absence of time urgency, and little need for location close to customer facilities. . . .

Differences in Country Costs and Skills: Factor costs generally vary across countries; this is particularly true in certain industries. The availability of particular skills also varies. Concentration of activities in low-cost or high-skill countries can increase productivity and reduce costs, but managers need to anticipate the danger of training future offshore competitors. . . .

Product Development Costs: Product development costs can be reduced by developing a few global or regional products rather than many national products. The automobile industry is characterized by long product development periods and high product development costs. One reason for the high costs is duplication of effort across countries. The Ford Motor Company's "Centers of Excellence" program aims to reduce these duplicating efforts and to exploit the differing expertise of Ford specialists worldwide. As part of the concentrated effort, Ford of Europe is designing a common platform for all compacts, while Ford of North America is developing platforms for the replacement of the mid-sized Taurus and Sable. This concentration of design is estimated to save "hundreds of millions of dollars per model by eliminating duplicative efforts and saving on retooling factories" (*Business Week,* 1987).

Governmental Drivers

Government globalization drivers depend on the rules set by national governments and affect the use of all global strategy levers.

Favorable Trade Policies: Host governments affect globalization potential through import tariffs and quotas, nontariff barriers, export subsidies, local content requirements, currency and capital flow restrictions, and requirements on technology transfer. Host government policies can make it difficult to use the global levers of major market participation, product standardization, activity concentration, and uniform marketing; they also affect the integrated-competitive moves lever. . . .

Compatible Technical Standards: Differences in technical standards, especially government-imposed standards, limit the extent to which products can be standardized. Often, standards are set with protectionism in mind. Motorola found that many of their electronics products were excluded from the Japanese market because these products operated at a higher frequency than was permitted in Japan.

Common Marketing Regulations: The marketing environment of individual countries affects the extent to which uniform global marketing approaches can be used. Certain types of media may be prohibited or restricted. For example, the United States is far more liberal than Europe about the kinds of advertising claims that can be made on television. The British authorities even veto the depiction of socially undesirable behavior. For example, British television authorities do not allow scenes of children pestering their parents to buy a product. . . .

Competitive Drivers

Market, cost, and governmental globalization drivers are essentially fixed for an industry at any given time. Competitors can play only a limited role in affecting these factors (although a sustained effort can bring about change, particularly in the case of consumer preferences). In contrast, competitive drivers are entirely in the realm of competitor choice. Competitors can raise the globalization potential of their industry and spur the need for a response on the global strategy levers.

Interdependence of Countries: A competitor may create competitive interdependence among countries by pursuing a global strategy. The basic mechanism is through sharing of activities. When activities such as production are shared among countries, a competitor's market share in one country affects its scale and overall cost position in the shared activities. Changes in that scale and cost will affect its competitive position in all countries dependent on the shared activities. Less directly, customers may view market position in a lead country as an indicator of overall quality. Companies frequently promote a product as, for example, "the leading brand in the United States." Other competitors then need to respond via increased market participation, uniform marketing, or integrated competitive strategy to avoid a downward spiral of sequentially weakened positions in individual countries.

In the automobile industry, where economies of scale are significant and where sharing activities can lower costs, markets have significant competitive interdependence. As companies like Ford and Volkswagen concentrate production and become more cost competitive with the Japanese manufacturers, the Japanese are pressured to enter more markets so that increased production volume will lower costs. Whether conscious of this or not, Toyota has begun a concerted effort to penetrate the German market: between 1984 and 1987, Toyota doubled the number of cars produced for the German market.

Globalized Competitors: More specifically, matching or preempting individual competitor moves may be necessary. These moves include expanding into or within major markets, being the first to introduce a standardized product, or being the first to use a uniform marketing program.

The need to preempt a global competitor can spur increased market participation. In 1986, Unilever, the European consumer products company, sought to increase its participation in the U.S. market by launching a hostile takeover bid for Richardson-Vicks Inc. Unilever's global archrival, Procter & Gamble, saw the threat to its home turf and outbid Unilever to capture Richardson-Vicks. With Richardson-Vicks's European system, P&G was able to greatly strengthen its European positioning. So Unilever's attempt to expand participation in a rival's home market backfired to allow the rival to expand participation in Unilever's home markets.

In summary, industry globalization drivers provide opportunities to use global strategy levers in many ways. Some industries, such as civil aircraft, can score high on most dimensions of globalization (Yoshino, 1986). Others, such as the cement industry, seem to be inherently local. But more and more industries are developing globalization potential. Even the food industry in Europe, renowned for its diversity of taste, is now a globalization target for major food multinationals.

Changes over Time

Finally, industry evolution plays a role. As each of the industry globalization drivers changes over time, so too will the appropriate global strategy change. For example, in the European major appliance industry, globalization forces seem to have reversed. In the late 1960s and early 1970s, a regional standardization strategy was successful for some key competitors (Levitt, 1983). But in the 1980s the situation appears to have turned around, and the most successful strategies seem to be national (Badenfuller et al., 1987).

In some cases, the actions of individual competitors can affect the direction and pace of change; competitors positioned to take advantage of globalization forces will want to hasten them. . . .

MORE THAN ONE STRATEGY IS VIABLE

Although they are powerful, industry globalization drivers do not dictate one formula for success. More than one type of international strategy can be viable in a given industry.

Industries vary across drivers: No industry is high on every one of the many globalization drivers. A particular competitor may be in a strong position to exploit a driver that scores low on globalization. . . . The hotel industry provides examples both of successful global and successful local competitors.

Global effects are incremental: Globalization drivers are not deterministic for a second reason: the appropriate use of strategy levers adds competitive advantage to existing sources. These other sources may allow individual competitors to thrive with international strategies that are mismatched with industry globalization drivers. For example, superior technology is a major source of competitive advantage in most industries, but can be quite independent of globalization drivers. A competitor with sufficiently superior technology can use it to offset globalization disadvantages.

Business and parent company position and resources are crucial: The third reason that drivers are not deterministic is related to resources. A worldwide business may face industry drivers that strongly favor a global strategy. But global strategies are typically expensive to implement initially even though great cost savings and revenue gains should follow. High initial investments may be needed to expand within or into major markets, to develop standardized products, to relocate value activities, to create global brands, to create new organization units or coordination processes, and to implement other aspects of a global strategy. The strategic position of the business is also relevant. Even though a global strategy may improve the business's long-term strategic position, its immediate position may be so weak that resources should be devoted to short-term, country-by-country improvements. Despite the automobile industry's very strong globalization drivers, Chrysler Corporation had to deglobalize by selling off most of its international automotive businesses to avoid bankruptcy. Lastly, investing in nonglobal sources of competitive advantage, such as superior technology, may yield greater returns than global ones, such as centralized manufacturing.

Organizations Have Limitations: Finally, factors such as organization structure, management processes, people, and culture affect how well a desired global strategy can be implemented. Organizational differences among companies in the same industry can, or should, constrain the companies' pursuit of the same global strategy. . . .

THE PROFESSIONAL CONTEXT

While most large organizations draw on a variety of experts to get their jobs done, there has been a growing interest in recent years in those organizations whose work, because it is highly complex, is organized primarily around experts. These range from hospitals, universities, and research centers to consulting firms, space agencies, and biomedical companies.

This context is a rather unusual one, at least when judged against the more traditional contexts discussed in previous chapters. Both its strategic processes and its structures tend to take on forms quite different from those presented earlier. Organizations of experts, in fact, seem to divide themselves into two somewhat different contexts. In one, the experts work in rapidly changing situations that demand a good deal of collaborative innovation (as in the biotechnology or semiconductor fields); in the other, experts work more or less alone in more stable situations involving slower-changing bodies of skill or knowledge (as in law, university teaching, and accounting). This chapter takes up the latter, under the label of the "professional" context; the next chapter discusses the former under the label of "innovation."

We open this chapter with a description of the type of organization that seems best suited to the context of the more stable application of expertise. Drawn from Mintzberg's work, primarily his original description of "professional bureaucracy," it looks at the structure of the professional organization, including its important characteristic of "pigeonholing" work, the management of professionals, the unusual nature of strategy in such organizations (drawing from a paper Mintzberg coauthored with Cynthia Hardy, Ann Langley, and Janet Rose), and some issues associated with these organizations.

The second article in this chapter, recently published in the *Sloan Management Review* and authored by Brian Quinn and his colleague Penny Paquette at the Dartmouth Amos Tuck School, focuses on the service sector, and especially changes that are now being rendered there as a result of technological developments. Not all service organizations fit into the professional context, by any stretch of the imagination, although many professional organizations do operate in the service sector, as will be evident from the examples of the first reading. Many services, such as retail banking, merchandise retailing, and fast-food restauranting, involve numerous unskilled jobs characteristic of the machinelike organizations described in the mature context. Nevertheless, many of the points made by Quinn and Paquette—about focusing on small units and empowering the operating people there, and about new organizational forms that invert the traditional pyramid, flatten the hierarchy, and create connections between relatively autonomous units —sound an awful lot like the professional form of organization described in the first reading. In other words, technological advances seem to have a professionalizing effect on many traditional machinelike services. And these advances seem to be rendering important changes in the more traditional professional services themselves, such as accounting and consulting. This reading, therefore, seems to provide us with glimpses of the professional organizations of the future.

Overall, these two readings suggest that the traditional concepts of managing and organizing simply do not work as we move away from conventional mass production—which has long served as the model for "one best way" concepts in management. Whether it be highly expert work in general or service work subjected to new technologies in particular, our thinking has to be opened up to very different needs.

● THE PROFESSIONAL ORGANIZATION*

BY HENRY MINTZBERG

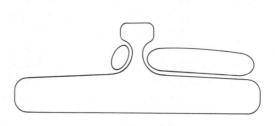

* Adapted from *The Structuring of Organizations* (Prentice Hall, 1979), Chap. 19 on "The Professional Bureaucracy"; also *Power In and Around Organizations* (Prentice Hall, 1983), Chap. 22 on "The Meritocracy"; the material on strategy formation from "Strategy Formation in the University Setting," coauthored with Cynthia Hardy, Ann Langley, and Janet Rose, in J. L. Bess (ed.) *College and University Organization* (New York University Press, 1984). A chapter similar to this one appeared in *Mintzberg on Management: Inside Our Strange World of Organizations* (Free Press, 1989).

An organization can be bureaucratic without being centralized. This happens when its work is complex, requiring that it be carried out and controlled by professionals, yet at the same time remains stable, so that the skills of those professionals can be perfected through standardized operating programs. The structure takes on the form of *professional* bureaucracy, which is common in universities, general hospitals, public accounting firms, social work agencies, and firms doing fairly routine engineering or craft work. All rely on the skills and knowledge of their operating professionals to function; all produce standardized products or services.

The Work of the Professional Operators

Here again we have a tightly knit configuration of the attributes of structure. Most important, the professional organization relies for coordination on the standardization of skills, which is achieved primarily through formal training. It hires duly trained specialists—professionals—for the operating core, then gives them considerable control over their own work.

Control over their work means that professionals work relatively independently of their colleagues but closely with the clients they serve—doctors treating their own patients and accountants who maintain personal contact with the companies whose books they audit. Most of the necessary coordination among the operating professionals is then handled automatically by their set skills and knowledge—in effect, by what they have learned to expect from each other. During an operation as long and as complex as open-heart surgery, "very little needs to be said [between the anesthesiologist and the surgeon] preceding chest opening and during the procedure on the heart itself . . . [most of the operation is] performed in absolute silence" (Gosselin, 1978). The point is perhaps best made in reverse by the cartoon that shows six surgeons standing around a patient on an operating table with one saying, "Who opens?"

Just how standardized the complex work of professionals can be is illustrated in a paper read by Spencer before a meeting of the International Cardiovascular Society. Spencer notes that an important feature of surgical training is "repetitive practice" to evoke "an automatic reflex." So automatic, in fact, that this doctor keeps a series of surgical "cookbooks" in which he lists, even for "complex" operations, the essential steps as chains of thirty to forty symbols on a single sheet, to "be reviewed mentally in sixty to 120 seconds at some time during the day preceding the operation" (1976:1179, 1182).

But no matter how standardized the knowledge and skills, their complexity ensures that considerable discretion remains in their application. No two professionals—no two surgeons or engineers or social workers—ever apply them in exactly the same way. Many judgments are required.

Training, reinforced by indoctrination, is a complicated affair in the professional organization. The initial training typically takes place over a period of years in a university or special institution, during which the skills and knowledge of the profession are formally programmed into the students. There typically follows a long period of on-the-job training, such as internship in medicine or articling in accounting, where the formal knowledge is applied and the practice of skills perfected. On-the-job training also completes the process of indoctrination, which began during the formal education. As new knowledge is generated and new skills develop, of course (so it is hoped) the professional upgrades his or her expertise.

339

All that training is geared to one goal, the internalization of the set procedures, which is what makes the structure technically bureaucratic (structure defined earlier as relying on standardization for coordination). But the professional bureaucracy differs markedly from the machine bureaucracy. Whereas the latter generates its own standards—through its technostructure, enforced by its line managers—many of the standards of the professional bureaucracy originate outside its own structure, in the self-governing associations its professionals belong to with their colleagues from other institutions. These associations set universal standards, which they ensure are taught by the universities and are used by all the organizations practicing the profession. So whereas the machine bureaucracy relies on authority of a hierarchical nature—the power of office—the professional bureaucracy emphasizes authority of a professional nature—the power of expertise.

Other forms of standardization are, in fact, difficult to rely on in the professional organization. The work processes themselves are too complex to be standardized directly by analysts. One need only try to imagine a work-study analyst following a cardiologist on rounds or timing the activities of a teacher in a classroom. Similarly, the outputs of professional work cannot easily be measured and so do not lend themselves to standardization. Imagine a planner trying to define a cure in psychiatry, the amount of learning that takes place in a classroom, or the quality of an accountant's audit. Likewise, direct supervision and mutual adjustment cannot be relied upon for coordination, for both impede professional autonomy.

The Pigeonholing Process

To understand how the professional organization functions at the operating level, it is helpful to think of it as a set of standard programs—in effect, the repertoire of skills the professionals stand ready to use—that are applied to known situations, called contingencies, also standardized. As Weick notes of one case in point, "schools are in the business of building and maintaining categories (1976:8). The process is sometimes known as *pigeonholing.* In this regard, the professional has two basic tasks: (1) to categorize, or "diagnose," the client's need in terms of one of the contingencies, which indicates which standard program to apply, and (2) to apply, or execute, that program. For example, the management consultant carries a bag of standard acronymic tricks: MBO, MIS, LRP, OD. The client with information needs gets MIS; the one with managerial conflicts, OD. Such pigeonholing, of course, simplifies matters enormously; it is also what enables each professional to work in a relatively autonomous manner.

It is in the pigeonholing process that the fundamental differences among the machine organization, the professional organization, and the innovative organization (to be discussed next) can best be seen. The machine organization is a single-purpose structure. Presented with a stimulus, it executes its one standard sequence of programs, just as we kick when tapped on the knee. No diagnosis is involved. In the professional organization, diagnosis is a fundamental task, but one highly circumscribed. The organization seeks to match a predetermined contingency to a standardized program. Fully open-ended diagnosis—that which seeks a creative solution to a unique problem—requires the innovative form of organization. No standard contingencies or programs can be relied upon there.

The Administrative Structure

Everything we have discussed so far suggests that the operating core is the key part of the professional organization. The only other part that is fully elaborated is the support staff, but that is focused very much on serving the activities of the operating core. Given the high cost of the professionals, it makes sense to back them up with as much support as possible. Thus, universities have printing facilities, faculty clubs, alma mater funds, publishing houses, archives, libraries, computer facilities, and many, many other support units.

The technostructure and middle-line management are not highly elaborated in the professional organization. They can do little to coordinate the professional work. Moreover, with so little need for direct supervision of, or mutual adjustment among, the professionals, the operating units can be very large. For example, the McGill Faculty of Management functions effectively with 50 professors under a single manager, its dean, and the rest of the university's academic hierarchy is likewise thin.

Thus, the diagram at the beginning of this chapter shows the professional organization, in terms of our logo, as a flat structure with a thin middle line, a tiny technostructure, but a fully elaborated support staff. All these characteristics are reflected in the organigram of a university hospital, shown in Figure 1.

Coordination within the administrative structure is another matter, however. Because these configurations are so decentralized, the professionals not only control their own work but they also gain much collective control over the administrative decisions that affect them—decisions, for example, to hire colleagues, to promote them, and to distribute resources. This they do partly by doing some of the administrative work themselves (most university professors, for example, sit on various administrative committees) and partly by ensuring that important administrative posts are staffed by professionals or at least sympathetic people appointed with the professionals' blessing. What emerges, therefore, is a rather democratic administrative structure. But because the administrative work requires mutual adjustment for coordination among the various people involved, task forces and especially standing committees abound at this level, as is in fact suggested in Figure 1.

Because of the power of their professional operators, these organizations are sometimes described as inverse pyramids, with the professional operators on top and the administrators down below to serve them—to ensure that the surgical facilities are kept clean and the classrooms well supplied with chalk. Such a description slights the power of the administrators of professional work, however, although it may be an accurate description of those who manage the support units. For the support staff—often more numerous than the professional staff, but generally less skilled—there is no democracy in the professional organization, only the oligarchy of the professionals. Such support units as housekeeping in the hospital or printing in the university are likely to be managed tightly from the top, in effect as machinelike enclaves within the professional configuration. Thus, what frequently emerges in the professional organization are parallel and separate administrative hierarchies, one democratic and bottom-up for the professionals, a second machinelike and top-down for the support staff.

The Roles of the Administrators of Professional Work

Where does all this leave the administrators of the professional hierarchy, the executive directors and chiefs of the hospitals and the presidents and deans of the universities? Are they powerless? Compared with their counterparts in the entrepreneurial and machine organizations, they certainly lack a good deal of power. But that is far from the whole story. The administrator of professional work may not be able to control the professionals directly, but he or she does perform a series of roles that can provide considerable indirect power.

FIGURE 1
Organization of a University Hospital

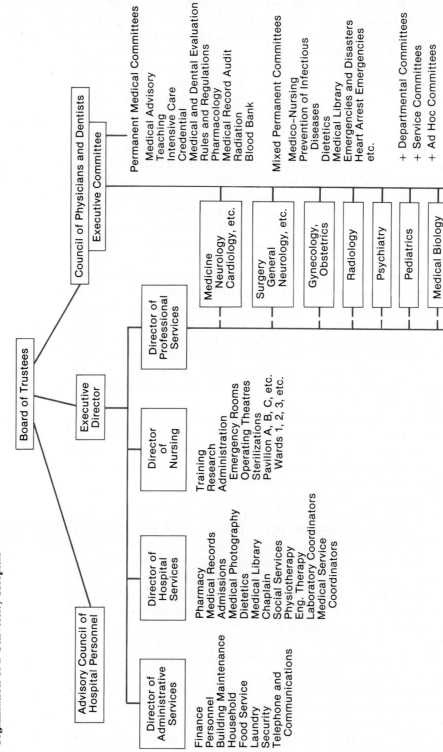

First, this administrator spends much time handling disturbances in the structure. The pigeonholing process is an imperfect one at best, leading to all kinds of jurisdictional disputes between the professionals. Who should perform mastectomies in the hospitals, surgeons who look after cutting or gynecologists who look after women? Seldom, however, can one administrator impose a solution on the professionals involved in a dispute. Rather, various administrators must often sit down together and negotiate a solution on behalf of their constituencies.

Second, the administrators of professional work—especially those at higher levels—serve in key roles at the boundary of the organization, between the professionals inside and the influencers outside: governments, client associations, benefactors, and so on. On the one hand, the administrators are expected to protect the professionals' autonomy, to "buffer" them from external pressures. On the other hand, they are expected to woo those outsiders to support the organization, both morally and financially. And that often leads the outsiders to expect these administrators, in turn, to control the professionals, in machine bureaucratic ways. Thus, the external roles of the manager—maintaining liaison contacts, acting as figurehead and spokesman in a public relations capacity, negotiating with outside agencies—emerge as primary ones in the administration of professional work.

Some view the roles these administrators are called upon to perform as signs of weakness. They see these people as the errand boys of the professionals, or else as pawns caught in various tugs of war—between one professional and another, between support staffer and professional, between outsider and professional. In fact, however, these roles are the very sources of administrators' power. Power is, after all, gained at the locus of uncertainty, and that is exactly where the administrators of professionals sit. The administrator who succeeds in raising extra funds for his or her organization gains a say in how they are distributed; the one who can reconcile conflicts in favor of his or her unit or who can effectively buffer the professionals from external influence becomes a valued, and therefore powerful, member of the organization.

We can conclude that power in these structures does flow to those professionals who care to devote effort to doing administrative instead of professional work, so long as they do it well. But that, it should be stressed, is not laissez-faire power; the professional administrator maintains power only as long as the professionals perceive him or her to be serving their interests effectively.

CONDITIONS OF THE PROFESSIONAL ORGANIZATION

The professional form of organization appears wherever the operating work of an organization is dominated by skilled workers who use procedures that are difficult to learn yet are well defined. This means a situation that is both complex and stable—complex enough to require procedures that can be learned only through extensive training yet stable enough so that their use can become standardized.

Note that an elaborate technical system can work against this configuration. If highly regulating or automated, the professionals' skills might be amenable to rationalization, in other words, to be divided into simple, highly programmed steps that would destroy the basis for professional autonomy and thereby drive the structure to the machine form. And if highly complicated, the technical system would reduce the professionals' autonomy by forcing them to work in multidisciplinary teams, thereby driving the organization toward the innovative form. Thus the surgeon uses a scalpel, and the accountant a pencil. Both must be sharp, but both are otherwise simple and commonplace instruments. Yet both allow their users to perform independently what can be exceedingly complex functions.

The prime example of the professional configuration is the personal-service organization, at least the one with complex, stable work not reliant on a fancy technical system. Schools and universities, consulting firms, law and accounting offices, and social work agencies all rely on this form of organization, more or less, so long as they concentrate not on innovating in the solution of new problems but on applying standard programs to well-defined ones. The same seems to be true of hospitals, at least to the extent that their technical systems are simple. (In those areas that call for more sophisticated equipment—apparently a growing number, especially in teaching institutions—the hospital is driven toward a hybrid structure, with characteristics of the innovative form. But this tendency is mitigated by the hospital's overriding concern with safety. Only the tried and true can be relied upon, which produces a natural aversion to the looser innovative configuration.)

So far, our examples have come from the service sector. But the professional form can be found in manufacturing too, where the above conditions hold up. Such is the case of the craft enterprise, for example the factory using skilled workers to produce ceramic products. They very term *craftsman* implies a kind of professional who learns traditional skills through long apprentice training and then is allowed to practice them free of direct supervision. Craft enterprises seem typically to have few administrators, who tend to work, in any event, alongside the operating personnel. The same would seem to be true for engineering work oriented not to creative design so much as to modification of existing dominant designs.

STRATEGY FORMATION IN THE PROFESSIONAL ORGANIZATION

It is commonly assumed that strategies are formulated before they are implemented, that planning is the central process of formulation, and that structures must be designed to implement these strategies. At least this is what one reads in the conventional literature of strategic management. In the professional organization, these imperatives stand almost totally at odds with what really happens, leading to the conclusion either that such organizations are confused about how to make strategy, or else that the strategy writers are confused about how professional organizations must function. I subscribe to the latter explanation.

Using the definition of strategy as pattern in action, strategy formation in the professional organization takes on a new meaning. Rather than simply throwing up our hands at its resistance to formal strategic planning, or, at the other extreme, dismissing professional organizations as "organized anarchies" with strategy-making processes as mere "garbage cans" (March and Olsen, 1976) we can focus on how decisions and actions in such organizations order themselves into patterns over time.

Taking strategy as pattern in action, the obvious question becomes, which actions? The key area of strategy making in most organizations concerns the elaboration of the basic mission (the products or services offered to the public); in professional organizations, we shall argue, this is significantly controlled by individual professionals. Other important areas of strategy here include the inputs to the system (notably the choice of professional staff, the determination of clients, and the raising of external funds), the means to perform the mission (the construction of buildings and facilities, the purchase of research equipment, and so on), the structure and forms of governance (design of the committee system, the hierarchies, and so on), and the various means to support the mission.

Were professional organizations to formulate strategies in the conventional ways, central administrators would develop detailed and integrated plans about these issues. This sometimes happens, but in a very limited number of cases. Many strategic issues come under the direct control of individual professionals, while others can be decided neither by individual professionals nor by central administrators, but instead require the participation of a variety of people in a complex collective process. As illustrated in Figure 2, we examine in turn the decisions controlled by individual professionals, by central administrators, and by the collectivity.

Decisions Made by Professional Judgment

Professional organizations are distinguished by the fact that the determination of the basic mission—the specific services to be offered and to whom—is in good part left to the judgment of professionals as individuals. In the university, for example, each professor has a good deal of control over what is taught and how, as well as what is researched and how. Thus the overall product-market strategy of McGill University must be seen as the composite of the individual teaching and research postures of its 1,200 professors.

That, however, does not quite constitute full autonomy, because there is a subtle but not insignificant constraint on that power. Professionals are left to decide on their own only because years of training have ensured that they will decide in ways generally accepted in their professions. Thus professors choose course contents and adopt teaching methods highly regarded by their colleagues, sometimes even formally sanctioned by their disciplines; they research subjects that will be

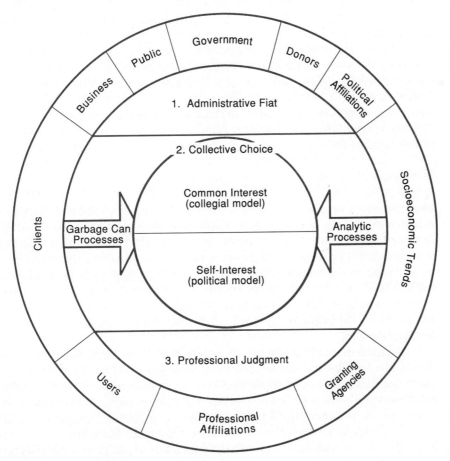

FIGURE 2
Three Levels of Decision Making in the Professional Organization

funded by the granting agencies (which usually come under professional controls); and they publish articles acceptable to the journals refereed by their peers. Pushed to the limit, then, individual freedom becomes professional control. It may be explicit freedom from administrators, even from peers in other disciplines, but it is not implicit freedom from colleagues in their own discipline. Thus we use the label "professional judgment" to imply that while judgment may be the mode of choice, it is informed judgment, mightily influenced by professional training and affiliation.

Decisions Made by Administrative Fiat

Professional expertise and autonomy, reinforced by the pigeonholing process, sharply circumscribe the capacity of central administrators to manage the professionals in the ways of conventional bureaucracy—through direct supervision and the designation of internal standards (rules, job descriptions, policies). Even the designation of standards of output or performance is discouraged by the intractable problem of operationalizing the goals of professional work.

Certain types of decisions, less related to the professional work per se, do however fall into the realm of what can be called administrative fiat, in other words, become the exclusive prerogative of the administrators. They include some financial decisions, for example, to buy and sell property and embark on fundraising campaigns. Because many of the support services are organized in a conventional top-down hierarchy, they too tend to fall under the control of the central administration. Support services more critical to professional matters, however, such as libraries or computers in the universities, tend to fall into the realm of collective decision making, where the central administrators join the professionals in the making of choices.

Central administrators may also play a prominent role in determining the procedures by which the collective process functions: what committees exist, who gets nominated to them, and so on. It is the administrators, after all, who have the time to devote to administration. This role can give skillful administrators considerable influence, however indirect, over the decisions made by others. In addition, in times of crisis administrators may acquire more extensive powers, as the professionals become more inclined to defer to leadership to resolve the issues.

Decisions Made by Collective Choice

Many decisions are, however, determined neither by administrators nor by individual professionals. Instead they are handled in interactive processes that combine professionals with administrators from a variety of levels and units. Among the most important of these decisions seem to be ones related to the definition, creation, design, and discontinuation of the pigeonholes, that is, the programs and departments of various kinds. Other important decisions here include the hiring and promotion of professionals and, in some cases, budgeting and the establishment and design of the interactive procedures themselves (if they do not fall under administrative fiat).

Decision making may be considered to involve the three phases of *identification* of the need for a decision, *development* of solutions, and *selection* of one of them. Identification seems to depend largely on individual initiative. Given the complexities of professional work and the rigidities of pigeonholing, change in this configuration is difficult to imagine without an initiating "sponsor" or "champion." Development may involve the same individual but often requires the efforts of collective task forces as well. And selection tends to be a fully interactive process, involving several layers of standing committees composed of professionals and administrators, and sometimes outsiders as well (such as government representatives). It is in this last phase that we find the full impact and complexity of mutual adjustment in the administration of professional organizations.

Models of Collective Choice

How do these interactive processes in fact work? Some writers have traditionally associated professional organizations with a *collegial* model, where decisions are made by a "community of individuals and groups, all of whom may have different roles and specialties, but who share common goals and objectives for the organization" (Taylor, 1983:18). *Common interest* is the guiding force, and decision making is therefore by consensus. Other writers instead propose a *political* model, in which the differences of interest groups are irreconcilable. Participants thus seek to serve their *self-interest,* and political factors become instrumental in determining outcomes.

Clearly, neither common interest nor self-interest will dominate decision processes all the time; some combination is naturally to be expected. Professionals may agree on goals yet conflict over how they should be achieved; alternatively, consensus can sometimes be achieved even where goals differ—Democrats do, after all, sometimes vote with Republicans in the U.S. Congress. In fact, we need to consider motivation, not just behavior, in order to distinguish collegiality from politics. Political success sometimes requires a collegial posture—one must cloak self-interest in the mantle of the common good. Likewise, collegial ends sometimes require political means. Thus, we should take as collegial any behavior that is *motivated* by a genuine concern for the good of the institution, and politics as any behavior driven fundamentally by self-interest (of the individual or his or her unit).

A third model that has been used to explain decision making in universities is the *garbage can.* Here decision making is characterized by "collections of choices looking for problems, issues and feelings looking for decision situations in which they may be aired, solutions looking for issues to which they might be an answer, and decision makers looking for work" (Cohen, March, and Olsen, 1972:1). Behavior is, in other words, nonpurposeful and often random, because goals are unclear and the means to achieve them problematic. Furthermore, participation is fluid because of the cost of time and energy. Thus, in place of the common interest of the collegial model and the self-interest of the political model, the garbage can model suggests a kind of *disinterest.*

The important question is not whether garbage can processes exist—we have all experienced them—but whether they matter. Do they apply to key issues or only to incidental ones? Of course, decisions that are not significant to anyone may well end up in the garbage can, so to speak. There is always someone with free time willing to challenge a proposal for the sake of so doing. But I have difficulty accepting that individuals to whom decisions are important do not invest the effort necessary to influence them. Thus, like common interest and self-interest, I conclude that disinterest neither dominates decision processes nor is absent from them.

Finally, *analysis* may be considered a fourth model of decision making. Here calculation is used, if not to select the best alternative, then at least to assess the acceptability of different ones. Such an approach seems consistent with the machine configuration, where a technostructure stands ready to calculate the costs and benefits of every proposal. But, in fact, analysis figures prominently in the professional configuration too, but here carried out mostly by professional operators themselves. Rational analysis structures arguments for communication and debate and enables champions and their opponents to support their respective positions. In fact, as each side seeks to pick holes in the position of the other, the real issues are more likely to emerge.

Thus, as indicated in Figure 2, the important collective decisions of the professional organization seem to be most influenced by collegial and political processes, with garbage can pressures encouraging a kind of haphazardness on one side (especially for less important decisions) and analytical interventions on the other side encouraging a certain rationality (serving as an invisible hand to keep the lid on the garbage can, so to speak!).

Strategies in the Professional Organization

Thus, we find here a very different process of strategy making, and very different resulting strategies, compared with conventional (especially machine) organizations. While it may seem difficult to create strategies in these organizations, due to the fragmentation of activity, the politics, and the garbage can phenomenon, in fact the professional organization is inundated with strategies (meaning patterning in its actions). The standardization of skills encourages patterning, as do the pigeonholing process and the professional affiliations. Collegiality promotes consistency of behavior; even politics works to resist changing existing patterns. As for the garbage can model, perhaps it just represents the unexplained variance in the system; that is, whatever is not understood looks to the outside observer like organized anarchy.

Many different people get involved in the strategy-making process here, including administrators and the various professionals, individually and collectively, so that the resulting strategies can be very fragmented (at the limit, each professional pursues his or her own product-market strategy). There are, of course, forces that encourage some overall cohesion in strategy too: the common forces of administrative fiat, the broad negotiations that take place in the collective process (for example, on new tenure regulations in a university), even the forces of habit and tradition, at the limit ideology, that can pervade a professional organization (such as hiring certain kinds of people or favoring certain styles of teaching or of surgery).

Overall, the strategies of the professional organization tend to exhibit a remarkable degree of stability. Major reorientations in strategy—"strategic revolutions"—are discouraged by the fragmentation of activity and the influence of the individual professionals and their outside associates. But at a narrower level, change is ubiquitous. Inside tiny pigeonholes, services are continually being altered, procedure redesigned, and clientele shifted, while in the collective process, pigeonholes are constantly being added and rearranged. Thus, the professional organization is, paradoxically, extremely stable at the broadest level and in a state of perpetual change at the narrowest one.

SOME ISSUES ASSOCIATED WITH THE PROFESSIONAL ORGANIZATION

The professional organization is unique among the different configurations in answering two of the paramount needs of contemporary men and women. It is democratic, disseminating its power directly to its workers (at least those lucky enough to be professional). And it provides them with extensive autonomy, freeing them even from the need to coordinate closely with their colleagues. Thus, the professional has the best of both worlds. He or she is attached to an organization yet is free to serve clients in his or her own way, constrained only by the established standards of the profession.

The result is that professionals tend to emerge as highly motivated individuals, dedicated to their work and to the clients they serve. Unlike the machine organization, which places barriers between the operator and the client, this configuration removes them, allowing a personal relationship to develop. Moreover, autonomy enables the professionals to perfect their skills free of interference, as they repeat the same complex programs time after time.

But in these same characteristics, democracy and autonomy, lie the chief problems of the professional organization. For there is no evident way to control the work, outside of that exercised by the profession itself, no way to correct deficiencies that the professionals choose to overlook. What they tend to overlook are the problems of coordination, of discretion, and of innovation that arise in these configurations.

Problems of Coordination

The professional organization can coordinate effectively in its operating core only by relying on the standardization of skills. But that is a loose coordinating mechanism at best; it fails to cope with many of the needs that arise in these organizations. One need is to coordinate the work of professionals with that of support staffers. The professionals want to give the orders. But that can catch the support staffers between the vertical power of line authority and the horizontal power of professional expertise. Another need is to achieve overriding coordination among the professionals themselves. Professional organizations, at the limit, may be viewed as collections of independent individuals who come together only to draw on common resources and support services. Though the pigeonholing process facilitates this, some things inevitably fall through the cracks between the pigeonholes. But because the professional organization lacks any obvious coordinating mechanism to deal with these, they inevitably provoke a great deal of conflict. Much political blood is spilled in the continual reassessment of contingencies and programs that are either imperfectly conceived or artificially distinguished.

Problems of Discretion

Pigeonholing raises another serious problem. It focuses most of the discretion in the hands of single professionals, whose complex skills, no matter how standardized, require the exercise of considerable judgment. Such discretion works fine when professionals are competent and conscientious. But it plays havoc when they are not. Inevitably, some professionals are simply lazy or incompetent. Others confuse the needs of their clients with the skills of their trade. They thus concentrate on a favored program to the exclusion of all others (like the psychiatrist who thinks that all patients, indeed all people, need psychoanalysis). Clients incorrectly sent their way get mistreated (in both senses of that word).

Various factors confound efforts to deal with this inversion of means and ends. One is that professionals are notoriously reluctant to act against their own, for example, to censure irresponsible behavior through their professional associations. Another (which perhaps helps to explain the first) is the intrinsic difficulty of measuring the outputs of professional work. When psychiatrists cannot even define the words *cure* or *healthy,* how are they to prove that psychoanalysis is better for schizophrenics than is chemical therapy?

Discretion allows professionals to ignore not only the needs of their clients but also those of the organization itself. Many professionals focus their loyalty on their profession, not on the place where they happen to practice it. But professional organizations have needs for loyalty too—to support their overall strategies, to staff their administrative committees, to see them through conflicts with the professional associations. Cooperation is crucial to the functioning of the administrative structure, yet many professionals resist it furiously.

Problems of Innovation

In the professional organization, major innovation also depends on cooperation. Existing programs may be perfected by the single professional, but new ones usually cut across the established specialties—in essence, they require a rearrangement of the pigeonholes—and so call for collective action. As a result, the reluctance of the professionals to cooperate with each other and the complexity of the collective processes can produce resistance to innovation. These are, after all, professional *bureaucracies,* in essence, performance structures designed to perfect given programs in stable environments, not problem-solving structures to create new programs for unanticipated needs.

The problems of innovation in the professional organization find their roots in convergent thinking, in the deductive reasoning of the professional who sees the specific situation in terms of the general concept. That means new problems are forced into old pigeonholes, as is excellently illustrated in Spencer's comments: "All patients developing significant complications or death among our three hospitals . . . are reported to a central office with a narrative description of the sequence of events, with reports varying in length from a third to an entire page." And six to eight of these cases are discussed in the one-hour weekly "mortality-morbidity" conferences, including presentation of it by the surgeon and "questions and comments" by the audience (1978:1181). An "entire" page and ten minutes of discussion for a case with "significant complications"! Maybe that is enough to list the symptoms and slot them into pigeonholes. But it is hardly enough even to begin to think about creative solutions. As Lucy once told Charlie Brown, great art cannot be done in half an hour; it takes at least 45 minutes!

The fact is that great art and innovative problem solving require *inductive* reasoning—that is, the inference of the new general solution from the particular experience. And that kind of thinking is *divergent;* it breaks away from old routines or standards rather than perfecting existing ones. And that flies in the face of everything the professional organization is designed to do.

Public Responses to These Problems

What responses do the problems of coordination, discretion, and innovation evoke? Most commonly, those outside the profession see the problems as resulting from a lack of external control of the professional and the profession. So they do the obvious: try to control the work through other, more traditional means. One is direct supervision, which typically means imposing an intermediate level of supervision to watch over the professionals. But we already discussed why this cannot work for jobs that are complex. Another is to try to standardize the work or its outputs. But we also discussed why complex work cannot be formalized by rules, regulations, or measures of performance. All these types of controls really do, by transferring the responsibility for the service from the professional to the administrative structure, is destroy the effectiveness of the work. It is not the government that educates the student, not even the school system or the school itself; it is not the hospital that delivers the baby. These things are done by the individual professional. If that professional is incompetent, no plan or rule fashioned in the technostructure, no order from any administrator or government official, can ever make him or her competent. But such plans, rules, and orders can impede the competent professional from providing his or her service effectively.

Are there then no solutions for a society concerned about the performance of its professional organizations? Financial control of them and legislation against irresponsible professional behavior are obviously in order. But beyond that, solutions must grow from a recognition of professional work for what it is. Change in the professional organization does not *sweep* in from new administrators taking office to announce wide reforms, or from government officials intent on bringing the professionals under technocratic control. Rather, change *seeps* in through the slow process of changing the professionals—changing who enters the profession in the first place, what they learn in its professional schools (norms as well as skills and knowledge), and thereafter how they upgrade their skills. Where desired changes are resisted, society may be best off to call on its professionals' sense of public responsibility or, failing that, to bring pressure on the professional associations rather than on the professional bureaucracies.

● TECHNOLOGY IN SERVICES: CREATING ORGANIZATIONAL REVOLUTIONS*

BY JAMES BRIAN QUINN AND PENNY C. PAQUETTE

Service technologies have radically reordered the power relationships, competitive environments, and leverageable opportunities in most industries—whether in services or manufacturing. In the process, they are obliterating long-held precepts about management itself and creating entirely new strategic, organizational, and control system options for achieving competitive advantage. What are some of the more important management insights from our research?

● Contrary to much popular dogma, well-managed service technologies can simultaneously deliver both *lowest cost outputs* and *maximum personalization and customization* for customers.

● In accomplishing this, enterprises generally obtain strategic advantage not through traditional economies of scale, but through *focusing on the smallest activity or cost units* that can be efficiently measured and replicated—and then *cloning and mixing these units* across as wide a geographical and applications range as possible.

● Instead of the dehumanization often experienced in other realms, well-implemented service automation actually *increases the independence* and value of lower-level jobs. At the same time, such automation *empowers contact people* to be much more responsive to customer needs.

● Such systems, when well implemented, frequently drive organizations toward entirely *new conceptual configurations*. These may assume "inverted pyramid," "infinitely flat," or "spider's web" characteristics in order to deliver outputs most effectively and flexibly to a widely distributed customer base.

● In the process, they often *disintermediate costly organizational bureaucracies,* dramatically *lower overhead costs, support rapid execution of strategies,* and substantially *increase the system's customer responsiveness.*

Creative use of technology in leading-edge companies has converted these concepts from theoreticians' fantasies into realistic strategic options for virtually any company.

OBTAINING BOTH CUSTOMIZATION AND LOWEST COST

Strategic dogmas exist that postulate an inherent conflict between obtaining lowest cost from a system and offering highest flexibility and customization (Porter, 1985). To achieve maximum value from service technologies, one must set these aside. By designing their systems properly, many well-run service companies both obtain optimal flexibility at the customer contact point and achieve maximum "production" efficiencies from constant repetition, experience curve effects, and cost-quality control. They accomplish this by first seeking the smallest possible core unit at which production can be replicated or repeated, then developing micromeasures to manage processes and functions at this level, and finally mixing these micro-units in a variety of combinations to match localized or individual customers' needs. What do these smallest replicable units look like? The nature of the unit, of course, varies by industry and by strategy.

• For Mary Kay Cosmetics or Tupperware, the sales presentation is such a unit; for accountants, audit check procedures, inventory control processes, or tax preparation subroutines may be critical; for lawyers, prepackaged documents, paragraphs, phrases, court opinions, or case briefings may be the leverageable unit. In financial services, elements of individual "transactions" (like buy/sell units, prices, times, names, customer codes, etc.) are core units; for information retrieval, it is the "key word"; for communications, it is the "packet" or the bit; and so on.

Early in the life cycle of many service industries, the smallest truly replicable unit seemed to be an individual office, store, or franchise location. Later, as volume increased, it often became possible for the parent to develop and replicate greater efficiencies within locations (Levitt, 1976). This was accomplished by managing and measuring critical performance variables at individual departmental, sales counter, activity, or stock-keeping unit (SKU) levels. Then the successful formula approaches of H&R Block, McDonald's, Mrs. Fields, and Pizza Hut pushed the repeatability unit to even smaller "micromanagement" levels. Replicating precisely measured activity cycles, personal selling approaches, inventory control patterns, ingredients, freshness and cooking cycles, counter display techniques, and cleanliness and maintenance procedures in detail became keys to success; lapses led to difficulties. So precise are many nationwide chains' measurement and feedback systems that their headquarters can tell within minutes when something goes wrong in a decentralized unit, and often precisely what the problem is.

Finally, in some industries—like banking, communications, structural design, or medical research—it has become possible to disaggregate the critical units of service production into packets, data blocks, or "bytes" of information. Accessing and combining such units on a large scale is emerging as the core activity in achieving flexibility and economies of scale on a level never before envisioned.

MANAGING AT THE MICRO-UNIT LEVEL

Most of the major strategic successes we observed in the use of service technologies came from defining and developing these replicability units and their associated micromeasures in careful detail. The exceptions were some large transportation companies (airlines or railroads) and utilities (electric power grids) that relied on more traditional economies from large-scale facilities. The ultimate purpose of focusing on the smallest replicable unit of operations, however, is not just the mass production benefit that standardization allows. Effectively combining these micro-units permits one to achieve the highest possible degrees of segmentation, strategic fine tuning, value-added, and customer satisfaction in the marketplace. Interestingly, the larger the organization, the more refined these replicability units may practically be—and the higher their leverage for creating value-added gains. Greater volume allows a larger company to collect more detail about its individual operating and market segments; analyze these data at more disaggregated levels; and experiment with more detailed segmentations in ways smaller concerns cannot. For example:

- American Express (AmEx) is the only major credit card company with a large travel service. By capturing in the most disaggregated possible form—essentially data bytes—the details that its various traveler, shopper, retailer, lodging, and transportation company customers put through its credit card and travel systems, AmEx can mix and match the patterns and capabilities of each group to add value for them in ways its competitors cannot. It can identify life-style changes (like marriage or moving) or match forthcoming travel plans with its customers' specific buying habits to notify them of special promotions, product offerings, or services AmEx's retailers may be presenting in their local or planned travel areas. From its larger information base AmEx can also provide more detailed information services to its two million retailer customers—like demographic and comparative analyses of their customer bases or individual customers' needs for wheelchair, pickup, or other convenience services. These can provide unique value for both consumer and retailer customers.

The key to micromanagement is breaking down both operations and markets into such detail that—by properly cross-matrixing the data—one can discern how a very slight change in one arena may affect some aspect of the other. The ability to micromanage, target, and customize operations in this fashion, because of the knowledge base that size permits, is becoming one of the most important uses of scale in services.

Critical to proper system design is conceptualizing the smallest replicable unit and its potential use in strategy as early as possible in system design. Summing disaggregated data later, if one so desires, is much easier than moving from a more aggregated system to a greater refinement in detail. And highly disaggregated data often capture unexpected experience patterns that summary data would obscure. Much of the later power and flexibility of American's SABRE, McKesson's ECONOMOST, or National Rental Car's EXPRESSWAY systems derived from making this choice correctly, while less successful competitors' systems did not.[1] Too many companies have chosen a larger replicability unit in order to save initial installation costs. In the process they have lost crucial detailed experience and segmentation data that should have become the core of their later strategies.

---

[1] McKesson's ECONOMOST system was planned from the beginning to collect such detailed information concerning item description, price, price changes, shelf location, sales rates, facings information, and so on, that the system could later be easily adapted for follow-on services like optimizing floor layouts, stock locations, reordering patterns, bill payments, accounting, credit, and insurance arrangements, market testing, and so on.

Well-designed technology systems for services not only increase efficiency, they empower employees to do their jobs better. Why is this so important in services? In most cases, a service must be produced simultaneously with its consumption—as a telephone call, a vacation, a restaurant meal, electrical energy, or a hospital stay would be. There is often no inventory potential, very little opportunity for later repair, and no resale market for the service. This means that much of a service's perceived value is created at the moment and place of contact. And the frontline person's willingness to handle that contact with diligence and flair is often critical to success of the enterprise.

Properly designed service technology systems allow relatively inexperienced people to perform very sophisticated tasks quickly—vaulting them over normal learning curve delays. Then by constant updating, the most successful technologies and systems automatically capture the highest potential experience curve benefits available in the entire system. This allows employees to take advantage of the total organization's constantly expanding capabilities, which they could not possibly learn first hand or be trained personally to execute. This is vital when so many service operations rely on entry-level, part-time, or relatively inexperienced workers to meet their needs at lowest cost. By increasing the value added per employee, the technologies also open possibilities for wage gains, as well as opportunities for many employees to own a profitable franchise or manage the very decentralized operations of automated service systems.

Interestingly, effective service automation generally encourages greater—rather than less—empowerment and decentralization at the contact level. This is true of both professional and more product-oriented service organizations—like restaurants, retailers, or postsale product support units. By routinizing the operating detail that it once took great effort to master, managers and workers can concentrate their attention on the more conceptual or personalized tasks only people can perform. An example will suggest how technology helps both decentralize and empower personnel in successful service organizations.

• Domino's Pizza, perhaps the fastest-growing food chain in history, encourages its local store managers to regard themselves as individual entrepreneurs. First, for each of its 4,500 highly decentralized outlets, industrial engineering and food science research automated the making of a pizza to as near a science as possible, eliminating much of the drudgery in such tasks, yet ensuring higher quality and uniformity. Then, finding that its store managers were still spending fifteen to twenty hours per week on paperwork, Domino's introduced NCR "minitower" systems at its stores to handle all of the ordering, payroll, marketing, cash flow, inventory, and work control functions. This freed store executives to perform more valuable supervisory, follow-up, menu experimentation, public relations, or customer service activities—expanding and elevating their management roles. Thus they could focus even more on founder Tom Monahan's goals: that they be independent entrepreneurs devoting themselves as much as possible to the company's highly developed customer service philosophies.

Some strategies, of course, call for more empowerment, some for more standardization of activity. Some service situations even require that technologies be used *primarily* to obtain uniformity, rather than flexibility. In some services, like bank accounting, film processing, or aircraft maintenance, one may actively discourage too much independence, because exactness and tight tolerances are required. Great service successes, however, generally exhibit a unique blend: a distinctly structured technology system and a carefully developed management style to support it. The subtle ways in which the two are developed and emphasized can lead to quite different market postures in the same industry.

• Federal Express (FedEx) has long emphasized the use of a friendly, people-oriented, entrepreneurial management style in conjunction with state-of-the-art technology systems. Its DADS (computer aided delivery) and COSMOS II (automated tracking) systems give FedEx maximum responsiveness. And its training programs, colorful advertising, decentralized operating style, and incentive systems stress the need to go to the limit personally in responding to customer needs and ensuring reliable, on-time delivery. By contrast, UPS has long utilized old-style trucks, hand sorting, lower-cost land transport, detailed time and motion study controls for its drivers, and a hard-headed control system that give it a lower cost—but considerably less customer responsive—market position. Both companies have been successful, FedEx by emphasizing "highest reliability and customer service" and UPS by emphasizing good service at low cost.

NEW ORGANIZATIONAL FORMS

In their efforts to gain the benefits of these two concepts—management at the micro-level and increased empowerment at the customer contact point—many service companies have developed strikingly new, and more effective, organizational modes. Several of the most important ones are described below.

Inverting the Organization

To the customer, the most important person in the company is very often the one at the point of contact. What happens in the usually brief one to three minutes of that contact will demonstrate—or destroy—for the customer all the value the company so expensively has sought to create through its product, quality, distribution, and advertising investments (Carlzon, 1987).

In some situations this consideration is so dominant that it has led to the concept of "inverting the organization" to make all systems and support staffs in the company "work for" the frontline person to deliver the company's full capabilities at the moment of customer contact. Managers in such enterprises try to make their organizations perform as if they were a series of pyramids focused on the frontline contact people. Some, like Toronto Dominion Bank and AIG, have formal organization charts with the customer at the top, the CEO at the bottom, and an inverted organization hierarchy in between.

Such techniques may be useful reminders, but it is really technology and an inversion of roles and attitudes that make such concepts work. The point person (e.g., a branch bank's customer service representative) cannot possibly know or control all the system details (investment options, differential interest rates, future values, etc.) necessary to deliver the organization's full power to the customer. Thus, successfully inverted organizations first capture and continuously update or monitor as many relevant service elements as possible by structuring data banks, "expert system" models, and interactive feedback and communication systems to make as much as possible of the firm's total expertise available instantly to the point person. Network technologies allow frontline personnel to call forth and cross-matrix whatever details their customers' specific needs may require—using collected micro-units of information either directly as data or indirectly to build unique solutions for customers even at the most remote locations. Within the data limits and decision rules defined by the system, nonroutine decisions are left as much as possible to local personnel. These individuals then call for help on those specialized issues they cannot handle themselves. And each person in the management hierarchy is expected to respond to this "order" for support.

As an interesting part of the inversion, it is usually the software or planning personnel (ordinarily considered "service" or "staff") who design "line" decisions. They do so by providing accessible answers to routinely asked questions or by simulating (through expert systems) many of the more sophisticated decisions line managers would normally make. To complete the inversion, intermediate line managers, rather than being order givers, become essentially expediters, information sources, and performance observers—roles frequently assumed to be "staff"—supporting the contact people. However, their other substantive line roles—particularly as arbiters of last resort for frontline personnel and as sensors of situations beyond the scope of the technological systems—take on even greater relative importance as routine activities decline. Because of the distortions that inevitably take place in human communication, eliminating the hierarchical layers between the central repository of information and the customer contact point becomes an important goal that a well-developed information technology system facilitates. When this occurs the few remaining line executives become even more important in their expanded roles—managing much wider areas of organizational contact and those more complicated issues where interpretation, intuition, creativity, and human motivation count.

"Infinitely Flat" Organizations

When technology is creatively implemented in services, companies often achieve other remarkable organizational configurations. For example, there now seems to be virtually no limit to the reporting span—the number of people reporting to one supervisor or center—that a service organization can make effective. While spans of twenty to fifty have become relatively common, spans of hundreds exist in some service organizations. Several examples will make the point.

• Shearson American Express's and Merrill Lynch's 310 to 480 domestic brokerage offices connect directly with their parents' central information offices for routine needs, yet can bypass the electronic system for personal access to individual experts in headquarters. In effect, technology permits the company to function in a coordinated fashion with the full power of a major financial enterprise, yet allows local brokers to manage their own small units independently. The result is to provide the most extensive possible local responsiveness and customization for the company's dispersed customer base.

• Federal Express, with 42,000 employees in more than 300 cities worldwide, has a maximum of only five organizational layers between its nonmanagement employees and its COO or CEO. Typical operating spans of control are 15–20 employees to one manager, with only 2.1 staff employees per million dollars in sales—about one-fifth the industry average. As many as 50 couriers are under the line control of a single dispatching center. FedEx's advanced DADS and COSMOS computer-communications capabilities allow it to coordinate its 21,000 vans nationwide to make an average of 720,000 "on call" stops per day. Because of its leading edge flight operations technologies and avionics controls, as many as 200 FedEx aircraft can be in the air simultaneously, but under the control of a single authority, should it become necessary to override flight plans because of weather or special emergencies.

There is no inherent reason that organizations cannot be made "infinitely flat"—in other words, with innumerable outposts guided by one central "rules-based" or "computer controlled inquiry" system. In designing service company systems, instead of thinking about traditional "spans of control," our study suggests that the terms "spans of effective cooperation," "communication spans," or "support spans" may have more meaning. By defining, routinizing, and automating operating parameters at their finest replicable level, companies can often obtain the thorough cost and quality controls they need for system coordination and productivity at each of many highly decentralized operating nodes. In these circumstances, the normal functions provided by personal hierarchical controls become almost irrelevant.

Extremely wide reporting spans work well when the following conditions exist: localized interactive contact is very important; each ultimate contact point or operations unit can operate independently from all others at its level; the critical relationship between decentralized units and the center is largely quantitative or informational; and the majority of the relationships with the information center can be routine or rules based. Although service units have generally pioneered such organizations, a few manufacturing enterprises have realized that the same characteristics occur in specific production situations and are beginning to implement similar approaches. The immediate economic impact of such systems is, of course, that they allow major investments in extremely sophisticated systems at the center, deliver this sophistication in highly customized form at remote points, eliminate overhead hierarchies, and add value (at lower unit costs) in both the center and the remote nodes. American Express—whose expertise at credit processing is so great that its competitors hire it to process their credit transactions—is one such example. AMRIS (described later) is another.

An often overlooked feature of these systems is the longer-term payoff potentials that carefully developed feedback loops from the decentralized nodes can offer to the center. By sophisticated segmentation and synthesis of data generated at the nodes—and the often much more detailed information about their customers they collect—the corporation's "information center" can develop a knowledge base with a power neither it nor any single outlet could possibly achieve alone. Aggregating and comparing detailed information from these sources, the center can often develop an ever-increasing set of higher value-added services and sell them back to its own nodes (or the latter's customers) to further increase its profits and those units' competitiveness. For example:

• American Airlines' parent recently created a sister company, AMR Information Services (AMRIS) to further leverage the knowledge, staff, facilities, and technologies its SABRE reservations system had built. Along with operating an offshore data entry business, AMRIS is entering a partnership with Hilton, Marriott, and Budget Rent-a-Car to handle their critical reservations and property management activities worldwide. AMRIS's system (called CONFIRM) will provide a single source with hundreds of remote nodes—in other words, a very flat organization—through which travel agents can make and confirm all desired reservations.

But CONFIRM will also provide its client industries with a much broader and deeper database to micromanage their yield strategies, for example, foreseeing unexpected shortfalls or special surges in occupancy or demand soon enough to target short-term promotional and pricing strategies. In time, comparative data across client companies will enable AMRIS to develop industrywide decision support models, further amplifying its own and its clients' competitive advantages. Yet each participant in this consortium (and their individual outlets) can operate as independently as they wish.

"Spider's Web" Organizations

When the highly dispersed nodes of service operations or customer contact must interact frequently, another startling organizational form begins to emerge. It is sometimes called a network, but is best described as a spider's web because of the light yet structured quality of its interconnections.

• Arthur Andersen and Company (AA&Co.,) a leader in applying technology to professional services, has to interlink its 40,000 knowledgeable professionals with thousands of clients, each with a mix of operations around the United States and in up to 200 other countries. The company's cumulative experience is growing so fast that, according to executives, "Even those in the know may not have the best answer to the totality of a complex question." Consequently, individuals in AA&Co. can no longer even rely on their personal knowledge of whom to call for information. So in addition to trying to capture the history of its contacts with major clients, keeping up electronically with changing IRS and FASB requirements, and attempting to catalogue where it has found solutions to particular problems, the firm is developing an electronic bulletin board to let any professional send out a query to the entire AA&Co. system to find useful solutions or knowledge that any other individual in the company may have for special problems.

The firm operates in a highly decentralized, real-time mode. Each local office is as independent as possible. Partners say that AA&Co.'s distinctive competency has become "empowering people to deliver better quality technology-based solutions to clients in a shorter time." Customers now look to the firm to deliver computer-based solutions to systems problems in a league competitive with EDS's and IBM's capabilities. Yet professionals who leave AA&Co. immediately lose access to its systems and accumulated experience.

Such open network formats increasingly characterize the way multinational or investment banks, financial or professional service companies, engineering and construction enterprises, research and health care, and accounting and advertising firms operate. Unlike the units of infinitely flat organizations, each of the nodes in the spider's web frequently needs, for effectiveness, to be in touch with the information or resources all other nodes contain. Within wide ranges, each node may function quite independently in serving a particular client base. However, in certain circumstances, the individual nodes may need to operate in a highly coordinated fashion to achieve strategic advantage for a specific purpose. To deal with this problem, companies with traditional organizational structures must resort to complex matrix organizations that allow the project leader to coerce resources, as needed, from the otherwise decentralized network. But this often creates very costly motivational, priority, turf, and transfer pricing issues. Others have found the flexibility, fast response, and opportunism of the spider's web concept so attractive that they have established entirely new management modes that allow it to operate.

CREATIVE MANAGEMENT FOR PROFITS

Managing these new organizational forms poses some interesting challenges. Yet we have observed some consistent patterns, problems, and benefits that seem to accompany development of these new modes. What are some of the most interesting themes?

Destruction of Bureaucracies

A common consequence of these new organizational strategies is their dramatic potential for reducing intermediate management—and other organizational—bureaucracies. This occurs in part because a customer's highly personalized perception of quality in services tends to demand as much customization at the point of sale as possible. Delivering reliably against this expectation requires that intermediate levels of interpretation or handling be avoided like the plague. Each transfer point or intermediary can introduce unintended errors, distort intentions, or create costly but unmeasured bureaucratic delays. Unfortunately, because the outputs of internal service functions are so difficult to measure, it is easy for such costs to balloon uncontrollably. Targeting internal, as well as external, service activities for substantial disintermediation (entire elimination of the function if possible) can lead to startling competitive gains, usually including more rapid response times and better service for customers.

- For major newspapers like *The New York Times,* electronic technologies are enabling editors and reporters to go directly to printable copy at their electronic work stations. While still in contact with their field sources, they can pretest spacings, enhance picture quality, and lay out entire pages without handling any hard copy. Through disintermediation of make up, type setting, and other proofing stages they cut costs, shorten cycle times, and deliver more current news to their customers. Electronic publishing also allows such newspapers to target the news for different localities, release multiple local editions on tight schedules, and serve their regional advertising customers more effectively. In many cases, outside suppliers like ADP Services (in payroll processing), ServiceMaster (in maintenance services), or Kelly Services (in temporary personnel services) can add more value and provide greater economies of scale through technology than any less specialized company can achieve internally. In these situations, a company will sacrifice competitive advantage if it does not outsource and eliminate as much of its internal bureaucracy as possible. Most overheads are merely services the company has chosen to produce internally. Approaching each such activity as a "make or buy" option (in light of new services technologies' potentials) will, at a minimum, stimulate creative strategic alternatives. In many cases it will lead to the dismantling of outmoded bureaucracies.

Leveraging and Keeping Key People

Many companies find that developing internal service technologies to a high level has become a critical factor in attracting, leveraging, and keeping key people. This is most obvious in the more professional service areas like research, design, engineering, finance, marketing, or public relations. In such fields, better qualified people will more readily join or stay with a company if it provides the most advanced technology systems for practicing their art. The concept has special power in independent professional service firms, where very talented people are essential but can easily move to other enterprises, often taking clients with them. Proper strategic use of technology in these situations increases the professionals' personal potentials within the firm—enabling higher billing rates and salaries—yet creates a dependency that ties them more tightly to the enterprise. Thus used, technology serves in both *offensive* and *defensive* roles.

- Advanced accounting, legal, consulting, and financial service houses use technology as a two-edged sword. First they capture and store updated regulations, legal opinions, and professional practice rules to ensure highest quality for their services. Then they attempt to automate their routine audit, client analysis, and repetitious operations (like contract boiler plate or tested clauses for public documents) and concentrate on the unique aspects of their clients' situations. This has progressed so far that some activities—like audit functions in CPA firms and portfolio or bubble chart analyses—that used to be the core offerings of many professional firms have become commodities with such low margins that they are often used primarily as promotions to obtain other business. As they are freed from overseeing these routine tasks, key people can benefit from the excitement of solving more challenging problems and from the higher revenues this allows. In fact, many professional services firms now find that the core of their distinctive competency lies in the accumulated knowledge in their databases and the capacity of their members to access and build solutions on those databases. The technology thus creates entry barriers for competitors, switching costs for clients, and (perhaps most important) switching costs for their own key personnel.

Successful use of technology in these situations is built around certain imperatives. First, the technology must leverage its users' personal capabilities and enhance their value to the greatest extent possible. Second, to capture the maximum benefits of the technology, quotes, billings, and internal controls need to shift from an hourly billing basis toward a value-added concept. Finally, while being simple to access, the technology's innards must be sufficiently complex that its reproduction becomes a genuine barrier to key individuals' leaving. This defensive consideration is especially critical for independent professional partnerships, but it is increasingly important in product-oriented companies where an individual's knowledge or contacts—for example, in research or marketing—are central to the enterprise's success.

Technology has also become strategically important in providing job satisfaction at all levels of service organizations. How well a company treats its key employees—whether they are high performing sales clerks, skilled technicians, or expensive professionals—will ultimately be reflected in how productive these employees are and how well they treat customers. Well-designed technology systems directly support desired motivational processes at all levels.

• For example, retail stores have found that some of the major benefits of their bar code scanning and price look-up systems come from a marked decrease in pricing and inventory identification errors and, even more important, a correspondingly improved morale among checkout personnel. Because there are no product identification errors, purchasing and stocking activities are more accurate, avoiding annoying stockouts and outdated merchandise. Checkout and salesclerks are less embarrassed by not knowing item descriptions or current prices, can speed up their service considerably (thus decreasing frustrated customers' antagonism), and have more time to spend on the more pleasant customer interactions they enjoy.

Precise and Swift Strategy Execution

Another important advantage accrues from proper exploitation of service technologies. As managers break their service production down to the smallest replicable units consistent with customers' varying needs, they must be able to measure performance in comparable detail. Assuming they install proper feedback mechanisms, this gives them the capability to execute their strategies quickly and precisely, maintaining a desired productivity, quality, and "product" mix even as demand fluctuates violently or new products are introduced.

• While insurance companies used to rewrite their offerings and rate books once or twice a year, they must now adjust to the constantly changing interest rates and offerings of other direct and functional competitors, like banks, money market funds, and the single-premium offers from brokerage houses. Insurance executives state flatly that their agents could not possibly understand or present the volatile complexity of their products without responsive on-line information connections with headquarters. Such connections are essential to calculate and immediately update the company's margins on each product, maintain desired spreads, and motivate agents to sell the most profitable current product mix.

Respondents in our study often asserted this theme: "In services, execution is everything. If you can't deliver what customers want, when they want it, with the personal touch they like, all your strategic thinking and investments won't amount to much. Our technology is one key factor in execution. The other is the management systems and culture that cause our people to react quickly and favorably to our offerings and to our customers' needs."

Managing Technologies and Attitudes

While many strategic analyses focus mostly on measurable economic factors, our study found that managing employee perceptions at the frontline level was among the most highly leverageable—and lowest-cost—activities service managers undertook. When strongly inculcated corporate values were made meaningful at the operating level, morale became higher, service levels improved, productivity went up, time horizons lengthened, increased delegation was possible, personal conflicts decreased, and control system costs dropped—all with high impacts on value added and profits. But it also turned out that a dual orientation toward technology and managing values was crucial. Together, in our sample, the two yielded some of the greatest successes in modern business history. But when one was ignored, disasters could happen.

• Many are familiar with the explosive growth Donald Burr created with his charismatic leadership of People Express. At first, the company's shared vision was fully communicated and internalized at virtually all levels of the organization. This and other personnel practices led to a highly committed, efficient, and responsive company. However, one of the reasons People Express failed was Mr. Burr's disdain, if not active dislike, for technology. Despite the pleading of some key people, People Express was not connected to the major automated reservation systems, key operations were not computerized, and flight services became ever more confused and difficult for passengers. Finally, other airlines with more sophisticated information about flight patterns and rate structures were able to chip away at People Express's niche without severe cost to themselves.

• By contrast, Wal-Mart stores, the last decade's fastest-growing and most profitable major retail chain, offers an excellent example of how the combination can be implemented well. Wal-Mart focuses its advanced technologies and all of its efficiency efforts on serving its customers better and lowering prices, not just on cost cutting or margin generating per se. To drive its customer-oriented value system, executives spend four to five days a week personally talking to customers and employees in the field, and then return for Friday/Saturday "idea sessions" to improve operations. To emphasize this orientation further, Wal-Mart often designates certain employees (who might otherwise have been displaced by technology or systems changes) as "people greeters" to increase customer satisfaction. It has also developed an extensive "Buy American Plan," which helps Wal-Mart's dominantly blue-collar customers by protecting their jobs. All these practices support the company's constantly reinforced theme that "serving the customer right is what makes profits" (Barrier, 1988).

The Company as a Voluntary Organization

Two of the most important strategic differences between large-scale services and manufacturing operations are the dependency of the entire system on the person at the contact point with the customer, and the very high degree of geographical dispersion among the points where the service is produced and delivered. The people who can and do create the greatest value in these situations are genuinely "volunteers"; they have often been described as "assets who walk out the door every night." And their skills, intrinsic attitudes, and knowledge are such that they rarely have to stay with the company unless they so choose. For a service company's core strategies to succeed, everyone in critical positions—especially those who deal directly with customers' concerns—must be in an environment where they want to perform well, and be trained and empowered to do so. Many of these people— often numbering in the thousands in large enterprises—tend to be at locations remote from the corporate center.

Realizing this, successful service companies focus on delivering empowering details—from required data to repair supplies—in a timely manner to key personnel and then cultivating their willingness and capabilities to use these to serve customers. In order to ensure maximum responsiveness at the contact point, however, one must also have the confidence that the frontline person will intuitively respond in the proper way when nonprogrammed situations occur. Empowerment with control entails many things. Critical among them are providing information, supplies, and performance measures with microprecision at the front-line level and paying special attention to values and attitude management—including the selection, indoctrination, skills training, and incentive processes converging on people at the point where the service is created and delivered.

One of the least glamorous services—hair dressing—shows dramatically how managing this combination can pay off.

• Visible Changes, in the fragmented hairdressing industry, achieves three and one-half times the turnover of its competitors, twice the average sales per customer, and almost four times the industry's average product sales in its outlets. Starting with hairdressers—who generally have no loyalty to their employers and see their profession as a low-paying dead end—Visible Changes tries to give its employees a sense of proprietorship, without stock equity. Employees make their own decisions, and always earn their rewards.

Nothing comes as a "benefit." People earn their health insurance from their sale of hair care products. They have to earn the right to go to advanced hair styling programs. But as a reward, hairdressers, when customers especially request them, receive a 35% commission and the right to raise service fees by up to 40%. Bonuses, based on performance ratings, can add another 10%, and profit sharing 15% more. A computer-based system helps measure and reward each individual's performance down to the finest detail; it maintains needed cost controls, points out where performance can be improved, and creates equity among individuals. The typical employee earns three times the industry's average wage.

The value of most service companies depends strongly on their managements' style and leadership qualities, the culture that management creates, and the way key people respond to these factors. No financial analysis of the "breakup" or "takeover" value of a service company means much without a realistic assessment of whether a new management could—and would—continue to build similar value through its people. To enhance a firm's market value, perhaps management should try to capitalize as much of a firm's uniqueness as possible into its operating systems and technologies, which are transferable on sale. But these will never quite capture that last, most important, ephemeral, and leverageable element in services—the skills and attitudes of key operating people and management.

KEY CHALLENGES

We have emphasized the reality and the success of these fascinating new organizational forms and strategies. Yet managements encounter many difficult issues in implementing them—particularly in settings where more traditional structures have enjoyed a long history. It is often easy to introduce a radical organization form in a well-conceived startup. Elsewhere, one can anticipate certain common complications.

- Intermediate management levels—whose very meaning is threatened by such configurations—will resist strongly, unless the firm's growth offers more productive havens.

- Especially in more professional service activities, those for whom information has been power will struggle against giving their newer colleagues access to client contacts, mentally stored solutions, or private files that have given senior members a competitive edge in the past.

- MIS people who have made their careers around large central computer systems often become unsettled centers of resistance when they realize that powerful desktop computers and decentralized networks will make their primary skills obsolescent and erode their power bases.

- Experienced line personnel may become frustrated and confused by the need to choose and compromise among the competing demands various important parties place on them.

By simplifying their organizations, companies can overcome many of these resistances while achieving much greater strategic focus. This article suggests that the opportunities for increased efficiency, flexibility, and responsiveness—with significantly lowered overheads—are very great. The question is no longer whether these potentials are real. The issue is whether, when, and how to begin moving toward those potentials—before or after one's competitors have seized the initiative.

13

THE INNOVATION CONTEXT

Although often seen as a high-technology event involving inventor-entrepreneurs, innovation may, of course, occur in high or low technology, product or service, large or small organizational situations. Innovation may be thought of as the *first reduction to practice* of an idea in a culture. The more radical the idea, the more traumatic and profound its impact will tend to be. But there are no absolutes. Whatever is most new and difficult to understand becomes the "high technology" of its age. As Jim Utterback of MIT is fond of pointing out, the delivery of ice was high technology at the turn of the century, later it was the production of automobiles. By the same token, fifty years from now, electronics and space stations may be considered mundane.

Our focus here, however, is not on innovation per se, but on the innovation *context,* that is the situation in which steady or frequent innovation of a complex nature is an intrinsic part of the organization and the industry segment of which it choses to operate. Such organizations depend, not just on a single entrepreneurial individual, but on teams of experts molded together for "intrapreneurship."

The innovation context is one in which the organization often must deal with complex technologies or systems under conditions of dynamic change. Typically, major innovations require that a variety of experts work toward a common goal, often led by a single champion or a small group of committed individuals. Much has been learned from research in recent years on such organizations. While this knowledge may seem less structured than that of previous chapters, several dominant themes have emerged.

This chapter opens with a description of the fifth of Mintzberg's structures, here titled the innovative organization, but also referred to as "adhocracy." This is the structure that, as noted, achieves its effectiveness by being inefficient. This reading probes into the unusual ways in which strategies evolve in the context of work that is both highly complex and highly dynamic. Here we see the full flowering of the notion of emergent strategy, culminating in a description of a "grass-roots" model of the process. We also see here a strategic leadership less concerned with formulating and then implementing strategies than managing a process through which strategies almost seem to *form* by themselves.

The second reading of this chapter, James Brian Quinn's "Managing Innovation: Controlled Chaos" (winner of the McKinsey prize for the best *Harvard Business Review* article of 1985), suggests how the spirit of adhocracy and strategy formation as a learning process can be integrated with some of the formal strategic processes of large organizations. To achieve innovativeness, other authors have advocated adhocracy with little or no reliance on planning. Quinn suggests that blending broad strategy planning with a consciously structured adhocracy gives better results. This reading also brings back the notion of "intrapreneurship," mentioned in the introduction to Chapter 9 on the entrepreneurial context. When it is successful, intrapreneurship—implying the stimulation and diffusion of innovative capacity throughout a larger organization, with many champions of innovations—tends to follow most of Quinn's precepts. As such, it seems to belong more to this context than the entrepreneurial one, which focuses on organizations highly centralized around the initiatives of their single leaders, whether or not innovative.

• THE INNOVATIVE ORGANIZATION*

BY HENRY MINTZBERG

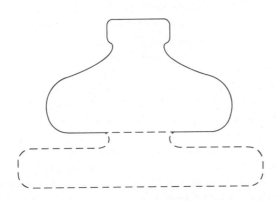

None of the organization forms so far discussed is capable of sophisticated innovation, the kind required of a high-technology research organization, an avant-garde film company, or a factory manufacturing complex prototypes. The

---

* Adapted from *The Structuring of Organizations* (Prentice Hall, 1979), Chap. 21 on the adhocracy; on strategy formation from "Strategy Formation in an Adhocracy," coauthored with Alexandra McHugh, *Administrative Science Quarterly* (1985: 160–197), and "Strategy of Design: A Study of 'Architects in Co-Partnership,' " coauthored with Suzanne Otis, Jamal Shamsie, and James A. Waters, in J. Grant (ed.), *Strategic Management Frontiers* (JAI Press, 1988). A chapter similar to this one appeared in *Mintzberg on Management: Inside Our Strange World of Organizations* (Free Press, 1989).

entrepreneurial organization can certainly innovate, but only in relatively simple ways. The machine and professional organizations are performance, not problem-solving types, designed to perfect standardized programs, not to invent new ones. And although the diversified organization resolves some problem of strategic inflexibility found in the machine organization, as noted earlier it too is not a true innovator. A focus on control by standardizing outputs does not encourage innovation.

Sophisticated innovation requires a very different configuration, one that is able to fuse experts drawn from different disciplines into smoothly functioning ad hoc project teams. To borrow the word coined by Bennis and Slater in 1964 and later popularized in Alvin Toffler's *Future Shock* (1970), these are the *adhocracies* of our society.

THE BASIC STRUCTURE

Here again we have a distinct configuration of the attributes of design: highly organic structure, with little formalization of behavior; specialized jobs based on expert training; a tendency to group the specialists in functional units for housekeeping purposes but to deploy them in small project teams to do their work; a reliance on teams, on task forces, and on integrating managers of various sorts in order to encourage mutual adjustment, the key mechanism of coordination, within and between these teams; and considerable decentralization to and within these teams, which are located at various places in the organization and involve various mixtures of line managers and staff and operating experts.

To innovate means to break away from established patterns. Thus the innovative organization cannot rely on any form of standardization for coordination. In other words, it must avoid all the trappings of bureaucratic structure, notably sharp divisions of labor, extensive unit differentiation, highly formalized behaviors, and an emphasis on planning and control systems. Above all, it must remain flexible. A search for organigrams to illustrate this description elicited the following response from one corporation thought to have an adhocracy structure: "[W]e would prefer not to supply an organization chart, since it would change too quickly to serve any useful purpose." Of all the configurations, this one shows the least reverence for the classical principles of management, especially unity of command. Information and decision processes flow flexibly and informally, wherever they must, to promote innovation. And that means overriding the chain of authority if need be.

The entrepreneurial configuration also retains a flexible, organic structure, and so is likewise able to innovate. But that innovation is restricted to simple situations, ones easily comprehended by a single leader. Innovation of the sophisticated variety requires another kind of flexible structure, one that can draw together different forms of expertise. Thus the adhocracy must hire and give power to experts, people whose knowledge and skills have been highly developed in training programs. But unlike the professional organization, the adhocracy cannot rely on the standardized skills of its experts to achieve coordination, because that would discourage innovation. Rather, it must treat existing knowledge and skills as bases on which to combine and build new ones. Thus the adhocracy must break through the boundaries of conventional specialization and differentiation, which it does by assigning problems not to individual experts in preestablished pigeonholes but to multidisciplinary teams that merge their efforts. Each team forms around one specific project.

Despite organizing around market-based projects, the organization must still support and encourage particular types of specialized expertise. And so the adhocracy tends to use a matrix structure: Its experts are grouped in functional units for specialized housekeeping purposes—hiring, training, professional communication, and the like—but are then deployed in the project teams to carry out the basic work of innovation.

As for coordination in and between these project teams, as noted earlier standardization is precluded as a significant coordinating mechanism. The efforts must be innovative, not routine. So, too, is direct supervision precluded because of the complexity of the work: Coordination must be accomplished by those with the knowledge, namely the experts themselves, not those with just authority. That leaves just one of our coordinating mechanisms, mutual adjustment, which we consider foremost in adhocracy. And, to encourage this, the organization makes use of a whole set of liaison devices, liaison personnel and integrating managers of all kinds, in addition to the various teams and task forces.

The result is that managers abound in the adhocracy: functional managers, integrating managers, project managers. The last-named are particularly numerous, since the project teams must be small to encourage mutual adjustment among their members, and each, of course, needs a designated manager. The consequence is that "spans of control" found in adhocracy tend to be small. But the implication of this is misleading, because the term is suited to the machine, not the innovative configuration: The managers of adhocracy seldom "manage" in the usual sense of giving orders; instead, they spend a good deal of time acting in a liaison capacity, to coordinate the work laterally among the various teams and units.

With its reliance on highly trained experts, the adhocracy emerges as highly decentralized, in the "selective" sense. That means power over its decisions and actions is distributed to various places and at various levels according to the needs of the particular issue. In effect, power flows to wherever the relevent expertise happens to reside—among managers or specialists (or teams of those) in the line structure, the staff units, and the operating core.

To proceed with our discussion and to elaborate on how the innovative organization makes decisions and forms strategies, we need to distinguish two basic forms that it takes.

The Operating Adhocracy

The *operating adhocracy* innovates and solves problems directly on behalf of its clients. Its multidisciplinary teams of experts often work under contract, as in the think-tank consulting firm, creative advertising agency, or manufacturer of engineering prototypes.

In fact, for every operating adhocracy, there is a corresponding professional bureaucracy, one that does similar work but with a narrower orientation. Faced with a client problem, the operating adhocracy engages in creative efforts to find a novel solution; the professional bureaucracy pigeonholes it into a known contingency to which it can apply a standard program. One engages in divergent thinking aimed at innovation, the other in convergent thinking aimed at perfection. Thus, one theater company might seek out new avant-garde plays to perform, while another might perfect its performance of Shakespeare year after year.

A key feature of the operating adhocracy is that its administrative and operating work tend to blend into a single effort. That is, in ad hoc project work it is difficult to separate the planning and design of the work from its execution. Both require the same specialized skills, on a project-by-project basis. Thus it can be difficult to distinguish the middle levels of the organization from its operating core, since line managers and staff specialists may take their place alongside operating specialists on the project teams.

Figure 1 shows the organigram of the National Film Board of Canada, a classic operating adhocracy (even though it does produce a chart—one that changes frequently, it might be added). The Board is an agency of the Canadian federal government and produces mostly short films, many of them documentaries. At the time of this organigram, the characteristics of adhocracy were particularly in evidence: It shows a large number of support units as well as liaison positions (for example, research, technical, and production coordinators), with the operating core containing loose concurrent functional and market groupings, the latter by region as well as by type of film produced and, as can be seen, some not even connected to the line hierarchy!

FIGURE 1
The National Film Board of Canada: An Operating Adhocracy (circa 1975; used with permission)
* *No lines shown on original organigram connecting Regional Programs to Studios or Filmmakers.*

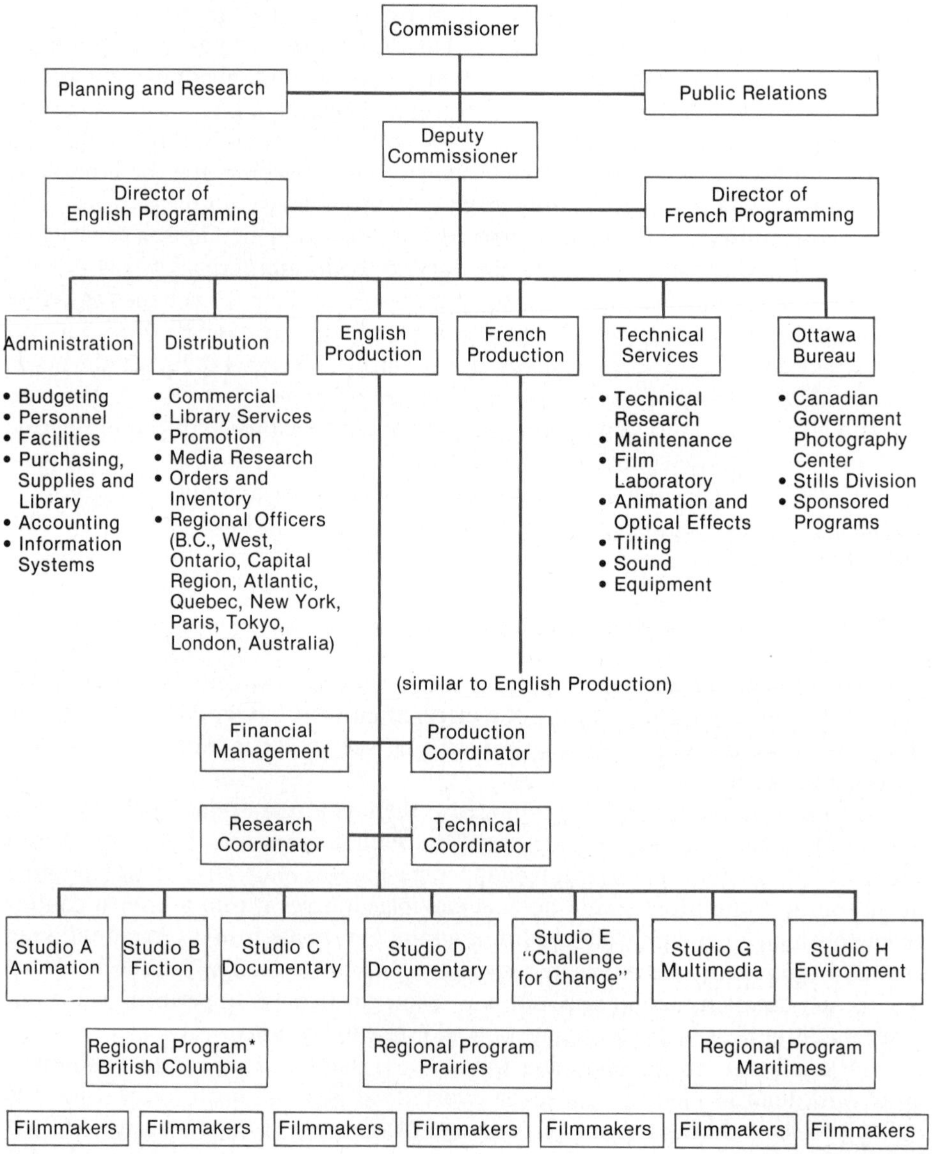

The second type of adhocracy also functions with project teams, but toward a different end. Whereas the operating adhocracy undertakes projects to serve its clients, the *administrative adhocracy* undertakes projects to serve itself, to bring new facilities or activities on line, as in the administrative structure of a highly automated company. And in sharp contrast to the operating adhocracy, the administrative adhocracy makes a clear distinction between its administrative component and its operating core. That core is *truncated*—cut right off from the rest of the organization—so that the administrative component that remains can be structured as an adhocracy.

This truncation may take place in a number of ways. First, when the operations have to be machinelike and so could impede innovation in the administration (because of the associated need for control), it may be established as an independent organization. Second, the operating core may be done away with altogether—in effect, contracted out to other organizations. That leaves the organization free to concentrate on the development work, as did NASA during the Apollo project. A third form of truncation arises when the operating core becomes automated. This enables it to run itself, largely independent of the need for direct controls from the administrative component, leaving the latter free to structure itself as an adhocracy to bring new facilities on line or to modify old ones.

Oil companies, because of the high degree of automation of their production process, are in part at least drawn toward administrative adhocracy. Figure 2 shows the organigram for one oil company, reproduced exactly as presented by the company (except for modifications to mask its identity, done at the company's request). Note the domination of "Administration and Services," shown at the bottom of the chart; the operating functions, particularly "Production," are lost by comparison. Note also the description of the strategic apex in terms of standing committees instead of individual executives.

The Administrative Component of the Adhocracies

The important conclusion to be drawn from this discussion is that in both types of adhocracy the relation between the operating core and the administrative component is unlike that in any other configuration. In the administrative adhocracy, the operating core is truncated and becomes a relatively unimportant part of the organization; in the operating adhocracy, the two merge into a single entity. Either way, the need for traditional direct supervision is diminished, so managers derive their influence more from their expertise and interpersonal skills than from formal position. And that means the distinction between line and staff blurs. It no longer makes sense to distinguish those who have the formal power to decide from those who have only the informal right to advise. Power over decision making in the adhocracy flows to anyone with the required expertise, regardless of position.

In fact, the support staff plays a key role in adhocracy, because that is where many of the experts reside (especially in administrative adhocracy). As suggested, however, that staff is not sharply differentiated from the other parts of the organization, not off to one side, to speak only when spoken to, as in the bureaucratic configurations. The other type of staff, however, the technostructure, is less important here, because the adhocracy does not rely for coordination on standards that it develops. Technostructure analysts may, of course, be used for some action planning and other forms of analysis—marketing research and economic forecasting,

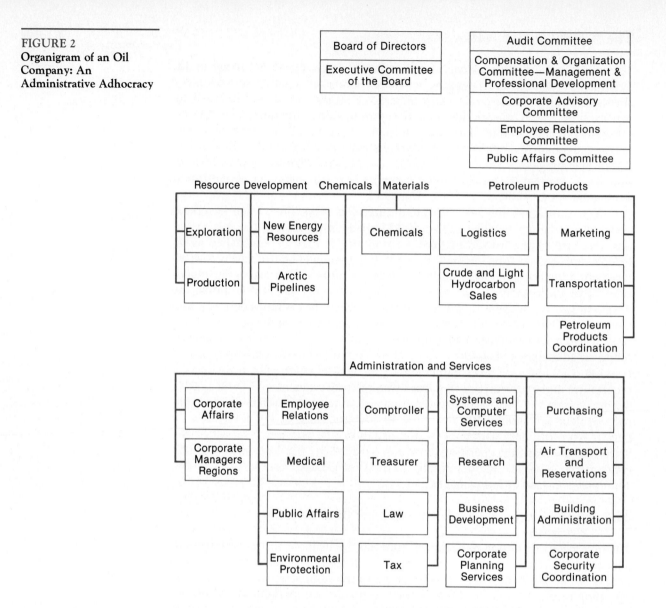

FIGURE 2
Organigram of an Oil Company: An Administrative Adhocracy

Board of Directors

Executive Committee of the Board

Audit Committee

Compensation & Organization Committee—Management & Professional Development

Corporate Advisory Committee

Employee Relations Committee

Public Affairs Committee

Resource Development   Chemicals   Materials   Petroleum Products

Exploration

New Energy Resources

Production

Arctic Pipelines

Chemicals

Logistics

Crude and Light Hydrocarbon Sales

Marketing

Transportation

Petroleum Products Coordination

Administration and Services

Corporate Affairs

Corporate Managers Regions

Employee Relations

Medical

Public Affairs

Environmental Protection

Comptroller

Treasurer

Law

Tax

Systems and Computer Services

Research

Business Development

Corporate Planning Services

Purchasing

Air Transport and Reservations

Building Administration

Corporate Security Coordination

for example—but these analysts are as likely to take their place alongside the other specialists on the project teams as to stand back and design systems to control them.

To summarize, the administrative component of the adhocracy emerges as an organic mass of line managers and staff experts, combined with operators in the operating adhocracy, working together in ever-shifting relationships on ad hoc projects. Our logo figure at the start of this chapter shows adhocracy with its parts mingled together in one amorphous mass in the middle. In the operating adhocracy, that mass includes the middle line, support staff, technostructure, and operating core. Of these, the administrative adhocracy excludes just the operating core, which is truncated, as shown by the dotted section below the central mass. The reader will also note that the strategic apex of the figure is shown partly merged into the central mass as well, for reasons we shall present in our discussion of strategy formation.

370

The top managers of the strategic apex of this configuration do not spend much time formulating explicit strategies (as we shall see). But they must spend a good deal of their time in the battles that ensue over strategic choices and in handling the many other disturbances that arise all over these fluid structures. The innovative configuration combines fluid working arrangements with power based on expertise, not authority. Together those breed aggressiveness and conflict. But the job of the managers here, at all levels, is not to bottle up that aggression and conflict so much as to channel them to productive ends. Thus, the managers of adhocracy must be masters of human relations, able to use persuasion, negotiation, coalition, reputation, and rapport to fuse the individualistic experts into smoothly functioning teams.

Top managers must also devote a good deal of time to monitoring the projects. Innovative project work is notoriously difficult to control. No MIS can be relied upon to provide complete, unambiguous results. So there must be careful personal monitoring of projects to ensure that they are completed according to specifications, on schedule and within budget (or, more likely, not excessively late and not too far in excess of cost estimates).

Perhaps the most important single role of the top management of this configuration (especially the operating adhocracy form) is liaison with the external environment. The other configurations tend to focus their attention on clearly defined markets and so are more or less assured of a steady flow of work. Not so the operating adhocracy, which lives from project to project and disappears when it can find no more. Since each project is different, the organization can never be sure where the next one will come from. So the top managers must devote a great deal of their time to ensuring a steady and balanced stream of incoming projects. That means developing liaison contacts with potential customers and negotiating contracts with them. Nowhere is this more clearly illustrated than in the consulting business, particularly where the approach is innovative. When a consultant becomes a partner in one of these firms, he or she normally hangs up the calculator and becomes virtually a full-time salesperson. It is a distinguishing characteristic of many an operating adhocracy that the selling function literally takes place at the strategic apex.

Project work poses related problems in the administrative adhocracy. Reeser asked a group of managers in three aerospace companies, "What are some of the human problems of project management?" Among the common answers: "[M]embers of the organization who are displaced because of the phasing out of [their] work . . . may have to wait a long time before they get another assignment at as high a level of responsibility" and "the temporary nature of the organization often necessitates 'make work' assignments for [these] displaced members." (1969:463) Thus senior managers must again concern themselves with a steady flow of projects, although in this case, internally generated.

CONDITIONS OF THE INNOVATIVE ORGANIZATION

This configuration is found in environments that are both dynamic and complex. A dynamic environment, being unpredictable, calls for organic structure; a complex one calls for decentralized structure. This configuration is the only type that provides both. Thus we tend to find the innovative organization wherever these conditions prevail, ranging from guerrilla warfare to space agencies. There appears to be no other way to fight a war in the jungle or to put the first man on the moon.

As we have noted for all the configurations, organizations that prefer particular structures also try to "choose" environments appropriate to them. This is especially clear in the case of the operating adhocracy. Advertising agencies and consulting firms that prefer to structure themselves as professional bureaucracies seek out stable environments; those that prefer the innovative form find environments that are dynamic, where the client needs are difficult and unpredictable.[1]

A number of organizations are drawn toward this configuration because of the dynamic conditions that result from very frequent product change. The extreme case is the unit producer, the manufacturing firm that custom-makes each of its products to order, as in the engineering company that produces prototypes or the fabricator of extremely expensive machinery. Because each customer order constitutes a new project, the organization is encouraged to structure itself as an operating adhocracy.

Some manufacturers of consumer goods operate in markets so competitive that they must be constantly changing their product offerings, even though each product may itself be mass produced. A company that records rock music would be a prime example, as would some cosmetic and pharmaceutical companies. Here again, dynamic conditions, when coupled with some complexity, drive the organization toward the innovative configuration, with the mass production operations truncated to allow for adhocracy in product development.

Youth is another condition often associated with this type of organization. That is because it is difficult to sustain any structure in a state of adhocracy for a long period—to keep behaviors from formalizing and thereby discouraging innovation. All kinds of forces drive the innovative configuration to bureaucratize itself as it ages. On the other hand, young organizations prefer naturally organic structures, since they must find their own ways and tend to be eager to innovate. Unless they are entrepreneurial, they tend to become intrapreneurial.

The operating adhocracy is particularly prone to a short life, since it faces a risky market which can quickly destroy it. The loss of one major contract can literally close it down overnight. But if some operating adhocracies have short lives because they fail, others have short lives because they succeed. Success over time encourages metamorphosis, driving the organization toward a more stable environment and a more bureaucratic structure. As it ages, the successful organization develops a reputation for what it does best. That encourages it to repeat certain activities, which may suit the employees who, themselves aging, may welcome more stability in their work. So operating adhocracy is driven over time toward professional bureaucracy to perfect the activities it does best, perhaps even toward the machine bureaucracy to exploit a single invention. The organization survives, but the configuration dies.

Administrative adhocracies typically live longer. They, too, feel the pressures to bureaucratize as they age, which can lead them to stop innovating or else to innovate in stereotyped ways and thereby to adopt bureaucratic structure. But this

---

[1] I like to tell a story of the hospital patient with an appendix about to burst who presents himself to a hospital organized as an adhocracy: "Who wants to do another appendectomy? We're into livers now," as they go about exploring new procedures. But the patient returning from a trip to the jungle with a rare tropical disease had better beware of the hospital organized as a professional bureaucracy. A student came up to me after I once said this and explained how hospital doctors puzzled by her bloated stomach and not knowing what to do took out her appendix. Luckily, her problem resolved itself, some time later. Another time, a surgeon told me that his hospital no longer does appendectomies!

will not work if the organization functions in an industry that requires sophisticated innovation from all its participants. Since many of the industries where administrative adhocracies are found do, organizations that survive in them tend to retain this configuration for long periods.

In recognition of the tendency for organizations to bureaucratize as they age, a variant of the innovative configuration has emerged—"the organizational equivalent of paper dresses or throw-away tissues" (Toffler, 1970:133)—which might be called the "temporary adhocracy." It draws together specialists from various organizations to carry out a project, and then it disbands. Temporary adhocracies are becoming increasingly common in modern society: the production group that performs a single play, the election campaign committee that promotes a single candidate, the guerrilla group that overthrows a single government, the Olympic committee that plans a single games. Related is what can be called the "mammoth project adhocracy," a giant temporary adhocracy that draws on thousands of experts for a number of years to carry out a single major task, the Manhattan Project of World War II being one famous example.

Sophisticated and automated technical systems also tend to drive organizations toward the administrative adhocracy. When an organization's technical system is sophisticated, it requires an elaborate, highly trained support staff, working in teams, to design or purchase, modify, and maintain the equipment. In other words, complex machinery requires specialists who have the knowledge, power, and flexible working arrangements to cope with it, which generally requires the organization to structure itself as an adhocracy.

Automation of a technical system can evoke even stronger forces in the same direction. That is why a machine organization that succeeds in automating its operating core tends to undergo a dramatic metamorphosis. The problem of motivating bored workers disappears, and with it goes the control mentality that permeates the structure; the distinction between line and staff blurs (machines being indifferent to who turns their knobs), which leads to another important reduction in conflict; the technostructure loses its influence, since control is built into the machinery by its own designers rather than having to be imposed on workers by the standards of the analysts. Overall, then, the administrative structure becomes more decentralized and organic, emerging as an adhocracy. Of course, for automated organizations with simple technical systems (as in the production of hand creams), the entrepreneurial configuration may suffice instead of the innovative one.

Fashion is most decidedly another condition of the innovative configuration. Every one of its characteristics is very much in vogue today: emphasis on expertise, organic structure, project teams, task forces, decentralization of power, matrix structure, sophisticated technical systems, automation, and young organizations. Thus, if the entrepreneurial and machine forms were earlier configurations, and the professional and the diversified forms yesterday's, then the innovative is clearly today's. This is the configuration for a population growing ever better educated and more specialized, yet under constant encouragement to adopt the "systems" approach—to view the world as an integrated whole instead of a collection of loosely coupled parts. It is the configuration for environments that are becoming more complex and more insistent on innovation, and for technical systems that are growing more sophisticated and more highly automated. It is the only configuration among our types appropriate for those who believe organizations must become at the same time more democratic and less bureaucratic.

Yet despite our current infatuation with it, adhocracy is not the structure for all organizations. Like all the others, it too has its place. And that place, as our examples make clear, seems to be in the new industries of our age—aerospace, electronics, think-tank consulting, research, advertising, filmmaking, petrochemicals—virtually all of which experienced their greatest development since World War II. The innovative adhocracy appears to be the configuration for the industries of the last half of the twentieth century.

STRATEGY FORMATION IN THE INNOVATIVE ORGANIZATION

The structure of the innovative organization may seem unconventional, but its strategy making is even more so, upsetting virtually everything we have been taught to believe about that process.

Because the innovative organization must respond continuously to a complex, unpredictable environment, it cannot rely on deliberate strategy. In other words, it cannot predetermine precise patterns in its activities and then impose them on its work through some kind of formal planning process. Rather, many of its actions must be decided upon individually, according to the needs of the moment. It proceeds incrementally; to use Charles Lindblom's words, it prefers "continual nibbling" to a "good bite" (1968:25).

Here, then, the process is best thought of as strategy *formation,* because strategy is not formulated consciously in one place so much as formed implicitly by the specific actions taken in many places. That is why action planning cannot be extensively relied upon in these organizations: Any process that separates thinking from action—planning from execution, formalization from implementation—would impede the flexibility of the organization to respond creatively to its dynamic environment.

Strategy Formation in the Operating Adhocracy

In the operating adhocracy, a project organization never quite sure what it will do next, the strategy never really stabilizes totally but is responsive to new projects, which themselves involve the activities of a whole host of people. Take the example of the National Film Board. Among its most important strategies are those related to the content of the hundred or so mostly short, documentary-type films that it makes each year. Were the Board structured as a machine bureacracy, the word on what films to make would come down from on high. Instead, when we studied it some years ago, proposals for new films were submitted to a standing committee, which included elected filmmakers, marketing people, and the heads of production and programming—in other words, operators, line managers, and staff specialists. The chief executive had to approve the committee's choices, and usually did, but the vast majority of the proposals were initiated by the filmmakers and the executive producers lower down. Strategies formed as themes developed among these individual proposals. The operating adhocracy's strategy thus evolves continuously as all kinds of such decisions are made, each leaving its imprint on the strategy by creating a precedent or reinforcing an existing one.

Strategy Formation in the Administrative Adhocracy

Similar things can be said about the administrative adhocracy, although the strategy-making process is slightly neater there. That is because the organization tends to concentrate its attention on fewer projects, which involve more people. NASA's Apollo project, for example, involved most of its personnel for almost ten years.

Administrative adhocracies also need to give more attention to action planning, but of a loose kind—to specify perhaps the ends to be reached while leaving flexibility to work out the means en route. Again, therefore, it is only through the making of specific decisions—namely, those that determine which projects are undertaken and how these projects unfold—that strategies can evolve.

Strategies Nonetheless

With their activities so disjointed, one might wonder whether adhocracies (of either type) can form strategies (that is, patterns) at all. In fact, they do, at least at certain times.

At the Film Board, despite the little direction from the management, the content of films did converge on certain clear themes periodically and then diverge, in remarkably regular cycles. In the early 1940s, there was a focus on films related to the war effort. After the war, having lost that raison d'être as well as its founding leader, the Board's films went off in all directions. They converged again in the mid-1950s around series of films for television, but by the late 1950s were again diverging widely. And in the mid-1960s and again in the early 1970s (with a brief period of divergence in between), the Board again showed a certain degree of convergence, this time on the themes of social commentary and experimentation.

This habit of cycling in and out of focus is quite unlike what takes place in the other configurations. In the machine organization especially, and somewhat in the entrepreneurial one, convergence proves much stronger and much longer (recall Volkswagenwerk's concentration on the Beetle for twenty years), while divergence tends to be very brief. The machine organization, in particular, cannot tolerate the ambiguity of change and so tries to leap from one strategic orientation to another. The innovative organization, in contrast, seems not only able to function at times without strategic focus, but positively to thrive on it. Perhaps that is the way it keeps itself innovative—by periodically cleansing itself of some of its existing strategic baggage.

The Varied Strategies of Adhocracy

Where do the strategies of adhocracy come from? While some may be imposed deliberately by the central management (as in staff cuts at the Film Board), most seem to emerge in a variety of other ways.

In some cases, a single ad hoc decision sets a precedent which evokes a pattern. That is how the National Film Board got into making series of films for television. While a debate raged over the issue, with management hesitant, one filmmaker slipped out and made one such series, and when many of his colleagues quickly followed suit, the organization suddenly found itself deeply, if unintentionally, committed to a major new strategy. It was, in effect, a strategy of spontaneous but implicit consensus on the part of its operating employees. In another case, even the initial precedent-setting decision wasn't deliberate. One film inadvertently ran longer than expected, it had to be distributed as a feature, the first for the organization, and as some other filmmakers took advantage of the precedent, a feature film strategy emerged.

Sometimes a strategy will be pursued in a pocket of an organization (perhaps in a clandestine manner, in a so-called "skunkworks"), which then later becomes more broadly organizational when the organization, in need of change and casting about for new strategies, seizes upon it. Some salesman has been pursuing a new market, or some engineer has developed a new product, and is ignored until the organization has need for some fresh strategic thinking. Then it finds it, not in the vision of its leaders or the procedures of its planners, not elsewhere in its industry, but hidden in the bowels of its own operations, developed through the learning of its workers.

What then becomes the role of the leadership of the innovative configuration in making strategy? If it cannot impose deliberate strategies, what does it do? The answer is that it manages patterns, seeking partial control over strategies but otherwise attempting to influence what happens to those strategies that do emerge lower down.

These are the organizations in which trying to manage strategy is a little like trying to drive an automobile without having your hands on the steering wheel. You can accelerate and brake but cannot determine direction. But there do remain important forms of control. First the leaders can manage the *process* of strategy-making if not the content of strategy. In other words, they can set up the structures to encourage certain kinds of activities and hire the people who themselves will carry out these activities. Second, they can provide general guidelines for strategy —what we have called *umbrella* strategies—seeking to define certain boundaries outside of which the specific patterns developed below should not stray. Then they can watch the patterns that do emerge and use the umbrella to decide which to encourage and which to discourage, remembering, however, that the umbrella can be shifted too.

A Grass-roots Model of Strategy Formation

We can summarize this discussion in terms of a "grass-roots" model of strategy formation, comprising six points.

1. *Strategies grow initially like weeds in a garden, they are not cultivated like tomatoes in a hothouse.* In other words, the process of strategy formation can be overmanaged; sometimes it is more important to let patterns emerge than to force an artificial consistency upon an organization prematurely. The hothouse, if needed, can come later.

2. *These strategies can take root in all kinds of places, virtually anywhere people have the capacity to learn and the resources to support that capacity.* Sometimes an individual or unit in touch with a particular opportunity creates his, her, or its own pattern. This may happen inadvertently, when an initial action sets a precedent. Even senior managers can fall into strategies by experimenting with ideas until they converge on something that works (though the final result may appear to the observer to have been deliberately designed). At other times, a variety of actions converge on a strategic theme through the mutual adjustment of various people, whether gradually or spontaneously. And then the external environment can impose a pattern on an unsuspecting organization. The point is that organizations cannot always plan where their strategies will emerge, let alone plan the strategies themselves.

3. *Such strategies become organizational when they become collective, that is, when the patterns proliferate to pervade the behavior of the organization at large.* Weeds can proliferate and encompass a whole garden; then the conventional plants may look out of place. Likewise, emergent strategies can sometimes displace the existing deliberate ones. But, of course, what is a weed but a plant that wasn't expected? With a change of perspective, the emergent strategy, like the weed, can become what is valued (just as Europeans enjoy salads of the leaves of America's most notorious weed, the dandelion!).

4. *The processes of proliferation may be conscious but need not be; likewise they may be managed but need not be.* The processes by which the initial patterns work their way through the organization need not be consciously intended, by formal leaders or even informal ones. Patterns may simply spread by collective action, much as plants proliferate themselves. Of course, once strategies are recognized as valuable, the processes by which they proliferate can be managed, just as plants can be selectively propagated.

5. *New strategies, which may be emerging continuously, tend to pervade the organization during periods of change, which punctuate periods of more integrated continuity.* Put more simply, organizations, like gardens, may accept the biblical maxim of a time to sow and a time to reap (even though they can sometimes reap what they did not mean to sow). Periods of convergence, during which the organization exploits its prevalent, established strategies, tend to be interrupted periodically by periods of divergence, during which the organization experiments with and subsequently accepts new strategic themes. The blurring of the separation between these two types of periods may have the same effect on an organization that the blurring of the separation between sowing and reaping has on a garden—the destruction of the system's productive capacity.

6. *To manage this process is not to preconceive strategies but to recognize their emergence and intervene when appropriate.* A destructive weed, once noticed, is best uprooted immediately. But one that seems capable of bearing fruit is worth watching, indeed sometimes even worth building a hothouse around. To manage in this context is to create the climate within which a wide variety of strategies can grow (to establish flexible structures, develop appropriate processes, encourage supporting ideologies, and define guiding "umbrella" strategies) and then to watch what does in fact come up. The strategic initiatives that do come "up" may in fact originate anywhere, although often low down in the organization, where the detailed knowledge of products and markets resides. (In fact, to be successful in some organizations, these initiatives must be recognized by middle-level managers and "championed" by combining them with each other or with existing strategies before promoting them to the senior management.) In effect, the management encourages those initiatives that appear to have potential, otherwise it discourages them. But it must not be too quick to cut off the unexpected: Sometimes it is better to pretend not to notice an emerging pattern to allow it more time to unfold. Likewise, there are times when it makes sense to shift or enlarge an umbrella to encompass a new pattern—in other words, to let the organization adapt to the initiative rather than vice versa. Moreover, a management must know when to resist change for the sake of internal efficiency and when to promote it for the sake of external adaptation. In other words, it must sense when to exploit an established crop of strategies and when to encourage new strains to displace them. It is the excesses of either—failure to focus (running blind) or failure to change (bureaucratic momentum)—that most harms organizations.

I call this a "grass-roots" model because the strategies grow up from the base of the organization, rooted in the solid earth of its operations rather than the ethereal abstractions of its administration. (Even the strategic initiatives of the senior management itself are in this model rooted in its tangible involvement with the operations.)

Of course, the model is overstated. But no more so than the more widely accepted deliberate one, which we might call the "hothouse" model of strategy formulation. Management theory must encompass both, perhaps more broadly labeled the *learning* model and the *planning* model, as well as a third, the *visionary* model.

I have discussed the learning model under the innovative configuration, the planning model under the machine configuration, and the visionary model under the entrepreneurial configuration. But in truth, all organizations need to mix these approaches in various ways at different times in their development. For example, our discussion of strategic change in the machine organization concluded, in effect, that they had to revert to the learning model for revitalization and the visionary model for turnaround. Of course, the visionary leader must learn, as must the learning organization evolve a kind of strategic vision, and both sometimes need planning to program the strategies they develop. And overall, no organization can function with strategies that are always and purely emergent; that would amount to a complete abdication of will and leadership, not to mention conscious thought. But none can function either with strategies that are always and purely deliberate; that would amount to an unwillingness to learn, a blindness to whatever is unexpected.

Environment Taking Precedence in the Innovative Organization

To conclude our discussion of strategy formation, as shown in Figure 3, in the innovative configuration it is the environment that takes precedence. It drives the organization, which responds continuously and eclectically, but does nevertheless achieve convergence during certain periods.[2] The formal leadership seeks somehow to influence both sides in this relationship, negotiating with the environment for support and attempting to impose some broad general (umbrella) guidelines on the organization.

If the strategist of the entrepreneurial organization is largely a concept attainer and that of the machine organization largely a planner, then the strategist of the innovative organization is largely a *pattern recognizer,* seeking to detect emerging patterns within and outside the strategic umbrella. Then strategies deemed unsuitable can be discouraged while those that seem appropriate can be encouraged, even if that means moving the umbrella. Here, then, we may find the curious situation of leadership changing its intentions to fit the realized behavior of its organization. But that is curious only in the perspective of traditional management theory.

FIGURE 3
**Environment Taking the
Lead in Adhocracy**

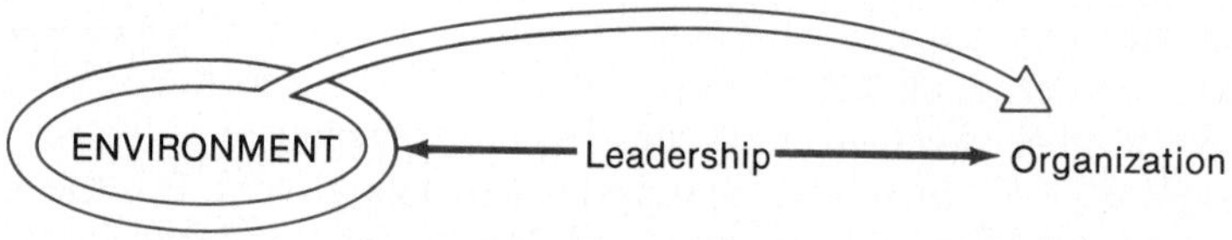

SOME ISSUES ASSOCIATED WITH THE INNOVATIVE ORGANIZATION

Three issues associated with the innovative configuration merit attention here: its ambiguities and the reactions of people who must live with them, its inefficiencies, and its propensity to make inappropriate transitions to other configurations.

---

[2] We might take this convergence as the expression of an "organization's mind"—the focusing on a strategic theme as a result of the mutual adjustments among its many actors.

Many people, especially creative ones, dislike both structural rigidity and the concentration of power. That leaves them only one configuration, the innovative, which is both organic and decentralized. Thus they find it a great place to work. In essence, adhocracy is the only structure for people who believe in more democracy with less bureaucracy.

But not everyone shares those values (not even everyone who professes to). Many people need order, and so prefer the machine or professional type of organization. They see adhocracy as a nice place to visit but no place to spend a career. Even dedicated members of adhocracies periodically get frustrated with this structure's fluidity, confusion, and ambiguity. "In these situations, all managers some of the time and many managers all the time, yearn for more definition and structure" (Burns and Stalker, 1966:122–123). The managers of innovative organizations report anxiety related to the eventual phaseout of projects; confusion as to who their boss is, whom to impress to get promoted; a lack of clarity in job definitions, authority relationships, and lines of communication; and intense competition for resources, recognition, and rewards (Reeser, 1969). This last point suggests another serious problem of ambiguity here, the politicization of these configurations. Combining its ambiguities with its interdependencies, the innovative form can emerge as a rather politicized and ruthless organization—supportive of the fit, as long as they remain fit, but destructive of the weak.

Problems of Efficiency

No configuration is better suited to solving complex, ill-structured problems than this one. None can match it for sophisticated innovation. Or, unfortunately, for the costs of that innovation. This is simply not an efficient way to function. Although it is ideally suited for the one-of-a-kind project, the innovative configuration is not competent at doing *ordinary* things. It is designed for the *extra*ordinary. The bureaucracies are all mass producers; they gain efficiency through standardization. The adhocracy is a custom producer, unable to standardize and so be efficient. It gains its effectiveness (innovation) at the price of efficiency.

One source of inefficiency lies in the unbalanced workload, mentioned earlier. It is almost impossible to keep the personnel of a project structure—high-priced specialists, it should be noted—busy on a steady basis. In January they may be working overtime with no hope of completing the new project on time; by May they may be playing cards for want of work.

But the real root of inefficiency is the high cost of communication. People talk a lot in these organizations; that is how they combine their knowledge to develop new ideas. But that takes time, a great deal of time. Faced with the need to make a decision in the machine organization, someone up above gives an order and that is that. Not so in the innovative one, where everyone must get into the act —managers of all kinds (functional, project, liaison), as well as all the specialists who believe their point of view should be represented. A meeting is called, probably to schedule another meeting, eventually to decide who should participate in the decision. The problem then gets defined and redefined, ideas for its solution get generated and debated, alliances build and fall around different solutions, until eventually everyone settles down to the hard bargaining over which one to adopt. Finally a decision emerges—that in itself is an accomplishment—although it is typically late and will probably be modified later.

The Dangers of Inappropriate Transition

Of course, one solution to the problems of ambiguity and inefficiency is to change the configuration. Employees no longer able to tolerate the ambiguity and customers fed up with the inefficiency may try to drive the organization to a more stable, bureaucratic form.

That is relatively easily done in the operating adhocracy, as noted earlier. The organization simply selects the set of standard programs it does best, reverting to the professional configuration, or else innovates one last time to find a lucrative market niche in which to mass produce, and then becomes a machine configuration. But those transitions, however easily effected, are not always appropriate. The organization came into being to solve problems imaginatively, not to apply standards indiscriminately. In many spheres, society has more mass producers than it needs; what it lacks are true problem solvers—the consulting firm that can handle a unique problem instead of applying a pat solution, the advertising agency that can come up with a novel campaign instead of the common imitation, the research laboratory that can make the really serious breakthrough instead of just modifying an existing design. The television networks seem to be classic examples of bureaucracies that provide largely standardized fare when the creativity of adhocracy is called for (except, perhaps, for the newsrooms and the specials, where an ad hoc orientation encourages more creativity).

The administrative adhocracy can run into more serious difficulties when it succumbs to the pressures to bureaucratize. It exists to innovate for itself, in its own industry. Unlike the operating adhocracy, it often cannot change orientation while remaining in the same industry. And so its conversion to the machine configuration (the natural transition for administrative adhocracy tired of perpetual change), by destroying the organization's ability to innovate, can eventually destroy the organization itself.

To reiterate a central theme of our discussion throughout this section: In general, there is no one best structure; in particular, there may be at a cost of something forgone, so long as the different attributes combine to form a coherent configuration that is consistent with the situation.

• MANAGING INNOVATION: CONTROLLED CHAOS*

BY JAMES BRIAN QUINN

Management observers frequently claim that small organizations are more innovative than large ones. But is this commonplace necessarily true? Some large enterprises are highly innovative. How do they do it? . . . This article [reports on a] $2\frac{1}{2}$ year worldwide study . . . [of] both well-documented small ventures and large U.S., Japanese, and European companies and programs selected for their innovation records. . . . More striking than the cultural differences among these companies are the similarities between innovative small and large organizations and among innovative organizations in different countries. Effective management of innovation seems much the same, regardless of national boundaries or scale of operations.

---

* Originally published in the *Harvard Business Review* (May–June, 1985); winner of the McKinsey prize for the best article in the *Review* in 1985. Copyright © 1985 by the President and Fellows of Harvard College; all rights reserved. Reprinted with deletions by permission of the *Harvard Business Review.*

There are ... many reasons why small companies appear to produce a disproportionate number of innovations. First, innovation occurs in a probabilistic setting. A company never knows whether a particular technical result can be achieved and whether it will succeed in the marketplace. For every new solution that succeeds, tens to hundreds fail. The sheer number of attempts—most by small-scale entrepreneurs—means that some ventures will survive. The 90% to 99% that fail are distributed widely throughout society and receive little notice.

On the other hand, a big company that wishes to move a concept from invention to the marketplace must absorb all potential failure costs itself. This risk may be socially or managerially intolerable, jeopardizing the many other products, projects, jobs, and communities the company supports. Even if its innovation is successful, a big company may face costs that newcomers do not bear, like converting existing operations and customer bases to the new solution.

By contrast, a new enterprise does not risk losing an existing investment base or cannibalizing customer franchises built at great expense. It does not have to change an internal culture that has successfully supported doing things another way or that has developed intellectual depth and belief in the technologies that led to past successes. Organized groups like labor unions, consumer advocates, and government bureaucracies rarely monitor and resist a small company's moves as they might a big company's. Finally, new companies do not face the psychological pain and the economic costs of laying off employees, shutting down plants and even communities, and displacing supplier relationships built with years of mutual commitment and effort. Such barriers to change in large organizations are real, important, and legitimate.

The complex products and systems that society expects large companies to undertake further compound the risks. Only big companies can develop new ships or locomotives; telecommunication networks; or systems for space, defense, air traffic control, hospital care, mass foods delivery, or nationwide computer interactions. These large-scale projects always carry more risk than single-product introductions. A billion-dollar development aircraft, for example, can fail if one inexpensive part in its 100,000 components fails.

Clearly, a single enterprise cannot by itself develop or produce all the parts needed by such large new systems. And communications among the various groups making design and production decisions on components are always incomplete. The probability of error increases exponentially with complexity, while the system innovator's control over decisions decreases significantly—further escalating potential error costs and risks. Such forces inhibit innovation in large organizations. But proper management can lessen these effects.

OF INVENTORS AND ENTREPRENEURS

A close look at innovative small enterprises reveals much about the successful management of innovation. Of course, not all innovations follow a single pattern. But my research—and other studies in combination—suggest that the following factors are crucial to the success of innovative small companies:

Need Orientation

Inventor-entrepreneurs tend to be "need or achievement oriented." They believe that if they "do the job better," rewards will follow. They may at first focus on their own view of market needs. But lacking resources, successful small entrepreneurs soon find that it pays to approach potential customers early, test their solutions in users' hands, learn from these interactions, and adapt designs rapidly. Many studies suggest that effective technological innovation develops hand-in-hand with customer demand (Von Hippel, 1982:117).

Experts and Fanatics

Company founders tend to be pioneers in their technologies and fanatics when it comes to solving problems. They are often described as "possessed" or "obsessed," working toward their objectives to the exclusion even of family or personal relationships. As both experts and fanatics, they perceive probabilities of success as higher than others do. And their commitment allows them to persevere despite the frustrations, ambiguities, and setbacks that always accompany major innovations.

Long Time Horizons

Their fanaticism may cause inventor-entrepreneurs to underestimate the obstacles and length of time to success. Time horizons for radical innovations make them essentially "irrational" from a present value viewpoint. In my sample, delays between invention and commercial production ranged from 3 to 25 years.[1] In the late 1930s, for example, industrial chemist Russell Marker was working on steroids called sapogenins when he discovered a technique that would degrade one of these, diosgenin, into the female sex hormone progesterone. By processing some ten tons of Mexican yams in rented and borrowed lab space, Marker finally extracted about four pounds of diosgenin and started a tiny business to produce steroids for the laboratory market. But it was not until 1962, over 23 years later, that Syntex, the company Marker founded, obtained FDA approval for its oral contraceptive.

For both psychological and practical reasons, inventor-entrepreneurs generally avoid early formal plans, proceed step-by-step, and sustain themselves by other income and the momentum of the small advances they achieve as they go along.

Low Early Costs

Innovators tend to work in homes, basements, warehouses, or low-rent facilities whenever possible. They incur few overhead costs; their limited resources go directly into their projects. They pour nights, weekends, and "sweat capital" into their endeavors. They borrow whatever they can. They invent cheap equipment and prototype processes, often improving on what is available in the marketplace. If one approach fails, few people know; little time or money is lost. All this decreases the costs and risks facing a small operation and improves the present value of its potential success.

Multiple Approaches

Technology tends to advance through a series of random—often highly intuitive—insights frequently triggered by gratuitous interactions between the discoverer and the outside world. Only highly committed entrepreneurs can tolerate (and even enjoy) this chaos. They adopt solutions wherever they can be found, unencum-

---

[1] A study at Battelle found an average of 19.2 years between invention and commercial production. Battelle Memorial Laboratories, "Science, Technology, and Innovation," Report to the National Science Foundation, 1973; also Dean (1974:13).

bered by formal plans or PERT charts that would limit the range of their imaginations. When the odds of success are low, the participation and interaction of many motivated players increase the chance that one will succeed.

A recent study of initial public offerings made in 1962 shows that only 2% survived and still looked like worthwhile investments 20 years later.[2] Small-scale entrepreneurship looks efficient in part because history only records the survivors.

Flexibility and Quickness

Undeterred by committees, board approvals, and other bureaucratic delays, the inventor-entrepreneur can experiment, test, recycle, and try again with little time lost. Because technological progress depends largely on the number of successful experiments accomplished per unit of time, fast-moving small entrepreneurs can gain both timing and performance advantages over clumsier competitors. This responsiveness is often crucial in finding early markets for radical innovations where neither innovators, market researchers, nor users can quite visualize a product's real potential. For example, Edison's lights first appeared on ships and in baseball parks; Astroturf was intended to convert the flat roofs and asphalt playgrounds of city schools into more humane environments; and graphite and boron composites designed for aerospace unexpectedly found their largest markets in sporting goods. Entrepreneurs quickly adjusted their entry strategies to market feedback.

Incentives

Inventor-entrepreneurs can foresee tangible personal rewards if they are successful. Individuals often want to achieve a technical contribution, recognition, power, or sheer independence, as much as money. For the original, driven personalities who create significant innovations, few other paths offer such clear opportunities to fulfill all their economic, psychological, and career goals at once. Consequently, they do not panic or quit when others with solely monetary goals might.

Availability of Capital

One of America's great competitive advantages is its rich variety of sources to finance small, low-probability ventures. If entrepreneurs are turned down by one source, other sources can be sought in myriads of creative combinations.

Professionals involved in such financings have developed a characteristic approach to deal with the chaos and uncertainty of innovation. First, they evaluate a proposal's conceptual validity: If the technical problems can be solved, is there a real business there for someone and does it have a large upside potential? Next, they concentrate on people: Is the team thoroughly committed and expert? Is it the best available? Only then do these financiers analyze specific financial estimates in depth. Even then, they recognize that actual outcomes generally depend on subjective factors, not numbers (Pence, 1982).

Timeliness, aggressiveness, commitment, quality of people, and the flexibility to attack opportunities not at first perceived are crucial. Downside risks are minimized, not by detailed controls, but by spreading risks among multiple projects, keeping early costs low, and gauging the tenacity, flexibility, and capability of the founders.

---

[2] Business Economics Group, W. R. Grace & Co., 1983.

Less innovative companies and, unfortunately, most large corporations operate in a very different fashion. The most notable and common constraints on innovation in larger companies include the following:

Top Management Isolation

Many senior executives in big companies have little contact with conditions on the factory floor or with customers who might influence their thinking about technological innovation. Since risk perception is inversely related to familiarity and experience, financially oriented top managers are likely to perceive technological innovations as more problematic than acquisitions that may be just as risky but that will appear more familiar (Hayes and Garvin, 1982:70; Hayes and Abernathy, 1980:67).

Intolerance of Fanatics

Big companies often view entrepreneurial fanatics as embarrassments or troublemakers. Many major cities are now ringed by companies founded by these "nonteam" players—often to the regret of their former employers.

Short Time Horizons

The perceived corporate need to report a continuous stream of quarterly profits conflicts with the long time spans that major innovations normally require. Such pressures often make publicly owned companies favor quick marketing fixes, cost cutting, and acquisition strategies over process, product, or quality innovations that would yield much more in the long run.

Accounting Practices

By assessing all its direct, indirect, overhead, overtime, and service costs against a project, large corporations have much higher development expenses compared with entrepreneurs working in garages. A project in a big company can quickly become an exposed political target, its potential net present value may sink unacceptably, and an entry into small markets may not justify its sunk costs. An otherwise viable project may soon founder and disappear.

Excessive Rationalism

Managers in big companies often seek orderly advance through early market research studies or PERT planning. Rather than managing the inevitable chaos of innovation productively, these managers soon drive out the very things that lead to innovation in order to prove their announced plans.

Excessive Bureaucracy

In the name of efficiency, bureaucratic structures require many approvals and cause delays at every turn. Experiments that a small company can perform in hours may take days or weeks in large organizations. The interactive feedback that fosters innovation is lost, important time windows can be missed, and real costs and risks rise for the corporation.

Inappropriate Incentives

Reward and control systems in most big companies are designed to minimize surprises. Yet innovation, by definition, is full of surprises. It often disrupts well-laid plans, accepted power patterns, and entrenched organizational behavior at high costs to many. Few large companies make millionaires of those who create such disruptions, however profitable the innovations may turn out to be. When control systems neither penalize opportunities missed nor reward risks taken, the results are predictable.

HOW LARGE INNOVATIVE COMPANIES DO IT

Yet some big companies are continuously innovative. Although each such enterprise is distinctive, the successful big innovators I studied have developed techniques that emulate or improve on their smaller counterparts' practices. What are the most important patterns?

Atmosphere and Vision

Continuous innovation occurs largely because top executives appreciate innovation and manage their company's value system and atmosphere to support it. For example, Sony's founder, Masaru Ibuka, stated in the company's "Purposes of Incorporation" the goal of a "free, dynamic, and pleasant factory . . . where sincerely motivated personnel can exercise their technological skills to the highest level." Ibuka and Sony's chairman, Akio Morita, inculcated the "Sony spirit" through a series of unusual policies: hiring brilliant people with nontraditional skills (like an opera singer) for high management positions, promoting young people over their elders, designing a new type of living accommodation for workers, and providing visible awards for outstanding technical achievements.

Because familiarity can foster understanding and psychological comfort, engineering and scientific leaders are often those who create atmospheres supportive of innovation, especially in a company's early life. Executive vision is more important than a particular management background—as IBM, Genentech, AT&T, Merck, Elf Aquitaine, Pilkington, and others in my sample illustrate. CEOs of these companies value technology and include technical experts in their highest decisions circles.

Innovative managements—whether technical or not—project clear long-term visions for their organizations that go beyond simple economic measures. . . . Genentech's original plan expresses [such a] vision: "We expect to be the first company to commercialize the [rDNA] technology, and we plan to build a major profitable corporation by manufacturing and marketing needed products that benefit mankind. The future uses of genetic engineering are far reaching and many. Any product produced by a living organism is eventually within the company's reach."

Such visions, vigorously supported, are not "management fluff," but have many practical implications.[3] They attract quality people to the company and give focus to their creative and entrepreneurial drives. When combined with sound internal operations, they help channel growth by concentrating attention on the ac-

---

[3] Thomas J. Allen (1977) illustrates the enormous leverage provided such technology accessors (called "gatekeepers") in R&D organizations.

tions that lead to profitability, rather than on profitability itself. Finally, these visions recognize a realistic time frame for innovation and attract the kind of investors who will support it.

Orientation to the Market

Innovative companies tie their visions to the practical realities of the marketplace. Although each company uses techniques adapted to its own style and strategy, two elements are always present: a strong market orientation at the very top of the company and mechanisms to ensure interactions between technical and marketing people at lower levels. At Sony, for example, soon after technical people are hired, the company runs them through weeks of retail selling. Sony engineers become sensitive to the ways retail sales practices, product displays, and nonquantifiable customer preferences affect success. . . .

From top to bench levels in my sample's most innovative companies, managers focus primarily on seeking to anticipate and solve customers' emerging problems.

Small, Flat Organizations

The most innovative large companies in my sample try to keep the total organization flat and project teams small. Development teams normally include only 6 or 7 key people. This number seems to constitute a critical mass of skills while fostering maximum communication and commitment among members. According to research done by my colleague, Victor McGee, the number of channels of communication increases as $n[2^{n-1}-1]$. Therefore:

For team size	=	1	2	3	4	5	6
Channels	=	1	2	9	28	75	186
		7	8	9	10	11	
		441	1016	2295	5110	11253	

Innovative companies also try to keep their operating divisions and total technical units small—below 400 people. Up to this number, only two layers of management are required to maintain a span of control over 7 people. In units much larger than 400, people quickly lose touch with the concept of their product or process, staffs and bureaucracies tend to grow, and projects may go through too many formal screens to survive. Since it takes a chain of yesses and only one no to kill a project, jeopardy multiplies as management layers increase.

Multiple Approaches

At first one cannot be sure which of several technical approaches will dominate a field. The history of technology is replete with accidents, mishaps, and chance meetings that allowed one approach or group to emerge rapidly over others. Leo Baekelund was looking for a synthetic shellac when he found Bakelite and started the modern plastics industry. At Syntex, researchers were not looking for an oral contraceptive when they created 19-norprogesterone, the precursor to the active ingredient in half of all contraceptive pills. And the microcomputer was born because Intel's Ted Hoff "happened" to work on a complex calculator just when Digital Equipment Corporation's PDP8 architecture was fresh in his mind.

Such "accidents" are involved in almost all major technological advances. When theory can predict everything, a company has moved to a new stage, from development to production. Murphy's law works because engineers design for what they can foresee; hence what fails is what theory could not predict. And it is rare that the interactions of components and subsystems can be predicted over the lifetime of operations. For example, despite careful theoretical design work, the first high performance jet engine literally tore itself to pieces on its test stand, while others failed in unanticipated operating conditions (like an Iranian sandstorm).

Recognizing the inadequacies of theory, innovative enterprises seem to move faster from paper studios to physical testing than do noninnovative enterprises. When possible, they encourage several prototype programs to proceed in parallel. . . . Such redundancy helps the company cope with uncertainties in development, motivates people through competition, and improves the amount and quality of information available for making final choices on scale-ups or introductions.

Developmental Shoot-outs

Many companies structure shoot-outs among competing approaches only after they reach the prototype stages. They find this practice provides more objective information for making decisions, decreases risk by making choices that best reflect marketplace needs, and helps ensure that the winning option will move ahead with a committed team behind it. Although many managers worry that competing approaches may be inefficient, greater effectiveness in choosing the right solution easily outweighs duplication costs when the market rewards higher performance or when large volumes justify increased sophistication. Under these conditions, parallel development may prove less costly because it both improves the probability of success and reduces development time.

Perhaps the most difficult problem in managing competing projects lies in reintegrating the members of the losing team. If the company is expanding rapidly or if the successful project creates a growth opportunity, losing team members can work on another interesting program or sign on with the winning team as the project moves toward the marketplace. For the shoot-out system to work continuously, however, executives must create a climate that honors high-quality performance whether a project wins or loses, reinvolves people quickly in their technical specialties or in other projects, and accepts and expects rotation among tasks and groups. . . .

Skunkworks

Every highly innovative enterprise in my research sample emulated small company practices by using groups that functioned in a skunkworks style. Small teams of engineers, technicians, designers, and model makers were placed together with no intervening organizational or physical barriers to developing a new product from idea to commercial prototype stages. In innovative Japanese companies, top managers often worked hand in hand on projects with young engineers. Surprisingly, *ringi* decision making was not evident in these situations. Soichiro Honda was known for working directly on technical problems and emphasizing his technical points by shouting at his engineers or occasionally even hitting them with wrenches!

The skunkworks approach eliminates bureaucracies, allows fast, unfettered communications, permits rapid turnaround times for experiments, and instills a high level of group identity and loyalty. Interestingly, few successful groups in my research were structured in the classic "venture group" form, with a careful balancing of engineering, production, and marketing talents. Instead they acted on an old truism: introducing a new product or process to the world is like raising a healthy child—it needs a mother (champion) who loves it, a father (authority figure with resources) to support it, and pediatricians (specialists) to get it through difficult times. It may survive solely in the hands of specialists, but its chances of success are remote.

Interactive Learning

Skunkworks are as close as most big companies can come to emulating the highly interactive and motivating learning environment that characterizes successful small ventures. But the best big innovators have gone even farther. Recognizing that the random, chaotic nature of technological change cuts across organizational and even institutional lines, these companies tap into multiple outside sources of technology as well as their customers' capabilities. Enormous external leverages are possible. No company can spend more than a small share of the world's $200 billion devoted to R&D. But like small entrepreneurs, big companies can have much of that total effort cheaply if they try.

In industries such as electronics, customers provide much of the innovation on new products. In other industries, such as textiles, materials or equipment suppliers provide the innovation. In still others, such as biotechnology, universities are dominant, while foreign sources strongly supplement industries such as controlled fusion. Many R&D units have strategies to develop information for trading with outside groups and have teams to cultivate these sources. Large Japanese companies have been notably effective at this. So have U.S. companies as diverse as Du Pont, AT&T, Apple Computer, and Genentech.

An increasing variety of creative relationships exist in which big companies participate—as joint venturers, consortium members, limited partners, guarantors of first markets, major academic funding sources, venture capitalists, spin-off equity holders, and so on. These rival the variety of inventive financing and networking structures that individual entrepreneurs have created.

Indeed, the innovative practices of small and large companies look ever more alike. This resemblance is especially striking in the interactions between companies and customers during development. Many experienced big companies are relying less on early market research and more on interactive development with lead customers. Hewlett-Packard, 3M, Sony, and Raychem frequently introduce radically new products through small teams that work closely with lead customers. These teams learn from their customers' needs and innovations, and rapidly modify designs and entry strategies based on this information.

Formal market analyses continue to be useful for extending product lines, but they are often misleading when applied to radical innovations. Market studies predicted that Haloid would never sell more than 5,000 xerographic machines, that Intel's microprocessor would never sell more than 10% as many units as there were minicomputers, and that Sony's transistor radios and miniature television sets would fail in the marketplace. At the same time, many eventual failures such as Ford's Edsel, IBM's FS system, and the supersonic transport were studied and planned exhaustively on paper, but lost contact with customers' real needs.

A STRATEGY FOR INNOVATION

The flexible management practices needed for major innovations often pose problems for established cultures in big companies. Yet there are reasonable steps managers in these companies can take. Innovation can be bred in a surprising variety of organizations, as many examples show. What are its key elements?

An Opportunity Orientation

In the 1981–1983 recession, many large companies cut back or closed plants as their "only available solution." Yet I repeatedly found that top managers in these companies took these actions without determining firsthand why their customers were buying from competitors, discerning what niches in their markets were growing, or tapping the innovations their own people had to solve problems. These managers foreclosed innumerable options by defining the issue as cost cutting rather than opportunity seeking. As one frustrated division manager in a manufacturing conglomerate put it: "If management doesn't actively seek or welcome technical opportunities, it sure won't hear about them."

By contrast, Intel met the challenge of the last recession with its "20% solution." The professional staff agreed to work one extra day a week to bring innovations to the marketplace earlier than planned. Despite the difficult times, Intel came out of the recession with several important new products ready to go—and it avoided layoffs.

Entrepreneurial companies recognize that they have almost unlimited access to capital and they structure their practices accordingly. They let it be known that if their people come up with good ideas, they can find the necessary capital—just as private venture capitalists or investment bankers find resources for small entrepreneurs.

Structuring for Innovation

Managers need to think carefully about how innovation fits into their strategy and structure their technology, skills, resources, and organizational commitments accordingly. A few examples suggest the variety of strategies and alignments possible:

Hewlett-Packard and 3M develop product lines around a series of small, discrete, freestanding products. These companies form units that look like entrepreneurial start-ups. Each has a small team, led by a champion, in low-cost facilities. These companies allow many different proposals to come forward and test them as early as possible in the marketplace. They design control systems to spot significant losses on any single entry quickly. They look for high gains on a few winners and blend less successful, smaller entries into prosperous product lines.

Other companies (like AT&T or the oil majors) have had to make large system investments to last for decades. These companies tend to make longterm needs forecasts. They often start several programs in parallel to be sure of selecting the right technologies. They then extensively test new technologies in use before making systemwide commitments. Often they sacrifice speed of entry for long-term low cost and reliability.

Intel and Dewey & Almy, suppliers of highly technical specialties to EOMs, develop strong technical sales networks to discover and understand customer needs in depth. These companies try to have technical solutions designed into customers' products. Such companies have flexible applied technology groups working close to the marketplace. They also have quickly expandable plant facilities and a cutting edge technology (not necessarily basic research) group that allows rapid selection of currently available technologies.

Dominant producers like IBM or Matsushita are often not the first to introduce new technologies. They do not want to disturb their successful product lines any sooner than necessary. As market demands become clear, these companies establish precise price-performance windows and form overlapping project teams to come up with the best answer for the marketplace. To decrease market risks, they use product shoot-outs as close to the market as possible. They develop extreme depth in production technologies to keep unit costs low from the outset. Finally, depending on the scale of the market entry, they have project teams report as close to the top as necessary to secure needed management attention and resources.

Merck and Hoffman-LaRoche, basic research companies, maintain laboratories with better facilities, higher pay, and more freedom than most universities can afford. These companies leverage their internal spending through research grants, clinical grants, and research relationships with universities throughout the world. Before they invest $20 million to $50 million to clear a new drug, they must have reasonable assurance that they will be first in the marketplace. They take elaborate precautions to ensure that the new entry is safe and effective, and that it cannot be easily duplicated by others. Their structures are designed to be on the cutting edge of science, but conservative in animal testing, clinical evaluation, and production control.

These examples suggest some ways of linking innovation to strategy. Many other examples, of course, exist. Within a single company, individual divisions may have different strategic needs and hence different structures and practices. No single approach works well for all situations.

Complex Portfolio Planning

Perhaps the most difficult task for top managers is to balance the needs of existing lines against the needs of potential lines. This problem requires a portfolio strategy much more complex than the popular four-box Boston Consulting Group matrix found in most strategy texts. To allocate resources for innovation strategically, managers need to define the broad, long-term actions within and across divisions necessary to achieve their visions. They should determine which positions to hold at all costs, where to fall back, and where to expand initially and in the more distant future.

A company's strategy may often require investing more resources in current lines. But sufficient resources should also be invested in patterns that ensure intermediate and long-term growth; provide defenses against possible government, labor, competitive, or activist challenges; and generate needed organizational, technical, and external relations flexibilities to handle unforeseen opportunities or threats. Sophisticated portfolio planning within and among divisions can protect both current returns and future prospects—the two critical bases for that most cherished goal, high price/earnings ratios.

AN INCREMENTALIST APPROACH

Such managerial techniques can provide a strategic focus for innovation and help solve many of the timing, coordination, and motivation problems that plague large, bureaucratic organizations. Even more detailed planning techniques may help in guiding the development of the many small innovations that characterize any successful business. My research reveals, however, that few, if any, major innovations result from highly structured planing systems. [Why?] . . .

The innovative process is inherently incremental. As Thomas Hughes says, "Technological systems evolve through relatively small steps marked by an occasional stubborn obstacle and by constant random breakthroughs interacting across laboratories and borders" (Hughes, 1984:83). A forgotten hypothesis of Einstein's became the laser in Charles Townes's mind as he contemplated azaleas in Franklin Square. The structure of DNA followed a circuitous route through research in biology, organic chemistry. X-ray crystallography, and mathematics toward its Nobel prize–winning conception as a spiral staircase of [base pairs]. Such rambling trails are characteristic of virtually all major technological advances.

At the outset of the attack on a technical problem, an innovator often does not know whether his problem is tractable, what approach will prove best, and what concrete characteristics the solution will have if achieved. The logical route, therefore, is to follow several paths—though perhaps with varying degrees of intensity—until more information becomes available. Now knowing precisely where the solution will occur, wise managers establish the widest feasible network for finding and assessing alternative solutions. They keep many options open until one of them seems sure to win. Then they back it heavily.

Managing innovation is like a stud poker game, where one can play several hands. A player has some idea of the likely size of the pot at the beginning, knows the general but not the sure route to winning, buys one card (a project) at a time to gain information about probabilities and the size of the pot, closes hands as they become discouraging, and risks more only late in the hand as knowledge increases. . . .

Chaos Within Guidelines

Effective managers of innovation channel and control its main directions. Like venture capitalists, they administer primarily by setting goals, selecting key people, and establishing a few critical limits and decision points for intervention rather than by implementing elaborate planning or control systems. As technology leads or market needs emerge, these managers set a few—most crucial—performance targets and limits. They allow their technical units to decide how to achieve these, subject to defined constraints and reviews at critical junctures.

Early bench-scale project managers may pursue various options, making little attempt at first to integrate each into a total program. Only after key variables are understood—and perhaps measured and demonstrated in lab models—can more precise planning be meaningful. Even then, many factors may remain unknown; chaos and competition can continue to thrive in the pursuit of the solution. At defined review points, however, only those options that can clear performance milestones may continue. . . .

Even after selecting the approaches to emphasize, innovative managers tend to continue a few others as smaller scale "side bets" or options. In a surprising number of cases, these alternatives prove winners when the planned option falls.

Recognizing the many demands entailed by successful programs, innovative companies find special ways to reward innovators. Sony gives "a small but significant" percentage of a new product's sales to its innovating teams. Pilkington, IBM, and 3M's top executives are often chosen from those who have headed successful new product entries. Intel lets its Magnetic Memory Group operate like a small company, with special performance rewards and simulated stock options. GE, Syntex, and United Technologies help internal innovators establish new companies and take equity positions in "nonrelated" product innovations.

Large companies do not have to make their innovators millionaires, but reward should be visible and significant. Fortunately, most engineers are happy with the incentives that Tracy Kidder (1981) calls "playing pinball"—giving widespread recognition to a job well done and the right to play in the next exciting game. Most innovative companies provide both. . . .

MATCH MANAGEMENT TO THE PROCESS

. . . Executives need to understand and accept the tumultuous realities of innovation, learn from the experiences of other companies, and adapt the most relevant features of these others to their own management practices and cultures. Many features of small company innovators are also applicable in big companies. With top-level understanding, vision, a commitment to customers and solutions, a genuine portfolio strategy, a flexible entrepreneurial atmosphere, and proper incentives for innovative champions, many more large companies can innovate to meet the severe demands of global competition.

MANAGING CHANGE

Strategy itself is really about continuity, not change: it is concerned with imposing stable patterns of behavior on an organization, whether these take the form of intentions in advance that become deliberate strategies or actions after the fact that fall into the consistent patterns of emergent strategies. But to manage strategy is frequently to manage change—to recognize when a shift of a strategic nature is possible, desirable, necessary, and then to act.

Managing such change is generally far more difficult than it may at first appear. The need for major strategic reorientation occurs rather infrequently, and when it does, it means moving from a familiar domain into a less well-defined future where many of the old rules no longer apply. People must often abandon the roots of their past successes and develop entirely new skills and attitudes. This is clearly a frightening situation—and often, therefore, the most difficult challenge facing a manager.

The causes of such change also vary, from an ignored steady decline in performance which ultimately demands a "turnaround" to a sudden radical shift in a base technology that requires a reconceptualization of everything the organization does; from the gradual shift into the next stage of an organization's "life cycle;" to the appearance of a new chief executive who wishes to put his or her particular stamp on the organization. The resulting strategic alignments may also take a variety of forms, from a shift of strategic position within the same industry to a whole new perspective in a new industry. Some changes require rapid transitions from one structural configuration to another, as in a machine organization that having diversified into new businesses suddenly switches to a divisionalized form of structure, while others are accompanied by slower structural change, as when a small entrepreneurial firm grows steadily toward a larger mature company. Each transition has its own management prerequisites and problems.

This chapter covers a number of these aspects of organizational change, presenting material on what evokes them in the first place, what forms they can take, and how they can and should be managed in differing situations. These readings appropriately cap the earlier chapters of this book: on strategy and its formation, structure and systems, power and culture, and the various contexts in which these come together. Major changes typically involve them all. Configuration, so carefully nurtured in earlier chapters, turns out to be a double-edged sword, promoting consistency on the one hand but sometimes discouraging change on the other.

We begin broadly and then focus, starting with some general theories of change in organizations and then consider views of how to manage crises brought on by change (or the lack of it) before closing with a specific set of ideas on how managers can deal with strategic change.

The first reading seeks to bring some closure to our discussion of the different configurations of structure presented in the last five chapters. Called "Beyond Configuration: Forces and Forms in Effective Organizations," it is, in a sense, Mintzberg's final chapter of his book on structure, except that it was written very recently, years after that book first appeared. It seeks to do just what its title says: make the point that while the different structural forms (configurations) of the last chapters can help us to make sense of, and to manage in, a complex world, there is also a need to go beyond configuration, to consider the nuanced linkages among these various forms. This he proposes be done by treating all the forms as a framework of forces that act on every organization and whose contradictions need to be reconciled. By so doing, we can begin to see the weaknesses in each form as well as the times when an organization is better off to design itself as a combination of two or more forms. Some organizations, to use a metaphor introduced in this reading, achieve greater effectiveness by playing "organizational LEGO"—creating their own form rather than letting themselves be put together like a jigsaw puzzle into a standard form. Finally, this reading discusses how the forces of ideology (representing cooperation—pulling together) and of politics (representing competition—pulling apart) work both to promote change and also to impede it, and how the contradictions among these two must also be reconciled if an organization is to remain effective in the long run.

Our second reading on managing the context of change considers the "unsteady pace of organizational evolution" in terms of distinct periods of "convergence" and "upheaval." Related to the literature on organizational life cycles, its three authors, Michael Tushman and William Newman of Columbia University's Graduate School of Business and Elaine Romanelli of Duke University's Fuqua School of Business, argue for what has also been referred to as a "quantum theory" or organizational change (Miller and Freisen, 1984). The essence of the argument is that organizations prefer to stay on course most of the time, accepting incremental changes to improve their strategies, processes, and structures, but that periodically they must submit to dramatic shifts in these—"strategic revolutions" of a sort—to realign their overall orientation.

This argument is obviously compatible with the earlier notion of configuration, which represents a form of alignment of strategy, structure, and processes that dictate a certain stability in an organization. But note that it differs from Quinn's concept of "logical incrementalism," introduced in Chapter 5, which argues for more of a gradual shift in strategic thinking as a way to achieve major change in an organization. There appears to be merit in both approaches and we shall return to some words of reconciliation between the two momentarily.

The next two readings share the quantum view, but approach it rather differently—one from the perspective of process and culture, the other from that of context and strategy. In "Responding to Crises," Starbuck, Greve, and Hedberg team up to explain why organizations need these dramatic revolutions—why they fall into crises, how they tend to cope with them, and how they should. This reading brings us back to the idea of culture, particularly why and how it acts as a deterrent to major strategic change, and discusses how a deeply engrained culture that is no longer viable might be changed. In fact, this paper reflects a most interesting body of research carried out in Sweden in the 1970s on the relationships between culture and strategy. (Two of the authors are Scandinavian—Arent Greve, an academic at the Bergen, Norway, business school, and Bo Hedberg, an ex-academic who now works for a Swedish banking federation—while the third, William Starbuck, is an American who teaches at the NYU Business School but who worked with the others in Europe.)

Starbuck and his colleagues deal with situations of quantum change—namely crisis—but their ideas nonetheless link up with those of Quinn as well, specifically on how to manage incrementally and above all how to work out difficulties through an interactive process of learning. This reading also challenges many conventional notions in management. For example, its final suggestion is that crises themselves can represent *opportunities* for those organizations prepared to exploit them. Often those who approach crises in this fashion earn critical strategic advantages in the next stage of their industry's development. Consider the emergence of entirely new dominant players in the deregulated transportation and financial services industries.

The next reading considers crises too—specifically organizations in need of "turnaround"—but very differently, more in the spirit of strategy analysis discussed in Chapter 4. Written by Charles Hofer, who teaches business policy at the University of Georgia, this reading considers various strategies that organizations can use to turn themselves around. In so doing, it introduces the important distinction between "operating" and "strategic" turnaround.

These last two readings, in suggesting very different approaches to managing crisis, reflect what are probably the two major themes today in the literature of organizational effectiveness. Picking up on a point made in Mintzberg's reading, we can call them "Porterian" and "Peterian," after Michael Porter, who argues that effectiveness resides in choosing the right strategy (positioning right), and Tom Peters, who believes it resides in carrying out the operations excellently no matter what the strategy (executing right). As Peter Drucker commented long ago, organizations may do the right things or they may do things right.

Finally, we close the chapter with James Brian Quinn's reading on "Managing Strategies Incrementally." Here he offers specific advice of various kinds on how managers can deal with the practical realities of creating change. While the previous readings have tended to look at organizations through telescopes, Quinn puts the exigencies of strategic change under a microscope—from the senior managers' perspective. In fact, while the others argue for the need to change the management in order to significantly change an organization, the Quinn reading shows how a management in place can render important strategic change. Consciously moving incrementally allows them to cope with many of the informational, political, motivational, and commitment problems that often inhibit or prevent change in large organizations. While Quinn's prescriptions do not appear as neat and orderly as those that show up in the "planned change" literature, they have direct relevance to managers who must deal in a complex, somewhat politicized world, that is, the real world of most large organizations. This reading also closes various loopholes by relating both the emergent and deliberate aspects of strategy formation to the various articles which dealt with the politics and social dynamics of change.

How can we reconcile Quinn's logical incrementalism with the ideas of those authors who promote the quantum view? Perhaps these views are not as contradictory as they seem. Consider three dimensions: (1) the specific aspects of the strategy change process that each considers, (2) the time frames of the two viewpoints, and (3) the types of organizations involved. Quinn's incrementalist view focuses on the processes going on in senior managers' minds as they help create new strategies. Because of the complexities involved, effective strategic thinking requires an incremental, interactive, learning process for all key players. The quantum approach, in contrast, focuses, not on the strategists' intentions so much as on the strategies actually pursued by the organization (referred to in Chapter 1 as the realized strategies of the organization). It is these that often seem to change in quantum fashion. It may be, therefore, that managers conceive and promote their intended strategies incrementally, but once that is accomplished they change their organizations in rapid, integrated leaps, quantum fashion.

But then again, each of these two approaches may also occur in their own situations. For example, quantum changes may more often take place in crisis situations, when top managements change, or when external environments compress time frames—often caused by technological or regulatory shifts. Incremental changes may, in contrast, be more common in large, healthy organizations with multiple power points. Most situations, however, are not "either-or" propositions. A program of radical change often takes place within a company where many other elements continue to perform along well-established norms.

BEYOND CONFIGURATION: FORCES AND FORMS IN EFFECTIVE ORGANIZATIONS*

BY HENRY MINTZBERG

Charles Darwin once made the distinction between "lumpers" and "splitters."[1] Lumpers categorize; they are the synthesizers, prone to consistency. Once they have pigeonholed something into one box or another, they are done with it. To a lumper in management, strategies are generic, structures are types, managers have a style (X, Y, Z, 9–9, etc.). Splitters nuance; they are the analyzers, prone to distinction. Since nothing can ever be categorized, things are never done with. To a splitter in management, strategies, structures, and styles all vary infinitely.

I believe a key to the effective organization lies in this distinction, specifically in its simultaneous acceptance and rejection (which themselves amount to lumping and splitting). Both are right and both are wrong. Without categories, it would be impossible to practice management. With only categories, it could not be practiced effectively.

For several years I worked as a lumper, seeking to identify types of organizations. Much as in the field of biology, I felt we in management needed some categorization of the "species" with which we dealt. We long had too much of "one best way" thinking, that every organization needed every new technique or idea that came along (like MBO or formal planning or participative management).

---

* Adapted from a chapter of this title in *Mintzberg on Management: Inside Our Strange World of Organizations* (Free Press, 1989); an article similar to this chapter was recently published in the *Sloan Management Review*.
[1] See F. Darwin (ed.), *The Life and Letters of Charles Darwin* (London: John Murray, 1887), p. 105.

Thus, in my books on structure and power, I developed various "configurations" of organizations. My premise was that an effective organization "got it all together" as the saying goes—achieved consistency in its internal characteristics, harmony in its processes, fit with its context.

But then, a student of mine, Alain Noël, came along and asked me a question that upset this nice lumping. He wanted to know whether I was intending to play "jigsaw puzzle" or "LEGO" with all the elements of structure and power that I described in those books. In other words, did I mean all these elements of organizations to fit together in set ways—to create known images—or were they to be used creatively to build new ones? I had to answer that I had been promoting jigsaw puzzle even if I was suggesting that the pieces could be combined into several images instead of the usual one. But I immediately began to think about playing "organizational LEGO." All of the anomalies I had encountered—all those nasty, well-functioning organizations that refused to fit into one or another of my neat categories—suddenly became opportunities to think beyond configuration. I could become a splitter too.

This reading is presented in the spirit of playing "organizational LEGO." It tries to show how we can use splitting as well as lumping to understand what makes organizations effective as well as what causes many of their fundamental problems.

FORMS AND FORCES

I shall refer to the configurations of organizations as *forms*. The original five of my structure book—here labeled entrepreneurial, machine, diversified, professional, and adhocracy—are laid out at the nodes of a pentagon, shown in Figure 1.

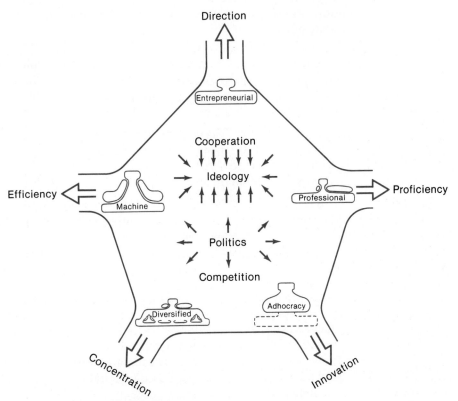

FIGURE 1
An Integrating Pentagon of Forces and Forms

Many organizations seem to fit naturally into one or another of these categories, *more or less.* We all know the small aggressive entrepreneurial firm, the perfectly machinelike Swiss hotel, the diversified conglomerate, the professional collegial university, the freewheeling intrapreneurial Silicon Valley innovator. But some organizations do not fit, much to the chagrin of the lumpers. And even many that may seem to, on closer examination reveal curious anomalies. It is difficult to imagine a more machinelike organization than McDonald's; why then does it seem to be rather innovative, at least in its own context? And why is it that whenever I mention to an executive group about a 3M or a Hewlett-Packard as innovative in form, someone from the audience leaps up to tell me about their tight control systems. Innovative adhocracies are not supposed to rely on tight controls.

All this of course pleases the splitters. "Come on, Henry," a colleague chided me recently, "in my consulting practice I never see any one of these forms. I can find all of them in all serious organizations." To him, organizations float around the inside of my pentagon; they never make it to any one node. In response, therefore, to the valid claims of the splitters, I recently added *forces* to the pentagon, shown as arrows emanating out from each of the forms. In other words, every form can be thought to represent a force too:

- First is the force for *direction,* represented by the entrepreneurial form, for some sense of where the organization must go. Without such direction—which today is apt to be called "strategic vision," years ago "grand strategy"—the various activities of an organization cannot easily work together to achieve common purpose.

- Next is the force for *efficiency,* represented by the machine form, for ensuring a viable ratio of benefits gained to costs incurred. Without some concern for efficiency, all but the most protected of organizations must eventually falter. Efficiency generally means standardization and formalization; often it reduces to economy. In current practice, it focuses on rationalization and restructuring, among other things.

- Across from the force for efficiency is the force for *proficiency,* represented by the professional form, for carrying out tasks with high levels of knowledge and skill. Without proficiency, the difficult work of organizations—whether surgery in the hospital or engineering in the corporation—just could not get done.

- Below efficiency is the force for *concentration,* represented by the diversified form, for individual units in an organization to concentrate their efforts on particular markets that it has to serve. Without such concentration, it becomes almost impossible to manage an organization that is diversified.

- At the bottom right of the pentagon is the force for *innovation,* represented by the adhocracy form. Organizations need central direction and focused concentration and they need efficiency and proficiency. But they also need to be able to learn, to discover new things for their customers and themselves—to adapt and to innovate.

I have so far left out the two forms from my book on power. We can certainly find examples of the missionary organization, as in the traditional Israeli kibbutz. Likewise, some regulatory agencies, sometimes even business corporations, become so captured by conflict for a time that they come to look like political organizations. But these forms are relatively rare, at least compared with the other five, and so I prefer to show them only as forces (placed in the middle of the pentagon for reasons to be discussed later).

- Ideology represents the force for *cooperation,* for "pulling together" (hence the arrows focus in toward the middle).
- And politics represents the force for *competition,* for "pulling apart" (hence the arrows flare out).

To recap to this point, we have two views of organizational effectiveness. One, for the lumpers, concentrates on a *portfolio of forms,* from which organizations are encouraged to choose if they wish to become effective. The other, for the splitters, focuses on a *system of forces,* with which organizations are encouraged to play in order to become effective.

The basis of my argument here is that both views are critical to the practice of management. One represents the most fundamental forces that act on organizations: All serious organizations experience all seven of them, at one time or another if not all the time. And the other represents the most fundamental forms that organizations can take, which some of them do some of the time. Together, as conceived on the pentagon, these forces and forms appear to constitute a powerful diagnostic framework by which to understand what goes on in organizations and to prescribe effective change in them.

My argument here will proceed as follows. First, I suggest that when one force dominates an organization, it is drawn toward a coherent, established form, described as *configuration.* That facilitates its management, but also raises the problem of *contamination,* which must be dealt with. When no one force dominates, the organization must instead function as a balanced *combination* of different forces, including periods of *conversion* from one form to another. But combination raises the problem of *cleavage,* which must also be dealt with. Both contamination and cleavage require the management of *contradiction,* and here the catalytic forces of the middle of the pentagon come into play: cooperation and competition both help to deal with it. But these two forces are themselves contradictory and so must be balanced as well. Put this all together and you get a fascinating game of jigsaw puzzle-cum-LEGO. It may seem difficult, but bear with me; reading it here will prove a lot easier than managing it in practice. And it may even help!

CONFIGURATION

When one force dominates the others, based on an organization's particular needs or perhaps just the arbitrary exercise of power, then we should look for the organization to fall close to one of the nodes, to take the form of one of our configurations, more or less. But these configurations are really pure types, what Max Weber once labeled "ideal types" (in Gerth and Mills, 1958). We must first ask whether they really do exist in practice.

In one sense, these configurations do not exist at all. After all, they are just words and pictures on pieces of paper, caricatures that simplify a complex reality. No serious organization can be labeled a pure machine or a pure innovator, and so on. On the other hand, managers who have to make decisions in their heads cannot carry reality around there either. They carry simplifications, called theories or models, of which these forms are examples. We must, therefore, turn to a second question: whether the forms are useful, real or not. And again I shall answer yes and no.

While no configuration ever matches a real organization perfectly, some do come remarkably close, as in the examples of the machinelike Swiss hotel or the freewheeling Silicon Valley innovator cited earlier. Species exist in nature in response to distinct ecological niches, likewise configurations evolve in human society to serve distinct needs. The Swiss hotel guest wants no surprises—no jack-in-the-box popping up when the pillow is lifted, thank you—just pure predictability, the efficiency of that wake-up call at 8:00, not 8:07. But in the niche called advertising, the client that gets no surprises may well take its business to another agency.

My basic point about configuration is simple: when the form fits, the organization is well advised to wear it, at least for a time. With configuration, an organization achieves a sense of order, of integration. There is internal consistency, synergy among processes, fit with the external context. It is the organization without configuration, much like the person without distinct character, that tends to suffer the identity crises.

Outsiders appreciate configuration; it helps them to understand an organization. We walk into a McDonald's and we know immediately what drives it, likewise a Hewlett-Packard. But more important is what configuration offers the managers: it makes an organization more manageable. With the course set, it is easier to steer, also to deflect pressures that are peripheral. No configuration is perfect—the professional one, for example, tends to belittle its clients and the machine one often alienates it workers—but there is something to be said for consistency. Closely controlled workers may not be happier than autonomous ones, but they are certainly better off than ones confused by quality circles in the morning and time study engineering in the afternoon. Better to have the definition and discipline of configuration than to dissipate one's energies trying to be all things to all people.

Moreover, much of what we know about organizations in practice applies to specific configurations. There may not be any one best way, but there are certainly preferred ways in particular contexts, for example time study in the machine organization and matrix structure in the innovative one.

Thus for classification, for comprehension, for diagnosis, and for design, configuration seems to be effective. But only so long as everything holds still. Introduce the dynamics of evolutionary change and, sooner or later, configuration becomes ineffective.

Contamination by Configuration

In harmony, consistency, and fit lies configuration's great strength. Also its debilitating weakness. The fact is that the dominant force sometimes dominates to the point of undermining all the others. For example, in a machine organization, the quest for efficiency can almost totally suppress the capacity for innovation, while in an adhocracy organization, it is the need to express some modicum of efficiency that often gets suppressed. I call this phenomenon *contamination,* although it might just as easily be called Lord Acton's dictum: among the forces of organizations too, power tends to corrupt and absolute power corrupts absolutely. For example, the story of medical care across the United States could well be described as the contamination of efficiency by proficiency. No one can deny the primacy of proficiency—who would go to a hospital that favors efficiency—but certainly not to the extent that it has been allowed to dominate.

Machine organizations recognize this problem when they put their research and development facilities away from head office, to avoid the contaminating effects of the central efficiency experts. Unfortunately, while lead may block X rays, there is no known medium to shield the effects of a dominant culture. The controller drops by, just to have a look: "What, no shoes?" Of course, the opposite case is also well known. Just ask the members of an innovative organization who's the most miserable person in adhocracy? Whenever I do this in a workshop with such an organization, the inevitable reply is a brief silence followed by a few smiles, then growing laughter as everyone turns to some poor person cowering in the corner. Of course, it's the controller, the victim of adhocracy's contamination. He or she may wear shoes, but that hardly helps him or her keep the lid on all the madness.

Contamination is another way of saying that a configuration is not merely a structure, not even merely a power system: each is a culture in its own right. Being machinelike or innovative is not just a way of organizing, it's a way of life!

Of course, given the benefits claimed for configuration, contamination may seem like a small price to pay for being coherently organized. True enough. Until things go out of control.

Configuration Out of Control

A configuration is geared not only to a general context but also to specific conditions—for example, a particular leader in an entrepreneurial organization, even a particular product and market in a machine one. Thus, when the need arises for change, the dominating force may act to hold the organization in place. Then other forces must come into play. But if contamination has worked its effects, the other forces are too weak. And so the organization goes out of control. For example, a machine organization in need of a new strategy may find available to it neither the direction of an entrepreneurial leader nor the learning of intrapreneurial subordinates. And so its internal consistency gets perpetuated while it falls increasingly out of touch with its context.

In addition, each configuration is also capable of driving itself out of control. That is to say, each contains the seeds of its own destruction. These reside in its dominating force, and come into play through the effects of contamination. With too much proficiency in a professional organization, unconstrained by the forces of efficiency and direction, the professionals become overindulged (as in many of today's universities), just as with too much technocratic regulation in a machine organization, free of the force for innovation, there arises an obsession with control (as in far too much contemporary industry and government).

My colleagues, Danny Miller and Manfred Kets de Vries (1987), have published an interesting book about *The Neurotic Organization.* They discuss organizations that become dramatic, paranoid, schizoid, compulsive, and depressive. In each case, a system that may once have been healthy has run out of control. Very roughly, I believe these five organizational neuroses correspond to what tends to happen to each of the five forms. The entrepreneurial organization tends to go out of control by becoming dramatic, as its leader, free of the other forces, takes the system off on a personal ego trip. The machine organization seems predisposed to compulsion once its analysts and their technocratic controls take over completely. Those who have worked in universities and hospitals well understand the collective paranoid tendencies of professionals, especially when free of the constraining forces of administration and innovation. I need not dwell on the depressive effects of that obsession with the "bottom line" in the diversified organization; the results on morale and innovation of the turning of the financial screws are now widely appreciated. As for the adhocracy organization, its problem is that while it must continually innovate, it must also exploit the benefits of that innovation. One requires divergent thinking, the other convergent. Other forces help balance that tension; without them, the organization can easily become schizoid.

In effect, each form goes over the edge in its own particular way, so that behaviors that were once functional when pursued to excess become dysfunctional.

This is easily seen on our pentagon. Remove all the arrows but one at any node, and the organization, no longer anchored, flies off in that direction.

Containment of Configuration

Thus I conclude that truly effective organizations do not exist in pure form. What keeps a configuration effective is not only the dominance of a single force but also the constraining effects of other forces. They keep it in place. I call this *containment*. For example, people inclined to break the rules may feel hard pressed in the machine organization. But without some of them, the organization may be unable to deal with unexpected problems. Similarly, administration may not be the strongest in the professional organization, but when allowed to atrophy, anarchy inevitably results as the absolute power of the professionals corrupts them absolutely. Thus, to manage configuration effectively is to exploit one form but also to reconcile the different forces. But how does the effective organization deal with the contradiction?

COMBINATION

Configuration is a nice thing when you can have it. Unfortunately, some organizations all of the time and all organizations some of the time cannot. They must instead balance competing forces.

Consider the symphony orchestra. Proficiency is clearly a critical force, but so too is direction: such an organization is not conceivable without highly skilled players as well as the strong central leadership of a conductor. The Russians apparently tried a leaderless orchestra shortly after their revolution, but soon gave it up as unworkable.

I shall use the word *combination* for the organization that balances different forces. In effect, it does not make it to any one node of the pentagon but instead finds its place somewhere inside.

How common are combinations as compared with configurations? To some extent the answer lies in the eyes of the beholder: what looks to be a relatively pure form to one person may look like a combination of forces to another. Still, it is interesting to consider how organizations appear to intelligent observers. For several years now, we have sent McGill MBA students out to study organizations in the Montreal area, having exposed them, among other things, to the five forms of organizations. At year end, I have circulated a questionnaire asking them to categorize the organization they studied as one of the forms, a combination of two or more, or neither. In just over half the cases—66 out of 123—the students felt that a single form fitted best. They identified 25 entrepreneurial, 13 machine, 11 diversified, 9 adhocracy, and 8 professional. All the rest were labeled combinations—seventeen different ones in all. Diversified machines were the most common (9), followed by adhocracy professionals (8), entrepreneurial professionals (6), and entrepreneurial machines (5).[2]

---

[2] The high incidence of entrepreneurial forms may be thought to reflect the students' bias toward studying small organizations, but I think not. There exist many more small organizations, in business and elsewhere, than large ones, usually entrepreneurial in nature. Of the larger ones, I would expect the machine form to predominate in any Western society. As for the incidence of combinations, I personally believe that the diversified and adhocracy forms are the most difficult to sustain (the former a conglomerate with no links between the divisions, the latter a very loose and freewheeling structure), and so these should be most common in hybrid combinations. Also some of the hybrids reflect common transitions in organizations, especially from the entrepreneurial to the machine form, as I shall discuss later.

Combinations themselves may take a variety of forms. They may balance just two main forces or several; these forces may meet directly or indirectly; and the balance may be steady over time or oscillate back and forth temporarily.

When only two of the five forces meet in rough balance, the organization might be described as a *hybrid* of two of our forms. This is the case of the symphony orchestra, which can be found somewhere along the line between the entrepreneurial and professional forms. Organizations can, of course, combine several of the forces in rough balance as well. In fact, five of the McGill student groups identified combinations of three forms and another a combination of four forms.

Consider Apple Computers. It seems to have developed under its founder, Steve Jobs, largely as an adhocracy organization, to emphasize new product development. The next CEO, John Sculley, apparently felt the need to temper that innovation with greater focus, to give more attention to efficiency in production and distribution. When I presented this framework at an executive program a couple of years ago, an employee of Apple Canada saw other things going on in his operation too: he added an entrepreneurial form in sales due to a dynamic leader, professional forms in marketing and training to reflect the skills there, and another adhocracy form in a new venture unit. Organizations that experience such multiple combinations are, of course, the ones that must really play LEGO.

Then there is the question of how the different forces interact. In some cases, they function on a direct steady basis; in others, they can be separated as to place or time. The combination in the symphony orchestra must be close and pervasive —leadership and professional skill meet regularly, face to face. In organizations like Apple, however, whose different units may reflect different forces, they can act somewhat independently of each other. In fact, some organizations are lucky enough to be able to achieve almost complete buffering between units representing different forces. In newspapers, for example, the more professional editorial function simply hands over its camera-ready copy to the machinelike plant for production, with little need for interaction.

Finally, in contrast to the combinations maintained on a steady-state basis are those that achieve balance in a dynamic equilibrium over time—power oscillates between the competing forces. In this regard, Richard Cyert and James March (1963) some years ago wrote about the "sequential attention to goals" in organizations, when conflicting needs are attended to each in their own turn—for example, a period of innovation to emphasize new product development followed by one of consolidation to rationalize product lines. (Might Apple Computers simply be in one of these cycles, the innovation of Jobs have been replaced by the consolidation of Sculley, or will Sculley himself be able to get the organization to balance these two forces?)

Cleavage in Combinations

Necessary as it may sometimes be, all is not rosy in the world of combination, however. If configuration encourages contamination, which can drive the organization out of control, then combination encourages *cleavage,* which can have much the same effect. Instead of one force dominating, two or more confront each other to the point of paralyzing the organization.

In effect, a natural fault line exists between any two opposing forces. Pushed to the limit, fissures begin to open up. In fact, Fellini made a film on exactly this with my favorite example. Called *Orchestra Rehearsal,* it is about musicians who revolt against their conductor, and so bring on complete anarchy, followed by paralysis. Only then do they become prepared to cooperate with their leader, who they realize is necessary for their effective performance.

But one need not turn to allegories to find examples of cleavage. It occurs commonly in most combinations, for example, in business in the battles between the R&D people who promote new product innovation and the production people in favor of stabilizing manufacturing for operating efficiency. Cleavage can, of course, be avoided when the different forces are separated in time or place, as in the newspaper. But not all organizations with combinations are so fortunate.

Combination of one kind or another is necessary in every organization. The nodes of our pentagon, where the pure configurations lie, are only points, imaginary ideals. Indeed, any organization that reaches one is already on its way out of control. It is the inside of the pentagon that has the space; that is where the effective organization must find its place. Some may fall close to one of the nodes, as configuration, more or less, while others may sit between nodes as combinations. But, ultimately, configuration and combination are not so very different, one representing more of a tilt in favor of one force over others, the other more of a balance between forces. In other words, there must always be the splitting of gray between the black and white of lumping. The question thus becomes again: how does the effective organization deal with the contradiction?

CONVERSION

So far our discussion has suggested that an organization finds its place in the pentagon and then stays there, more or less. But, in fact, few organizations get the chance to stay in one place forever: their needs change, and they must therefore undergo *conversion* from one configuration or combination to another.

Any number of external changes can cause such a conversion. An innovative organization may chance upon a new invention and decide to settle down in machine form to exploit it. Or a previously stable market may become subject to so much change that machine forms must become innovative. Some conversions are, of course, temporary, as in a machine organization in trouble that becomes entrepreneurial for a time to allow a forceful leader to impose new direction on it (usually called "turnaround"). This seems to describe Chrysler's experience when Iacocca first arrived, also that of SAS when Carlzon took over.

Cycles of Conversion

Of particular interest here is another type of conversion, however, somewhat predictable in nature because it is driven by forces intrinsic to the organization itself. Earlier I discussed the seeds of destruction contained in each configuration. Sometimes they destroy the organization, but other times they destroy only the configuration, driving the organization to a more viable form. For example, the entrepreneurial form is inherently vulnerable, dependent as it is on a single leader. It may work well for the young organization, but with aging and growth a dominant need for direction may be displaced by that for efficiency. Then conversion to the machine form becomes necessary—the power of one leader must be replaced by that of administrators.

The implication is that organizations often go through stages as they develop —*if* they develop—possibly sequenced into so-called life cycles. In fact, I have placed the forces and forms on the pentagon to reflect the most common of these, with the simple, earlier stages near the top and the more complex ones lower down.

What appears to be the most common life cycle, especially in business, occurs around the left side of the figure. Organizations generally begin life in the entrepreneurial form, because start-up requires clear direction and attracts strong leaders. As they grow and develop, many settle into the machine form to exploit increasingly established markets. But with greater growth, established markets eventually become saturated, and that often drives the organization to diversify its markets and then divisionalize its structure, taking it finally to the bottom left of our pentagon. Those organizations highly dependent on expertise, however, will instead go down the right side of the pentagon, using the professional form if their services are more standardized or the adhocracy form if these are more creative. (Some adhocracy organizations eventually settle down by converting to the professional form, where they can exploit the skills they have developed, a common occurrence, for example, in the consulting business.)

Ideology is shown above politics on the pentagon because it tends to be associated with the earlier stages of an organization's life, politics with the later ones. Any organization can, of course, have a strong culture, just as any can become politicized. But ideologies develop rather more easily in young organizations, especially with charismatic leadership in the entrepreneurial stage, whereas it is extremely difficult to build a strong and lasting culture in a mature organization. Politics, in contrast, typically spreads as the energy of a youthful organization dissipates with age and its activities become more diffuse. In fact, time typically blunts ideology as norms rigidify into procedures and beliefs become rules; then political activity tends to rise in its place. Typically, it is the old and spent organizations that are the most politicized; indeed, it is often their political conflict that finally kills them.

Cleavage in Conversion

Conversions may be necessary, but that does not make them easy. Some are, of course; they occur quickly because a change is long overdue, much as a supersaturated liquid, below the freezing point, solidifies the moment it is disturbed. But most conversions require periods of transition, prolonged and agonizing, involving a good deal of conflict. Two sides battle, usually an "old guard" committed to the status quo challenged by a group of "Young Turks" in favor of the change. As Apple Computer grew large, for example, a John Sculley intent on settling it down confronted a Steve Jobs who wished to maintain its freewheeling style of innovation.

As the organization in transition sits between its old and new forms, it becomes, or course, a form of combination, with the same problems of cleavage. Given that the challenge is to the very base of its power, there can be no recourse to higher authority to reconcile the conflict. Once again, then, the question arises: how does the effective organization deal with the contradiction?

CONTRADICTION

The question of how to manage contradiction has been the concluding point of each of the sections of this reading. I believe the answer lies in the two forces in the center of our pentagon. Organizations that have to reconcile contradictory forces, especially in dealing with change, often turn to the cooperative force of ideology or the competitive force of politics. Indeed, I believe that these two forces themselves represent a contradiction that must be managed if an organization is not to run out of control.

I have placed these two forces in the middle of the pentagon because I believe they commonly act in ways different from the other five. It is true that each can dominate an organization, and so draw it toward a missionary or political form, but more commonly I believe that these forces act differently. While the other forces tend to infiltrate parts of an organization (for example, direction in senior management, efficiency in accounting), and so isolate them, these tend instead to *infuse* the entire organization. Thus I refer to them as *catalytic,* noting that one tends to be centripetal, drawing behavior inwards toward a common core , and the other centrifugal, driving behavior away from any central place. I shall argue that both can act to promote change, also to prevent it, either way sometimes rendering an organization more effective, sometimes less.

Cooperation Through Ideology

Ideology represents the force for cooperation in an organization, for collegiality and consensus. People "pull together" for the common good—"we" are in this together.

I use the word ideology here to describe a rich culture in an organization, the uniqueness and attractiveness of which binds the members tightly to it. They commit themselves personally to the organization and identify with its needs.

Such an ideology can infuse any form of organization. It is often found with the entrepreneurial form, because, as already noted, organizational ideologies are usually created by charismatic leaders. But after such leaders move on, these ideologies can sustain themselves in other forms too. Thus we have the ideological machine that is McDonald's and the ideological adhocracy built up by Messrs. Hewlett and Packard. And one study some years ago (Clark, 1970) described "distinctive" colleges, such as Swarthmore and Antioch—professional forms infused with powerful ideologies.

Ideology encourages the members of an organization to look inward—to take their lead from the imperatives of the organization's own vision, instead of looking outward to what comparable organizations are doing. (Of course, when ideology is strong, there are no comparable organizations!) A good example of this is Hewlett Packard's famous "next bench syndrome"—that the product designer receives his or her stimulus for innovation, not from the aggregations of marketing research reports, but from the need of a particular colleague at the next bench.

This looking inward is represented by the direction of the halo of the arrows of cooperation on the pentagon. They form a circle facing inward, as if to shield the organization from outside influences. Organizational ideology above all draws people to cooperate with each other, to work together to take the organization where all of them, duly indoctrinated into its norms, believe it must go. In this sense, ideology should be thought of as the spirit of an organization, the life force that infuses the skeleton of its formal structure.

One important implication of this would appear to be that the infusion of an ideology renders any particular configuration more effective. People get fired up to pursue efficiency or proficiency or whatever else drives the organization. When this happens to a machine organization—as in a McDonald's, very responsive to its customers and very sensitive to its employees—I like to call it a "snappy bureaucracy." Bureaucratic machines are not supposed to be snappy, but ideology changes the nature of their quest for efficiency. This, of course, is the central message of the Peters and Waterman (1982) book, *In Search of Excellence,* that effectiveness is achieved, not by opportunism, not even by clever strategic positioning, but by a management that knows exactly what it must do ("sticks to its knitting") and then does it with the fervor of religious missionaries ("hands on, value driven").

There seems to be another important implication of this: ideology helps an organization to manage contradiction and so to deal with change. The different forces no longer need conflict in quite the same way. As an organization becomes infused with ideology, parts that reflect different forces can begin to pull together. As a result, forces that normally dominate or oppose each other begin to work together, thereby reducing contamination and cleavage and so facilitating adaptation.

I have always wondered why it is that McDonald's, so machinelike, is so creative in its advertising and new product development. Likewise, if 3M and Hewlett Packard really do conform largely to the adhocracy model, why do they have those tight control systems? I suspect we have the answer here. Their strong cultures enable these organizations to reconcile forces that work against each other in more ordinary organizations. People behind these different forces develop a grudging respect for one another: when it matters, they actively cooperate for the common good. "Old Joe, over there, that nut in R&D: we in production sometimes wonder about him. But we know this place could never function without him." Likewise in the great symphony orchestra, the musicians respect their conductor because they know that without him they could never produce beautiful music.

Such organizations can more easily reconcile their opposing forces because what matters to their people is the organization itself, not any of its particular parts. If it is IBM you believe in over and above marketing finesse or technical virtuosity per se, then when things really matter you will suspend your departmental rivalries to enable IBM to adapt. Great organizations simply pull together when they have to, because they are rooted in great systems of beliefs.

In his popular book, *Competitive Strategy,* Michael Porter (1980) warns about getting "stuck in the middle" between a strategy of "cost leadership" and one of "differentiation" (one representing the force for efficiency, the other including quality as well as innovation). How, then, has Toyota been able to produce such high-quality automobiles at such reasonable cost? Why didn't Toyota get stuck in the middle?

I believe that Porter's admonition stems from the view, prevalent in American management circles throughout this century and reflected equally in my own case for configuration, that if an organization favors one particular force, then others must suffer. If the efficiency experts have the upper hand, then quality gets slighted; if it is the elite designers who get their way, productive efficiency must lag; and so on. This may be true so long as an organization is managed as just a collection of different parts—a portfolio of products and functions. But when the spirit of ideology infuses the bones of its structure, an organization takes on an integrated life of its own and contradictions get reconciled. In Toyota, for example, one has the impression that each individual is made to feel like the embodiment of the entire system, that no matter what job one does, it helps to make Toyota great. Is that not why the assembly workers are allowed to shut down the line: each one is treated as a person capable of making decisions for the good of Toyota. Thus the only thing that gets stuck in the middle at Toyota is the conventional management thinking of the West!

I have so far discussed the reconciliation of contradictory forces between people and units. But even more powerful can be the effect of reconciling these forces within individuals themselves. That is what the concept of infusion really means. It is not the researchers who are responsible for innovation, not the accountants for efficiency; everyone internalizes the different forces in carrying out his or her own job. In metaphorical terms, it is easy to change hats in an organization when all are emblazoned with the same insignia.

Limits to Cooperation

Overall, then, ideology sounds like a wonderful thing. But all is not rosy in the world of culture either. For one thing, ideologies are difficult to build, especially in established organizations, and difficult to sustain once built. For another thing, established ideologies can sometimes get in the way of organizational effectiveness.

The impression left by a good deal of current writing and consulting notwithstanding, ideology is not there for the taking, to be plucked off the tree of management technique like just another piece of fashionable fruit. As Karl Weick has argued, "A corporation doesn't *have* a culture. A corporation *is* a culture. That's why they're so horribly difficult to change (in Kiechel, 1984:11). The fact is that there are no procedures for building ideologies, no five easy steps to a better culture. At best, those steps overlay a thin veneer of impressions that washes off in the first political storm; at worst, they destroy whatever is left of prevailing cultural norms. I believe that effective ideologies are built slowly and patiently by committed leaders who establish compelling missions for their organizations, nurture them, and care deeply about the people who perform them.

But even after an ideology is established, the time can come—indeed usually does eventually—when its effect is to render the organization ineffective, indeed sometimes to the point of destroying it. This is suggested in the comment above that ideologies are "so horribly difficult to change."

Just as I argued that ideology promotes change, by allowing an organization to reconcile contradictory forces, now I should like to argue the opposite. Ideology discourages change by forcing everyone to work within the same set of beliefs. In other words, strong cultures are immutable: they may promote change within themselves but they themselves are not to be changed. Receiving "the word" enables people to ask all kinds of questions but one: the word itself must never be put into question.

I can explain this in reference to two views of strategy, as position and as perspective. In one case, the organization looks down to specific product-market positions (as depicted in Michael Porter's work), in the other it looks up to a general philosophy of functioning (as in Peter Drucker's earlier writings about the "concept of a business"). In this regard, I like to ask people in my management seminars whether Egg McMuffin was a strategic change for McDonald's. Some argue yes, of course, because it brought the firm into the breakfast market. Others dismiss this as just a variation in product line, pure McDonald's, just different ingredients in a new package. Their disagreement, however, concerns not the change at McDonald's so much as their implicit definition of strategy. To one, strategy is position (the breakfast market), to the other it is perspective (the McDonald's way). The important point here is that change *within* perspective—change at the margin, to new position—is facilitated by a strong culture, whereas change *of* perspective—fundamental change—is discouraged by it. (Anyone for McDuckling à l'Orange?) The very ideology that makes an organization so adaptive within its niche undermines its efforts to move to a new niche.

Thus, when change of a fundamental nature must be made—in strategy, structure, form, whatever—the ideology that may for so long have been the key to an organization's effectiveness suddenly becomes its central problem. Ideology becomes a force for the status quo; indeed, because those who perceive the need for change are forced to challenge it, the ideology begins to breed politics!

To understand this negative effect of ideology, take another look at the pentagon. All those arrows of cooperative ideology face inward. The halo they form may protect the organization, but at the possible expense of isolating it from the outside world. In other words, ideology can cause the other forces to atrophy: direction comes to be interpreted in terms of an outmoded system of beliefs, forcing efficiency, proficiency, and innovation into ever narrower corners. As the other arrows of the figure disappear, those of ideology close in on the organization, causing it to *implode.* That is how the organization dominated by the force of ideology goes out of control. It isolates itself and eventually dies. We have no need for the extreme example of a Jonestown to appreciate this negative consequence of ideology. We all know organizations with strong cultures that, like that proverbial bird, flew in ever diminishing circles until they disappeared up their own rear ends!

Competition through Politics

If the centripetal force of ideology, ostensibly so constructive, turns out to have a negative consequence, then perhaps the centrifugal force of politics, ostensibly so destructive, may have a positive one.

Politics represents the force for competition in an organization, for conflict and confrontation. People pull apart for their own needs. "They" get in our way.

Politics can infuse any of the configurations or combinations, exacerbating contamination and cleavage. Indeed, both problems were characterized as intrinsically conflictive in the first place; the presence of politics for other reasons simply encourages them. The people behind the dominant force in a configuration—say, the accountants in a machine organization or the experts in a professional one—lord their power over everyone else, while those behind each of the opposing forces in a combination relish any opportunity to do battle with each other to gain advantage. Thus, in contrast to a machinelike Toyota pulling together is the Chrysler Iaccoca entered pulling apart; the ideology of an innovative Hewlett-Packard stands in contrast to the politics of a NASA during the *Challenger* tragedy; for every "distinctive" college there are other "destructive" ones.

Politics is generally a parochial force in organizations, encouraging people to pursue their own ends. Infusing the parts of an organization with the competitive force of politics only reinforces their tendency to fly off in different directions. At the limit, the organization dominated by politics goes out of control by *exploding.* Nothing remains at the core—no central direction or even set of concentrations and no integrating ideology, and therefore, no directed effort at efficiency or proficiency or innovation.

In this respect, politics may be a more natural force than ideology in organizations. That is to say, organizations left alone seem to pull apart rather more easily than they pull together. Getting a system of human beings to cooperate, on the other hand, seems to require continual effort on the part of a dedicated management.

Benefits of Competition

But we cannot dismiss politics as merely divisive. The constructive role that politics can play in an organization is suggested by the very problems of ideology. If pulling together discourages people from addressing fundamental change, then pulling apart may become the only way to ensure that happens.

Change is fundamental to an organization because it upsets the deeply rooted status quo. Most organizations have such a status quo, reinforced especially by the forces of efficiency, proficiency, and ideology, all designed to promote development within an established perspective. Thus, to achieve fundamental change in an organization, particularly one that has achieved configuration and more so when that is infused with ideology, generally requires challenge of the established forces, and that means politics. In the absence of entrepreneurial or intrapreneurial capabilities, and sometimes despite them, politics may be the only force available to stimulate the change. The organization must, in other words, pull apart before it can again pull together. Thus, it appears to be an inevitable fact of life in today's organizations that a great deal of the most significant change is driven, not by managerial insight or specialized expertise or ideological commitment, let alone the procedures of planning, but by political challenge.

I conclude that both politics and ideology can promote organizational effectiveness as well as undermine it. Ideology infused into an organization can be a force for revitalization, energizing the system and making its people more responsive. But that same ideology can also hinder fundamental change. Likewise, politics often impedes necessary change and wastes valuable resources. But it can also promote important change that may be available in no other way, by enabling those who realize the need for it to challenge those who do not. There thus remains one last contradiction to reconcile in our story, between ideology and politics themselves.

Combining Cooperation and Competition

My final point is that the two catalytic forces of ideology and politics are themselves contradictory forces that have to be reconciled if an organization is to remain truly effective in the long run. Pulling together ideologically infuses life energy into an organization; pulling apart politically challenges the status quo; only by encouraging both can an organization sustain its viability. The centripetal force of ideology must contain and in turn be contained by the centrifugal force of politics. That is how an organization can keep itself from imploding or exploding —from isolating itself, on one hand, and going off in all directions, on the other. Moreover, maintaining a balance between these two forces—in their own form of combination—can discourage the other forces from going out of control. Ideology helps secondary forces to contain a dominant one; politics encourages them to challenge it. All of this—politics tempering the insularity of ideology, ideology restraining the divisiveness of politics, and both helping to limit the destructive power of the other forces—is somewhat reminiscent of that old children's game (with extended rules!): paper (ideology) covers scissors (politics) and can also help cover rocks (the force for efficiency), while scissors cut paper and can even wedge rocks out of their resting places.

Let me turn one last time to the arrows of the pentagon to illustrate. Imagine first the diverging arrows of competition contained within the converging circle of cooperation. Issues are debated and people are challenged, but only within the existing culture. The two achieve an equilibrium, as in the case of those Talmudic scholars who fight furiously with each other over the interpretation of every word in their ancient books yet close ranks to present a united front to the outside world. Is that not the very behavior we find in some of our most effective business corporations, IBM among others? Or reverse the relationship and put the arrows pulling apart outside those of the halo pulling together. Outside challenges keep a culture from closing it on itself.

Thus, I believe that only through achieving some kind of balance of these two catalytic forces can an organization maintain its effectiveness. That balance need not, however, be one of steady state. Quite the contrary, I believe it should constitute a dynamic equilibrium over time, to avoid constant tension between ideology and politics. Most of the time, to be preferred is the cooperative pulling together of ideology, contained by a healthy internal competition, so that the organization can pursue its established perspective with full vigor. But occasionally, when fundamental change becomes necessary, the organization has to be able to pull apart vigorously through the competitive force of politics. That seems to be the best combination of these two forces.

COMPETENCE

To conclude, what makes an organization truly effective? Two views tend to dominate much of the current management literature. I like to call them "Peterian" and "Porterian." Tom Peters implores managers to "stick to their knitting" and to be "hands on, value driven," among other best ways, while Michael Porter insists that they use competitive analysis to choose strategic positions that best match the characteristics of their industries. To Porter, effectiveness resides in strategy, while to Peters it is the operations that count—executing any strategy with excellence.

While agreeing that being effective depends on doing the right thing as well as doing things right, as Peter Drucker put it years ago, I believe we have to probe more deeply to find out what really makes an organization truly effective. We need to understand what takes it to a viable strategy in the first place, what makes it excellent there, and how some organizations are able to sustain viability and excellence in the face of change.

Let me close the reading by summarizing five increasingly developed views of organizational effectiveness.

Convergence: First is the *convergence* hypothesis. "One best way" is its motto, the single lens its image. There is a proper way to view, and so to design, an organization. This is usually associated with the machine form. A good structure is one with a rigid hierarchy of authority, with spans of control no greater than six, with heavy use of strategic planning, MIS, and whatever else happens to be in the current fashion of the rationalizers. In *In Search of Excellence,* in contrast, Peters and Waterman argued that ideology was the key to an organization's success. While we cannot dismiss this hypothesis—sometimes there *are* proper things to do in most if not all organizations—we must take issue with its general thrust. Society has paid an enormous price for "one best way" thinking over the course of this century, on the part of all its organizations that have been drawn into using what is fashionable rather than functional. We need to look beyond the obvious, beyond the convergence hypothesis.

Congruence: Beyond convergence is the *congruence* hypothesis, "it all depends" being its motto, the buffet table its image. Introduced in organization theory in the 1960s, it suggests that running an organization is like choosing dinner from such a table—a little bit of this, a little bit of that, all selected according to specific needs. Organizational effectiveness thus becomes a question of matching a given set of internal attributes, treated as a kind of portfolio, with various situational factors. The congruence hypothesis has certainly been an improvement, but like a dinner plate stacked with an old assortment of foods, it has not been good enough.

Configuration: And so the *configuration* hypothesis was introduced. "Getting it all together" is its motto, the jigsaw puzzle its image, the lumpers its champions. Design your organization as you would do a jigsaw puzzle, fitting all the pieces together to create a coherent, harmonious picture. There is certainly reason to believe that organizations succeed in good part because they are consistent in what they do; they are certainly easier to manage that way. But, as we have seen, configuration has its limitations too.

Contradiction: While the lumpers may like the configuration hypothesis, splitters prefer the *contradiction* hypothesis. Manage the dialectic, the dynamic tension, is their call, perhaps "to each his own" their motto, the tug of war their image. They point to the common occurrence of combinations and conversions, where organizations are forced to manage contradictory forces. This is an important hypothesis, together with that of configuration (in their own dynamic tension) certainly an important clue to organizational effectiveness. But still it is not sufficient.

Creation: The truly great organization transcends all of the foregoing while building on it to achieve something more. It respects the *creation* hypothesis. Creativity is its forte, "understand your inner nature" is its motto, LEGO its image. The most interesting organizations live at the edges, far from the logic of conventional organizations, where as Raphael (1976:5–6) has pointed out in biology (for example, between the sea and the land, or at the forest's edge), the richest, most varied, and most interesting forms of life can be found. These organizations invent novel approaches that solve festering problems and so provide all of us with new ways to deal with our world of organizations.

• CONVERGENCE AND UPHEAVAL: MANAGING THE UNSTEADY PACE OF ORGANIZATIONAL EVOLUTION*

By Michael L. Tushman, William H. Newman, and Elaine Romanelli

A snug fit of external opportunity, company strategy, and internal structure is a hallmark of successful companies. The real test of executive leadership, however, is in maintaining this alignment in the face of changing competitive conditions.

Consider the Polaroid or Caterpillar corporations. Both firms virtually dominated their respective industries for decades, only to be caught off guard by major environmental changes. The same strategic and organizational factors which were so effective for decades became the seeds of complacency and organization decline.

Recent studies of companies over long periods show that the most successful firms maintain a workable equilibrium for several years (or decades), but are also able to initiate and carry out sharp, widespread changes (referred to here as reorientations) when their environments shift. Such upheaval may bring renewed vigor to the enterprise. Less successful firms, on the other hand, get stuck in a particular pattern. The leaders of these firms either do not see the need for reorientation or they are unable to carry through the necessary frame-breaking changes. While not all reorientations succeed, those organizations which do not initiate reorientations as environments shift underperform.

This reading focuses on reasons why for long periods most companies make only incremental changes, and why they then need to make painful, discontin-

---

* Originally published in the *California Management Review* (Fall 1986). Copyright © 1986 by The Regents of the University of California. Reprinted with deletions by permission of the *Review.*

uous, system-wide shifts. We are particularly concerned with the role of executive leadership in managing this pattern of convergence punctuated by upheaval. . . .

The task of managing incremental change, or convergence, differs sharply from managing frame-breaking change. Incremental change is compatible with the existing structure of a company and is reinforced over a period of years. In contrast, frame-breaking change is abrupt, painful to participants, and often resisted by the old guard. Forging these new strategy-structure-people-process consistencies and laying the basis for the next period of incremental change calls for distinctive skills.

Because the future health, and even survival, of a company or business unit is at stake, we need to take a closer look at the nature and consequences of convergent change and of differences imposed by frame-breaking change. We need to explore when and why these painful and risky revolutions interrupt previously successful patterns, and whether these discontinuities can be avoided and/or initiated prior to crisis. Finally, we need to examine what managers can and should do to guide their organizations through periods of convergence and upheaval over time. . . .

The following discussion is based on the history of companies in many different industries, different countries, both large and small organizations, and organizations in various stages of their product class's life-cycle. We are dealing with a widespread phenomenon—not just a few dramatic sequences. Our research strongly suggests that the convergence/upheaval pattern occurs within departments at the business-unit level . . . and at the corporate level of analysis. . . . The problem of managing both convergent periods and upheaval is not just for the CEO, but necessarily involves general managers as well as functional managers.

PATTERNS IN ORGANIZATIONAL EVOLUTION: CONVERGENCE AND UPHEAVAL

Building on Strength: Periods of Convergence

Successful companies wisely stick to what works well. . . .

. . . convergence starts out with an effective dovetailing of strategy, structure, people, and processes. . . . The formal system includes decisions about grouping and linking resources as well as planning and control systems, rewards and evaluation procedures, and human resource management systems. The informal system includes core values, beliefs, norms, communication patterns, and actual decision-making and conflict resolution patterns. It is the whole fabric of structure, systems, people, and processes which must be suited to company strategy (Nadler and Tuchman, 1986).

As the fit between strategy, structure, people, and processes is never perfect, convergence is an ongoing process characterized by incremental change. Over time, in all companies studied, two types of converging changes were common: fine-tuning and incremental adaptations.

- *Converging change: Fine-tuning*—Even with good strategy-structure-process fits, well-run companies seek even better ways of exploiting (and defending) their missions. Such effort typically deals with one or more of the following:

  - *Refining* policies, methods, and procedures.
  - Creating *specialized units and linking mechanisms* to permit increased volume and increased attention to unit quality and cost.

- *Developing personnel* especially suited to the present strategy—through improved selection and training, and tailoring reward systems to match strategic thrusts.
- Fostering individual and group *commitments* to the company mission and to the excellence of one's own department.
- Promoting *confidence* in the accepted norms, beliefs, and myths.
- *Clarifying* established roles, power, status, dependencies, and allocation mechanism.

The fine-tuning fills out and elaborates the consistencies between strategy, structure, people, and processes. These incremental changes lead to an ever more interconnected (and therefore more stable) social system. Convergent periods fit the happy, stick-with-a-winner situations romanticized by Peters and Waterman (1982).

- *Converging change: Incremental adjustments to environmental shifts*—In addition to fine-tuning changes, minor shifts in the environment will call for some organizational response. Even the most conservative of organizations expect, even welcome, small changes which do not make too many waves.

A popular expression is that almost any organization can tolerate a "ten percent change." At any one time, only a few changes are being made; but these changes are still compatible with the prevailing structures, systems, and processes. Examples of such adjustments are an expansion in sales territory, a shift in emphasis among products in the product line, or improved processing technology in production.

The usual process of making changes of this sort is well known: wide acceptance of the need for change, openness to possible alternatives, objective examination of the pros and cons of each plausible alternative, participation of those directly affected in the preceding analysis, a market test or pilot operation where feasible, time to learn the new activities, established role models, known rewards for positive success, evaluation, and refinement.

The role of executive leadership during convergent periods is to reemphasize mission and core values and to delegate incremental decisions to middle-level managers. Note that the uncertainty created for people affected by such changes is well within tolerable limits. Opportunity is provided to anticipate and learn what is new, while most features of the structure remain unchanged.

The overall system adapts, but it is not transformed.

Converging Change: Some Consequences: For those companies whose strategies fit environmental conditions, convergence brings about better and better effectiveness. Incremental change is relatively easy to implement and ever more optimizes the consistencies between strategy, structure, people, and processes. At AT&T, for example, the period between 1913 and 1980 was one of ever more incremental change to further bolster the "Ma Bell" culture, systems, and structure all in service of developing the telephone network.

Convergent periods are, however, a double-edged sword. As organizations grow and become more successful, they develop internal forces for stability. Organization structures and systems become so interlinked that they only allow compatible changes. Further, over time, employees develop habits, patterned behaviors begin to take on values (e.g., "service is good"), and employees develop a sense of competence in knowing how to get work done within the system. These self-reinforcing patterns of behavior, norms, and values contribute to increased organizational momentum and complacency and, over time, to a sense of organizational history. This organizational history—epitomized by common stories, heroes, and standards—specifies "how we work here" and "what we hold important here."

This organizational momentum is profoundly functional as long as the organization's strategy is appropriate. The Ma Bell ... culture, structure, and systems—and associated internal momentum—were critical to [the] organization's success. However, if (and when) strategy must change, this momentum cuts the other way. Organizational history is a source of tradition, precedent, and pride which are, in turn, anchors to the past. A proud history often restricts vigilant problem solving and may be a source of resistance to change.

When faced with environmental threat, organizations with strong momentum

- may not register the threat due to organization complacency and/or stunted external vigilance (e.g., the automobile or steel industries), or

- if the threat is recognized, the response is frequently heightened conformity to the status quo and/or increased commitment to "what we do best."

For example, the response of dominant firms to technological threat is frequently increased commitment to the obsolete technology (e.g., telegraph/telephone; vacuum tube/transistor; core/semiconductor memory). A paradoxical result of long periods of success may be heightened organizational complacency, decreased organizational flexibility, and a stunted ability to learn.

Converging change is a double-edged sword. Those very social and technical consistencies which are key sources of success may also be the seeds of failure if environments change. The longer the convergent periods, the greater these internal forces for stability. This momentum seems to be particularly accentuated in those most successful firms in a product class ... in historically regulated organizations ... or in organizations that have been traditionally shielded from competition. ...

On Frame-Breaking Change

Forces Leading to Frame-Breaking Change: What, then, leads to frame-breaking change? Why defy tradition? Simply stated, frame-breaking change occurs in response to or, better yet, in anticipation of major environmental changes—changes which require more than incremental adjustments. The need for discontinuous change springs from one or a combination of the following:

- *Industry discontinuities*—Sharp changes in legal, political, or technological conditions shift the basis of competition within industries. *Deregulation* has dramatically transformed the financial services and airlines industries. *Substitute product technologies* ... or *substitute process technologies* ... may transform the bases of competition within industries. Similarly, the emergence of industry standards, or *dominant designs* (such as the DC-3, IBM 360, or PDP-8) signal a shift in competition away from product innovation and towards increased process innovation. Finally, *major economic changes* (e.g., oil crises) and *legal shifts* (e.g., patent protection in biotechnology or trade/regulator barriers in pharmaceuticals or cigarettes) also directly affect bases of competition.

- *Product life-cycle shifts*—Over the course of a product class life cycle, different strategies are appropriate. In the emergence phase of a product class, competition is based on product innovation and performance, where in the maturity stage, competition centers on cost, volume, and efficiency. Shifts in patterns of demand alter key factors for success. For example, the demand and nature of competition for mini-computers, cellular telephones, wide-body aircraft, and bowling alley equipment was transformed as these products gained acceptance and their product classes evolved. Powerful international competition may compound these forces.

• *Internal company dynamics*—Entwined with these external forces are breaking points within the firm. Sheer size may require a basically new management design. For example, few inventor-entrepreneurs can tolerate the formality that is linked with large volume. . . . Key people die. Family investors may become more concerned with their inheritance taxes than with company development. Revised corporate portfolio strategy may sharply alter the role and resources assigned to business units or functional areas. Such pressures especially when coupled with external changes, may trigger frame-breaking change.

Scope of Frame-Breaking Change: Frame-breaking change is driven by shifts in business strategy. As strategy shifts so too must structure, people, and organizational processes. Quite unlike convergent change, frame-breaking reforms involve discontinuous changes throughout the organization. These bursts of change do not reinforce the existing system and are implemented rapidly. . . . Frame-breaking changes are revolutionary changes *of* the system as opposed to incremental changes *in* the system.

The following features are usually involved in frame-breaking change:

• *Reformed mission and core values*—A strategy shift involves a new definition of company mission. Entering or withdrawing from an industry may be involved; at least the way the company expects to be outstanding is altered. . . .

• *Altered power and status*—Frame-breaking change always alters the distribution of power. Some groups lose in the shift while others gain. . . . These dramatically altered power distributions reflect shifts in bases of competition and resource allocation. A new strategy must be backed up with a shift in the balance of power and status.

• *Reorganization*—A new strategy requires a modification in structure, systems, and procedures. As strategic requirements shift, so too must the choice of organization form. A new direction calls for added activity in some areas and less in others. Changes in structure and systems are means to ensure that this reallocation of effort takes place. New structures and revised roles deliberately break business-as-usual behavior.

• *Revised interaction patterns*—The way people in the organization work together has to adapt during frame-breaking change. As strategy is different, new procedures, work flows, communication networks, and decision-making patterns must be established. With these changes in work flows and procedures must also come revised norms, informal decision-making/conflict-resolution procedures, and informal roles.

• *New executives*—Frame-breaking change also involves new executives, usually brought in from outside the organization (or business unit) and placed in key managerial positions. Commitment to the new mission, energy to overcome prevailing inertia, and freedom from prior obligations are all needed to refocus the organization. A few exceptional members of the old guard may attempt to make this shift, but habits and expectations of their associations are difficult to break. New executives are most likely to provide both the necessary drive and an enhanced set of skills more appropriate for the new strategy. While the overall number of executive changes is usually relatively small, these new executives have substantial symbolic and substantive effects on the organization. . . .

Why All at Once?: Frame-breaking change is revolutionary in that the shifts reshape the entire nature of the organization. Those more effective examples of frame-breaking change were implemented rapidly. . . . It appears that a piecemeal approach to frame-breaking changes gets bogged down in politics, individual resistance to change, and organizational inertia. . . . Frame-breaking change requires discontinuous shifts in strategy, structure, people, and processes concurrently—or at least in a short period of time. Reasons for rapid, simultaneous implementation include:

- *Synergy* within the new structure can be a powerful aid. New executives with a fresh mission, working in a redesigned organization with revised norms and values, backed up with power and status, provide strong reinforcement. The pieces of the revitalized organization pull together, as opposed to piecemeal change where one part of the new organization is out of synch with the old organization.

- *Pockets of resistance* have a chance to grow and develop when frame-breaking change is implemented slowly. The new mission, shifts in organization, and other frame-breaking changes upset the comfortable routines and precedent. Resistance to such fundamental change is natural. If frame-breaking change is implemented slowly, then individuals have a greater opportunity to undermine the changes and organizational inertia works to further stifle fundamental change.

- Typically, there is a *pent-up need for change*. During convergent periods, basic adjustments are postponed. Boat rocking is discouraged. Once constraints are relaxed, a variety of desirable improvements press for attention. The exhilaration and momentum of a fresh effort (and new team) make difficult moves more acceptable. Change is in fashion.

- Frame-breaking change is an inherently *risky and uncertain venture*. The longer the implementation period, the greater the period of uncertainty and instability. The most effective frame-breaking changes initiate the new strategy, structure, processes, and systems rapidly and begin the next period of stability and convergent change. The sooner fundamental uncertainty is removed, the better the chances of organizational survival and growth. While the pacing of change is important, the overall time to implement frame-breaking change will be contingent on the size and age of the organization.

Patterns in Organization Evolution: This historical approach to organization evolution focuses on convergent periods punctuated by reorientation—discontinuous, organizationwide upheavals. The most effective firms take advantage of relatively long convergent periods. These periods of incremental change build on and take advantage of organization inertia. Frame-breaking change is quite dysfunctional if the organization is successful and the environment is stable. If, however, the organization is performing poorly and/or if the environment changes substantially, frame-breaking change is the only way to realign the organization with its competitive environment. Not all reorientations will be successful. . . . However, inaction in the face of performance crisis and/or environmental shifts is a certain recipe for failure.

Because reorientations are so disruptive and fraught with uncertainty, the more rapidly they are implemented, the more quickly the organization can reap the benefits of the following convergent period. High-performing firms initiate reorientations when environmental conditions shift and implement these reorientations rapidly. . . . Low-performing organizations either do not reorient or reorient all the time as they root around to find an effective alignment with environmental conditions. . . .

EXECUTIVE LEADERSHIP AND ORGANIZATION EVOLUTION

Executive leadership plays a key role in reinforcing systemwide momentum during convergent periods and in initiating and implementing bursts of change that characterize strategic reorientations. The nature of the leadership task differs sharply during these contrasting periods of organization evolution.

During convergent periods, the executive team focuses on *maintaining* congruence and fit within the organization. Because strategy, structure, processes, and systems are fundamentally sound, the myriad of incremental substantive decisions can be delegated to middle-level management, where direct expertise and information resides. The key role for executive leadership during convergent periods is to reemphasize strategy, mission, and core values and to keep a vigilant eye on external opportunities and/or threats.

Frame-breaking change, however, requires direct executive involvement in all aspects of the change. Given the enormity of the change and inherent internal forces for stability, executive leadership must be involved in the specification of strategy, structure, people, and organizational processes *and* in the development of implementation plans. . . .

The most effective executives in our studies foresaw the need for major change. They recognized the external threats and opportunities, and took bold steps to deal with them. . . . Indeed, by acting before being forced to do so, they had more time to plan their transitions.

Such visionary executive teams are the exceptions. Most frame-breaking change is postponed until a financial crisis forces drastic action. The momentum, and frequently the success, of convergent periods breeds reluctance to change. . . .

. . . most frame-breaking upheavals are managed by executives brought in from outside the company. The Columbia research program finds that externally recruited executives are more than three times more likely to initiate frame-breaking change than existing executive teams. Frame-breaking change was coupled with CEO succession in more than 80% of the cases. . . .

There are several reasons why a fresh set of executives are typically used in company transformations. The new executive team brings different skills and a fresh perspective. Often they arrive with a strong belief in the new mission. Moreover, they are unfettered by prior commitments linked to the status quo; instead, this new top team symbolizes the need for change. Excitement of a new challenge adds to the energy devoted to it.

We should note that many of the executives who could not, or would not, implement frame-breaking change went on to be quite successful in other organizations. . . . The stimulation of a fresh start and of jobs matched to personal competence applies to individuals as well as to organizations.

Although typical patterns for the when and who of frame-breaking change are clear—wait for a financial crisis and then bring in an outsider, along with a revised executive team, to revamp the company—this is clearly less than satisfactory for a particular organization. Clearly, some companies benefit from transforming themselves before a crisis forces them to do so, and a few exceptional executives have the vision and drive to reorient a business which they nurtured during its preceding period of convergence. The vital tasks are to manage incremental change during convergent periods; to have the vision to initiate and implement frame-breaking change prior to the competition; and to mobilize an executive which can initiate and implement both kinds of change.

CONCLUSION

. . . Managers should anticipate that when environments change sharply

- Frame-breaking change cannot be avoided. These discontinuous organizational changes will either be made proactively or initiated under crisis/turnaround conditions.
- Discontinuous changes need to be made in strategy, structure, people, and processes concurrently. Tentative change runs the risk of being smothered by individual, group, and organizational inertia.
- Frame-breaking change requires direct executive involvement in all aspects of the change, usually bolstered with new executives from outside the organization.
- There are no patterns in the sequence of frame-breaking changes, and not all strategies will be effective. Strategy and, in turn, structure, systems, and processes must meet industry-specific competitive issues.

Finally, our historical analysis of organizations highlights the following issues for executive leadership:

- Need to manage for balance, consistency, or fit during convergent period.
- Need to be vigilant for environmental shifts in order to anticipate the need for frame-breaking change.
- Need to manage effectively incremental as well as frame-breaking change.
- Need to build (or rebuild) a top team to help initiate and implement frame-breaking change.
- Need to develop core values which can be used as an anchor as organizations evolve through frame-breaking changes (e.g., IBM, Hewlett-Packard).
- Need to develop and use organizational history as a way to infuse pride in an organization's past and for its future.
- Need to bolster technical, social, and conceptual skills with visionary skills. Visionary skills add energy, direction, and excitement so critical during frame-breaking change. . . .

• RESPONDING TO CRISIS*

BY WILLIAM H. STARBUCK, ARENT GREVE, AND BO L. T. HEDBERG

For nearly 50 years, Facit was regarded as a successful manufacturer of business machines and office furnishings. Facit grew until it operated factories in twenty cities and it maintained sales units in fifteen countries. Employment reached

---

* Originally published in the *Journal of Business Administration* (Spring 1978). Reprinted with deletions by permission of the *Journal of Business Administration*.

14,000. Suddenly, this success metamorphosed into impending disaster. For three consecutive years, gross profits were negative and employment and sales declined. Plants were closed or sold. Again and again, top managers were replaced and the managerial hierarchy was reorganized. Consultants were called in: they recommended that more operations should be closed and more employees should be fired. But after numerous meetings, the top managers could not decide whether to do what the consultants recommended. . . .

Facit . . . exemplifies organizations which encounter crises. Crises are times of danger, times when some actions lead toward organizational failure. . . .

Based on several case studies of organizations facing crises, this article explains what makes some organizations especially prone to encounter crises, it describes how organizations typically react to crises, and it prescribes how organizations ought to cope with crises.

WHY DO CRISES OCCUR?

One initial conjecture was that crises originate as threatening events in organizations' environments. A competing conjecture was that crises originate from defects within organizations themselves. Analyses of actual crises suggest that both conjectures are partly true and both are partly false. Organizations facing crises do perceive the crises as having originated in their environments. For example, Facit's top managers attributed many difficulties to temporary depressions of the firm's economic environment, and they often complained about the fierceness of market competition. At first, Facit's top managers thought that electronic calculators would replace mechanical calculators only very gradually; later, they saw electronic calculators as a technological revolution that was progressing too quickly for Facit to adapt to it (Starbuck and Hedberg, 1977).

And it was, in fact, true that national economic growth was sometimes faster and sometimes slower. There were indeed competing firms that were wooing Facit's customers. Electronic calculators actually did challenge and ultimately replace mechanical calculators. So the observations of Facit's top managers had bases in reality. But one would have to be quite gullible to accept such reasons as completely explaining Facit's crises.

Organizations' perceptions are never totally accurate. Organizations decide, sometimes explicitly but often implicitly, to observe some aspects of their environments and to ignore other aspects. They also interpret, in terms of their current goals, methods and competences, what they do observe. Such interpretation is evident in the statements about electronic calculators by Facit's top managers.

There are special reasons to question the perceptions of the top managers in organizations facing crises. If crises result partly from defects within organizations, these defects could distort the organizations' perceptions. Because distorted perceptions appear in all organizations, it may be overstatement to say that distorted perceptions are alone sufficient to cause crises. However, perceptual distortions do seem to contribute to crises by leading organizations to take no actions or inappropriate actions. . . .

Defects in organizations not only affect perceptions; they also affect the realities that are there to be perceived. Organizational defects are translated into environmental realities when organizations choose their immediate environments—by choosing suppliers, product characteristics, technologies or geographic locations—or when they manipulate their environments—by advertising, training employees, conducting research or negotiating cooperative agreements (Starbuck, 1976). . . .

Talk of organizational defects can, however, easily create misimpressions about the differences between those organizations which encounter crises and those which avoid crises. The organizations which encounter crises do not have qualitatively unusual characteristics, and they are not fundamentally abnormal. Probably the great majority of organizations have the potential to work themselves into crises, and the processes which produce crises are substantially identical with the processes which produce successes (Hedberg et al., 1976).

LEARNING/PROGRAMMING

These ironies arise from how organizations learn and from how they use their successes. The key process for organizational learning is programming: when organizations observe that certain activities appear to succeed, they crystallize these activities as standardized programs. These programs are built into the formalized roles assigned to organizations' members. Both programs and roles make activities consistent across different people and across different times. Programs generate activities that resemble those leading to good results in the past, and they do so efficiently. Organizations respond quickly to most environmental events because these events activate previously learned programs. Programs also loosen organizations' connections to their environments. Because environmental events fall into equivalence classes according to which programs they activate, organizations fail to perceive many of the small differences among environmental events. Because organizations indoctrinate their members and train them to perform roles, organizations fail to accommodate or utilize many of the differences among members who are recruited at various times in diverse locations (Nystrom et al., 1976).

Programming often facilitates success, and success always fosters programming. Success also produces slack resources and opportunities for buffering—both of which allow organizations to loosen their connections to their environments (Cyert and March, 1963; Thompson, 1967). Customers are clustered into equivalence classes, and products are standardized. Raw materials and products are stored in inventories, work activities are smoothed, and work schedules are stretched out into the future. Programs and roles are added rather frequently and discarded less frequently. Technologies are frozen by means of large capital investments. . . .

Programming, buffering, and slack resources are tools that cut on two sides. On one side, these tools enable organizations to act autonomously—to choose among alternative environments, to take risks, to experiment, to construct new environmental alternatives—and autonomous actions are generally prerequisites for outstanding successes. But on the other side, these tools render organizations less sensitive to environmental events. Organizations become less able to perceive what is happening, so they fantasize about their environments, and it may happen that realities intrude only occasionally and marginally on these fantasies. Organizations also become less able to respond to the environmental events they do perceive. . . .

WHAT REACTIONS DO CRISES EVOKE?

Explaining Crises Away

It seems that conventional accounting reports, and the ideology asserting that such reports should be bases for action, are among organizations' major liabilities. The more seriously organizations attend to their accounting reports, the more likely they are to encounter crises, and the more difficulty they have coping with crises.

Accounting reports are intentionally historical: at best they indicate what happened during the previous quarter, and even recent reports are strongly influenced by purchases of goods and equipment dating back many years and by inventories of unsalable products and obsolete components. The formats of accounting reports change very slowly. Accounting reports also intentionally focus upon formalized measures of well observed phenomena; the measures are always numerical, the importances of phenomena are appraised in monetary units, and the observations are programmatic. Much of the content in every report is ritualized irrelevance.

... The organizations which take their accounting reports very seriously are assuming that their worlds change slowly—that precedents are relevant to today's actions, that tomorrow's environments will look much like yesterday's, that current programs and methods are only slightly faulty at most (Hedberg and Jönsson, 1978; Thompson, 1967). Such organizations devote few resources to monitoring and interpreting unexpected environmental events; they do not tolerate redundant, ostensibly inessential activities; they guide their development by means of systematic long-range planning. ...

All of these characteristics make it difficult for organizations to see unanticipated threats and opportunities. Many unanticipated events are never perceived at all; others are only perceived after they have been developing for some time. Then when unanticipated events are perceived, these characteristics introduce perceptual errors. One consequence is that organizations overlook the earliest signs that crises are developing. ...

Those organizations which are strongly wedded to their pasts, naturally enough, fear rapid changes. They expect abrupt changes to produce undesirable consequences. This logic is often reversed when undesirable events occur: the undesirable events are hypothesized to be the consequences of rapid changes. The early signs of crises are attributed to the organizations' injudicious efforts to change—new markets, capital investments, inexperienced personnel, or product innovations. Such interpretations imply that no remedies are needed beyond prudent moderation, because performances will improve automatically as operations stabilize.

The idea that organizations ought to be stable structures also fosters another rationalization for early signs of crises—that poor performances result from transient environmental pressures such as economic recessions, seasonal variations in consumption, or competitors' foolish maneuvers. This rationale implies that no major strategic reorientations are called for; to the contrary, the current strategic experiments ought to terminate. Organizations decide that temporary belt-tightening is needed, together with some centralization of control and restraints on wasteful entrepreneurial ventures, but these are portrayed as beneficial changes that focus attention on what is essential (Beer, 1974; Nystrom et al., 1976; Thompson, 1967). ...

... Managers who have helped to formulate strategies ... resist strategic reorientations in order to retain power and status, and they try to persuade themselves and others that their strategies are appropriate ... [they] may launch propaganda campaigns that deny the existence of crises. These propaganda efforts always include distortions of accounting reports: accounting periods are lengthened, depreciation charges are suspended, gains from sales or reevaluations of assets are included with operating profits. ...

Facit's top managers made numerous efforts to persuade stockholders, employees, and the public that no crises existed, that the crisis was not serious, or that the crisis had ended. When poor performance first intruded into Facit's accounting reports, the top managers explained that this poor performance was the temporary product of currency devaluations and fierce competition. "Facit is well equipped to meet future competition. . . . Improvement is underway, but has not affected this year's outcome." Later, as the crisis deepened, Facit's managing director was replaced several times: each new managing director reported sadly that the situation was actually worse than his predecessor had publicly admitted, but he was happy to be able to announce that the nadir had been passed and the future looked rosy. Again and again, Facit's top managers announced that their firm was in sound condition and that improved performances were imminent; the chairman of the board and the managing director made such announcements even while they were secretly negotiating to sell the firm. After two years of serious difficulties, when plants were being closed, when hundreds of employees were losing their jobs, and when the top managers were privately in despair, the top managers announced that they intended to expand Facit's product line by sixty percent (Starbuck and Hedberg, 1977). . . .

Living in Collapsing Palaces

The organizations which encounter crises resemble palaces perched on mountaintops that are crumbling from erosion. Like palaces, these organizations are rigid, cohesive structures that integrate elegant components. Although their flawless harmonies make organizational palaces look completely rational—indeed, beautiful —to observers who are inside them, observers standing outside can see that the beauty and harmony rest upon eroding grounds.

Organizational palaces are rigid because their components mesh so snugly and reinforce their neighbors. Perceptions, goals, capabilities, methods, personnel, products, and capital equipment are like stone blocks and wooden beams that interlock and brace each other. There are no chinks, no gaps, and no protruding beams because careful reason has guided every expansion and remodeling. Rationality is solidified in integrated forms that are very difficult to move: the components which blend smoothly in one arrangement fit badly in another, components which mesh tightly must be moved simultaneously, and movements fracture tight junctions. So the inhabitants' first reactions to crises are to maintain their palaces intact—they shore up shaky foundations, strengthen points of stress, and patch up cracks—and their palaces remain sitting beautifully on eroding mountaintops.

However, shoring up affords only temporary remedies against crumbling mountains, and eventually, the palaces themselves start falling apart. People begin to see that the top managers have been making faulty predictions: doubts arise that the top managers know how to cope with the crises, and the top managers usually end up looking like incompetent liars. Idealism and commitments to organizational goals fade; cynicism and opportunism grow; uncertainty escalates (Jönsson and Lundin, 1977; Kahn et al., 1964; Vickers, 1959). But cuts and reorganizations stir up power struggles that undermine cooperation. . . .

Two or three years after Facit's crisis became obvious, the top managers reached a state of paralysis. The managerial hierarchy had been reorganized repeatedly. Several small plants had been closed, and the main office-furnishings plant had been sold. But the situation had continued to get worse and worse. . . .

At this point, Electrolux bought Facit and achieved a dramatic turnaround. Eight-hundred employees were laid off right away, but these people were being rehired within three months. It was discovered that Facit possessed a large, unfilled demand for typewriters: a mechanical-calculator plant was converted to typewriters, and the typewriter plants were expanded The demand for office furnishings was also found to exceed production capacity. Facit's research had developed electronic calculators, small computers, and computer terminals which had never been marketed aggressively; substantial demands existed for these products. During the second year after Electrolux stepped in, Facit's employment went up 10%, production increased 25%, and Facit earned a profit.

Facit's turnaround was made possible by the disintegration that preceded it. The impediments to learning usually grow very strong in organizations. Because organizations are intricate, they fear that changes would produce unforeseen disadvantages. Because organizations are logically integrated, they expect changes to initiate cascades of further changes. Because organizations are rational, they buttress their current programs and roles with justifying analyses. These impediments to learning grow strongest in the organizational palaces that emphasize rational analyses, reliable information, and logical consistency. Palaces have to be taken apart before they can be moved to new locations, and organizations have to unlearn what they now know before they can learn new knowledge. Organizations have to lose confidence in their old leaders before they will listen to new leaders. Organizations have to abandon their old goals before they will adopt new goals. Organizations have to reject their perceptual filters before they will notice events they previously overlooked. Organizations have to see that their old methods do not work before they will invent and use new methods (Cyert and March, 1963; Hedberg, 1981; Nystrom et al., 1976).

Unfortunately, crisis-ridden organizations may learn that their old methods do not work, and yet they may not learn new methods which do work.

HOW TO COPE WITH CRISES

Crises are dangerous, by definition. After crises have fully developed, organizations face serious risks of failure. To eliminate these risks is often difficult, and the remedies bring pain to some people. Consequently, the best way to cope with crises is to evade them.

Avoiding Excesses

. . . case studies suggest that many organizations adhere too strictly to those prescriptions which favor rationality, reliability, formality, logical consistency, planning, agreement, stability, hierarchical control and efficiency. All of these properties can bring benefits when they appear in moderation: organizations need some rationality, some formality, some stability, and so on. But excessive emphases on these properties turn organizations into palaces—palaces on eroding mountaintops. Organizations also need moderate amounts of irrationality, unreliability, informality, inconsistency, spontaneity, dissension, instability, delegation of responsibility, and inefficiency. These properties help to keep perceptions sharp, they disrupt complacency, and they nurture experimentation and evolutionary change (Hedberg et al., 1976; Miller and Mintzberg, 1974).

One sensible operating rule is that whenever organizations adopt one prescription, they should adopt a second prescription which contradicts the first. Contradictory prescriptions remind organizations that each prescription is a misleading oversimplification that ought not be carried to excess. For example, organizations should work toward consensus, but they should also encourage dissenters to speak out; organizations should try to exploit their strategic strengths, but they should also try to eliminate their strategic weaknesses; organizations should formulate plans, but they should also take advantage of unforeseen opportunities and they should combat unforeseen threats. It is as if each prescription   425

presses down one pan of a balance: matched pairs of prescriptions can offset each   _____
other and keep a balance level. . . .

But balancing prescriptions is a defensive tactic that cannot rescue the organizations which already face crises. These organizations have been defending themselves—unsuccessfully—too long; they need to go on the offensive. The remainder of this article prescribes how organizations can terminate their crises and begin to rebuild themselves in viable forms.

Replacing Top Managers

When Electrolux took over Facit, it promptly fired all of Facit's top managers. This is exactly what Electrolux should have done. If Electrolux had not taken such drastic action, its intervention would probably have failed. . . .

Indiscriminate replacements of entire groups of top managers are evidently essential to bringing organizations out of crises. The veteran top managers ought to be replaced even if they are all competent people who are trying their best and even if the newcomers have no more ability, and less direct expertise, than the veterans. . . .

[In crises,] remedies are needed urgently. Perhaps the greatest need is for dramatic acts symbolizing the end of disintegration and the beginning of regeneration. Because propaganda and deceit have been rife, these symbolic acts have to be such that even skeptical observers can see they are sincere acts; and because the top managers represent both past strategies and past attempts to deceive, these symbolic acts have to punish the top managers. In addition, however, the organizations need new perceptions of reality, fresh strategic ideas, and revitalization. Since no one really knows what strategies will succeed, new strategies have to be discovered experimentally. Experimenting depends upon enthusiasm and willingness to take risks; people must have confidence their organizations can surmount new challenges and exploit discoveries. Experimenting also depends upon seeing aspects of reality which have been unseen and upon evaluating performances by criteria that differ from past criteria. . . .

. . . replacements of one or two top managers at a time are not enough. Such gradual replacements happen spontaneously while crisis-ridden organizations are disintegrating: if gradual replacements were sufficient to end crises, the crises would already have ended. But when top managers are replaced gradually, the newcomers are injected into ongoing, cohesive groups of veterans, and the newcomers exert little influence on these groups, whereas the groups exert much influence on the newcomers.

Group cohesion also impedes the veteran's own efforts to adopt remedies. Each member of a group is constrained by the other members' expectations, and cohesion draws these constraints tight. A group as a whole may bind itself to its current methods even though everyone in the group is individually ready to change; when a group includes one or two members who actively resist change, these resisters can control what happens. . . .

Rejecting Implicit Assumptions

One reason groups of top manages find change difficult is that many of the assumptions underlying their perceptions and behaviors are implicit ones. Explicit assumptions can be readily identified and discussed, so people can challenge these assumptions and perhaps alter them. But implicit assumptions may never be seen by the people who make them, and these unseen assumptions may persist indefinitely. . . .

Experimenting with Portfolios

. . . In order to escape from crises, organizations have to invest in new markets, new products, new technologies, new methods of operating, or new people. Diversification plays the same role in these investments as it does in other investments: expected returns are traded for protection against mistaken predictions. . . .

But crisis-ridden organizations find it difficult to pursue several alternatives simultaneously because they lack resources. Not many organizations start to develop alternatives while they are still [affluent]. . . .

Managing Ideology

Top managers are often the villains of crises. They are the real villains insofar as they steer their organizations into crises and insofar as they intensify crises by delaying actions or taking inappropriate actions. And they are symbolic villains who have to be replaced before crises end. But top managers are also the heroes when their organizations escape from crises. They receive the plaudits, and they largely deserve the plaudits because their actions have been the crucial ones.

Sometimes top managers contribute to escapes from crises by inventing new methods and strategies. Top managers have the best chance to do this effectively in small organizations . . . because small organizations do not make sharp demarcations among managers at different levels and they do not sharply distinguish managers from staff analysts. However, even in small organizations, the top managers should beware of relying on their own strategy-making skills. In large organizations where top management is a specialized occupation, it is generally a mistake for the top managers to act as strategy makers. . . .

. . . when top managers are occupied with strategy making, they are not doing the more important work which is their special responsibility: managing ideology. The low-level and middle managers do attend to ideological phenomena to some extent, but they focus their attentions upon visible, physical phenomena—the uses of machines, manual and clerical work, flows of materials, conferences, reports, planning documents such as schedules and blueprints, or workers' complaints. Top managers have the complementary responsibility: although they have to attend to visible, physical phenomena to some extent, they should concentrate their attentions on ideological phenomena such as morale, enthusiasm, beliefs, goals, values, and ideas. Managing ideology is very difficult because it is so indirect —like trying to steer a ship by describing the harbor toward which the ship should sail. But managing ideology is also very important because ideological phenomena exert such powerful effects upon the visible, physical phenomena.

Electrolux's turnaround of Facit was wrought almost entirely by managing ideology (Starbuck and Hedberg, 1977). Except for the replacements of top managers, Electrolux left Facit's organization largely alone. Electrolux did loan Facit approximately two million dollars so that actions would not have to be taken solely out of financial exigency, but this was a small sum in relation to the size of the company. What Electrolux did was to reconceptualize Facit and Facit's environment. Electronic calculators were no longer a technological revolution that was leaving Facit behind: Facit was making and selling electronic calculators. Typewriters and office furnishing became key product lines instead of sidelines to calculators. Competition stopped being a threat and became a stimulus. As Electrolux's managing director put it: "Hard competition is a challenge; there is no reason to withdraw." A newspaper remarked: "Although everything looks different today, the company is still more or less managed by the same people who were in charge of the company during the sequence of crises. It is now very difficult to find enough people to recruit for the factories. . . . All the present products emanate from the former Facit organization, but still, the situation has changed drastically." . . .

Facit . . . [is an organization that has] rediscovered the truth of an ancient, Chinese insight. The Chinese symbol for crisis combines two simpler symbols, the symbol for danger and the one for opportunity. Crises are times of danger, but they are also times of opportunity. . . .

● DESIGNING TURNAROUND STRATEGIES*

BY CHARLES W. HOFER

At some time in their history, most successful organizations suffer stagnation or decline in their performance. . . . Nevertheless, the Western ethic that "one must grow or die" causes psychological problems in such instances, much as the onset of middle age does in many individuals. . . .

This article will discuss turnarounds and turnaround strategies in business organizations. . . . [It will examine] turnarounds at the business-unit level. Its focus will be prescriptive rather than descriptive. Specifically, it will (1) analyze the nature of business-level turnaround situations, (2) discuss the types of turnaround strategies that are possible at this level, (3) present an analytical framework for deciding what type of turnaround strategy should be used in particular situations, and (4) discuss how to design and implement the various aspects of the indicated turnaround strategy.

THE NATURE OF TURNAROUND SITUATIONS

There are two factors that are important in describing turnaround situations. They are (1) the areas of organizational performance affected and (2) the time criticality of the turnaround situation.

In terms of organizational performance, the types of turnarounds that have been pursued and studied most frequently are those involving declines in organizational efficiency and/or profitability. Such declines usually have been measured by declining net income after taxes, although net cash flow and earnings per share have also been used.

The types of turnaround receiving next highest priority have been those involving stagnation or declines in organizational size or growth. The reason for such attention derives partly from the obvious link between size, growth, and net income, partly from the Western myth that one must grow or die, and partly from research findings linking profitability to relative market share. . . .

The third type of turnarounds to receive substantial management attention in the 1980s have been those involving poor organizational asset utilization. Such turnaround efforts have not received as much publicity or research attention as the

---

first two, however, primarily because they have been pursued by firms that are performing reasonably well in terms of profits and growth. Thus, poor performance with respect to asset utilization does not *appear* to pose the same threat to organizational or management survival as poor performance in the former areas. Furthermore, such asset utilization turnaround strategies usually have not been discussed by the firms pursuing them outside of their management councils, primarily for competitive reasons. Asset utilization turnarounds are likely to receive far greater attention from top management in the late 1980s and early 1990s than they have to date, however, because the combination of reasonable profits and poor asset utilization provides an open invitation to corporate takeover and greenmail specialists. . . . Despite (or perhaps because of) such threats, it is still likely that most asset utilization turnaround efforts will continue to be pursued with a low profile.

The second characteristic of turnaround situations that is important to the design of effective turnaround strategies is the time criticality of the firm's current situation. If there is imminent danger to survival, it is almost always necessary to make an operational response to the situation in the near term even though a strategic response may eventually follow. The reason for this is the lengthy time delay that usually exists between the taking of a strategic action and the response that accompanies it. When the threat to organizational survival is not imminent (i.e., when there is some time to respond in a variety of ways), then it is possible to "customize" the turnaround strategy to the specific situation involved.

TYPES OF TURNAROUND STRATEGIES

There are two broad types of turnaround strategies that may be followed at the business-unit level: strategic turnarounds and operating turnarounds.

Strategic turnarounds are of two types: those that involve a change in the organization's strategy for competing in the same business, and those that involve entering a new business or businesses. The latter involve questions of corporation portfolio strategy and will not be discussed further here. Strategies for saving the existing business may be further subdivided according to the nature of the competitive position change desired, and by the core skills and competitive weapons around which the strategy is built. Most such strategic turnarounds can be classified into one of three categories:

1. Those that seek to move to a larger strategic group in the industry involved
2. Those that seek to compete more effectively within the business' existing strategic group through the use of different (or substantially modified) competitive weapons and core skills
3. Those that seek to move to a smaller strategic group in the industry involved

In terms of competitive weapons and core skills, most strategic turnarounds involve switches in the ways firms seek to achieve differentiation or cost effectiveness, rather than switches from a differentiation strategy to a cost effectiveness strategy, or vice versa.

Operating turnarounds are usually one of four types, none of which involves changing the firm's business-level strategy. These are nonstrategic turnarounds that emphasize: (1) increased revenues, (2) decreased costs, (3) decreased assets, or (4) a balanced combination of two or more of the preceding options. It should be noted that these categories could also be used to describe strategic turnarounds. In strategic turnarounds, though, the focus is on the strategy changes sought, with the performance produced being a derivative of the strategy change. In operating turnarounds, by contrast, the focus is on the performance targets, and any actions that can achieve them are to be considered whether they make good long-run strategic sense or not.

In practice, the distinction between strategic and operating actions and turnarounds becomes blurred because actions that substantially decrease assets also often require a change in strategy to be most effective, and so on. The distinction is still relevant, however, because of the different priorities attached to short-term versus long-term actions and trade-offs in the two types of strategies.

SELECTING THE TYPE OF TURNAROUND STRATEGY TO BE FOLLOWED

In trying to decide what type of turnaround strategy should be pursued in a particular situation, three questions should be asked:

1. Is the business worth saving? More specifically, can the business be made profitable in the long run, or is it better to liquidate or divest it now? And, if it is worth saving, then,
2. What is the current operating health of the business?
3. What is the current strategic health of the business?

Although one occasionally encounters turnarounds that involve long time horizons, the vast majority of turnaround situations involve severe constraints on the time available for action. In fact, in most turnaround situations there is some imminent danger to the firm's survival. For this reason, one must first check the current operating health of the business as longer-term considerations will be irrelevant if the firm goes bankrupt in the near term. For this same reason, the first step in assessing a firm's current operating health is an analysis of its current financial condition. The purpose of such analysis is to determine: (1) how probable it is that the firm may go bankrupt in the near term, (2) how much time it has to make needed changes before it goes bankrupt, (3) the magnitude of the turnaround needed to avoid bankruptcy, and (4) the financial resources that could be raised in the short term to aid in the battle. Once this analysis is completed, similar analyses must be conducted of the firm's current market, technological, and production positions in order to complete the determination of its current operating health.

After these analyses are completed, the task of selecting the optimal type of turnaround strategy can begin. In general, such optimal strategies will depend on the firm's current operating and strategic health. . . . If both are weak, then liquidation is probably the best option unless the firm has no other businesses in which it could invest. In the latter case, a combined operating/strategic turnaround with very tight controls might be possible. With a weak operating position and a moderate or strong strategic position, an operating turnaround strategy is usually needed, although divesture is also reasonable if the corporation has other businesses in which it might invest.

When the business is strong operationally but weak strategically, then a strategic turnaround is almost always indicated although the firm may have a grace period in which to decide what it will do. When both operating and strategic health are strong, turnaround strategies are seldom needed unless it is to improve asset utilization, which may sometimes lag. The approach to use for improving asset utilization in such cases will normally depend on the firm's current strategic health.

Once a business has selected the type of broad turnaround strategy it should use, that is, strategic or operating, it then needs to select the more specific aspects of its turnaround strategy. The details of these action plans will depend, of course, on the exact nature of the industry in which the business competes and on its strengths and weaknesses vis-à-vis its major competitors in that industry.

THE NEED FOR NEW TOP MANAGEMENT

Before discussing any specific turnaround options, though, one nearly universal generalization must be made. It is the "fact" that almost all successful turnarounds require the replacement of the business's current top management. There is, of course, no law written in stone that says a firm's current top management team cannot supervise a successful turnaround. Usually, however, the old management has such a strong set of beliefs about how to run the business in question, many of which must be wrong for the current problems to have arisen, that the only way to get a new view of the situation is to bring in new top management. There will, of course, be some exceptions to this generalization as there are to all generalizations. Nonetheless, in over 95% of the cases cited by Kami and Ross (1973) and by Schendel, Patton, and Riggs (1976), a change in top management did accompany a successful turnaround. Thus, one can say that a successful turnaround will require, almost without exception, either a change in top management or a substantial change in the behavior of the existing management team. Moreover, increasing evidence from the experiences of General Electric and other similar multi-industry companies indicates that different general managers are skilled at different types of tasks. Consequently, the new top management team should be selected to the degree possible with the skills appropriate to the type of turnaround strategy that will need to be followed. For instance, an entrepreneurial strategist should be chosen if a high-growth, strategic turnaround is to be pursued, while a hard-nosed, experienced cost cutter should be selected if an operating turnaround with a major cost-reduction effort is to be pursued.

STRATEGIC TURNAROUNDS

Strategic turnarounds are appropriate when the business has an average or strong current operating position, but a lost position strategically. Although it is possible that the business could be weak in its strategic technological, production, or financial positions (situations which usually produce declines in profits and ROI) but not its market share, such is not usually the case. Instead, most strategic turnarounds involve situations in which there has been a major decline in both sales and share position, and possibly even a change in the strategic group in which the business competes. Consequently, the principal method of differentiating among strategic turnarounds is according to the magnitude of the share reversal or strategic group change sought. Three options are possible: (1) a maintenance of the business's current share and/or strategic group position accompanied by a refocusing of the business on one or more easily defensible product-market segments or niches within the strategic group selected; (2) one-level shifts in share and strategic group position,[1] that is, movement from a dropout position to a follower position or from a follower position to a competitor position or from a competitor position to a leader position; or (3) two-level shifts in share and strategic group position, that is, from a dropout position to a competitor position or from a follower position to a leader position.

Usually, however, two-level shifts in share and strategic group position, or even one-level shifts that involve attempting to secure the leadership position, are not possible unless the business has unusual strategic resources that it has failed to exploit as well as access to discretionary strategic funds 50 to 100% more than it could normally generate on its own. (One such source is a corporate parent that is willing to fund heavy investments in areas of relative competitive advantage over moderately long periods of time, such as Phillip Morris was willing to do with Miller's.) The only other times when shifts of such magnitude are possible are (1) when the current leader slips, (2) when there is a major change in stage of product-market evolution, or (3) when the turnaround firm is the former leader who had recently fallen.

Normally, therefore, the choice of a strategic turnaround strategy is between a one-level shift in share and strategic group position (which might involve moving from fifth, sixth, or seventh position to a second, third, or fourth position in the industry), and a segmentation or niche strategy within the business' current strategic group. Again, unless the business has unusual resources or there is a shift in stage of product-market evolution, the segmentation/niche type strategy will normally be more profitable in terms of ROI, earnings per share, and other similar asset utilization measures of organizational performance. However, segmentation/niche strategies usually provide little or no opportunity for eventually seizing leadership in the industry involved and will usually produce lower total dollar sales and net income than a successful one-level share and strategic group shifting turnaround strategy—unless the segments selected for the new focus grow substantially. Most businesses, therefore, usually try strategic turnarounds that involve seeking higher dollar sales through one-level shifts in share and strategic group position, with a possible, even though remote, opportunity for seizing leadership should competitors slip or environmental challenges change.

Optimally, a strategic turnaround should attempt to combine the best features of both these approaches; that is, it should seek segmentation, but in such a way that overall sales and share would increase because of the strategic position or group change. Such an optimum strategic turnaround is usually not possible, however, unless there is a newly emerging segment to the market, and even then the turnaround business must be able to develop superior products for that segment, as well as upgrading its competences in the other functional areas important for serving that segment. Moreover, to be able to maintain any headstart it might get on its competitors, the firm involved needs to be able to differentiate itself from its key competitors in some relatively enduring way—a most difficult task if its competitors have superior resources.

The major conclusion that can be drawn from industry practice to date is that too much attention is given to strategic turnarounds that involve one-level increases in share and strategic group position, and not enough to strategic turnarounds that involve segmentation and niche hunting.

---

[1] Theoretically it would be possible, at least in some industries, to make a one-level shift in share position within the *same* strategic group. Practically, however, almost all efforts to achieve one- or two-level shifts in share position require a change in the strategic group in which the business competes.

There are four different types of operating turnaround strategies that are possible:

1. Revenue-increasing strategies
2. Cost-cutting strategies
3. Asset-reduction strategies
4. Combination strategies

While these turnaround strategies might seem to correspond in some ways to the three different types of strategic turnarounds noted above, attempts to make such a correspondence are really misleading since the correspondence is more one of results than of means, and as a consequence, usually exists only in the short term. A comparison of a typical strategic turnaround involving a one-level shift in the strategic group in which the firm competes with a typical revenue-increasing operating turnaround should help illustrate the differences. In the former instance, the business involved would normally develop a new line of products, alter the basic character of its production system, invest heavily in R&D, possibly even change its methods of distribution, and be slightly overstaffed in anticipation of future growth. In addition, that growth would start slowly since the efforts being undertaken are long-term ones. Later, however, the growth rate would take off for a period of several years before it slowed as the firm reached its new position.

In a typical revenue-generating operating turnaround, however, the firm would keep its existing line of products, although it might supplement these with products that it used to make but had discontinued—provided there was some indication this action would boost current sales. Also, the business might produce some products totally unrelated to its principal business if these required little start-up expense and helped utilize its facilities more fully in the short-term. In addition, both R&D and staffing would be at moderate or low levels relative to sales, while some major marketing efforts, such as price cutting, increased advertising, or increased direct sales calls, would be undertaken to stimulate current sales. One other difference would also exist. In a strategic turnaround designed to move a business to a larger strategic group, few activities would be undertaken that were not directly related to the business's long-term strategic thrust. At the same time, substantial attention would be given to *all* of the key success factors critical to the future health of the business. In a revenue-increasing operating turnaround, by contrast, almost total attention would be focused on short-term, revenue-generating actions with little or no attention to the other areas of the business. Moreover, several of the revenue-generating actions undertaken in such an operating turnaround might have no bearing on the long-term strategic health of the business. In short, strategic and operating turnarounds are really substantially different in character, even though there sometimes appears to be a similarity in the short-term results they produce.

Because of the primary focus on short-term operating actions, the first step in any operating turnaround should be to identify the resources and skills that the business will need to implement its long-term strategy so that these can be protected in the short-term action program that will follow. Once these resources have been identified, the type of operating turnaround strategy to be followed should be selected based primarily on the firm's current break-even position. . . .

If the firm is close to its current break-even point . . . but has high direct labor costs, high fixed expenses, or limited financial resources, then cost-cutting turn-around strategies are usually preferable because moderately large short-term decreases in fixed costs are usually possible and because cost-cutting actions take effect more quickly than revenue-generating actions. On the other hand, if the business is extremely far below its break-even point . . . then the only viable option is usually an asset-reduction turnaround strategy, especially if the business is close to bankruptcy. . . . If the firm's sales fall between the above ranges . . . then the most effective operating turnarounds usually involve revenue-generating or asset-reduction strategies, because in such circumstances there is usually no way to reduce costs sufficiently to reach a new break-even, and time and resources are typically not adequate to attempt a combination turnaround strategy. The choice between revenue-generating and asset-reduction strategies in such situations depends primarily on the longer-term potential of the business after turnaround, and the criticalness of the firm's current financial position. . . .

No matter what type of operating turnaround strategy is followed, though, the limited financial resources and time urgency associated with most operational turnaround situations require that particular attention be given to all actions that will have a major cash flow impact on the business in the short term. As a consequence, actions such as collecting receivables, cutting inventories, increasing prices when possible, focusing on high-margin products, stretching payables, decreasing wastage, and selling off surplus assets should almost always be pursued. . . .

SUMMARY AND CONCLUSIONS

Before closing, three other points deserve repeating. First, before starting any turnaround, an explicit calculation should be made to determine whether the turnaround effort will be worth it. Too often firms embark on turnaround efforts as a knee-jerk reaction to the myth that nothing can be worse than failure, that is, liquidation. Such is not the case, though, and in many instances, stockholders, employees, and other organizational stakeholders would be better served if management faced up to the true prospects and benefits of long-run survival and decided to liquidate the business for what it is worth now.

Second, before embarking on a strategic turnaround, an explicit investigation should be made of the conditions in the industry involved, and, in particular, of its competitive structure and stage of evolution. The reason for such analysis is quite simple. It is that industry structure is not uniformly flexible at all points in time. Thus, there are times when strategic changes abound within an industry. During such periods, shifts in relative competitive position occur moderately often. Consequently, during such times strategic turnarounds are relatively easy and inexpensive. At other times, however, it is almost impossible to make major shifts in competitive position with the resources available to most firms in the industry. During these periods, strategic turnarounds should not be attempted unless the organization has access to substantial outside resources or unless there are special circumstances, such as a competitor asleep at the switch, that provide unique opportunities in an otherwise barren situation.

Finally, it should be noted that the ideas presented in this article are based on limited research and study. It is, therefore, likely that some of them will be modified (or elaborated on) by future research.

• MANAGING STRATEGIES INCREMENTALLY*

BY JAMES BRIAN QUINN

MANAGING INCREMENTALISM

... [A section of the reading on "logical incrementalism" in Chapter 5 of this text states the logic for incremental management of strategies. But specifically] how can one proactively manage in this mode? One executive provided perhaps the most articulate short statement of the overall approach:

> Typically you start with a general concern, vaguely felt. Next, you roll an issue around in your mind until you think you have a conclusion that makes sense for the company. Then you go out and sort of post the idea without being too wedded to its details. You then start hearing the arguments pro and con, and some very good refinements of the idea usually emerge. Then you pull the idea in and put some resources together to study it so it can be put forward as more of a formal presentation. You wait for "stimuli occurrences" or "crises," and launch pieces of the idea to help in these situations. But they lead toward your ultimate aim. You know where you want to get. You'd like to get there in six months. But it may take three years, or you may not get there at all. And when you do get there, you don't know whether it was originally your own idea—or somebody else had reached the same conclusion before you and just got you on board for it. You never know.

Because of differences in organizational form, management style, and the content of individual decisions, no single paradigm holds for all strategic decisions (Quinn, 1977). But my study suggests that [many] executives [in large companies] tend to utilize somewhat similar incremental processes as they manage complex strategy shifts. [Some summary] glimpses follow:

Leading the Formal Information System

Rarely do the earliest signals for strategic change come from the company's formal horizon scanning, planning or reporting systems. Instead, initial sensing of needs for major strategic changes is often described as "something you feel uneasy about," "inconsistencies" or "anomalies" (Normann, 1977) between the enterprise's current posture and some general perception of its future environment (Mintzberg et al., 1976). Effective managers establish multiple credible internal and external sources to obtain objective information about their enterprise and its surrounding environments (Wrapp, 1967). They use these networks to short-circuit all the careful screens their organizations build up "to tell the top only what it wants to hear" (Argyris, 1977). They actively search beyond their organization's formal information systems, deeming the latter to be too historical, tradition oriented or extrapolative to pinpoint needed basic changes in time. For example,

---

* Originally published in modified form in *Omega: The International Journal of Management Science* (1982). Copyright © James Brian Quinn, all rights reserved. Adapted and reprinted by courtesy of *Omega*.

434

To avoid their own natural biases, executives who are aggressively seeking new potential opportunities or threats make sure their networks include people who look at the world quite differently from the dominating culture of the enterprise. Some companies have structured "devil's advocates" into their planning processes for this purpose. Others have undertaken "aggressor company" exercises to stimulate how intelligent aggressors could best attack their patents, markets, or desired future positions. Still others—like Xerox—have commissioned groups of known independent thinkers to make special studies, with the extensive help of outside consultants and authorities, to ensure top managers view changing environments analytically and creatively.

Building Organizational Awareness

This may be essential when key players do not have enough information or psychological stimulation to voluntarily change their past action patterns or to investigate options creatively. At early stages, successful change managers seem to consciously generate and consider a broad array of alternatives (Wrapp, 1967). While tapping the "collective wit" of the organization, they try to build awareness and concern about new issues. They assemble objective data to argue against preconceived ideas or blindly followed past practices. Yet they want to avoid prematurely threatening power centers that might kill important changes before potential supporters really know what is at stake and can bring broader interests to bear. At this stage, management processes are rarely directive. Instead they are likely to involve studying, challenging, questioning, listening, talking to creative people outside ordinary decision channels, generating options, but purposely avoiding irreversible commitments (Gilmore, 1973). . . .

Executives may want their colleagues to be more knowledgeable about . . . major issues and help think through ramifications clearly before taking specific actions. They want to avoid being the prime supporter of a losing idea or having the organization attack or slavishly adopt "the boss's solution" and having to change it as more evidence becomes available. Even though top executives may not have in mind specific solutions to an emerging problem they can proactively guide early steps in intuitively desired directions by defining the issues staffs investigate, selecting the people who make the investigations, and controlling the reporting process. They may not terminate this "diagnostic phase" (Mintzberg et al., 1976) until they have identified potential proponents and opponents of various positions and are sure that enough people will "get on board" to make a solution work.

Building Credibility/Changing Symbols

Symbols may help managers signal to the organization that certain types of changes are coming, even when specific solutions are not yet in hand. Knowing they cannot communicate directly with the thousands who must carry out a strategy, many executives purposely undertake a few highly visible symbolic actions which wordlessly convey complex messages they could never communicate as well, or as credibly, in verbal terms. Through word of mouth the informal grapevine can amplify signals of a pending change [with a power] no formal communication could (Rhenman, 1973). . . . Organizations often need such symbolic moves, or decisions they regard as symbolic, to verify the intention of a new strategy or to build credibility behind one in its initial stages. Without such actions people may interpret even forceful verbiage as mere rhetoric and delay their commitment to new thrusts.

Legitimizing New Viewpoints

[Strategy development] will often involve planned delays, since top managers may purposely create discussion forums or allow slack time [so that] their organizations can talk through threatening issues, work out the implications of new solutions, or gain an improved information base that permits new options to be evaluated objectively in comparison with more familiar alternatives. Because of familiarity, solutions which arise out of executives' prior experiences are perceived as having lower risks (or potential costs) than newer alternatives that are more attractive when viewed objectively. In many cases, strategic concepts which are at first strongly resisted can gain acceptance and positive commitment simply by the passage of time and open discussion of new information—when executives do not exacerbate hostility by pushing them too fast from the top (Cyert et al., 1958). Many top executives, planners, and change agents consciously arrange for such "gestation periods" and find that the concept itself is frequently made more effective by the resulting feedback and acceptance. . . . For example,

> When William Spoor took over as CEO as Pillsbury, one of the biggest issues he faced was whether to stay in or get out of the Pillsbury Farms' chicken business. Management was deeply split on the question. Spoor asked all key protagonists for position papers and purposely commissioned two papers on each side for the Board. He invited consultants' views and visited Ralston Purina, which had undergone a similar divestiture. He got an estimate from Lehman Brothers as to the division's value. All this went to the Board which debated the issue for months. A key event occurred when Lehman found a potential European buyer at a good price. Finally, when the vote was taken only one person—Pillsbury Farms' original champion—voted for retention.

Tactical Shifts and Partial Solutions

These are typical steps in developing a new overall strategic posture [when] early problem resolutions [need] to be partial, tentative, or experimental. Beginning moves are often handled as mere tactical adjustments in the enterprise's existing posture and as such they encounter little opposition. Executives can often obtain agreement to a series of small programs when a broad objective change would encounter too much opposition. Such programs allow the guiding executive to maintain the enterprise's ongoing strengths while shifting momentum—at the margin—toward new needs (Cyert and March, 1963). At this stage, top executives themselves may not yet comprehend the full nature or extent of the strategic shifts they are beginning. They can still experiment with partial new approaches without risking the viability of the total enterprise, while their broad early steps can legitimately lead to a variety of different success scenarios. . . .

As events unfurl, the solutions to several initially unrelated problems tend to flow together into a new synthesis. When possible, strategic logic (risk minimization) dictates starting broad initiatives that can be flexibly guided in any of several possible desirable directions (Wrapp, 1967).

Broadening Political Support

Broadening political support for emerging new thrusts is frequently an essential and consciously proactive step in major strategy changes. Committees, task forces or retreats tend to be favored mechanisms. By selecting such groups' chairmen, membership, timing, and agenda the guiding executive can largely influence and predict a desired outcome, yet nudge other executives toward a consensus. The careful executive, of course, still maintains complete control over these "advisory" processes through his various influence and veto potentials. In addition to facilitating smooth implementation, many managers report that interactive consensus building also improves the quality of the strategic decisions themselves and helps achieve positive and innovative assistance when things otherwise would go wrong.

Overcoming Opposition

Overcoming opposition is almost always necessary at some stage. Careful executives realize that they must deal with the support the preceding strategy had. They try not unnecessarily to alienate managers from the earlier era, whose talents they may need in future ventures, through a frontal assault on old approaches. Instead, they persuade individuals toward new concepts whenever possible, coopt or neutralize serious opposition if necessary (Sayles, 1964), or move through zones of indifference (Barnard, 1938) where early changes will not be disastrously opposed. Under the best circumstances, they find "no lose" situations that activate all important players positively towards new common goals. . . .

Successful executives tend to honor [and even stimulate] legitimate differences in views concerning even major directions and note that initial opponents often thoughtfully shape new strategies in more effective directions. Some may become active supporters as new information emerges to change their views. But consensus is not always possible. Strong minded executives sometimes disagree to the point where they must be moved to positions of less influence or stimulated to leave. And timing can dictate very firm top level direction at key junctures.

Consciously Structured Flexibility

Flexibility is essential in dealing with the many "unknowables" in the total environment. One cannot possibly predict the precise form or timing of all important threats and opportunities the firm may encounter. Logic dictates therefore that managers purposely design flexibility into their organizations and have resources ready to deploy incrementally as events demand. This requires

1. proactive horizon scanning to identify the general range, scale, and impact of the opportunities and threats the firm is most likely to encounter
2. creating sufficient resource buffers, or slacks, to respond as events actually do unfurl
3. developing and positioning "champions" who will be motivated to take advantage of specific opportunities as they occur
4. shortening decision lines between such persons and the top for rapid system response.

These—rather than precapsuled (and shelved) programs to respond to stimuli which never occur quite as expected—are the keys to real contingency planning. . . . With such flexible patterns designed into the strategy the enterprise is proactively ready to move on those thrusts that by their very nature may have to evolve incrementally.

Trial Balloons and Systematic Waiting

These are often the next steps for prepared strategists. As Roosevelt awaited a critical event like Pearl Harbor, [company] strategists may have to wait patiently for the proper option or precipitating event to appear. For example,

> The availability of desired acquisitions or real estate may depend upon a death, divorce, fiscal crisis, management change, or erratic economic break. Technological advances may await new knowledge, inventions, or lucky accidents. Or planned market entries may not be wise until new legislation, trade agreements or competitive shake outs occur. Very often the optimum strategy depends on the timing and sequence of such random events. For example the timing and nature of SDS Inc.'s availability was a proximate cause of both the date and results of this first Xerox entry into computers.

Executives may also consciously launch trial concepts . . . [like Mr. Spoor's "Super Box"] in order to attract options and concrete proposals. Usually these trial balloons are phrased in very broad contextual terms. Without making a commitment to any specific solution, the executive activates the organization's creative abilities. This approach keeps the manager's own options open until substantive alternatives can be evaluated against each other and against concrete current realities. And it prevents practical line managers from rejecting desirable strategic shifts because they are forced to compare "paper options" against what they see as well-defined, urgent needs.

Creating Pockets of Commitment

This may be necessary for entirely new strategic thrusts. The executive may encourage exploratory projects to test options, create necessary skills or technologies, or build commitment for several possible options deep within the organization. Initial projects may be kept small, partial, or ad hoc, not forming a comprehensive program or seeming to be integrated into a cohesive strategy. At this stage guiding executives may merely provide broad goals, a proper climate and flexible resource support, without being identified with specific projects (Soelberg, 1967). In this way they can avoid escalating attention to any one solution too soon or losing personal credibility if it fails. But they can stimulate those options which lead in desired directions, set higher hurdles for those that do not or quietly have them killed some levels below to maintain their own flexibility. Executives can then keep their own options open, control premature momentum, openly back only winners, and select the right moment to blend several successful thrusts into a broader program or concept (Witte, 1972). They can delay their own final decisions on a total thrust until the last moment, thus obtaining the best possible matchup between the company's capabilities, psychological commitments, and changing market needs. . . .

Crystalizing Focus

Crystalizing focus at critical points in the process is, of course, vital. Sometimes executives will state a few key goals at an early stage to generate action or cohesion in a difficult or crisis situation. But for reasons noted, guiding executives often purposely keep early goal statements vague and commitments broad and tentative (Quinn, 1977). Then as they develop information or consensus on desirable thrusts, they may use their prestige or power to push or crystalize a particular formulation. Despite adhering to the rhetoric of specific goal setting, most executives in my study were careful not to state many new strategic objectives in concrete terms until they had carefully built consensus among key players. To do otherwise might inadvertently centralize their organizations, preempt interesting options, provide a common focus for otherwise fragmented opposition, or cause the organization to undertake undesirable actions just to carry out a stated commitment. Because the net direction of an organization's goals ultimately reflects a negotiated balance among the imperatives felt by the dominant executive coalition (Perrow, 1961) and the most important power centers and stakeholders in the enterprise, the last thing an executive wants is to weaken his or her position by creating an unintended counter coalition. When to crystalize viewpoints and when to maintain open options is one of the true arts of strategic management. . . .

Formalizing Commitment

This is the final step in formulation. As partial consensus emerges, the guiding executive may crystalize events by stating a few broad goals in more specific terms for internal consumption. Finally when sufficient general acceptance exists and the timing is right, the decision may appear in more public pronouncements. For example, as General Mills divested several of its major "old line" divisions its annual reports began to state these as moves "to concentrate on the company's strengths" and "to intensify General Mills' efforts in the convenience foods field," statements which it would have been unwise or impolitic to make until many of the actual divestitures had taken place and a new management coalition and consensus had emerged.

As each major new thrust comes into focus, strategic managers ensure that some individual(s) feel responsible for its execution. Plans are locked into programs or budgets, and control and reward systems are aligned to reflect intended strategic emphases (Cohen and Cyert, 1973). Since so much has been written on this subject, I will avoid details here.

Continuing Dynamics and Mutating Consensus

[Unfortunately, old crusades can quickly become a] new conventional wisdom and the organization [can] fail to prepare itself for new concerns and concepts. In trying to build commitment, executives often surround themselves with people who strongly identify with the new strategy. These supporters can rapidly become systematic screens against new views. Even as the organization arrives at its new consensus, guiding executives must move to ensure that this too does not become inflexible. Effective strategic managers therefore immediately introduce new foc[i] and stimuli at the top to begin mutating the very strategic thrusts they have just solidified—a most difficult but essential psychological task. . . .

Not a Linear Process

While generation of a strategy generally flows along the sequence presented, stages are by no means orderly or discrete. Few executives manage the process through all phases linearly. . . . The strategy's ultimate development [usually] involves a series of nested partial decisions (in each strategic area) interacting with similar decisions in all other areas and with a constantly changing resource base. Pfiffner (1960) has aptly described the process as "like fermentation in biochemistry, rather than an industrial assembly line." The validity of a strategy lies not in its pristine clarity or rigorously maintained structure, but in its capacity to capture the initiative, to deal with unknowable events, to redeploy and concentrate resources as new opportunities and thrusts emerge, and thus to use resources most effectively toward selected goals.

Each major segment of a strategy is likely to be in a different phase of its development—from initial awareness to . . . ultimate commitment—at any given moment. The real integration of all these components into a total enterprise strategy takes place primarily in the minds of individual top executives. Some portions of the strategy may be seen the same way by all, but each executive may legitimately perceive the overall balance of goals and thrusts slightly differently. Some differences may be openly expressed as issues to be resolved when new information becomes available; others may remain unstated, hidden agendas to emerge at later dates; still others may be masked by accepting a broad statement of intention that accommodates many divergent views within its seeming consensus—while a more specific statement might be divisive. Events often move almost imperceptibly from awareness, to concern, to experiments, to options, to partial acceptance, to momenta, to consensus, to formal reinforcement. The process is so continuous that it may be hard to discern the particular point in time when specific clear-cut decisions are made.

INTEGRATING THE STRATEGY

Nevertheless, the total pattern of actions, though incremental, does not remain piecemeal in well-managed organizations. Effective executives constantly reassess the total organization, its capacities and needs as related to surrounding environment. . . .

Concentrating on a Few Key Thrusts

Strategic managers constantly seek to distil out a few (six to ten) "central themes" that draw the firm's diverse existing activities and new probes into common cause. Once identified, these help maintain focus and consistency in the strategy. They make it easier to discuss and monitor intended directions. In ideal circumstances, these themes can be converted into a matrix of strategic "thrusts" or "missions" cutting across divisional plans and dominating other criteria used to rank divisional commitments (see Quinn, 1980). Each division's plans have to show *enough* effort to accomplish its share of each thrust, even though this means overriding short-term present-value or rate-of-return rankings on projects within the division (Pfeffer et al., 1976). Texas Instruments and General Electric Company have provided some well-publicized formal models for doing this. Unfortunately, few companies seem able to implement such complex planning systems without generating voluminous paperwork, large planning bureaucracies and undesirable rigidities in the plans themselves. . . .

Coalition Management

[Nevertheless,] at the heart of all controlled strategy development lies coalition management. Top managers operate at a confluence of pressures from: stockholders, environmentalists, government bodies, customers, suppliers, distributors, producing units, marketing groups, technologists, unions, special issue activities, individual employees, ambitious executives, and so on, where knowledgeable people of good will can easily disagree on a proper balance of actions. In response to changing pressures and coalitions among these groups, the top management team continuously forms and reforms its own coalitions aligned around specific decisions. These represent various members' different values and interests concerning the particular issue at hand and are sources of constant negotiations and implied bargains among the leadership group (Sayles, 1964).

Most major strategic moves tend to assist some interests—and executives' careers—at the expense of others. Consequently, each set of interests can serve as a check on the others and thus help maintain the breadth and balance of the overall strategy. Some managements try to ensure that all important [polities] have representation or access at the top. And the guiding executive group may continuously adjust the number, power, or proximity of these access points to maintain a desired balance and focus (Zaleznik, 1970). People selection and coalition management are the ultimate controls top executives have in guiding and coordinating their companies' strategies.

15

THINKING STRATEGICALLY

We have made no secret of our intention in this text to upset many accepted and cherished notions about how organizations are supposed to work: what their strategies are supposed to be and how they are supposed to be formed, how structure and systems are supposed to coincide with these, and how managers are supposed to get their jobs done. We hope that we have succeeded not only in bringing conventional beliefs into question, but also in helping to replace them with broader, more insightful and useful ways to think about these phenomena.

The two readings we bring together in this last chapter on "thinking strategically" have been included to maintain this tone, but also to close with admonitions we believe are important for students about to embark on the world of organizations and management.

Tom Peters, the most popular of today's management "gurus," opens by warning about the whole idea of strategy. Don't think that just because you have *thought* it through you are through. Peters emphasizes that "execution is strategy," that it is in the hard work of *doing it*—something almost impossible to teach in a management school—that organizations succeed. As he stresses, it is in all those "boring" little details that the real effectiveness of an organization lies, and these depend on the distinctive competence that the organization builds up only slowly and carefully. Carrying beyond his best-seller *In Search of Excellence,* Peters presents its message for strategic management, and this served to admonish the management student from taking the excitement of managing the "big picture" too seriously. A good point for anyone finishing a course on the strategy process!

Finally, Sterling Livingston ends this text on a point that is important for everyone finishing an education in management in general: you are not finished, indeed you have barely begun. Livingston wrote this article many years ago, but the only thing dated about it is its gender. All managers-to-be, male and female, would be well warned to take its vital message seriously. Writing from his own experiences as a manager and entrepreneur as well as professor at the Harvard Business

School, Livingston cities evidence on the lack of association between how well a student does in business school and his or her later success on the job. He offers sage advice on how managers can learn from their own first hand experiences on the job, and on what kinds of people are suitable to becoming successful managers in the first place.

The message is clear, simple, and poignant: you have learned important things in school but that alone does not prepare you to manage an organization. A little humility can only help anyone who graduates from a business school today!

• STRATEGY FOLLOWS STRUCTURE: DEVELOPING DISTINCTIVE SKILLS*

BY THOMAS J. PETERS

. . . strategy follows structure. Distinctive organizational performance, for good or ill, is almost entirely a function of deeply engrained repertoires. The organization, within its marketplace, *is* the way it *acts* from moment to moment—not the way it thinks it *might* act or *ought* to act. Larry Greiner recently noted,

> Strategy evolves from inside the organization—not from its future environment. . . . Strategy is a deeply engrained and continuing pattern of management behavior that gives direction to the organization—not a manipulable and controllable mechanism that can easily be changed from one year to the next. Strategy is a nonrational concept stemming from the informal values, traditions, and norms of behavior held by the firm's managers and employees—not rational, formal, logical, conscious and predetermined thought processes engaged in by top executives. Strategy emerges out of the cumulative effect of many informal actions and decisions taken daily over the years by many employees—not a "one shot" statement developed exclusively by top management for distribution to the organization. (1983:13)

Of course we understand, at one level, exactly what Greiner is saying; few would disagree with it. At the same time, however, we more often than not manage as if the principal variable at our command—in order to bring about an adjustment to a changing environment—is the "strategy lever."

EXECUTION IS STRATEGY

SAS (Scandinavian Air System) [in the early 1980s] completed a monumental "strategic turnaround." In a period of 18 months, amid the worst recession in 40 years, it went from a position of losing $10 million a year to making $70 million a year (on $2 billion in sales), and virtually the entire turnaround came at the direct expense of such superb performers as SwissAir and Lufthansa. The "strategy" (he calls it "vision") of SAS's Jan Carlzon was "to become the premiere business person's airline." Carlzon is the first to admit that it is a "garden variety" vision: "It's everyone's aspiration. The difference was, we executed." Carlzon describes SAS as having shifted focus from "an aircraft orientation" to a "customer orientation," adding that, "SAS *is* the personal contact of one person in the market and one per-

---

* Originally published in the *California Management Review* (Spring 1984). Copyright © 1984 by The Regents of the University of California. Reprinted with deletions by permission of the *Review*.

son at SAS." He sees SAS as "50 million 'moments of truth' per year, during each of which we have an opportunity to be distinctive." That number is arrived at by calculating that SAS has 10 million customers per year, each one comes in contact with five SAS employees on average, which leads to a product of 50 million "opportunities."

Perdue Farms sells chickens. In the face of economists' predictions for over 50 consecutive years (according to Frank Perdue), Perdue Farms has built a three-quarter-billion-dollar business. Margins exceed that of its competitors by 700 or 800%. . . . Frank Perdue argues, and a careful analysis of his organization would lead one to argue, that his magic is simple: "If you believe there's absolutely no limit to quality [remember we're talking about roasters, not Ferraris] and you engage in every business dealing with total integrity, the rest [profit, growth, share] will follow automatically. . . ."

A colleague of mine once said, "Execution *is* strategy." The secret to success of the so-called excellent companies that Bob Waterman and I looked at, and the ones that I have looked at since, is almost invariably mundane execution. The examples—small and large, basic industry or growth industry— are too numerous to mention: Tupperware, Mary Kay, Stew Leonard's, Mrs. Field's Cookies, W. L. Gore, McDonald's, Mars, Perdue Farms, Frito-Lay, Hewlett-Packard, IBM, and on it goes.

My reason for belaboring this point is to suggest that, above all, the top performers—school, hospital, sports team, business—are a *package of distinctive skills.* In most cases, one particularly distinctive strength—innovation at 3M, J&J, or Hewlett-Packard; service at IBM, McDonald's, Frito-Lay, or Disney; quality at Perdue Farms, Procter & Gamble, Mars, or Maytag—and the distinctive skill— which in all cases is a product of some variation of "50 million moments of truth a year"—are a virtual unassailable barrier to competitor entry or serious encroachment. David Ogilvy quotes Mies van der Rohe as saying of architecture, "God is in the details" (1983:101). Jan Carlzon of SAS puts it this way, "We do not wish to do one thing a thousand percent better, we wish to do a thousand things one percent better." Francis G. (Buck) Rodgers, IBM's corporate marketing vice-president, made a parallel remark, "Above all we want a reputation for doing the little things well." And a long-term observer of Procter & Gamble noted, "They are so thorough, it's boring." The very fact that excellence has a "thousand thousand little things" as its source makes the word "unassailable" (as in "an unassailable barrier to entry") plausible. No trick, no device, no sleight of hand, no capital expenditure will close the gap for the also rans.

DISTINCTIVE COMPETENCE—THE FORGOTTEN TRAIL

The focus on execution, on distinctive competence is indeed not new. Philip Selznick, as far as I can determine, talked about it first:

> The term "organization" suggests a certain bareness, a lean, no-nonsense system of consciously coordinated activities. It refers to an *expendable tool,* a rational instrument engineered to do a job. An "institution," on the other hand, is more nearly a natural product of social needs and pressures—a responsive adaptive organism. The terms institution, organizational character, and distinctive competence all refer to the same basic process—the transformation of an engineered, technical arrangement of building blocks into a purposive social organization. (1957:5)

Early thinking about strategy, which was the focus of my MBA schooling a dozen years ago at Stanford, was driven by the industry standard: Edmund P. Learned and others's (1965) textbook, *Business Policy.* The focus of strategy making at that point was clearly on analyzing and building distinctive competences.

In the years since Selznick and Learned and others, the focus on distinctive competence has been downgraded. Analysis of strategic position within a competitive system has all but butted out concern with the boring details of execution (which sum up to that elusive competence). Presumably the "people types" (the OB faculty) take care of such mundane stuff. The experience curve, portfolio manipulation, competitive cost position analysis, and the like have reigned supreme for the last decade or so.

I have no problem with the usefulness of any of these tools. Each is vital, and a few of them, indeed, were used very thoughtfully or regularly just a dozen years ago. However, we seem to have moved (rushed?) from a position of "implementation without thought" (analyzing structures on the basis of span of control, rather than on the basis of external forces) to "thought without implementation." We have reached a wretched position in which Stanford, annually voted by the business school deans as America's leading business school (and thus the world's), has only *three* of 91 elective MBA courses focusing on the making (manufacturing policy) or selling (sales management) functions of business.[1] This distortion of priorities was poignantly brought home to me late last school year. A local reporter attended my last class (an elective based on *In Search of Excellence*) and asked my students if the course had been useful. One student, quoted in the subsequent article, tried to say the very most complimentary thing he could: "It's great. Tom teaches all that soft, intangible stuff—innovation, quality, customer service—that's not found in the hard P&L or balance statements." Soft? Hard? Has that youngster got it straight or backwards—is there a problem here? . . .

As best I can determine, there are only *three* truly distinctive "skill packages" . . .

Total Customer Satisfaction: . . . As Ted Levitt begins in his . . . very readable book, *The Marketing Imagination,* "There is no such thing as a commodity" (1983:72). The often slavish devotion to the experience curve effect is not responsible for our forgetting all of this counter evidence, to be sure. Making more (selling at a lower price to gain share) in order to achieve a barrier to entry via lowest subsequent industry cost is certainly not a bad idea. It's a great one. But the difficulty seems to be the unintended resultant *mind-set.* As one chief executive officer noted to me, "We act as if cost—and thus price—is the only variable available these days. In our hell bent rush to get cost down, we have given all too short shrift to quality and service. So we wake up, at best, with a great share and a lousy product. It's almost always a precarious position that can't be sustained." Also, I suspect, the relative ease of gaining dominant market position—first in the United States, and then overseas—by most American corporations in the 1950s through the 1970s (pre-OPEC, pre-Japan) led institutions to take their eye off the service and quality ball. The focus was simply on making a lot of it for ever-hungry markets. Moreover, this led to the executive suite dominance by financially trained executive-administrators, and the absence of people who were closer to the product (and thus the importance of quality and service)—namely, salespersons, designers, and manufacturers. . . .

Continuous Innovation: The second basic skill trait is the ability to constantly innovate. Virtually all innovations—from miracle drugs, to computers, to air-

---

[1] "Course Descriptions for Electives Taught in the 1983–84 Academic Year," Stanford University Graduate School of Business. [Peters later adds that 34 courses focus on accounting, finance, and decision analysis.]

planes, to bag size changes at Frito-Lay, to menu item additions at McDonald's—come from the wrong person, in the wrong division, of the wrong company, in the wrong industry, for the wrong reason, at the wrong time, with the wrong set of end-users. The assumption behind most planning systems, particularly the highly articulated strategic planning systems of the seventies, was that we could plan our way to new market successes. The reality differs greatly. Even at the mecca of planning systems, General Electric, the batting average of strategic planning was woefully low. In the 1970s (when planners were regularly observed walking on water at Fairfield), GE's major innovative, internally generated business successes—for example, aircraft engines, the credit business, plastics, and the information services company—came solely as a product of committed, somewhat irrational (assumed, inside, to be crazy) champions. When Jack Welch became GE's chairman in 1980—ending a 30-year reign by accountants—he moved to enhance entrepreneurship. One of his first steps was to reduce the corporate planning staff by more than 80 percent. The most truly innovative companies—Hewlett-Packard, the Raychem Corporation, 3M, Johnson & Johnson, PepsiCo, and the like—clearly depend upon a thoroughly innovative climate. Radical decentralization marks Johnson & Johnson. Both J&J and IBM (via its new Independent Business Unit structure) gives the innovating unit a Board of Directors with an explicit charter to "ignore the strictures of formal planning systems and to keep the bureaucrats out of the hair of the inventors." 3M is simply a collection of skunkworks. . . .

. . . A most unlikely vital company is U.S. Shoe, yet the entrepreneurial vigor of this billion-and-a-half-dollar company is extraordinary. A recent *Fortune* article attributed its success to "superior market segmentation." The next issue of *Fortune* carried a letter to the editor from the son of the founder which rebutted that argument: "My father's real contribution was not superior market segmentation. Rather, he created a beautiful corporate culture which encouraged risk taking. . . ."

All Hands: The third and final regularly found skill variable is the sine qua non that goes hand in glove with the first two. Superior customer service, quality, and courtesy (total customer satisfaction) is not a product of the executive suite—it's an all hands effort. Constant innovation from multiple centers is similarly not the domain of a handful of brilliant thinkers at the top. Thus, virtually all of these institutions put at the head of their corporate philosophies a bone-deep belief in the dignity and worth and creative potential of *all* their people. Said one successful Silicon Valley chief executive officer recently, "I'll tell you who my number one marketing person is. It's that man or woman on the loading dock who decides *not* to *drop* the box into the back of the truck." Said another, "Doesn't it follow that if you wish your people to treat your customers with courtesy that you must treat your people with courtesy?" Many sign up for these three virtues, but only the truly distinguished companies seem to practice them regularly.

COMMON THREAD: THE ADAPTIVE ORGANISM

These three skills—and these three alone—are virtually the *only* effective sources of sustainable, long-term competitive advantage. Notice that each suggests the essence of an adaptive organism. The organization that provides high perceived value—service, quality, courtesy—invariably does so by constantly listening and adapting to its customers' needs. The innovative company is similarly radically focused on the outside world. And the expectation that all people will contribute creatively to their jobs—receptionist and product designer alike—means similarly that each person is a source of external probing and a basis for constant renewal, fulfillment, and adaptation. These organizations, then, are alive and are excited—in both the "attuned" and the "enthusiastic" sense of that word. Moreover, such organizations are in the process of constant redefinition. The shared values surrounding these skills—customer listening and serving, constant innovation, and expecting all people to contribute—are rigid. But, paradoxically, the rigid values/skills are in service of constant externally focused adaptation and growth.

The excellent companies—chicken makers to computer makers—use their skills as the basis for continually reinventing adaptive strategies—usually on a decentralized basis—to permit them to compete effectively in both mature and volatile youthful markets. Skills, in a word, *drive* strategy in the best companies.

SKILLS VERSUS STRATEGY

I tend to see the word strategy, in the sense that it's currently taught in the business schools (or practiced by the leading consultants), as *not* having much meaning at the corporate or sector level at all, but as being the appropriate domain of the strategic business unit or other form of decentralized unit (the IBU at IBM, the division of Hewlett-Packard or J&J, the merchant organization at Macy's). To return to our 7-S model, this is the classic case for what we have constantly called "soft is hard." The driving variable in the model, which creates the preconditions for *effective* strategizing, is, above all, skills. Strategy is the dependent variable, operable at a lower level in the business.

We view the constantly innovating, constantly customer-serving organization as one that continually *discovers* new markets and new opportunities. The notion of the learning organization, the adapting organization, the discovering organization, reigns supreme. . . . By contrast, we watch the traditional "strategists" fall into the abyss time and again. Because a market looks good on paper, they believe the company should take it on. Yet they invariably underestimate the executional effort (skill base) required to do extremely well at *anything*.

PROACTIVE LEADERSHIP

If there is some sense to all the above, what then is the leader's role? If not master strategist, then what? He or she becomes, above all, a creator or shaper or keeper of skills. . . .

Above all the leader's role becomes proactive rather than reactive. . . . The important people are those that view their prime role as protecting the champions from the silliness of inertial bureaucracies. . . . Sam Walton, founder of the remarkably successful WalMart Corporation, says, "The best ideas have always come and will always come from the clerks. The point is to seek them out, to listen, and to act. . . .

ENTHUSIASTS, PASSION, AND FAITH

Let's really stray afield from the world of traditional definitions of strategy formulation. Ray Kroc says, "You gotta be able to see the beauty in a hamburger bun." Recall that Debbie Fields of Mrs. Field's Cookies says, "I am not a business woman, I am a cookie person." Sam Walton loves retailing. From Steve Jobs to Famous Amos, the creators of effective organizations are unabashed *enthusiasts.* Bill Hewlett and Dave Packard had a passion for their machines. Herman Lay had a passion for his potatoes. Forrest Mars loved factories. Marvin Bower of McKinsey loved his clients. John Madden loved linebackers. The love was transmitted and transmuted into excitement, passion, enthusiasm, energy. These virtues infected an entire organization. They created the adaptive organization—the organization aimed externally, yet depending upon the full utilization of each of its people. This seemingly simple-minded definition of effective strategy for the ages even holds in mature organizations. The fervor with which Procter & Gamble revered quality has now been passed down through many generations. The "salesman's bias" of an IBM and 3M has similarly been maintained several generations beyond the founder. The passionate belief that the dominant skill reigns supreme is at the heart of business success. . . .

So where does all this leave us? The world of experience curves, portfolios, and 4-24 box matrices has led us badly astray. George Gilder notes in *Wealth and Poverty,*

> Economists who attempt to banish chance through methods of rational management also banish the only source of human triumph. The inventor who never acts until statistics affirm his choice, the businessman who waits until the market is proven—all are doomed to mediocrity by their trust in a spurious rationality. (1981:264)

The devilish problem is that there is nothing wrong with any of these strategy tools. In fact, each one is helpful! I think of the same thing in the area of quality: quality circles, automation, and statistical quality control are extraordinarily powerful tools—but *if and only if* a bone-deep belief in quality comes first. Given the 145-year tradition at Procter & Gamble, the tools are then helpful. Absent the faith, passion, belief, value, and skill, the tools become just one more manifestation of bureaucracy—another attempt to patch a fundamental flaw with a bureaucratic band-aid. . . .

But we should never forget for a moment that the analytic models are not neutral. Any analyst worth his salt, with anything from a decision tree to a portfolio analysis, can shoot down any idea. Analysts are well-trained naysayers, professional naysayers. Yet it turns out that only passion, faith, and enthusiasm win. Passion can also lead to losses—many of them, of that there is no doubt. Yet there is no alternative. We simply can't plan our way to certain success. John Naisbitt, *Megatrends* author, asserts: "Strategic planning turned out to be an orderly, rational way to efficiently ride over the edge of the cliff." I think he's not far off. Above all, the winning companies that we've observed—small and large, regulated or unregulated, mature or new—are ruled by somewhat channeled passion in pursuit of distinctive skill building and maintenance.

• MYTH OF THE WELL-EDUCATED MANAGER*

BY J. STERLING LIVINGSTON

How effectively a manager will perform on the job cannot be predicted by the number of degrees he holds, the grades he receives in school, or the formal management education programs he attends. Academic achievement is not a valid yardstick to use in measuring managerial potential. Indeed, if academic achievement is equated with success in business, the well-educated manager is a myth.

Managers are not taught in formal education programs what they most need to know to build successful careers in management. Unless they acquire through

---

* Originally published in the *Harvard Business Review* (January–February 1971). Copyright © by the President and Fellows of Harvard College; all rights reserved. Reprinted with deletions by permission of the *Harvard Business Review.*

their own experience the knowledge and skills that are vital to their effectiveness, they are not likely to advance far up the organizational ladder.

Although an implicit objective of all formal management education is to assist managers to learn from their own experience, much management education is, in fact, miseducation because it arrests or distorts the ability of managerial aspirants to grow as they gain experience. Fast learners in the classroom often, therefore, become slow learners in their executive suite.

Men who hold advanced degrees in management are among the most sought after of all university graduates. Measured in terms of starting salaries, they are among the elite. Perhaps no further proof of the value of management education is needed. Being highly educated pays in business, at least initially. But how much formal education contributes to a manager's effectiveness and to his subsequent career progress is another matter.

Professor Lewis B. Ward (1970) of the Harvard Business School has found that the median salaries of graduates of that institution's MBA program plateau approximately 15 years after they enter business and, on the average, do not increase significantly thereafter. While the incomes of a few MBA degree holders continue to rise dramatically, the career growth of most of them levels off just at the time men who are destined for top management typically show their greatest rate of advancement.

Equally revealing is the finding that men who attend Harvard's Advanced Management Program (AMP) after having had approximately 15 years of business experience, but who—for the most part—have had no formal education in management, earn almost a third more, on the average, than men who hold MBA degrees from Harvard and other leading business schools.

Thus the arrested career progress of MBA degree holders strongly suggests that men who get to the top in management have developed skills that are not taught in formal management education programs and may be difficult for many highly educated men to learn on the job. . . .

UNRELIABLE YARDSTICKS

Lack of correlation between scholastic standing and success in business may be surprising to those who place a premium on academic achievement. But grades in neither undergraduate nor graduate school predict how well an individual will perform in management.

After studying the career records of nearly 1,000 graduates of the Harvard Business School, for example, Professor Gordon L. Marshall concluded that "academic success and business achievement have relatively little association with each other" (Marshall, 1964). In reaching this conclusion, he sought without success to find a correlation between grades and such measures of achievement as title, salary, and a person's own satisfaction with his career progress. (Only in the case of grades in elective courses was a significant correlation found.)

Clearly, what a student learns about management in graduate school, as measured by the grades he receives, does not equip him to build a successful career in business.

Scholastic standing in undergraduate school is an equally unreliable guide to an individual's management potential. Professor Eugene E. Jennings of the University of Michigan has conducted research which shows that "the routes to the top are apt to hold just as many or more men who graduated below the highest one third of their college class than above (on a per capita basis)" (1967:21).

A great many executives who mistakenly believe that grades are a valid measure of leadership potential have expressed concern over the fact that fewer and fewer of those "top-third" graduates from the better-known colleges and universities are embarking on careers in business. What these executives do not recognize, however, is that academic ability does not assure that an individual will be able to learn what he needs to know to build a career in fields that involve leading, changing, developing, or working with people.

Overreliance on scholastic learning ability undoubtedly has caused leading universities and business organizations to reject a high percentage of those who have had the greatest potential for creativity and growth in nonacademic careers.

This probability is underscored by an informal study conducted in 1958 by W. B. Bender, Dean of Admissions at Harvard College. He first selected the names of 50 graduates of the Harvard class of 1928 who had been nominated for signal honors because of their outstanding accomplishments in their chosen careers. Then he examined the credentials they presented to Harvard College at the time of their admission. He found that if the admission standards used in 1958 had been in effect in 1928, two thirds of these men would have been turned down. (The proportion who would have been turned down under today's standards would have been even higher.)

In questioning the wisdom of the increased emphasis placed on scholastic standing and intelligence test scores, Dean Bender asked, "Do we really know what we are doing?"[1]

There seems to be little room for doubt that business schools and business organizations which rely on scholastic standing, intelligence test scores, and grades as measures of managerial potential are using unreliable yardsticks.

Career Consequences

.. **Arrested Progress and Turnover:** Belief in the myth of the well-educated manager has caused many employers to have unrealistic performance expectations of university graduates and has led many employees with outstanding scholastic records to overestimate the value of their formal education. As a consequence, men who hold degrees in business administration—especially those with advanced degrees in management—have found it surprisingly difficult to make the transition from academic to business life. An increasing number of them have failed to perform up to expectations and have not progressed at the rate they expected.

The end result is that turnover among them has been increasing for two decades as more and more of them have been changing employers in search of a job they hope they "can make a career of." And it is revealing that turnover rates among men with advanced degrees from the leading schools of management appear to be among the highest in industry.

As Professor Edgar H. Schein of the Massachusetts Institute of Technology's Sloan School of Management reports, the attrition "rate among highly educated men and women runs higher, on the average, than among blue-collar workers hired out of the hard-core unemployed. The rate may be highest among people coming out of the better-known schools" (1969:95). Thus over half the graduates of MIT's master's program in management change jobs in the first three years, Schein further reports, and "by the fifth year, 73% have moved on at least once and some are on their third and fourth jobs" (p. 90).

---

[1] Quoted in Anthony G. Athos and Lewis B. Ward, "Corporations and College Recruiting: A Study of Perceptions" (unpublished study prepared for the Division of Research, Harvard Business School), p. 14.

Personnel records of a sample of large companies I have studied similarly revealed that turnover among men holding master's degrees in management from well-known schools was over 50% in the first five years of employment, a rate of attrition that was among the highest of any group of employees in the companies surveyed.

The much publicized notion that the young "mobile managers" who move from company to company are an exceptionally able breed of new executives and that "job-hopping has become a badge of competence" is highly misleading. While a small percentage of those who change employers are competent managers, most of the men who leave their jobs have mediocre to poor records of performance. They leave not so much because the grass is greener on the other side of the fence, but because it definitely is brown on their side. My research indicates that most of them quit either because their career progress has not met their expectations or because their opportunities for promotion are not promising.

In studying the career progress of young management-level employees of an operating company of the American Telephone & Telegraph Company, Professors David E. Berlew and Douglas T. Hall of MIT found that "men who consistently fail to meet company expectations are more likely to leave the organization than are those who turn in stronger performances" (1964:36).

I have reached a similar conclusion after studying attrition among recent management graduates employed in several large industrial companies. Disappointing performance appraisals by superiors is the main reason why young men change employers.

"One myth," explains Schein, "is that the graduate leaves his first company merely for a higher salary. But the MIT data indicate that those who have moved on do not earn more than those who have stayed put" (p. 90). Surveys of reunion classes at the Harvard Business School similarly indicate that men who stay with their first employer generally earn more than those who change jobs. Job-hopping is not an easy road to high income; rather, it usually is a sign of arrested career progress, often because of mediocre or poor performance on the job.

WHAT MANAGERS MUST LEARN

One reason why highly educated men fail to build successful careers in management is that they do not learn from their formal education what they need to know to perform their jobs effectively. In fact, the tasks that are the most important in getting results usually are left to be learned on the job, where few managers ever master them simply because no one teaches them how.

Formal management education programs typically emphasize the development of problem-solving and decision-making skills, for instance, but give little attention to the development of skills required to find the problems that need to be solved, to plan for the attainment of desired results, or to carry out operating plans once they are made. Success in real life depends on how well a person is able to find and exploit the opportunities that are available to him, and, at the same time, discover and deal with potential serious problems before they become critical.

Problem Solving

Preoccupation with problem solving and decision making in formal management education programs tend to distort managerial growth because it overdevelops an individual's analytical ability, but leaves his ability to take action and to get things done underdeveloped. The behavior required to solve problems that already have been discovered and to make decisions based on facts gathered by someone else is quite different from that required to perform other functions of management.

On the one hand, problem solving and decision making in the classroom require what psychologists call "respondent behavior." It is this type of behavior that enables a person to get high grades on examinations, even though he may never use in later life what he has learned in school.

On the other hand, success and fulfillment in work demand a different kind of behavior which psychologists have labeled "operant behavior." Finding problems and opportunities, initiating action, and following through to attain desired results require the exercise of operant behavior, which is neither measured by examinations nor developed by discussing in the classroom what someone else should do. Operant behavior can be developed only by doing what needs to be done.

Instruction in problem solving and decision making all too often leads to "analysis paralysis" because managerial aspirants are required only to explain and defend their reasoning, not to carry out their decisions or even to plan realistically for their implementations. Problem solving in the classroom often is dealt with, moreover, as an entirely rational process, which, of course, it hardly ever is.

As Professor Harry Levinson of the Harvard Business School points out: "The greatest difficulty people have in solving problems is the fact that emotion makes it hard for them to see and deal with their problems objectively" (1070:109–110).

Rarely do managers learn in formal education programs how to maintain an appropriate psychological distance from their problems so that their judgments are not clouded by their emotions. Management graduates, as a consequence, suffer their worst trauma in business when they discover that rational solutions to problems are not enough; they must also somehow cope with human emotions in order to get results.

Problem Finding

The shortcomings of instruction in problem solving, while important, are not as significant as the failure to teach problem finding. As the research of Norman H. Mackworth of the Institute of Personality Assessment and Research, University of California, has revealed "the distinction between the problem-solver and the problem-finder is vital" (1969:242).

Problem finding, Mackworth points out, is more important than problem solving and involves cognitive processes that are very different from problem solving and much more complex. The most gifted problem finders, he has discovered, rarely have outstanding scholastic records, and those who do excel academically rarely are the most effective problem finders. . . .

. . . the [skill managers] need cannot be developed merely by analyzing problems discovered by someone else; rather, it must be acquired by observing firsthand what is taking place in business. While the analytical skills needed for problem solving are important, more crucial to managerial success are the perceptual skills needed to identify problems long before evidence of them can be found by even the most advanced management information system. Since these perceptual skills are extremely difficult to develop in the classroom, they are now largely left to be developed on the job.

A manager's problem-finding ability is exceeded in importance only by his opportunity-finding ability. Results in business, Peter F. Drucker reminds us, are obtained by exploiting opportunities, not by solving problems. Here is how he puts it:

> All one can hope to get by solving a problem is to restore normality. All one can hope, at best, is to eliminate a restriction on the capacity of the business to obtain results. The results themselves must come from the exploitation of opportunities.... "Maximization of opportunities" is a meaningful, indeed a precise, definition of the entrepreneurial job. It implies that effectiveness rather than efficiency is essential in business. The pertinent question is not how to do things right, but how to find the right things to do, and to concentrate resources and efforts on them. (1964:5).

Managers who lack the skill needed to find those opportunities that will yield the greatest results, not uncommonly spend their time doing the wrong things. But opportunity-finding skill, like problem-finding skill, must be acquired through direct personal experience on the job.

This is not to say that the techniques of opportunity finding and problem finding cannot be taught in formal management education programs, even though they rarely are. But the behavior required to use these techniques successfully can be developed only through actual practice.

A manager cannot learn how to find opportunities or problems without doing it. The doing is essential to the learning. Lectures, case discussions, or text books alone are of limited value in developing ability to find opportunities and problems. Guided practice in finding them in real business situations is the only method that will make a manager skillful in identifying the right things to do.

Natural Management Style

Opportunities are not exploited and problems are not solved, however, until someone takes action and gets the desired results. Managers who are unable to produce effective results on the job invariably fail to build successful careers. But they cannot learn what they most need to know either by studying modern management theories or by discussing in the classroom what someone else should do to get results.

Management is a highly individualized art. What style works well for one manager in a particular situation may not produce the desired results for another manager in a similar situation, or even for the same manager in a different situation. There is no one best way for all managers to manage in all situations. Every manager must discover for himself, therefore, what works and what does not work for him in different situations. He cannot become effective merely by adopting the practices or the managerial style of someone else. He must develop his own natural style and follow practices that are consistent with his own personality.

What all managers need to learn is that to be successful they must manage in a way that is consistent with their unique personalities. When a manager "behaves in ways which do not fit his personality," as Rensis Likert's managerial research has shown, "his behavior is apt to communicate to his subordinates something quite different from what he intends. Subordinates usually view such behavior with suspicion and distrust" (1969:90).

Managers who adopt artificial styles or follow practices that are not consistent with their own personalities are likely not only to be distrusted, but also to be ineffective. It is the men who display the "greatest individuality in managerial be-havior," as Edwin E. Ghiselli's studies of managerial talent show, who in general are the ones "judged to be best managers" (1969:236).

Managers rarely are taught how to manage in ways that are consistent with their own personalities. In many formal education and training programs, they are in fact taught that they must follow a prescribed set of practices and adopt either a "consultative" or "participative" style in order to get the "highest productivity, lowest costs, and best performance" (Likert, 1969:11).

The effectiveness of managers whose personalities do not fit these styles often is impaired and their development arrested. Those who adopt artificial styles typi-cally are seen as counterfeit managers who lack individuality and natural styles of their own.

Managers who are taught by the case method of instruction learn that there is no one best way to manage and no one managerial style that is infallible. But un-like students of medicine, students of management rarely are exposed to "real" people or to "live" cases in programs conducted either in universities or in in-dustry.

They study written case histories that describe problems or opportunities dis-covered by someone else, which they discuss, but do nothing about. What they learn about supervising other people is largely secondhand. Their knowledge is de-rived from the discussion of what someone else should do about the human prob-lems of "paper people" whose emotional reactions, motives, and behavior have been described for them by scholars who may have observed and advised man-agers, but who usually have never taken responsibility for getting results in a busi-ness organization.

Since taking action and accepting responsibility for the consequences are not a part of their formal training, they neither discover for themselves what does—and what does not—work in practice nor develop a natural managerial style that is consistent with their own unique personalities. Managers cannot discover what practices are effective for them until they are in a position to decide for themselves what needs to be done in a specific situation, and to take responsibility both for getting it done and for the consequences of their actions.

Elton Mayo, whose thinking has had a profound impact on what managers are taught but not on how they are taught, observed a quarter of a century ago that studies in the social sciences do not develop any "skill that is directly useful in human situations" (1945:19). He added that he did not believe a useful skill could be developed until a person takes "responsibility for what happens in particular human situations—individual or group. A good bridge player does not merely conduct post mortem discussions of the play in a hand of contract; he takes re-sponsibility for playing it" (p. 32).

Experience is the key to the practitioner's skill. And until a manager learns from his own firsthand experience on the job how to take action and how to gain the willing cooperation of others in achieving desired results, he is not likely to ad-vance very far up the managerial ladder.

NEEDED CHARACTERISTICS

Although there are no born natural leaders, relatively few men ever develop into effective managers or executives. Most, in fact, fail to learn even from their own experience what they need to know to manage other people successfully. What, then, are the characteristics of men who learn to manage effectively?

The answer to the question consists of three ingredients: (1) the need to manage, (2) the need for power, and (3) the capacity for empathy. In this section of the article, I shall discuss each of these characteristics in some detail.

The Need to Manage

This first part of the answer to the question is deceptively simple: only those men who have a strong desire to influence the performance of others and who get genuine satisfaction from doing so can learn to manage effectively. No man is likely to learn how unless he really wants to take responsibility for the productivity of others, and enjoys developing and stimulating them to achieve better results.

Many men who aspire to high-level managerial positions are not motivated to manage. They are motivated to earn high salaries and to attain high status, but they are not motivated to get effective results through others. They expect to gain great satisfaction from the income and prestige associated with executive positions in important enterprises, but they do not expect to gain much satisfaction from the achievements of their subordinates. Although their aspirations are high, their motivation to supervise other people is low.

A major reason why highly educated and ambitious men do not learn how to develop successful managerial careers is that they lack the "will to manage." The "*way* to manage," as Marvin Bower has observed, usually can be found if there is the "*will* to manage." But if a person lacks the desire, he "will not devote the time, energy, and thought required to find the way to manage" (1966:6).

No one is likely to sustain for long the effort required to get high productivity from others unless he has a strong psychological need to influence their performance. The need to manage is a crucial factor, therefore, in determining whether a person will learn and apply in practice what is necessary to get effective results on the job.

High grades in school and outstanding performance as an accountant, an engineer, or a salesman reveal how able and willing a person is to perform tasks he has been assigned. But an outstanding record as an individual performer does not indicate whether that person is able or willing to get other people to excel at the same tasks. Outstanding scholars often make poor teachers, excellent engineers often are unable to supervise the work of other engineers, and successful salesmen often are ineffective sales managers.

Indeed, men who are outstanding individual performers not uncommonly become "do-it-yourself" managers. Although they are able and willing to do the job themselves, they lack the motivation and temperament to get it done by others. They may excel as individual performers and may even have good records as first-line managers. But they rarely advance far up the organizational hierarchy because, no matter how hard they try, they cannot make up through their own efforts for mediocre or poor performance by large numbers of subordinates.

Universities and business organizations that select managerial candidates on the basis of their records as individual performers often pick the wrong men to develop as managers. These men may get satisfaction from their own outstanding performance, but unless they are able to improve the productivity of other people, they are not likely to become successful managers.

Fewer and fewer men who hold advanced degrees in management want to take responsibility for getting results through others. More and more of them are attracted to jobs that permit them to act in the detached role of the consultant or specialized expert, a role described by John W. Gardner (1965) as the one preferred increasingly by university graduates. . . .

As Charlie Brown prophetically observed in a "Peanuts" cartoon strip in which he is standing on the pitcher's mound surrounded by his players, all of whom are telling him what to do at a critical point in a baseball game: "The world is filled with people who are anxious to act in an advisory capacity." Educational institutions are turning out scholars, scientists, and experts who are anxious to act as advisers, but they are producing few men who are eager to lead or take responsibility for the performance of others.

Most management graduates prefer staff positions in headquarters to line positions in the field or factory. More and more of them want jobs that will enable them to use their analytical ability rather than their supervisory ability. Fewer and fewer are willing to make the sacrifices required to learn management from the bottom up; increasingly, they hope to step in at the top from positions where they observe, analyze, and advise but do not have personal responsibility for results. Their aspirations are high, but their need to take responsibility for the productivity of other people is low.

The tendency for men who hold advanced degrees in management to take staff jobs and to stay in these positions too long makes it difficult for them to develop the supervisory skills they need to advance within their companies. Men who fail to gain direct experience as line managers in the first few years of their careers commonly do not acquire the capabilities they need to manage other managers and to sustain their upward progress past middle age.

"A man who performs nonmanagerial tasks five years or more," as Jennings discovered, "has a decidedly greater improbability of becoming a high wage earner. High salaries are being paid to manage managers (1967:15). This may well explain in part why the median salaries of Harvard Business School graduates plateau just at the time they might be expected to move up into the ranks of top management.

The Need for Power

Psychologists once believed that the motive that caused men to strive to attain high-level managerial positions was the "need for achievement." But now they believe it is the "need for power," which is the second part of the answer to the question: What are the characteristics of men who learn to manage effectively? . . .

Power seekers can be counted on to strive hard to reach positions where they can exercise authority over large numbers of people. Individual performers who lack this drive are not likely to act in ways that will enable them to advance far up the managerial ladder. They usually scorn company politics and devote their energies to other types of activities that are more satisfying to them. But, to prevail in the competitive struggle to attain and hold high-level positions in management, a person's desire for prestige and high income must be reinforced by the satisfaction he gets or expects to get from exercising the power and authority of a high office.

The competitive battle to advance within an organization, as Levinson points out, is much like playing "King of the Hill" (1969:53). Unless a person enjoys playing that game, he is likely to tire of it and give up the struggle for control of the top of the hill. The power game is a part of management, and it is played best by those who enjoy it most.

The power drive that carries men to the top also accounts for their tendency to use authoritative rather than consultative or participative methods of management. But to expect otherwise is not realistic. Few men who strive hard to gain and hold positions of power can be expected to be permissive, particularly if their authority is challenged.

Since their satisfaction comes from the exercise of authority, they are not likely to share much of it with lower-level managers who eventually will replace them, even though most high-level executives try diligently to avoid the appearance of being authoritarian. It is equally natural for ambitious lower-level managers who have a high need for power themselves to believe that better results would be achieved if top management shared more authority with them, even though they, in turn, do not share much of it with their subordinates.

One of the least rational acts of business organizations is that of hiring managers who have a high need to exercise authority, and then teaching them that authoritative methods are wrong and that they should be consultative or participative. It is a serious mistake to teach managers that they should adopt styles that are artificial and inconsistent with their unique personalities. Yet this is precisely what a large number of business organizations are doing; and it explains, in part, why their management development programs are not effective.

What managerial aspirants should be taught is how to exercise their authority in a way that is appropriate to the characteristics of the situation and the people involved. Above all, they need to learn that the real source of their power is their own knowledge and skill, and the strength of their own personalities, not the authority conferred on them by their positions. They need to know that overreliance on the traditional authority of their official positions is likely to be fatal to their career aspirations because the effectiveness of this kind of authority is declining everywhere —in the home, in the church, and in the state as well as in business.

More than authority to hire, promote, and fire is required to get superior results from most subordinates. To be effective, managers must possess the authority that comes with knowledge and skill, and be able to exercise the charismatic authority that is derived from their own personalities.

When they lack the knowledge or skill required to perform the work, they need to know how to share their traditional authority with those who know what has to be done to get results. When they lack the charisma needed to get the willing cooperation of those on whom they depend for performance, they must be able to share their traditional authority with the informal leaders of the group, if any exist.

But when they know what has to be done and have the skill and personality to get it done, they must exercise their traditional authority in whatever way is necessary to get the results they desire. Since a leader cannot avoid the exercise of authority, he must understand the nature and limitations of it, and be able to use it in an appropriate manner. Equally important, he must avoid trying to exercise authority he does not, in fact, possess.

The Capacity for Empathy

Mark Van Doren once observed that an educated man is one "who is able to use the intellect he was born with: the intellect, and whatever else is important" (1967:13). At the top of the list of "whatever else is important" is the third characteristic necessary in order to manage other people successfully. Namely, it is the capacity for empathy or the ability to cope with the emotional reactions that inevitably occur when people work together in an organization.

Many men who have more than enough abstract intelligence to learn the methods and techniques of management fail because their affinity with other people is almost entirely intellectual or cognitive. They may have "intellectual empathy" but may not be able to sense or identify the unverbalized emotional feelings which strongly influence human behavior (Paul, 1967:155). They are emotion-blind just as some men are color-blind.

Such men lack what Normal L. Paul describes as "affective empathy" (p. 155). And since they cannot recognize unexpressed emotional feelings, they are unable to learn from their own experience how to cope with the emotional reactions that are crucial in gaining the willing cooperation of other people.

Many men who hold advanced degrees in management are emotion-blind. As Schein has found, they often are "mired in the code of rationality" and, as a consequence, "undergo a rude shock" on their first jobs (p. 92). After interviewing dozens of recent graduates of the Sloan School of Management at MIT, Schein reported that "they talk like logical men who have stumbled into a cell of irrational souls," and he added,

> At an emotional level, ex-students resent the human emotions that make a company untidy. . . . [Few] can accept without pain the reality of the organization's human side. Most try to wish it away, rather than work in and around it. . . . If a graduate happens to have the capacity to accept, maybe to love, human organization, this gift seems directly related to his potential as a manager or executive" (p. 90).

Whether managers can be taught in the classroom how to cope with human emotions is a moot point. There is little reason to believe that what is now taught in psychology classes, human relations seminars, and sensitivity training programs is of much help to men who are "mired in the code of rationality" and who lack "affective empathy."

Objective research has shown that efforts to sensitize supervisors to the feelings of others not only often have failed to improve performance, but in some cases have made the situation worse than it was before (see Fleishmann et al., 1955). Supervisors who are unable "to tune in empathically" on the emotional feelings aroused on the job are not likely to improve their ability to emphathize with others in the classroom (Paul, pp. 150–157).

Indeed, extended classroom discussions about what other people should do to cope with emotional situations may well inhibit rather than stimulate the development of the ability of managers to cope with the emotional reactions they experience on the job.

CONCLUSION

Many highly intelligent and ambitious men are not learning from either their formal education or their own experience what they most need to know to build successful careers in management.

Their failure is due, in part, to the fact that many crucial managerial tasks are not taught in management education programs but are left to be learned on the job, where few managers ever master them because no one teaches them how. It also is due, in part, to the fact that what takes place in the classroom often is miseducation that inhibits their ability to learn from their experience. Commonly, they learn theories of management that cannot be applied successfully in practice, a limitation many of them discover only through the direct experience of becoming a line executive and meeting personally the problems involved.

Some men become confused about the exercise of authority because they are taught only about the traditional authority a manager derives from his official position—a type of authority that is declining in effectiveness everywhere. A great many become innoculated with an "antileadership vaccine" that arouses within them intense negative feelings about authoritarian leaders, even though a leader cannot avoid the exercise of authority any more than he can avoid the responsibility for what happens to his organization.

Since these highly educated men do not learn how to exercise authority derived from their own knowledge and skill or from the charisma of their own personalities, more and more of them avoid responsibility for the productivity of others by taking jobs that enable them to act in the detached role of the consultant or specialized expert. Still others impair their effectiveness by adopting artificial managerial styles that are not consistent with their own unique personalities but give them the appearance of being "consultative" or "participative," an image they believe is helpful to their advancement up the managerial ladder.

Some managers who have the intelligence required to learn what they need to know fail because they lack "whatever else is important," especially "affective empathy" and the need to develop and stimulate the productivity of other people. But the main reason many highly educated men do not build successful managerial careers is that they are not able to learn from their own firsthand experience what they need to know to gain the willing cooperation of other people. Since they have not learned how to observe their environment firsthand or to assess feedback from their actions, they are poorly prepared to learn and grow as they gain experience.

Alfred North Whitehead once observed that "the secondhandedness of the learned world is the secret of its mediocrity" (Whitehead, 1929:79). Until managerial aspirants are taught to learn from their own firsthand experience, formal management education will remain secondhanded. And its secondhandedness is the real reason why the well-educated manager is a myth.

BIBLIOGRAPHY FOR READINGS

ABELL, D.F., *Defining the Business: The Starting Point of Strategic Planning.* Englewood Cliffs, N.J.: Prentice Hall, 1980.

ABERNATHY, W.J. & K. WAYNE, "Limits on the Learning Curve," *Harvard Business Review,* September–October 1974: 109–119.

ACKERMAN, R.W., *The Social Challenge to Business.* Cambridge, MA: Harvard University Press, 1975.

ADVISORY COMMITTEE ON INDUSTRIAL INNOVATION: FINAL REPORT. Washington, D.C.: U.S. Government Printing Office, 1979.

AGUILAR, F.J., *Scanning the Business Environment.* New York: Macmillan, 1967.

ALLEN, M.P., "The Structure of Interorganizational Elite Cooptation: Interlocking Corporate Directorates," *American Sociological Review,* 1974: 393–406.

ALLEN, S.A., "Organizational Choices and General Management Influence Networks in Divisionalized Companies," *Academy of Management Journal,* 1978: 341–365.

ALLISON, G.T., *Essence of Decision: Explaining the Cuban Missile Crisis.* Boston: Little, Brown, 1971.

ANSOFF, H.I., *Corporate Strategy: An Analytic Approach to Business Policy for Growth and Expansion.* New York, McGraw-Hill, 1965.

ARGYRIS, C., "Double Loop Learning in Organizations," *Harvard Business Review,* September–October 1977: 115–125.

ASTLEY, W.G., & C.J. FOMBRUN, "Collective Strategy: Social Ecology of Organizational Environments," *Academy of Management Review,* 1983: 576–587.

BACON, J., *Corporate Directorship Practices: Membership and Committees of the Board.* Conference Board and American Society of Corporate Secretaries, Inc., 1973.

———, & J.K. BROWN, *Corporate Directorship Practices: Role, Selection and Legal Status of the Board.* New York: The Conference Board, 1975.

BADEN FULLER, C., et al., "National or Global? The Study of Company Strategies and the European Market for Major Appliances," London Business School Centre for Business Strategy, Working Paper series no. 28 (June 1987).

BARNARD, C.I., *The Functions of the Executive.* Cambridge, Mass.: Harvard University Press, 1938.

BARREYRE, P.Y., "The Concept of 'Impartition' Policy in High Speed Strategic Management." Working Paper, Institut d'Administration des Entreprises, Grenoble, 1984.

———, & M. CARLE, "Impartition Policies: Growing Importance in Corporate Strategies and Applications to Production Sharing in Some World-Wide Industries." Paper Presented at Strategic Management Society Conference, Paris, 1983.

BARRIER, M., "Walton's Mountain," *Nation's Business,* April 1988: 18–26.

BARTLETT, C.A., & S. GHOSHAL, "Managing Across Borders: New Strategic Requirements," *Sloan Management Review,* Summer 1987: 7–17.

BATY, G.B., W.M. EVAN, & T. W. ROTHERMEL, "Personnel Flows as Interorganizational Relations," *Administrative Science Quarterly,* 1971: 430–443.

BAUER, R. A., I. POOL, & L.A. DEXTER, *American Business and Public Policy.* New York: Atherton Press, 1968.

BAUMBACK, C., & J. MANCUSO, *Entrepreneurship and Venture Management.* Englewood Cliffs, N.J.: Prentice Hall, 1975.

BECKER, G., *Human Capital.* New York: National Bureau of Economic Research, 1964.

BEER, S., *Designing Freedom.* Toronto: CBC Publications, 1974.

BENNIS, W.G. & P.L. SLATER, *The Temporary Society.* New York: Harper & Row, 1964.

BERLEW, D.E. & D.T. HALL, "The Management of Tension in Organization: Some Preliminary Findings," *Industrial Management Review,* Fall 1964: 31–40.

BERNSTEIN, L., "Joint Ventures in the Light of Recent Antitrust Developments," *The Antitrust Bulletin,* 1965: 25–29.

BETTIS, R. A., "Performance Differences in Related and Unrelated Diversified Firms," *Strategic Management Journal,* 1981: 379–394.

BOSTON CONSULTING GROUP, *Perspectives on Experience.* Boston, 1972.

——, *Strategy Alternatives for the British Motorcycle Industry.* London: Her Majesty's Stationery Office, 1975.

BOULDING, K. E., "The Ethics of Rational Decision," *Management Science,* 1966: 161–169.

BOWER, J. L., "Planning within the Firm," *The American Economic Review,* 1970: 186–194.

BOWMAN, E.H., "Epistemology, Corporate Strategy, and Academe," *Sloan Management Review,* Winter 1974: 35–50.

BRAYBROOKE, D., "Skepticism of Wants, and Certain Subversive Effects of Corporations on American Values," in S. Hook, ed., *Human Values and Economic Policy.* New York: New York University Press, 1967.

—— & C.E. LINDBLOM, *A Strategy of Decision: Policy Evaluation as a Social Process.* New York: Free Press, 1963.

BRENNER, S.N. & E.A. MOLANDER, "Is the Ethic of Business Changing?" *Harvard Business Review,* January–February 1977: 57–71.

BROOK, P., *The Empty Space.* Harmondsworth, Middlesex: Penguin Books, 1968.

BROOM, H.N., J.G. LONGENECKER & C.W. MOORE, *Small Business Management.* Cincinnati, OH: Southwest, 1983.

BRUNSSON, N., "The Irrationality of Action and Action Rationality: Decisions, Ideologies, and Organizational Actions," *Journal of Management Studies,* 1982(1): 29–44.

BUCHELE, R. B., *Business Policy in Growing Firms.* San Francisco, CA: Chandler, 1967.

BURNS, T., "Micropolitics: Mechanisms of Institutional Change," *Administrative Science Quarterly.* December 1961: 257–281.

—— & G.M. STALKER, *The Management of Innovation,* 2d ed. London: Tavistock, 1966.

BUSINESS WEEK. "Japan's Strategy for the 80's," December 14, 1981: 39–120.

——. "The Hollow Corporation," March 3, 1986: Supplement.

BUZZELL, R. D., B.T. GALE, & R.G.M. SULTAN, "Market Share—A Key to Profitability," *Harvard Business Review,* January–February 1975: 97–106.

CARLZON, J., *Moments of Truth.* New York: Ballinger Press, 1987.

CHANDLER, A.D., *Strategy and Structure: Chapters in the History of the Industrial Enterprise.* Cambridge, Mass.: M.I.T. Press, 1962.

CHANNON, D.F., "The Strategy, Structure and Financial Performance of the Service Industries," Working Paper, Manchester Business School, 1975.

CHEIT, E.F., "The New Place of Business: Why Managers Cultivate Social Responsibility," in E.F. Cheit, ed., *The Business Establishment.* New York: John Wiley, 1964.

CHRISTENSON, C.R., K.R. ANDREWS, & J.L. BOWER, *Business Policy: Text and Cases.* Homewood, Ill.: Richard D. Irwin, 1978.

CLARK, B.R., *The Distinctive College: Antioch, Reed and Swarthmore.* Chicago: Aldine, 1970.

——, "The Organizational Saga in Higher Education," *Administrative Science Quarterly,* 1972: 178–184.

CLARK, R.C., *The Japanese Company.* New Haven: Yale University Press, 1979.

COHEN, K.J. & R.M. CYERT, "Strategy: Formulation, Implementation and Monitoring," *The Journal of Business,* 1973: 349–367.

—— & J.P. OLSEN, "A Garbage Can Model of Organizational Choice," *Administrative Science Quarterly,* 1972: 1–25.

COHN, T., & R.A. LINDBERG, *How Management is Different in Small Companies.* New York: American Management Association, 1972.

COLE, A.H., Business Enterprise in Its Social Setting. Cambridge, Mass.: Harvard University Press, 1959.

COLE, R.E., *Japanese Blue Collar: The Changing Tradition.* Berkeley: University of California Press, 1971.

——, *Work, Mobility and Participation.* Berkeley: University of California Press, 1979.

COPEMAN, G.H., *The Role of the Managing Director.* London: Business Publications, 1963.

COYNE, K.P., "Sustainable Competitive Advantage," *Business Horizons,* January–February 1986: 54–61.

CROZIER, M., *The Bureaucratic Phenomenon.* Chicago: University of Chicago Press, 1964.

CVAR, M.R., "Case Studies in Global Competition," in M.E. Porter, ed., *Competition in Global Industries.* Boston: Harvard Business School Press, 1986.

CYERT, R.M., W. R. DILL, & J.G. MARCH, "The Role of Expectations in Business Decision Making," *Administrative Science Quarterly,* 1958: 307–340.

CYERT, R.M. & J.G. MARCH, *A Behavioral Theory of the Firm.* Englewood Cliffs, N.J.: Prentice Hall, 1963.

DAVIS, R.T., *Performance and Development of Field Sales Managers.* Boston: Harvard Business School, 1957.

DELBECQ, A. & A.C. FILLEY, *Program and Project Man-*

agement in a Matrix Organization: A Case Study. Madison, Wis.: University of Wisconsin, 1974.

DOERINGER, P. & M. PIORE, *Internal Labor Market and Manpower Analysis.* Lexington, Mass.: Lexington Books, 1971.

DOUGLAS, S.P., & Y. WIND, "The Myth of Globalization," *Columbia Journal of World Business,* Winter 1987: 19–29.

DRUCKER, P.F., *The Practice of Management.* New York: Harper & Row, 1954.

———, *Management: Tasks, Responsibilities, Practices.* New York: Harper & Row, 1974.

———, "Clouds Forming Across the Japanese Sun," *Wall Street Journal,* July 13, 1982.

EDWARDS, J.P., "Strategy Formulation as a Stylistic Process," *International Studies of Management and Organization,* Summer 1977: 13–27.

ELECTRONIC BUSINESS, "Services Get the Job Done," September 15, 1988: 87–90.

EPSTEIN, E.M., *The Corporation in American Politics.* Englewood Cliffs, N.J.: Prentice Hall, 1969.

———, "The Social Role of Business Enterprise in Britain: An American Perspective; Part II," *The Journal of Management Studies,* 1977: 281–316.

ESSAME, H., *Patton: A Study in Command.* New York: Charles Scribner's Sons, 1974.

EVERED, R., *So What Is Strategy?* Working Paper, Naval Postgraduate School, Monterey, 1980.

FARAGO, L., *Patton: Ordeal and Triumph.* New York: I. Obolensky, 1964.

FIRSIROTU, M., "Strategic Turnaround as Cultural Revolution: The Case of Canadian National Express," doctoral dissertation, Faculty of Management, 1985.

FLEISHMANN, E.A., E.F. HARRIS, & H.E. BURT, *Leadership and Supervision in Industry: An Evaluation of Supervisory Training Program.* Columbus, Ohio: The Ohio State University, 1955.

FOCH, F., *Principles of War,* translated by J. DeMorinni. New York: AMS Press, 1970. First published London: Chapman & Hall, 1918.

FORRESTER, J. W., "Counterintuitive Behavior of Social Systems," *Technology Review,* January 1971: 52–68.

FRANKLIN, B., *Poor Richard's Almanac.* New York: Ballantine Books, 1977. First Published, Century Company, 1898.

FRIEDMAN, M., *Capitalism and Freedom.* Chicago: University of Chicago Press, 1962.

———, "A Friedman Doctrine: The Social Responsibility of Business is to Increase its Profits," *The New York Times Magazine,* September 13, 1970.

GALBRAITH, J.K., *American Capitalism: The Concept of Countervailing Power.* Boston: Houghton Mifflin, 1952.

———, *The New Industrial State.* Boston: Houghton Mifflin, 1967.

GALBRAITH, J. R., *Organization Design.* Reading, Mass.: Addison-Wesley, 1977.

———, "Strategy and Organization Planning." *Human Resource Management,* 1983: 63–77.

——— & D. NATHANSON, *Strategy Implementation.* St. Paul, Minn.: West Publishing, 1978.

GARDNER, J.W., "The Anti-Leadership Vaccine," in *Carnegie Corporation of New York Annual Report,* 1965.

GARSON, G.D., "The Codetermination Model of Worker's Participation: Where Is It Leading?" *Sloan Management Review,* Spring 1977: 63–78.

GERTH, H.H., & C. WRIGHT MILLS, eds., *From Max Weber: Essays in Sociology.* New York: Oxford University Press, 1958.

GHISELLI, E.E., "Managerial Talent," in D. Wolfe, ed., *The Discovery of Talent.* Cambridge, Mass.: Harvard University Press, 1969.

GILDER, G., *Wealth and Poverty.* New York: Basic Books, 1981.

GILMORE, F.F., "Overcoming the Perils of Advocacy in Corporate Planning," *California Management Review,* Spring 1973: 127–137.

GLUECK, W. F., *Business Policy and Strategic Management.* New York: McGraw Hill, 1980.

GOSSELIN, R., *A Study of the Interdependence of Medical Specialists in Quebec Teaching Hospitals.* Ph.D. thesis, McGill University, 1978.

GREEN, P., *Alexander the Great.* New York: Frederick A. Praeger, 1970.

GREINER, L.E., "Evolution and Revolution as Organizations Grow," *Harvard Business Review,* July–August 1972: 37–46.

———, "Senior Executives as Strategic Actors," *New Management,* Vol. 1, no. 2, Summer 1983.

GRINYER, P.H., & J.C. SPENDER, *Turnaround—Management Recipes for Strategic Success.* New York: Associated Business Press, 1979.

GROSS, W., "Coping with Radical Competition," in A. Gross & W. Gross, eds., *Business Policy: Selected Readings and Editorial Commentaries,* pp. 550–560. New York: Ronald Press, 1967.

GUEST, R.H., "Of Time and The Foreman," *Personnel,* May 1956: 478–486.

HAITANI, K., "Changing Characteristics of the Japanese Employment System," *Asian Survey,* 1978: 1029–1045.

HAMERMESH, R.G., M.J. ANDERSON, JR. & J.E. HARRIS, "Strategies for Low Market Share Business," *Harvard Business Review,* May–June 1978: 95–102.

HART, B.H.L., *Strategy.* New York: Frederick A. Praeger, 1954.

HATTORI, I., "A Proposition on Efficient Decision-Making in Japanese Corporation," *Management Japan,* Autumn 1977: 14–20.

HAYES, R.H. & W. J. ABERNATHY, "Managing Our Way to Economic Decline," *Harvard Business Review,* July–August 1980: 67–77.

———— & D.A. GARVIN, "Managing as if Tomorrow Mattered," *Harvard Business Review,* May–June 1982: 70–79.

HAZAMA, H., "Characteristics of Japanese-Style Management," *Japanese Economic Studies,* Spring–Summer 1978: 110–173.

HEDBERG, B.L.T., "How Organizations Learn and Unlearn," in P.C. Nystrom and W.H. Starbuck, eds., *Handbook of Organizational Design,* Volume 1. New York: Oxford University Press, 1981.

———— & S.A. JÖNSSON, "Designing Semi-confusing Information Systems for Organizations in Changing Environments," *Accounting Organizations and Society,* 1978: 47–64.

————, P.C. NYSTROM, & W.H. STARBUCK, "Camping on Seesaws: Prescriptions for a Self-designing Organization," *Administrative Science Quarterly,* 1976: 41–65.

HICKSON, D.J., C.A. LEE, R.E. SCHNECK & J.M. PENNINGS, "A Strategic Contingencies' Theory of Intraorganizational Power," *Administrative Science Quarterly,* 1971: 216–229.

HIRSCH, P.M., "Organizational Effectiveness and the Institutional Environment," *Administrative Science Quarterly,* 1975: 327–344.

HOFER, C.W. & D. SCHENDEL, *Strategy Formulation: Analytical Concepts.* St. Paul, Minn.: West Publishing, 1978.

HOSMER, A., "Small Manufacturing Enterprises," *Harvard Business Review,* November–December 1957: 111–122.

HOUSE OF REPRESENTATIVES, Staff Report to the Antitrust Subcommittee of the Committee on the Judiciary, *Interlocks in Corporate Management,* Washington, D.C.: U.S. Government Printing Office, 1965.

HOUT, T., M.E. PORTER & E. RUDDEN, "How Global Companies Win Out," *Harvard Business Review,* September–October 1982: 98–108.

HUGHES, T., "The Inventive Continuum," *Science 84,* November 1984.

HUNT, R.G., "Technology and Organization," *Academy of Management Journal,* 1970: 235–252.

IACOCCA, L., with W. NOVAK, *Iacocca: An Autobiography.* New York: Bantam Books, 1984.

IMAI, K., I. NONAKA & H. TAKEUCHI, "Managing the New Product Development Process: How Japanese Companies Learn and Unlearn," in K.B. Clark, R.H. Hayes, and C. Lorenz, eds., *The Uneasy Alliance.* Boston: Harvard Business School Press, 1985.

IRVING, D., *The Trail of the Fox.* New York: E.P. Dutton, 1977.

JACOBS, D., "Dependency and Vulnerability: An Exchange Approach to the Control of Organizations," *Administrative Science Quarterly,* 1974: 45–59.

JAMES, D.C., *The Years of MacArthur, 1941–1945.* Boston: Houghton Mifflin, 1970.

JANIS, I., *Victims of Group Think.* Boston: Houghton Mifflin, 1972.

JAY, A., *Management and Machiavelli.* New York: Penguin Books, 1970.

JENKINS, C., *Power at the Top.* Westport, Conn.: Greenwood Press, 1976.

JENNINGS, E.E., *The Mobile Manager.* Ann Arbor: University of Michigan, 1967.

JOHNSON, S.C., & C. JONES, "How to Organize for New Products," *Harvard Business Review,* May–June 1957: 49–62.

JOMINI, A.H., *Art of War,* translated by G.H. Mendell and W.P. Craighill. Westport, Conn.: Greenwood Press, 1971. Original Philadelphia: J. B. Lippincott, 1862.

JÖNSSON, S.A. & R.A. LUNDIN, "Myths and Wishful Thinking as Management Tools," in P.C. Nystrom and W.H. Starbuck eds., *Prescriptive Models of Organizations.* Amsterdam: North-Holland, 1977.

JORDAN, W.A., "Producer Protection Prior Market Structure and the Effects of Government Regulation," *Journal of Law and Economics,* 1972.

KAGONO, T., I. NONAKA, K. SAKAKIBARA & A. OKUMURA, *Strategic vs. Evolutionary Management: A. U.S.–Japan Comparison of Strategy and Organization.* Amsterdam: North-Holland, 1985.

KAHN, R. L., D.M. WOLFE, R.P. QUINN, J.D. SNOEK, & R.A. ROSENTHAL, *Organizational Stress.* New York: John Wiley, 1964.

KAMI, M.J. & J.E. ROSS, *Corporate Management in Crisis: Why the Mighty Fall.* Englewood Cliffs, N.J.: Prentice Hall, 1973.

KANO, T., "Comparative Study of Strategy, Structure and Long-Range Planning in Japan and in the United States," *Management Japan,* 1980(1): 20–34.

KATZ, R.L., *Cases and Concepts in Corporate Strategy.* Englewood Cliffs, N.J.: Prentice Hall, 1970.

————, "Time and Work: Towards an Integrative Perspective," in B.M. Staw and L.L. Cummings, eds., *Research in Organizational Behavior,* Vol. 1. Greenwich, Conn.: JAI Press, 1980.

KIDDER, T., *The Soul of a New Machine.* Boston: Little, Brown, 1981.

KIECHEL, W., III, "Sniping at Strategic Planning (interview with himself)," *Planning Review,* May 1984: 8–11.

KONO, T., "Comparative Study of Strategy, Structure and Long-Range Planning in Japan and in the United States," *Management Japan,* Spring 1980: 20–34.

KOTLER, P., & R. SINGH, "Marketing Warfare in the 1980s," *Journal of Business Strategy,* Winter 1981: 30–41.

KOTTER, J.P., & L.A. SCHLESINGER, "Choosing Strategies for Change," *Harvard Business Review,* March–April 1979: 106–114.

KUHN, T., *The Structure of Scientific Revolutions.* Chicago: University of Chicago Press, 1970.

LAND, E., "People Should Want More from Life . . . ," *Forbes,* June 1, 1975.

LAPIERRE, L., "Le changement stratégique: Un rêve en quête de réel." Ph.D. Management Policy course paper, McGill University, Canada, 1980.

LEARNED, E.P., C.R. CHRISTIANSEN, K.R. ANDREWS & W.D. GUTH, *Business Policy: Text and Cases.* Homewood, IL: Richard D. Irwin, 1965.

————, D.N. ULRICH, & D.R. BOOZ, *Executive Action.* Boston: Harvard Business School, 1951.

LENIN, V.I., *Collected Works of V.I. Lenin,* edited and annotated. New York: International Publishers, 1927.

LEVINSON, H., "On Becoming a Middle-Aged Manager," *Harvard Business Review,* July–August 1969: 51–60.

————, *Executive Stress.* New York: Harper & Row, 1970.

LEVITT, T., "Marketing Myopia," *Harvard Business Review,* July–August 1960: 45–56.

————, "Why Business Always Loses," *Harvard Business Review,* March–April 1968: 81–89.

————, "Industrialization of Service," *Harvard Business Review,* September–October 1976: 63–74.

————, "Marketing Success Through Differentiation—of Anything," *Harvard Business Review,* January–February 1980: 83–91.

————, "The Globalization of Markets," *Harvard Business Review,* May–June 1983: 92–102.

————, *The Marketing Imagination.* New York: Free Press, 1983.

LEWIN, K., *Field Theory in Social Science.* New York: Harper & Row, 1951.

LIKERT, R., *New Patterns of Management.* New York: McGraw-Hill, 1969.

LINDBLOM, C.E., "The Science of 'Muddling Through,'" *Public Administration Review,* 1959: 79–88.

————, *The Policy-Making Process.* Englewood Cliffs, N.J.: Prentice Hall, 1968.

LITTLE, A.D., INC., *"Transportation Planning in the District of Columbia, 1955–65: A Review and Critique,"* Report to The Policy Advisory Committee to the District Commissioners. Washington, D.C.: U.S. Government Printing Office, 1966.

LODGE, G.C., *The New American Ideology.* New York: Alfred A. Knopf, 1975.

LOHR, S., "Japan Struggling With Itself," *New York Times,* June 13, 1982.

MACAVOY, P.W., *The Economic Effects of Regulation.* Cambridge, MA: M.I.T Press, 1965.

MACMILLAN, I.C., "Seizing Competitive Initiative," *Journal of Business Strategy,* Spring 1982: 43–57.

————, "Preemptive Strategies," *Journal of Business Strategy,* Fall 1983: 16–26.

————, & P.E. JONES, "Designing Organizations to Compete," *Journal of Business Strategy,* Spring 1984: 11–26.

————, M. MCCAFFERY & G. VAN WIJK, "Competitors' Responses to Easily Imitated New Products—Exploring Commercial Banking Product Introductions," *Strategic Management Journal,* 1985: 75–86.

MACE, M.L. & G.G. MONTGOMERY, *Management Problems of Corporate Acquisitions.* Boston: Harvard Business School, 1962.

MACHIAVELLI, N., *The Prince, and the Discourses.* New York: Modern Library, 1950.

MACKWORTH, N.H., "Originality," in D. Wolfe, ed., *The Discovery of Talent.* Cambridge, Mass.: Harvard University Press, 1969.

MAGEE, J.F., "Decision Trees for Decision Making," *Harvard Business Review,* July–August, 1964: 126–138.

————, *Desirable Characteristics of Models in Planning,* a paper delivered at the Symposium on the role of Economic Models in Policy Formulation, sponsored by the Department of Housing and Urban Development, Office of Emergency Planning, National Resource Evaluation Center, Washington, D.C., October, 1966.

MAJONE, G., "The Use of Policy Analysis," in *The Future and the Past: Essays on Programs,* Russell Sage Foundation Annual Report, 1976–1977.

MAO TSE-TUNG, *Selected Military Writings, 1928–1949.* San Francisco: China Books, 1967.

MARCH, J.G. & J.P. OLSEN, *Ambiguity and Choice in Organizations.* Bergen, Norway: Universitetsforlaget, 1976.

————, & H.A. SIMON, *Organizations.* New York: John Wiley, 1958.

MARSHALL, G.L., *Predicting Executive Achievement.* Ph.D. thesis, Harvard Business School, 1964.

MARTIN, L.C. "How Beatrice Foods Sneaked Up On $5 Billion," *Fortune,* April 1976: 119–129.

MATLOFF, M. & E.M. SNELL, *Strategic Planning for Coalition Warfare (1941–42).* Washington, D. C.: Office of Chief of Military History, Department of the Army, 1953.

MAYO, E., *The Social Problems of an Industrial Civilization.* Boston: Harvard Business School, 1945.

MCCLELLAND, D.C., "The Two Faces of Power," *Journal of International Affairs,* 1970: 29–47.

MCDONALD, J., *Strategy in Poker, Business and War.* New York: W.W. Norton, 1950.

MCINTYRE, S.H., "Obstacles to Corporate Innovation," *Business Horizons,* January–February 1982: 23–28.

MECHANIC, D., "Sources of Power of Lower Participants in Complex Organizations," *Administrative Science Quarterly,* 1962: 349–364.

464

MILLER, D., & P.H. FRIESEN, "Archetypes of Strategy Formulation," *Management Science,* May 1978: 921–933.

_____, *Organizations: A Quantum View.* Englewood Cliffs, N.J.: Prentice Hall, 1984.

_____, & M. KETS DE VRIES, *The Neurotic Organization.* San Francisco: Jossey-Bass, 1984.

_____, *Unstable at the Top.* New York: New American Library, 1987.

_____, & H. MINTZBERG, *Strategy Formulation in Context: Some Tentative Models.* Working Paper, McGill University, 1974.

MINTZBERG, H., "Research on Strategy-Making," *Academy of Management Proceedings,* 1972: 90–94.

_____, *The Nature of Managerial Work.* New York: Harper & Row, 1973.

_____, "Strategy Making in Three Modes," *California Management Review,* Winter 1973b: 44–53.

_____, "The Manager's Job: Folklore and Fact," *Harvard Business Review,* July–August 1975: 49–61.

_____, "Generic Strategies: Toward a Comprehensive Framework," *Advances in Strategic Management,* Vol. 5, pp. 1–67. Greenwich, CT: JAI Press, 1988.

_____, D. RAÌSINGNANÌ, & A. THÉORÊT, "The Structure of 'Unstructured' Decision Processes," *Administrative Science Quarterly,* 1976: 246–275.

_____ & J.A. WATERS, "Tracking Strategy in an Entrepreneurial Firm," *Academy of Management Journal,* 1982: 465–499.

_____, "Of Strategies, Deliberate and Emergent," *Strategic Management Journal,* 1985: 257–272.

MONTGOMERY, B.L., *The Memoirs of Field-Marshal The Viscount Montgomery of Alamein.* Cleveland: World Publishing, 1958.

MORITANI, M., *Japanese Technology: Getting the Best for the Least.* Tokyo: Simul Press, 1981.

MOYER, R.C., "Berle and Means Revisited: The Conglomerate Merger," *Business and Society,* Spring 1970: 20–29.

NADLER, D.A. & E.E. LAWLER, III, "Motivation—A Diagnostic Approach," in J.R. Hackman, E.E. Lawler, III, and L.W. Porter, eds., *Perspective on Behavior in Organizations.* New York: McGraw-Hill, 1977.

NADLER, D., & M.L. TUSHMAN, *Strategic Organization Design.* Homewood, IL: Scott Foresman, 1986.

NAISBITT, J., *Megatrends.* New York: Warner Books, 1982.

NAPOLEON, I., "Maximes de Guerre," in T.R. Phillips, ed., *Roots of Strategy.* Harrisburg, Pa.: Military Service Publishing, 1940.

NATHANSON, D. & J. CASSANO, "Organization Diversity and Performance," *The Wharton Magazine,* Summer 1982: 18–26.

NEUSTADT, R.E., *Presidential Power: The Politics of Leadership.* New York: John Wiley, 1960.

NONAKA, I., "Creating Organizational Order out of Chaos: Self-Renewal in Japanese Firms," *California Management Review,* Spring 1988: 57–73.

NORMANN, R., *Management for Growth,* translated by N. Adler. New York: John Wiley, 1977.

NYSTROM, P.C., B.L.T. HEDBERG, & W.H. STARBUCK, "Interacting Processes as Organization Designs," in R.H. Kilmann, L.R. Pondy, & D.P. Slevin, eds., *The Management of Organization Design,* Vol. 1. New York: Elsevier North-Holland, 1976.

OGILVY, D., *Ogilvy on Advertising.* New York: Crown, 1983.

OHMAE, K., *The Mind of the Strategist.* New York: McGraw-Hill, 1982.

ONO, H., "Nihonteki Keiei Shisutemu to Jinji Kettei Shisutemu," ("Japanese Management System and Personnel Decisions,") *Soshiki Kagaku,* 1976: 22–32.

OUCHI, W.G., "Market, Bureaucracies and Clans," *Administrative Science Quarterly,* 1980: 129–140.

_____, *Theory Z.* Reading, Mass.: Addison-Wesley, 1981.

_____, & A.M. JAEGER, "Type Z Organization: Stability in the Midst of Mobility," *Academy of Management Review,* 1978: 305–314.

_____, W.G., & B. JOHNSON, "Types of Organizational Control and Their Relationship to Emotional Well Being," *Administrative Science Quarterly,* 1978: 293–317.

PARSONS, T., *Structure and Process in Modern Societies.* Glencoe, Ill.: Free Press, 1960.

PASCALE, R.T., "Perspectives on Strategy: The Real Story Behind Honda's Success," *California Management Review,* Spring 1984: 47–72.

PAUL, N.L., "The Use of Empathy in the Resolution of Grief," in *Perspective in Biology and Medicine.* Chicago: University of Chicago Press, 1967.

PENCE, C.C., *How Venture Capitalists Make Venture Decisions.* Ann Arbor, Mich.: UMI Research Press, 1982.

PERROW, C., "The Analysis of Goals in Complex Organizations," *American Sociological Review,* 1961: 854–866.

_____, *Organizational Analysis: A Sociological Review.* Belmont, Calif.: Wadsworth, 1970.

_____, *Complex Organizations: A Critical Essay,* New York: Scott, Foresman, 1972.

PETERS, T.J., "A Style for All Seasons," *Executive,* Summer 1980: 12–16.

_____, & R.H. WATERMAN, *In Search of Excellence: Lessons from America's Best Run Companies.* New York: Harper & Row, 1982.

PFEFFER, J., "Size and Composition of Corporate Boards of Directors: The Organization and its Environment," *Administrative Science Quarterly,* 1972a: 218–228.

———, "Merger as a Response to Organizational Interdependence," *Administrative Science Quarterly,* 1972b: 382–394.

———, "Size, Composition and Function of Hospital Boards of Directors: A Study of Organization-Environment Linkage," *Administrative Science Quarterly,* 1973: 349–364.

———, "Administrative Regulation and Licensing: Social Problem or Solution?" *Social Problems,* 1974: 468–479.

———, *Management as Symbolic Action: The Creation and Maintenance of Organizational Paradigms.* Working Paper, Stanford University, 1979.

———, & H. LEBLEBICI, "Executive Recruitment and the Development of Interfirm Organizations," *Administrative Science Quarterly,* 1973: 449–461.

———, & P. NOWAK, "Patterns of Joint Venture Activity: Implications for Antitrust Policy," *The Antitrust Bulletin,* 1976: 315–339.

———, "Joint Ventures and Interorganizational Interdependence," *Administrative Science Quarterly,* 1976b: 398–418.

———, *Organizational Context and Interorganizational Linkages Among Corporations.* Working Paper, University of California at Berkeley, no date.

———, & H. LEBLEBICI, "The Effect of Uncertainty on the Use of Social Influence in Organizational Decision-Making," *Administrative Science Quarterly,* 1976: 227–245.

PFIFFNER, J.M., "Administrative Rationality," *Public Administration Review,* 1960: 125–132.

PHILLIPS, T.R. ED., *Roots of Strategy.* Harrisburg, Pa.: Military Service Publishing, 1940.

PORTER, M.E., *Competitive Strategy: Techniques for Analysing Industries and Competitors.* New York: Free Press, 1980.

———, *Competitive Advantage: Creating and Sustaining Superior Performance.* New York: Free Press, 1985.

———, "Generic Competitive Strategies," in M.E. Porter, *Competitive Advantage,* pp. 34–46. New York: Free Press, 1985.

———, "From Competitive Advantage to Corporate Strategy," *Harvard Business Review,* May–June 1987: 43–59.

———, "Competition in Global Industries: A Conceptual Framework," in M.E. Porter, ed., *Competition in Global Industries.* Boston: Harvard Business School Press, 1986.

POSNER, B., & B. BURLINGHAM, "The Hottest Entrepreneur in America," *Inc.,* January 1988, 44–58.

POSNER, R.A., "Theories of Economic Regulation," *Bell Journal of Economics and Management Science,* 1974: 335–358.

PRICE, J.L., "The Impact of Governing Boards on Organizational Effectiveness and Morale," *Administrative Science Quarterly,* 1963: 361–378.

PUCIK, V., "Getting Ahead in Japan," *The Japanese Economic Journal,* 1981: 970–971.

———, "Promotions and Intra-organizational Status Differentiation Among Japanese Managers," *The Academy of Management Proceedings,* 1981: 59–63.

PURKAYASTHA, D., *"Note on the Motocycle Industry—1975."* Copyrighted Case, Harvard Business School, 1981.

QUINN, J.B., "Strategic Goals: Process and Politics," *Sloan Management Review,* Fall 1977: 21–37.

———, *Strategies for Change: Logical Incrementalism.* Homewood, Ill.: Richard D. Irwin, 1980.

RAPHAEL, R., *Edges.* New York: Alfred A. Knopf, 1976.

REESER, C., "Some Potential Human Problems in the Project Form of Organization," *Academy of Management Journal,* 1969: 459–467.

REID, S.R., *Mergers, Managers, and the Economy.* New York: McGraw-Hill, 1968.

RHENMAN, E., *Organization Theory for Long-Range Planning.* New York: John Wiley, 1973.

ROHLEN, T.P., *For Harmony and Strength: Japanese White-collar Organization in Anthropological Perspective.* Berkeley: University of California Press, 1974.

ROSNER, M., *Principle Types and Problems of Direct Democracy in the Kibbutz.* Working Paper, Social Research Center on the Kibbutz, Givat Haviva, Israel, 1969.

ROSS, I., "How Lawless are the Big Companies?" *Fortune,* December 1, 1980: 56–64.

ROSSOTTI, C.O., *Two Concepts of Long-Range Planning.* Boston: The Management Consulting Group, The Boston Safe Deposit & Trust Company, no date.

RUMELT, R.P., *Strategy, Structure and Economic Performance.* Boston: Harvard Business School, 1974.

———, "A Teaching Plan for Strategy Alternatives for the British Motocycle Industry," in *Japanese Business: Business Policy.* New York: The Japan Society, 1980.

———, "Diversification Strategy and Profitability," *Strategic Management Journal,* 1982: 359–370.

SAHLMAN, W.A., & H.H. STEVENSON, "Capital Market Myopia," *Journal of Business Venturing,* Winter 1985: 7–30.

SAKIYA, T., "The Story of Honda's Founders," *Asahi Evening News,* June–August, 1979.

———, *Honda Motor: The Men, The Management, The Machines.* Tokyo, Japan: Kadonsha International, 1982.

SALTER, M.S., & W.A. WEINHOLD, *Diversification Through Acquisition.* New York: Free Press, 1979.

SAYLES, L.R., *Managerial Behavior: Administration in Complex Organizations.* New York: McGraw-Hill, 1964.

———, "How Graduates Scare Bosses," *Careers Today,* January, 1969.

466

SCHELLING, T.C., *The Strategy of Conflict,* 2nd. ed. Cambridge, MA: Harvard University Press, 1980.

SCHENDEL, D.G., R. PATTON, & J. RIGGS, "Corporate Turnaround Strategies: A Study of Profit Decline and Recovery," *Journal of General Management,* Spring 1976: 3–11.

SCOTT, W.E., "Activation Theory and Task Design," *Organizational Behavior and Human Performance,* September 1966: 3–30.

SELZNICK, P., *TVA and the Grass Roots.* Berkeley: University of California Press, 1949.

———, *Leadership in Administration: A Sociological Interpretation.* New York: Harper & Row, 1957.

SHUBIK, M., *Games for Society, Business, and War: Towards a Theory of Gaming.* New York: Elsevier, 1975.

SIMON, M.A., "On the Concept of Organizational Goals," *Administrative Science Quarterly,* 1964–1965: 1–22.

SMITH, L., "The Boardroom Is Becoming a Different Scene," *Fortune,* May 8, 1978: 150–88.

SMITH, W.R., "Product Differentiation and Market Segmentation as Alternative Marketing Strategies," *Journal of Marketing,* July 1956: 3–8.

SOLZHENITSYN, A., "Why The West Has Succumbed to Cowardice," *The Montreal Star: News and Review,* June 10, 1978.

SPEER, A., *Inside the Third Reich.* New York: Macmillan, 1970.

SPENCER, F.C., "Deductive Reasoning in the Lifelong Continuing Education of a Cardiovascular Surgeon," *Archives of Surgery,* 1976: 1177–1183.

SPENDER, J.-C., *Industry Recipes: The Nature and Sources of Managerial Judgement.* London: Basil Blackwell, 1989.

STARBUCK, W.H., "Organizations and Their Environments," in M.D. Dunnette, ed., *Handbook of Industrial and Organizational Psychology.* Chicago: Rand McNally, 1976.

STARBUCK, W.H. & B.L.T. HEDBERG, "Saving an Organization from a Stagnating Environment," in H.B. Thorelli, ed., *Strategy + Structure = Performance.* Bloomington: Indiana University Press, 1977.

THE STATE OF SMALL BUSINESS, A REPORT TO THE PRESIDENT. Washington, D.C.: U.S. Government Printing Office, 1984.

STERN, L.W., B. STERNTHAL, & C.S. CRAIG, "Managing Conflict in Distribution Channels: A Laboratory Study," *Journal of Marketing Research,* 1973: 169–179.

STEVENSON, H.H., "Defining Corporate Strengths and Weaknesses," *Sloan Management Review,* Spring 1976: 51–68.

STEVENSON, W., *A Man Called Intrepid: The Secret War.* New York: Harcourt Brace Jovanovich, 1976.

STEWART, R., *Managers and Their Jobs.* London: Macmillan, 1967.

STIGLER, G.J., "The Theory of Economic Regulation," *Bell Journal of Economics and Management Science,* 1971: 3–21.

SUN TZU, *The Art of War,* translated by S.B. Griffith. New York: Oxford University Press, 1963. Original 500 B.C.

TAKEUCHI, H., & I. NONAKA, "The New New Product Development Game," *Harvard Business Review,* January–February 1986: 137–146.

TAYLOR, W.H., "The Nature of Policy Making in Universities," *The Canadian Journal of Higher Education,* 1983: 17–32.

TECHNOLOGICAL INNOVATION: ITS ENVIRONMENT AND MANAGEMENT. Washington, D.C.: U.S. Government Printing Office, 1967.

THOMPSON, J.D., *Organizations in Action.* New York: McGraw-Hill, 1967.

THOMPSON, V.A., *Modern Organizations.* New York: Alfred A. Knopf, 1961.

TILLES, S., "How to Evaluate Corporate Strategy," *Harvard Business Review,* July–August 1963: 111–121.

TIME. "The Most Basic Form of Creativity," June 26, 1972.

TOFFLER, A., *Future Shock.* New York: Bantam Books, 1970.

TREGOE, B., & I. ZIMMERMAN, *Top Management Strategy.* New York: Simon & Schuster, 1980.

TSUJI, K., "Decision-Making in the Japanese Government: A Study of Ringisei," in R.E. Wards, ed., *Political Development in Modern Japan,* Princeton: Princeton University Press, 1968.

TSURUMI, Y., *Multinational Management: Business Strategy and Government Policy.* Cambridge, Mass.: Ballinger, 1977.

TUCHMAN, B.W., *The Guns of August.* New York: Macmillan, 1962.

VANCIL, R.F., "Strategy Formulation in Complex Organizations," *Sloan Management Review,* Winter 1976: 1–18.

———, & P. LORANGE, "Strategic Planning in Diversified Companies," *Harvard Business Review,* January–February 1975: 81–90.

VAN DOREN, M., *Liberal Education,* Boston: Beacon Press, 1967.

VARNER, V.J. & J.I. ALGER, EDS., *History of the Military Art: Notes for the Course.* West Point, N.Y.: U.S. Military Academy, 1978.

VICKERS, G., "Is Adaptability Enough?" *Behavioral Science,* 1959: 219–234.

VOGEL, E., *Japan as Number One.* Cambridge, Mass.: Harvard University Press, 1979.

VON BÜLOW, D.F., *The Spirit of the Modern System of War,* translated by C.M. deMartemont. London: C. Mercier, 1806.

VON CLAUSEWITZ, C., *On War,* translated by M. Howard

and P. Paret. Princeton, N.J.: Princeton University Press, 1976.

VON HIPPEL, E., "Get New Products From Customers," *Harvard Business Review,* March–April 1982: 117–122.

VON NEUMANN, J. & O. MORGENSTERN, *Theory of Games and Economic Behavior.* Princeton, N.J.: Princeton University Press, 1944.

WARD, L.B., *Analysis of 1969 Alumni Questionnaire Returns.* Unpublished Report, Harvard Business School, 1970.

WATERMAN, R.H., JR., T.J. PETERS & J.R. PHILLIPS, "Structure is Not Organization," *Business Horizons,* June 1980: 14–26.

WEBER, M., "The Three Types of Legitimate Rule," translated by H. Gerth, in A. Etzioni, ed., *A Sociological Reader on Complex Organizations.* New York: Holt, Rinehart and Winston, 1969.

WEICK, K.E., "Educational Organizations as Loosely Coupled Systems," *Administrative Science Quarterly,* 1976: 1–19.

WESTLEY, F., & H. MINTZBERG, "Visionary Leadership and Strategic Management," *Strategic Management Journal,* 1989: 17–32.

WHEELWRIGHT, S.C., "Japan—Where Operations Really are Strategic," *Harvard Business Review,* July–August 1981: 67–74.

WHITE, T.H., *In Search of History: A Personal Adventure.* New York: Warner Books, 1978.

WHITEHEAD, A.N., *Aims of Education and Other Essays.* New York: Macmillan, 1929.

WHYTE, W.F., *Street Corner Society.* Chicago: University of Chicago Press, 1955.

WILLIAMSON, O.E., *Markets and Hierarchies: Analysis and Antitrust Implications.* New York: Free Press, 1975.

———, *The Economic Institutions of Capitalism.* New York: Free Press, 1985.

WISE, D., "Apple's New Crusade," *Business Week,* November 26, 1984.

WITTE, E., "Field Research on Complex Decision-Making Processes—The Phase Theorem," *International Studies of Management and Organization,* Summer 1972: 156–182.

WODARSKI, J.S., R.L. HAMBLIN, D.R. BUCKHOLDT, & D.E. FERRITOR, "Individual Consequences versus Different Shared Consequences Contingent on the Performance of Low-Achieving Group Members," *Journal of Applied Social Psychology,* 1973: 276–290.

WOO, C., & A. COOPER, "Strategies of Effective Low Share Businesses," *Strategic Management Journal,* 1981: 301–318.

WORTHY, J.C., "Organizational Structure and Employee Morale," *American Sociological Review,* 1950: 169–179.

———, *Big Business and Free Men.* New York: Harper & Row, 1959.

WRAPP, H.E., "Good Managers Don't Make Policy Decisions," *Harvard Business Review,* September–October 1967: 91–99.

WRIGLEY, L., "Diversification and Divisional Autonomy," DBA dissertation, Graduate School of Business Administration, Harvard University, 1970.

YOSHINO, M., *Japan's Managerial System.* Cambridge, Mass.: MIT Press, 1968.

YOSHINO, M.Y., "Global Competition in a Salient Industry: The Case of Civil Aircraft," in M.E. Porter, ed., *Competition in Global Industries.* Boston: Harvard Business School Press, 1986.

YOUNG, D., *Rommel: The Desert Fox.* New York: Harper & Row, 1974.

ZALD, M.N., "Urban Differentiation, Characteristics of Boards of Directors and Organizational Effectiveness," *American Journal of Sociology,* 1967: 261–272.

———, & M.A. BERGER, "Social Movements in Organizations: Coup d'Etat, Insurgency, and Mass Movements," *American Journal of Sociology,* 1978.

ZALEZNIK, A., "Power and Politics in Organizational Life," *Harvard Business Review,* May–June 1970: 47–60.

SUBJECT INDEX

474

NAME INDEX

478